Consumer finance
The consumer experience

CONSUMER FINANCE
THE CONSUMER EXPERIENCE

David J. Ward, Ph.D.
Associate Professor of Finance

Robert M. Niendorf, Ph.D.
Associate Professor of Finance

both of
The University of Wisconsin–Oshkosh

1978

RICHARD D. IRWIN, INC.
Homewood, Illinois 60430

Irwin-Dorsey Limited Georgetown, Ontario L7G 4B3

ISBN 0-256-02035-3
Library of Congress Catalog Card No. 77–085803

Printed in the United States of America

1 2 3 4 5 6 7 8 9 0 MP 5 4 3 2 1 0 9 8

To Judy and Carol

Preface

In recent decades, the American consumer has faced enormous changes in the marketplace. Improvements in technology and corporate marketing strategies have resulted in thousands of new products, services, and brands, all of which have complicated the consumer's spending decisions. Rapid price inflation has seriously eroded purchasing power and strained many budgets. Consumer advocates and government regulators have questioned the safety and usefulness of many products, and consumers have been bombarded with product recalls, health warnings, and general uncertainty.

The consumer has also had to cope with what seems to be a never-ending stream of crises and shortages. While the energy crisis looms largest, predicted shortages of water may be equally significant. Given the magnitude of these crises, we often overlook other recent shortages and minor crises. Lumber, paper, bread, beef, cocoa, sugar, and coffee have each been the subject of either real or imagined shortages. With each crisis the consumer has had to cope with rising prices and has often had to adjust spending habits.

There is very little to indicate that this rate of change will slow in the future. If anything, it almost seems that you, the consumer, had best be prepared for even greater and more rapid changes. Under such conditions, your most effective tool will be the ability to make intelligent decisions.

As you read this book, you will find that our approach to managing personal finances emphasizes the importance of decision making and that we have focused on crucial points overlooked in some traditional personal finance texts. Specifically, the following are key features in our approach:

1. Our text recognizes the importance of consumer behavior in managing personal finances. In Chapter 4 and other parts of our text, we point out how businesses attempt to capitalize on your behavior in selling their goods. Using the information we provide about con-

sumer research and consumer behavior models, you should be able to combat irrational and subtle promotional appeals designed to separate you from your dollars.

2. Our text deals with *all* the vital consumer spending areas. We emphasize the importance of decision processes to help you in spending for food, clothing, housing, appliances, and autos. These areas consume the bulk of your dollars and thus deserve close consideration.

3. Our text develops a Consumer Decision Model which ties together the four sections of the book and focuses on the importance of decision making in managing personal finances. The decision model allows for great variation in the influences and desires of individual consumers.

4. The final section of our text uses the theme of financial planning to tie together the many aspects of consumer finance. Most texts introduce you to budgeting in an early chapter and then delve into spending, credit, and investments without ever coming back to how budgeting and financial planning can be used to integrate what you've learned in succeeding chapters. Our text introduces you to budgeting in Chapters 1 and 2 and then uses the final two chapters to tie together the setting of goals and priorities, budgeting, spending, and financing through an analysis of your financial condition and the preparation of a personal balance sheet and budget.

We are especially grateful to Eugene Dunham, Virginia Commonwealth University; Thomas Herzing, University of Wisconsin–Oshkosh; Dean Robert Pierce, Central Missouri State University; Theodore Mah, Diablo Valley College; and Grant Wells, Ball State University, for their thorough reviews and incisive suggestions during the preparation of the manuscript.

Special recognition must go to Carol Niendorf, who has been instrumental in the completion of this book.

January 1978

David J. Ward
Robert M. Niendorf

Contents

section one

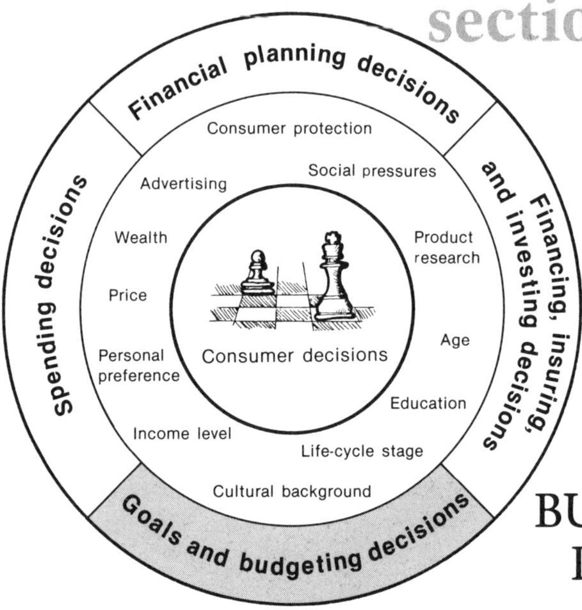

GOALS AND BUDGETING DECISIONS

Over 200 years ago, the noted economist Adam Smith declared, "The consumer is King!" That statement summarized his belief that the success of almost all economic activity lay in the hands and pocketbooks of consumers. In Smith's theory, consumers make spending decisions that best serve their own needs, in what Smith termed enlightened self-interest. In making these decisions, consumers determine which products will succeed and which will fail. Thus, the consumer holds great economic power and determines the fate of most business ventures.

Yet another view of the consumer is contained in the writings of modern consumer activists such as Vance Packard and Ralph Nader. To them, the consumer is anything *but* a king. Rather, the consumer is more like a pawn being manipulated to the advantage of big business. This consumer is often overwhelmed by mass merchandising techniques, slick advertising, and selling gimmicks that create unwanted needs for many products. In this view of the consumer, the consumer is the servant, not the master of the economic system.

Well, which is it? Are you and I the kings or the pawns? Do we as consumers have any choice in the matter? What can we do to determine our fate?

The central idea of this book is that you can become the king. But in order to do that, you must understand the general framework and environment within which all consumers operate. This first section of the book emphasizes the need to understand the nature and behavior of consumers and the influences and pressures that come to bear on each of them. This understanding serves as a means of helping choose an appropriate plan for managing personal finances. The primary aim of this approach is to provide you with information that allows you to develop individual methods and styles of consumption that are harmonious with personal goals and objectives.

This section of the text looks at the consumer from two viewpoints. The first two chapters are concerned with the general nature of consumers and how they make decisions. Chapter 1 analyzes national spending patterns and then contrasts these average patterns with the variety of spending patterns and desires that occur within the typical life cycle. This first chapter concludes with a general consumer decision model that focuses on the major decision areas facing all consumers.

Chapter 2 carries on the theme of consumer decisionmaking by examining how a budget can be a major aid in making better spending decisions. The budgeting emphasis in this chapter is on the individuality of consumers and the need for a flexible approach to budgeting. The chapter concludes by examining two very practical approaches to budgeting that should be of assistance to consumers who prefer a more structured approach to spending.

The final two chapters in this section focus on the realities of the consumer's marketplace. The general theme, "consumer beware," is developed in Chapter 3 as the issue of consumer fraud is examined. The chapter explains not only how you may be deceived or swindled but also how you can avoid or counteract fraudulent or deceitful schemes.

A more subtle side of the manipulation of consumers is dealt with in Chapter 4. This chapter focuses on the use of consumer behavior as a prime marketing strategy of mass merchandisers. The chapter also develops the idea that you can benefit from knowing about these techniques by taking account of them in making spending decisions.

Decisions in a consumer economy

1

OBJECTIVES

This chapter focuses on the importance of consumer decisionmaking in determining personal financial success or failure. After thoroughly reading and discussing this chapter, you should be able to:

. . . Explain the basic elements of the Consumer Decision Model.
. . . Describe the average national spending patterns of consumers.
. . . Recognize differences in spending patterns among consumers.
. . . Explain the economic life cycle of individuals and families.

Early in 1971, one of the most powerful corporations in the world admitted defeat. E. I. du Pont de Nemours & Co., a multi-billion-dollar firm, announced that it was withdrawing its product Corfam from the consumer market. The cause of this defeat was consumer refusal to accept shoes made of Corfam, a manmade substitute for leather. Du Pont had spent millions of dollars and years of research in an attempt to produce and market profitably this new line of shoe material. Despite its great corporate strength and its success in marketing hundreds of other products, du Pont was forced to withdraw from this market and take a loss estimated at $100 million.

An even greater example of rejection by consumers occurred in the late 1950s when Ford Motor Company introduced the Edsel. In its short life, which began in 1957 and ended in 1959, the Edsel was a catastrophic financial failure. Estimates of losses run as high as $350

Reprinted by special permission from the Ford Motor Company.

million. Yet the Edsel had been scientifically designed and marketed to appeal to the American automobile-buying public.

Edsel and Corfam are just two examples of product failures in recent decades. But both failures stand as important signposts in the history of the American economy. They show what happens when the American consumer decides not to buy a product. More importantly, both signal a change that has occurred in our economic system over the last three decades: it is becoming evident that the purchasing decisions of consumers hold the key to the success and failure of the American economy. In the words of Adam Smith, the modern consumer is indeed King!

CONSUMER DECISIONS

While it is true that our decisions to buy or not to buy hold the key to the success of millions of products and services, it is also true that our individual decisions determine our own financial success or failure. Our spending decisions, career and education choices, and similar consumer decisions are reflected in our satisfaction as consumers and our overall financial success.

It's not too hard to find examples of how we as consumers have made some poor decisions. Evidence of poor decisionmaking can be found in the increasing number of bankruptcies filed by American consumers. Bankruptcy is the most severe form of financial distress. A straight bankruptcy is a legal action taken by a consumer which asks a court to discharge that individual's debts because there is no hope of repaying them. As Exhibit 1–1 shows, bankruptcies have increased sharply since World War II and continue to run at very high

EXHIBIT 1–1
Nonbusiness bankruptcies filed selected years—1940–1976

Year	*Number of bankruptcies filed*
1940	39,076
1945	11,051
1950	25,040
1955	50,219
1960	97,750
1965	163,413
1966	175,924
1967	191,729
1968	181,266
1969	169,500
1970	178,202
1971	182,249
1972	164,737
1973	155,707
1974	168,767
1975	224,354
1976	211,238

Source: *Tables of Bankruptcy Statistics,* Administrative Office of the United States Courts, Annual Report, June 30, 1976.

levels. One should also remember that bankruptcies are the tip of the iceberg. For every case of bankruptcy there are at least twenty other families and individuals who are delinquent on loan payments or having other financial difficulties. As a rule of thumb, in any one year between 3 percent and 6 percent of U.S. families have serious financial problems.[1]

The financial difficulties of others serve as important warnings that any of us can fall into the same kind of trouble. As most of us will admit, we want more than we can afford. We must learn to decide what is most important and to direct our money to meeting our most important objectives. The key to avoiding financial difficulties and to getting more for our money is to become better decisionmakers.

THE CONSUMER'S ENVIRONMENT

In our role as consumers, we make decisions in an economy that has grown more complex. The array of products directed toward us has increased rapidly. Today we are buying campers, snowmobiles, stereos, portable TVs, CB radios, and countless other items that

[1] *Family Credit Counseling—An Emerging Community Service* (New York: Family Service Association of America, 1967).

EXHIBIT 1–2
Total personal income in the United States, 1929–1976 (in $ billions)

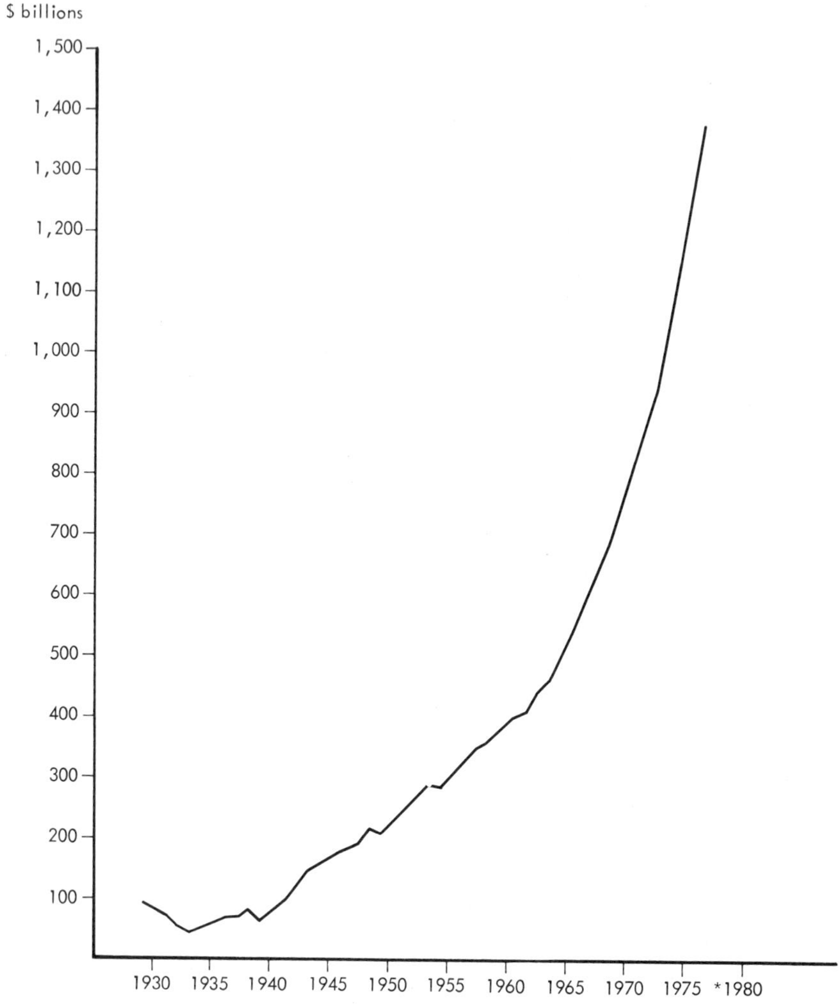

* Department of Commerce estimates—monthly data seasonally adjusted totals at annual rates.

Source: *Historical Statistics of the United States, Colonial Times to 1970, Part I,* U.S. Bureau of the Census Series F144–162, p. 234; *The Survey of Current Business,* July, 1974, vol. 54, no. 7, p. 15 and October, 1976, vol. 55, no. 10, p. 11; *Federal Reserve Bulletin.*

weren't previously available in mass supply at reasonable prices or weren't even produced twenty years ago. Thus we have many more outlets competing for our dollars, and spending decisions and priorities are that much more complex.

Consumers have also been affected by a tremendous growth in personal income (see Exhibit 1–2). This increased income has complicated each of our lives by providing more uncommitted or discretionary dollars than ever before. Previous generations of American consumers had to use the bulk of their income for essentials such as food, clothing, and shelter. Their spending decisions were quite confined and obvious. By comparison, today's consumer has money to spend beyond the essentials of life and must decide how to spend this discretionary income in an economy that offers a limitless variety of products and services.

The consumer is also affected by complex selling techniques designed to stimulate demands for goods and services. Much has been made of Madison Avenue advertising and the hidden persuaders designed to appeal to our subconscious desires. While much of this talk is probably overdone, sophisticated selling techniques may well influence some consumers and make rational spending decisions much more difficult.

Coupled with better selling techniques has been a trend toward more consumer credit which has made it easier for consumers to get financially overextended. Exhibit 1–3 shows this tremendous growth in consumer credit in recent years. Easier credit has led many consumers to buy more than their incomes can support. This ability to overbuy stems largely from open access to credit, which allows the consumer to spend today and pay out of tomorrow's income. Unfortunately, tomorrow's income may not be enough to take care of all the bills that must be paid.

While increased product choice, more discretionary income, sophisticated selling techniques, and easier credit are major factors in complicating the consumer's life, there are other factors that may influence consumers. For example, social pressures from friends, relatives, or coworkers may influence some consumers in their spending decisions. Education, cultural background, and age may also play a role in consumer decisions.

The list of factors that influence decisions will be unique to each consumer. Taken together, these factors form the general environment within which we make decisions. The decisions we make as consumers can be categorized into four general areas: goals and budgeting decisions; spending decisions; financing, insuring, and investing decisions; and financial planning decisions.

EXHIBIT 1–3
Consumer installment credit outstanding for selected years from 1920–1976 (in $ millions)

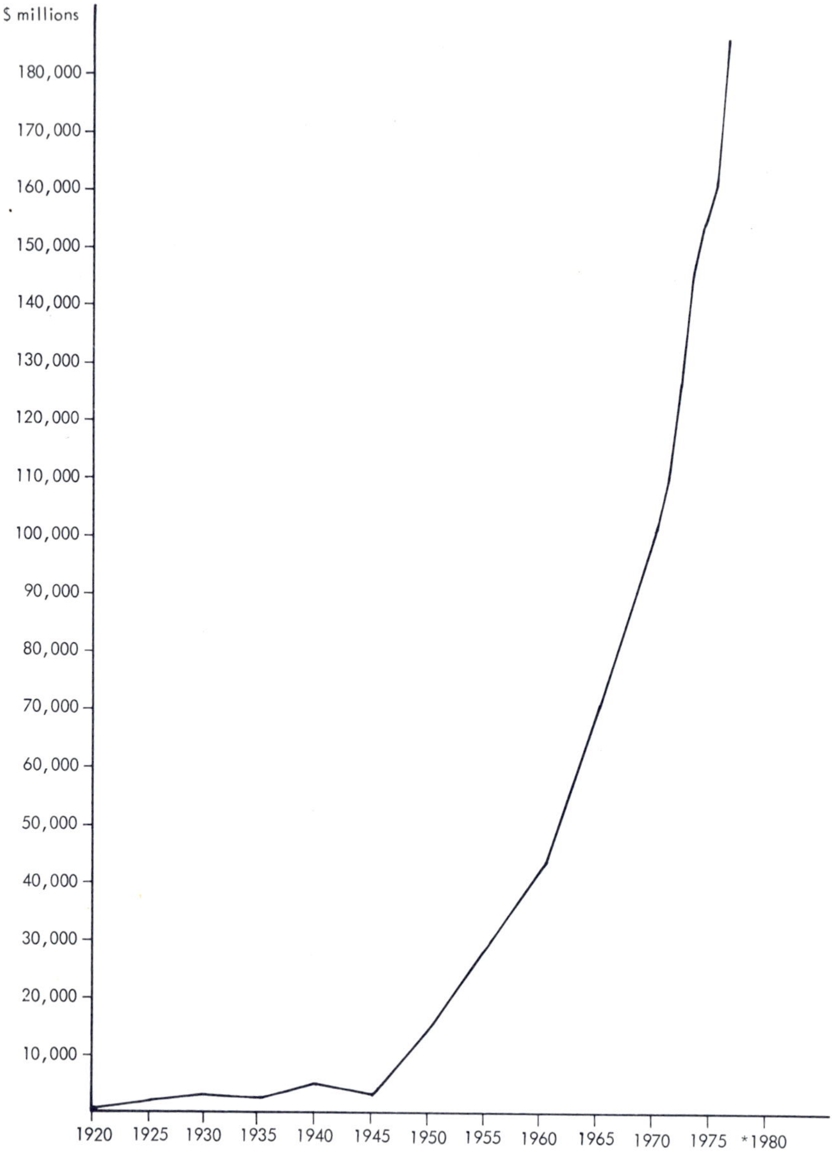

* As of May 31, 1976.

Source: *Historical Statistics of the United States, Colonial Times to 1970, Part II,* U.S. Bureau of the Census, Series X547–550, p. 1009; *Federal Reserve Bulletin,* March, 1977.

Goals and budgeting decisions

These decisions establish the general direction and priorities of a consumer's spending and savings plan. Goals are what a consumer wants to accomplish: "I want to own a summer vacation home." Priorities establish the relative importance of all goals; for example, owning a summer home is less important than eating every day. Budgeting decisions involve setting up a financial plan that will carry out the consumer's goals.

Spending decisions

These decisions are generally made after the consumer has established spending goals and priorities and through this process has decided to buy particular goods and services. For example, a consumer may decide that a new automobile is the number one spending priority for next year. The consumer will then consider spending decisions relative to the make or brand of car, the best available price, and the appropriate dealer in order to get the most car for the money spent.

Financing, insuring, and investing decisions

Consumers must make decisions on how to finance spending and where to invest savings. The consumer must decide how to finance each purchase (credit vs. cash) and must also consider financial protection (insurance) for both people and property. Financial decisions must also be made in determining the appropriate investment outlets for savings.

Financial planning decisions

These decisions involve longer range considerations to meet possible future events. For example, consumers should consider the need for effective plans to deal with future tax problems, retirement, and the orderly transfer of assets at death. To deal with these future possibilities, the consumer must often make decisions well in advance of these anticipated events.

THE CONSUMER DECISION PROCESS

One view of the process of making consumer decisions is contained in Exhibit 1–4. In this model, decisions are ongoing, interrelated

EXHIBIT 1–4
The consumer decision model

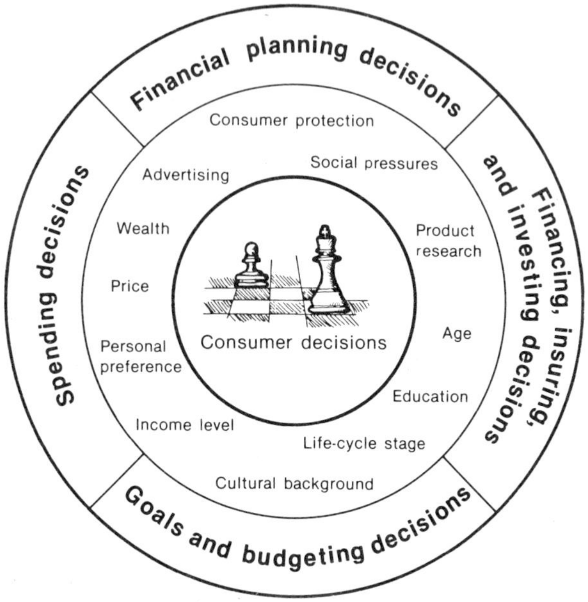

events. For example, spending decisions (buying a new stereo) relate to the goal decisions of a consumer (how important is a stereo?) as well as financing decisions (is there enough cash or credit to finance the purchase?). To illustrate this interrelatedness, major decision areas are connected by the outer ring on our model.

The inner ring on the model identifies some of the factors that may influence these decisions. These factors form the decision environment or "influence ring," which will tend to vary from consumer to consumer. For example, one consumer may be heavily influenced by advertising while another may ignore advertising but pay heed to price considerations.

The Consumer Decision Model draws together the key elements in the consumer's decisionmaking process. It also focuses attention upon the importance of our decisions in achieving orderly personal finances. As we progress through the text we will examine the key consumer decisions and the factors that may influence those decisions with the primary purpose of improving decisionmaking ability.

One part of being a better decisionmaker is to become familiar with how other consumers spend their personal income. To do that, we can begin to look at how consumers as a group spend their money and how individual consumers can differ in their spending habits.

WHERE DOES IT GO?

In 1976 consumers earned a whopping $1,375,300,000,000 in personal income (see Exhibit 1–2). How did consumers dispose of this? What sort of spending decisions did consumers make? In short, where did it all go?

General consumer spending patterns

Broadly speaking, the personal income of consumers is spent in three ways. First, consumers must spend some money for **taxes** to support federal, state, and local governments. This tax money would include payments for income taxes, sales taxes, property taxes, Social Security taxes, and other miscellaneous taxes such as federal excise taxes.

A second area of spending, which takes the bulk of the consumer's money, is **personal consumption expenditures** including durables, nondurables, and services. *Durables,* sometimes called hard goods, are items that are used or consumed gradually over a period of time. For example, with appropriate maintenance an automobile can normally be used for many years. Other durables include furniture, appliances, and houses. *Nondurables,* by contrast, are items that are used up or consumed in a short period of time or in a single use. Probably the most common example of a nondurable is food, which is normally consumed within days or weeks of purchase. Other nondurables include certain textiles, petroleum products, and personal articles such as toiletries and cosmetics.

A portion of personal consumption expenditures is devoted to buying services. *Services* represent someone else's labor. Normally, services are purchased for convenience or because we need specialized or professional expertise that someone else has. The services of the plumber, housekeeper, lawyer, doctor, and dentist all represent useful labors that we purchase in the normal course of life.

A third type of spending represents consumer commitments to future financial goals through **savings.** This money is usually invested with the purpose of earning some form of return such as interest income or capital growth. The bulk of individual investment funds goes into savings accounts at various financial institutions. In addition to deposits at financial institutions, consumers hold common stocks, bonds, mutual funds, and other forms of investments.

Consumer expenditures in these three main areas of taxes, personal consumption, and savings are classified as either *nondiscretionary* or *discretionary*. Nondiscretionary expenditures are purchases that the consumer must make to provide basic goods and services or to fulfill legal obligations or debts. For example, a large part of the money spent on food is required simply to stay alive. Similarly, most of us must spend money on shelter, clothing, utilities, and other such basics. Money spent to pay taxes or to repay installment loans also represents nondiscretionary expenditures. The common thread in all of these expenditures is that the consumer has little choice or discretion.

By contrast, discretionary expenditures are purchases in which the consumer has great freedom or discretion. Most nonessential spending on luxuries is discretionary; camping trailers, sports cars, stereos, and similar items are examples.

The division of personal income of consumers in the various spending areas in any one year will depend upon many things including existing economic conditions. For example, when the economy is in a recession, consumers tend to save a higher percentage of their income and to restrict nonessential expenditures. By contrast, when the economy is booming, consumers tend to have more income and spend a higher percentage on nonessential items. With this possible variation in mind, Exhibit 1–5 illustrates the division of personal income for 1976.

EXHIBIT 1–5
Distribution of personal income in the United States in 1976 (in $ billions)

Personal taxes		$ 193.6
Personal consumption		
Durables	$156.5	
Nondurables	440.4	
Services	482.8	$1,079.7
Investments		76.5
Other		25.5
Total personal income		$1,375.3

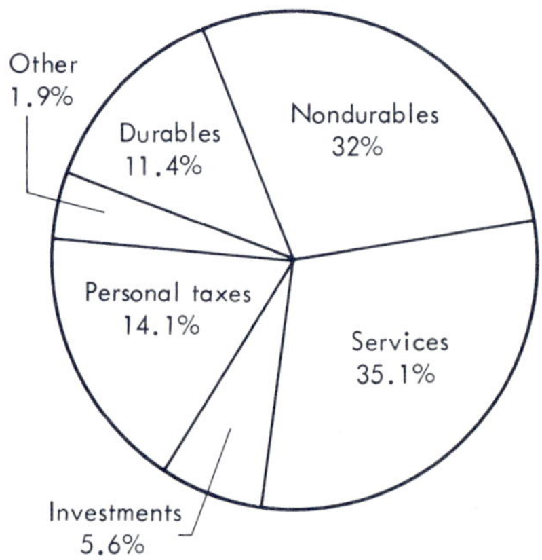

Source: *The Federal Reserve Bulletin*, March 1977.

Individual consumer spending patterns

Perhaps more important than the year-to-year variation in consumer spending on the national level is a recognition that consumer spending within any one year varies widely among individual consumers. As most of us will recognize from observation, each of us has a unique spending pattern. These differences in spending tend to be caused by three primary factors: income level, life-cycle stages, and personal preference.

Income level. Perhaps the most important factor influencing spending is income level. Generally speaking, at higher income levels there is more money available for discretionary expenditures. By contrast, consumers with lower incomes must concentrate their spending on basics such as food and clothing. The contrasted spending patterns of families with different levels of income are shown in Exhibit 1–6. In general, the lower the level of income, the larger the percentage consumers must allocate to food and medical care, while higher income budgets allocate a larger percentage to items such as housing, taxes, and other family consumption items.

Life-cycle stage. Another factor that influences spending patterns is the consumer's stage in the life cycle. The idea of a life cycle, while somewhat imprecise and open to interpretation, suggests that people progress through life in some sort of orderly series of stages. From the standpoint of human growth and development, we all pass from infancy to early childhood, then on to adolescence, adulthood, middle age, and old age.

For each stage in the life cycle, there seems to be a distinct pattern of spending as illustrated in Exhibit 1–7. Significant consumption begins in adolescence, and it is primarily aimed at nondurables (food, records, clothing) and services (movies and recreational activities). Typically, adolescents progress to a young singles stage where significant consumption of durables (automobiles) and services (higher education, personal services) begins to take place. At the end of this stage, one of two life stages follows. The majority of people marry and rear children, and in the process they are heavy consumers of durables and nondurables. Those who choose not to marry follow the single

EXHIBIT 1–6
Comparative spending for selected items: Autumn 1976 urban family budgets for a family of four

	Lower level budget	*Higher level budget*
Income	$10,041	$23,759
Percentage spent on:		
Food	29.9%	20.4%
Housing	19.6	24.5
Medical care	8.9	4.0
Clothing	8.0	7.0
Transportation	7.6	7.7
Taxes	14.2	23.0
Other	11.8	13.4

Source: "Family Budgets—Urban Areas—Autumn 1976" (Washington, D.C.: United States Department of Labor, 1977).

EXHIBIT 1–7
Personal consumption expenditure patterns for average urban family income

Percentage of consumption expenditures for	Stages in the life cycle						
			Married with children			Older couples	
	Young singles	*Young marrieds*	*Under 6 yrs. old*	*6–17 years old*	*Oldest over 18 years*	*55–64 years*	*65–74 years*
Food	21.8	19.4	22.3	25.8	23.4	24.2	25.2
Tobacco	1.7	2.0	1.9	1.8	1.6	1.8	1.4
Alcoholic beverages	3.7	2.1	1.3	1.5	1.7	1.6	1.5
Housing (shelter, utilities, furnishings)	24.4	32.8	33.4	28.7	24.2	29.4	31.9
Clothing	13.7	9.5	8.8	11.3	12.1	8.6	7.0
Personal care	2.8	2.7	2.6	2.9	2.8	2.8	2.8
Medical care	3.4	5.8	6.8	6.1	5.8	8.1	10.0
Recreation	6.0	4.6	4.1	4.5	4.4	3.3	2.6
Reading	1.0	.9	.8	.9	.8	1.0	1.1
Education	2.3	.9	.6	1.0	3.2	.3	.1
Transportation	18.2	18.0	16.2	13.6	16.5	15.6	13.6
Other expenditures	1.1	1.3	1.2	1.9	3.4	3.3	2.6
Total	100.0	100.0	100.0	100.0	100.0	100.0	100.0

Source: Adapted from *Bureau of Labor Statistics Report* 237–38, Supplement 2, Part A, pp. 10, 12, and 17.

career pattern, and they tend to spend heavily on durables and nondurables while also spending significant amounts on services and savings. From a consumption standpoint, both of these life stages merge in middle age, at which point spending on services such as education and on nondurables such as clothing tends to rise while spending on durables tends to fall. In the final stages of economic life—retirement and old age—there is emphasis on spending for medical and other services, with less emphasis on spending for most nondurables and durables.

Indications of the existence of these spending differences at various stages of life can be found in a number of studies of consumer finances. For example, the Survey Research Center of the University of Michigan periodically measures consumer spending and, as Exhibit 1–8 shows, these surveys point up significant differences in spending

EXHIBIT 1–8
Ownership and purchasing in 1970 by age of head of family

Age of family head	*Own a home*	*Own at least one car*	*Own two or more cars*	*Own certificates of deposit*	*Have checking account*	*Purchased household durables (1969)*
Younger than 25	12%	82%	15%	2%	32%	51%
25–34	48	88	26	3	25	57
35–44	72	89	38	5	28	53
45–54	74	90	44	7	30	47
55–64	77	80	27	11	36	39
65 or older	71	60	10	17	39	25

Source: *1970 Survey of Consumer Finances*, Survey Research Center, Institute for Social Research, The University of Michigan.

at various stages of the life cycle. Note the contrast in spending on durables and savings (certificates of deposit) as two obvious differences that occur.

Personal preference. A final factor that influences the pattern of consumer expenditures is personal preference. While it is a very difficult factor to quantify, casual observation of our own spending patterns compared with other family members, with neighbors, or with national averages will probably reveal significant differences. While one consumer may spend heavily on a vacation home, another may prefer to spend money on travel, yet both may have similar incomes and be in the same life cycle group.

SUMMARY

Consumer decisions determine the economic success or failure of most businesses. These decisions are equally important to consumers themselves because the quality of those decisions will reflect on the consumer's personal financial success or failure.

The Consumer Decision Model illustrates the general nature of consumer decisions and the major decisions consumers must make. These major decisions involve goals, priorities and budgets, spending, financing, and financial planning. The model demonstrates that these decisions are interrelated and that there are many influences that come to bear on consumers when they make these decisions.

Part of the process of becoming a better consumer decisionmaker involves recognizing the general spending pattern of consumers and the differences in spending patterns among individual consumers. The differences among consumers may relate to a number of factors. The stage of the economic life cycle is quite important. Level of income may also be a factor. Other factors including personal preference may also be key factors in a consumer's spending pattern.

APPENDIX 1–A

Selected family characteristics and weekly expenditures by region, all urban and rural families and single consumers, United States survey of consumer expenditures —Diary, July 1972–June 1973

		Region			
	Total	*Northeast*	*North central*	*South*	*West*
Selected family characteristics					
No. of families (000s)	71,163	16,921	19,558	21,938	12,746
Average					
Family size	2.9	2.9	2.9	2.9	2.8
Income before taxes	$9,081	$9,113	$9,323	$8,326	$9,969
Age of head (years)	47.8	48.7	47.6	47.9	46.7
No. children under 18	1.0	1.0	1.0	1.0	0.9
No. persons 65 and over	0.3	0.3	0.3	0.3	0.3
No. vehicles owned	1.3	1.1	1.3	1.3	1.4
Selected family expenditures					
Total food, excluding alcoholic beverages	$30.32	$33.92	$30.15	$27.67	$30.39
Food at home, total	22.17	24.92	21.98	20.83	21.12
Food away from home, total	8.15	9.00	8.17	6.84	9.27
Selected nonfood expenditures					
Gasoline	6.36	6.09	6.43	6.26	6.81
Gas and electricity	5.25	5.15	6.15	4.87	4.67
Other fuels	.92	1.90	.70	.70	.33
Personal care services	1.30	1.45	1.30	1.20	1.28
Personal care products	1.48	1.50	1.41	1.45	1.60
Nonprescriptive drugs and medical supplies	1.12	1.09	1.16	1.12	1.11
Housekeeping supplies	2.52	2.68	2.59	2.31	2.54

Source: U.S. Department of Labor, Bureau of Labor Statistics.

DISCUSSION QUESTIONS

1. How do more sophisticated selling techniques and easy access to credit make the consumer's decision process more complex?
2. Distinguish between a consumer's goals and a consumer's priorities.
3. Explain how a consumer's spending and financing decisions may be interrelated.
4. In the Consumer Decision Model, how does the "influence ring" allow for the individuality of consumers as decisionmakers?
5. Explain the difference between discretionary and nondiscretionary expenditures. Drawing upon your own experience, list three discretionary and three nondiscretionary expenditures you have made in the last few months.
6. According to the life cycle expenditures shown in Exhibit 1–7, which group of individuals spends the most (percentagewise) on alcoholic beverages? How would you explain this fact?
7. Again drawing upon Exhibit 1–7, contrast and explain the expenditure patterns of young marrieds with those of older couples, aged 65–74.

CASE PROBLEMS

1. Differences in spending patterns among consumers may be caused by many factors. Age and stage in the life cycle have already been mentioned as important factors. Another factor that should not be overlooked is the impact of geography or region. The table in the Appendix is drawn from the 1972–73 Consumer Expenditure Survey.

   After examining these figures, analyze the differences in income and consumption patterns and indicate why these differences may exist.

2. Gerri and John Forsythe are newly married and are setting up their household. Both Gerri and John have just graduated from college and both have jobs. Their combined income is $23,000 per year and the outlook for promotions and salary increases is good. Gerri and John have decided to map out their spending for the next year. They sat down and discussed the matter and arrived at the following budget:

Food	$ 1,800
Rent	3,600
Utilities	960
Car payments	2,400
Furniture payments	2,400
Gasoline	500
Personal care items	400
Entertainment	1,000
Clothing	550
Medical care	300
Insurance	800

Social Security taxes	1,400
Federal taxes	4,100
State income tax	800
Savings	1,990
Total	$23,000

Assuming Gerri and John can live within this budget, how would they compare with the national pattern for urban families (Exhibit 1–6)? Where there are differences between their budget and the national pattern, what explains these differences?

SELECTED READINGS

"Consumers and Economic Recovery," University of Michigan Survey *Intellect* 104 (April 1976), pp. 486–87.

Dolphin, Robert D., Jr. *An Analysis of Economic and Personal Factors Leading to Consumer Bankruptcy.* East Lansing, Michigan: Michigan State University Press, 1965.

Duncan, Greg J., and Morgan, James N., eds. *Five Thousand American Families—Patterns of Economic Progress.* Vol. I–IV. Ann Arbor, Michigan: Institute for Social Research, 1976.

National Consumer Finance. *Finance Facts Yearbook.* Washington, D.C., annual.

Sherwin, Sidney. *What to Do When Your Bills Exceed Your Paycheck.* Englewood Cliffs, N.J.: Prentice-Hall, Inc., 1974.

Budgeting for consumers

2

OBJECTIVES

The chapter deals with the importance of budgeting in the consumer's financial plans. After thoroughly reading and discussing this chapter you should be able to:

. . . Identify the basic principles involved in the flexible approach to budgeting.

. . . Identify and *apply* the basic budgeting techniques as developed by the Institute of Life Insurance and the U.S. Department of Agriculture.

For most consumers, life holds two imponderables—losing weight and balancing a budget. The latter is a common yet troublesome issue with millions of consumers. As we pointed out in the last chapter, the failure to control expenditures often leads to serious financial problems. And the prime tool used to control spending is a financial plan—a budget.

The idea of budgeting or even the mention of the word "budget" often has a negative effect on people. Budgeting seems to be thought of in terms of restrictions and controls. The following definitions from Webster's Third New International Dictionary illustrate the popular usage of the word "budget":

budget: 3b a plan for the coordination of resources (as of money and manpower) and expenditures [a good family budget keeps something in reserve for emergencies];

3c the amount of money available, required, or assigned to a particular purpose in or as if in a budget [a minimum weekly budget for a family of five] [trying to operate efficiently on a budget of less than $3,000][1]

[1] By permission. From *Webster's Third New International Dictionary,* © 1971 by G. & C. Merriam Co., Publishers of the Merriam-Webster Dictionaries.

It is interesting to note the usages suggested in Webster's Third. Budget is associated with a "reserve for emergencies." It is also associated with the words "minimum" and "efficiently." Both these associations seem to have a negative overtone.

The negative connotation of budgeting is unfortunate because budgeting is a key tool to improving consumer decisionmaking. Budgeting is a goal-oriented planning process that improves the consumer's awareness of his or her financial position, thereby helping to avoid financial problems. Our approach to budgeting in this chapter will stress a positive, flexible approach to budgeting that can help you make decisions on spending and income.

FACTORS DETERMINING INCOME LEVEL

A key part of the budget is determining how much money you have to spend. For most of us, the largest part of our spendable money comes from working at a job or profession. Many people may also derive spendable funds from savings income or investment income. They may also choose to spend the accumulated capital in their savings and investment accounts.

Income from a job is generally the main source of our spending money, and it is an important decisionmaking area. Many of our decisions as consumers will affect our present and future income level.

Education and income level

Your decision to continue your education beyond high school has increased your projected lifetime earnings. Experts estimate that lifetime earnings of a college graduate will be considerably higher than

EXHIBIT 2–1
Estimated lifetime earnings for men and women for selected ages and educational attainments, 1972*

	Years of school completed							
	8		*9–11*		*12*		*16 or more*	
Age	*Men*	*Women*	*Men*	*Women*	*Men*	*Women*	*Men*	*Women*
20–24 . . .	$210,703	$146,568	$253,674	$151,883	$304,792	$170,275	$466,945	$228,677
25–29 . . .	211,791	135,104	248,384	140,110	298,102	158,287	475,444	219,745
30–34 . . .	201,327	120,490	230,869	125,116	276,750	142,171	458,683	202,358
35–39 . . .	178,908	105,392	205,316	109,470	247,752	125,201	419,053	181,069
40–44 . . .	150,413	89,428	174,021	92,952	212,975	107,126	365,032	157,839

* In arriving at projected lifetime incomes, this study did not project annual rates of gain in productivity.

Source: U.S. Department of Health, Education, and Welfare, Social Security Administration, *Research and Statistics Note No. 12,* May 20, 1972.

those of a high school graduate. Exhibit 2–1 illustrates the difference in the projected lifetime incomes of men and women by educational level.[2] As you can see from these statistics, projected income increases with the level of education. The gap between high school and college graduates has narrowed in recent years, but the differences reflected in Exhibit 2–1 are still quite large.

Education and income stability

Education is an important determinant of the stability of family income. Although education levels beyond high school have been the standard for some time for many of the professional occupations, other occupations now require more than the high school diploma. Employers increasingly demand better-trained employees. Young people who do not get a good education in preparation for work will find the going more difficult in the years ahead. During the mid-1970s when unemployment rates were at their highest since the Great Depression of the 1930s, those workers with less education experienced higher unemployment. Exhibit 2–2 shows that the unemployment rate for workers generally declines as the level of education increases. The low levels of unemployment for those who have completed a college education indicates that most college graduates enjoy a stable income over their work lives.[3]

EXHIBIT 2–2
Unemployment rates of workers by age and level of educational attainment (March, 1976)

	Age		
Education	*16–24*	*25–54*	*55 and over*
Elementary			
Less than 8 years	20.3%	9.0%	8.8%
8 Years	29.2	8.1	7.7
High school			
1–3 Years	22.6	9.0	6.0
4 Years	14.8	6.2	5.1
College			
1–3 Years	9.1	4.4	4.4
4 Years	6.4	2.4	2.0

Source: Special Labor Force Report 193, "Educational Attainment of Workers, March 1976," U.S. Department of Labor, Bureau of Labor Statistics, Washington, D.C., 1976.

---

[2] U.S. Department of Health, Education, and Welfare, Social Security Administration, *Research and Statistics Note No. 12,* May 20, 1972.

[3] Bureau of Labor Statistics, *Occupational Outlook Handbook,* 1976–77 Edition, pp. 18–19.

Two-income families

While many people have increased their incomes through more training and education, many have taken another route to increasing the family income. The "man of the house" is no longer the sole means of support. Instead, both spouses are bringing home paychecks. Exhibit 2–3 shows this growth in working spouses, and it shows that

EXHIBIT 2–3
Working spouses for selected years

Year	*Husbands*	*Wives*
1947	29,865,000	6,502,000
1951	31,968,000	8,750,000
1955	32,207,000	10,021,000
1959	32,928,000	11,516,000
1963	34,305,000	13,303,000
1967	35,963,000	15,189,000
1971	36,620,000	17,445,000
1975	37,788,000	19,835,000

Source: "The Outlook," *The Wall Street Journal,* Feb. 2, 1976, p. 1.

the number of working wives has increased by 205 percent from 1947 to 1975, while the number of working husbands has increased by only 27 percent in this same period.

The reasons for this change in the source of family income are not altogether clear. To some extent, social movements such as women's liberation may play a part. Higher prices for housing and automobiles and larger tax burdens may be a factor. The need for more money to finance leisure-time activities or a higher level of material goods may also be a factor. Whatever the real factors may be, the working wife has had a tremendous influence on the family income. The average U.S. family income has grown by 208 percent from 1954 to 1974. By contrast, the average earnings of all U.S. workers have grown only 140 percent. The difference between these two figures is largely due to income provided by working wives.

A FLEXIBLE APPROACH TO BUDGETING

We said at the outset of this chapter that we would stress a flexible and positive approach to budgeting. Part of the idea of flexibility stems from the belief that people do differ in their spending patterns and life styles. Thus it is likely that people may choose different ways of budgeting.

Given these likely differences, we've chosen to explore the idea of budgeting from the standpoint of some general principles that should apply to most people. Before we explore these general principles, it is important to lay the groundwork for successful budgeting by looking at the importance of having personal financial goals.

Goals in budgeting

The process of setting goals or objectives centers on the question "What do I (we) want?" In answering that question most people quickly realize that they want an unlimited number of things. They also find that some of their goals are short-term ("I want a new frying pan") and are easily achieved today or tomorrow, while others are long-term goals ("I want to retire to a condominium in Arizona") that will take years to achieve. Finally, they realize that as they go through the various stages of the life cycle their goals may change.

One way of setting goals is to make a list of all the items that seem important in terms of spending. Using this list, a ranking of items by importance can be obtained by assigning priorities to each item. This ranking can then serve as an important measure of an individual's goals.

An example of this technique used on a broad scale can be seen in Exhibit 2–4, which is taken from the 1974 Youth Survey conducted for the American Council of Life Insurance (formerly the Institute of Life Insurance). The responses were drawn from a national probability sample of 2,510 persons between the ages of 14 and 25. The responses show the relative importance of a number of items that represent potential areas of spending. The responses would seem to indicate that as a group, young people feel that owning a home and having a pension plan are important spending priorities, while owning a dishwasher or color TV is relatively unimportant.

The exhibit also shows that people may differ greatly in what they consider to be important. For example, while 59 percent of the respondents indicated that owning a home was a necessity, at least seven percent considered this item as relatively unimportant. It would appear that the data shown in Exhibit 2–4 support the idea that individuals have widely varying spending objectives.

Some basic principles of budgeting

Many texts in the field of personal finance lay out relatively rigid guidelines for budgeting. They may suggest, for example, that each spending item such as food or clothing should be a specific percent-

EXHIBIT 2–4

Relative spending priorities in 1974 of people between the ages of 14 and 25 (by degree of importance of 12 items)

	A necessity			*Important but not necessity*			*Relatively unimportant*		
	Total	*Mar-ried*	*Single*	*Total*	*Mar-ried*	*Single*	*Total*	*Mar-ried*	*Single*
Your own home	59%	63%	58%	33%	30%	34%	7%	7%	8%
A pension plan	57	66	55	30	25	31	9	9	9
A savings account of at least $5,000	43	37	45	48	52	44	11	10	10
Life insurance amounting to at least $50,000	40	35	42	38	45	35	19	19	19
A college education	38	25	42	41	45	40	20	30	17
A new car	30	25	31	48	44	49	22	31	20
An air-conditioned home	14	13	15	35	38	35	49	48	50
An opportunity to travel abroad	13	6	15	45	34	48	40	59	36
A stereo system	13	5	15	39	33	40	48	62	44
A master's degree	12	8	14	44	39	45	42	54	39
A color TV	12	9	12	34	32	34	54	59	53
A dishwasher	9	5	10	27	28	27	64	68	63

Source: *Youth 1974: Finance-Related Attitudes,* American Council of Life Insurance.

age of take-home income. This method is then used to draw up a line-by-line spending plan that is held out as the primary example of what people *on the average* actually should spend.

While this approach has some merit, we find that it does not take into account factors such as the vast differences in income, geographical locale, stage of life, and personal preference that make it difficult to neatly label and categorize each of us. We are therefore suggesting that the process of budgeting be approached from a more general point of view. We think that an individual or family budget should be based upon a set of general budgeting principles that might include the following:

Successful and effective personal budgets must begin with an active plan and planning process. Large and successful organizations in government and business realize that budgeting is essential to their continued success. Typically the budgeting process is formalized into a printed document that lays out the overall spending plan and possible deviations in spending that may be necessary. Usually this spending plan is agreed upon after discussion or debate among department heads or others who are in positions of responsibility.

Personal budgeting should not be an exception to this process. Some kind of written budget, even in very general terms, is needed to serve as a permanent reminder of the general direction of personal spending plans. Communication and agreement among the spenders in the family unit is essential in arriving at that plan. As we previously suggested, this communication process can start with goal setting, and then it might naturally flow into a more detailed discussion of spending plans. The advantage of this approach is that all who are party to the budget will then know what the overall plan is and should be able to tailor their spending to fit the general spending pattern.

Individual and family budgets must begin with realistic spending levels for the basics or essentials of life. Studies by agencies such as the Family Service Association of America have found that the largest portion of a consumer's dollar is necessarily committed to the essentials of life such as food, clothing, shelter, and transportation. While the extent of this commitment may vary with many of the factors we have discussed, these basic or nondiscretionary expenditures may consume 75 to 100 percent of personal income.

Depending upon personal preferences, considerable variation in basic expenditures may be possible. For example, while the Department of Labor suggests that a low-income urban family budget calls for 30 percent of its total family consumption to be devoted to food, the actual consumption figure may be above or below that percentage, with the variation determined by how important the quality, variety, and quantity of food is to the family.[4]

Whatever the final individual decision may be on these basic items, spending on essentials must be in line with real costs. To imagine, for example, that food costs might be held down to five percent of family consumption expenditures (that would be $480 a year for an urban family of four with a low-level budget) is simply unrealistic. One study by the Family Service Association of America determined that many people justified spending in other areas by cutting planned basic spending to unrealistically low levels.[5] The result of this kind of planning was eventual financial difficulty when spending on basics had to rise to meet current needs and this new commitment plus existing required payments exceeded the available income.

Once the basics have been provided for, the spending of discretionary income should be related to meeting high-priority spending objectives by immediate and direct commitment of discretionary funds. Setting goals is a worthless exercise unless goals really mean something in terms of a spending commitment. The willingness to fulfill goals, especially long-term goals, is weakened by a natural human tendency toward short-term goal gratification. In short, the desire to reach a lesser objective that can be attained today frequently scuttles a much more important objective that takes longer to reach.

This natural tendency toward instant gratification is aided by the advertising and marketing techniques used to sell products. These techniques frequently encourage "impulse spending." Impulse spending is the process of spending with little or no thought or planning, and marketers frequently take advantage of this natural urge by placing impulse items in areas where customers may be tempted to buy on impulse, e.g., cigarettes and candy around cash registers and checkout areas. Impulse spending is often aided and abetted by the consumer's own poor judgment. Drawing upon the Family Service Association study, "poor judgment" was listed as an important reason why families overspent and thus went into debt.[6]

The solution to this problem lies in controlling the commitment of discretionary dollars. Discretionary income should be directly and immediately committed to fulfilling objectives. Any time lag between the receipt of income and spending on objectives increases the possibility that this income will be spent on something else. To avoid this

---

4 "Family Budgets—Urban Areas—Autumn 1976," U.S. Department of Labor, Bureau of Labor Statistics.

5 *Family Credit Counseling—An Emerging Community Service* (New York: Family Service Association of America, 1967), p. 20.

6 *Family Credit Counseling—An Emerging Community Service*, p. 19.

possibility, the spender should commit the money, perhaps *even before it is received.* For example, a payroll deduction can be used to commit money into a savings account or savings bond, thus avoiding any delay in spending on the most important objectives. By directing the money into a special account (and innumerable separate accounts may be established) the spender is also putting money into an earmarked fund, which should help maintain the commitment to a particular spending goal.

The process of budgeting must seek to control spending not only from current income and savings but from all spending sources, especially those generated through short-term credit. Spending can come from existing savings and income and it can also come from credit that sellers are willing to grant to buyers. With the abundance of credit sources now available to consumers, this problem of controlling the total sources of spending power takes on added meaning. An inability or unwillingness to control debt inevitably leads to financial distress.[7]

It should of course be recognized that at certain stages in the life cycle, spending demands will exceed income. Much of this spending will buy the family's permanent possessions including a house or automobile. These expenditures may require financing through credit and this will result in the need to commit future income to repay borrowed money.

There must, however, come a point where overspending by using credit leads to debt that future income cannot repay. As a general guideline, any time installment and short-term debt payments exceed 20 percent of gross income, a consumer may be heading for trouble. Such a guideline takes into account the fact that expenditures on nondiscretionary items such as food, clothing, and shelter will typically be equal to 80 to 85 percent of total income. While this may vary with individual situations, it would seem that committing future income to paying off debt must be related to the level of spending on basic or essential items in present and future years.

Budgeting plans should be prepared to cope with adverse, normal, and windfall situations. Most of us tend to think of budgeting in terms of one financial plan that is agreeable to all parties. That one plan is usually based upon "normal" or average future events. But what if you are suddenly beset with problems such as unemployment or disability? And on the other hand, what if you receive a windfall such as an unexpected inheritance?

What we are suggesting is that any budget really should consist of

---

[7] *Family Credit Counseling—An Emerging Community Service,* p. 19.

three budgeting levels. The first budget would describe spending under normal circumstances. The second would describe spending under adverse conditions. The final level would describe budgeting given the best possible outcomes in life.

While most of our suggested principles of budgeting are aimed at normal situation budgets, we do feel that considerable attention should be focused on the adverse situation budget. Adverse situations such as unemployment and health problems have been shown to be primary causes of increased debt and eventual financial distress.[8]

One approach to planning for adverse situations is to construct a minimum budget to see what bare-bones expenses would have to be met just to survive. These expenses can then be compared with expected income and revenue from insurances, savings, social programs, and other sources. If there is a gap between expenses and income, this would of course show a need to revise your minimum expenditures or to provide additional sources of income during periods of adversity. An example of this type of planning is shown in Exhibit 2–5.

EXHIBIT 2–5
Minimum budget approach assuming total disability of one spouse

Minimum budget expenditures		*Expected income and revenue sources*		*Gap between minimum expenditures and expected income to be filled by*	
Food	$ ______	Sick Pay	$ ______	Additional insurance	$ ______
Shelter	______	Disability insurance	______	Spouse returning to work	______
Health Care	______	Savings	______	Total	$ ______
Insurance	______	Social Security	______		
Debt repayment	______	Etc.	______		
Etc.	______	Total	$ ______		
Total	$ ______				

The process of planning a budget is wasted unless there is followup and control. Comparing planned to actual spending is a crucial step in making a budget work. The followup on a budget should be designed to measure how well the budget objectives are being met. In most cases it will also be a time to revise and rethink budgeting goals or spending patterns.

A practical approach to checking on the budget is to review monthly cash and credit expenditures. Cash expenditures can usually be made through a checking account, which leaves the cancelled check as an evidence of spending. Credit purchases can be tallied by examining

---

[8] *Family Credit Counseling—An Emerging Community Service,* pp. 18–19.

charge slips or monthly billing statements. The objective in examining these purchases will be to trace total spending to see how your spending conforms to your budget goals.

The tracing of spending may show that what you have set as a goal is really not that important. On the other hand, you may find that your impulse spending or short-term goal achievement is preventing you from reaching more important objectives. In either case, adjustments in your spending plan may be frequent, and the entire budgeting process should be viewed as one that involves regular reassessment.

PRACTICAL APPROACHES TO BUDGETING

For some people, a spending plan may take the form of spending money without much planning. This usually leads to spending as bills arrive or as impulses arise with a subsequent lack of money near the end of a pay period. Others may use a more disciplined budgeting arrangement, in which they informally anticipate future spending and set aside money to pay these amounts. Still others may have an elaborate month-by-month or day-by-day budget that is formally laid out on paper. Each of the above methods may work and have merit for the individuals involved. What follows, however, is an attempt to present a more formal and disciplined budgeting process that can be used in your own financial planning.

The basic ideas behind budgeting are certainly not new. There have been many textbooks, pamphlets, films, and other materials that detail how you should budget your money. For this reason, we have not tried to develop a "new" approach to a topic that has been explored thousands of times. Rather, we will look at budgeting as presented by two reputable sources and then try to see the similarities in these approaches.

American Council of Life Insurance approach to budgeting

The American Council of Life Insurance has for many years promoted the need for sound personal financial planning. The Council has published a number of short pamphlets on the subject including one entitled "Money—A Woman's Guide to Financial Planning," which suggests a five-step approach to budgeting.[9] This approach is outlined in Exhibit 2–6.

---

[9] "Money—A Woman's Guide to Financial Planning" (New York: American Council of Life Insurance, July 1974).

EXHIBIT 2–6
Budget plan recommended by the American Council of Life Insurance

My money plan for ____________________
(year)

STEP 1. My income

Annual take-home pay (gross salary less taxes, group pension, group life insurance and group health insurance contributions and other deductions)	$ ______
Other income (interest, dividends, etc.)	+ ______
Total annual income with which I have to work	$ ______
Weekly or monthly income (annual total divided by 52 or 12)	$ ______

STEP 2. Payments I have to meet (figure first on an annual basis)

Rent or mortgage	$ ______
Other housing expenses (taxes, major repairs, insurance, etc.)	______
Electricity, heat, gas, water, telephone	______
Church and contributions	______
Life insurance	______
Health insurance	______
Other insurance (auto, liability, etc.)	______
Major clothing	______
Additional income taxes (not already withheld)	______
Property and local taxes	______
Loan or installment payments	______
	+ ______
Annual total of payments I have to meet	$ ______
I'll set aside weekly or monthly (total amount divided by 52 or 12)	$ ______

EXHIBIT 2–6 (*continued*)

STEP 3. My emergency fund

My emergency fund goal is	$ ______
I'll add weekly or monthly until I reach this goal	$ ______

STEP 4. Day-to-day expenses
(weekly or monthly estimates)

Food	$ ______
Other clothing	______
Household incidentals (maintenance and minor repairs, laundry, cleaning, etc.)	______
Transportation and work expenses	______
Professional expenses (dues, publications, meetings, etc.)	______
Newspapers, magazines, other club dues, recreation, etc.	______
Regular medical expenses	______
Personal allowances	______
	+ ______
Total day-to-day expenses	$ ______

STEP 5. Summary

Total weekly or monthly income minus	$ ______
Total weekly or monthly outgo (Total set aside for payments I have to meet and for emergency fund plus total day-to-day expenses)	– ______
Balance For regular savings, investments or special goal	$ ______

This five-step approach begins after you have thought about your goals and assessed where you are, financially. Following these preliminaries, step one consists of **figuring your income.** This means that you should figure out how much money you'll make in the next week, month, or year. Income from a job, pension benefits, investment income, and interest on savings represent typical sources of money you will have to manage. This estimate should be as realistic as possible. Overly generous estimates of future income may lead to future financial problems when the anticipated income does not materialize.

Step two of the Council's approach is to **calculate how much you will spend on regular fixed items.** These items, which are sometimes referred to as "set-asides," are usually larger essential expenditures for goods, services, and debt repayment. Examples of set-asides include rent, mortgage payments, installment loan payments, telephone and utility bills, church and other contributions, insurance premiums, and taxes. Because these fixed expenditures tend to be larger monthly and annual payments, you may have to set aside a portion of each paycheck to accumulate enough money to meet these expenditures.

A third step in this approach involves the **creation of an emergency fund**. The purpose of this is to establish a reserve to pay for expenses that crop up unexpectedly and cannot be deferred. A breakdown of the family auto, a major illness, a major expense for a hot water heater, furnace, or appliance—all of these represent events that may create an instant need for cash. The target amount for the emergency fund and the amount of periodic payment to that fund are decisions that the individual consumer must make.

Step four in this budgeting method requires an **allocation of money to be spent on day-to-day expenses.** These day-to-day items represent both essential and nonessential spending on items such as transportation, food, clothing, household expenses, and entertainment. The consumer can by definition control the nonessential spending and can thus determine the final level of spending for such items. The consumer can also control essential spending at least to some degree. That is, while spending on an item such as food is essential, we can decide whether to eat steak or hamburger (that is, spend more or less on food).

Step five involves a **determination of any leftover funds** by totaling your income and then subtracting the money spent on necessities, the emergency fund, and day-to-day items, i.e., in steps two, three and four. The amount in step five represents a balance which you can then commit to special goals. Step five is also the point at which you can reconsider the whole plan and perhaps decide to go back and adjust various spending levels.

U.S. Department of Agriculture approach to budgeting

We can compare the Council's approach to budgeting with one suggested by the United States Department of Agriculture.[10] The USDA method of budgeting consists of the following three steps:

Step One—Estimating funds available for spending. In addition to estimating the money income of each wage earner in the family unit, the USDA suggests that income in kind and money from financial reserves be considered. Income in kind consists of the goods and services you receive as the result of your own labor, as barter or trade with someone else, or other non-cash benefits. Raising your own food and job-related fringe benefits such as health insurance are common examples of income in kind. By totaling income and income in kind, you should get an accurate estimate of your real income and this may help you in budgeting your cash income.

Step Two—Estimating expenditures. The process of estimating future spending begins by examining past expenses. With this background, the consumer can look at regular expenditures for necessities such as food and shelter, irregular expenditures on essentials such as medical checkups and seasonal fuel costs, unexpected large bills caused by emergencies, and all other miscellaneous living expenses such as entertainment and weekly spending allowances. Part of the suggested planning includes the spreading of payments for big expenditures by the wise use of credit.

Another part of the USDA approach suggests consideration of set-asides for future financial goals. "Set-asides," in this scheme of things, means a weekly or monthly amount of savings that is set aside to meet future goals. For example, post-secondary education for children at a technical school or university may represent a long-term goal that you should begin to meet long before the actual expenditures are to be made.

Step Three—Comparing income and expenditures. Up to this point, income and expenditures have not been compared to see if they are in balance. When income exceeds expenditures, the consumer can decide to increase the level of expenses or increase savings and emergency accounts.

The tougher situation occurs when expenditures exceed income. One way to solve this problem is to cut expenses by reducing consumption, eliminating some spending, or spreading out the larger

---

10 Alice Hanson Jones, "Helping Families Manage Their Finances," Agricultural Research Service, U.S. Department of Agriculture, Revised June 1968.

expenses. A second approach may be to increase spendable funds by taking on a second job, having both spouses work, using credit, or drawing on cash reserves. You should remember that the use of credit is simply an advance against future income, and thus credit reduces future spendable income.

As you can see, the three-step approach of the USDA is quite similar to the five-step budgeting process of the American Council of Life Insurance. Their common points include a provision for estimating income, provision for emergencies, estimating expenditures and comparing expenditures to income.

Major problems in budgeting

The practical approaches to budgeting we have just discussed make it look quite easy. But in carrying out any approach to budgeting, you should be aware of some problems you may encounter.

Price recognition. In the first chapter of our book, we discussed a family economic life cycle in which spending priorities undergo changes from one phase of the cycle to another. For example, young married couples devote more money to savings and leisure-time activities. As these changes take place, we may find that we are unfamiliar with the new set of products and their prices. Thus we may not have adequate price recognition skills (the ability to judge the relative cost of an item) and this may cause budgeting problems. For example, a young couple planning marriage may greatly underestimate the cost of housing, food, and utilities because they haven't had much experience in buying these items. This may lead to serious financial problems when their income doesn't cover the anticipated expenses.

To show problems of price recognition on an everyday level, we can turn to the Fernandes study published in *The Progressive Grocer*.[11] This study dealt with the level of price recognition for basic grocery items. Both buyers and nonbuyers of these products were asked to estimate the prices of 44 items that consumers commonly bought.

The results of this study, shown in Exhibit 2–7, indicate that nonbuyers had a poor perception of actual retail prices and on the average estimated the correct price 20 percent of the time. While buyers of the product did better than nonbuyers (buyers estimated the correct price 29 percent of the time on the average), the buyers were correct in their estimates less than one third of the time.

This study would seem to show that consumers often lack a clear

---

[11] "How Customers' Estimates Compare with Actual Prices," *The Progressive Grocer*, November 1974. See also "The Price is Important . . . But Seldom Remembered," *The Progressive Grocer*, January 1977.

EXHIBIT 2–7

Comparison of customers' estimates of prices with actual retail prices on selected items

Product (ranked in order of buyer's correct estimates)	*Buyer's estimates*			*Nonbuyer's estimates*		
	Correct price (±5%)	*Lower*	*Higher*	*Correct price (±5%)*	*Lower*	*Higher*
Marlboro Cigarettes (Kings, carton)	71%	3%	26%	36%	18%	46%
Land-O-Lakes Butter (1 pound)	54	12	34	41	16	43
Scott Paper Towels (1 roll, 100 sq. ft.)	52	28	20	34	38	19
Fab Detergent (Giant 49 oz.)	50	24	26	21	43	45
Private Label Coffee (1 lb.)	47	35	18	20	31	49
Private Label Fruit Cocktail (16 oz.)	46	37	17	25	48	27
Private Label Orange Drink (46 oz.)	42	47	11	26	37	37
Pillsbury Hungry Jack Pancake Mix (32 oz.)	41	17	42	14	30	56
Carnation Evaporated Milk (13 oz.)	38	42	20	23	46	31
Heinz Catsup (14 oz.)	37	34	29	32	20	48
SOS Soap Pads (10 count)	32	21	47	10	16	74
Private Label Canned Milk (13 oz.)	31	50	19	16	56	28
Morton Chocolate Cream Pie	29	31	40	10	5	85
B & M Baked Pea Beans (28 oz. can)	28	29	43	19	46	35
Breck Regular Shampoo (11 oz.)	28	30	42	20	56	24
Kraft Miracle Whip Salad Dressing (quart)	28	57	15	29	52	19
Del Monte Fruit Cocktail (17 oz.)	26	21	53	24	21	55
Coca-Cola (8-pack 12 oz. cans)	26	54	20	13	79	8
Dixie Cup 5 oz. refills (100 count)	26	33	41	27	40	33
Armour Bacon (1 pound sliced)	25	48	27	21	48	31
Ken-L-Ration Dog Food (15.5 oz.)	17	57	26	12	25	63
Private Label Apple Sauce (25 oz.)	16	57	27	14	43	43
Milk Bone Biscuits (26 oz.)	15	43	42	9	24	67
Green Giant Niblets Corn (12 oz.)	15	19	66	17	7	76
Pillsbury Best XXXX Flour (5 lbs.)	14	33	53	28	31	41
Private Label Frozen Orange Juice (6 oz.)	14	16	70	9	26	65
Kellogg's Corn Flakes (12 oz.)	12	6	82	7	2	91
Crest Toothpaste (3 oz.)	10	43	47	11	31	58
Maxwell House Instant Coffee (6 oz.)	9	66	25	6	67	27
Saran Wrap (100 sq. ft.)	8	43	49	21	49	30
Average of all items included in the study	**29**	**38**	**33**	**20**	**36**	**44**

Source: "How Customers' Estimates Compare with Actual Prices," *The Progressive Grocer*, November 1974.

perception of prices. Such a lack of recognition at key points in the life cycle may well be the foundation for financial disaster. For example, if young singles marry without sufficient education on the price of items that they will be consuming, budget problems may develop. A change from a life-style where clothes, cars, and entertainment items are dominant to one where food, housing, and insurance are dominant requires some adjustment.

One suggestion we would offer to all consumers is that price recognition abilities can be improved by comparison shopping and by less impulsive buying. Time to think over and evaluate prices will lead to more careful decisions and a better recognition of prices.

Changes in income. A second major problem with which most consumers must deal involves planning for changes in income. Changes in income may be associated with transitions in the life cycle. When an individual retires from the work force, there is a change in the source and amount of income. Usually, the individual must be prepared to get along on less income. Another change that frequently occurs arises when a young married couple loses the wife's income during the child-bearing years. At this point, the loss in income must somehow be made up by changes in spending or a drawdown of family reserves. Decreases in the income level may result from other unexpected events such as illness, disability, layoff, or accident.

Whatever the source of change in income, the consumer must be prepared to deal with such eventualities. One solution may be to build up an emergency fund as suggested in the budgeting approaches we examined earlier in this chapter. A second answer may be to provide some form of insurance against the most severe changes.

Adjusting to traumatic life changes. One of the most traumatic transitions in the life cycle is from married status to that of a widower or widow. The death of a spouse ranks as one of the most severe psychological shocks that a person experiences in a lifetime.

As with most transitions in the life cycle, the death of a spouse can produce difficult budgeting problems. The severity of these problems depends on the age of the surviving spouse, his or her experience in family finances, and the general stage of family development. Probably the most difficult of these special budgeting problems will beset a widow aged 25–40 who has not been directly involved in the family finances and who has responsibility for several young children.

The result of this situation is indeed an unhappy one. The widow is faced with the loss of the breadwinner and thus a likely change in the source of income. New income sources may include Social Security, life insurance death benefits, and family assets. At the same time, the widow faces immediate spending decisions as well as crucial long-term spending plans. All this will likely be faced in a state of shock that may last several months. To compound the problem, the young widow must make spending decisions she has never faced. What then are the solutions to such a problem?

One solution is to avert the situation by making sure that both spouses understand and experience the family finances. For many couples, this may mean a periodic reversal in family management roles. Each spouse should have experience in each area of spending. Thus, perhaps the husband may try to handle food shopping while the wife takes charge of financing, insurance, or budgeting.

For those who face these problems, there are some stopgap solutions. One is to seek expert financial advice. This may be done by contacting a banker or family financial counselor. Another solution may be to join an organization of widows or widowers. One such organization is NAIM, an organization of widows that has nationwide chapters under the sponsorship of the Catholic Family Life Program and is open to persons of all faiths.

As with any special problem area, death of a spouse is best dealt with before it occurs. A good family budgeting plan that spreads experience among both spouses and a proper estate plan are the best tools to deal with the problem before it happens.

SUMMARY

An orderly approach to budgeting should include a look at an individual's income. Income from a job is generally the main source of spendable funds. The level and stability of income is strongly related to the level of an individual's educational attainment. Another factor that is increasingly important to family income has been a trend toward two incomes in family units with both spouses holding jobs.

Once the consumer has an idea of present and potential income, there is a need to establish direction in the budgeting process. A goal-oriented approach to budgeting encourages the needed positive direction within which the budgeting process can proceed.

The idea of budgeting is designed to coordinate resources and spending in light of personal financial goals and priorities. The flexible approach to budgeting emphasizes the fact that personal budgets may differ widely depending upon individual spending priorities. This flexibility should be tempered by the following basic principles:

1. Budgeting involves an active planning process.
2. Realistic spending levels for nondiscretionary or basic expenditures must be set.

3. Discretionary spending objectives are best met with a direct commitment of discretionary funds.
4. Effective budgeting must seek to coordinate all spending resources, especially consumer credit.
5. Budget planning should include plans for a number of possible events or outcomes.
6. Follow-up and control must be part of the budgeting process.

The budgeting process should be thought of as an ongoing process or cycle. Part of that process should include a regular cycle that allows for adjustments in income estimates, spending goals, budget plans, and spending habits of individual consumers.

For those who want more specific budget patterns, the American Council of Life Insurance and the USDA have developed some basic approaches to budgeting. The Council's method uses a five-step approach to budgeting while the USDA technique emphasizes three basic steps.

Finally, all this material on budgeting should be viewed in relation to the several major problems consumers may encounter as they budget. Problems such as recognizing prices, changes in income, and traumatic changes in life situation may add to the complexity of budgeting one's finances.

DISCUSSION QUESTIONS

1. An analysis of spending priorities is very important to the establishment of a good working personal budget. Compare and contrast your own priorities with those in Exhibit 2–4. You may wish to expand this survey of priorities by constructing a different list of spending items and/or expanding your survey of priorities to a large group of people.
2. How can individual spending preferences and priorities come into conflict with nondiscretionary expenditures when budgeting personal income? What evidence is there that this conflict may lead to financial difficulties for consumers?
3. Explain why the budgeting process must help you plan the use of not only current income but also other spending sources such as installment credit and savings.
4. According to the data presented in Exhibit 2–1, what is the value of four or more years of education beyond the 12 years of elementary and high school education? Is there any apparent difference in this value for men versus women? If so, can you explain the difference?
5. Explain the American Council of Life Insurance approach to budgeting. In this approach, how are nondiscretionary (necessity) expenditure amounts determined?

6. Explain the three-step USDA approach to budgeting. What is the meaning of the term "set-asides"? Is there a comparable component to set-asides in the American Council of Life Insurance method of budgeting? Explain.

CASE PROBLEMS

1. Judy and George Sanderson have decided that they need some help in budgeting. Over the last few months, they have had some difficulty meeting their financial obligations. They are particularly distressed because both Judy and George hold fulltime jobs, and with a combined income of $21,000 they expected to be saving some money. In reviewing their expenditures, Judy and George found that certain items just had to be paid. Their utility bills average $95 a month and the family food bill runs $60 a week. The mortgage payment is $300 a month and they must set aside $100 a month for property taxes. Their annual federal income tax bill is $3,200, and they pay $1,300 annually in Social Security taxes. Life, health and property insurance payments amount to $110 per month. The Sandersons make installment payments on an auto and some living room furniture, which total $180 per month. Monthly expenditures on clothing run $80 and personal care items amount to $15 a week. Entertainment and miscellaneous expenditures average $100 a month. Judy and George are trying to save $100 a month toward a vacation home and they are also building an emergency fund at the rate of $50 a month.

   Using either the five-step American Council of Life Insurance approach or the three-step USDA approach, lay out a monthly budget for the Sandersons based upon their current expenditure patterns.

2. Using the figures given in Case Problem 1, compare Judy and George's expenditure patterns with the national average.

   Are there significant differences between the Sandersons' expenditures and the national averages? If so, what might account for these differences?

SELECTED READINGS

"A Five-Year Plan for Managing Your Money," *Changing Times,* The Kiplinger Magazine, October 1973.

"The Executive's Personal Budget," *Business Week* (Personal Business Supplement), February 2, 1974, pp. 67–73.

"A Guide to Budgeting for the Young Couple." Washington, D.C.: U.S. Government Printing Office, Public Documents Department, 1973.

"Reaching Your Financial Goals." Published as part of the *Money Management Library.* Chicago: Household Finance Corporation, 1971.

Consumer protection

3

OBJECTIVES

This chapter discusses consumer fraud and the need for consumer protection in the context of the broader issue of the consumer movement. After thoroughly reading and discussing the chapter you should be able to:

. . . Identify and describe common types of fraudulent schemes that victimize consumers.

. . . Trace the major events in the rise of the consumer movement.

. . . Recognize the role of local, state, and federal consumer protection agencies in protecting and informing consumers.

. . . Describe how to file a consumer complaint effectively.

. . . Discuss the responsibilities of consumers in creating an atmosphere of fairness in the business world.

There is rarely a consumer among us who has not been annoyed or angered about some purchase. The source of this dissatisfaction may lie in the product or service that failed to live up to expectations. Or, it may lie in the failure of a dealer or manufacturer to stand behind a product or service when we have a complaint. Yet another source of complaint may be the fact that we have been swindled out of our money.

Whatever the cause of the complaint, we are often frustrated in trying to get a satisfactory settlement when something goes wrong. In order to avoid such situations, we must learn how to deal with a complaint, or better yet, to avoid the problem in the first place.

CONSUMER FRAUD

In the famous words of P. T. Barnum, "There's a sucker born every minute." It is something less than flattering to think of ourselves as "suckers," yet in the minds of some unscrupulous persons who wish to defraud us this is exactly how we appear. They see us as a source of a fast buck—an easy mark.

Our purpose in this section is not to look at consumers as suckers, but rather to look at some of the fraudulent schemes used on consumers and the reasons for the success of these practices. By using false advertising and other unscrupulous practices, promoters are able to bilk the American consumer out of millions of dollars per year. The best defense against these fraudulent schemes is to be able to recognize them before you have been taken in. There are various types of fraudulent schemes used to separate consumers from their money. While new frauds are constantly being dreamed up, they are usually variations on three basic types of fraud: the something-for-nothing fraud, high-pressure sales fraud, and mail fraud.

SOMETHING-FOR-NOTHING FRAUDS

The basic appeal of the something-for-nothing fraud is that a product or service is offered free or at a very low price relative to its "real" value. It appears to be such a fantastic opportunity for such a ridiculously low price that there is no way to lose. Somehow, though, a way always seems to appear.

A swindler from Miami has provided the secret of success for anyone in the swindling profession. He said, "Find somebody looking for an edge, trying to get something for nothing. Ideally, the mark should be greedy enough to think about larceny but not quite smart enough to steal anything himself."[1] Examples of the something-for-nothing fraud include bait-and-switch, big winner, referral sales, and investment schemes.

Bait-and-switch

The bait-and-switch fraud is exactly what the name implies—bait the consumer with an unbelievable offer and then disparage the offer in favor of a more expensive item. The bait is an item advertised at a very attractive price. The intent is not to sell the advertised item but rather to get the consumer into the store where the seller can make a

[1] Pete Axthelm, "Art of the Swindler," *Newsweek*, June 30, 1975, p. 42.

strong pitch for a more expensive model. The switch can occur in many ways but often involves a demonstration that clearly points out the inferiority of the advertised item. It may be a vacuum cleaner that doesn't pick up dirt, a car that won't start, or meat that is dried out and generally unappetizing in appearance. Other switches may be made under the pretense that all of the advertised items have been sold or have not yet arrived but a more expensive product or model is readily available.

When it is obvious that the shopper is dissatisfied with the advertised item, the salesperson will suggest another product or model in place of the inferior product. Appearances and demonstrations of this model are successful. The consumer is then encouraged to buy the switch item because it's far superior to the advertised model. Not only is the quality higher, but the price is usually much higher—it may even be higher than the price for the same item at a competitor's store down the street.

The consumer should be aware of the warning signs of the bait-and-switch fraud. First, there is usually an ad promising to deliver goods at an unusually low price, an opportunity to get something for next to nothing. Second, in the store demonstration the salesperson emphasizes the low quality of the advertised model relative to other models available. Another warning sign is that the seller indicates that the advertised item is out of stock or has not arrived for the sale and then proceeds to push a "better" model. One method of testing the sincerity of the seller is to ask for a "rain check" that can be redeemed at the special price when the advertised item is in stock. If the salesperson is reluctant to give you a rain check, be careful.

If the merchant fully intends to sell the advertised item, care will be taken so that quantities, appearances, and demonstrations favorably promote the product. Businesses keep their good reputations by having satisfied customers.

The consumer must be wary of the bait-and-switch fraud but shouldn't confuse it with the legitimate practice known in the selling trade as "trading up." Trading up means that the salesperson points out the advantages of a higher priced model without degrading the advertised model. The difference between the two selling methods is that the advertised model is a good value and there is an intent to sell it. The choice of which model best meets your needs is up to you.

The big winner

Another of the something-for-nothing frauds is the free offer to contest winners. These contests are a means by which the seller is able to get the names and addresses of people who are interested in getting something for nothing by signing up for a drawing to be held at some future date. The winner of the drawing gets a "free" product. Usually there are several prizes so that the odds of "winning" are attractive enough to get you to register. When the drawing is completed, everyone is a winner, or so it seems. Other big winner techniques use telephone quizzes, in-person delivery of a coupon for a free gift, or the mailing of coupons for a free gift, with no apparent strings attached.

The fraud in the big winner approach is that the free prize requires the purchase of an accessory essential to the use of the prize. This accessory is usually priced high enough to cover more than the purchase price of the accessory and the "free" prize. A comparison to the cost of a similar item from a reputable dealer usually will show that a better product is available at a lower total cost. The big winner technique is frequently used to sell items such as sound systems, sewing machines, water softeners, cookware, and furniture.

To illustrate the big winner technique, suppose that you are shopping and happen to register in a contest sponsored by Euphoria Music. Within a few days you receive a telephone call from Euphoria indicating that you are the winner of a new tape deck. All you must do is pick it up by closing time today. In a state of euphoria, you rush to the store and approach a salesperson to claim your prize. Of course the salesperson recognizes your name immediately as the grand prize winner. The salesperson shows you around to explain the advantages of a truly good sound system. At the end of the tour you are shown your prize. However, your deck will need special speakers, which only Euphoria manufactures, at a sale price of only $200 per speaker. Because you are the grand prize winner, Euphoria will sell you the pair of speakers plus ten tapes for only $439. If you do not have the cash, easy credit terms are available.

It is now very clear to you that the tape deck is not very useful without the speakers or tapes. And, as the salesperson continues to point out, how could you possibly get a better deal than a "free" tape deck, for only the price of the speakers. But the so-called "free" prize may end up costing you much more than you might have spent at a reputable dealer for a comparable system.

Referral sales schemes

Referral sales are generally standard and legitimate sales techniques in which the salesperson asks each customer for names of other potential customers. Then the salesperson calls on these names and in turn asks for more potential client names.

The referral sales technique can become part of a consumer fraud scheme when it is used to lead customers into believing they can lower the purchase price of an item by giving names of potential customers. The salesperson will promise a cash rebate to you for each referred customer who buys the product. The seller indicates that these rebates will reduce your purchase price even to the extent of totally paying for the item purchased. If no rebates materialize, however, you are stuck with the full price of the product. Such schemes are often used with high-priced items such as encyclopedias, home improvements, or vacuum cleaners with extra special features. A home improvement seller may use a variation of this scheme by offering to make yours the model house that will be used to sell siding to others. Obviously, with all of the potential sales in the area, your siding will cost you very little or nothing at all. Sellers usually indicate, however, that the most you can earn is the cost of your siding. After all, you can't expect more than that, can you?

Such schemes are used by fly-by-night firms that stay in a territory only long enough to get the quick and easy sales and then move on to new ground. They use the referral technique to hide the overpricing of the product they handle. They also fail to mention that a similar referral offer is made to every customer so that in a given area, the chain of referrals can soon exceed the area's population. Finally, they usually fail to provide a satisfactory product or service for customers.

Unbelievable tours

"Super Bowl 'Deal' Real Super Swindle" was a headline on January 19, 1976, the day after the Super Bowl game between the Pittsburgh Steelers and the Dallas Cowboys in Miami. Some Steeler fans had been sold package deals costing $375 to $800 each for transportation, lodging, and a guaranteed ticket to the game. No tickets ever showed up, but some 5,000 Steeler fans watched the game in Miami anyway—on television in their hotel rooms. As one of the fans commented, "It sounded too good to be true at the beginning—a guaranteed ticket to the game. I guess it *was* too good."

Other tours may also provide much less than was originally promised. Instances where tour planes are up to 24 hours late in taking off are not uncommon. This reduces an eight-day tour to a seven-day tour, but rarely reduces the price. Dealing with reputable travel agencies is the best defense against such schemes.

Whenever an opportunity of this type appears to be too good to be true, it probably is.

Investment frauds

A millionaire! It's easy. All you have to do is invest a few dollars and in a short time they will grow into millions. Opportunities to get rich quick are also something-for-nothing frauds. Consumers are attracted by the chance to realize great wealth with what appears to be little chance of loss.

A wide variety of land schemes fall into this category. Many of the schemes involve the sale of land in a vacation or retirement area such as Florida or Arizona. Con artists have frequently used the appeal of Florida's climate to defraud the unwary investor. Investors have purchased land that they have never seen from a salesperson who assured them it was an ideal way to invest their money. Such land, if it exists at all, often turns out to be at the bottom of a lake or in an uninhabitable swamp. In other cases real estate developers have failed to say in their advertising that certain essential utilities and services, such as fire protection and an adequate water supply, were not readily available.

Persons considering the purchase of land should first investigate the reputation of the promoter and whether there are any hidden costs for improvements and services that are not included in the advertised price. Before buying, inspect the lot to determine whether it meets your needs.

Securities offer another opportunity for the con artist to get rich at the expense of the unwary investor. Many schemes have been exposed in the past that verify that the investment opportunity was too good to be true. One of the most infamous swindlers of this type was a Bostonian named Charles Ponzi.

Ponzi became well known in 1920 when he promised $1.40 in 90 days for every $1 invested. This offer attracted capital at a spiraling rate and made him a multimillionaire in a year. Ponzi's scheme consisted of using the new investors' money to repay the old investors. Before his scheme collapsed he had $15 million and control of a Boston bank.

A more recent version of the Ponzi scheme was uncovered in Home-Stake Production Co., a Tulsa-based tax-shelter drilling company. Shares of this company were sold to investors desiring a means to reduce their taxes. Many well-known athletes, politicians, businessmen, actors and actresses, and even attorneys were included in the list of investors. Some of them invested more than $500,000 in the company, which allegedly painted irrigation pipes to look like oil lines and drilled 500-foot oil wells where there was no oil.

Investment frauds are usually very well organized. They promise to provide the something for nothing that the investors are searching for. As with the other schemes of this type, the end result is designed to provide the unwary investor with "nothing for something."

HIGH-PRESSURE SALES FRAUDS

High-pressure salespeople depend upon their ability to dominate and intimidate the consumer. Tactics such as fatigue, fear, or the now-or-never approach are used by these salespeople.

Fatigue

A seller employing this technique depends upon the ability to dominate the situation for such a long period of time that you finally wear down and sign a sales contract just to end the sales pitch. For example, a high-pressure salesperson may call on you to sell you encyclopedias. You really don't want any encyclopedias, but because you are too polite or timid to ask the salesperson to leave, the sales talk continues into the night. After several hours you begin to tire and in a weak moment you sign the sales agreement. This approach may be used to sell pots and pans, cutlery, insurance, mutual fund shares, and a host of other products and services.

Fear

Fear is an effective tactic for selling items about which consumers have little expertise but for which they have a great need. Salespeople employing this technique defraud you by making you believe that something disastrous will happen to you or your family if their product or service is not purchased.

An example of this fraud is the furnace inspection scheme, which begins with an offer for a free inspection of your chimney and furnace. In the course of the inspection, you may be told that the furnace is faulty. At that point the inspector has the furnace parts spread on the floor and informs you that the furnace is in such bad condition that it cannot be put back together safely. The inspector does not want to be responsible for any explosion that could occur if you continue to use this furnace. Through the use of such scare tactics, you may be induced to sign a contract for a new furnace that just happens to be readily available. That "new" furnace may be a rebuilt furnace that is really no better than your current model.

These home improvement and other scare schemes are a constant source of abuse, especially for the senior citizen or the infirm consumer. The initial scare is always followed by an offer to help by selling the product or service that appears to be needed. The scheme is also used to sell services such as chimney repairs or termite control. After all, who wants mortar mice (which do not exist) in the chimney or a brick falling on your head or that of a neighbor or visitor? Or, what if termites are eating your house away with you inside it?

To add insult to injury, many of these schemes use fine print clauses to trap the consumer. When you sign the papers for the work to be done, you may sign a contract for the work and a statement of job completion even when the work has not yet begun. These documents are then usually sold to a third party, such as a bank.

Fortunately, recent changes in the law are making it harder to operate fear frauds. Prior to May, 1976, when a new Federal Trade Commission rule went into effect, you could have been forced to pay for the work even if it were unsatisfactory or not done. Since that date, the holder of the sales contract (the bank or other third party) is also responsible for the quality of the work, and the consumer may be able to recover the purchase price from the holder of the sales contract if the product is unsatisfactory or fraudulently represented.

Now or never

Another fraudulent sales technique is to attempt to close the sale by indicating that the price quoted expires within a very short time. Thus the consumer believes that there will be no other chance to buy at what appears to be a bargain price.

Various reasons are given by the sales representative for the need to complete the sale now. Some will say that they have this special offer that is made only to new customers on the first call. Others may indicate that because a sales contest in which they are competing ends tonight, they are willing to sell at this low price so they can win some prize. Presumably when the contest ends, the price goes up.

One can contrast this technique to the practice of reputable businesses, which are usually willing to sell the item at the price quoted immediately or at some later point in time. There is no attempt made to force a quick decision that may result in a dissatisfied customer.

MAIL FRAUDS

American consumers are swindled out of more than $100 million per year through mail-order frauds. Consumer complaints in this area are increasing and the U.S. Postal Inspection Service, which is officially responsible for prosecuting such frauds, has reported a steady mail-order fraud increase in the 1960s and 1970s.

Exhibit 3–1 shows the number of criminal investigations of mail fraud made by the U.S. Postal Inspection Service during the fiscal year 1976.

EXHIBIT 3–1
Criminal investigations of mail fraud by Postal Inspection Service (fiscal year 1976)

Complaints received	135,717
Investigations completed	5,793
Questionable promotions discontinued	2,786
Convictions obtained	1,458
Fines imposed	$1,588,174
Restitution	$8,530,564

Source: U.S. Postal Service.

Many mail frauds are possible because of the ease of obtaining a mailing list and because of the unwillingness of many consumers to admit that they have been "had." Mailing lists are available for purchase from many companies that are in the business of preparing such lists. In addition, it is possible in many states to purchase mailing lists from state government agencies such as the department of motor vehicle registration.

Some common mail frauds include work-at-home schemes, chain letters, sales of franchises, and failure to furnish promised merchandise.

Failure to furnish promised merchandise

The most common mail order fraud is failure to furnish merchandise. Very often the promoters are small operators with very little capital and they must wait until orders and money are received so that they can buy the merchandise advertised. Even in cases where there is an intent to deliver, delivery time may be unreasonably delayed. Or, in some cases, the shipment to consumers is not made until authorities begin to investigate.

Fraudulent promoters know that if the price charged for an undelivered product is under $5, many consumers will not bother to file an official complaint. Thus the promoters are able to continue bilking consumers until there are enough complaints filed with authorities to enable them to investigate.

A Federal Trade Commission rule states that you have a right to know when you can expect your merchandise to be shipped. If an advertisement says that the manufacturer will rush the product to you in less than a week, the manufacturer must comply. If there is no shipping period stated by the seller, you have a right to have the merchandise shipped to you within 30 days. When the merchandise is not shipped as promised, you have the right to cancel your order and to receive a refund of the full amount you paid. The seller must mail your refund within seven business days after you cancel your purchase.

Sales of franchises

A franchise is simply the right to handle a brand-name product or service. Generally a franchise holder is given the right to act as an exclusive dealer for the product or service in a given geographic area. The dealer has to pay the franchise-issuing company for this privilege. Payment may be a lump sum, a percentage of sales, or it may be tied into a promise to purchase all needed supplies from the issuer of the franchise. Franchise holders expect a good profit in return for the purchase of the franchise, and many franchise arrangements have turned into very profitable businesses. Some notably successful franchises in recent years include McDonald's and Kentucky Fried Chicken.

Because of the popularity of franchises, swindlers and con artists have been attracted to this concept. Their fraudulent schemes include selling franchises for products with little or no chance of success. The best defense against these frauds is to investigate thoroughly any franchise offer and to seek legal advice. Contact the Better Business Bureau in your area and in the franchiser's home city for information on the reliability of the franchiser. Should you decide to go into a franchise, have an attorney who specializes in handling franchises inspect the contract before you sign.

Chain letters

At one time or another, nearly everyone has received a chain letter from a "friend." In most cases these friendly greetings are actually illegal under federal law: any scheme involving payment of something of value for a chance of winning a prize is regarded as a lottery and is illegal under the federal lottery statute.

Chain letters are fraudulent, in addition to being illegal, in that they promise geometric rewards if the chain is not broken. To illustrate, suppose you receive a chain letter asking you to send a money order for $2 to the person whose name appears on the top of the list. Then you are asked to cross off the top name, add your name at the bottom of the list, and send a copy of the letter to five friends. If everyone keeps the chain going and there are five names on the list, when your name reaches the top you should receive $6,250 from 3,125 people. If there are ten names on the list when your name reaches the top, you should receive $19,531,250. In addition to the tremendous banking problem you may have, the mathematical problem becomes apparent: within a short time this geometric progression exceeds the population of the United States.

A recent chain letter scheme called the "Spirit of '76 Invest in America Plan" required people to send two U.S. savings bonds costing $18.75 each to people higher up on the list. People were dazzled with the possibility of a $38,400 quick return on a $37.50 investment. Participants in the chain became very angry when the attorney general of Maryland denounced the scheme on a radio talk show, because they felt he could cause the chain to be broken.[2]

Chain letters always collapse before they reach their full potential, and the only people who benefit from them are those who start the chain. Chain letters, like many other frauds, are a sure trap for those who want "something for nothing."

Work-at-home schemes

The work-at-home scheme is often promoted through a direct mailing. In return for some nominal amount, $1 or so, promoters offer to supply information on how you can earn money by working at home. Often when this information arrives, it contains little except general statements about the plan with an offer to provide the training, equipment, or details for the project, all for an additional fee of $5–$20 or more.

Many of these schemes include promises to purchase any salable items produced by the home worker in excess of those that can be sold locally. However, the definition of what constitutes salable goods may change between the time the original offer is made and the time workers actually have something to sell. Promoters may find many excuses not to purchase any of the goods produced by the home worker.

A middle-aged couple in Illinois who wished to get into the Bicentennial spirit paid $2,495 for equipment needed to produce red, white, and blue Bicentennial mementoes in their home. What began as a dream ended as a nightmare when the promoter delayed delivery of

---

[2] *The Wall Street Journal,* April 19, 1976, p. 1.

the plaster needed for the plaques. Then, the market that was promised never developed. And finally, U.S. officials claimed that the plaque's design violated the copyright on the Bicentennial Emblem. The attorney general estimated that in Illinois alone 80 persons lost $250,000 in this work-at-home scheme.[3]

As with other frauds, the appeal of these schemes is the dream that you may get rich quick or get something for nothing. Only the promoters benefit from the scheme, however. They may receive hundreds of thousands of $1 bills for the initial information.

Any work-at-home scheme should be viewed with suspicion. This is especially true if it promises large returns or requires the purchase of anything from the promoter in order to operate the work-at-home business.

CONSUMERISM: THE CONSUMER RESPONDS

What we have discussed so far presents a bleak picture to most consumers. The marketplace seems to be full of unscrupulous individuals who are ready to take advantage of the unwary.

Further deepening the gloom of this picture is the increased complexity of being a consumer. Rapidly advancing technology has created a great increase in the flow of new or "improved" products into the marketplace. This has made it all but impossible for the consumer to keep fully informed. For example, how can consumers differentiate between the performance of upright and canister vacuum cleaners, the various qualities of the multitudes of fabric blends, the braking systems on automobiles, the performance of side-by-side or top-mounted refrigerator-freezers, etc., etc., etc.? The consumer is faced with a large variety of products, considerable price variation among sellers of a single product, and a multitude of sales promotion offers. In combination, these factors place the consumer at a great disadvantage and make informed consumer choices, or decisions, exceedingly difficult.

In recent decades, consumers have responded to these conditions by becoming more militant. This has given rise to a movement known as consumerism. A broad definition of consumerism is that it represents an organized movement by consumers for the purpose of protecting their rights by acting through government, business, and private organizations.[4] The definition implies that consumers seek to protect themselves by working through existing channels and by seeking new institutions to protect the purchaser's welfare. Consumerism is an

[3] *The Wall Street Journal*, April 19, 1976, p. 1.

[4] C. Glenn Walters, *Consumer Behavior*, 3d ed. (Homewood, Ill.: Richard D. Irwin, Inc., 1978), pp. 427–28.

emphatic rejection of the *caveat emptor* (let the buyer beware) doctrine in favor of a *caveat venditor* (let the seller beware) doctrine, which makes the seller more responsible for a product or service after a sale.

HISTORY OF AMERICAN CONSUMERISM

Consumer movements may seem to be a phenomenon originating in the past decade. In fact the consumer movement has intensified in the last few years, but an examination of the history of consumerism shows that its roots go far back in our history.

Grangers—1880s

The advocacy of consumer rights peaked in three periods prior to the movement started in the 1960s. The first one came after the Civil War. At that time there was a thrust for regulatory action brought about by farmers through the Granger Movement. Grangers wanted regulation of unfair pricing structures used by the railroads. In the landmark Wabash case, the Supreme Court decided that railroads that were involved in interstate commerce could be regulated by the federal government.[5] Discriminatory pricing was declared illegal. This 1886 decision provided impetus for the passage of the Interstate Commerce Act of 1887, which became a precedent for an independent regulatory commission, the Interstate Commerce Commission, which was to look out for the consumer's interest in interstate commerce.

Pure food—1900s

In the early 20th century consumer activism peaked again. This time instead of unfair economic practices, it was against abuses in the wholesomeness of food and the safety of medicine. Farmers were again the major advocates, perhaps for reasons of self-interest as much as consumer needs. By the early 1900s, many people had moved to the cities from the farm, and they soon became dependent on farmers to provide their food needs. Farmers sought greater regulation to protect their business interests by prohibiting the sale of imitation or unwholesome food.

A crusader of the period was a doctor named Harvey W. Wiley. Dr. Wiley was the Chief Chemist of the United States Department of Ag-

---

[5] *Wabash, St. Louis, and Pacific Railway Co.* v. *Illinois,* 188 U.S. 557 (1886).

riculture. His findings, that five percent of the food sold was adulterated, were badly misquoted when published. Published reports indicated that Dr. Wiley found 90 percent of the food sold was adulterated. Needless to say, this caused a real stir among consumers. Many consumer advocacy groups were formed and they pushed for a pure food and drug act.

The pressure for this regulation was increased by the publication of Upton Sinclair's book, *The Jungle.* This book exposed the filth in the meat-packing industry and shocked the whole country, including President Theodore Roosevelt. President Roosevelt sent investigators to corroborate the conditions described in the book. Validation of the facts exposed by Sinclair resulted in the passage of both the Pure Food and Drug Act of 1906 and the Meat Inspection Act. It took the combined efforts of an active consumer movement and muckraking journalists during an era of progressivism to bring all of this about.

Food and drugs—1930s

The next peak in the consumer movement occurred during the troubled 1930s. A great Depression and the New Deal brought about consumer activism with the rise of an advocate named Rexford G. Tugwell. Tugwell was an assistant secretary of agriculture and a member of President Franklin D. Roosevelt's "Brain Trust."

Tugwell investigated and attempted to revise the existing food and drug laws, especially the labeling of toxic dangers of drug medication and cosmetics. The result was the passage of the 1938 federal Food, Drug and Cosmetics Act.

Consumer activity subsided when the United States became involved in World War II and people became concerned in the war effort. The rationing of foodstuffs, restrictions on driving, and disappearance of new appliances from the market were all accepted as a part of the military crusade, and in a Spartan "make-do" atmosphere, the voice of consumerism fell to a whisper.

Consumerism—1960s and 1970s

In the early 1960s a new surge in consumer awareness initiated a consumerism movement that has lasted longer than any of its predecessors. Consumer advocates were voicing growing dissatisfaction with federal regulatory agencies. Agencies had begun their duties with vigor; however, they often were caught up in handling individual cases and lost much of their clout as promoters of the public interest.

Loss of clout was commonly followed by a reduction in enforcement and sometimes a reduction in the funding of the agency. As the existing agencies weakened their enforcement, they often ended up promoting the interests of an industry rather than regulating that industry.

The weakening of these regulatory agencies and the ever-increasing complexity of the marketplace led to a number of consumer problems. One problem that was highly visible and caused a great deal of interest was product safety. Unsafe automobiles, highly flammable children's nightwear, and toys with sharp fasteners were examples of products that consumer advocates sought to remove or improve. The issue of product safety became an important catalyst to a broader based consumer movement.

Consumer Bill of Rights

John F. Kennedy was the first president to take a stand on consumer issues when he delivered the 1962 Consumer Message to Congress. In that message he proclaimed four basic rights of consumers:

1. *The right to safety.* Consumers have a right to be protected against the marketing of goods which are hazardous to health or life.
2. *The right to be informed.* President Kennedy declared it is the right of the consumer "to be protected against fraudulent, deceitful, or grossly misleading information, advertising, labeling, or other practices, and to be given the facts needed to make an informed choice."
3. *The right to choose.* Consumers have a right to be assured that wherever possible they should have access to a variety of products and services at competitive prices.
4. *The right to be heard.* It is the right of consumers to be assured that their voice is heard when government policy decisions are made.

In addition to the stimulus provided by the Consumer Bill of Rights and the general dissatisfaction with regulating agencies, it is thought that the consumer movement gained impetus for two other reasons. First, it was good politics. It coincided with a politician's "career maintenance" by attracting a great deal of publicity. Second, investigative reporting by the news media focused attention on many vital consumer issues.

By the late 1960s consumerism was a popular cause with officials of the government, better business bureaus, performers, academicians, and even some businesses. The usually fragmented movement began to show signs of organization. By 1969, about two thirds of the states had consumer leagues or similar organizations.[6]

Personalities associated with the consumer movement during this time included Ralph Nader, Vance Packard, Rachel Carson, and John Kenneth Galbraith. Consumer concern about such issues as the quality of life, the exploitation of limited resources, social injustice, and costs of the Vietnam War led these people to publish books exposing the violation of the presumed rights of the consumer.[7] A communication system far superior to that of past consumer movement periods enabled consumer experts to add impetus to the consumer movement by informing millions of consumers.

CONSUMER PROTECTION AGENCIES

Consumer advocacy has resulted in the organization of agencies to help the consumer pursue complaints about products or services. Agencies presently exist at the local, state, and federal levels. We emphasize that consumers can usually resolve problems by face-to-face contact with the seller. Personal contact with reputable business people will usually lead to an equitable settlement of legitimate consumer grievances.

When this first level of recourse fails, consumers should turn to local and state consumer organizations for assistance in solving problems. Local and state agencies are generally convenient to contact (there is often less "red tape" than in dealing with federal agencies) and are funded by tax dollars so you bear no direct cash costs.

Local and state consumer protection agencies

All fifty states now have a bureau of consumer protection or a similar agency. These agencies are commonly found in the state justice department, attorney general's office, or in the state department of agriculture. The powers of these organizations vary greatly from state to state, but in general such agencies have an overall charge to protect consumer interests.

---

[6] Robert O. Herrmann, *The Consumer Movement in Historical Perspective.* (University Park, Pa.: Department of Agricultural Economics and Rural Sociology, 1970), pp. 2–31.

[7] Ralph Nader, *Unsafe at any Speed* (New York: Grossman, 1965); Vance Packard, *The Hidden Persuaders* (New York: D. McKay Co., 1957); Rachel Carson, *Silent Spring* (Boston: Houghton Mifflin, 1962); John Kenneth Galbraith, *The Affluent Society,* 2d ed. (Boston: Houghton Mifflin, 1969).

Assisting these overall consumer agencies are a host of other state commissions and departments designed to look out for the consumer's interest. For example, **state insurance commissions** were formed years ago by states to regulate the operations of insurance companies. These state commissions regulate the rates charged for many types of insurance coverage, periodically audit insurance companies to assure financial soundness, and handle complaints and inquiries by consumers concerning all kinds of insurances.

Each of the fifty states has a **public service commission** that regulates the rates and operations of the electric, gas, water, and telephone companies. This agency also handles complaints and inquiries by consumers regarding adequacy of these services and the rates charged.

Another powerful state agency is the **banking commission.** This commission regulates the various financial institutions including the state commercial banks, savings and loan associations, finance companies, and credit unions. Some states have a separate commission for each of the financial institutions.

Most states regulate professionals such as accountants, attorneys, brokers, pharmacists, and morticians by creating **licensing boards or bureaus.** Consumer problems with a member of a licensed profession can usually be solved rapidly with the aid of the appropriate agency.

Other state regulators include **real estate boards,** which handle consumer problems with real estate transactions; **securities commissions,** which deal with consumer complaints associated with the sale of securities and investments; and **state departments of agriculture,** which are responsible for the regulation of weights and measures, the wholesomeness of food, and the processing of meats and dairy products.

On the local level, many counties and municipalities have created organizations that represent the consumer's interest. **Public health agencies** generally regulate the sanitation of businesses that serve the public, especially in the areas of health care and food preparation. The **county district attorney** handles consumer complaints where criminal activities such as consumer frauds are involved. These and a variety of other local governmental organizations may be of assistance to the consumer in resolving complaints.

Local and state private agencies

One of the best known of the local private agencies involved in protecting consumers from unfair business practices is the **Better Business Bureau (BBB).** The Advertising Men's League of New York organized the National Better Business Bureau in 1911 to fight dishonesty in the advertising of products. Within a year, similar groups were formed in most major cities. In 1914, the group in Minneapolis hired a full-time secretary for their organization. Minneapolis is thus considered to be the birthplace of the local Better Business Bureau, although the agency name was not coined until 1916.[8] The Better Business Bureaus of today have multiple aims:

To protect the buying power of the consumer;
To encourage honesty in business;
To inform the public on how to do business so the consumer can buy intelligently and gain maximum satisfaction from his purchases.[9]

Better Business Bureaus are organized and supported by local businesses. As a result, they can afford to antagonize neither the supporting businesses nor the consumers they serve. Because the BBB has no policing authority, it must depend upon voluntary compliance on the part of the business community.

Chamber of Commerce. Even though the BBB is the oldest of the private agencies, it is not available in all cities. In the absence of a BBB, consumers may go to the local chamber of commerce. Chambers of commerce are much like the BBB in that they are supported by local businesses. They keep records of complaints about businesses and often help consumers solve problems with businesses.

Federal government agencies

On the national level there are over forty agencies or departments that are responsible for protecting consumer interests. These federal agencies seek to protect the consumer by regulating the group or industry over which they have specific authority. This regulatory role makes these agencies quite inaccessible to the ordinary citizen. As a result, Ralph Nader and other consumer advocates have sharply criticized the agencies for working more closely with the regulated industry than with the consumer. Advocates believe that the close contact between the regulator and the regulated may cause the regulator to lose sight of the main reason for its existence—namely, to protect the interests of the consumers, whom they rarely meet.

It is impractical for federal agencies to handle all of the individual complaints of consumers. This is better done at the state and local level. Instead, these federal agencies work with organized groups such as business, labor, and agriculture for the good of all consumers. In addition to the regulatory role, however, several agencies have set up

---

8 *Consumer's Buying Guide* (New York: Rutledge Books, Inc., and The Benjamin Company, Inc., 1969), pp. 10–11.

9 *Consumer's Buying Guide*, pp. 13–14.

departments of consumer affairs, consumer relations, or consumer services to act on individual consumer complaints. The following agencies have major responsibilities on behalf of consumers.

Federal Trade Commission. The Federal Trade Commission (FTC) was created around the turn of the twentieth century to combat problems that had occurred with monopolies and trusts. More recently, it has aided consumers by halting unfair business practices such as false, misleading, or deceptive advertising, labeling, and packaging of nonfood items. The FTC can issue cease-and-desist orders to violators in order to stop undesirable practices, or it may require sellers of deceptively advertised products to make positive public statements regarding product limitations. In addition, it is the FTC that has the major responsibility for the enforcement of the Truth-in-Lending Law, which protects consumers in lending and credit transactions.

Food and Drug Administration. The Food and Drug Administration (FDA) is a part of the Department of Health, Education, and Welfare. The FDA has jurisdiction over the safety and health aspects of products such as food, cosmetics, drugs, and medical devices.

Office of Consumer Affairs. The Office of Consumer Affairs (OCA) was originally established as the President's Committee on Consumer Interests, and it reported directly to the President. The OCA has now been placed within the Department of Health, Education, and Welfare. It serves as a coordinator for the consumer activities of all federal agencies. Although the OCA has no power of redress, if enough letters relating to the same problem are sent to it by consumers, action by some federal agency will usually be initiated.

Consumer Product Safety Commission. The Consumer Product Safety Commission (CPSC) was established by the Consumer Product Safety Act of 1972 with immense powers to regulate the production and sale of potentially hazardous consumer products. It can set safety standards or actually ban the production and sale of products that it deems hazardous. Hazardous products that are already on the market may be seized and removed from the market.

The purposes for creating the CPSC, as stated in the Act, are:

1. To protect the public against unreasonable hazards associated with consumer products;
2. To assist consumers in evaluating the comparative safety of consumer products;
3. To develop uniform safety standards for consumer products and to minimize conflicting state and local regulations; and
4. To promote research and investigation into the causes and prevention of product-related deaths, illnesses, and injuries.

Members of the commission are appointed by the President with confirmation by the Senate for seven-year terms. The independence of these commissioners is strengthened in that they cannot be removed from their positions for any cause other than neglect of duty or malfeasance in office.

Consumers with concerns about the safety of products have access to the commission directly through a WATS telephone line or by writing directly to the commission in Washington, D.C.

Consumer Protection Agency. The Consumer Protection Agency (CPA) was created in 1974 to serve as the advocate of the consumer's interests in issues before federal agencies and courts. In addition, the CPA is to serve as the focal point in government to handle complaints by consumers. These complaints are referred to the proper agencies with the power to take action. Unlike the CPSC, which has sweeping powers, the CPA itself does not have any power to take action against violators. However, the centralization of consumer complaints is intended to make government more responsive to consumer concerns.

National industry information and complaint centers

Assistance with consumer complaints is also provided through the establishment of national industry-backed information and complaint centers. Four Consumer Action Panels (CAPS) are currently operating in the following product areas in cooperation with the Office of Consumer Affairs:

1. **MACAP** (Major Appliances Consumer Action Panel) is sponsored jointly by the Association of Home Appliance Manufacturers, Gas Appliance Manufacturers Association, American Retail Federation, and the National Retail Merchants Association. The panel consists of consumer representatives who are entirely independent of the appliance industry.
2. **CRICAP** (Carpet and Rug Industry Consumer Action Panel) provides educational material to consumers, listens to consumer complaints, and helps to find the best solutions for the consumer.
3. **FICAP** (Furniture Industry Consumer Action Panel) is made up of experts whose aim is to track down causes of complaints about furniture and to investigate ways to prevent recurrence of the defects that brought forth the complaints.
4. **AUTOCAP** (Automobile Consumer Action Panel) is made up of local and state panels organized under the auspices of the National Automobile Dealers Association.

Recover your losses—File a complaint

Careful analysis and selection when buying products or services will decrease the chances of having problems. Problems can arise, however, and you may find yourself trying to recover your loss. A well-developed approach to filing a complaint is most likely to result in a satisfactory solution.

Preparing to file a complaint. When preparing a complaint you will need to have complete details of the purchase, the source of dissatisfaction, and what you consider to be needed to correct the problem. Purchase details such as receipts, service invoices, hang tags, warranties, care labels, etc., are needed to establish the date and source of purchase of the product or service. Carefully think through and describe your problem so that you do a good job of presenting your case. Finally, know whether you want a refund (if the seller gives them) or an exchange for a new product. If it is a service, decide whether you want the work redone or just a refund.

Presenting a complaint. A complaint can best be filed by starting at the local level and moving up to the state and national levels if necessary. If these agencies cannot help, you may have to take legal action. The levels through which a complaint should move are illustrated in Exhibit 3–2.

Local level. First, go back to the person or business that sold you the product or service and explain exactly what is wrong. Chances are very good that the problem will be taken care of right then and there.

If for some reason your contact with the seller does not produce satisfactory results, the next step is to write directly to the manufacturer. Your letter should state concisely all of the facts concerning the complaint. The product involved should be properly identified as to make, model, and serial number, if there is one, and you should enclose copies (not originals) of bills, receipts, letters, and any other material that has a bearing on the purchase and adjustment activity with the dealer. Then describe the problem and state exactly what type of adjustment you want. Be sure to include your name and address; many complaints go unanswered because the persons filing the complaint do not identify themselves.

If this letter fails to produce satisfactory results within two weeks, it is time to step up to the next level by contacting your nearest Better Business Bureau or Chamber of Commerce for help. If a professional service is involved, a contact with the local society, which usually has an ethics committee, can bring fast action.

Many newspapers offer a consumer complaint investigation service in which they publish the results of specific complaints, along with

EXHIBIT 3–2
The route to resolving consumer complaints

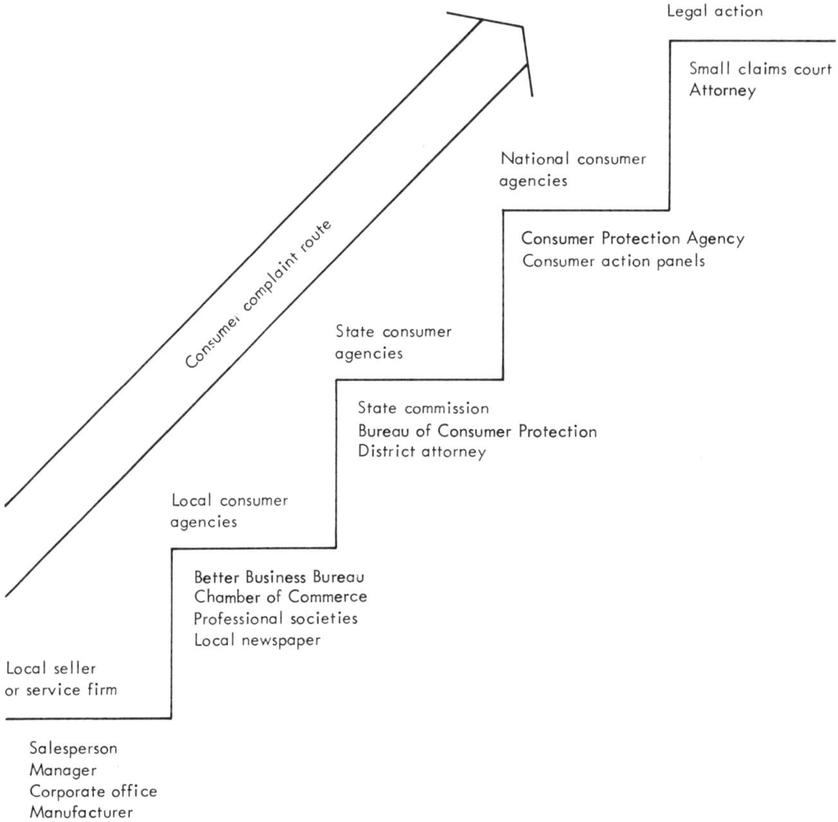

the name of the dealer or product. These are often quite effective in reaching a satisfactory adjustment. Contact major newspapers in your area regarding this service.

State level. If your efforts on the local level do not bring about a satisfactory adjustment, contact your state bureau of consumer protection or the appropriate state commission or bureau. Again, you should make a clear statement of the facts, including the results of your prior contacts at the local level.

National level. The next step is to make contact with national groups. Write to the CAP concerned and relate all of the details. This panel will notify the manufacturer and request that measures be taken to solve the problem. Additional assistance may be obtained by dealing with federal agencies that represent the consumer interest for the product or service involved.

Legal action. As a last resort, it may be necessary to take legal action against the business firm.

Small claims courts. Small claims courts are available in most states for consumers who have not been able otherwise to resolve complaints. These courts have several advantages over the regular courts. First, the costs are usually lower. In most states, you are required to pay a small filing fee, \$4 to \$5, to initiate the suit. Often, because of the informal atmosphere of the court, you can act on your own and do not need to hire an attorney—another cost saving. A second advantage is the prompt settlement. The judge often hears the case within a few days or weeks, thereby giving you prompt satisfaction rather than the one- to five-year wait involved in cases heard in higher courts.

Most small claims courts will not handle cases that involve more than a specified amount, such as \$500. However, because many consumer complaints involve amounts less than this maximum, it is not a serious disadvantage.

Other court action. If your case cannot be heard in small claims court, it is possible to take it to the regular courts. This usually means that you need to get an attorney. This action not only costs you more money, but also costs you more time. There are often long delays.

Any court action should be considered only as a last resort. You must be certain that the claim is worth the time and cost involved in a legal suit.

CONSUMERISM AND CONSUMER BEHAVIOR

Consumer advocacy groups are ever on the lookout for changes that American consumers *ought* to want. Much of the action that has been taken, including legislation at all levels of government, is intended to protect consumers from those things from which they *should* be protected. Yet when we observe the behavior of many consumers, it becomes increasingly clear that they do not seem to want the things or the protection many advocates think that they should want.

Examples abound of the difference between the ways in which consumers actually behave and the way in which advocates feel they should behave. One of these examples can be found in the strong consumer advocate demand for control of environmental quality. Consumer advocates have maintained consistent pressure for products that do not add to the pollution of the environment. Because the automobile is a major contributor to air pollution, federal legislation was passed imposing standards for automobile emissions. As a result low-lead and unleaded gasolines were developed; these are believed to reduce air pollution. Initial sales of these gasolines, however, were very low. Even though consumers *should* want to use them exclusively, they do not use them.

Several reasons may account for the failure of consumers to behave as the advocates think they should when buying gasoline. First, purchasing gasoline may be a habitual decision, and we as consumers simply continue to purchase the same gasoline as always. Second, we may feel that the use of leaded gasoline in our own auto is not serious enough to result in a pollution problem. A third possible reason for shunning the low-lead or unleaded gasoline is that it costs us more than does leaded gasoline. Even though we are concerned about the quality of the environment, we are not so concerned that we will pay a higher price for gasoline.

Another example of consumers' failing to behave as advocates think they should is the unsuccessful "Diamond Lane" highway experiment conducted in the Los Angeles area. A special lane going each direction on a freeway was designated for use only by buses or by autos with three or more passengers to encourage the use of public transportation or car pooling. Use of the lane was so sparse that a court ordered the experiment ended on August 13, 1976, so that all autos could use the "Diamond Lane" and help to relieve traffic congestion.

Issues in consumerism

The consumerism movement has without question improved the consumer's lot. Businesses recognize the need for improvement in consumer products and their distribution to consumers. But in light of the differences between the observed behavior of many consumers and the manner in which advocates feel they should behave, there are some questions about how far the consumerism movement should go in controlling the marketplace.

Control of consumer choice. Some aspects of the consumerism movement have worked toward limiting the variety of products firms can offer for sale. Such limiting is rationalized by saying that businesses have excessive power over consumers by creating imagined needs for new products. Therefore, some governmental control is necessary to protect the consumer. A basic issue raised is "Who has the right to determine which products are offered to consumers?"

Many advocates appear to assume that consumers must be forced to do the things that are "best" for them. Many would seek to control the number of product models or package sizes in order to protect the consumer interest.

On the other hand, there are those who believe that the control of consumer choice can and should be achieved not by legislation but rather by educating consumers to make better decisions.

Environmental goals. Consumers and their advocates have become greatly concerned with the quality of our environment, and rightly so. However, one task that appears to be Herculean in size is to define acceptable environmental goals. Consumers must balance the levels of pollution they can tolerate against the economic impact of pollution control on their community or on their desire for goods and services.

A recent example of such a decision involved U.S. Steel. In 1972 U.S. Steel decided that it would be more economical to replace two open-hearth furnaces than to equip them with the required pollution controls. The old furnaces were emitting 3,000 tons of pollutants into the air of Jefferson County, Alabama, each year. When the deadline of June 30, 1976, for closing the furnaces was approaching, the new furnaces were not yet ready to begin operation. As a result, U.S. Steel sought to have the Environmental Protection Agency extend the deadline for one year. U.S. Steel mustered the support of those concerned with the jobs that would be lost if the furnaces were closed. Offering support for U.S. Steel were the United Steelworkers Union, two senators, two congressmen, and Alabama's governor. U.S. Steel's bid to continue the operation of these furnaces was not successful. According to U.S. Steel, 300 jobs were eliminated.[10]

Product safety. The demand for safety of life and health is an important aspect of the current consumerism movement. Consumer concern about safety is manifested in complaints, legislation requiring safety standards for product manufacturers, and in suits brought against suppliers of "unsafe" products. Greater safety, however, generally means greater cost for the product. In the case of higher safety standards and accordingly higher costs of automobiles, consumers did not behave as many advocates believed they should have. Safety features such as seat belts were not used, and in some cases warning systems were made inoperable.

The issue is to determine an acceptable level of safety consistent with consumer desires. Are consumers better served by laws requiring high safety standards, thereby increasing the cost and perhaps decreasing the number of consumers who are able to purchase the product?

BUSINESS CONSUMERISM AND CONSUMER CONSUMERISM

The previous sections of this chapter discuss almost exclusively the responsibility of businesses in providing products and services for the

[10] *The Wall Street Journal*, August 9, 1976, p. 1.

consuming public in an atmosphere of fairness. There has been no consideration of the possibility that consumers have responsibilities to businesses to provide a similar atmosphere. We as consumers should not accept the position that because *some* businesses have exploited the consumer, it is now time for the consumer to "rip off" the businesses.

While we must be concerned with the rights of the consumer, we all know of instances where consumers have displayed conduct that could be considered at best unethical. Such actions range from "oversights" to outright thievery, but it is the principle that is important. A discount store in a large eastern U.S. city conducted an experiment in which it purposely overcharged 20 customers 40 cents and undercharged another 20 customers by 40 cents. Eighteen of those overcharged called attention to the matter, but only two of those who were undercharged "noticed."

Retailers who have liberal return policies are often victims of "unfair consumer practices." Consumers will purchase an item at a sale price at one store and try to return it to another store for a refund at their regular price. Then there was the well-dressed woman who drove to a high-priced suburban store in her very expensive automobile and purchased, on credit, a $250 dress. She took the dress to her dressmaker. Several days later she returned to the dressmaker and picked up the original dress and her $50 copy. She took the original back to the store, sales slip in hand, and said she had changed her mind. She "permitted" the store to credit the full purchase price to her account.

An even more obvious abuser is the consumer who buys an expensive dress or suit on Saturday, wears it to an event on Saturday evening, then returns it to the store on Monday for a refund.

The practice of "tag-switching" is considered to be theft in most states, yet many consumers continue the practice. Switching tags makes a $50 sweater into a $15 bargain. Supermarket managers say there is nothing so weird as watching a shopper wearing a mink coat switch the tag from chuck steak to a package of sirloin steak. Or watching a shopper replacing the medium-size eggs in a carton with large-size eggs from another carton to save seven cents.

Hotels and motels have problems maintaining their inventory of towels, sheets, ashtrays, draperies, shower curtains, and even the paintings and TV sets, which are bolted to the wall or floor.

Some hospitals have found that many patients are almost as likely to take home the sheets from their beds as they are to take home their pills.

Airlines are unable to explain why the luggage that they "lose" is always genuine leather and always contains $350 suits from Saks Fifth

Avenue. Passengers rarely lose old, inexpensive luggage containing medium-priced clothing. One major airline estimates that only about one third of the claims for lost baggage are legitimate.

Other consumers "rip off" auto insurance companies by obtaining inflated estimates for the repair of damages from minor accidents. Some drivers will abandon their car that refuses to move under its own power and go home to report to the police that the car has been stolen. After it has been "found," the owner insists that it was in perfect running condition before it was "stolen." Insurance adjusters agree that it is not easy to prove that the owner is dishonest, but many of these "stolen" vehicles have obviously been very poorly maintained.[11]

After reviewing these unethical and illegal consumer practices, you will perhaps agree that if we are to have an atmosphere of fairness in the business world, we as consumers must accept our share of the responsibility. One way to evaluate the ethics of an act would be to ask two simple questions: "Would I do this to a friend?" and "Am I willing to have this done to me?" Legislation can provide a framework within which consumers and businesses can operate, but an atmosphere of fairness can be created only when consumers and business people accept their respective shares of the responsibility.

SUMMARY

The purpose of this chapter is to examine the issue of consumer fraud and the need for consumer protection as part of the organized movement known as consumerism.

An understanding of common consumer frauds will help you to recognize and avoid fraudulent offers. Something-for-nothing frauds include the bait-and-switch, the big winner, referral sales, unbelievable tours, and investment frauds. All offer an apparent road to riches at little or no cost to the consumer. You should recognize that when the opportunity looks too good to be true, it probably is.

A second type of fraud uses high-pressure sales techniques. The high-pressure salesperson attempts to sell a product or service by dominating the consumer through tactics of fatigue, fear, or urgency of decision. You should then recognize that a comparable, or even better quality, product or service is probably available from a reputable dealer at a lower cost.

Mail frauds are a third type of scheme used to bilk the consumer.

---

[11] Barbara Katz, "Reverse Rip-Offs: Consumers Who Cheat Business People," *Media and Consumer*, vol. 2, no. 1, January 1974.

The most common mail frauds involve chain letters, a variety of work-at-home schemes, sales of franchises, and failure to furnish the promised merchandise. Many of these are variations of the something-for-nothing frauds. As with other "opportunities," claims and promises that appear to be unbelievable usually are.

Consumerism is a term commonly used today to refer to the organized movement to protect the rights of consumers. The present movement has lasted longer than any other consumer movement in American history. Present-day consumer advocates act through government, business, and private organizations for things they believe the consumer *should* want. However, consumer actions often indicate that what advocates feel consumers should want and what they actually do want are not always the same.

Issues in the consumerism movement include the control of choices available to consumers, responsibility for environmental quality, and the safety and quality of products available for the consumer.

Consumers recognize rather quickly the responsibilities of the business community in providing an atmosphere of fairness. It is doubtful, however, that such an atmosphere will exist until consumers also recognize their responsibilities to eliminate the "unfair consumer practices" now used by many consumers.

DISCUSSION QUESTIONS

1. Why are the something-for-nothing fraudulent schemes successful?
2. Describe the bait-and-switch fraud. What are the warning signs of the scheme?
3. Explain the "big winner" fraud. Give some examples. How can you avoid being trapped by this scheme?
4. Describe the characteristics and warning signs of sales referral and investment schemes.
5. Explain the tactics used in high-pressure sales frauds. Drawing upon your own experiences, describe actual high-pressure sales.
6. During what periods of American history has consumer advocacy activity peaked? What were the causes and conditions that encouraged consumer movements?
7. What are the major criticisms of federal regulatory agencies as protectors of the consumer's interest?
8. Do consumers always want what consumer advocates feel they should want? Give some examples.
9. Discuss ways in which President Kennedy's consumer bill of rights affected the swing from *caveat emptor* to *caveat venditor*. Is the consumer entitled to these rights? Explain.

CASE PROBLEM

Susan Hartwell purchased a used 1975 Chevrolet Impala from Goodwill Gus's Used Car Company. Susan carefully examined the car prior to purchase and asked whether the car had ever been in an accident. Goodwill Gus assured her that the car was in mint condition and that he would guarantee parts and labor for 30 days or 1,000 miles.

About 40 days after purchasing the car, Susan began to hear strange sounds from the engine and drive-train. Within several days the car quit running and Susan was told at a repair shop that the engine block and transmission were damaged beyond repair. In the opinion of the mechanic, this damage appeared to have been caused by an automobile accident in which the car had suffered extensive damage.

Susan immediately went to see Goodwill Gus. Gus politely told her that he hadn't known of any previous accident. Furthermore he explained that the 30-day guarantee had expired and he could do nothing further to help her.

How should Susan proceed with her complaint?

What consumer organizations could help her at the local, state, and national level?

SELECTED READINGS

Cohen, Dorothy. "Remedies for Consumer Protection: Prevention, Restitution, or Punishment," *Journal of Marketing,* vol. 39, no. 4 (October 1975), pp. 24–31.

Engel, James F.; Kollat, David T.; and Blackwell, Roger D. "Consumerism." Chap. 25, in *Consumer Behavior,* 2d ed. New York: Holt, Rinehart, and Winston, Inc., 1973.

Feldman, Laurence P. *Consumer Protection: Problems and Prospects,* St. Paul, Minnesota: West Publishing Co., 1976.

Rosenbloom, Joseph. *Consumer Complaint Guide, 1976.* New York: Macmillan Information Corp., 1976.

Sanford, David. *Who Put the Con in Consumer?* New York: Liveright, 1972.

Walters, C. Glenn. "The Consumerism Movement." Chapter 21 in *Consumer Behavior: Theory and Practice,* 3d ed. Homewood, Ill.: Richard D. Irwin, Inc., 1978.

The consumer in the marketplace

4

OBJECTIVES

This chapter examines how businesses may use consumer behavior to help market products and how consumers can learn to make better spending decisions by being aware of such techniques. After thoroughly reading and discussing this chapter you should be able to:

. . . Identify and explain the basic models of consumer behavior as portrayed in the rational consumer model, the habitual consumer model, the symbolic consumer model, and the social consumer model.

. . . Explain the typical process of consumer purchasing decisions as illustrated in the composite consumer behavior model.

. . . Identify and explain modern marketing techniques that draw on consumer behavior to influence consumer purchases.

. . . Explain how the consumer can use the knowledge of consumer behavior to improve purchasing decisions.

What do the following things have in common? Faded blue jeans. Digital watches. Tennis rackets. Kentucky Fried Chicken. CB radios. "Jaws." Earth shoes. Miniature calculators. Leisure suits. Vans. Disney World.

As you probably guessed, these things have one important thing in common: they have been commercial successes that were accepted by American consumers. While each item has enjoyed success for varying periods of time, each product or service has appealed to consumers and caused them to spend part of their income.

We could just as easily compile another list of things that consumers rejected. The Edsel, 3-D movies, Salvo detergent, the World Football League, light whiskey, and lettuce-based cigarettes are just a few items that consumers did not buy. You and many other consumers have long forgotten most of these products or never realized they even existed, but it is interesting to speculate as to why these items were not successful. The fact that some products and services are accepted by consumers while others are not raises an interesting question: What determines whether or not the consumer accepts and, more importantly, buys an item?

American businesses have spent hundreds of millions of dollars trying to answer that question. In recent years, their search has focused on the concept of consumer behavior. They have scientifically studied the behavior of consumers to learn why they buy. The results of that research are evident in the advertising, packaging, and other merchandising techniques now being used to persuade consumers to buy particular products. For example, the color and texture of packaging for products is carefully researched: it is no accident that products being sold primarily to women often use red and pink packaging colors. Similarly, many products sold to men are wrapped in shades of blue or green on the theory that these colors appeal primarily to the male consumer.

The use of consumer behavior techniques by businesses is consistent with a contemporary approach known as the "marketing concept." According to this concept, marketers should offer only those goods and services that appeal to *existing* consumer wants and needs. Consumer research is seen by the business as one way of finding and delineating those needs and wants so that the appropriate goods and services are available to consumers.

While this marketing concept is consistent with the business community's goals of serving people and making a profit, is this concept always beneficial to consumers? For example, some critics have suggested that much of the consumer behavior research is used to develop advertising that creates *imagined* wants and needs. Others claim that consumer behavior techniques capitalize on the consumer's fear of rejection by emphasizing common hygiene problems such as bad breath and in turn trying to sell their products as a quick cure to these problems. As we look at the question of consumer behavior and its use in marketing products to consumers, we can see both positive and negative interpretations of this technique. Whatever the final outcome of this debate, it is the consumer who must still function in the marketplace. To the extent that consumer behavior techniques affect the consumer's decisions to purchase goods and services, the study of these techniques and their effect on consumers is an important issue. If by studying consumer behavior, the consumer can understand how it affects his or her buying decisions, then perhaps the consumer can make better decisions in the marketplace.

MODELS OF CONSUMER BEHAVIOR

Much of the research into consumer behavior has been devoted to constructing comprehensive models of consumer behavior. The object of this sort of research is to assemble a theory or theories about how consumers approach the process of buying goods and services. Research has revealed that there are a number of types of behavior that can be used as consumer behavior models. It should, of course, be kept in mind that the summary of these basic models that follows greatly simplifies some very complex theories.

The rational consumer model

One of the first and most basic models of consumer behavior is that of the rational consumer. The rational consumer model stems from the writings of the classical economists Adam Smith[1] and Alfred Marshall.[2] According to Smith and Marshall, the consumer is basically a rational being, whose buying decisions are the result of rational and conscious economic deliberations. The rational consumer seeks to spend income in such a way as to get the most satisfaction for each dollar spent.

The purchase of an automobile provides an interesting example of how the rational consumer might try to get the most from each dollar spent. The rational consumer is likely to be interested in the engineering and durability of an auto. These factors combined with the best price are likely to deliver the most economical transportation for our rational consumer. In the process of buying, the rational consumer will assign little value to color, styling (unless styling might have economic value), or the image (sexy, luxurious, etc.) a particular car might have. The essence of rational consumption is the process of deliberating before purchasing.

The habitual consumer model

A marketing model that involves the deliberative process to a lesser degree is the habitual consumer model. The habitual consumer model is based upon the belief that people are creatures of habit. Once they

---

[1] Adam Smith, *An Inquiry into the Nature and Causes of the Wealth of Nations,* 1776.

[2] Alfred Marshall, *Principles of Economics, 1890* (London: The Macmillan Company, 1927).

purchase a product they like, they will probably purchase that product time and again out of loyalty to the product and/or its brand name.

The habitual model has its roots in the work of the Russian psychologist Ivan Pavlov. Pavlov designed and tested an experiment in which he rang a bell before he fed a dog. The dog became so conditioned to being fed after hearing the bell that he would salivate upon hearing the bell whether or not he was supplied with food. From this experiment, Pavlov concluded that learning was largely a process of association and that conditioned responses were a major component of behavior.

From the standpoint of consumer behavior, the habitual model explains purchasing decisions in terms of brand habits or loyalties. Through promotional efforts, the manufacturer attempts to get customers to try its brand in the hope that the customer will be satisfied, thus developing a positive association between satisfaction and the product or brand name. Because of this positive association, it is much more probable that the consumer will again purchase this brand when the occasion arises.

Some companies seek to generalize this consumer response by placing a common, or "family" brand on all of their products. For instance, when the Chevrolet division of General Motors finally decided to introduce a subcompact to compete with foreign imports and domestic competitors, they chose to call the car Chevette. This name traded on the brand loyalty and positive response that millions of Chevrolet owners had with other Chevrolet models and the name Chevrolet.

Even stronger brand loyalty approaches can be found among food processors. Brand names such as "Libby," "Hunt's" and "Del Monte" are used to market a wide variety of food products. Almost all these food producers emphasize the central brand name rather than developing distinct individual product names. Libby, for example, used a slogan which urged consumers to look for "Libby, Libby, Libby on the Label, Label, Label." The implications of brand loyalty in using this type of slogan are obvious.

The symbolic consumer model

A third view of the consumer can be found within the symbolic consumer model. This model is based upon the theories of Sigmund Freud. Freud believed that the key to human behavior lay in the complex human psyche. The psyche was believed to be composed of the id, a source of strong drives and urges; the ego, a conscious planning center for finding outlets for drives and urges; and the super-ego, which channeled instinctive drives into socially approved outlets. In

Freud's view, the meaning of human behavior was not obvious to the casual observer, and almost all human behavior had far deeper meanings with frequent sexual overtones.

Though Freud's ideas have been substantially refined, criticized, and developed, the idea of the symbolic consumer is still apparent in the marketplace. The symbolic model assumes that consumers are motivated by symbols and attitudes as well as economic factors. The presence of this symbolism can best be seen in the advertising for certain cosmetic products. For example, Noxzema shave creams have used the athlete Joe Namath as well as several lovely young ladies and the theme "Take it off" as an approach to marketing. The use of the dashing athlete with women clustered about him has obvious sexual overtones that may appeal to the symbolic consumer.

Social consumer model

A final model that has symbolic elements is the social consumer model. This model stems from the writings of Thorstein Veblen.[3] Veblen viewed human beings as primarily social animals whose behavior was strongly influenced by cultural background. Veblen viewed consumption as a reaction to peer and social group standards with consumers striving to consume in a manner that would bring them acceptance in higher social groups. Veblen related this concept to the consumption patterns of the leisure class, whose consumption of status symbols and taste for the theater and the arts were viewed as prestige-seeking behavior. One of the more folksy and common applications of the Veblen model is contained in the saying, "Keeping up with the Joneses." The social consumption model is implicit in this saying, and it suggests that consumer buying behavior is heavily influenced by cultural and social surroundings.

Social influences have been found to be a powerful force in consumer behavior. The members of the "country club" set who drive a Mercedes Benz may be seeking peer approval. Similarly, a college professor who buys a compact car is reacting to the same influences, though to a somewhat different reference group. The first instance would be termed conspicuous by Veblen. The second demonstrates that purchase behavior may be influenced by social reference groups without being conspicuous in the Veblenian sense. The college student planning a party for Friday night is heavily influenced by friends' preferences in deciding what brand of beer to have in the keg. While

---

[3] Thorstein Veblen, *The Theory of the Leisure Class* (New York: The Macmillan Co., 1899).

the brand of beer may be highly visible, it would not be an example of what Veblen would call "conspicuous consumption." Nonetheless, conspicuous or not, consumers are influenced by social peer pressures in much of their purchase behavior.

A composite consumer model

The four basic consumer behavior models we've reviewed so far cover a broad spectrum of the research on consumer behavior. There are hundreds of variations of these basic four models, but none of them, any more than the models we've examined, can possibly describe the total behavior of any one consumer. Each model does provide useful insights into consumer behavior that may be combined into the composite model of consumer behavior shown in Exhibit 4–1.

EXHIBIT 4–1
A composite consumer behavior model

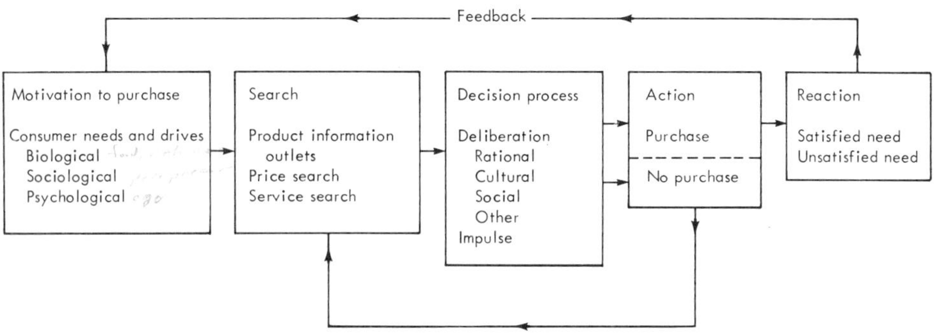

One of the most important elements of all of these behavior models is the feedback mechanism that delivers information upon which buying decisions are based. This feedback comes from our experiences when we go out to make a purchase. In the cases where we make a purchase, the feedback might consist of a subsequent evaluation of the usefulness, durability, and performance of the product. In the case of no purchase, the feedback might contain information that helped to halt the purchase action, such as price constraints. All feedback information, whether positive or negative, is added to the store of information to be used later in a buying decision. In this sense most consumer models are dynamic and active, for there is the constant possibility of change and growth in the information used in decision making.

We might look at the consumer behavior model in Exhibit 4–1 and apply it to the purchase of a new color television set. To begin with, there must be some motivation to purchase; motivational factors might include the fact that you don't have a color TV but would like one or the fact that new color TVs have features such as electronic game attachments, which you feel would add to your entertainment. We should be aware that the motivation to buy might come from a combination of factors, such as an unexpected bonus check, a visit to a shopping center, and the suspicion that your color picture tube is about to go.

Once the motivation is present, the consumer may move to the search stage. In this stage the consumer gathers information about the product and the possible places where the product might be bought. Researching product information might include looking into product testing reports such as *Consumer's Report* or searching through government testing data. Looking for the best place to buy might include a price search at discount, catalog, and conventional retail stores to determine which outlet will offer the best service and the cheapest price. We should recognize that some consumers may not engage in a search stage, but may simply decide to buy something on the spot based upon impulse. Also, some products such as toothpicks or salt may not require a search stage because they are standard low-cost items.

Following the deliberation process, the consumer moves to the action stage. When the consumer decides to buy, the purchase is then evaluated in the reaction stage and important information or feedback is gathered. For example, perhaps the color TV you now own doesn't give you a good, sharp picture and requires frequent repair. On the other hand, your long satisfaction with your present set may make you inclined to buy the same brand of TV when you replace the set.

A second possible stage in the decision process is not to purchase the color TV. This may be caused by price considerations, a lack of time to go shopping, or other factors. In this case the need to have a color TV goes unfilled and the consumer will generally return to the search or decision stage.

This example of the applied consumer model shows the general process of consumer behavior and suggests that each consumer can have unique consumer behavior models. The point of the whole model is to illustrate an organized display of how we as consumers generally operate. From this model we may be able to learn more about ourselves and our behavior in order to improve our purchasing decisions.

CONSUMER BEHAVIOR: A CONSUMER'S TOOL

The idea of studying consumer behavior to become a more knowledgeable consumer has support from a number of points of view. One school of thought is well represented by Vance Packard's book *The Hidden Persuaders.*[4] The central theme of Packard's book is that consumers are manipulated in their economic lives. The opening paragraph of his book illustrates this theme:

> This book is an attempt to explore a strange and rather exotic new area of American life. It is about the way many of us are being influenced and manipulated—far more than we realize—in the patterns of our everyday lives. Large-scale efforts are being made, often with impressive success, to channel our unthinking habits, our purchasing decisions, and our thought processes by the use of insights gleaned from psychiatry and the social sciences. Typically these efforts take place beneath our level of awareness; so that the appeals which move us are often, in a sense, 'hidden.'[5]

Packard's book fueled a tremendous controversy that is still with us today. Essentially his book and others that followed raised moral questions about using "the insights gleaned from psychiatry and the social sciences" to influence the lives of millions of consumers. One example of the moral questions raised was the commercial exploitation of human doubts and miseries to sell some products. In this appeal, sellers play upon the human fear of social rejection. Biologically common human traits such as bad breath and body odor are portrayed as culprits in the social rejection of both the young and old. The seller of course offers a solution to this difficult and embarrassing situation in the form of a socially acceptable, sweet-smelling product. Thus, in recent years, such products as deodorants and mouthwashes have been sold on the human doubt appeal.

Packard's attack on the "hidden persuaders" provides an important reason for consumers to study their own behavior. If we as consumers are being manipulated, then we should certainly be aware of the various appeals that may be directed toward us. And, as Vance Packard suggests, perhaps we will want to develop a "recognition reflex" as a way of combating the manipulation. The idea of a recognition reflex suggests that consumers should become aware of the subtle appeals used by the sellers of goods and services so they can sort out the irrational appeals and make better decisions. This, of course, does not rule

---

[4] Copyright © 1957 by Vance Packard. From the book *The Hidden Persuaders,* published by David McKay Company, Inc. Reprinted by permission of the publisher.

[5] *The Hidden Persuaders,* p. 3.

out the possibility that we will recognize when our irrational impulses are being played upon, yet choose to follow irrational impulses anyway. In this case, as—we hope—with all buying decisions, behavior becomes an act of informed will in which consumers are aware of all the facts and are free to act as they please.

Quite a different reason for a better understanding of consumer behavior is advanced by George Katona in his book *The Powerful Consumer.*[6] Katona contends that consumers should understand how their behavior affects the stability of the economy:

> Instead of arguing that there is too much manipulation of consumers, a good case might be made for the thesis that they are not manipulated enough in the sense of not being helped to acquire sufficient information and knowledge. No doubt progress has been made in the fight against the instability of our economy, but undoubtedly again much further progress is needed if we are to accelerate improvement in the standard of living of the masses and avoid occasional substantial losses in production as well as human suffering through widespread unemployment. We have pointed to certain tendencies in consumer behavior which counteract instability in the economy. To attempt to influence consumers so that they should better understand their function and make better use of their power is a task for leaders of public opinion.[7]

Katona advances the position that more knowledge about consumer behavior in the hands of consumers will lead to more responsible buying decisions. This argument suggests that knowing about consumer behavior is in the best self-interest of the consumer who is, after all, a member of the economic system and thus has a stake in its stability.

THE SUPERMARKET: A CASE STUDY IN CONSUMER BEHAVIOR

One of the best ways of studying consumer behavior is to look at that behavior from the standpoint of the seller of products and services. By examining the marketing technique of the seller, we are able to gain insight into how those techniques capitalize on the consumer's behavior.

An interesting example of the use of consumer behavior marketing techniques can be found in the modern food supermarket. The supermarket is a seller with whom the consumer has frequent contact. A study of supermarket selling strategy takes the form of store layout, product display techniques, and pricing policies.

---

[6] George Katona, *The Powerful Consumer* (New York: McGraw-Hill, 1960).

[7] *The Powerful Consumer,* p. 245.

Overall supermarket layout

An ideal layout and display plan for a supermarket is one that successfully combines the shopping-selling points of view of both the consumer and the retailer. The consumer looks for a store in which food shopping may be done with the least effort and confusion. At the same time, food retailers strive for maximum sales by exposing the greatest number of shoppers to the greatest number of products. Store layout has become a much-studied subject in an effort to provide a layout from which both the consumer and the retailer can benefit.

Supermarkets are designed to create a favorable first impression on the shopper and to make shopping as simple as possible. An atmosphere is created that makes the shopper more receptive to the various selling appeals used throughout the store.

The study of consumer behavior indicates that store sales can be increased by increasing the amount of time that shoppers spend in the store and also by increasing the number of items to which they are exposed. As a result, the overall layout has been designed to guide shoppers past as many items as possible at a leisurely pace.

The typical supermarket layout, as shown in Exhibit 4–2, greets the consumer with either the bakery goods or the produce, depending upon which entrance they use. In some stores a delicatessen may be substituted for or included in the first view facing the shopper. Both of these areas will encourage the shopper to browse and examine the items on display.

A leisurely pace through the store enables shoppers to observe and shop more of the items displayed. Frequently used means of slowing the consumer's pace include free coffee, music, and wider aisles so that the shopper does not feel crowded. Wider aisles are especially used in the high-profit areas such as the meats, vegetables, and dairy products.

Supermarket shoppers have effectively shown their dislike for complicated store layouts—they just don't shop them. A study conducted by *Progressive Grocer* indicates the behavior of shoppers when faced with an alcove as part of the layout. Exhibit 4–3 shows that many shoppers do not even go into the alcove area. In actual traffic figures, the ice cream freezer located in front of the alcove is passed by 75 out of every 100 shoppers (position "A") while only 27 out of every 100 shoppers are attracted into the alcove (position "B"). Such shopper behavior is undesirable for the retailer because the products displayed in the alcove are not heavily exposed to traffic. Therefore, sales may suffer.

EXHIBIT 4–2
Typical supermarket layout

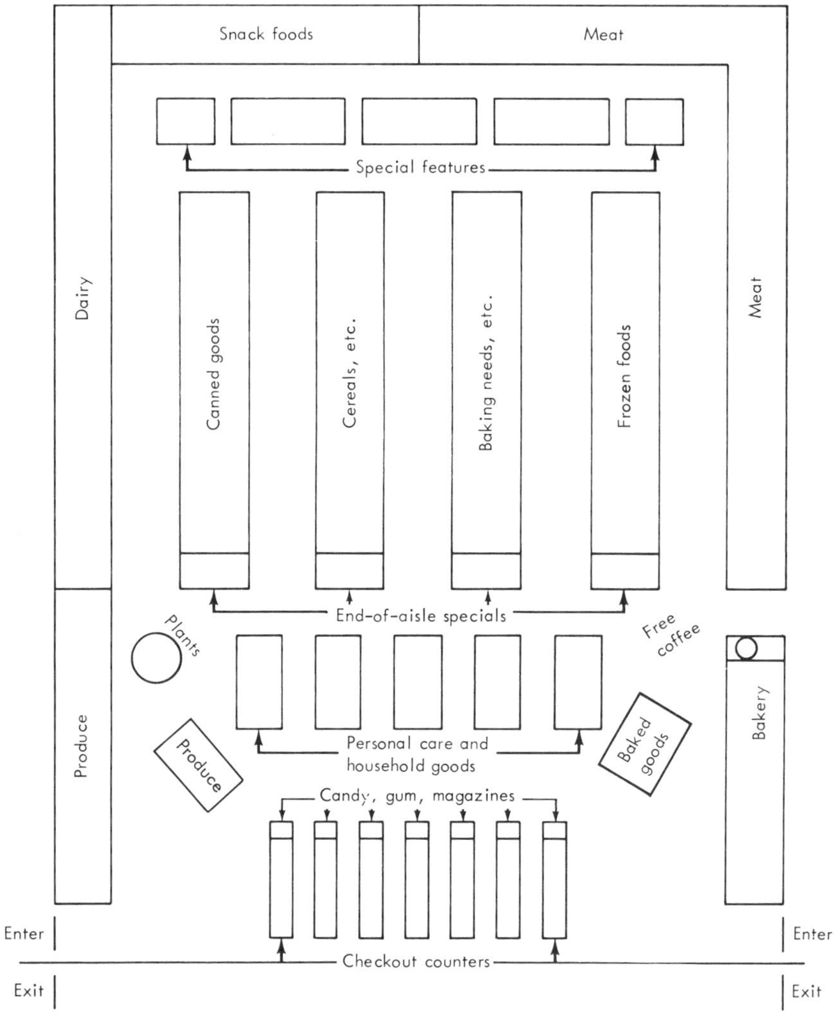

Shopper traffic in a supermarket is heaviest around the perimeter of the store. This is partially caused by the definition of the direction of traffic flow from the entrance of the store. Usually the flow is directed toward a perimeter aisle from which the shopper can branch out into other aisles.

The perimeters are usually dominated by the most popular items in the supermarket—the produce, dairy products, meat, frozen food, and bakery departments. Consumers are strongly attracted to these

EXHIBIT 4–3
Supermarket layout with alcove

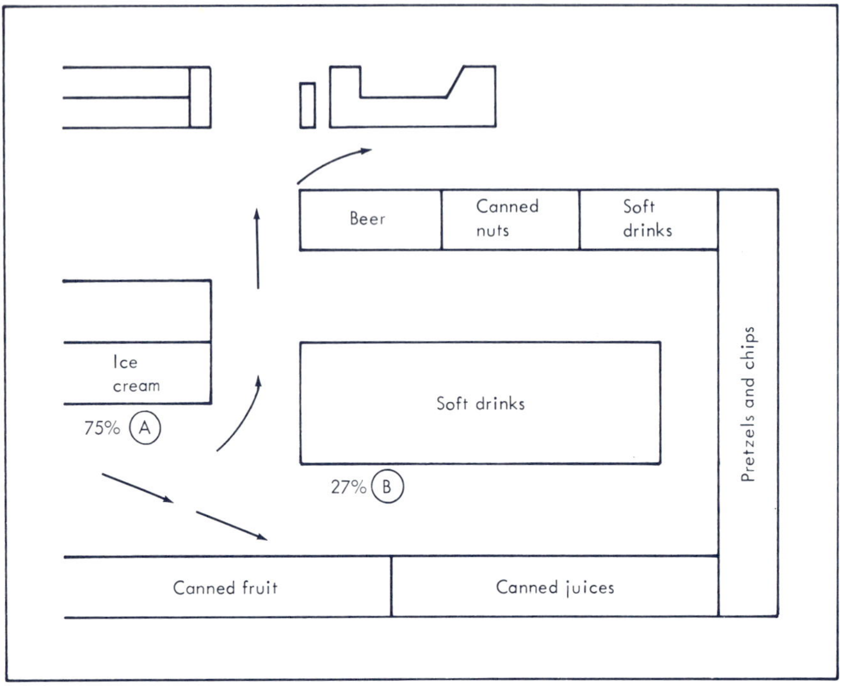

Source: *Consumer Dynamics* (New York: Progressive Grocer, 1971), p. K77.

items and usually pay less attention to items displayed across the aisles. For example, data from *Progressive Grocer's* study (Exhibit 4–4) showed that 75 percent of the customers shopped the dairy products (position "A") but only 49 percent shopped the canned fruit juices (position "B") located approximately eight feet away across the aisle.

Even when the product displayed across the aisle is from the same department, a drop in traffic occurs. Position "C" of the meat display is shopped by 78 percent of the customers, but a refrigerated meat case, position "D" across the aisle, receives the attention of only 32 percent of the shoppers.

Yet another layout technique involves the display of a wide array of lower priced items at the entrances to the supermarket checkout counter. These items are largely personal items such as razor blades, cigarettes, candy, batteries, magazines and other items that may catch the shopper's eye. This technique takes advantage of the checkout line delay to promote casual, nondeliberative impulse spending.

An important goal of supermarket layout is the encouragement of

EXHIBIT 4–4
Cross-aisle shopping behavior—dissimilar products

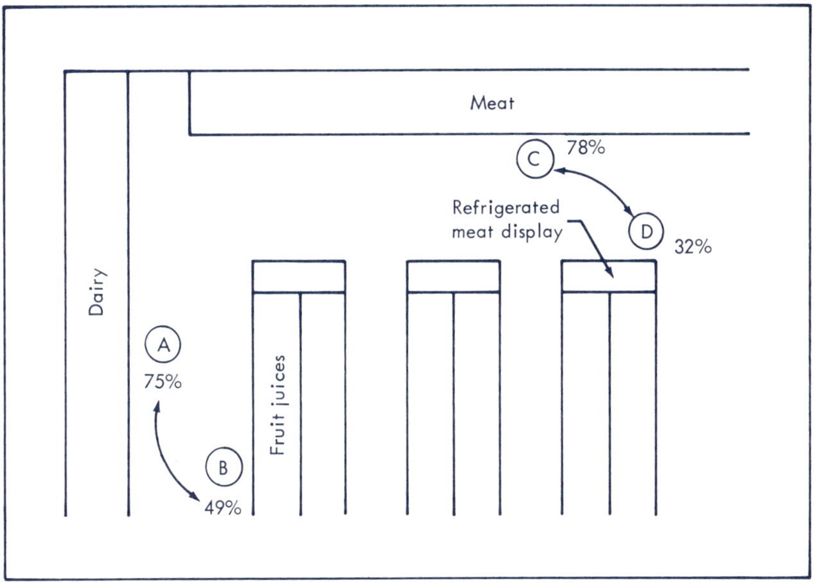

Source: *Consumer Dynamics* (New York: Progressive Grocer, 1971), p. K78.

impulse buying. In a study of the effect of the placement of impulse items, *Progressive Grocer* found that it is to the greatest advantage of the supermarket to place these items in heavy traffic areas. Exhibit 4–5 summarizes the effect of location on sales of candy and health and beauty aids.[8] The placement of the impulse product groups across from each other in a low traffic area, as in store A, was very ineffective. However, placement of these items in heavy traffic areas as in

EXHIBIT 4–5
Influence of location on purchase of impulse items

			Per 100 customers	
Store	*Products*	*Location*	*No. passing*	*No. buying*
A	Health and beauty aids	Midstore across from candy	20	5
B	Health and beauty aids	Perimeter next to dairy department	59	22
A	Candy	Midstore across from health and beauty aids	20	4
B	Candy	Midstore next to coffee and crackers	43	20

Source: *Consumer Dynamics* (New York: Progressive Grocer, 1971), p. K81.

[8] Consumer Dynamics (New York: Progressive Grocer, 1971), pp. K80–81.

store B proved to be much more successful. A larger percentage of the shoppers passed and purchased the items in store B than in store A.

Retailers attempt to capitalize on these observed patterns of consumer behavior with respect to store layout. In most supermarkets, layout is supplemented with devices such as special displays or pricing to gain greater product exposure.

Display of food in the supermarket

Overall layout of the supermarket concentrates on the general arrangement of products in the store, while display of food concentrates on increasing supermarket sales by attractively presenting products. The success of display techniques depends upon two factors. First, supermarkets are self-service stores in which the shopper chooses most goods without the aid of a sales clerk. Overall layout and arrangement must make up for the lack of a sales clerk by encouraging consumers to move through the aisles at a leisurely pace so they are attracted to the various displays. Second, special displays work best when they are used to promote items that the shopper might not ordinarily buy. For example, displays of impulse items or slow-moving frozen food items can greatly increase sales.

The display technique used for the food products depends upon such characteristics as perishability, bulk, packaging, and attractiveness. Special displays usually highlight products through the use of unusual display containers, prime locations, and/or visual aids. These special techniques complement the usual shelving and pricing techniques used throughout the store.

You should be aware that the items in the special displays may or may not be bargains. Special displays do not always mean reduced prices. Many store managers will tell you that simply placing an item in a special display will usually increase the immediate sales of that item, even if the price is increased for the special display.

Special displays are used by supermarkets for many reasons, such as:

1. Decoration. These displays can be used to enhance the appearance of the store.
2. To increase impulse buying.
3. To increase sales of related line products.
4. To clear out obsolete or slow-moving items.
5. To give a "bargain" appearance.[9]

---

[9] Rom J. Markin, *The Supermarket: An Analysis of Growth, Development and Change* (Pullman, Washington: Washington State University Press, 1968), p. 99.

Techniques that illustrate such use of special displays include the end-of-aisle, point-of-purchase, and dump basket displays.

End-of-aisle displays are those placed at the ends of a selling counter. This technique is widely used in a self-service store to expose the consumer to the displayed product for a longer period of time. As the consumer turns to go to another aisle, end-of-aisle displays provide a greater opportunity for impulse buying.

Point-of-purchase display refers to the use of signs, banners, streamers, merchandise displayers, etc. These tools are used to call attention to the product or group of related products. There may be a meat counter display of pork and sauerkraut or an end-of-aisle display featuring noodles with tuna to suggest use in casseroles. Such devices may indeed stimulate a need for the associated product or may jog the shoppers' memory to purchase the displayed items. A study published in the *Progressive Grocer* reported that customers do increase purchases of items displayed as related products.

The use of a *jumbled basket* of goods is another effective display method used by supermarkets. Goods that have been "dumped" into the basket give the impression of bargain items. These goods may or may not represent bargains. They may simply be items that have moved slowly in the past or that are a special purchase by the store.

Effectiveness of special display techniques. A series of tests of the effectiveness of special display techniques was reported in *Progressive Grocer* magazine. The tests involved the pairing of similar supermarkets and comparing results in the store using special display techniques with those in the store that continued displaying products as usual. Some results of these tests can be summarized as follows:

1. Point-of-purchase displays of related items sold as much as 418 percent more when in combination than when the same items were displayed separately elsewhere in the store.
2. Displays featuring interdepartmental tie-ins also increased sales. For example, in stores displaying instant tea and fresh lemons, sales of these products were greater than in stores displaying them separately.
3. Special displays of new health and beauty aid products resulted in sales of from 100 percent to 400 percent more than normal shelf displays.[10]

[10] "How In-Store Merchandising Can Boost Sales," *Progressive Grocer*, October 1971, pp. 94–97; "How the Basics of Special Display Affect Sales and Profits," *Progressive Grocer*, January 1971, pp. 34–45; "How to Make Displays More Sales Productive," *Progressive Grocer*, February 1971, pp. 34–45.

While it is still not determined whether such displays actually increase the amounts of these products consumed or the stocks held by consumers simply increase, there is little question that consumers' shopping behavior patterns are influenced by the displays.

Pricing practices

Supermarket pricing policies are designed to increase the overall profit of the store. This must be done within the competitive limits of the food industry. That is, pricing policies that result in "price wars" are not desirable and therefore, most supermarket managers will adjust pricing policies to stay in line with competition.

Price is an important and effective means of maintaining an image. Consumers look to prices to tell them something about the quality of an item. As such, pricing is used by supermarkets to attract and to sell to consumers.

Retailers have found that pricing a product too low leads to reduced sales. Consumers apparently believe that there is something wrong with the product and refuse to buy it. It appears that consumers have acceptable ranges of prices in their minds and they hesitate to buy if the price of the item is outside this range.

Consumer reaction to pricing policy is also important for new products introduced to the market. In his book *Food Retailing,* L. B. Darrah makes a similar observation for the introduction of new products.

> Normally, manufacturers desire to reduce prices of new products below the relatively fixed prices at which they eventually hope to sell them in an effort to encourage sales and develop customers for the products. However, if an initial price is set at 52¢ and then, after the introductory period, raised to 59¢, a tremendous amount of customer resistance develops to the change, and sales decline sharply. Experience has taught that setting the initial price at 59¢, then encouraging sales by providing customers with coupons good for 7¢, leads to introductory sales without incurring the resistance to the problem of raising prices. Similarly, other firms will maintain a fixed retail price and provide purchasing incentives through special cents-off-the-regular-price deals to customers during the introductory period. This procedure has the same advantages as the coupon arrangement and is less expensive to operate.[11]

Pricing techniques often used by retailers include leader prices, odd pricing, and multiple-unit pricing.

Leader pricing. Leader pricing can be defined as purposely pricing items at levels that will not in themselves contribute the most to the

[11] L. B. Darrah, *Food Marketing,* Revised Printing. (New York: The Ronald Press Company, 1971), pp. 147–148.

store's profits, but by attracting a large number of shoppers to the store overall profits are increased. Many states have Unfair Sales Practices Acts prohibiting the use of loss leaders because it is considered to be an unfair competitive practice. Generally, these acts require some prescribed minimum markup above retailer cost of the merchandise sold.

Consumers who come in for the price leader items are guided through the store past several thousand other items that are offered at normal prices. It is expected that the sales and profits of the nonleader items will increase more than enough to offset the reduced profit from the leader items. The effectiveness of leader pricing requires that the consumer be able to recognize the bargain price. Therefore, the leader items must be goods that consumers buy often. Items frequently used as leaders include meat, poultry, dairy products, coffee, etc. Consumers buy these products regularly and are familiar with their regular prices.

Odd pricing. Odd pricing means that the seller uses odd numbers rather than round numbers. The frequent use of odd pricing would seem to indicate that sellers believe there is some psychological advantage in the practice. Even during periods of increasing costs, supermarkets may hesitate to increase prices immediately to an even cent. They may wait until the price can be raised to the next odd cent before making the change.

The use of odd numbers presents a bargain image for many products, since it implies that prices have been cut to the minimum. Popular odd prices include nines such as 19 cents, 29 cents, 49 cents, and 99 cents. However, ones, threes, and sevens are also popular odd price figures.

Multiple-unit pricing. Multiple-unit pricing refers to the practice of pricing items in quantities of more than one unit. As a result of this pricing technique consumers are tempted to purchase more than one unit because the cost per item at the multiple price is slightly less than the price of a single unit. For example, if canned peas are priced at two for 89 cents, the price per can if bought at the multiple price is 44.5 cents while the single can will cost 45 cents.

Supermarkets attempt to use multiple prices that are easy for the consumer to understand, such as two for 29 cents, three for 89 cents. In order to present the intended bargain image, the total price of the units will usually be less than one dollar. Manufacturers of some products have strongly encouraged retailers to use the multiple pricing technique by packaging items in multiples.

Multiple pricing is most commonly used on heavily purchased items such as canned fruits and vegetables and fresh vegetables. When faced with products that are priced in multiples, you must decide whether the quantity involved is appropriate for your usage within a reasonable time. It is doubtful whether a few cents saved in buying several units of a product is really worthwhile if it takes you several months to use the product. In fact, the savings may be offset by storage costs for the extra items.

Supermarket researchers have found that consumers seem to expect and be willing to buy certain products in multiples, but if other items are priced in multiples, sales may actually decline. An experiment reported by the *Progressive Grocer* indicated that this was the case.[12] A summary of the results of the study, involving a panel of matched supermarkets over a six-month period, are shown in Exhibit 4–6.

EXHIBIT 4–6
Effects of multiple-unit pricing in supermarkets

Item	*Price of item* *Old*	*New*	*Sales volume* *Old*	*New*	*Percentage change*
Switching from single-unit to multiple unit					
Catsup, 14 oz.	24¢ ea.	2 for 47¢	11	15	+36%
Aluminum foil, 25 ft.	25¢ ea.	2 for 49¢	34	47	+38
Macaroni and cheese, 7¼ oz.	15¢ ea.	3 for 44¢	8	14	+75
Mustard, 9 oz.	17¢ ea.	2 for 33¢	34	39	+15
Onion sauce, 6 oz.	27¢ ea.	2 for 53¢	10	11	+10
Switching from multiple-unit to single unit					
Mustard, 9 oz.	2 for 37¢	19¢ ea.	69	50	−28
Macaroni and cheese, 7¼ oz.	2 for 43¢	22¢ ea.	75	54	−28
Catsup, 14 oz.	2 for 49¢	25¢ ea.	28	18	−36
Frozen peas, 10 oz.	2 for 43¢	22¢ ea.	32	29	− 9
Salt, 26 oz.	2 for 25¢	13¢ ea.	32	23	−28
Switching from one multiple to another					
Frozen corn, 10 oz.	2 for 43¢	3 for 65¢	19	15	−21
Dog food, 15½ oz.	2 for 29¢	7 for $1	24	60	+150
Catsup, 14 oz.	2 for 47¢	3 for 72¢	15	11	−27
Macaroni and cheese, 7¼ oz.	2 for 43¢	3 for 64¢	6	7	+17

Source: "How Multiple-Unit Pricing Helps . . . and Hurts," *Progressive Grocer*, June 1971, p. 55.

When the store changed from single-unit to multiple-unit pricing, the quantity of each product sold increased by as much as 75 percent,

[12] "How Multiple-Unit Pricing Helps . . . and Hurts," *Progressive Grocer*, June 1971, pp. 52–58.

while when prices were changed from multiple-unit to single-unit pricing, quantities sold decreased. The results indicate that consumers do respond to multiple pricing for many products.

THE CONSUMER AND CONSUMER BEHAVIOR

The supermarket case study shows an example of the importance of consumer behavior in the marketing of goods and services. Marketers simply try to appeal to consumer traits or impulses in order to sell their products.

From the standpoint of the consumer, a number of things about consumer behavior should be apparent. First, the consumer should realize that every purchase involves some type of decision process. The four basic models reviewed earlier in the chapter show a number of ways the buying decision could come about. It is unlikely that any of us as consumers exactly fits any one model; rather, we tend to blend behaviors, one time buying very deliberately, another time buying on impulse. This is not to say that deliberate behavior is right while non-deliberative behavior is wrong. It simply says that there are a number of approaches and that consumers should recognize all of the aspects of the decision process. Once consumers are aware of this fact, they may wish to evaluate the individual models and decide which basic type of behavior is best.

A second point that should be understood is that many of the marketing techniques we've discussed may not work on all consumers. The marketing research done on Corfam and the Edsel illustrates that the analysis of the consumer is a challenging task that occasionally falls short of its goal. Therefore, much of the criticism leveled at the Madison Avenue approach to advertising should be viewed with the realization that a good deal of advertising strategy is not effective.

SUMMARY

The primary purpose of this chapter has been to explain the importance and usefulness of understanding consumer behavior. The general types of consumer behavior are shown in the four basic consumer models. The rational consumer model stresses deliberation before purchase. The habitual model indicates that purchasing behavior is a process of association and learned responses. The symbolic consumer model contends that the economic activity of consumers has deeper meaning within the context of the human psyche. Finally, the social consumer model points to consumption as a function of social status.

Each type of consumer model serves as a potential target for marketing strategy. Within a typical arena of economic activity such as a supermarket, a number of techniques may be used to stimulate buying. Store layout, product display, and pricing techniques represent some of the appeals to the consumer's purse.

Finally, consumer behavior should be considered in light of its potential value to consumers. Knowledge in this area may improve the consumer's decision processes and may have an immense influence on the consumer and the entire economy.

DISCUSSION QUESTIONS

1. Thorstein Veblen described the "conspicuous consumption" of the leisure class of his day. Explain the concept of conspicuous consumption and describe present-day examples.
2. Explain the role of feedback in the composite consumer model.
3. John Johnson, a rational type consumer, and Sam Swinger, a symbolic type consumer, are contemplating the purchase of new cars. Based on the general behavior patterns associated with the rational and symbolic consumers, describe the factors each of these consumers might consider in this type of purchasing decision.
4. How does supermarket layout encourage impulse buying? From your own shopping experience, do other stores such as discount and drug stores use impulse buying display techniques? Explain.
5. Explain how the multiple-unit pricing of supermarket products is designed to influence shoppers. Again drawing upon your shopping experience, do other types of retailers follow this practice?
6. Explain the concept of a recognition reflex as set forth by Vance Packard. How is the recognition reflex useful in evaluating promotional techniques that involve subtle or hidden appeals that play upon a consumer's behavior?
7. Explain why high-volume products such as dairy and snack foods are generally located near the back of a supermarket.

CASE PROBLEMS

1. While store layout and product packaging are good examples of how marketers take advantage of consumer behavior, the area of advertising is also full of appeals to consumers. Many consumer critics claim that advertising is full of "hidden persuaders" that unnecessarily create needs or images in the minds of consumers and in general promote nondeliberative, unwanted consumption. In short, advertising is frequently viewed as a negative influence on the consumer decision process.

   To examine this issue, locate three ads that feature automobiles, beer, and/or cigarettes. Current news magazines such as *Time, Newsweek,* and

U.S. News are good sources for such ads. When you have collected these ads, carefully analyze them for "hidden persuaders."

Do the ads suggest appeals to any of the four basic consumer models? Do you detect any hidden appeals? In your mind, do these ads promote deliberative and rational purchasing or nondeliberative, image-oriented purchasing?

2. The supermarket example in this chapter illustrates how store layout is designed to take advantage of consumer behavior. The techniques used in the supermarket are also used in other types of retail stores. This is particularly true of discount department stores, which have enjoyed enormous popularity among consumers.

A typical discount store layout is shown below. Examine this layout and compare it to discount stores in which you shop.

On the basis of this layout and your own shopping experience, explain how the discount store layout attempts to capitalize on consumer behavior. In particular, how do discount stores take advantage of traffic flow and impulse shopping habits?

Typical discount store layout

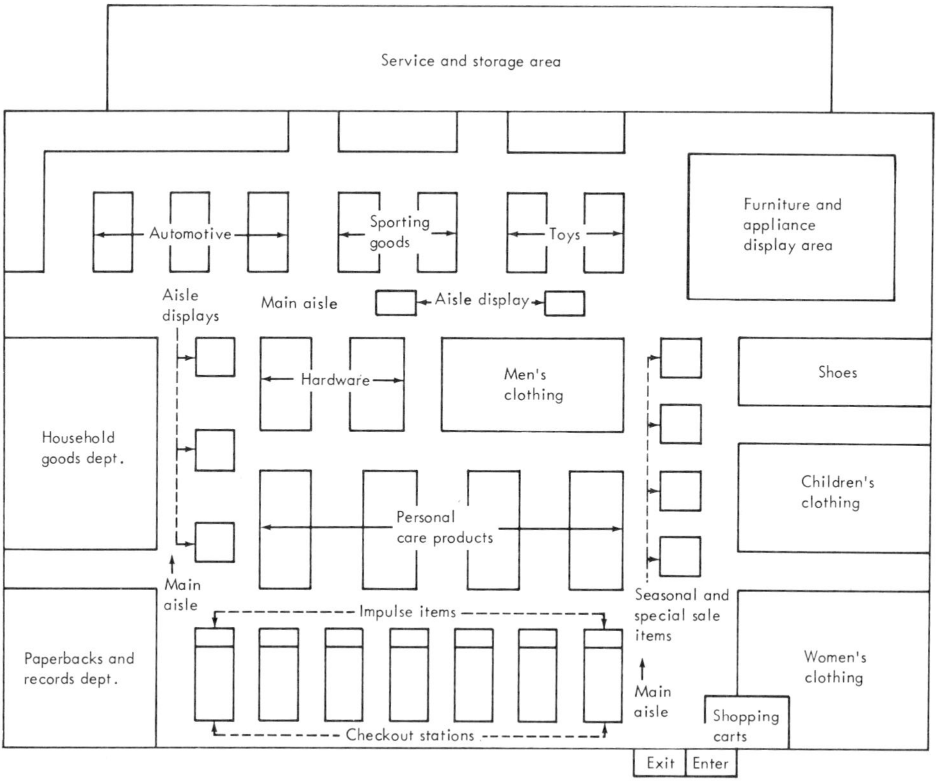

SELECTED READINGS

Howard, John A., and Ostlund, Lyman E., eds. *Buyer Behavior: Theoretical and Empirical Foundations.* New York: Alfred A. Knopf, Inc., 1973.

Kassarjian, Harold H., and Thomas S. Robertson. *Perspectives in Consumer Behavior,* Revised. Glenview, Ill.: Scott Foresman and Company, 1973.

Kerby, Joe Kent. *Consumer Behavior.* New York: Dun-Donnelley Publishing Corp., 1975.

Packard, Vance. *The Hidden Persuaders.* New York: David McKay Co., Inc., 1957.

Walters, C. Glenn. *Consumer Behavior: Theory and Practice,* 3d ed. Homewood, Ill.: Richard D. Irwin, 1978.

section two

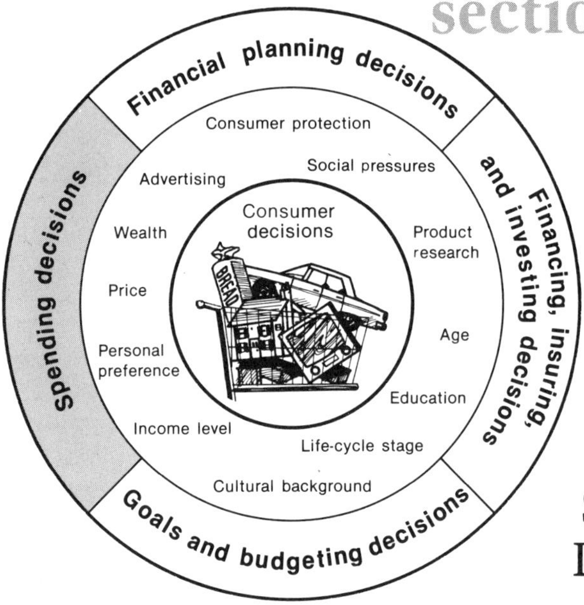

SPENDING DECISIONS

The major portion of consumer spending is used to buy life's essentials. On the average, American consumers spend 75 percent of their incomes on housing, food, transportation, and clothing.

The large amount of money spent on these essentials highlights the importance of making good decisions. The chapters in this section are devoted to improving these spending decisions by examining some of the crucial factors that influence consumer spending plans. For example, Chapter 5 explores the strategies and shopping techniques that help consumers get more for their dollars by recognizing the importance of planning before purchasing the everyday items.

Chapter 6 looks into purchasing decisions for big-ticket items such as appliances. Among the issues raised in this chapter is the need to consider the effect of operating costs and maintenance costs in making purchases of TVs, refrigerators, and other appliances.

Chapter 7 delves into the issue of transportation and the consumer's expensive affair with the automobile. This analysis points out the transportation alternatives available to the consumer and looks at the operating costs of different size automobiles over varying periods of time.

Chapter 8 concludes this section by dealing with consumer expenditures on housing. This chapter probes the issue of renting versus buying housing, and it also covers the basic steps in purchasing a home.

Nondurables: The everyday expenditures

5

OBJECTIVES

This chapter looks at ways in which you, the consumer, can get the greatest satisfaction from the dollars you spend on everyday items such as food and clothing. After thoroughly reading and discussing this chapter, you should be able to:

. . . Explain the basic strategies and tools that consumers can use to improve food buying decisions.

. . . Discuss the importance of legislation as a means of providing consumer protection and information in buying food.

. . . Describe the major elements to consider in buying clothing.

Consumers use 39 percent of their annual disposable income to buy nondurable goods.[1] In 1976 this amounted to $459.8 billion. Nondurables include those goods that, because of their nature, have short useful lives. Food and clothing are major nondurable goods that must be replaced frequently.

Data on consumer spending patterns were first published in 1857 by a German statistician named Engel. Generalizations from these data have become known as "Engel's Laws." Engel noted that as income changed, spending patterns also changed. For example, one of Engel's Laws states that as income increases, the *percentage* spent for food decreases. (The food expenditure in dollars increases, but as a

1 *Federal Reserve Bulletin.*

percentage of family income it decreases.) Such a conclusion is as valid today as it was some 120 years ago.

The study of consumer behavior in Chapter 4 showed that shoppers' buying decisions may be influenced by factors such as store layout, product display techniques, product brands, pricing strategies, and acceptance standards set by peer groups. Sellers use their knowledge about consumer behavior to influence consumer decisionmaking. Consumers must therefore become aware of the effect of these seller strategies on their decisionmaking process.

CONSUMERS IN THE FOOD MARKET

Food is a nondurable good that must of necessity be purchased regularly and in quantities that provide the nutrition needed for good health. Food-buying decisions often reflect the personal values and tastes as well as the nutritional needs of the family. History has shown that while the type of food purchased may vary with the level of income, food purchases are continued under the worst economic conditions. Because food is essential to life, your decision relates to which foods should be purchased rather than whether food should be purchased. Food expenditures, while essential, can be controlled without sacrificing nourishment and attractiveness of meals.

Average American families spend nearly 19 percent of their disposable income on food. Disposable personal income (DPI) is the income consumers have available to spend; that is, their take-home pay. DPI can be calculated by deducting income taxes—federal, state, and local—from gross income.

In 1976, food expenditures totaled $224.5 billion. Of this amount, almost $186.9 billion was spent for food used at home. Food purchases for home use, as shown in Exhibit 5–1, decreased as a percentage of disposable income from 20 percent in 1960 to 15.8 percent in 1976. This means that while the cost of food has been increasing, family disposable income has been increasing at a faster rate.

In spite of what these averages indicate, there is evidence that some consumers suffered much more from the increased food costs than others. A 1973–74 survey of food price changes in one major American city indicated that many of the price increases had a greater effect on the middle-to-low-income consumers than on the upper-income group because of the differences in the types of food eaten. For example, during this period the price of porterhouse steak increased by only one percent and sirloin steak decreased by six percent. During the same period the price of dried beans increased by 208 percent and the prices of other staples also rose sharply: parboiled rice, +61 percent;

EXHIBIT 5–1
Food expenditures in relation to disposable personal income for 1960, 1965–1976

		Disposable personal income spent for food					
		Total		*Use at home*		*Use away from home*	
Year	*DPI ($ Billion)*	*($ Billion)*	*Percentage of DPI**	*($ Billion)*	*Percentage of DPI**	*($ Billion)*	*Percentage of DPI**
1960	$ 350.0	$ 82.3	23.51%	$ 70.1	20.03%	$12.2	3.49%
1965	473.2	100.9	21.32	85.8	18.13	15.1	3.14
1966	511.9	108.5	21.20	92.0	17.97	16.5	3.22
1967	546.5	111.0	20.31	93.6	17.13	17.4	3.18
1968	590.0	118.5	20.08	99.7	16.90	18.8	3.19
1969	634.4	124.1	19.56	104.1	16.41	20.0	3.15
1970	685.9	142.2	20.73	118.6	17.29	23.6	3.44
1971	742.8	146.5	19.72	122.0	16.42	24.5	3.30
1972	801.3	157.2	19.62	130.6	16.30	26.6	3.32
1973	901.7	176.7	19.60	146.8	16.28	29.9	3.32
1974	982.9	199.6	20.31	166.4	16.93	33.2	3.38
1975	1080.9	209.5	19.38	175.2	16.21	34.3	3.17
1976	1181.7	224.5	19.00	186.9	15.82	37.6	3.18

* May not add to total percentage of DPI because of rounding.

Source: U.S. Bureau of the Census, *Statistical Abstract of the United States,* 1970 and 1976; National Consumer Finance Association; U.S. Bureau of Economic Analysis, *Survey of Current Business,* January, 1977; *Federal Reserve Bulletin.*

EXHIBIT 5–2
Food plans that families of different sizes and incomes can usually afford

Family income (after taxes)	Number of persons in family					
	1	2	3	4	5	6
$2,000 to $4,000	Thrifty or low-cost	*	*	*	*	*
$4,000 to $6,000	Low-cost	Low-cost	*	*	*	*
$6,000 to $8,000	Moderate-cost	Moderate-cost	Low-cost	Low-cost	*	*
$8,000 to $10,000	Moderate-cost or Liberal	Moderate-cost	Moderate-cost	Low-cost	Low-cost	*
$10,000 to $15,000	Liberal	Moderate-cost or Liberal	Moderate-cost or Liberal	Moderate-cost	Low-cost or Moderate-cost	Low-cost
$15,000 to $20,000	Liberal	Liberal	Liberal	Moderate-cost or Liberal	Moderate-cost	Moderate-cost
$20,000 and over	Liberal	Liberal	Liberal	Liberal	Moderate-cost or Liberal	Moderate-cost or Liberal

* Most families of this size will require a plan that is less costly than the low-cost plan. One such plan is the thrifty plan developed by USDA.

Source: Adapted from U.S. Department of Agriculture, *Survey of Consumer Expenditures.*

vegetable oil, +61 percent; quick-cooking rice, +41 percent; and margarine, +40 percent.[2]

Estimating food costs

Because consumers differ, there is no dollars-and-cents answer to the amount of money that should be spent for food. Nutritionists and food economists of the United States Department of Agriculture have developed food cost estimates for three basic food plans. Costs of these plans—low-cost, moderate-cost, and liberal—reflect buying practices of different income levels and family sizes. A fourth plan, the thrifty plan, is a guide for families that have very little money for food and families eligible for government assistance programs such as food stamps.

An estimate of weekly food costs in these plans is made by following these steps. First, select the food plan from Exhibit 5–2 that best suits the family situation. Choose the column that shows the family size and move downward to the income level. Notice that the income level reflects income *after taxes;* that is, disposable rather than gross income. The plans listed in the exhibit reflect the average cost of food for the selected family size and income. For example, a family of four with after-tax income of $12,000 would probably find the moderate-cost plan best suited to its needs.

The second step is to estimate the average cost of the food plan for the family. Exhibit 5–3 presents an estimate of food costs for a family of four with parents in the 20–54 years age range and a teenage boy and teenage girl. These costs assume all meals and snacks are prepared at home for all members of the family. The estimated cost of food using the moderate-cost plan is $70.20 per week or $304.40 per month.

EXHIBIT 5–3
Estimated food costs for a family of four persons

	Weekly	*Monthly*
Woman (20–54 yrs.)	$15.70	$ 68.20
Man (20–54 yrs.)	19.50	84.30
Girl (12–19 yrs.)	15.60	67.80
Boy (15–19 yrs.)	19.40	84.10
Total	$70.20	$304.40

Source: U.S. Department of Agriculture, Agricultural Research Service, Consumer and Food Economics Institute, April 1977.

[2] *The Milwaukee Journal,* July 29, 1974, p. 8.

If there are more or fewer than four members of the family the costs shown in Exhibit 5–3 must be adjusted. Adjustments to the per-person cost suggested are as follows: for a one-person family, add 20 percent; two-person, add 10 percent; three-person, add 5 percent; five- or six-person, subtract 5 percent; and seven-or-more-person family, subtract 20 percent. As the family size decreases, certain economies from purchasing in family-size quantities are not available and thus the cost per person increases. The reverse of this explains why individual food costs decrease as the family size increases.

Amounts actually spent by families will ordinarily differ from these estimates, which are intended only as guidelines, not limits. In general, spending either much more or less than the estimate indicates that more attention may be needed in the planning and selection of food. Overspending indicates that you may not be getting the most food value for your dollar, while underspending may indicate that you may be sacrificing variety of food items used in meal planning. The important point is that you should analyze the reason the difference exists.

Spending on food should reflect the priority of family needs. Factors such as the types of foods selected, geographic location, use of prepared mixes or scratch foods, use of frozen or canned foods, effort spent in planning and shopping, and the importance placed on food in relation to other family needs can explain differences in spending.

CONSUMER STRATEGY FOR FOOD SHOPPING

Rapidly rising food prices have made consumers far more aware of the importance of getting as much as possible for each food dollar. This requires the development of a decisionmaking strategy to help the shopper evaluate appeals made by retailers and to take advantage of shopping opportunities when they present themselves. Development of such a strategy requires careful advance planning and careful selection on the shopping trip.

Advance planning and timing

Advance planning of food needs will result in the development of a shopping list. The use of such a list is a must in that it enables the shopper to identify specific items and quantities desired. Planning should be flexible enough, however, to permit substitution of items if special purchase opportunities are available. A list enables the shopper to avoid overbuying on impulse. Shoppers purchase more of both necessary and unnecessary items when proper planning has not been done before the shopping trip. As a result, they have less money available for other needs and pleasures. Planning what to buy and buying what you have planned is the key to success in stretching the food dollar.

The timing of food shopping is also important because many food prices tend to vary within any week. Supermarkets usually advertise end-of-week specials featuring price reductions for meats, poultry, and produce on Thursday, Friday, and Saturday. Researchers have discovered that over 75 percent of grocery sales in supermarkets occur between Thursday and Saturday as a result of the specials advertised and the paydays for many shoppers.[3] Supermarkets often promote specials early in the week in an attempt to get shoppers to spread their shopping over more than one visit. Careful planning of meals makes it possible to also take advantage of the early-in-the-week specials.

Private brands or national brands?

Many supermarkets offer their own private brand of food items on the shelves alongside the national brands. It is entirely possible that the only difference between the private and national brands is the name on the label. Private brands are often processed in national brand plants and then are labeled differently at the end of the production line.

Processors, supermarket managers, and government officials involved with food regulation agree that the nutritional value of private brands and national brands is comparable. There are only rare instances when there are noticeable differences in quality between private and national brands. Products that are most similar include margarine, grade AA butter, peanut butter, jams, jellies, preserves, bread, milk, and eggs.[4]

Prices of private brand goods are typically lower than their national brand counterparts. Price differences between private and national brands may vary depending upon such things as the season, size of the store, or location of the supermarket.

To estimate the difference in prices of national brands and private brands, prices of two market baskets of 28 heavy-selling supermarket items, differing only by brand name, were compared. The survey included five chain supermarkets in the Midwest. Results as summarized in Exhibit 5–4 show that prices of national brands averaged 25.8 percent higher than prices of private brands. However, on some

---

[3] *Consumer Dynamics* (New York: Progressive Grocer, 1971), p. K104.

[4] William B. Mead, "What's in a Name Brand?" *Money*, February 1974, pp. 40–42.

EXHIBIT 5–4
Comparison of retail prices on national and private brands of selected supermarket products

Product	*Price Difference**
Bacon (1 lb.)	21.2%
Bread–white (1½ lb.)	21.4
Butter–grade AA (1 lb.)	8.3
Cake mix–yellow (18½ oz.)	13.9
Chicken dinner–frozen (11½ oz.)	23.2
Coffee–ground (1 lb.)	10.1
Cola (12-oz. can)	65.0
Corn–canned whole kernel (17 oz.)	27.0
Corn–frozen whole kernel (10 oz.)	43.2
Crackers–grahams (1 lb.)	26.6
Crackers–saltines (1 lb.)	16.1
Flour (5 lbs.)	14.3
Frankfurters (1 lb.)	34.1
Gelatin dessert	18.0
Ice cream (½ gal.)	50.4
Jelly–grape (18 oz.)	39.2
Liquid dish detergent (32 oz.)	57.2
Margarine (1 lb.)	47.0
Mayonnaise (32 oz.)	21.1
Milk (1 gal.)	1.8
Orange juice–frozen (6 oz.)	40.3
Paper towels (jumbo roll)	12.7
Peaches–canned (16 oz.)	6.7
Peanut butter (18 oz.)	51.5
Salad oil–vegetable (48 oz.)	13.9
Soup–condensed tomato (10¾ oz.)	13.0
Toilet tissue (4-pack)	10.6
Tunafish–canned (6½ oz.)	13.6
Average price difference	25.8

* As percentage of private brand price.

Source: Robert M. Niendorf, "Pricing Strategies of Private Brands," unpublished manuscript.

products the price differences were much greater than the average; for example, 57 percent on liquid dish detergent, 65 percent on cola, 50 percent on ice cream, 40 percent on frozen orange juice, 51 percent on peanut butter, and 47 percent on margarine.[5]

Supermarket shoppers can conserve their food dollars by carefully comparing prices of the different brands. When shoppers become too attached to a brand name, they fail to compare prices. It is possible in many supermarkets for a shopper to be able to substitute private brands for half of the purchases. This substitution would result in a

[5] Robert M. Niendorf, "Pricing Strategies of Private Brands," unpublished manuscript. University of Wisconsin—Oshkosh, 1977.

decrease in grocery costs of nearly 13 percent. This means that for a family of four with teenage children on the moderate-cost food plan discussed earlier in the chapter, it may be possible to decrease food costs by about $475 per year through the use of private brands.

Unit pricing information

Unit pricing is a system whereby the seller provides the price per standard measure or weight (pint, quart, gallon, ounce, or pound) in addition to the price per package. Consumer advocates favor the use of unit pricing systems because it makes it possible for shoppers more easily to compare the prices of items in differing sized containers or packages. For example, to compare accurately the prices of a 3¼-ounce package selling for $1.10 with that of a 4¾-ounce package selling for $1.43 requires knowing the cost per ounce. Unit pricing labels would show you the unit prices of these packages, $0.34 and $0.30 per ounce respectively, along with the package price. Based on the per-ounce cost, you can then make a more informed purchasing decision.

In some states, unit pricing of many of the items in the supermarket is required by law. Supermarkets in many other states have voluntarily adopted a method of unit pricing. The effectiveness of such a system in aiding shoppers to get the most for each food dollar is as yet undetermined. One study showed that it is entirely possible that consumers in the low-income groups do not or are not able to make as much use of unit prices as do other shoppers. In fact, shoppers in the low-income-area stores paid higher unit prices where the unit price information was available than where the unit prices were not shown. Medium- and high-income groups chose lower unit prices when given unit price information.[6] When the unit price information is available to all consumers, it can be effective in improving the use of the food dollar only if shoppers learn to use it.

Use of food-buying clubs

Food-buying clubs reduce food costs by pooling the individual purchase orders of club members, buying in large quantities from wholesalers, and then distributing the goods to the club members. This procedure can result in lower food costs because the club members eliminate some of the handling and marketing costs charged by food retailers. For example, food clubs save advertising and display costs and if club members are willing to contribute their labor in the buy-

---

[6] Hans R. Isakson and Alex R. Maurizi, "The Consumer Economics of Unit Pricing," *Journal of Marketing Research*, Vol. 10, August 1973, pp. 277–285.

ing, distributing, and recordkeeping work, they save many of the labor costs incurred by the food retailer.

An important factor in the success of a food-buying club is its selectivity of items to be purchased. Club members are often unhappy when the hoped-for savings do not result because the items bought through the club are items that are featured as specials at nearby supermarkets. If food-buying clubs stick largely to items such as prepackaged meats, canned soda, private brands of canned goods, and nonfood items such as cleaning and washing products, there is a greater chance that savings will be realized.[7]

CONSUMER PROTECTION IN THE FOOD INDUSTRY

Consumer protection in the food industry appears in a variety of forms. Generally, these protective instruments are the result of competition in the food industry or of legislation.

Competition—The consumer's friend

Since the early days of self-service supermarkets, supermarket managers have made a continuous and constant effort to attract the consumer to their store. Retailers have found that one of the most effective ways to attract shoppers to stores is to offer goods for sale at lower prices. A major way to cut prices is to cut back services offered to the consumer. Consumers are willing to select, assemble, and mark prices on their own food items if the price is lower than a "full-service" grocery store. Because of this price competition among the retail grocers in a community, consumers can generally be assured that retailers have goods available at a reasonable price. However, strong competitive pressures may result in the use of certain practices such as mislabeling and shortweighting, which are not in the best interest of the consumer. As a result, laws have been passed by governmental units to protect the consumer.

Legislation

Laws have been passed to protect the consumer and to provide information that will make shopping easier. These laws cover a wide range of topics such as standards for packing and labeling of food

[7] Jean Ende and Clifford Earl, *Buy It Right!* (New York: E. P. Dutton & Co., Inc., 1974), pp. 41–44; Sidney Margolius, *The Consumer's Guide to Better Buying,* Revised Edition (New York: Pocket Books, 1972), pp. 89–90.

items as well as standards that food products must meet to qualify for a given grade rating.

The Fair Packaging and Labeling Act, 1966 (FPLA). As a result of the passage of the FPLA, certain information is required to appear in a prominent manner on all food labels. The label that you see in Exhibit 5–5 illustrates the four kinds of information required by the FPLA.

EXHIBIT 5–5

By permission, Del Monte Corporation.

First, all labels are required to contain an identity statement, which must include the common food name and the form that is contained in the package; e.g., sliced, ground, whole. Such information must appear on the principal display panel of the package.

Second, the net contents of the package must be displayed on the lower 30 percent of the label. The weight must be presented first in ounces for items weighing between one and four pounds or one pint to one gallon. This is followed by the appropriate whole units written in parentheses such as pound-ounce or quart-pint combinations.

Third, the label must include a list of the ingredients contained in the package. The order of presentation in the list must be according to predominance by weight. There are two exceptions: 1) The list is not required when a product meets the standard of identity; that is, it has been prepared according to formulas specified by law. Standards of identity have been fixed by the United States Food and Drug Administration for foods such as ice cream, ice milk, sherbet, canned fruits and vegetables, breads, jams, jellies, preserves, oleomargarine, and canned or frozen shellfish. As a result, labels on these items do not include a complete listing of the ingredients. 2) A listing of ingredients is not required if the product name identifies the single ingredient in the package; e.g., packaged dried peas.

The fourth piece of information required on the package label is the name, address, and zip code of the firm responsible for the product. This refers to the manufacturer, packer, or distributor of the item.

FDA labeling regulations. As of January 1, 1974, the United States Food and Drug Administration's (FDA) nutrition labeling regulations went into effect. The effect of this law on food labels can be seen by examining Exhibit 5–5. Labeling is required if any nutrient is added or if a nutritional claim is made for the food either in the labeling or in any advertising of the product. Information must be on a per-serving basis and include serving size, calories, protein, fat, carbohydrates, and the percentage of the U.S. recommended daily allowance of seven important vitamins and minerals.

Consumer Food Act of 1976. The purpose of the Consumer Food Act of 1976 is twofold: (1) to provide consumers with greater assurance that the food they eat is safe and wholesome, and (2) to prevent the deception of shoppers by requiring comprehensive and informative food labeling. This act upgrades the nation's food safety and sanitation programs by requiring food recall coding, by providing a national registration program for food processors, and by extending the FDA's inspection authority to include records kept by food processors. Under this act food manufacturers are required to provide complete food ingredient information, open dating information, and information about the nutritional value of food products in a uniform manner.[8]

Federal inspection regulations. Food inspection and food grading are distinctly different and should not be confused. Inspection stamps or labels that appear on many fresh and processed products tell the consumer that the food is safe and unadulterated. For example, under the Wholesome Meat Act of 1967, federal or federally approved inspection is required in all food-processing plants that sell products in interstate or foreign commerce. Inspection is made by federal inspectors unless the state has developed inspection programs that are equal to the federal ones. The purple stamp that appears on the fat of all meat shipped interstate says, "U.S. Inspected and Passed." This stamp assures the consumer that the meat is from a healthy animal and that the plant in which it was processed has met the health and safety standards.

---

[8] *Consumer Food Act of 1976* (Washington, D.C.: U.S. Government Printing Office).

Federal grading regulations. Grading of food products is intended to permit you easily to identify the quality of a product through the use of a system of grade letters, numbers, or names. Unfortunately, this system is very confusing because of the proliferation of grade indicators used by manufacturers, packers, and distributors. Unless you are familiar with the system used by a store, you have no way of knowing whether an item on special marked "Grade—fantastic" is a high-quality item for a low price or low-quality item with a fancy name featured at a high price.

As a result, many consumers depend upon the grading system of the U.S. Department of Agriculture. Such grading classifications are established by setting minimum standards to which the product quality must conform.

U.S. OFFICIAL GRADES AS GUIDES FOR CONSUMERS

The Agricultural Marketing Act of 1946 and related acts have provided the authority under which the USDA has issued grade standards for more than three hundred farm and food products in the basic four foods. These include meats and poultry (excluding pork), milk and milk products, and fruits and vegetables. Food grains are also graded, but the foods into which they are processed, such as flour and cereal, are not graded.

The use of the federal grading standards by processors or packers is not required by federal law. Some states or municipalities, however, may require the use of federal grading standards for products sold within their boundaries. Officially graded products are labeled with an appropriate stamp or marking on the label of the package such as the purple shield stamp "USDA Prime" on beef.

Whenever grade labels appear on products they assure the consumer of a certain minimum quality. Packers or processors may not include an official grade on the label unless it actually meets the federal standards. The use of "Grade A" on an egg carton, even excluding the "USDA" or "US" prefix, is considered a violation of the Food, Drug, and Cosmetics Act unless the eggs meet the federal standards.

Product grading gives you added information to use when making a purchase decision. This, of course, is true only if you are able to understand the grading system that is used. Because prices of lower grade food are often below those of higher grades, you can save money by buying the grade that best meets your needs. For example, chicken for a casserole can be of a lower grade than that used for roasting. Examples of food grading stamps are shown in Exhibit 5–6.

EXHIBIT 5–6
Guides to food quality

Eggs

Fresh fruits and vegetables

Meat

Poultry

Processed fruits and vegetables (and related products)

Butter, cheddar cheese

Meat, poultry, and fish

Meat, including poultry and fish, accounts for 30 to 35 cents of each food dollar spent by an average family. Therefore, as a food group, meat is usually the costliest part of the meal. The range in prices of different types, grades, and cuts of meat is great. This means that in addition to knowing what type and cut of meat is desired, selection of the right grade will also result in savings.

USDA grades—Meat. Consumers who shop by grades may feel more confident with USDA grades than with the grading system used by individual processors or stores. USDA grading is usually done at the slaughterhouse, packing house, or wholesale outlet. The quality grade classification predicts the eating quality of meat. Eating quality is indicated by factors such as contour and fat covering of the carcass, marbling of fat, texture, color, firmness of the meat, and the age of the animal. Grades used in the classification of beef, veal, and lamb from high to low are as follows: USDA prime, USDA choice, USDA good, USDA standard, USDA commercial, and USDA utility.

In general, the higher grades of meat have more marbling (fat throughout the lean meat) with a creamy white fat covering, indicating that the animal was grain-fed rather than range-fed. Meat in the upper three grades comes almost exclusively from young animals. Choice-grade meat is one of the most commonly sold grades in the supermarket. Lower-grade meat, particularly utility grade, is found in the supermarket in the form of processed products such as ground meat, bologna, or frankfurters, in which meat grade is not designated.

USDA grades—Poultry. As with meat, government inspection for wholesomeness of poultry is required, but grading is voluntary. Such inspection standards are intended to protect the consumer by making sure that only healthy birds are processed and that the processing is done under sanitary conditions.

The USDA grade levels for poultry are indicated as U.S. Grade A, B, and C. Grade A birds will have a good shape and appearance with a well-developed layer of fat under the skin and will be relatively free of defects. Grade B and C chickens, though less attractive in appearance, have the same nutritional value as Grade A birds. These chickens are usually sold to processors for use in other chicken products such as chicken soup and pot pies. Therefore, chickens sold in the supermarkets are nearly always Grade A.

Fish and fish products. The United States has no mandatory inspection or grading requirements for fish and fish processing. Government inspection of fish and shellfish is available to fisheries and processors who desire it through the Bureau of Commercial Fisheries. As yet, less than 25 percent of the fresh or processed fish sold in the United States is covered by inspection. Fish products that have been processed in an inspected plant may carry an appropriate inspection symbol. Grade labeling is not required, however, even of officially inspected and graded products.

Milk and milk products

After meat, milk and milk products take the biggest cut out of the average family's food dollar—20–25 cents. Nearly all the milk available to the consumer has been processed under the U.S. Public Health Service Milk Ordinance standards, which have been adopted by most cities and states. In contrast to the USDA quality grade standards, the USPHS standards are largely standards of wholesomeness. The law provides quality standards for three grades of raw milk (A, B, and C) and three grades of fluid milk—Grade A, pasteurized; Grade B, pasteurized; and Grade C, pasteurized.

Science has as yet been unable to discover a substitute for milk.

There are, however, forms of milk that are less expensive than fluid whole milk. These forms include those containing less fat—two percent, one percent, or skim—evaporated or dry. You can get more for your milk dollar by selecting the form of milk that best meets particular needs for drinking or cooking.

Milk products. Butter and cheese are sold largely on the basis of grade. Established standards for each define levels of eating quality.

The grade labeling requirements for butter differ from those for meat products; processors may label butter as Grade AA without the U.S. prefix even though the butter has not been graded by a federal butter grader or according to federal standards. Such a grade label reflects the standards of the manufacturer or distributor.

States may require the grading of butter according to their adopted standards. Such grade labels may contain the state name as the prefix rather than U.S.

When the state name or U.S. prefix are not found in the grade label, the consumer must rely on the distributor's reputation for the quality contained in the product.

Eggs

Eggs are sold on the basis of quality, grade, and size. It is important to know that the grade and the size have no relation to each other but do have an effect on the prices charged.

Grade is a measure of quality. Standards of quality relate to the appearance of the egg and its suitability to various methods of cooking. They define such factors as thickness of the albumen, condition of the yolk, and the condition of the shell. The higher grade eggs, AA and A, are more expensive and are usually preferred for frying, poaching, or boiling. The less expensive lower grades, B and C, can also be used for these purposes but are usually used for scrambling, cooking, or baking.

Fruits and vegetables

Grading of fruits and vegetables by producers and processors is voluntary. Twelve consumer-level standards have been established by the U.S. Department of Agriculture for about eighty fresh fruits and vegetables ranging from "anise, sweet" to "watermelons." Standards are established for each product. They define factors such as shape, color, maturity, size, and absence of defects.

The typical range of grades for the fruits and vegetables includes U.S. Fancy, U.S. No. 1, and U.S. No. 2. The main trading grade for most of the products is U.S. No. 1. Grade names for processed fruits and vegetables are U.S. Grades A, B, and C.

Voluntary inspection and grading standards established by the U.S. Department of Agriculture are supplemented by regulatory standards under the federal Food, Drug and Cosmetic Act. These standards are administered by the Food and Drug Administration of the U.S. Department of Health, Education, and Welfare. The act provides for three kinds of regulatory standards for products in interstate commerce: standards of fill of container, standards of identity, and standards of minimum quality.

FDA standards of fill of container establish the relationship of water or air and product in a container. They are intended to prevent deception through the sale of water in place of food.

Standards of identity established by the FDA indicate what a food product is—that is, what a product must be to be labeled "preserves." Products with labels that may mislead the consumer—such as "raspberry spread" made from a little fruit and a lot of water, pectin, sugar, artificial coloring and flavoring, and a few seeds—have been eliminated from the market. The FDA standards of identity provide that when there are optional ingredients in addition to those required, they must be listed on the label.

Food products that do not meet the FDA minimum quality standards must be labeled as such. Statements such as "Below Standard in Quality; Good Food—Not High Grade," "Below Standard in Quality; Excessively Broken," or "Below Standard in Quality; Excessive Peel" may be used. Consumers rarely see a product with a substandard label.

Standards of quality that are established for a product by the USDA are consistent with those of the FDA. The minimum requirements for the lowest USDA grade are set at least as high as the minimum required by the FDA. USDA grades for canned tomatoes, for example, are U.S. Grades A, B, and C. Grade C is comparable to the FDA's minimum standard of quality.[9]

Bread and cereals

Official grades are not available for processed breads and cereals because processed grain products are not graded. Grading standards are applied to food grains, however, as a result of the U.S. Grain Standards Act of 1970. Standards are established on the basis of factors such as moisture content, freedom from defective kernels, weight, size, etc.

---

[9] U.S. Department of Agriculture, *USDA Grade Standards for Food—How They are Developed and Used* (Washington, D.C.: U.S. Government Printing Office, January 1973).

CONSUMERS IN THE CLOTHING MARKET

Clothing acts as a kind of "sign language" that influences first impressions formed by others. Whether we like it or not, people are constantly making these judgments about us, just as we are about others. These first impressions may be false, unfair, and inaccurate, or they may be quite accurate. However, the fairness and accuracy of the judgments do not matter, for they are formed anyway. Because of the strong psychological effect that clothing can have, it is important to understand the role it plays in the achievement of a desired image and relationship with others.

Consumer clothing needs

For most people, clothing satisfies more than the need for warmth and comfort. It can also make them look more attractive, help them feel part of a group, provide social status or prestige, give them individuality, or satisfy the need for creative self-expression. Satisfaction of one of these needs may require that an individual compromise the satisfaction of other needs. It may be necessary, for example, to sacrifice warmth or comfort in order to gain social approval, which comes from conforming to group fads and fashions.

Peer group approval. Clothing is a frequent source of disagreement between parents and children. Because of a difference in the emphasis on the needs to be satisfied by clothing, parents and children may disagree on fashions. The patched jeans and sandals approved by a child's peer group may not be consistent with the parents' values of appearance. However, parents who insist on frilly dresses when all the other little girls are wearing denim pants and cotton T-shirts may unknowingly exclude their child from acceptance by her peer group.

Establishment of identity. While conformity to group norms provides for social approval, we all feel the need to distinguish ourselves from others.

At every stage of your development, clothes can help establish an identity for yourself and for those with whom you interact. Many roles in life can be carried off successfully only with the aid of the proper dress. Bankers who look like rock singers may have difficulty convincing associates of their financial wisdom. The degree to which people choose clothes that "fit" their roles—whether they be teachers, business managers, salespersons, or university presidents—will influence the effectiveness of their performance.

Many Americans also recognize that "proper" appearance and dress are the keys to association with the "right crowd." Such associations have been known to open doors to professional opportunities, job advancement, and prestige that would otherwise not have been available. One researcher studied the effect of dress on the evaluation of character and executive ability of persons pictured. The test included showing pictures of three persons to business executives in hundreds of American corporations. The three persons were pictured in three types of clothing designated by the researcher as 1) expensive, well-tailored but high-fashion; 2) conservative upper middle class; and 3) lower middle class. Eighty-eight percent of the executives gave highest ratings to the person in the upper middle class attire.

In a separate experiment, the same researcher tested the effectiveness of two raincoats: a beige raincoat, designated as upper middle class, and a black raincoat, designated as lower class. He attempted personally to deliver sets of papers to the officer in charge at 25 business offices selected at random. When he was wearing the black raincoat his task took a day and a half, but when wearing the beige raincoat he delivered all of the papers in a single morning.[10]

Status and prestige. Fashion is a powerful force in human nature that cannot be ignored. Individual needs for status and prestige are often closely related to an individual's need to display the latest in fashion.

Self-expression. As evidenced by the increasing sales of yard goods and sewing machines, people are expressing themselves by making their own clothing. In many situations, making clothing has a stronger psychological base than an economic one.

Clothing needs—A complex system. It is clear that our clothing needs are influenced by many factors. Buying decisions are seldom simple and rarely made on completely rational grounds. People must determine their needs and the order of priority of these needs. For example, if the need for status and prestige is more important than physical comfort or warmth, then the clothing selection process should reflect these priorities because it will bring the greatest need satisfaction.[11]

Planning and selecting clothing to meet needs

Clothing expenditures for the family have averaged about nine percent of disposable personal income during the past ten years. In 1975 consumers spent over $90 billion on clothing and accessories. Such

[10] John T. Molloy, *Dress for Success* (New York: Peter H. Wyden, Inc., distributor for David McKay, Inc., 1975).

[11] Marilyn J. Horn, "Carrying It Off in Style! The Role of Clothing," *Handbook for the Home,* U.S. Department of Agriculture, 1973, pp. 316–319.

large outlays for clothing easily justify the time spent on careful planning and selection to enable the consumer to get the greatest satisfaction for the amount of money spent. Because it is rarely possible to build an entirely new wardrobe, start with what you have and determine what is necessary to meet your needs.

A clothing inventory will help to determine the items needed to complete your wardrobe. As you plan the items to be added to your wardrobe, consider the following factors to increase the satisfaction derived from your clothing:

Choose basic styles that can be dressed up or down for different occasions. A tailored suit or dress can be casual or dressy depending on the accessories used.

Plan around one or two basic color groups so clothes will go well together. If most of your clothing belongs to the same color family such as browns, oranges, and golds, you can mix and match more garments and accessories.

Choose accessories to go with different outfits. One pair of shoes and one handbag can go with a number of dresses. One shirt and tie can be worn with several suits.

Use mix-and-match separates to extend your wardrobe. Three sweaters and three pairs of slacks or three blouses and three skirts, if they go together, can be interchanged to make nine outfits.

Look for versatile garments that you can wear most of the year or year around.

Avoid novelty or high fashion in garments that are to be worn often or over a long period of time. Extreme clothing designs usually do not stay in fashion long.

Decide how much time and money you are willing to give to clothing care. Do garments require ironing, hand or machine washing, or drycleaning?[12]

When to buy

Purchasing clothing during sale periods can help to reduce the cost of building and maintaining a wardrobe. When shopping sales you should be aware of two things: first, the kind of merchandise that is on sale. Merchandise that has been purchased especially for the sale is generally of lower quality than the seller's regular merchandise. Sec-

[12] This information taken from the Money Management Institute booklet titled *Your Clothing Dollar* printed by the Money Management Institute of Household Finance Corporation, Chicago, Illinois.

ond, the sale price relative to the regular price. Generally, at least 20 percent should be marked off the price of clothing, but you may find savings of 30 to 50 percent from the regular price.

Retailers usually have sales at various times ranging from the celebration of anniversaries to end-of-month clearance sales. The timing of these sales varies from seller to seller, and therefore you must watch carefully for these special sales. There are traditional times of the year, however, when certain types of clothing are on sale. Examples of the types of clothing and the months for traditional sales are shown in Exhibit 5–7. It generally breaks down to two times of the year: end of year, such as December, January, and February, and mid-year including June, July, and September. The two best months to shop for general clothing, including shoes, are January and July.

EXHIBIT 5–7
Traditional timing of clothing sales

Women's dresses	*Coats*	*General clothing*	*Shoes*	*Men's and boys' suits and coats*
April	February	January	January	January
June	November	March	July	August
November	December	July		December
		September		

Post-season results

Even the best plan is not perfect. What appeared to be a good idea at the beginning of the season may not work out as expected. As a result of such problems in planning a wardrobe, a post-season review should be made to determine which items did not meet your needs and which items performed better than expected. Such information should serve as a good basis for planning next year's wardrobe by pointing out items that may be desirable but not essential and thereby enabling you to increase the satisfaction from each clothing dollar spent.

SUMMARY

Nondurables include any products with short useful lives. Food and clothing are major nondurable goods: clothing is often used up in a single season while food is used at an even faster pace. Careful planning and selection are required in order to get the greatest satisfaction for the money spent. Consumer expenditure decisions may be influenced by strategies used by food and clothing retailers.

Shoppers can stretch their food dollars by carefully planning and selecting their food purchases. Preparation of a shopping list encourages planning of meals and purchasing only the food items needed. Such planning reduces the number of items purchased on impulse.

Private-label goods offer a saving over national brands with no apparent sacrifice of food value. Unit pricing information enables shoppers to purchase the quantity needed at the lowest available price. Food-buying clubs may save money by enabling a group of shoppers to purchase large quantities.

Competition within the food industry has encouraged producers and retailers to make food items available at reasonable prices. Because of undesirable practices that developed, however, such as mislabeling and poor sanitation conditions, federal and state legislation has been passed to help protect the consumer.

Consumers are protected by legislative requirements for the grading and inspection of food products. While most federal grading programs are voluntary, the inspection programs are required to assure wholesomeness of food products. Product grades generally indicate the eating quality of the food items. Higher grade foods cost more than the lower grades. Thus, selection of proper grades to meet your food needs can result in lower food cost.

Clothing satisfies psychological as well as physiological needs. Needs for warmth and comfort are often compromised when the need for peer approval, establishment of identity, status and prestige, and for self-expression are considered. Planning a wardrobe must reflect your priorities of these needs. Careful wardrobe planning must be followed by thoughtful selection to provide clothes that will be worn and will meet clothing needs. Careful timing of purchases can save from 20 to 50 percent in the cost of building and maintaining a wardrobe. A follow-up evaluation at the end of the season is essential to provide useful information on the wearability of selected clothing items and is invaluable for future wardrobe planning.

DISCUSSION QUESTIONS

1. Explain why the rapid price increases of food have had different effects on families with low income and those with high income.
2. On the basis of the discussion in the text and your own shopping experience, compare the cost of national and private brands of supermarket products. Estimate the amount of possible annual savings in food cost for your family if you substitute private brands for 50 percent of the products purchased.
3. Why is unit pricing information valuable for the shopper?
4. How do food-buying clubs work? How can they save money for members?

5. What information is required to appear on food labels by the Fair Packaging and Labeling Act of 1966? How do the FDA labeling regulations supplement this information? Explain how to use this information.
6. What does a federal inspection seal tell a consumer about the food product? How does this differ from the information provided by USDA grading systems?
7. Describe the communicative power of clothing. How can clothing be used to meet both the psychological and physiological needs of the consumer? Make a list of your needs to be satisfied by clothing. Identify the needs in terms of those discussed in the chapter (e.g., peer group approval) and then rank them in order of your priorities.
8. Describe a logical approach to making clothing purchase decisions that enable you to get the greatest satisfaction from each dollar spent. Why is the post-season evaluation helpful in your future decisionmaking?

CASE PROBLEMS

1. Sue Peterson and Betsy Lane are both university students. They are planning to share an apartment during their senior year and prepare their own meals there. Sue and Betsy are in the process of estimating their food costs and have asked you for help. Their incomes will be very low; they work part-time during the school year and full-time during summers, earning $1,200 each after taxes. Each of their families will be helping them financially by paying their tuition, books, and one-half of their rent. Their families have incomes that enable them to follow a moderate-cost food plan. (See Appendix on pp. 116–17 for food cost estimates.)

   a. Which food plan is likely to be appropriate for these college students? Does the guide given in Exhibit 5–2 necessarily apply to students?

   b. Based upon USDA estimates shown in Exhibit 5–3 provide an estimate of food costs for the academic year (nine months).

2. As part of his household responsibility, Tony Fazio does the grocery shopping for his family of four, including two young children. One of the items on his list is canned peaches. After locating the canned fruit display, Tony is faced with a selection of brand names and container sizes and finds the following:

Prices of canned peaches of private and national brand in different container sizes

	16-oz	*29-oz.*	*106-oz.*
Private brand	$0.39	$0.53	$2.19
National brand	0.43	0.58	2.40

   a. Which container would you expect to have the lowest unit cost? Discuss.

   b. Is the lowest unit price necessarily an indication of the best buy?

APPENDIX

Cost of food at home estimated for food plans at four cost levels, April 1977, U.S. average*

Sex–age groups	Cost for one week				Cost for one month			
	Thrifty plan†	*Low-cost plan*	*Moderate-cost plan*	*Liberal plan*	*Thrifty plan†*	*Low-cost plan*	*Moderate-cost plan*	*Liberal plan*
Families								
Family of 2:‡								
20–54 years	$23.40	$30.90	$38.70	$46.40	$101.60	$133.50	$167.80	$201.30
55 years and over	21.20	27.70	34.20	40.90	91.70	119.80	148.20	177.40
Family of 4:								
Couple, 20–54 years and children—								
1–2 and 3–5 years	33.10	43.00	53.80	64.50	143.50	186.30	232.90	279.40
6–8 and 9–11 years	39.80	51.90	65.10	78.00	172.40	224.40	282.00	338.40
Individuals§								
Child:								
7 months to 1 year	4.80	5.90	7.20	8.50	20.70	25.40	31.00	36.70
1–2 years	5.40	6.80	8.50	10.10	23.20	29.70	36.60	43.60
3–5 years	6.40	8.10	10.10	12.20	27.90	35.20	43.80	52.80
6–8 years	8.20	10.60	13.30	15.90	35.40	45.80	57.50	69.00
9–11 years	10.30	13.20	16.60	19.90	44.60	57.20	72.00	86.40

Male:								
12–14 years	10.90	14.00	17.60	21.10	47.40	60.60	76.10	91.20
15–19 years	12.00	15.50	19.40	23.40	52.10	67.00	84.10	101.30
20–54 years	11.70	15.40	19.50	23.40	50.70	66.60	84.30	101.60
55 years and over	10.50	13.70	17.00	20.40	45.30	59.20	73.50	88.60
Female:								
12–19 years	9.80	12.60	15.60	18.70	42.60	54.70	67.80	81.00
20–54 years	9.60	12.70	15.70	18.80	41.70	54.80	68.20	81.40
55 years and over	8.80	11.50	14.10	16.80	38.10	49.70	61.20	72.70
Pregnant	12.20	15.60	19.30	22.90	52.80	67.80	83.60	99.30
Nursing	12.90	16.50	20.70	24.50	55.80	71.70	89.50	106.30

* Assumes that food for all meals and snacks is purchased at the store and prepared at home. Estimates for each plan were computed from quantities of foods published in the Winter 1976 (thrifty plan) and Winter 1975 (low-cost, moderate-cost, and liberal plans) issues of *Family Economics Review*. The costs of the food plans were first estimated using prices paid in 1965–66 by households from USDA's Household Food Consumption Survey with food costs at four selected levels. These prices are updated by use of "Estimated Retail Food Prices by Cities" released monthly by the Bureau of Labor Statistics.

† Coupon allotment in the Food Stamp Program based on this food plan.

‡ Ten percent added for family size adjustment. (See § below.)

§ The costs given are for individuals in 4-person families. For individuals in other size families, the following adjustments are suggested: 1-person—add 20 percent; 2-person—add 10 percent; 3-person—add 5 percent; 5-or-6-person—subtract 5 percent; 7-or-more-person—subtract 10 percent.

Source: U.S. Department of Agriculture, Agricultural Research Service, Consumer and Food Economics Institute, Hyattsville, Maryland 20782.

3. The clothing that people wear communicates to others.

   Describe the clothing that you would expect the following persons to wear:

   a. *President of the United States*
   b. *Chancellor or president of a university*
   c. *Bank vice-president*
   d. *Accountant*
   e. *University student*
   f. *Teacher*
   g. *Clergy*
   h. *Politician*

SELECTED READINGS

Chambers, Raymond. *Buyer's Handbook: A Guide to Defensive Shopping,* Englewood Cliffs, N.J.: Prentice-Hall, Inc., 1976.

Cross, Jennifer. *Supermarket Trap: The Consumer and the Food Industry,* rev. ed. Bloomington, Indiana: Indiana University Press, 1976.

Molloy, John T. *Dress for Success.* New York: Peter H. Wyden, Inc., 1975.

Parsons, Frank A. *Psychology of Dress.* Detroit: Gale Research Co., 1975.

U.S. Department of Health, Education, and Welfare. *Consumer Nutrition Knowledge Survey, Report II, 1975,* Washington, D.C.: U.S. Government Printing Office, 1976 (DHEW Publication No. FDA 76–2059).

Big ticket decisions: Consumer durables

6

OBJECTIVES

Buying a consumer durable usually involves spending a lot of money on a product you'll have to live with for several years. Before making a selection, it is important to gather information and compare features and facts such as total lifetime costs of these products. After thoroughly reading and discussing this chapter you should be able to:

. . . Identify common sources of product information.

. . . Illustrate the use of the life-cycle cost concept when making product cost comparisons.

. . . Describe a rational decision process for the purchase of durable goods.

Buying big ticket items poses a challenge to every consumer. As the amount of money involved rises, we worry more about making the "right" decision. On major durable items including TVs, refrigerators, ranges, sofas, dishwashers, clothes washers and dryers, and vacuum cleaners, we all tend to shop around to learn more about available products. This decision process is often quite informal and we may not plan it ahead of time. As a result, buying decisions can become hit-or-miss.

Making sure that you consider all the relevant factors in buying these items is an important part of becoming a better consumer. The typical durable means a large outlay for the purchase price, followed by operating and maintenance costs during the time you own and get the benefits from the product. Not only do these products put large demands on income, they also use our limited natural resources.

When making a buying decision, you should think about both the costs and the long-term demands for electricity, gas, and water created by the use of the durable good.

This chapter suggests a method for making rational buying decisions about durables that takes into account all relevant costs and benefits. A rational decision is one that results in, or is expected to result in, the greatest satisfaction for the family. Thus different families may make different decisions, all of which may be rational depending upon their circumstances. It should be stressed that our decision process does not attempt to provide pat answers to problems of consumer choice. Rather, it is a method that aids in making a rational decision.

As we examine the purchase of durables, keep in mind that houses and cars can also be classified as durables. Because of their relative importance in the consumer's budget, we will devote the next two chapters to these topics.

If making the right decision when you buy durables is important, developing a logical decision process is equally important. One view of that process is illustrated in Exhibit 6–1. In this process the decision to purchase involves five major steps: (1) recognizing a need, (2) researching the product, (3) shopping, (4) making the actual purchasing decision, and (5) evaluating the decision after the purchase.

EXHIBIT 6–1
Purchase decisions for consumer durable goods

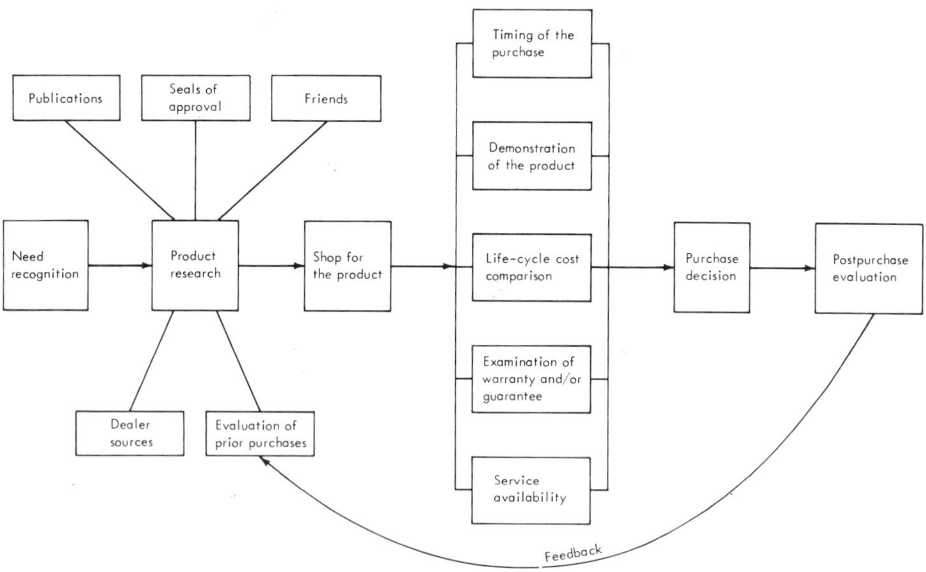

NEED RECOGNITION

In a rational buying process, the decision to buy durables begins when you recognize a need for these items. Your recognition of a need will usually occur for one of these reasons: you desire the convenience or service of something you don't presently own; or, you need to replace an item you now own. In either case, your recognition spurs the need to buy a particular product.

The need for goods that you don't presently own may be stimulated in several ways. In the case of young married couples or persons who are setting up households, certain major items such as a range or furniture are necessary to running the household. Other items may not be necessities and in fact may be luxuries that are purchased for convenience, entertainment, or personal enjoyment.

Replacement of existing durable goods in the household may result from the wearing out of old appliances or from the changing needs of the family. For example, it may be necessary to buy a new refrigerator because the old one no longer operates. This may result in a crisis purchase, where the need for a replacement dominates all other considerations and must be satisfied before life can return to normal. On the other hand, the degree of urgency would be much less if the family simply needed a larger refrigerator because of an increased storage-space requirement.

PRODUCT RESEARCH

Product research should be an important stage in the right purchasing decision. In this stage you can learn which features you want to include or exclude from the items you buy. Product research should also include general information on the safety and usefulness of products as well as specific information on brand names and models.

Product research can be expensive if you consider all of the direct and indirect costs involved. Direct costs include the cost of product information publications and telephone calls, transportation costs for trips to various retailers, and the value of your time spent shopping.

Indirect costs may be more difficult to measure than direct costs. You may incur certain psychological costs such as frustration, tension, and annoyance while fighting traffic, finding a parking space, waiting to be waited on, or dealing with incompetent salespeople.

The product research step involves a trade-off in costs and benefits. You should search for additional information as long as costs are offset by the benefits derived. You can justify a greater research effort when: (1) the expenditure is large relative to the family income, (2) research is easily and inexpensively done, (3) the price of the product does not necessarily indicate the quality of the item, and (4) there are large differences between the operating and maintenance costs of various brands and models. For example, the purchase of a refrigerator-freezer represents a large outlay for most families. Such a large expenditure calls for a thorough search to determine the size required for the family, the features (manual or automatic defrost, automatic icemaker, etc.), the model (top-bottom or side-by-side), the average cost of repairs and maintenance, and the cost of operation (some models cost twice as much to operate as others with the same amount of usable space).

The search process will reveal general product information (the operating costs of all refrigerators) and specific product information (the operating costs of a Frigidaire refrigerator). Common sources of product information include publications, seals of approval, friends, visits to retail stores, and your own past experiences.

Publications

Many publications are available that contain both general and specific product information. Objectivity of information is very important in the evaluation of products. Publications whose support comes from the manufacturers of the products evaluated should be viewed more as advertising than as unbiased research. Publications that are independent of manufacturers are those published by the U.S. government and by private, nonprofit testing and rating agencies.

U.S. government publications. One source of general product information is U.S. government documents published by the General Services Administration. Government research findings on safety features, specifications, and desirable or undesirable features to look for are published without reference to specific brands. As a result, these publications are useful for general information only. But this information is valuable because it may help you identify which of the sizes or optional features will best meet your needs.

Private nonprofit testing and rating agencies. When you are in the market to buy big ticket items, you are faced with a large number of brands and models to choose from. Except for the general information about durables you find in the government publications, much of the information available on these products is sponsored by someone with a vested interest in the item, commonly manufacturers or retailers. In such sources there is a certain amount of "puffing" in the claims.

Reliable and unbiased information on the specific brands and models of durables is available from consumer-financed, nonprofit testing and rating agencies. These agencies are independent of manufacturers and other product representatives. They are financed solely by the consumers who subscribe to their publications, and they neither accept advertising nor permit manufacturers or dealers to make commercial use of their findings or ratings.

Consumers' Research Magazine. One of the consumer-financed testing and rating agencies is Consumers' Research, Inc. (CR). CR publishes monthly issues of *Consumers' Research Magazine* containing the results of laboratory research on the quality of specific products.

Product ratings by CR are based upon the performance of the item under testing conditions or in some cases upon the judgments of qualified, unbiased experts. Products are placed in one of the three following rating groups: *A*, recommended on the basis of quality or performance; *B*, intermediate with respect to quality and performance; and *C*, not recommended. With the exception of cars, quality ratings are completely independent of the price of the product. For some of the large, expensive products, CR often uses test results from manufacturers who sign affidavits that the items were randomly selected and typical of those on the market.

Testing of products is expensive and therefore CR is not able to test as many products or models as subscribers would like. As a result, sometimes you may not find a rating for a brand or model that you are considering. This omission of brands or models should not be used as any indication of judgment of quality or lack thereof.

Consumer Reports. Consumer's Union of the United States, Inc. (CU), chartered in New York in 1936, is another consumer-financed agency. Income is derived solely from the sale of its publications, including *Consumer Reports.* In addition, expenses of occasional research projects of a public service nature may be met in part by nonrestrictive, noncommercial grants and fees. CU accepts no advertising or product samples and is obliged to no commercial interest. Neither ratings nor reports may be used in advertising or for any commercial use. This restriction is backed up by the threat of legal action against any violator, a threat CU has carried out in the courts.

The purposes of CU, as stated in its charter, are to provide consumers with information and counsel on consumer goods and services, to give information on all matters relating to the expenditure of the family income, and to initiate and cooperate with individual and group efforts seeking to create and maintain decent living standards.

Samples of the products tested by CU are obtained by 85 shoppers located in 60 different cities scattered about the U.S. These shoppers go to retail stores and, without identifying themselves as CU shoppers, purchase the desired item at retail price and send it to CU. These products are then subjected to controlled laboratory tests and expert judgments to determine ratings, which are independent of product price. The highest rating is given when CU judges the test sample to be of high overall quality and clearly superior to other tested models. This rating is "Acceptable," indicated by a check (√) beside the brand name. The lowest rating given by CU is "Not Acceptable," which is assigned to products that have performed poorly or proven unsafe during the testing. "Best Buy" ratings are given to products that are expected to offer more quality per dollar than other "Acceptable" products in that set of ratings.

Seals of approval

Seals of approval originated in the 1920s. The implication was that the product bearing the seal had met at least the minimum standards for the tests made on the product. At one time, out of some 1,400 trade associations, 700 issued seals of approval. Often standards for these seals were not based upon safety, quality, or any other relevant standard. Most of the meaningless seals of approval are now gone and the seals of approval used today do have certain meanings that you may find useful.

American National Standards Institute. The American National Standards Institute (ANSI), formerly the American Standards Association, is a national coordinating institution for voluntary standards. ANSI issues a seal of approval for products that meet its standards. Professional groups concerned with standardization may cooperate through ANSI in recognizing, establishing, and improving standards used by industry, consumers, and governmental agencies. Many of the standards developed by ANSI organizations have been and are being written into law by federal, state, and local governmental bodies. An example of such action relates to the mobile home industry. The ANSI Standard A 119.1 pertaining to mobile home construction was first written into law by many of the states and is contained in the National Housing Act of 1974. All mobile homes manufactured after February, 1976, are required to conform to these standards.

The American Gas Association. The seal of the American Gas Association (AGA) indicates that the gas appliance was manufactured by a member of the Association who had met certain minimum standards of utility, durability, and safety of gas burners and gas equipment. The Association is financed by manufacturers of gas appliances. A seal of "Certified Performance" may be used by members whose products meet additional standards of efficiency, convenience, and performance.

While the seal may indicate that the standards have been met, lack of a seal may simply indicate that the manufacturer is not a member of AGA rather than noncompliance with their standards. This is always a problem with association seals. By and large, though, if you purchase a gas appliance, you should look for the AGA seal.

Underwriters' Laboratories. Underwriters' Laboratories (UL) is a nonprofit testing organization sponsored by insurance companies. It tests the safety of electrical appliances of manufacturers and makes spot checks of products purchased on the open market. Periodically, representatives of UL visit and inspect the production facilities of manufacturers. The UL seal is a mark of safety and makes no claim for the quality of a product.

In purchasing electrical appliances, you should make certain that both the cord and the appliance have the UL seal. Approval of the cord does not mean that the appliance itself has met UL standards.

Other seals. Other seals, some of which are associated with publications or professional health associations, do appear on products or in advertising. Before you place any confidence in them, make certain you understand what the seals stand for. In some cases, the seal means only that the manufacturer paid for the seal or for advertising space in the publication; it means nothing with respect to product quality or safety.

Sellers as sources of information

Consumers can also obtain information from those who are selling a product. Although the information is biased in favor of the seller's product, it can point out how the product can meet your needs.

Major sources of seller-dominated product information include advertisements and visits to retail outlets.

Advertisements. Advertisements provide the consumer with information about the features of various models, prices, uses of the product, brand and model comparisons, etc. Studies indicate that consumer use of advertising as a source of product information varies a great deal among products. Of the consumers who purchased major durable goods, 21 percent said that they had obtained information from reading advertisements and circulars.[1]

Visits to retailers. You may also get information about goods by visiting retail outlets. Consumers use retailers as a source of informa-

[1] James F. Engel, David T. Kollat, and Roger D. Blackwell, *Consumer Behavior*, 2d ed. (New York: Holt, Rinehart and Winston, Inc., 1973), p. 388.

tion about price, quality, performance, style and appearance of the product, product features, service facilities, and/or conditions of sale. You should keep in mind that information provided by retailers may be biased because of their interest in making a sale.

This search method is quite expensive in terms of direct and indirect costs because of transportation cost and the time required to make a personal visit. As a result, you should probably use other sources of information before you visit the retailer so that you know what information the retailer can provide to help you make your purchase decision.

Friends

Comments from friends about their experiences with various brands, models, and features can be very useful in the decisionmaking process. By discussing these experiences it is possible to learn from their successes as well as from their mistakes. For example, suppose you need a new refrigerator-freezer and are wondering what features it should have. The experience of others may help you decide whether such features as an ice dispenser in the door, an air purification system, a fingerprint-free door finish, and rearrangable shelves are worth the higher purchase and operating cost.

Evaluation of prior purchases

Another important input into the decisionmaking process is your past experience with products you have owned. Take advantage of your own experience. What brands, models, or features have you been satisfied with? Which were you dissatisfied with? What new or additional features would you find useful?

PRODUCT SHOPPING

After you have researched the products and have identified the features required to meet your needs, the next stage in the purchasing process is shopping. There are five factors to consider for successful shopping: timing of purchase, demonstration, cost comparison, warranty/guarantee, and service.

Timing of purchase

Timing is important: most durables are placed on sale at certain times during the year. In situations where it is possible to postpone the purchase until these periods, you can save on the purchase. Exhibit 6–2 shows the typical annual sales periods for selected durables. In addition to these times, some retailers have holiday or anniversary sales or special-purpose sales such as beat-the-tax or changes of model year.

EXHIBIT 6–2
Selected month-by-month bargains for durables

Month	Items
January	Small appliances; furniture
February	Furniture; carpeting; home furnishings
May	Home furnishings; television; air conditioning; carpeting
June	Television; refrigerators; furniture
July	Furniture; refrigerators; washing machines; other appliances
August	Furniture
October	Major appliances; furniture; home furnishings
November	Major appliances; home furnishings

Product demonstration

When shopping for durables, you should request a demonstration so you can see the product in operation. You should operate the product before buying so you know how it feels to operate the unit, not just how it looks when someone else operates it.

Cost comparison

An analysis of the costs of a durable must include the purchase price, energy cost, and maintenance cost for the entire useful life of the product. The importance of each of these cost components differs for various products because of differences in design and frequency of use. To illustrate, service cost is more important for the TV set than for the refrigerator because of its greater electrical complexity. On the other hand, operating costs are more important for the refrigerator than for the TV set because the refrigerator uses energy for 24 hours a day. Your evaluation of durables should include an examination of each of the cost components in light of its role in influencing the life-cycle cost.

A study conducted at the Massachusetts Institute of Technology found the components of the life-cycle costs for refrigerators and color TV sets to be as presented in Exhibit 6–3.[2] According to the study, if

[2] Massachusetts Institute of Technology, *The M.I.T. Report, Consumer Appliances: The Real Cost* (Washington, D.C.: The National Science Foundation, 1974), p. 13.

EXHIBIT 6–3
Components of life-cycle costs for refrigerators and color TV*

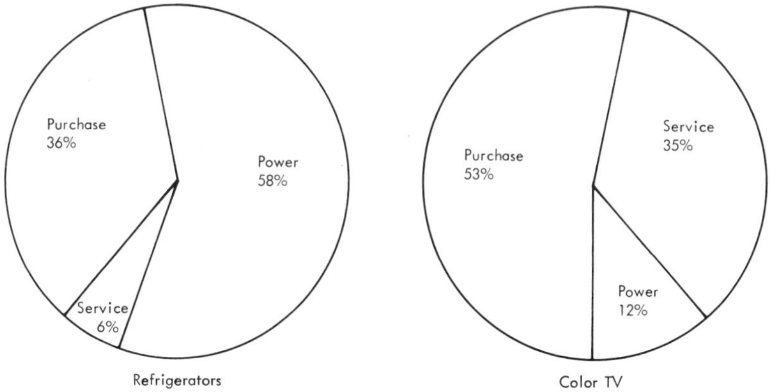

* Based on the year 1972 and discounted to time of purchase.
Source: *The M.I.T. Report, Consumer Appliances: The Real Cost*, p. 13.

you buy a refrigerator for $400, expect to pay an additional $67 for maintenance and $644 for energy over its life cycle (these figures were based upon costs in effect at the time of the study). Thus, the costs for maintaining and operating the appliance are 177 percent greater than the purchase price.

Purchase price. When you are shopping for durables, purchase price becomes the most obvious cost to consider because of the large outlay involved. But, as shown in the MIT study, changing energy and maintenance costs could make it the smallest portion of the life-cycle cost. Refrigerators are an especially good example of the decreasing importance of the purchase price. In the early 1920s, when refrigerators came into fairly wide use, you had to pay about $700 for a nine-cubic-foot unit. By the early 1940s the price had dropped to about $250 for a similar refrigerator. Now, a refrigerator costing about $250 has 14 cubic feet, or 56 percent more space. In addition, the current models include many new features and better-quality materials than their earlier counterparts.

Energy costs. Energy costs are a subject of much discussion throughout the world. The ever-rising cost of energy is increasingly important as a component of the life-cycle costs, particularly for those appliances that use large amounts of energy.

Electrical energy consumers are classified in terms of the purpose for which energy is used, such as residential, commercial, or industrial. Residential consumers use slightly less than one third of all electrical energy sold to ultimate consumers in the United States. Much of this is used for the operation of household appliances.

Durable household goods that use large amounts of electricity include refrigerators, water heaters, and household lighting, followed by others including TV. The energy requirement for a TV set has declined over the past ten years, primarily because of conversion to solid-state construction of color sets. However, the total energy consumed by TV sets has increased greatly during the same ten-year period because of the increased number of TV sets owned.

Energy consumed by refrigerators has nearly quadrupled over the past 20 years to over four kilowatt-hours (kwh) per day. Increased energy use is accounted for largely by increased size and by added features (frostless models, which require heating and then recooling the storage space; icemakers, etc.). If your frostless refrigerator-freezer has 19 cubic feet of space, at five cents per kwh of electricity you could be paying as much as $1,500 for electrical energy during the 14-year average life of the refrigerator.

Exhibit 6–4 provides a basis for estimating the monthly cost of energy for many electrical products in the home. The cost shown is based upon an average of 5 cents per kwh; your kwh cost may be higher or lower depending upon your locality.

You can estimate the energy cost of your own electrical products. Monthly utility bills are determined by the kilowatt (1,000 watts) hours of electricity used. Look on the serial plate for the wattage of the appliance. Multiply the wattage by the number of hours the appliance is operated during a month. Next, divide by 1,000 to determine kilowatt hours. Multiply the number of kilowatt hours by the electric rate and you will have an estimate of the monthly cost of electricity for each appliance.

For example, suppose that your four-slice toaster has a wattage of 1,650 and that it is used about six minutes per day or three hours per month. You can estimate the monthly energy cost as follows:

1. Wattage = 1,650
2. Wattage × hours = watt-hours
   1,650 × 3 = 4,950
3. Watt hours ÷ 1,000 = kilowatt-hours
   4,950 ÷ 1,000 = 4.95
4. Kilowatt-hours × kilowatt rate = monthly cost of operation
   4.95 × $0.05 = $0.248 or 24.8 cents.

Prospects for savings in the life-cycle costs of appliances seem better when we consider possible changes in design and efficiency than when we consider any decrease in energy cost. Appliances that use electricity for heating or cooling purposes probably will become more efficient as energy costs rise. This may be achieved through trade-offs in design and construction by using materials that would increase the

EXHIBIT 6–4
Estimates of average cost of home electrical usage*

Appliance	Wattage	Hrs. used per month	Kwh used per month	Monthly cost
Food preparation				
Blender	300	3	1	$ 0.05
Coffee maker	894	10	9	0.45
Dishwasher	1,201	25	30	1.50
Frying pan	1,196	8	9	0.45
Mixer	127	8	1	0.05
Oven, Microwave (only)	1,450	11	16	0.80
Range, with oven†	12,200	8	98	4.90
Range, with self-cleaning oven†	12,200	8	101	5.05
Toaster	1,146	3	3	0.15
Waste disposal	445	7	3	0.15
Food preservation				
Freezer (15–21 cu. ft.)				
Chest type, manual defrost	342	322	110	5.50
Upright type, manual defrost	342	322	110	5.50
Upright, frostless	440	377	166	8.30
Refrigerator-freezer,				
Manual def., 10–15 cu. ft.	—	—	58	2.90
Auto. def., 16–18 cu. ft.	—	—	150	7.50
Auto. def., 20 cu. ft. and up	—	—	158	7.90
Laundry				
Clothes dryer	4,856	17	83	4.15
Iron (hand)	1,100	4	5	0.25
Washing mach. (auto.)	512	18	9	0.45
Water heater‡	2,475	142	352	17.60
Water heater, quick recovery‡	4,474	90	401	20.05
Comfort conditioning				
Air conditioner (room)	860	285	245	12.25
Blanket (winter)	177	119	21	1.05
Dehumidifier (summer)	257	245	63	3.15
Fan, attic (summer)	370	262	97	4.85
Fan, circulating (summer)	88	159	14	0.70
Home entertainment				
Radio	71	99	7	0.35
Radio/record player	109	83	9	0.45
Television				
Black and white, tube	100	180	18	0.90
B&w, solid state	45	180	8	0.40
Color, tube type	240	183	44	2.20
Color, solid state	145	183	27	1.35

* It should be noted that usage of some electrical appliances—such as ovens, and entertainment appliances—varies from season to season. Differences in usage are not reflected unless noted.

† Usage estimated with oven and all range units on at the same time.

‡ Seasonal changes in the temperature of cold water supplies result in greater energy consumption during winter months than during summer months.

Source: Edison Electric Institute, EEI-Pub. #75–61.

purchase price but would decrease the life-cycle energy cost by a greater amount.

For example, one of the possibilities for reducing heat leakage in refrigerators is through the use of polystyrene insulation rather than continuing to use fiberglass. According to the MIT study, such a change would increase the purchase price but it would decrease energy costs so that life-cycle costs could be decreased by about ten percent.[3]

Energy costs could be further decreased by making changes in motor and condenser efficiencies. Some of the proposed changes have already been made in some refrigerators. If these changes, in addition to the insulation change, were made in design and construction, estimated energy use could be reduced from 210 watts to 97 watts for a 15-cubic-foot, self-defrost refrigerator. In one year this would mean a reduction in electrical usage from 1840 kwh to 850 kwh. The saving in energy cost is estimated to be more than double the added increase in purchase price required to cover the added improvements.[4]

Comparative operating costs for specific brands and models of appliances are provided by *Consumers' Research Magazine.* These costs are estimates based upon the results of their tests of the specific products.

Consumer Reports does not provide specific operating cost estimates, but it does indicate those brands and models that appear to be more efficient than average and those that are quite inefficient.

Expected increases in the cost of energy make operating costs an important factor in the decision process. Future energy costs are projected to rise by 8 to 12 percent per year. As a result, owning an inefficient appliance will become more and more expensive. To illustrate, suppose that the present annual energy costs for regular and superefficient models of refrigerators are $115 and $80, respectively. As energy costs rise, the annual cost difference of $35 will increase.

As shown in Exhibit 6–5, if energy costs rise 8 percent per year the difference in the annual energy cost at the end of year 5 is $51. By the end of the average life of the refrigerators the annual difference will be $103. Should the annual energy price rise by 12 percent, the added energy cost will go to $62 and $171 for years 5 and 14 respectively. For the average useful life, energy cost differences total $915 and $1,270 for the 8 percent and 12 percent rates, respectively. Such

[3] Massachusetts Institute of Technology, *The M.I.T. Report, Consumer Appliances: The Real Cost* (Washington, D.C.: National Science Foundation, 1974), p. 20.

[4] Massachusetts Institute of Technology, *The Productivity of Servicing Consumer Durable Products* (Washington, D.C.: National Science Foundation, 1974), pp. 195–96.

EXHIBIT 6–5
Projected energy cost differences

Years in future	Value of difference in energy cost with annual energy cost increases of: 8%	12%
Present	$ 35	$ 35
5	51	62
10	76	109
14*	103	171
Total (Years 1–14)	$915	$1,270

* Average life of a refrigerator.

large differences in energy cost can easily justify higher purchase prices for the more efficient units.

Maintenance costs. Maintenance costs account for an amazingly large portion of the life-cycle costs of many durables—especially those that have more complex design. As shown in Exhibit 6–3, TV set owners can expect to pay nearly two thirds as much for maintenance as for the purchase price of the set (36 percent of life cycle cost). That is, if you buy a TV set for $500, you should expect to pay about $340 in maintenance costs over its estimated ten-year average life.

The maintenance cost segment of the life-cycle cost depends upon two things: the cost per service call and the service incidence rate. The cost per TV service call has nearly doubled in the past ten years. It is expected that by 1980 the average cost per repair will be about $50. The situation is much the same for refrigerators, except that the average repair cost is slightly less than that for color TV.

Fortunately, service incidence rates have shown a declining trend for both TVs and refrigerators. It is difficult to measure the service incidence after the warranty period has expired and the consumer pays the repair costs, but estimates of incidence indicate that for color TV you can expect an average of one repair per year for at least the first two years of ownership and an increasing number of repairs as the set gets older. For refrigerators the service-incidence rate is higher during the first year than for the second through fifth years of ownership, and then increases as age takes its toll.

The net result of the increasing service cost per repair and the declining service incidence rate has been that the maintenance cost component has been decreasing slightly in the life-cycle costs of both of the above durables. Considering that maintenance accounts for 35 percent of the life-cycle costs for a color TV, this is welcome news for consumers.

Redesign or changes in construction materials that are expected to increase the efficiency of energy use or reduce the service incidence rate will result in higher purchase prices for durables. However, these changes should reduce the life-cycle cost of the durable, thereby providing greater satisfaction for the dollar of income spent. As consumers we should become more aware of the importance of life-cycle costs and shop for energy-efficient and low maintenance units. If we don't, manufacturers will hesitate to make any changes that affect purchase price and place them at a competitive disadvantage. For example, in 1973 Philco introduced its Cold Guard line of refrigerators for which it was claimed that energy use could be 10 to 35 percent below that for competing lines. Company representatives said the consumers could be shown that the energy cost savings in the first two years would offset the higher purchase price of the unit, but consumers were unwilling to pay the higher purchase price. As a result, these refrigerators are no longer made.[5] If we as consumers do not show our concern for energy conservation through our shopping practices, governmental units will likely do it for us through some type of legislative action such as has already occurred in gas mileage and pollution standards for automobiles.

An example of life-cycle cost comparison. A comparison of the purchase, energy, and maintenance costs of refrigerator-freezers illustrates the importance of selecting a unit on the basis of life-cycle costs. *Consumers' Research Magazine* has estimated the energy cost and average purchase price for refrigerator-freezers manufactured by several makers. Exhibit 6–6 presents estimated life-cycle costs of several brands and models (side-by-side and top-mount freezers) studied by CR.

An important part of the life-cycle cost comparison lies in the column headed "Life-Cycle Costs per Usable Cubic Foot." This is the cost for usable space, not just manufacturer's stated volume rating. Standards used by most refrigerator-freezer manufacturers are based upon recommendations by the Association of Home Appliance Manufacturers (AHAM). AHAM standards for capacity measurement state that the AHAM rating ". . . is not intended to provide a means of measuring the food-storage capacity, but rather to provide a uniform means of rating the size. . . ."[6] A comparison of the manufacturers'

[5] "Distributors Bring Back the Crosley Appliance," *Business Week*, January 31, 1977, p. 92.

[6] *Consumers' Research Magazine*, November 1973, p. 12.

EXHIBIT 6–6
Estimated life-cycle costs for side-by-side and top-mount refrigerator-freezers (14-year life)

	Mfr. vol. rating (cu. ft.)	*Approx. usable capacity (cu. ft.)*	*Approx. purch. price*	*Energy cost (room temp. 90° F; $0.05 per kwh)*	*Approx. maintenance cost (6% life-cycle cost)*	*Life-cycle cost*	*Life-cycle cost per usable cu. ft.*
Side-by-side							
Amana	22.3	18.0	$815	$1,613	$155	$2,583	$144
Coldspot	19.1	14.1	533*	1,310	118	1,961	139
General Electric	18.8	14.7	730	1,310	130	2,170	148
Gibson	19.0	15.5	600	1,386	127	2,113	136
Hotpoint	19.0	14.7	709	1,310	129	2,148	146
Kelvinator	19.0	15.1	690	1,487	139	2,316	153
Whirlpool	22.2	16.5	770	1,537	147	2,454	149
Top-mount freezer							
Amana	18.2	14.4	590	1,462	131	2,183	152
Coldspot	15.1	12.1	413*	924	85	1,422	117
General Electric	15.6	12.0	510	1,210	110	1,830	152
Gibson	17.0	14.1	430	1,218	105	1,753	124
Hotpoint	15.7	12.6	510	1,226	111	1,847	147
Kelvinator	17.0	14.1	460	1,058	97	1,615	115
Whirlpool	17.1	14.0	470	1,008	94	1,572	112

* Includes estimated shipping cost of $23.

Source: Adapted by special permission from *Consumers' Research Magazine,* August 1976 and September 1976.

capacity ratings and the actual usable food-storage capacities as measured by CR shows that any resemblance must be accidental. Measured usable capacities for all of the models tested by CR ranged from 17 to 26 percent less than the manufacturers' volume ratings.

You must, therefore, look to the comparison of life-cycle cost per unit of usable space to aid you in selecting the unit that will provide the needed storage capacity at the lowest life-cycle cost.

For example, suppose you have decided that you need a unit that has 14 or 15 cubic feet of space. A comparison of the life-cycle cost per usable cubic foot of space would show that the Whirlpool top-mount has the lowest cost at $112, while the Kelvinator side-by-side has the highest cost of $153 per usable cubic foot.

Warranty/guarantee

When you are buying a major durable good you want to know what maintenance costs you will have to pay and under what conditions manufacturers will stand behind their products.

As might be expected, warranty service costs are included as a part of the purchase cost—remember "there is no such thing as a *free* lunch." In the TV industry, for example, the MIT study found that in the early 1960s when there was a 90-day, parts-only warranty, the cost accounted for about one percent of the purchase price of a set. Since 1969 the one-year labor and parts warranty has been almost industrywide. The cost of such a warranty accounts for as much as ten percent of the purchase price.[7]

In an effort to gain a competitive advantage, manufacturers are attempting to reduce their warranty costs by increasing the reliability of their products during the warranty period. These developments benefit you by encouraging the manufacturer to use higher quality components, which last longer and thus reduce total maintenance cost. However, there are still several problem areas with warranties that can cost you money.

One of these problems was pointed out by a statement from the Presidential Task Force on Appliance Warranties and Service in 1969, which said that "it is fair to state that in some instances the exclusions, disclaimers, and exceptions so diminished the obligations of the manufacturer that it was deceptive to designate the document as a warranty."

Upgrading the warranty. In 1975 the Magnuson-Moss Warranty–

[7] Massachusetts Institute of Technology, *The M.I.T. Report, Consumer Appliances: The Real Cost* (Washington, D.C.: The National Science Foundation, 1974), p. 15.

Federal Trade Commission Improvement Act (Public Law 93-637) was passed by Congress to provide consumers with better warranties on products costing $15 or more. One of the purposes of this law is to provide minimum disclosure standards for product warranties. These standards require that the items in the written warranty must be in words or phrases that would not mislead a reasonable, average consumer as to the nature or scope of the warranty. Among the major items to be included in a warranty are the following:

1. Names and addresses of the warrantors;
2. Who is covered;
3. Products or parts covered;
4. What the warrantor will do in case of a product failure, at whose expense, and for what time period;
5. Step-by-step procedure the customer must follow in order to get warranty service;
6. Authorized service centers;
7. Information about procedures to follow for any informal dispute settlement; and
8. Parts and properties of the product not covered.

The Act does not require warranties for consumer products, but if product warranties are made these standards must be met.

Your warranty responsibility. Even though a warranty is written and issued, the consumer needs to understand what it means. When you examine a warranty you should look for and understand several points:

1. Determine whether a defective product will be repaired or replaced. If it is to be repaired, find out who is responsible for fixing the product (the seller, the manufacturer, or an authorized service agency), where the product must be delivered, and who pays for shipping charges, parts, and labor. Will a substitute be available while the defective product is being repaired? At whose expense? When it is to be replaced, who is responsible and who pays shipping charges?

2. Know how long the guarantee covering parts, labor, transportation, etc., is in effect. Some parts may be covered longer than others and some may be excluded from coverage.

3. Determine whether there are any limitations on the warranty. Is the warranty good only in the continental U.S. or North America? What happens if you move to Alaska or Hawaii? Is accidental damage or damage as a result of acts of God covered? Is the use limited to the home?

4. Make certain that all promises are written. Verbal promises made by a seller cannot be enforced. If you are promised double your

money back if you are not satisfied for any reason, get it in writing; otherwise, don't count on it.

5. Make certain that you keep your bill of sale showing the purchase date and product serial number. Return any registration cards by the date specified. Lack of either of these bits of information often voids the warranty.

A second problem area in controlling warranty costs is the so-called education service call caused by consumer ignorance rather than by failure of the product. You can help to lower product life-cycle costs by becoming better informed about the operation of products. Consumers forget to plug the appliance into a live wall socket or they fail to operate or adjust the unit according to instructions. Such calls result in increased warranty costs for all consumers; they are estimated to account for 30 percent of all warranty service.[8]

Service facilities

As we discussed above, you must expect to pay for maintenance as a part of the life-cycle costs of a durable. For major durables, dealers are often responsible for providing a service facility to take care of such maintenance needs.

You will need to know the extent of the dealer's service capacity. Many dealers give preferential treatment to consumers who purchase the product from them. In fact, many dealers will service only appliances that they have sold.

Maintenance agreements. Some sellers offer special maintenance agreements for appliances they sell. In a maintenance agreement, also known as a service contract, the seller promises to provide repairs needed on a specific appliance for a specified time. In return, the buyer pays a flat fee for the time period covered, whether the appliance needs repairs or not. Most agreements are for total service, which means they cover all labor and parts required for the repairs.

An advantage of a service contract is that you are able to plan for appliance repair costs and can thereby avoid unexpected repair bills. In this way, the maintenance agreement is like an insurance policy; that is, for the payment of a fixed amount you can have someone else take the risk of repair costs. However, there are some cautions to observe with regard to maintenance contracts. Some sellers claim it is desirable to have the service contract even during the first year when many of the repair costs are covered by the warranty. This indicates

[8] Massachusetts Institute of Technology, *The Productivity of Servicing Consumer Durable Products* (Washington, D.C.: National Science Foundation, 1974), p. 93.

that the profitability of the contracts in the earlier years is very attractive to the seller. Unfortunately, the cost of these contracts rises sharply each year or so as the appliance gets older and as a result many consumers drop the contract just when they could reasonably expect to begin to benefit from it. Maintenance contracts are not even available for older appliances, for which you most need this protection, unless you have had a contract since the appliance was new.

Exhibit 6–7 shows the costs, rounded to the nearest dollar, of the maintenance agreements on a washer and a color TV offered by one of the national retailers. Annual costs are shown for a six-year period, but it is possible to get a lower rate if you take the contract for a two- or three-year term. These two appliances were selected because of the importance of maintenance costs in their life-cycle costs.

EXHIBIT 6–7
Typical maintenance agreement costs

	Years						*6-Year*
	1	*2*	*3*	*4*	*5*	*6*	*total*
Washer (purchase price $330)	$30	$30	$35	$40	$45	$ 45	$225
Color TV (purchase price $500)	$55	$55	$65	$85	$95	$100	$455

Source: Author survey, 1977.

It is clear from Exhibit 6–7 that the cost of the service contract goes up rapidly as the appliance gets older. For the six years shown, the total cost for washer and TV maintenance agreements is $225 and $455 respectively. If we suppose that the cost of the service contract on the TV goes up ten percent per year for years 6 through 10 (the average life of a TV), the total maintenance agreement cost rises to $966. This is nearly double the original purchase price of the set.

Using the information shown in Exhibit 6–3, the estimated life-cycle cost of the above TV is as follows:

	*Percentage of total**	*Amount*
Purchase price	53	$500
Energy	12	113
Service	36	340
Total		$943

* Percentages do not add to 100 because of rounding.

Service costs under the maintenance contract are greater than the total expected life-cycle cost for a color TV and are nearly triple the expected life maintenance cost for the set.

You can provide your own appliance maintenance fund by making monthly deposits of about one-third the monthly cost of a service contract in a special account. When repairs are necessary the money will be on hand to pay for the service calls. Any excess in this account can be used when it is necessary to replace the appliance.

PURCHASE DECISION

A purchase decision is the next logical step following the recognition of a need, research of the products available to satisfy the need, and a conscientious shopping effort.

The decision reached should reflect the acuteness of the need and your financial ability to satisfy it. You may find that the cost of the product exceeds the capacity of your income. To illustrate, suppose that an in-home demonstration of a new color TV set is unsatisfactory because of poor video reception. If the reception problem would require a new antenna system, this added cost must be considered as part of the price to be paid. The added cost of the antenna may mean that the cash outlay will exceed the family's capacity. Acceptable alternative decisions may be either not to purchase the TV at this time or to substitute a less expensive model.

POST-PURCHASE EVALUATION

The preceding steps of the decisionmaking framework may lead to the actual purchase of a product. But the process does not end at this stage, because there is a need to evaluate the decision and the decisionmaking process used. It is through the evaluation of past purchasing decisions that we may learn from our experiences. Following the purchase decision, you can expect to experience either: (1) a feeling of satisfaction with the decision or (2) conflicting feelings resulting in dissatisfaction. If viewed as a continuum, complete satisfaction can be thought of as being at one extreme and complete dissatisfaction at the other. Most post-purchase feelings will be somewhere between these two extremes.

No matter what the outcome, the post-purchase evaluation is important. Satisfaction with your purchase serves to reinforce both the recent decision and the decisionmaking process. As a result, future decisions will probably be made in a similar way. If there is doubt or dissatisfaction with the decision, you can still benefit from an evaluation. In this case, you should learn from your experience and avoid similar mistakes in the future.[9]

SUMMARY

A rational decision process is one that leads the decisionmaker through a logical sequence of steps from recognizing the need for a product, to gathering information, to making the purchasing decision and evaluating it.

The need for a product may evidence itself as a replacement or as a desire for a product not presently owned.

Product research helps you determine the product features that meet your needs. Important information about products, of general or specific nature, is available from publications, seals of approval, retailers, friends, and your own past experience.

After you have identified the features that are required, the next step is shopping. The five factors to consider when shopping are: timing of purchase, product demonstration, cost comparison (with emphasis on the life-cycle cost), warranty/guarantee, and service facilities.

A purchase decision is based upon the priority of the need satisfaction, the information gathered, and the financial ability to satisfy the need.

After the decision has been made it is important to evaluate it and the decisionmaking process used. You can expect the greatest satisfaction from your decision if you have carefully considered all of the stages in the decision process.

DISCUSSION QUESTIONS

1. What is meant by "rational decision"? Is the same decision rational for all families? Explain.
2. Describe a decision process for making rational purchase decisions.
3. What conditions give rise to need recognition? Are all needs of the same urgency? Explain.
4. Describe the two types of costs involved in the product research process.
5. Describe the type of product information available from private nonprofit testing and rating agencies. How does this information relate to that available from U.S. government publications?

---

[9] For a more detailed discussion of consumer conflict, see James F. Engel, David T. Kollat, and Roger D. Blackwell, *Consumer Behavior*, 2d ed. (New York: Holt, Rinehart and Winston, Inc., 1973), pp. 529–543.

6. What is the value of seals of approval to decisionmaking consumers? Are all seals equally valuable?
7. Define "life-cycle cost." Why is life-cycle cost important when making a purchase decision? Are each of the components in the life-cycle cost of equal importance for all durables? Explain and give examples.

CASE PROBLEM

Julio and Maria are planning to be married next month. In shopping for a 15-cubic-foot refrigerator-freezer they have found a standard model and a new energy-saving model.

The standard refrigerator-freezer that is available has a selling price of $400. Cost of service and power for the unit are expected to be the average as determined by the MIT study. The energy-saving refrigerator-freezer sells for $525 and has several construction and design changes that have been made in order to make it operate more efficiently. While the standard model requires 610 watts the new model requires only 275 watts. Lifetime service cost for the energy-saving model is estimated to be no greater than the service cost for the standard model.

Which of these models should they select?

SELECTED READINGS

Margolius, Sidney. *The Consumer's Guide to Better Buying,* Revised Edition. New York: Simon & Schuster, Inc., 1972, pp. 146–246.

Klamkin, Charles. *How to Buy Major Appliances.* Chicago: H. Regnery Co., 1973.

Autos: The American way

7

OBJECTIVES

Transportation can be supplied by the family and/or by a public system. Choosing a mode of transportation requires a careful comparison of the costs of each of the alternatives. After carefully reading and discussing this chapter you should be able to:

. . . Describe the role of the automobile in meeting the American family's transportation needs.
. . . Explain the concept of life-cycle cost as it applies to automobiles.
. . . Evaluate the alternative of leasing an auto.
. . . Evaluate purchasing a used auto vs. a new auto.

Automobile transportation is a way of life for the American family today. In 1977, the nation's more than 111 million autos were driven just over 1.1 trillion miles.[1]

Mass ownership of cars is responsible for changing our patterns of recreation, increasing our standard of living, and developing more conveniences and services. The development of giant shopping centers, drive-in movies and restaurants, parks, and tourist attractions has been possible only because we are able to reach these new locations easily in our autos.

Most families view car ownership as a necessity, not just a convenience. Owning a car enables us to live farther from our places of work and in places where other forms of transportation are not available. As a necessity, the auto is given high priority on the list of needs to be satisfied by the family income.

---

[1] U.S. Department of Transportation.

OWNERSHIP OF AUTOMOBILES

Ownership of autos has been increasing steadily. In 1950, cars were owned by nearly 60 percent of all American families. By 1975, about 80 percent of the families owned at least one vehicle, a percentage that has been stable since 1965. In addition to the increase in the number of single-car owners, there has been a marked increase in two- and three-car families. About eight percent of the families owned two or more cars in 1950. By 1975, this percentage had increased to about 33 percent. This means that as of 1975, 12 out of 15 U.S. families owned at least one car and 5 of the same 12 families had two or more vehicles.[2]

The number of autos owned increases as income increases. As shown in Exhibit 7–1, 36 percent of all families with incomes under

EXHIBIT 7–1
Automobile ownership by family income level

Family income before taxes	*Percentage of families owning at least one vehicle*	*Number of vehicles per family*
Average	79	1.2
Less than $3,000	36	0.4
$ 3,000–3,999	54	0.6
$ 4,000–4,999	58	0.7
$ 5,000–5,999	68	0.8
$ 6,000–6,999	73	0.9
$ 7,000–7,999	79	1.0
$ 8,000–9,999	85	1.1
$10,000–11,999	90	1.2
$12,000–14,999	93	1.4
$15,000–19,999	96	1.6
$20,000–24,999	96	1.8
$25,000 and over	94	1.9

Source: U.S. Department of Labor, Bureau of Labor Statistics, Report 455–3, 1976, pp. 14–15.

$3,000 own at least one car, while 94 percent of all families with annual incomes above $25,000 own at least one car. As the level of family income increases, the average number of vehicles owned also increases. Lower income families apparently travel less and are more dependent upon means of transportation other than the family car.

---

[2] U.S. Department of Labor, Bureau of Labor Statistics. Press Release, May 15, 1975.

Need for automobiles

The reasons for owning an auto vary among consumers. Some people's main need is for convenient transportation while others own an auto for status recognition or prestige.

A family's need for an auto as a means of transportation is affected by the existence of alternatives such as public transportation. In some large cities it may be possible completely to satisfy transportation needs through mass transit. Where good mass transit systems are not available, the family must rely more heavily on the auto. Even where public transportation is available some families may rely on cars because of the greater convenience they offer.

Owning an auto means committing yourself to definite expenses such as depreciation, operating and repair costs, insurance, taxes, and licenses. Therefore, a rational evaluation of the family's needs for a car requires that consideration be given to the size, body type, and options required to satisfy transportation and status needs. The cost of buying and operating a car increases as the number of options and the size of the car increase.

THE COST OF TRANSPORTATION[3]

Rising family income and increased leisure time have led to greater spending for transportation. Approximately eight percent of the average family take-home pay is spent for transportation. The importance of transportation is indicated by the fact that transportation costs are exceeded only by those for food and housing.[4]

Automobile operating cost

Many consumers think of an auto's cost in terms of purchase price alone. As is the case with any durable, the purchase price is only the first outlay in a long series of cash outflows over the life of the car. Yet, not many car buyers realize how much it costs to own and operate an automobile. The U.S. Department of Transportation, in a 1976 study, found that the owner of a standard-size auto in the suburban Baltimore area will spend about 17.9 cents per mile to drive and maintain it over a ten-year, 100,000-mile estimated life. In ten years

[3] Much of this section is based on *Cost of Operating an Automobile*, U.S. Department of Transportation, Federal Highway Administration, Office of Highway Planning, Highway Statistics Division, April 1976.

[4] *Autumn 1976 Urban Family Budgets*, U.S. Department of Labor, Bureau of Labor Statistics.

EXHIBIT 7–2

Comparison of costs of operating a standard, compact, and subcompact automobile in 1972, 1974, and 1976*

	Standard size cents per mile				*Compact size cents per mile*				*Subcompact size cents per mile*			
	1972	*1974*	*1976*	*Percentage increase 1972–76*	*1972*	*1974*	*1976*	*Percentage increase 1972–76*	*1972*	*1974*	*1976*	*Percentage increase 1972–76*
Depreciation	4.4	4.2	4.9	11.4	2.7	2.9	3.8	40.7	2.1	2.3	3.2	52.4
Maintenance, accessories, parts and tires	2.6	3.4	4.2	61.5	2.2	2.7	3.4	54.5	2.1	2.5	3.1	47.6
Gas and oil (excluding taxes)	2.1	3.2	3.3	57.1	1.8	2.6	2.5	38.9	1.4	2.0	1.8	28.6
Garage, parking, tolls	1.8	2.0	2.2	22.2	1.8	2.0	2.1	16.7	1.8	2.0	2.1	16.7
Insurance	1.4	1.6	1.7	21.4	1.3	1.5	1.6	23.1	1.2	1.5	1.5	25.0
State and federal taxes	1.3	1.5	1.6	23.1	1.0	1.2	1.2	20.0	0.8	0.9	0.9	12.5
Total cost	13.6	15.9	17.9	31.6	10.8	12.9	14.6	35.2	9.4	11.2	12.6	34.0

* Costs based on new cars operating over a ten-year, 100,000-mile life.

Source: *Cost of Operating an Automobile,* U.S. Department of Transportation, 1972, 1974, and 1976.

EXHIBIT 7–3
Automobile operating costs—bases for estimates

Item	*Standard size automobile*	*Compact size automobile*	*Subcompact size automobile*
Automobile description	1976 model 4-door sedan Equipped with: V-8 engine, automatic transmission, power steering and brakes, air conditioning, tinted glass, radio, clock, white stripe radial tires, wheel covers, remote control left-hand mirror, and body protective moulding. Purchase price: $4,899.	1976 model 2-door sedan Equipped with: 6-cylinder engine, automatic transmission, power steering and brakes, radio, vinyl top, wheel covers, tinted glass, remote control left-hand mirror and body protective moulding. Purchase price: $3,865	1976 model 2-door sedan Equipped with: standard equipment plus radio, wheel covers, and body protective moulding. Purchase price: $3,224.
Repairs and maintenance	Includes routine maintenance such as lubrications, repacking wheel bearings, flushing cooling system, and aiming headlamps; replacement of minor parts such as spark plugs, fan belts, radiator hoses, distributor cap, fuel filter, and pollution control equipment; minor repairs such as brake jobs, water pump, carburetor overhaul, and universal joints; and major repairs such as a complete "valve job." Costs were calculated using 1976 parts prices and a $13.50 per hour labor rate.		
Replacement tires	It was assumed that 3 new regular tires and 4 new snow tires would be purchased during the lives of the standard and subcompact size cars, and 7 new regular tires and 4 new snow tires would be purchased during the life of the compact car.		
Accessories	It was assumed that extra wheels and floor mats would be purchased the first year, seat covers the sixth year, and miscellaneous items totalling $2.65 each year.		

Gasoline	Consumption rate of 15 miles per gallon and a gasoline price of 60.9 cents per gallon including taxes were used.	Consumption rate of 21 miles per gallon and a gasoline price of 60.9 cents per gallon including taxes were used.	Consumption rate of 29 miles per gallon and a gasoline price of 60.9 cents per gallon including taxes were used.
Oil	Consumption at a rate of 1 gallon of oil for every 167 gallons of gasoline and a price of $1.06 per quart were used.	Consumption at a rate of 1 gallon of oil for every 119 gallons of gasoline and a price of $1.06 per quart were used.	Consumption at a rate of 1 gallon of oil for every 95 gallons of gasoline and a price of $1.06 per quart were used.
Insurance	Coverage includes $50,000 combined public liability ($15,000/$30,000 bodily injury, and $5,000 property damage), $2,500 personal injury protection, uninsured motorist coverage, and full comprehensive coverage for the 10-year period. Deductible collision insurance was assumed for the first 5 years ($100 deductible).		
Garaging, parking, and tolls	Includes monthly charges of $12.00 for garage rental or indirect cost of the owner's garaging facility, and a toll average of $6.88 per year; plus parking fee averages of $70.00 per year for standard size cars, and $60.00 per year for compact and subcompact size cars. Parking fees and toll fee averages were assigned in proportion to annual travel.		
Taxes	Includes federal excise taxes on tires (10 cents per pound), lubricating oil (6 cents per gallon), and gasoline (4 cents per gallon); plus the Maryland tax on gasoline (9 cents per gallon), titling tax (4 percent of retail price), sales tax (4 percent of retail items), and registration fee ($20.00 for 3,700 pounds or less shipping weight, or $30.00 for vehicles over 3,700 pounds).		

Source: *Cost of Operating an Automobile,* U.S. Department of Transportation, 1976.

the total cost is $17,900, many times the original average purchase price of $4,899. In fact the purchase price is only 27.4 percent of the estimated total life-cycle cost of this car.

Auto operating costs have risen substantially in recent years. Much of the increase in operating costs between 1972 and 1976 (see Exhibit 7–2) is the result of greatly increased prices for petroleum products, maintenance, accessories, parts, and tires.

Operating costs do vary by the size of the car. Owners of a 1976 compact car can expect to spend about 14.6 cents per mile, or $14,561.46, over its ten-year life. An owner of a 1976 subcompact car can count on spending 12.6 cents per mile, or $12,638.35, for using the subcompact for ten years. While these operating costs are less than those for the standard-size car, they have increased by about 35 percent between the 1972 and 1976 model years.

Basis for cost estimates

Descriptions of the vehicles, repairs, maintenance, replacements, insurance, etc., used by the U.S. Department of Transportation in its study are shown in Exhibit 7–3. The accessories included on each size are those that nationwide sales records show to be typical for that group. For example, these records show that 90 percent or more of the 1976 model standard- and compact-size cars had power steering, over 95 percent had automatic transmissions, 80 percent had radios, and 89 percent of the standard-size cars had air conditioning. For the subcompacts the number with power steering was negligible, 27 percent had air conditioning, 60 percent had automatic transmissions, and 77 percent had radios.

Operating costs. The operating costs are calculated on the basis of a ten-year, 100,000-mile estimated life. Each car is assumed to be purchased new, without a trade-in, at a price that represents an average discount from sticker price. Annual mileage is decreased over the life of the car because as a car gets older it is driven fewer miles each year and tends to be used as a second car. Even though an average automobile passes through three or more owners during its life, no adjustments in cost were made for change-of-ownership fees. The four major operating costs include depreciation, maintenance and repair, gasoline, and tires.

Depreciation. We can define depreciation as the loss in value of the car during the time it is owned. This loss occurs for three main reasons: (1) passage of time, (2) the number of miles driven, and (3) mechanical and physical deterioration. National vehicle dealer groups issue car value books that give the average values of used cars by geographic areas. These values reflect the loss in value as a result of depreciation.

Formerly the total cost of depreciation for compact and subcompact cars was exceeded by the total cost of gasoline, including taxes. However, rapidly increasing purchase prices for these autos and some improvement in gas mileage now makes the cost of depreciation greater than the cost of gasoline for the ten-year life.

The age of a car is generally a more important factor than is mileage in determining depreciation. Estimates of the percentage of depreciation that occurs in each of the ten years are shown in Exhibit 7–4. For the standard-size car, about 53 percent of the dollar depreciation occurs in the first three years; the remaining 47 percent is spread over the last seven years of life. Depreciation on the smaller cars is more evenly distributed throughout their years of use. At the end of three years, compacts have depreciated by 38 percent while subcompacts have depreciated by only 34 percent.

EXHIBIT 7–4
Estimated percent depreciation by year for a standard, compact, and subcompact automobile over a ten-year, 100,000-mile life

Age (years)	*Standard*	*Compact*	*Subcompact*
1	24.98%	13.99%	12.01%
2	15.38	13.00	11.01
3	13.09	11.51	10.98
4	9.58	10.50	10.69
5	6.99	10.00	10.32
6	6.29	9.84	10.00
7	6.00	9.24	9.69
8	6.00	8.02	9.22
9	6.00	7.40	8.59
10	5.69	6.50	7.49
Total	100.00%	100.00%	100.00%

Source: Adapted from *Cost of Operating an Automobile*, U.S. Department of Transportation, April 1976.

Because new cars are driven more miles than older cars, the depreciation on a per-mile basis is held down the first few years. For example, for the standard-size car purchased for $4,899, the depreciation cost in the first year is $1,215 spread over 14,500 miles, or 8.4 cents per mile. By the end of the second year the car has been driven 27,500 miles and the depreciation totals $1,963, or 7.1 cents per mile. As the car gets older the depreciation decreases, but the outlay for maintenance and repairs increases.

Maintenance and repairs. Safe travel on today's limited-access, high-speed highways requires a well-maintained vehicle. As a car ages it becomes increasingly difficult and expensive to keep it in satisfactory operating condition. Labor charges are a major factor in the high cost of maintenance and repair; charges of $13 per hour or more are not unusual. However, there are large differences in maintenance and repair costs in different parts of the country. Minor maintenance and repairs may be done by the owner of the compact and subcompact models, but they are very difficult on the standard-size automobile.

Gasoline and oil. Expenditures for gas and oil alone, including state and federal taxes, during the ten-year life of each of the cars will be $4,232 for the standard, $3,072 for the compact, and $2,256 for the subcompact. Even ignoring probable price increases over the ten-year period, these petroleum products will cost from 76 percent for the subcompact, to 86 percent for the standard, of the purchase price of the car. Chances that gasoline prices will ever return to pre-1973 levels are so remote as to be nonexistent. Rather, gas prices can be expected to continue to increase and thus increase the life-cycle cost of an auto.

Tires. When a car is driven 100,000 miles there are 400,000 miles of tire wear. The Department of Transportation study assumed that radial tires were mounted on the standard and subcompact cars. Therefore, these autos would wear out the five original tires and require seven replacements each for a total cost of $470 for the standard and $365 for the subcompact car. The 1976 compact models were not typically delivered with radial tires, so it was assumed that fiberglass bias-belted tires were used. Compact-size cars are assumed to require 11 replacement tires at a total cost of $411.

Automobile financing costs. Auto financing charges are not included in the calculation of operating costs by the U.S. Department of Transportation. However, they can easily be computed for given auto sales prices and interest rates.

In buying a car, you may have two alternatives: either pay interest on money borrowed from a bank or other financial institution or buy the car from savings and forego the interest that the money would have earned. Either way, you pay a cost above the ordinary purchase price.

Exhibit 7–5 shows a comparison of the auto financing costs for a 36-month loan covering two-thirds of the purchase price of the car. If the purchase is financed by a withdrawal of savings rather than by borrowing, the amount withdrawn is assumed to be redeposited in 36 equal monthly installments to the savings account where it will earn 5½ percent. A summary of the effect on financing charges on the life-

EXHIBIT 7–5
Comparison of automobile financing costs for a loan and for using savings

Type of auto	Financing costs	
	Loan at 10%	*Withdrawn savings**
Standard	$533	$296
Compact	420	233
Subcompact	339	181

* Assumes a 5½ percent return on savings accounts.

Source: *Cost of Operating an Automobile,* U.S. Department of Transportation, April 1976.

cycle cost of a car is shown in Exhibit 7–6. There can be important cost differences in alternative methods of financing a new car purchase. The merits of various credit plans will be discussed in Chapter 9.

EXHIBIT 7–6
Estimated life-cycle costs of owning an automobile, including financing, over ten-year, 100,000-mile life

	Borrowing at 10%		*Withdraw savings (5½ %)*	
	Total	*Cents per mile*	*Total*	*Cents per mile*
Standard	$18,412	18.41	$18,175	18.18
Compact	14,981	14.98	14,794	14.79
Subcompact	12,977	12.98	12,819	12.82

Source: Adapted from *Cost of Operating an Automobile,* U.S. Department of Transportation, April 1976.

BUY AND HOLD OR TRADE?

A question that often arises is whether you should buy a car and hold it until it has essentially no resale value, or trade every year or so. There is no answer that fits everyone, because families have differing needs and money considerations. Vehicle style, size, interior decor, mechanical features, or availability of money will be factors in your decision. There are, however, larger issues that you should examine first—matters of trading or keeping an auto, leasing or buying, purchasing a new or used vehicle, and so on.

Effect of trading on transportation costs

The cost study by the U.S. Department of Transportation shows that depreciation costs incurred by the "annual trader" over a ten-year period on a standard-size car amount to about $12,150 (ten times the first-year depreciation). Trading every two years would cost about $9,815 in depreciation; trading every three years would cost about $9,015 for the same 10-year period. Exhibit 7–7 shows that even

EXHIBIT 7–7
Operating costs per mile for a standard-size 1976 automobile over ten-year, 100,000-mile life assuming decreasing mileage per year

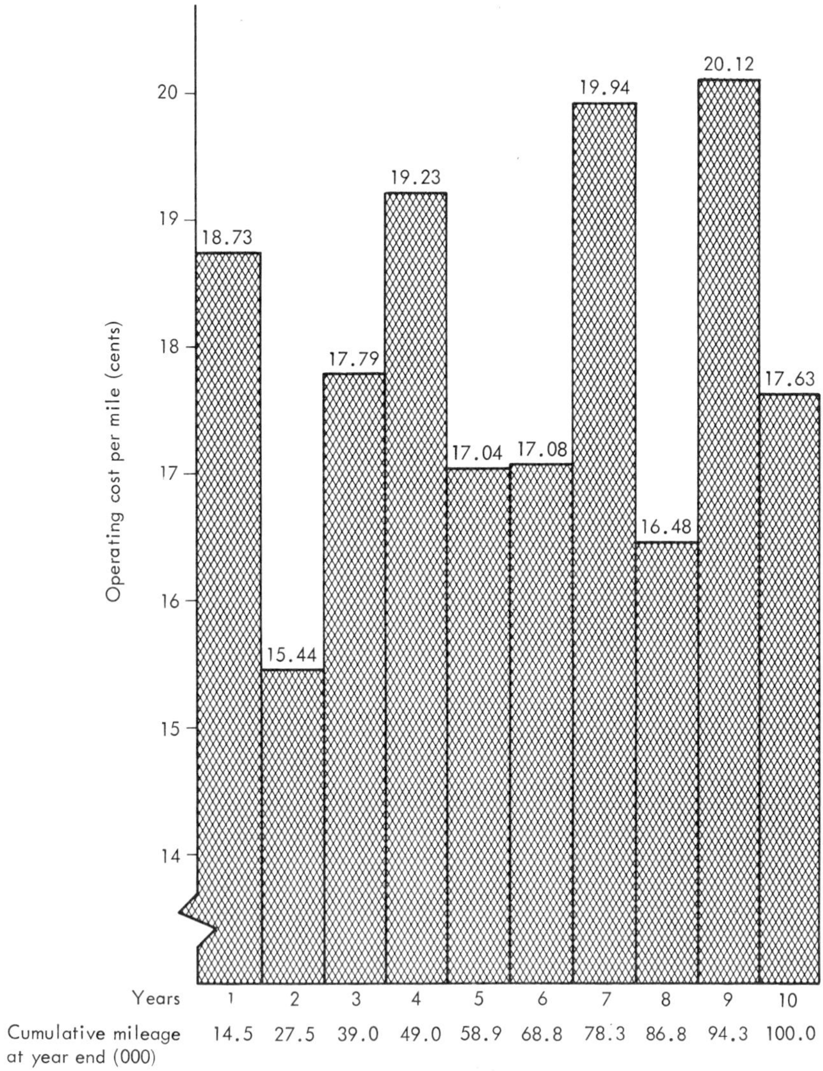

Source: Adapted from *Cost of Operating an Automobile*, U.S. Department of Transportation, Federal Highway Administration, April 1976.

though the depreciation costs for a standard-size car decrease as it gets older, operating costs per mile are higher in years 4, 7, and 9 than in the first year, mainly because of increased maintenance and repairs and decreasing annual mileage. Higher mileage costs for these years could be avoided by trading just before these years. Trading the car at the end of the sixth year and 68,800 miles and buying a new one would enable you to travel 100,000 miles at a lower cost than holding one car for the entire period. The cost of operating a standard-size car for six years and 68,800 miles is $12,072. If a new car is used for the remaining 32,200 miles, the cost is $5,560, for a 100,000-mile total cost of $17,632. This is $247 less than the cost of holding one car for the entire 100,000 miles. This calculation assumes that you drive the car fewer miles each year it is owned.

If you drive 10,000 miles each year for ten years rather than decreasing your use each year as assumed by the U.S. Department of Transportation, holding one car for the 100,000 miles costs less than trading for another car during the ten-year period. The total cost of buying and holding one car is $17,879. If you trade at the end of year 6 for a new car to be driven the remaining 40,000 miles, the total cost of 100,000 miles using the two cars is $18,893. This is largely the result of the greatly reduced depreciation cost per mile in the later years of the life of the auto. Cost per mile for the first 10,000 miles is 24.42 cents (see Exhibit 7–8), 12.15 cents of which is depreciation. For the next eight years, the mileage cost ranges from 16.27 cents to 18.85 cents and then drops to 15.07 cents per mile in the tenth year. Early trading of an auto means that you forego the use of the auto when the cost per mile is lowest.

An obvious difficulty in trying to use these estimates to determine when to trade in a car is that a person's annual car use may tend to be quite constant from year to year. If you drive 14,500 miles each year, by the end of the third year you will have driven 43,500 miles instead of the 39,000 miles estimated by the Transportation Department study. Thus, costs for maintenance and repairs, tires, etc., can be expected to be higher for this three-year-old car than for the average car of its age. Or, if you drive 10,000 miles per year, maintenance, repairs, tires, gasoline, etc., will cost less; however, depreciation will not change significantly.

The total vehicle cost per mile is lower for high-mileage drivers, because depreciation in the early years of a car's life is determined more by age than by miles; and because some of the annual costs, such as garaging and insurance, do not vary in proportion to mileage. These are known as fixed costs; their total amount is constant regardless of whether the auto is used. A low-mileage driver incurs about

EXHIBIT 7–8
Operating costs per mile for a standard-size 1976 automobile over ten-year, 100,000-mile life, assuming constant mileage per year

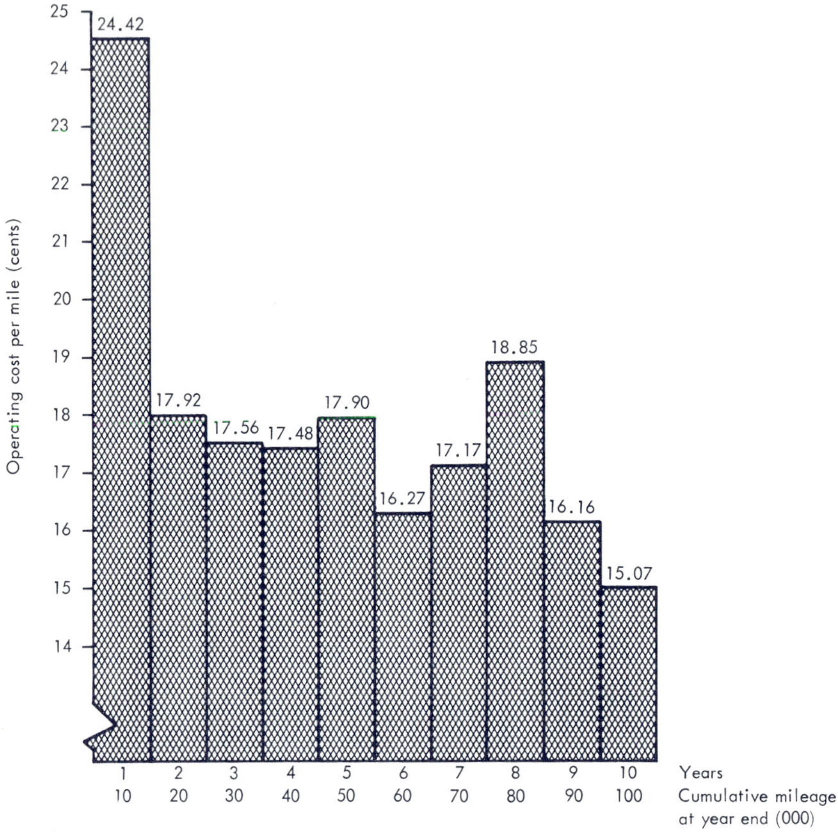

Source: Adapted from *Cost of Operating an Automobile,* U.S. Department of Transportation, 1976.

the same total depreciation and insurance costs, but they are distributed over fewer miles and result in a higher cost per mile. Insurance rates reflect commuting distance to work, but they do not vary directly with total miles driven.

Once you determine your vehicle-use pattern, you can analyze your costs and decide when it will be most advantageous to trade your car. The high-mileage driver may find some repairs and tire replacements moved to earlier years than those assumed by the U.S. Department of Transportation. Of course, comfort, dependability, and appearance are important to many car owners and do influence the automobile trading decision.

Should you consider a used car?

If after considering the purchase of a car you are hesitant about spending so much money for a new one, maybe you should consider buying a "pre-owned" vehicle. Lower purchase prices and much-reduced depreciation are the main advantages over new cars. In return, however, you often must give up the appearance of a new car and be ready to pay higher maintenance and repair costs for a used car.

Some people feel that used cars are available because the previous owners were unhappy with them. While this may be true, people do trade cars for reasons not related to the performance of the car. A carefully chosen used car can provide many miles of transportation, often for a much lower cost than a new car.

A comparison of transportation costs for new and used cars in Exhibit 7–9 indicates that operating costs are lower for the used car. This represents a saving of 3.04 cents per mile over the 30,000 miles. The costs shown are based upon the estimated operating costs of a full-size 1976 car. It is assumed that the family travels 10,000 miles per year and keeps the car, whether purchased new or used, for three years. During this period the operating costs that differ by the greatest amounts are depreciation, repairs and maintenance, and financing.

Depreciation costs shown reflect a 53 percent decrease in value of the auto during the first years of the auto's useful life. The buyer of a three-year-old used car incurs much lower depreciation costs during the next three years.

EXHIBIT 7–9
Comparison of total operating costs, plus financing, for new and used automobiles over a three-year, 30,000-mile life

	*New car**	*Used car†*
Depreciation	$2,600	$1,112
Repairs and maintenance	447	1,331
Replacement tires and accessories	82	129
Gasoline and oil	1,009	1,009
Garage, parking, and tolls	663	663
Insurance	614	504
State and federal taxes	380	418
Financing costs (before taxes)	533	249
Total cost	$6,328	$5,415
Cost per mile (cents)	21.09 cents	18.05 cents

* U.S. Department of Transportation, *Cost of Operating an Automobile.* Standard-Size Auto, April 1976, Years 1–3.

† U.S. Department of Transportation, *Cost of Operating an Automobile.* Standard-Size Auto, April 1976, Years 4–6.

Source: *Cost of Operating an Automobile,* U.S. Department of Transportation, April 1976.

Repairs and maintenance increase as the age and mileage on a car increase. Our example assumes that the used car has 39,000 miles at the time of purchase. If the used car has fewer than 39,000 miles at the time of purchase, the repair and maintenance costs could be lower than the estimates shown.

The assessment of financing cost assumes a three-year, ten percent loan on two-thirds of the purchase price. The assumed purchase price for the new car is $4,899 and the depreciated book value is $2,299 for the used car. Presumably, both cars can be sold for their depreciated values at the end of the three-year period.

ALTERNATIVES TO AUTO OWNERSHIP

An alternative to borrowing money to buy a car is to borrow the car. In return for the use of the car you agree to pay a monthly fee for a specified period of time. This arrangement is known as *leasing.* You are the *lessee* and the lender of the car is known as the *lessor.*

Automobile leasing

There are two basic forms of auto leases, open-end and closed-end. An open-end lease, also referred to as a "finance lease," involves a monthly payment over the life of the lease in addition to paying for all maintenance and other operating and nonoperating costs. The amount of the monthly lease payment is based upon the purchase price of the car and an estimated, guaranteed (by the lessee) value of the car at the end of the lease period. If at the end of the lease period the car can be sold for more than this guaranteed amount, the lessee receives the excess amount. However, any deficiency must be made up by the lessee. The lessee takes the risk of changes in the used-car market. If the lessee does not like the condition of the used-car market at the end of the lease period, the lease can be extended and the car kept on lease.

With a closed-end lease, the lessee simply agrees to make a monthly payment, which may or may not cover other auto costs, and to return the car in acceptable condition at the end of the lease period. The lessor absorbs any gain or loss on the disposal of the car.

Because the lessee guarantees the terminal value of the car, an open-end lease usually requires smaller monthly payments than does a closed-end lease.

Cost comparison of leasing and owning. The decision to lease a car or to borrow the money and buy the car can be made through a comparison of the costs involved with each. As an example we can use the standard-size car described in Exhibit 7–3.

The car may be acquired by borrowing the money to buy or through a closed-end lease. Suppose that an amount equal to two-thirds of the purchase price can be borrowed at an annual rate of ten percent for 36 months. Equal monthly payments are required to repay the loan.

Operating costs shown in Exhibit 7–10 are based upon the U.S. Department of Transportation estimates and are to be paid by the owner or lessee. These costs, except for depreciation and registration, will be identical regardless of the method used to acquire the auto.

EXHIBIT 7–10
Estimated total costs of owning and of leasing a standard-size automobile for a three-year period

	Owning	*Leasing*
Costs excluding taxes:		
Depreciation	$2,600.00	$ 0.00
Repairs and maintenance	772.00	772.00
Replacement tires	83.20	83.20
Gasoline	1,245.39	1,245.39
Oil	43.41	43.41
Insurance	614.00	614.00
Garaging, parking, tolls, etc.	722.83	722.83
Taxes:		
State: Gasoline	234.00	234.00
Registration	90.00	0.00
Federal: Gasoline and oil	104.63	104.63
Tires	4.06	4.06
Total of operating costs	$6,513.52	$3,823.52
Financing or lease:		
Interest foregone on downpayment of $1,633	$ 216.00	$ 0.00
Financing charges on balance of $3,266	425.36	0.00
Lease payments	0.00	5,024.52
Total finance or lease costs	$ 641.36	$5,024.52
Total costs	$7,154.88	$8,848.04
Estimated cost advantage of owning for the three-year period	$1,693.16	

Source: Owning costs based on *Cost of Operating an Automobile,* U.S. Department of Transportation, April 1976. Lease estimates based on average lease costs quoted to author by auto leasing firms.

Costs of owning. Exhibit 7–10 shows the total cost of owning and operating an auto, including the financing of the purchase. These costs include not only the actual outlays for the downpayment and repayment of balance plus interest, but also the interest foregone during the three-year period by making the downpayment. If an amount equal to the downpayment were deposited to earn 5½ percent in a savings account for the three-year period, it would earn about $216 after paying income taxes at an assumed rate of 20 percent ($1,633 ×

0.055 × 3 × 0.80). In addition, 36 monthly payments of $105.49 each are required to repay the loan balance of $3,266.

It is necessary to adjust the amount of interest paid because it is a deductible item for income tax purposes, assuming you itemize deductions.[5] If you are in the 20 percent marginal tax bracket, the net after-tax cost of the interest paid is $425.36 ($531.70 × .80). The total cost of owning the car for the three years is $7,154.88.

Cost of leasing. The cost of leasing differs from the cost of owning because the lessee does not incur the depreciation or registration costs, nor is a cash downpayment required at the beginning of the lease period. However, the lessee's monthly payments are $139.57 and thus they exceed in amount the monthly payments made by owners. A disadvantage of leasing is that at the end of the lease period the auto belongs to the lessor.

There are no income tax adjustments for lease payments because lease payments for family transportation are not allowable as itemized deductions.

Cost Comparison. A comparison of the total costs of owning and leasing shown in Exhibit 7–10 indicates a cost advantage of $1,693.16 for owning. Because of the higher costs usually associated with leasing, it is not an attractive way for a family to meet its transportation needs.

Although we do not discuss it, leasing may be advantageous to those people who can deduct the lease cost as a professional or business expense for tax purposes. Because most consumers do not fit in that category when providing for personal transportation needs, we have left out this discussion. However, if you are in a high tax bracket and use an auto extensively for business, you should look at the after-tax cost in comparing leasing and owning.

Alternative—Public transit systems

The availability and quality of public transportation are topics of much discussion in most cities today. On the one hand, there is the perceived social need to increase the use of mass transportation systems in order to conserve our resources and reduce pollution. On the other hand, public transportation systems are being criticized for the quantity or quality of their service. As a result, many consumers seem to feel that the cost of inconveniences such as transferring lines or waiting for the bus or train is greater than the cost of operating a private auto. Because of this "cost," they continue using private autos to

---

[5] Taxes will be discussed in greater detail in Chapter 16.

commute to work even with public transportation available. Continued use of the auto may also be the result of habit. In any case, the selection of a mode of transportation should include a comparison of relative costs.

Cost comparison—An example. It is very difficult to compare the cost of operating a private auto with the cost of using public transportation if the comparison is to consider any factors other than time and out-of-pocket costs. Benefits to be obtained from the transportation—getting from home to the job—can be assumed to be identical regardless of the mode used. The question becomes one of getting there at the least cost.

To illustrate the selection decision process, consider the example in Exhibit 7–11. Shown there are the estimated out-of-pocket and time costs for the private auto and for public transportation using the following assumptions. First, the car is owned for family purposes and is available for the trip to the job. Thus, only the costs that vary with the mileage driven are included in this calculation. The variable cost of 8.63 cents per mile for the 20-mile round trip by auto is based upon the U.S. Department of Transportation estimates for the cost of operating standard-size cars. A separate cost is included for parking and tolls incurred in traveling to and from the job.

EXHIBIT 7–11
An example of relative costs for private and public transportation

	Private auto	*Public transportation*
Out-of-pocket costs		
Operating costs at 8.63 cents per mile (trip of 10 miles each way)*	$1.73	—
Parking and tolls	3.00	—
Fare	—	$1.00
Total	$4.73	$1.00
Time		
Waiting for public vehicle (5 min. each way)	—	10
Walking time: home to pickup point	—	10
Walking time: pickup point to job site	—	10
Walking time: parking lot to job site	15	—
Time spent in vehicle for 20-mile round trip	50	70
Total time door-to-door (minutes)	65	100
Value of time at $4 per hour	$4.33	$6.67
Total cost of trip	$9.06	$7.67

* Ten-year average cost from U.S. Department of Transportation, *Cost of Operating an Automobile, 1976.*

Second, an average wait of five minutes is spent for each trip on the public vehicle in order to allow for variation in vehicle time schedules.

In addition, it is assumed that it is a five-minute walk from the rider's home to the public vehicle pickup point and a five-minute walk from the destination stop to the job location. The auto driver takes seven minutes to walk from the parking lot to the job location. The parking fee and tolls for the auto are $3 per day.[6] Finally, assume that time spent in transit is valued at $4 per hour.

Based on these estimates, the use of the public vehicle is $1.39 per day cheaper than the use of the private auto if time costs are considered. For the 260 working days in a year (52 weeks × 5 days per week) this would mean a cost savings of $361 per year. However, small changes in the assumptions could reverse this decision. For example, if parking is provided by the employer, the cost of using the auto would be less than the cost of using a public vehicle. Or, the use of a compact or subcompact auto would reduce the out-of-pocket auto costs.

Other cost factors. It should be recognized that this cost comparison does not consider other factors that favor the private auto, such as privacy, flexibility, and convenience; nor does it reflect the large governmental subsidies for auto travel, which place public transportation at a competitive disadvantage.

Many economists believe that the current level of subsidization of auto travel will not encourage car drivers to begin using public transportation. Presently, car owners do not directly pay the full cost of driving an auto. Costs of street maintenance and repairs, snow removal, traffic controls, and police are commonly paid out of city tax revenues. Even on-street parking spaces can be "rented" by auto drivers for a pittance relative to the true value of the property. Urban commuters pay only a small percentage of the costs of driving their cars in the city. As a result, mass transit will probably not be very successful in solving transportation problems until auto drivers are required to bear more of the full cost of auto travel.

AUTOMOBILE REPAIRS

It has been estimated that consumers spend over $30 billion of their income each year for auto maintenance and repairs. A check with the Better Business Bureau, American Automobile Association, or similar organization will quickly reveal that there are frightening numbers of incompetent and dishonest auto mechanics who defraud unsuspecting and vulnerable consumers. During 1972 the diagnostic clinic of the Automobile Club of Missouri rechecked more than 1,000

[6] Average 1977 downtown parking fees for 50 cities across the United States are shown in Appendix B. The study was conducted by Runzheimer and Company, Inc.

autos that had been repaired by mechanics. They found that nearly 29 percent of the repairs were not satisfactory or were not done but charged for. The average bill for the incompetent or fraudulent repairs was $127. The survey was repeated in 1974. This time they found nearly 38 percent of the work to be unsatisfactory. Car owners paid an average of $148 for these repairs. In New York City, reporters for the *New York Times* removed a small part from an auto that otherwise worked perfectly. They took the car to 24 repair shops with the explanation that the car didn't work right. Of the 24 shops, only eight were able to repair it—one did it without charge. Seven other shops offered estimates ranging from $199.95 to $345 for the repair.[7] For a consumer, the difficulty is finding the honest and competent mechanic and avoiding the charlatans.

The estimated cost of maintenance and repairs increases as the car gets older and has traveled more miles, as shown in Exhibit 7–12. Parts wear out, and their replacement requires the services of someone who is knowledgeable. While many do-it-yourself mechanics may be able to change oil and spark plugs, fewer are able to change points or rebuild carburetors. Thus, because of our dependence on the auto for transportation, sooner or later we are all at the mercy of the auto repair industry.

EXHIBIT 7–12
Estimated maintenance and repair costs for first five years

Size of auto	Maintenance and repair costs*				
	Year 1	*Year 2*	*Year 3*	*Year 4*	*Year 5*
Standard	$157.05	$199.95	$414.67	$548.03	$406.52
	(1.08)	(1.54)	(3.60)	(5.48)	(4.11)
Compact	$139.33	$234.68	$296.88	$386.04	$397.98
	(0.96)	(1.81)	(2.58)	(3.86)	(4.02)
Subcompact	$126.12	$190.82	$167.73	$436.97	$370.54
	(0.87)	(1.47)	(1.46)	(4.37)	(3.74)

* Figures in parentheses represent cents per mile based upon estimated miles driven per year.

Source: *Cost of Operating an Automobile*, U.S. Department of Transportation, April 1976.

Selecting a mechanic

One way to improve your chances of getting competent service is to find a shop that employs mechanics certified through the National Institute for Automotive Service Excellence. Through this Institute's

[7] "How to Find a Good Mechanic," *Consumer Reports*, April 1976, pp. 199–204.

EXHIBIT 7–13
Indexes relative to automobile repair costs, 1967–1977

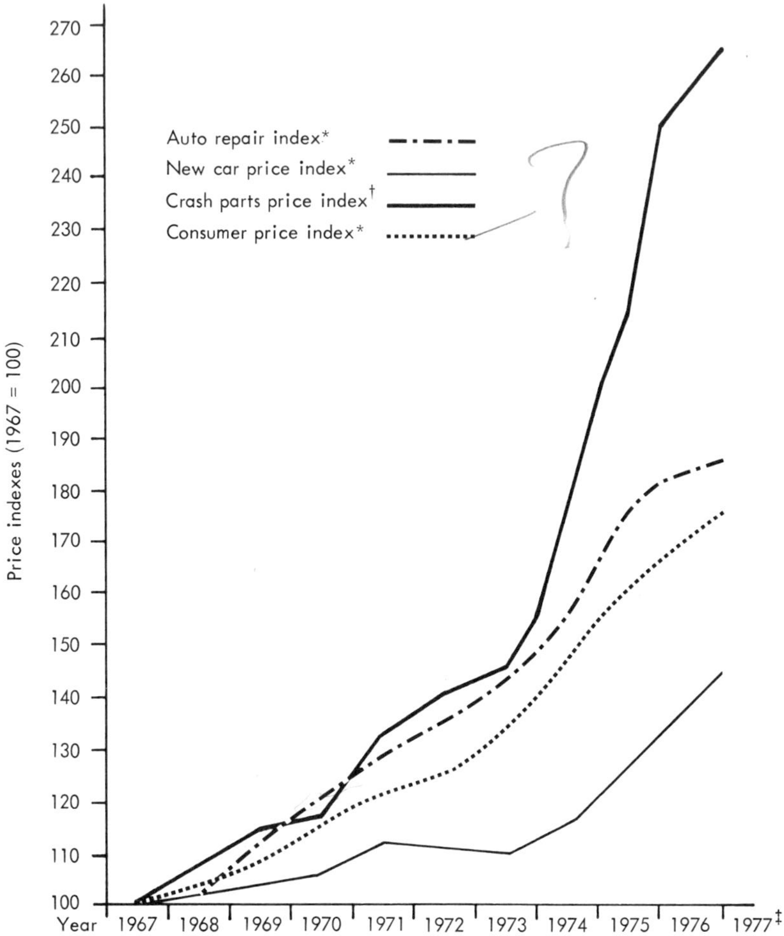

* U.S. Department of Labor, Bureau of Labor Statistics.

† State Farm Crash Parts Price Index.

‡ State Farm Crash Parts Price Index (preliminary, January 1977).

Source: State Farm Mutual Automobile Insurance Co., *The Crash Parts Price Index,* October 1976.

voluntary certification program, mechanics may take tests prepared by the Educational Testing Service of Princeton, New Jersey. A battery of four exams is used to certify the mechanics as competent to perform specific repairs on an automobile.

Another important source of information on auto repairs and

service is your friends. If they have been treated fairly and have received competent service at a shop, chances are you will have the same experience.

Once you find an honest, competent mechanic, continue to take your car to that person for service. The mechanic will get to know what work has been done and needs to be done on your car. Because of the labor cost involved in tearing down an engine, it may be possible to repair several things while the car is apart at a much lower cost than doing each repair separately.

High repair costs

The cost of auto repairs has increased steadily as a result of increased charges for labor and rapidly rising prices for parts.

A cost study conducted by the American Mutual Insurance Alliance showed that it would cost $19,979 to replace all the parts on a 1976 standard-size car. The factory list price of this same car was $4,438. The significance of this is that damage to less than one fourth of the car will cost more to repair than the car is worth. For example, suppose that the car used in this study is involved in a crash and 25 percent of its parts must be replaced. Repair costs will be $4,995 (0.25 × $19,979), or $557 more than the factory list price of a new car.[8]

Changes in the cost of auto repairs, replacement parts, and the cost of new cars are shown in Exhibit 7–13 along with changes in the consumer price index. During the period 1967 to 1977, the cost of auto repairs has increased by 82.5 percent; the cost of replacement "crash parts" (those parts that are typically repaired or replaced as a result of an accident rather than as a matter of maintenance) has increased by nearly 165 percent; the consumer price index increased by 74.3 percent.[9] Such rapid increases in prices make it difficult for consumers to maintain their levels of satisfaction for transportation.

OPPORTUNITIES TO SAVE ON AUTOMOBILE OPERATING COSTS

As indicated in the preceding discussion, auto operating costs require a large portion of family income. To keep these costs as low as

[8] *The National Underwriter*, Property and Casualty Insurance Edition, April 9, 1976, p. 2. See also *Cost of Automobile Crash Parts* (hearings before a Committee on Commerce, United States Senate, 94th Congress, 2d session), (Washington, D.C.: U.S. Government Printing Office, 1976).

[9] State Farm Mutual Automobile Insurance Company, *The Crash Parts Index*, October 1976, p. 3.

possible, the following opportunities are available to nearly all families.

Tire selection and care

Using radial tires instead of bias-ply tires provides longer tire life, particularly in over-the-road driving. The original cost of the radials is higher, but the longer life and the increased gas mileage, 5 to 7 percent, will easily make up the difference. Proper tire inflation also adds to their life. Pressure should be checked regularly. For long trips that involve carrying luggage, it may be wise to add up to two pounds of pressure per tire.

Carpools

Carpools can provide adequate transportation in most cases, and cut car costs. One study by the Federal Highway Administration concluded that forming a two-person carpool saved from $366 to $581 per year per person, depending upon the size of the car driven. Expanding the carpool to four members resulted in an annual saving per person of $847 when a standard-size car was used, $635 per person with a compact, and $528 per person when a subcompact car was used for a 30-mile commuting distance.[10]

Finance costs

Shopping for money to finance the auto purchase is worthwhile. Finance costs can be reduced even further if money is accumulated in a savings account, then used to pay cash for the auto. The use and cost of credit is discussed in Chapter 9.

Maintenance and repairs

Regular maintenance of an auto contributes to lower operating costs. For example, a well-tuned engine uses fuel efficiently.

Careful reading of the new car warranty and full use of every promised service can save substantial costs. If warranty-based repairs are put in writing, and a copy is retained by the owner, this record may be useful in determining responsibility for any repairs requested but not completed before the warranty expires.

---

[10] *Carpool Savings Analysis*, Federal Highway Administration, December 1975.

Additional costs may be saved when you make as many minor repairs and replacements as possible rather than paying mechanic's wages to have them done.

Insurance

Insurance suited to particular use patterns and reduced rates for a good safety record are economical. Reduced rates are also often available for second cars and for cars used in a carpool. Chapter 11 includes a more detailed discussion of auto insurance.

SOCIAL COSTS OF AUTOMOBILES

Owning and operating a car involves more than just operating expenses. Until recently car owners were quite unaware of, and certainly did not pay, the social costs of auto transportation. People, particularly those living in large cities such as Los Angeles, Chicago, and New York, have now become painfully aware of the social costs—especially air pollution. The exhaust fumes of autos are believed to account for about 60 percent of the air pollution in American cities today.

The social costs of auto ownership can no longer be ignored. As a result, the users of cars are being required to pay more of the full cost of owning and operating their autos. Though the pollution control and safety devices required on new cars reduce emissions and increase the owners' security, they add considerably to purchase costs and often raise life-cycle costs in terms of more repairs or greater gas consumption.

Another social cost that must be dealt with is the traffic congestion resulting from the large number of cars in use. The U.S. Department of Transportation reports that in 1977 there were over 111 million registered cars in the United States—more than one car for each two persons. Congestion in cities, on bridges, and at intersections results in social costs such as time lost by everyone involved.

Society also pays for auto transportation by having the beauty of the landscape covered with concrete or blacktop in order to have a place to drive and park cars. The increasing number of cars seems to have created an insatiable need to expand these facilities, often with little regard to the nonaesthetic monsters created in the process. Highways cover roughly one percent of the total area of the 50 states, an area about the size of the state of Indiana. Some 14 to 15 percent of the land in metropolitan areas is devoted to streets, and the percentage is even higher in central business districts.[11]

Our capitalistic system would indicate that the obvious solution lies in the pocketbook. When auto owners are required to pay the full cost of owning and operating a car, they will re-evaluate their priorities and seek alternative means of transportation. If a higher fee is charged to cross a bridge during peak traffic hours, some drivers will arrange to cross during off-peak periods and thereby reduce congestion. If gas taxes or tolls are increased to support the building and maintenance of the highways, people may arrange carpools to reduce the cost for each person. Such an action would not only reduce congestion but also gas usage and highway space required.

Until we get to the point where such a pricing system can be implemented, we, as members of society, are likely to continue subsidizing auto travel through payment of taxes, aesthetic discomfort, and breathing polluted air.

SUMMARY

As is indicated by auto ownership information, the auto has become a necessity in today's family life. Two- and three-car families are becoming common, especially among the middle and upper income groups. Alternative means of family transportation are not likely to replace cars until auto owners are required to bear the full cost of auto transportation.

The major auto operating expenses include depreciation, maintenance and repairs, and gasoline. Operating costs are highest per mile for the average car, as described by the U.S. Department of Transportation, in years 4, 7, and 9 of the estimated ten-year life. This varies, however, depending upon the use patterns of different families.

Alternatives to owning an auto may be more convenient and less costly. Auto leasing offers one alternative to owning a car. Generally, a comparison of costs will show that there is a cost advantage to owning an auto. Public transit should also be considered as a possible option in filling transportation needs.

Auto repairs can be very costly. The best approach to auto repairs is to find a competent, honest auto mechanic to do all of the work on your car.

In considering the cost of autos, we must all be aware of social costs. Society pays a great cost in the form of pollution, aesthetic discomforts, and taxes in order that car owners may operate their vehicles.

---

[11] U.S. Department of Transportation, *National Transportation Trends and Choices* (Washington, D.C.: U.S. Government Printing Office, 1977), pp. 89–90.

APPENDIX A

Estimated cost of operating a compact-size 1976 model automobile*

Item	First year (14,500 miles) Total cost	First year Cost per mile†	Second year (13,000 miles) Total cost	Second year Cost per mile†	Third year (11,500 miles) Total cost	Third year Cost per mile†	Fourth year (10,000 miles) Total cost	Fourth year Cost per mile†	Fifth year (9,900 miles) Total cost	Fifth year Cost per mile†
Costs excluding taxes										
Depreciation	$ 536.00	3.70¢	$ 498.00	3.83¢	$ 441.00	3.83¢	$ 402.00	4.02¢	$ 383.00	3.87¢
Repairs and maintenance	139.33	.96	234.68	1.81	296.88	2.58	386.04	3.86	397.98	4.02
Replacement tires	20.23	.14	18.14	.14	30.55	.27	48.05	.48	43.34	.44
Accessories	7.59	.05	7.07	.05	6.55	.06	6.05	.06	6.02	.06
Gasoline	330.74	2.28	296.52	2.28	262.31	2.28	228.10	2.28	225.81	2.28
Oil	14.84	.10	13.78	.10	14.84	.13	13.78	.14	19.08	.19
Insurance	199.00	1.38	187.00	1.44	187.00	1.63	173.00	1.73	173.00	1.75
Garaging, parking, tolls, etc.	240.98	1.66	230.94	1.78	220.91	1.92	210.88	2.11	210.21	2.12
Total	1,488.71	10.27	1,486.13	11.43	1,460.04	12.70	1,467.90	14.68	1,458.44	14.73
Taxes and fees										
State:										
Gasoline	62.10	.43	55.71	.43	49.32	.43	42.84	.43	42.39	.43
Registration	20.00	.14	20.00	.15	20.00	.17	20.00	.20	20.00	.20
Titling	154.60	1.06	—	—	—	—	—	—	—	—
Sales	7.28	.05	10.95	.09	13.95	.12	18.16	.18	18.66	.19
Subtotal	243.98	1.68	86.66	.67	83.27	.72	81.00	.81	81.05	.82
Federal:										
Gasoline	27.60	.19	24.76	.19	21.92	.19	19.04	.19	18.84	.19
Oil	.21	—	.20	—	.21	—	.19	—	.27	—
Tires	1.25	.01	1.12	.01	1.89	.02	2.97	.03	2.68	.03
Subtotal	29.06	.20	26.08	.20	24.02	.21	22.20	.22	21.79	.22
Total taxes and fees	273.04	1.88	112.74	.87	107.29	.93	103.20	1.03	102.84	1.04
Total of all costs	1,761.75	12.15	1,598.87	12.30	1,567.33	13.63	1,571.10	15.71	1,561.28	15.77

APPENDIX A *(continued)*

Item	Sixth year (9,900 miles)		Seventh year (9,500 miles)		Eighth year (8,500 miles)		Ninth year (7,500 miles)		Tenth year (5,700 miles)		Totals and averages for ten years (100,000 miles)	
	Total cost	*Cost per mile*†	*Total cost*	*Cost per mile*†	*Total cost*	*Cost per mile*†	*Total cost*	*Cost per mile*†	*Total cost*	*Cost per mile*†	*Total cost*	*Cost per mile*†
Costs excluding taxes:												
Depreciation	$ 377.00	3.81¢	$ 354.00	3.73¢	$ 307.00	3.61¢	$ 283.00	3.77¢	$249.00	4.37¢	$ 3,830.00	3.83¢
Repairs and maintenance	405.32	4.10	618.16	6.51	293.95	3.46	132.41	1.77	56.25	.99	2,961.00	2.96
Replacement tires	49.90	.51	53.74	.56	48.08	.57	42.42	.57	32.75	.57	387.20	.39
Accessories	12.16	.12	11.77	.12	10.82	.13	9.84	.13	8.13	.14	86.00	.09
Gasoline	225.81	2.28	216.69	2.28	193.88	2.28	171.07	2.28	130.01	2.28	2,280.94	2.28
Oil	19.08	.19	21.20	.22	19.08	.22	20.14	.27	13.78	.24	169.60	.17
Insurance	135.00	1.36	135.00	1.42	135.00	1.59	135.00	1.80	135.00	2.37	1,594.00	1.59
Garaging, parking, tolls, etc.	210.21	2.12	207.54	2.19	200.85	2.36	194.16	2.59	182.12	3.20	2,108.80	2.11
Total	1,434.48	14.49	1,618.10	17.03	1,208.66	14.22	988.04	13.18	807.04	14.16	13,417.54	13.42
Taxes and fees:												
State:												
Gasoline	42.39	.43	40.68	.43	36.45	.43	32.13	.43	24.39	.43	428.40	.43
Registration	20.00	.20	20.00	.21	20.00	.24	20.00	.26	20.00	.35	200.00	.20
Titling	—	—	—	—	—	—	—	—	—	—	154.60	.16
Sales	19.46	.20	28.19	.30	14.88	.17	8.19	.11	4.43	.07	144.15	.14
Subtotal	81.85	.83	88.87	.94	71.33	.84	60.32	.80	48.82	.85	927.15	.93
Federal:												
Gasoline	18.84	.19	18.08	.19	16.20	.19	14.28	.19	10.84	.19	190.40	.19
Oil	.27	—	.30	—	.27	—	.29	—	.19	—	2.40	—
Tires	3.11	.03	3.32	.04	2.98	.04	2.63	.04	2.02	.04	23.97	.02
Subtotal	22.22	.22	21.70	.23	19.45	.23	17.20	.23	13.05	.23	216.77	.21
Total taxes and fees	104.07	1.05	110.57	1.17	90.78	1.07	77.52	1.03	61.87	1.08	1,143.92	1.14
Total of all costs	1,538.55	15.54	1,728.67	18.20	1,299.44	15.29	1,065.56	14.21	868.91	15.24	14,561.46	14.56

* This estimate covers the total costs of a medium priced, compact size, 2-door sedan, purchased for $3,865, operated 100,000 miles over a 10-year period, then scrapped for $35. Baltimore area prices, considered to be in the middle range, were used.

† Where costs per mile are less than 1/20 cent, a dash (—) appears in the column.

Source: U.S. Department of Transportation, Federal Highway Administration, *Cost of Owning and Operating an Automobile, 1976.*

APPENDIX B

Average 1977 downtown parking fees for selected U.S. cities (based on monthly rates)

	Average downtown parking fees	
	Annually	*Monthly*
New York (Manhattan) NY	$1,127	$93.91
Boston, MA	709	59.06
Washington, DC	692	57.70
Houston, TX	622	51.87
Chicago, IL	578	48.19
Philadelphia, PA	564	47.03
New Orleans, LA	537	44.78
Pittsburgh, PA	535	44.57
San Francisco, CA	526	43.81
Baltimore, MD	508	42.34
Columbus, OH	451	37.60
Cleveland, OH	443	36.92
Honolulu, HI	426	35.52
Miami, FL	401	33.45
Minneapolis, MN	399	33.29
Tampa, FL	390	32.51
Harrisburg, PA	385	32.08
Cincinnati, OH	383	31.95
Detroit, MI	383	31.93
Seattle, WA	364	30.32
Dallas, TX	360	30.00
Milwaukee, WI	358	29.87
Nashville, TN	347	28.88
Omaha, NE	344	28.70
Atlanta, GA	335	27.95
Denver, CO	325	27.11
Worcester, MA	317	26.40
Los Angeles, CA	308	25.65
Providence, RI	305	25.40
Spokane, WA	303	25.23
Dayton, OH	302	25.14
Rochester, NY	300	25.02
Jacksonville, FL	298	24.80
Albany, NY	296	24.67
Kansas City, MO	295	24.62
Indianapolis, IN	295	24.60
St. Louis, MO	291	24.21
Wilmington, DE	290	24.18
Buffalo, NY	286	23.82
Des Moines, IA	284	23.68
Louisville, KY	283	23.60
Portland, OR	282	23.50
Syracuse, NY	282	23.50
Richmond, VA	278	23.20
Toledo, OH	275	22.90
Tulsa, OK	273	22.73
Memphis, TN	268	22.34
Birmingham, AL	268	22.33
Madison, WI	264	22.00
San Diego, CA	258	21.47

Source: Runzheimer and Company, Inc.

DISCUSSION QUESTIONS

1. Discuss the role of the automobile in meeting family transportation needs. How is this role affected by the level of family income?
2. Mass transit systems are encouraged and discouraged at the same time by governmental actions toward energy conservation, pollution control, and by heavily subsidizing auto travel. Discuss.
3. Define the term "depreciation." Why does it occur? Do cars of different sizes depreciate at the same rates? Give examples.
4. Describe what a car owner can expect to happen to maintenance expense as the car gets older.
5. Which costs of operating a car are fixed costs (remain the same whether or not the car is driven) and which are variable?
6. Explain why the operating costs per mile, from the Department of Transportation Study, reach high points in years 4, 7, and 9. How do these changing costs affect the buyer of a used automobile?
7. What is leasing? What are the two basic types of leases available?
8. What is meant by the term "social costs"? Who pays these costs?

CASE PROBLEMS

1. Kelly Flanagan is planning to purchase a new compact car. She plans to keep the car for four years and then replace it with another new one. Kelly estimates that she will drive 49,000 miles during the four years.

   Estimate the average cost per mile that Kelly can expect to pay if she follows her plan. Assume that the cost estimates of the U.S. Department of Transportation shown in Appendix A apply.

2. John Rawlins commutes 20 miles one way to work each day. In an effort to keep his costs down, he is considering the use of public transportation rather than the family car. John estimates that his time spent commuting is worth $5 per hour.

   In an effort to determine the out-of-pocket costs and time spent, John has kept records for one week for each mode of transportation. He has found that his bus fare is $2 for the round trip. It takes three minutes to walk from his home to the bus stop where his average wait is five minutes. Upon reaching his destination stop after a 45-minute ride John spends three minutes walking to his place of work. When he returns home he spends the same total time in transit.

   When John drives the family compact-model car to work it takes an average of 40 minutes to travel from home to the parking lot. Parking and tolls cost $2.50 per day. He then must walk for five minutes to reach his job. The return trip home takes the same length of time. See Appendix A for estimated operating costs.

   How should John travel to and from his job? Why?

3. Clayton Williams, a 21-year-old student, wishes to compare the costs of owning a new vs. used compact automobile. He has obtained the cost estimates from the U.S. Department of Transportation (Appendix A) as a basis for his comparison. Clayton's driving patterns do not match those used in the Department of Transportation estimates, however, in that he drives 14,000 miles per year. Present plans are that Clayton will keep whichever car he purchases for four years.

   After doing some shopping around, Clayton has found that he can buy a new compact for $3,865 or he could purchase a two-year-old used compact with 20,000 miles for $2,831. Financing is available for 90 percent of the purchase price at an annual percentage rate of 12 percent for 36 months. Total financing costs are $745.30 and $545.38 for the new and used cars, respectively. (Hint: Assume that the estimated costs shown in Appendix A are valid for both cars.)

   a. What are the total estimated operating costs for the four years if Clayton owns a new car? For the used car? Compare the cost per mile for each car.

   b. Which car should Clayton purchase? Are there factors other than cost that should be considered? Explain.

SELECTED READINGS

Consumer Guide. *Complete Guide to Used Cars.* New York: Signet, annual editions.

Consumer Guide. *New Car Price Guides.* New York: Signet, annual editions.

Consumer Reports (Special Automobile Issue), annual publication, usually in April.

Ende, Jean, and Earl, Clifford J. *Buy it Right!* New York: E. P. Dutton & Co., Inc., 1974, pp. 62–72.

"Making Mass Transit Work," *Business Week,* February 16, 1974 (no. 2318), pp. 74–80.

Engel, Lyle K. *Auto Repair Frauds.* New York: Arco Publishing Co., Inc., 1976.

U.S. Department of Transportation. *National Transportation Trends and Choices,* Washington, D.C.: U.S. Government Printing Office, 1977.

Family housing: Rent or buy?

8

OBJECTIVES

Housing decisions require the careful consideration of housing needs and the costs of satisfying these needs either by buying or renting. After thoroughly reading and discussing this chapter you should be able to:

. . . Explain the role of housing in satisfying human needs.
. . . Identify the relationship between family housing status, family income, and family size.
. . . Describe the advantages and disadvantages of owning and of renting housing.
. . . Compare the costs of owning with the costs of renting housing.
. . . Describe the advantages and disadvantages of owning co-op housing, mobile homes, and condominiums.

One of your most important spending decisions involves money spent on housing. Housing costs, on the average, will consume 25 to 35 percent of your annual income. As a result, careful consideration is required to ensure that you receive the greatest satisfaction possible from the income you spend on housing. Decisions on housing expenditures call for careful analysis of housing needs and dollars available to fill those needs.

DETERMINANTS OF FAMILY HOUSING NEEDS

Needs, life-styles, goals, and aspirations vary greatly from one family to another. A variety of housing forms is needed to meet these varying requirements. You can best decide how to meet your own housing needs if you first analyze how families are similar and how they tend to differ in their needs.[1]

Common needs for housing

Several housing needs are common to all people. Among the common needs are shelter from the elements, health and sanitation, and a place to keep possessions. Space is needed for the basic activities such as preparing meals, eating, sleeping, and entertaining. Filling these common needs is an important factor in choosing housing. You should analyze these needs, keeping in mind that your priorities for each may differ from the priorities of others.

Varying needs for housing

In addition to these common housing needs there are needs that, though less well understood, are of a social nature, such as the need for privacy and the need to interact with others. Family situations and personal needs also have an effect on decisions for housing.

Family situation. Housing needs are greatly affected by your stage in the family life cycle. Space needs increase as children grow and mature and then decrease as the family reaches the "empty nest" stage.

Housing needs vary from family to family as well as from stage to stage. For example, one family with school-age children may place a high priority on location near selected schools, while another may wish to locate near a recreation site such as a lake. Senior families may be more concerned with privacy or with easy access to community facilities. As the family's situation changes, so do its needs and priorities; thus families often change housing to better meet their needs.

Personal preferences. We all need to think well of ourselves. We evaluate ourselves in terms of the way in which we think others feel toward us or perceive us. We are often judged on the basis of the clothing we wear, the cars we drive, and the houses we live in. Factors such as these influence our self-concept, and our choice of housing will often reflect our desire for self-esteem, our need for privacy, our wish to interact with others, our need to feel we belong, our need to feel we control our environment, and our desire to be creative.

An analysis of your needs and priorities will lay the foundation for your selection of the best housing form you can afford.

---

[1] Much of the following section is based on James Montgomery, "A Complex of Factors Determines our Family Housing Requirements," *Handbook for the Home*, U.S. Department of Agriculture, 1973, pp. 92–97.

TO RENT OR TO BUY

At some time in your life, you are likely to be faced with providing housing for yourself and your family. In so doing you will have the choice of renting or buying housing.

Historically, a majority of people have chosen to buy housing. In the late 19th century, about half of the families in the United States owned their own homes. During the Great Depression of the 1930s, home ownership declined to about 44 percent of the families. Following the Depression the proportion of homeowners increased to about 62 percent by 1960, and the survey of consumer expenditures conducted by the U.S. Department of Labor for 1972–73 indicates that about 60 percent of American families own homes.

Whether a family should rent or buy a dwelling can only be answered by investigating the advantages, costs, and limitations of the various housing alternatives available for both renters and buyers. Housing decisions should take into account both the family's financial ability and the priorities of its needs.

The U.S. Department of Labor Consumer Survey indicates that income level, family size, and the age of the family head have an effect on home ownership. Exhibit 8–1 shows that as the level of income rises, the percentage of homeowners increases. Families in the lower income levels tend to rely more on renting as a means of satisfying

EXHIBIT 8–1
Selected U.S. family housing characteristics by income (all urban and rural families and single consumers, 1973)

	*Housing status**		
Family income before taxes	*Home owner*	*Renter*	*Other or not reported*
Less than $3,000	35%	63%	2%
$3,000–3,999	41	56	3
$4,000–4,999	46	51	3
$5,000–5,999	50	44	5
$6,000–6,999	50	47	3
$7,000–7,999	47	51	2
$8,000–9,999	50	45	6
$10,000–11,999	57	37	6
$12,000–14,999	69	25	6
$15,000–19,999	75	18	6
$20,000–24,999	79	15	6
$25,000 and over	85	11	3
Income incompletely reported	64	31	5
Total	59	36	5

* Percentages may not add to 100 because of rounding.

Source: U.S. Department of Labor, Bureau of Labor Statistics, Report 455-3, 1976, pp. 14–15.

housing needs. As family income increases, the proportion of homeowners increases from 35 percent for those with annual incomes under $3,000 to 85 percent for families with annual incomes over $25,000.

The proportion of those owning homes also appears to be related to family size. This is explained in part by the fact that rental housing may not be readily available to meet the needs of large families. Exhibit 8–2 shows that while 34 percent of the single-person families own their homes, 74 percent of the families with five persons are homeowners.

EXHIBIT 8–2
Selected U.S. family housing characteristics by family size (all urban and rural families and single consumers, 1973)

Number of persons in family	*Housing status**		
	Home owner	*Renter*	*Other or not reported*
1	34%	63%	2%
2	63	32	5
3	61	32	7
4	70	24	6
5	74	21	5
6 or more	76	21	3
All families	59	36	5

* Percentages may not add to 100 because of rounding.

Source: U.S. Department of Labor, Bureau of Labor Statistics, Report 455-3, 1976, p. 29.

The age of the family head is also a factor in home ownership, as shown in Exhibit 8–3. Young families are more dependent on renting to meet housing needs. This may be explained by the fact that young

EXHIBIT 8–3
Selected U.S. family housing characteristics by age of family head (all urban and rural families and single consumers, 1973)

Age of family head (years)	*Housing status**		
	Home owner	*Renter*	*Other or not reported*
22	9%	85%	6%
29	40	50	10
39	68	27	5
49	74	24	3
59	75	23	2
73	67	31	2

* Percentages may not add to 100 because of rounding.

Source: U.S. Department of Labor, Bureau of Labor Statistics, Report 455-3, 1976, p. 49.

families usually have limited financial resources and a strong need for mobility. As the average age of the head of the family increases from 22 years to 59 years, the proportion of those owning homes rises from 9 to 75 percent. The most rapid increases take place when the head of family is still fairly young.

Advantages of renting

Today you can rent nearly any kind of housing including single-family houses, condominiums, cooperative units, mobile homes, duplexes and apartments. Renting a dwelling has some advantages over owning:

1. The amount of money tied up by the renter is usually much smaller than that required to own a home. Some renters may be required to make security deposits equal to one to three months' rent, but this is still usually much less than a downpayment on a home.[2]
2. Renters have greater flexibility than homeowners. Many leases can be terminated by giving 30 days' notice to the landlord or forfeiting the deposit—a small cost relative to a sales commission on a home. Renters do not then have the problem of disposing of a house; they simply move.
3. Renters are freed of most of the maintenance responsibilities that homeowners must face. The landlord usually cares for the yard and maintains the property (including, in most cases, the appliances if they are furnished).
4. Because rental units come in smaller sizes than single-family houses, they better meet some families' needs. For example, a young family that seeks a small housing unit for financial reasons will more likely find a small, one-bedroom apartment than a similar size house.
5. Apartment complexes often provide facilities that renters could not afford if they purchased their home. Some complexes provide tennis courts, swimming pools, or golf courses for their tenants.
6. Renting enables you to plan exactly how much you will spend for housing for the duration of the lease. Unexpected costs of home ownership, such as a new water heater or plumbing repairs, are paid by the landlord.
7. Renters don't have the cost of selling a home.

---

[2] A security deposit is money required by the landlord to ensure that a tenant will pay for any damage caused or to ensure the payment of rent. The deposit is returned to the tenant after the lease has been terminated if there is no damage to be repaired.

Disadvantages of renting

1. As a renter, you usually do not get the tax advantage of deductions for items such as interest on the mortgage and real estate taxes paid, even though the rent you paid to the landlord is used to cover these expenses.[3]
2. Your entire rental payment is an expense. You are not building any ownership (equity) with your rental payment.
3. In a rental property you must contend with other renters and the landlord. In some situations it may be difficult to maintain good relations with them.
4. You may have to sacrifice privacy if you rent. A homeowner will usually have more privacy, or will be more at liberty to provide for it, than will a renter.
5. Rent may increase over time, generally whenever the lease is up for renewal. Some leases may even allow for rent increases during the term of the lease.

Advantages of buying

1. Owning a home may add to the family's self-esteem. For many families home ownership provides a feeling of pride and of belonging to a community, a feeling often lacking for renters. This is one of the home ownership advantages that cannot be expressed in monetary terms.
2. An advantage that can be expressed in dollars and cents is the relative stability of the mortgage payment over long periods of time. Most mortgages provide for fixed monthly payments.
3. Owners build up equity with a part of their mortgage payment. A portion of each payment is a repayment of borrowed money and represents an increasing ownership value.
4. Homeowners can benefit from a general increase in the value of the home during the period of ownership. Suppose you purchase a $50,000 home in a good location. You get a nine percent mortgage, make a $10,000 downpayment, and your home increases in value at a rate of five percent each year. Your home would increase in value by $2,500 ($0.05 \times \$50,000$) in the first year. If you then sold your home this would result in a return of $2,500 on an

---

[3] The treatment of the property tax deduction has been modified in some states for some rental situations so the renter is able to derive some tax benefits. If you are a renter, consult with an income tax specialist for the proper treatment of your situation.

investment of $10,000, or a 25 percent annual rate of return. (However, as your actual investment increases because of loan repayment, the return declines in subsequent years). While renters do not have to make the downpayment, it would be difficult to find acceptable investments that would yield such a high rate of return.

5. Tax benefits are available to the homeowner which are not available to the renter. As discussed below and in Chapter 16, these benefits can be substantial, depending upon your level of taxable income.

Disadvantages of buying

1. A disadvantage of buying a home is the need for money to make the downpayment and to pay closing costs. Closing costs include legal fees and fees you must pay to get financing. These outlays may drain your financial resources to a dangerously low level and leave you in a very vulnerable position in case of an emergency. This disadvantage should receive serious thought in the decision to buy.
2. Home buyers have less flexibility than renters. It is costly to sell a home; commissions of about seven percent of the selling price must be paid to the realtor plus one to three percent, or more if VA/FHA discount points are involved, in closing costs. It is quite likely that, if housing is needed for a period of less than three years, buying can be a costly (losing) investment.
3. Housing values can decline. It is unwise always to assume inflation in housing values. The demand and supply of homes in various price ranges and geographic locations fluctuate. To illustrate, the construction of freeways has been credited with enabling people to move out of the cities into the suburbs. This shift has greatly affected the housing values in the cities.

Estimating costs of renting

Being able to compare the cost of renting and buying is an important part of sound financial planning. It is very difficult to compare the costs of renting and buying because the value received for the rental payment on a one-bedroom apartment may be quite different from the value received from the mortgage payment on a three-bedroom house. Thus any comparison of costs should be based upon comparable housing units.

Rental cost usually includes more than just the monthly rent payment; the renter may have expenses that are specified in the rental agreement. This agreement is a legal document known as a lease agreement (of which Exhibit 8–4 is an example) designed to protect both parties by carefully specifying the rights and responsibilities of each. Because such agreements can be enforced in the courts, it is very important that the renter understand every word contained therein before signing. Verbal agreements not covered in the lease are worthless—so if changes are required, make sure they are written in the lease before you sign. Misunderstandings about clauses in the lease may result in a greatly increased cost of renting either by making the renter responsible for unusual maintenance or other charges or through unreasonable penalty charges for such minor things as nailholes from hanging pictures on walls.

Rent. Rent is the most obvious part of the monthly rental costs. The exact amount and the date on which it is due (e.g., the fifteenth of each month) should be clearly stated in the lease. There may be a penalty of up to five percent for late rent payments, making it more important to pay the rent on time. Frequently the landlord will require the prepayment of the first and last month's rent at the time the lease is signed. This is to protect the landlord if the renter moves out before the end of the lease. If you may be required to move on short notice for any reason, forfeiture of the prepaid rent can increase your cost of renting.

In estimating the monthly rental outlay, you should know what happens when the original term of the lease expires. For example, you must know whether the lease becomes renewable on a month-to-month basis or whether a new lease must be negotiated. You also should know how the monthly rent will be determined for the new lease period.

Security deposit. A security deposit is money held by the landlord to pay for any damage repair required on the rental unit in preparing for the next people to move in. The specific arrangement for the return of this deposit should be clearly spelled out in the lease. When the lease expires, all or part of the deposit may be returned if you have taken reasonable care of the property. In any case, regardless of how clean the unit is when you move out, a cleaning charge is often assessed. The final decision on the amount to be returned is left to the landlord. If there is substantial disagreement on the amount returned, small claims courts often provide a satisfactory solution.

To protect yourself from unwarranted damage charges, you should require that the landlord prepare and sign a written check-in list that notes any existing damage or wear and tear. Then when you move out you should have a check-out list which notes any damage or wear and

EXHIBIT 8–4
Typical rental lease agreement

Parties to Lease

It is mutually agreed this date by and between .... Lessor, and .... Lessee, that:

Description of Premises

Lessor does hereby lease to Lessee the following described premises in the .... of ...., County of ...., and State of ...., to-wit: ....

Term of Lease

for the term of .... beginning on the .... day of ...., 19.........., and ending on the .... day of ...., 19.........., Lessee paying therefor

Rent **Rent Payment Date** **Place of Payment**

the sum of $.................................... per month on the .... day of each month of this lease with the first payment due and owing on the .... day of ...., 19.........., payments to be made at .... or at such other place as Lessor may designate in writing.

Renewal of Lease for Like Term **Notice to Termin. Lease**

(EITHER CLAUSE "A" OR "B" MUST BE STRICKEN)

A. This lease shall stand, without notice from either party, renewed on identical terms for a like successive period unless either party shall at least forty-five (45) days before the expiration of the lease notify the other in writing to the contrary However, the Lessor must at least 15 days but not more than 30 days prior to the time specified for giving the notice as herein set forth notify the Lessee in writing of the above provision for automatic renewal or extension.

OR

Renewal of Lease Without Notice On Month to Month

B. This lease shall stand without notice from either party renewed on identical terms, except that it shall be a month-to-month tenancy, and in the event neither clause is stricken, this clause shall be controlling in this lease.

Assignment of Lease

Lessee shall not assign this lease, nor sublet said premises or any part thereof, without prior written consent of Lessor.

Security Deposit

Lessee agrees that security deposit in the amount of ($....................................) .... Dollars shall be held by .... and if held by Agent
(Insert Name of Lessor or Agent)

Written Demand for Return of Security Deposit **Lessor to Furnish Written Statement of Damages** **Lessor's Obligation For Failure to Return Deposit**

said security deposit shall be held in Agent's trust account. Said deposit shall be refunded to Lessee in the event the premises are left in the condition called for by this lease, upon Lessee furnishing Lessor with written demand for said security deposit, which demand shall include Lessee's new address. Lessor shall furnish Lessee with written statement of conditions causing forfeiture of all or part of security deposit within ten (10) days after Lessee vacates premises or Lessor receives said demand, whichever shall be later, or Lessor shall be deemed to have waived any claims against security deposit. Any damage caused by Lessee, normal wear and tear excepted, shall be repaired by Lessor and the cost thereof deducted from said security deposit. Should such security deposit be unreasonably withheld, Lessor agrees to pay and discharge all reasonable costs, attorneys' fees and expenses that shall be paid or incurred by Lessee in recovering such deposit.

Lessee Has Examined Premises **Defects Noted by Lessee** **Notice Required**

Lessee has examined and knows the condition of said premises, and has received same in good order and repair, except as herein otherwise specified, and no representations as to the condition or repair thereof have been made by Lessor or his Agent prior to, or at the execution of this lease, that are not herein expressed or endorsed hereon. Lessee shall have five (5) days after date of occupancy to notify Lessor or Lessor's Agent in writing of any defects or needed repairs in said premises or else shall be deemed to have received said premises in good order and repair.

Insurance by Lessee

It is the responsibility of Lessee to provide insurance coverage for his personal property.

When Lessee to Vacate

Lessee agrees to vacate premises at the end of said term, and deliver the keys to Lessor.

Lessor's Right to Show or Repair Premises

Lessor may, at reasonable and proper times, with prior notice, enter and show said premises to persons wishing to rent or purchase same, or to make such repairs as Lessor may deem necessary.

Lessor's Right to Post for Rent Sign

Lessor may, within two (2) months next preceding the expiration of said term, place the usual "FOR RENT" notice on said premises, and Lessee shall not interfere with same.

Abandonment by Lessee **Lessee's Liability**

If Lessee shall abandon or vacate said premises before the expiration of said term, Lessor shall make reasonable efforts to rent same and shall apply the money therefrom to the rent due, or to become due, on this lease and Lessee shall remain liable for any deficiency and agrees to pay same.

Disposal of Lessee's Property Left on Premises

If Lessee shall leave any property on said premises, Lessor shall have right to dispose of said property without liability thirty (30) days after Lessee vacates, or abandons, said premises.

Restrictions On Use of Premises **Lessee Not to Violate Fire Policy**

Premises herein leased and every part thereof shall, during said term, be used only for residential purposes by Lessee and his immediate family or .... and Lessee will not permit said premises to be used for any immoral or unlawful purpose, or purpose that will injure the reputation of same or the building of which they are a part, and will not use or keep in or about said premises any article or thing which would in any way affect the validity of the Standard Fire Insurance Policy of the State of ....

Pets and Animals

Lessee shall not keep in or about said premises any live animals, reptiles, or birds (except: ....)

Parties to Obey Laws

Lessee and Lessor shall obey all lawful orders, rules and regulations of all governmental authorities.

Lessee to Keep Prem. Clean

Lessee shall keep said premises in a clean and tenantable condition.

Lessee to Keep Premises In Good Repair

Lessee shall keep said premises in as good repair as same are in at the commencement of said term, normal use and wear and damage by accidental fire excepted and Lessee shall be liable for all acts of negligence by Lessee and guests.

Windows

Lessee shall keep the glass in the windows and storms clean.

Signs Prohibited

Lessee shall not paint upon, attach, exhibit or display in or about said premises any signs or placards, without written consent of Lessor.

Written Consent for Alterations or Redecorat.

Lessee shall not alter, or redecorate said premises without prior written consent of Lessor. All alterations to said premises shall remain for the benefit of Lessor, unless otherwise provided in said consent.

Lessee Liable for Damage for Fastening to Premises **Nothing to Be Attached to Exterior**

Lessee shall not drive nails, tacks, screws or apply other fasteners on or into any of the walls, ceilings, floors or woodwork of said premises, or allow same to be done without written consent of Lessor or his Agent and in any case Lessee agrees to be responsible for any damage done and will pay for same. Nothing whatsoever shall be attached or affixed either to exterior of said building or any part thereof, whether permanent or otherwise, without written consent of Lessor or his Agent. Lessor is hereby authorized to remove, at the expense of Lessee, anything so attached or affixed without written consent.

Lessee Liab. Minor Repairs **Lessor Liable Major Repairs** **Lessee May Terminate Lease**

Lessee shall be liable for maintenance and minor repairs to the premises. Any necessary replacements and major repairs shall be at the expense of Lessor. If Lessor fails to take care of any replacements or major repairs after ten (10) days written notice, delivered to Lessor personally or mailed by Certified Mail, Lessee may declare the lease terminated and vacate the premises without any further liability for the rent set forth in this lease.

Damage by Fire

In case said premises shall be partially damaged by fire, or other casualty, same shall be repaired as soon as reasonably possible by and at the expense of Lessor. In case the damage is so extensive as to render the premises untenantable, the rent shall cease until same is repaired; and this lease may be terminated at the option of either Lessee or Lessor and the rent prorated to the date of said damage.

Lessor Not Liable for Damage

Lessor shall not be liable for any damage occasioned by failure to keep said premises in repair, and shall not be liable for any damage done or occasioned by or from plumbing, gas, water, steam or other pipes, or sewerage, or the bursting, leaking or running of any cistern, tank, washstand, water closet, or waste pipe in, above, upon or about said building or premises nor for damage occasioned by water, snow or ice being upon or coming through the roof, skylight, trap door or otherwise, or for any damage arising from acts or neglect of co-tenants or other occupants of same building.

EXHIBIT 8–4 *(continued)*

Who Pays for Water and Sewer — During said term Less........... shall pay all water and/or sewer charges levied against the premises herein leased at the time such charges become due and payable.

Lessee to Pay Gas & Elec. — During said term Lessee shall pay all gas and electric bills at the time such bills become due and payable.

Notice of Breach of Lease — Should Lessee neglect or fail to perform and observe any of the terms of this lease, Lessor shall give Lessee written notice of such breach, delivered to Lessee personally or mailed by Certified Mail requiring the Lessee to remedy the breach or vacate the premises on or before a date at least 5 days after the giving of the notice (except if such breach is for failure to pay rent in which case the 5 day or 14 day statutory notice may be used) and if the Lessee fails to comply with such notice the Lessor may

Failure to Correct Breach — declare this lease terminated and institute action to expel Lessee from premises without limiting liability of Lessee for the rent due or to become due under this lease.

If a tenant under a lease for more than one year fails to pay rent when due, or commits waste, or breaches any other covenant or condition of his lease, the tenancy is terminated if the landlord gives the tenant notice requiring him to pay the rent, repair the waste, or otherwise comply with the lease on or before a date at least 30 days after the giving of the notice, and if the tenant fails to comply with the notice.

Lessee to Pay Attorney Fees — Lessee agrees to pay all reasonable costs, attorneys' fees and expenses that shall be paid or incurred by Lessor in enforcing this lease.

Definition of Lessor and Lessee — The terms "Lessor" and "Lessee" when used herein shall be taken to mean either singular or plural, masculine or feminine, as the case may be, and the provisions of this instrument shall bind the parties and their heirs, personal representatives, successors and assigns.

Special Conditions — ....

....

....

....

....

Date of Execution — IN WITNESS WHEREOF, The said parties have hereunto set their hands and seals this.............................. day of ...., 19..........

Signature of Parties

Signed and Sealed in Presence of — LESSEE ....(SEAL)

....(SEAL)

....(SEAL)

LESSOR ....(SEAL)

....(SEAL)

....(SEAL)

GUARANTY

Guaranty by Third Party — For value received and in consideration of Lessor making this lease, the undersigned hereby guarantees the payment of the rent and the performance of the covenants thereof by Lessee.

Date of Guaranty — IN WITNESS WHEREOF, The undersigned have hereunto set their hands and seals this.............................. day of ...., 19..........

Signatures of Guarantors

Signed and Sealed in Presence of

....(SEAL)

....(SEAL)

ASSIGNMENT, ACCEPTANCE AND CONSENT

Assignment of Lease and Guaranty of Lessee on Assignment — Lessee hereby assigns all his right, title and interest in and to the within lease to.. and in consideration of the consent to the assignment by Lessor, he guarantees the performance by said Assignee of all obligations of Lessee.

In consideration of the above assignment and the written consent of Lessor, Assignee hereby assumes all obligations of Lessee in said lease.

Lessor's Consent to Assignment — LESSOR HEREBY CONSENTS TO THIS ASSIGNMENT AND ACCEPTANCE

Date of Assignment — IN WITNESS WHEREOF, The parties have hereunto set their hands and seals this.............................. day of ...., 19..........

Signatures of Parties to Assignment

Signed and Sealed in Presence of — ....(SEAL) Lessee

....(SEAL) Lessee

....(SEAL) Assignee

....(SEAL) Assignee

....(SEAL) Lessor

....(SEAL) Lessor

TO

Lease

Lease of ....

Location ....

Total Rent, - - $..........................

Rent per month, - $..........................

Expires ...., 19

tear on the date you leave. These lists protect against unwarranted charges and changes in management; a new manager may not be aware of any deals or understandings you made with the previous manager.

Other expenses. In addition to the amount of rent and security deposit, the lease should state specifically who pays for expenses such as utilities, heat, repairs, and insurance. The more closely the rental unit approximates an individual house, the more likely the renter will be responsible for other expenses. In any case, renters can expect to pay for electricity and fuel for heat and hot water as well as for insurance on their own belongings. The landlord will usually pay for normal repairs and maintenance of the property.

Restrictions. Most landlords put very definite restrictions on the use of their property. The lease should state clearly any rules related to things such as pets, children, overnight guests, painting walls, hanging things on walls, subleasing, and use of radio, television, or musical instruments.

Estimating costs of owning

One of the most common mistakes made by people buying a house is to greatly underestimate the initial and monthly outlay by considering only the downpayment and monthly payments of interest and principal on the mortgage. It is essential to keep in mind that other items have to be paid and can add up to a large amount. Before you buy, be sure that your estimates include *all* of the costs that you will have to pay.

Outlays required for buying a home may be one-time or regular running costs. One-time outlays include closing costs, the downpayment, and moving expenses, while the recurring outlays include maintenance, heat and utilities, taxes and insurance, and mortgage payments.

Closing costs. The term "closing costs" generally refers to all of the charges paid for obtaining the mortgage loan and transferring real estate title. While the person paying the closing costs may vary from situation to situation, all or a major part of the closing costs are usually paid by the buyer. These costs are usually higher than the buyer expects them to be, especially if this is the first home a buyer has purchased.

The Real Estate Settlement Procedures Act of 1974 (RESPA) was passed to protect the buyer in the closing or settlement process. RESPA covers most residential mortgage loans used to finance the purchase of one- to four-family properties. It was not designed to set the prices of settlement services, but instead requires the lender to provide you with information prior to the settlement date to take the mystery out of the settlement process. With this information you can "shop" for settlement services and make informed decisions.

Items paid to obtain a loan are those fees that lenders charge to process, approve, and make the mortgage loan, such as a loan origination fee, loan discount, and appraisal fee. Title charges cover a variety of services performed by the lender or others for handling and supervising the settlement transaction. These items vary because of the diversity in practice from area to area, but items most often incurred include title search, title insurance, attorney fees, recording fees, and escrow fees.

Loan origination fees cover the lender's administrative costs in processing the loan. Often expressed as a percentage of the loan, the fee will vary among lenders and from locality to locality. The fee generally ranges from one half percent to one percent of the mortgage amount.

Loan discount, often called "points," is a one-time charge used to adjust the lender's return on the loan to what present market conditions demand. Mortgage discount points are discussed in greater detail below as part of home financing.

An *appraisal fee* pays for a statement of property value for the lender by an independent appraiser or by a member of the lender's staff. This charge varies greatly from transaction to transaction and from area to area but usually ranges from $50 to $200 on single-family houses.

Title insurance has been developed to protect against loss to the lender and buyer in the event that a future claim arises from a flaw not found by the title search. Lenders may require title insurance and buyers will find it wise to take out the insurance. The buyer's policy should cover the cost of the property, not just the amount of the loan, in order to protect any equity in the property.

A buyer of title insurance pays a single premium at the time the policy is issued. The policy remains in force for as long as the insured owns the property. Premiums for title insurance are based on the valuation of the property; as the property value increases, the cost of added coverage decreases. An example of premium rates for title insurance is shown in Exhibit 8–5. Rates are usually approved by a state insurance commission and tend to vary from state to state.

Using the premium rates shown in Exhibit 8–5, the premium for a home valued at $40,000 would be $243 [$68 + (35 × $5)]. This amount may be lower if the seller of the property has title insurance. In that case, a lower rate, known as a reissue rate, is available for the buyer.

EXHIBIT 8–5
Premium rates for title insurance—An example

Property value covered	Premium
Up to $5,000	$68 (minimum premium)
Next $45,000	$5 per $1,000
Next $50,000	$4.25 per $1,000
Next $1,900,000	$3 per $1,000

Title insurance continues to protect you even after you sell your property. If a claim arises in the future regarding your rights to the title you transferred, the title insurance continues to protect you.

Attorney's fees are often charged even if you do not hire your own attorney, because the lending institution may require you to pay a fee for its lawyer to handle the closing or to give advice concerning the title. It is a good idea to hire an attorney who represents only you in the transaction, because no other attorney is responsible solely or primarily for protecting your interests.

States have laws that require the recording of real estate transactions with the county clerk, for which a *recording fee* is charged. Public record of change of ownership or creditor claims on the property is used to provide notice to anyone concerned about the status of the title. The buyer should be sure to have the deed recorded to protect his or her right to the property. Generally lenders involved will require the deed to be recorded to protect their first mortgage (their "lien").

In many states there is a tax collected on the transfer of titles and mortgages. This tax can range from $1.10 per $1,000 of value to about $8 per $1,000 depending upon the state.

Escrow accounts are separate or independent accounts set up "in trust" to hold funds for closing costs, insurance premiums, and property taxes. Lenders often require the borrowers to have escrow accounts to cover the payment of real estate taxes and insurance on the property. Borrowers make the periodic contributions, usually as part of the monthly mortgage payment, and the funds go into the escrow account, from which the escrow agent makes the payments for the taxes and insurance.

Downpayment. The downpayment is the initial amount of money the buyer puts up toward the purchase price of a home. The minimum amount is typically a part of the financing arrangement, but some buyers want to make a larger downpayment in order to reduce the principal amount to be borrowed or to obtain a lower interest rate. You must keep in mind that too large a downpayment can put undue strain on family finances by reducing the amount available to cover such costs as moving expenses, draperies, and other furnishings needed in a new home.

Maintenance. Maintenance costs are frequently ignored by the buyer when estimating costs. Remember that like everything else your house will wear out as it gets older, and to keep it in good shape you will need to pay for maintenance and repairs. The average frame house needs painting every three to five years. To prevent damage to the house interior from water leakage, roofs need replacing in 15 to 25 years, depending upon the roofing material. The heating, electrical, and plumbing systems will need repairs or replacement from time to time. As the house gets older you will be spending more and more on maintenance and repairs of both the outside and inside.

At present-day prices even a minor job can require a substantial amount of money. Because of the great differences between localities, types of construction, construction materials, personal tastes, etc., it is nearly impossible to estimate maintenance and repair costs. The U.S. Department of Commerce has estimated annual maintenance costs as averaging between three fourths and one percent of the home's value. Remember, these costs usually are not spread evenly over the life of the house but rather come in "lumps" such as new siding, new roof, or redecorating or remodeling the interior.

If your purchase requires you to join a neighborhood association, dues and periodic assessments may be significant expense items. Such associations are formed for the purpose of providing maintenance of "common areas" shared by the neighborhood.

Heat and utilities. You will have to pay the heating and utility bills. Amounts of energy used will vary depending upon climate, insulation, and the extent to which automatic appliances are used. In estimating the expenses for energy, check with your lender, the local utility companies, or other homeowners in the area.

Taxes and insurance. Real estate taxes will have to be paid each year, whether in a lump sum or over a period specified by the taxing unit. It is not uncommon for property taxes to cost 1½ to four percent of a home's value. These costs, as discussed above, may be paid monthly or semiannually by the homeowner as part of the regular payment to the lender and held in escrow by the lending institution. Whenever possible, you should place these payments in interest-bearing accounts.

Mortgage payments. More than 90 percent of the families who purchase homes use mortgage loans. A mortgage is a legal document which specifies that should the borrower (mortgagor) not fulfill the agreement, the title of the property will pass (via foreclosure) to the lender as full or partial settlement of the debt. Inability or failure of the borrower to make the required mortgage payment gives the lender the right to begin foreclosure proceedings. The lender may resell the property in order to recover any money due.

The monthly mortgage payment includes an amount for the interest due as well as an amount for the repayment of the principal. This method of repaying the loan may be used in two ways—the *direct reduction* and the *fund* plans. Payments are fixed in amount under both plans but the difference lies in how the payments are used.

Under the fund plan, an amount to repay the principal is accumulated in a fund, usually a savings account at the institution granting the loan. When this fund plus the interest earned on the account deposits equals the amount of the loan, the principal is repaid. However, because the principal is not decreased until the end of the payment period, the annual amount of interest required on the loan does not decrease. Even though this interest cost on the principal is partially offset by the interest earned on the accumulating fund, the rate paid on the mortgage is greater than the rate earned in the savings account.

As a result, the direct reduction method is preferred. Under this plan, the principal is amortized over the term of the mortgage; that is, a portion of each monthly payment reduces the principal amount. As the principal decreases, the amount of interest also decreases. Thus, each month a smaller portion of the fixed payment goes for interest and a larger portion goes for principal reduction.

A comparison of the fund and direct reduction plans is shown in Exhibit 8–6. The example assumes that you are purchasing a $25,000 home. The lender requires a 20 percent downpayment, leaving a balance of $20,000 to be financed for 25 years at eight percent.

The fund plan will require monthly interest of $133.33 because of the constant principal balance. To provide for the repayment of the $20,000 principal at the end of 300 months (25 years), $33.53 must be placed in the accumulation fund each month at a five percent interest rate. Thus, the total monthly payment required is $166.86.

Under the direct reduction plan, it should be noted that the principal balance decreases over time until at the end of the 300-month period it is zero. While the monthly payment remains constant over the life of the loan, the amount for interest decreases until in the 197th month it is less than the amount for principal reduction.

Monthly payments for the direct reduction plan are lower than for the fund plan because of the decreasing principal over the life of the loan. In total, the direct reduction plan requires an outlay of $46,298.02 while the fund plan requires $50,059 to retire the 25-year, eight percent, $20,000 mortgage. As you can see, the amount of interest paid under both plans exceeds the amount of principal retired.

The amount of the monthly mortgage payment depends upon three

EXHIBIT 8–6

Comparison of monthly payments for fund and direct reduction plans on a 300-month (25-year), $20,000 mortgage at 8 percent interest

	Payment in month								
Type of plan	*12*	*24*	*36*	*48*	*60*	*120*	*240*	*300*	*Total*
Fund plan									
Monthly payment	$ 166.86	$ 166.86	$ 166.86	$ 166.86	$ 166.86	$ 166.86	$ 166.86	$ 166.86	$50,059.00
Interest payment	133.33	133.33	133.33	133.33	133.33	133.33	133.33	133.33	40,000.00
Principal payment	33.53	33.53	33.53	33.53	33.53	33.53	33.53	33.53	10,059.00
Fund accumulation (5%) at end of period	411.71	844.48	1,299.40	1,777.59	2,280.24	5,206.61	13,781.69	20,000.00	
Direct reduction plan									
Monthly payment	154.37	154.37	154.37	154.37	154.37	154.37	154.37	141.42*	46,298.02
Interest payment	131.73	129.85	127.82	125.61	123.23	107.97	51.38	00.93	26,298.02
Principal payment	22.64	24.52	26.55	28.76	31.14	46.40	102.99	140.49	20,000.00
Principal balance	19,738.01	19,454.28	19,147.00	18,814.20	18,453.79	16,150.17	7,604.88	00.00	

* A payment of $141.42 in the final month of the repayment period repays the balance of the loan plus interest. Payments of $154.37 are required in each of the other 299 months.

factors—principal amount, interest rate on the loan, and the length of time for repayment. As illustrated in Exhibit 8–7 for the direct reduction method, for a given payment period, higher interest rates require higher monthly payments to cover the added amount of interest that must be paid. As the payment period is increased from 10 to 30 years the amount of the monthly payment decreases because less principal is repaid each month. Adjusting the length of the payment period is an often-used means of changing the monthly amounts required for mortgage payments to meet the borrower's ability to repay.

EXHIBIT 8–7
Monthly payments required to amortize a $1,000 loan (direct reduction method)

Payment period (years)	*Interest rate*						
	7%	*7½%*	*8%*	*8½%*	*9%*	*9½%*	*10%*
10	$11.61	$11.87	$12.13	$12.40	$12.67	$12.94	$13.22
15	8.99	9.27	9.56	9.85	10.14	10.45	10.75
20	7.75	8.06	8.37	8.68	9.00	9.33	9.66
25	7.07	7.39	7.72	8.05	8.40	8.74	9.09
30	6.65	6.99	7.34	7.69	8.05	8.41	8.78

Tax benefits of ownership. Although there are a multitude of costs that bombard the homeowner, there are also certain tax benefits available to homeowners who are able to itemize deductions. Out of the yearly costs for your $25,000 home you can use interest charges and real estate taxes as itemized deductions on your income tax return, thus decreasing the amount of income on which you must pay tax. For example:

Deductible costs for the first year are:

Real estate taxes (3 percent of cost) ...	$ 750
Interest on mortgage*	1,590
Total deduction	$2,340

* Total interest paid in months 1–12.

The tax benefit of the deduction will vary with your tax rate. To illustrate:

Tax rate	*Deduction*	*Tax saving*
15%	$2,340	$351
20%	$2,340	$468
33%	$2,340	$772

Tax benefits are clearly more valuable at higher incomes because the tax rates increase as the taxable income increases. These benefits are realized when you calculate the amount of income tax you must pay. However, home buyers must remember that while tax benefits decrease their net costs, the amounts of the monthly cash outlays are not changed.

In summary, when estimating the monthly home ownership outlays required, you must be careful to consider outlays for maintenance, heat and utilities, and taxes and insurance in addition to the mortgage payments. Ignoring these required outlays may encourage you to purchase a home beyond your means and this may lead to financial problems.

SELECTING RENTAL HOUSING

If after comparing advantages and disadvantages and costs of renting and owning your decision is to rent, your next step is to carefully select housing to meet your needs. You cannot take all of the guesswork out of house hunting. No matter how carefully you investigate beforehand, there are bound to be some surprises—good and bad—after you move into an apartment or a house.

The checklist for apartments in Exhibit 8–8 can help you judge and compare different apartments, houses, and living quarters to find the best home for you. Based on your overall spending plan, establish a price range so that you will not waste time looking at housing that is beyond your means.

As you read through the checklist, check the features that are most important to you and your family. Compare those features in several houses or apartments before you make your decision.

BUYING A HOME

Decisions made during the process of buying a home should follow a logical sequence such as the one discussed in Chapter 6 (see Exhibit 6–1). The process should follow a carefully prepared plan that begins with a statement of priorities of the family housing needs and then proceeds through the search, inspection, appraisal, purchase, and financing stages of the decision process.

The housing search

Searching for housing includes identifying your housing needs and then locating available houses to meet these needs. Because of the

EXHIBIT 8–8
Checklist for apartments

Building and grounds

- ☐ Attractive, well-constructed building
- ☐ Good maintenance and upkeep
- ☐ Clean, well-lighted and uncluttered halls, entrances, stairs
- ☐ Reliable building management and supervision
- ☐ Attractive landscaping with adequate outdoor space for tenants
- ☐ Locked entrances, protected from outsiders
- ☐ Clean, attractive lobby

Services and facilities

- ☐ Laundry equipment
- ☐ Parking space (indoor or outdoor)
- ☐ Receiving room for packages
- ☐ Convenient trash collection and disposal
- ☐ Adequate fire escapes
- ☐ Storage lockers
- ☐ Locked mail boxes
- ☐ Elevators
- ☐ Engineer on call for emergency repairs
- ☐ Extras—window washing, decorating, maid service, shops, doorman

Living space in the apartment

- ☐ Adequate room sizes and storage space
- ☐ Convenient floor plan
- ☐ Suitable wall space for furniture
- ☐ Soundproof. Listen for talking, footsteps, plumbing and equipment noise from other apartments or hallways.
- ☐ Attractive decorating and fixtures
- ☐ Pleasant views
- ☐ Windows located to provide enough air, light and ventilation
- ☐ Agreeable size, type and placement of windows
- ☐ Windows with blinds, shades, screens and storm windows
- ☐ Easy cleaning and maintenance
- ☐ Attractive, easy-to-clean floors
- ☐ Furnished appliances in good condition
- ☐ Clean, effective heating, thermostatically controlled
- ☐ Up-to-date wiring
- ☐ Conveniently placed electric outlets
- ☐ Well-fitted doors, casings, cabinets and built-ins
- ☐ Extras—air conditioning, carpeting, dishwasher, disposer, fireplace, patio

Source: This information taken from the Money Management Institute booklet titled YOUR HOUSING DOLLAR printed by the Money Management Institute of Household Finance Corporation, Chicago, Illinois.

usual financial constraints, it is unlikely that all of these needs can be satisfied. Therefore, the process should be directed toward housing within an acceptable price range that best meets the family's needs.

Most families searching for homes use the services of a real estate broker who brings buyer and seller together. Real estate brokers are licensed by the state in which they do business after they have passed qualifying exams and have had some specified minimum of experience. A broker can assist greatly in your search for a home, especially if you are unfamiliar with the area. A competent broker can provide information about taxes, zoning, future development plans, public transportation, schools, shopping facilities, and sources of financing. Using the information that you give about your housing needs, the broker will attempt to find the best house available for you. In any case, be sure that the broker you select is reputable and active in your desired purchase location. Good places to check on the reputation of a broker are the Better Business Bureau, lending agencies, and the local board of realtors.

Physical inspection

Before buying a home, you'll want to inspect it carefully for structural soundness and general condition. The physical inspection of the house and lot involves more than the appearance: it requires special attention to the exterior and interior structures and building materials, the utility systems, and location of the lot and home.

Exterior and interior. Quality of materials and carpentry are crucial to a structurally sound home. High-quality construction is likely to result in lower maintenance costs for the homeowner.

Part of the physical inspection of the internal construction should include a check on insulation. Considering rapidly rising heating and cooling costs, insulation is becoming much more significant. In a study made for the Federal Energy Administration, the National Bureau of Standards found that few of the nation's 40 million homes built before 1960 are adequately insulated. Also, over half of those built more recently are deficient.

If you have an average-size uninsulated frame house, heated with oil and located in the colder area of the country, you may be spending up to $200 per year for heat lost through the roof. A layer of 3½ inches of high-quality insulation batting between the joists in the ceiling could reduce this loss to about $50 a year. Six inches of insulation will reduce the loss even further. Careful inspection of the insulation increases in importance as the cost of energy increases.

Utility systems. It is not easy to estimate how long the utility systems will last. An older home may be very sound structurally, but have obsolete electrical, plumbing, heating, or cooling systems. The utility systems of newer houses, if they have met area building codes, are probably adequate for current living standards. There are enough exceptions to this, however, to require a careful inspection of the size of installation. To illustrate, in areas of the country where the winters are cold, an adequate heating system is a necessity. A good guideline for furnace capacity is 35,000 BTUs per bedroom in the house—although 50,000 is even better. Some builders may install smaller units, resulting in an overburdened, unsafe, or short-lived heating system.

Lot and location. Physical inspection should include a look at the housing site or lot to determine if it meets your needs. It has often been said that the three most important factors to consider when selecting a house are "location, location, and location." This emphasizes the effect of the future of the area in which a property is located on the present and potential value of the home and the eventual satisfaction realized by the buyer.

A glance at the inspection checklist shown in Exhibit 8–9 will indicate items to be inspected. It is difficult to evaluate many of these points unless you are an expert, or at least knowledgeable, on the subject. Consequently, when you have found the house you wish to buy, it is usually best to supplement your evaluation by hiring a professional house inspector to prepare a complete assessment of the

EXHIBIT 8–9
Checklist for houses

Outside house and yard

- ☐ Attractive, well-designed house
- ☐ Suited to natural surroundings
- ☐ Lot of the right size and shape for house and garage
- ☐ Suitable use of building materials
- ☐ Compatible with houses in the area
- ☐ Attractive landscaping and yard
- ☐ Good drainage of rain and moisture
- ☐ Dry, firm soil around the house
- ☐ Mature, healthy trees—placed to give shade in summer
- ☐ Convenient, well-kept driveway, walks, patio, porch
- ☐ Yard for children
- ☐ Parking convenience—garage, carport or street
- ☐ Distance between houses for privacy
- ☐ Sheltered entry—well-lighted and large enough for several to enter the house together
- ☐ Convenient service entrance

Outside construction

- ☐ Durable siding materials—in good condition
- ☐ Solid brick and masonry—free of cracks
- ☐ Solid foundation walls—six inches above ground level—eight inches thick
- ☐ Weather stripped windows and doors
- ☐ Noncorrosive gutters and downspouts, connected to storm sewer or splash block to carry water away from house
- ☐ Copper or aluminum flashing used over doors, windows and joints on the roof
- ☐ Screens and storm windows or Thermopane glass
- ☐ Storm doors

Inside construction

- ☐ Sound, smooth walls with invisible nails and taping on dry walls; without hollows or large cracks in plaster walls
- ☐ Well-done carpentry work with properly fitted joints and moldings
- ☐ Properly fitted, easy-to-operate windows
- ☐ Level wood floors with smooth finish and no high edges, wide gaps or squeaks
- ☐ Well-fitted tile floors—no cracked or damaged tiles—no visible adhesive
- ☐ Good possibilities for improvements, remodeling, expanding
- ☐ Properly fitted and easy-to-work doors and drawers in built-in cabinets
- ☐ Dry basement floor with hard smooth surface
- ☐ Adequate basement drain
- ☐ Sturdy stairways with railings, adequate head room—not too steep
- ☐ Leakproof roof—in good condition
- ☐ Adequate insulation for warmth, coolness and soundproofing

EXHIBIT 8–9 *(continued)*

Living space

- ☐ Convenient floor plan and paths from room to room
- ☐ Convenient entry with foyer and closet
- ☐ Convenient work areas (kitchen, laundry, workshop) with adequate drawers, cabinets, lighting, work space, electric power
- ☐ Private areas (bedrooms and bathrooms) located far enough from other parts of the house for privacy and quiet
- ☐ Social areas (living and dining rooms, play space, yard, porch or patio) convenient, comfortable, large enough for family and guests
- ☐ Rooms conveniently related to each other—entry to living room, dining room to kitchen, bedrooms to baths
- ☐ Adequate storage—closets, cabinets, shelves, attic, basement, garage
- ☐ Suitable wall space and room size for your furnishings
- ☐ Outdoor space convenient to indoor space
- ☐ Windows located to provide enough air, light and ventilation
- ☐ Agreeable type, size and placement of windows
- ☐ Usable attic and/or basement space
- ☐ Possibilities for expansion
- ☐ Attractive decorating and fixtures
- ☐ Extras—fireplace, air conditioning, porches, new kitchen and baths, built-in equipment, decorating you like

Source: This information taken from the Money Management Institute booklet titled YOUR HOUSING DOLLAR printed by the Money Management Institute of Household Finance Corporation, Chicago, Illinois.

condition of the house and lot. By hiring a reputable professional you can be assured of getting the best evaluation possible from an independent third party. It is usually quite easy to find an inspector by contacting members of professional appraisers' organizations, discussed below, the Nationwide Real Estate Inspectors Service, Inc., or the National Home Inspection Service. The latter two companies have offices in the larger metropolitan areas and act as inspectors, but not as appraisers. These professionals generally charge from $50 to $250 for their service, but considering the investment to be made it is money well spent.

Price appraisal

Estimating the value of a house and property is difficult, but very important for a home buyer. Because a home means such a large expenditure you must be sure that you are getting reasonable value for your money. Three approaches that may be used to estimate the value of the property are market value, cost value, and income value. A professional appraiser uses these methods and you can too.

Market value. The market value method consists of comparing the price asked for your prospective purchase with prices of similar homes in the same general location. You will want to know not only asking prices of these homes but also the prices at which similar homes have been sold recently. By knowing the prices on comparable sales, you can judge the value of a home and the reasonableness of the seller's asking price.

Another source for judging a fair market value of a house is to ask lenders for an appraisal. Because the lending institution must be assured that the property will serve as proper security for a loan, it will make an appraisal, which is paid for by the buyer. Experienced lenders will know more than an average person about the values and trends of the various locations. The lender will charge $50 to $200 for the appraisal, but in return the potential buyer knows whether the price of the property is reasonable.

Cost value. Cost value methods of valuation are based upon estimating the price of building an equal amount of living space of equal quality. This method is somewhat complicated for the average consumer and should be used only after doing some basic research on local building costs.

Get information on building costs by asking lenders, contractors, or builders' suppliers. You will find that the construction cost per square foot of living space varies with the type of construction (brick, frame, etc.) as well as with the climate. North central and northeastern states have higher building costs because of the colder temperatures in winter. A very rough but useful measure of cost is to calculate cost per square foot by dividing the sale price of the home by its area in square feet. Clearly this guide includes the value of the lot as well as various qualities of the home, including the grade of building materials and extras like pools or large garages.

What this guide gives you, though, is a common base for comparing similar homes. If homes you like sell for $24.50 per square foot of house living space (excluding garages and unfinished basements and using exterior wall measurements) and the seller/builder wants $25.25, you have an indication that you may be paying too much. If the house is desirable, for whatever reason, you may use your comparison to "bargain" the price down.

Average (median) costs of new site-built homes have been increasing. Exhibit 8–10 shows that, according to the U.S. Department of Commerce, the cost of construction per square foot of living space has increased from $13.45 in 1969 to $23.50 in 1976. This is an increase of nearly 75 percent over the seven-year period.

With these cost estimates and the size of house involved you can estimate the basic value of the house—if it is in new condition. Homes that are not new need adjustments in their cost value. For example, costs of required exterior and interior repairs such as new screens, new roof, painting, doors, etc., must be deducted. Even if the house does not

EXHIBIT 8–10
Costs and sizes of new homes*

Year	Cost† (per sq. ft.)	Median area (sq. ft.)	Median sales price‡
1969	$13.45	1,585	$25,600
1970	13.95	1,400	23,400
1971	14.55	1,415	25,200
1972	15.35	1,460	27,600
1973	17.10	1,540	32,500
1974	19.00	1,565	35,900
1975	20.75	1,560	39,300
1976	23.50	1,560	44,200

* Excludes homes built for rent or by individuals.
† Excludes value of improved lot.
‡ Includes land.
Source: U.S. Department of Commerce, Bureau of the Census.

require repairs and is in top condition the cost value should be reduced if the house is functionally or economically obsolete.

Functional obsolescence is a term meaning old-fashioned or outmoded. An example would be a home electrical system too small for modern use even though at the time the house was built the system was considered adequate. For example, houses built in the 1950s frequently had 60–80 amp service, but today 150–250 is normal because many electrical appliances require the larger electrical installation. Other examples of functional obsolescence include inadequate plumbing and fixtures and heating system.

When the equipment in the home is obsolete, it can be replaced. But, when the house itself is outmoded—having small, poorly designed rooms and storage space—changes can be made only at considerable expense.

Economic obsolescence refers to decrease in value as a result of deterioration of the location. However, improvement in an area can increase the value of the home.

An important part of the value of a home is the land on which it is built. Local lenders or realtors can give an estimate of the current value of the lot. The market value method could also be used for an estimate of the lot's value.

Improvements such as landscaping, patio, finished basement, or finished attic may also increase the value of the property. But all improvements may not be desirable for all people. For example, a family with very young children may not want a swimming pool in the backyard. For them the cost of removing the pool or installing a protective cover over it would reduce the value of the property.

The total of the house, the lot, and any improvements, all after adjustment as suggested above, will give an estimate of the cost value of the property.

Income value. Income or other benefits expected from ownership is another measure of value of property. The income value method is generally more appropriate when estimating the value of commercial or business property, but it can also be applied to residential property. The method requires an estimate of the rental income of the property and an adequate rate of return on the owner's investment.

One useful method of valuation based upon the income concept is the gross rent multiplier (GRM). GRM is a method of converting monthly gross rent into an estimate of market value through multiplying the periodic rent by some multiplier. To estimate the multiplier for market value, analyze the relationship between the estimated or actual rent and the selling prices of houses similar to those you are considering. Estimates or actual monthly rentals can be obtained from realtors who are familiar with rental property in the area.

Suppose that your market analysis is as shown in Exhibit 8–11. The GRM of 134 can be applied to an estimated monthly rent for a home you are considering.

EXHIBIT 8–11
Estimate of gross rent multiplier

House	*Selling price* ÷	*Monthly rental* =	*GRM*
1	$31,500	$240	131
2	33,700	255	132
3	34,300	250	137
4	30,600	225	136
Average	$32,525	$242.50	134

One major weakness of GRM is that it ignores differences in maintenance and operating costs for different types of construction, etc., in that gross rent is used rather than net rent. GRM also ignores any differences in the remaining lives of homes compared. In spite of these weaknesses, however, GRM can serve as a useful tool if it is carefully and intelligently applied. It should be used as only one of the estimates of value to justify a final judgment of market value.

An example of valuation. To illustrate the valuation methods described, suppose that you are considering the purchase of a one-story home with three bedrooms and a family room with a fireplace. The house is three years old and contains 1,600 square feet. It is located in a newly developed area that is zoned for residential use. The lot is 100 feet by 100 feet. Other houses in the area are similar in size and age and are occupied by upper-middle-income families. You have evaluated the features of the house and its location and have determined that it meets your family housing needs. The seller is asking $44,500.

Your investigation indicates that similar houses in the area have recently been sold for from $36,500 to $38,000, although these houses did not have fireplaces and were on 85 by 100 foot lots.

A dealer in builders' supplies has told you that a house of this type currently costs $24 per square foot to build. Improved 100 by 100 foot (quarter-acre) lots in the area are selling for $5,000. Because the house is three years old it has a lower value than an equivalent new house. Suppose that the expected life of the house is fifty years. Three years' depreciation would amount to about $2,304. Using the cost value method, an estimated value would be $41,096 [(1,600) ($24) – $2,304 + $5,000].

The GRM method can also be applied. Realtors indicate that the rent on a similar house would be $280 per month. Your analysis of the present average multiplier indicates that 135 is reasonable. Using these estimates would result in an estimated value of $37,800 for the house.

You now have estimates of the value of your prospective purchase ranging from $36,500 to $41,096. These estimates provide an objective basis upon which to decide how much you are really willing to pay for the house.

Professional appraisal. To help settle the question of how much to pay for the house, you may want it appraised by a qualified professional appraiser. The appraiser's report will cover the value and condition of the house and lot, the economic trend of the neighborhood, and the condition of the housing market in general.

Consumers should seek experienced appraisers who have the appropriate qualifications recognized by professional appraiser societies. Designations providing such assurance include RA, MAI, SRA, SREA, and ASA. Recognition as an RA (Residential Appraiser) or MAI (Member of the Appraisal Institute) indicates that the appraiser meets the standards established by the American Institute of Real Estate Appraisers. The SRA designates an appraiser as a Senior Residential Appraiser; SRPA, Senior Real Property Appraiser; and SREA, Senior Real Estate Analyst, all of which are designations of the Society of Real Estate Appraisers. ASA indicates the holder is a senior member of the American Society of Appraisers. Most ASA's are in real estate, but the Society also includes appraisers who specialize in fine arts, stamps, etc.[4]

Appraisals are also available from VA or FHA units. The VA and

[4] American Institute of Real Estate Appraisers, 155 East Superior Street, Chicago, Illinois 60611; Society of Real Estate Appraisers, 7 South Dearborn Street, Chicago, Illinois, 60603; American Society of Appraisers, P.O. Box 17265, Washington, D.C. 20041.

FHA appraisals are usually somewhat less expensive than private appraisals and also serve as a good estimate of the value of the property.

When taken together, these different methods of estimating the value of a house can give an objective estimate of the value of the property under consideration. However, the term "value" is not strictly an economic term. Some people pay premiums for features that are psychologically satisfying, but have no functional value (decor, hardwood trim, cathedral ceilings, carved plaster, French windows). When making a housing purchase decision, it is important to recognize that portion of the value which is of an economic nature and that portion which is of a psychological nature. This will help you decide the maximum that you are willing to pay for the house. The actual price paid will be determined through a negotiated bidding process between you and the seller.

Purchase

When you and the seller have agreed upon a purchase price, you will be asked to supply "earnest money," which is a deposit made with the offer to purchase in order to show the seriousness of the offer.

The offer-to-purchase agreement is the legal document signed by the buyer and seller that specifically states the terms and conditions of purchase. An agreement can be cancelled only if one or more of the terms are not fulfilled. Therefore, be sure you are satisfied with all of the terms and conditions in the agreement *before* you sign. Carefully preparing this document will avoid bitter disagreements between buyer and seller on items such as price, each party's share of the taxes due, special assessments, financing, property and furnishings covered, payment for title search and insurance, escape clauses for buyer and seller, and closing date. Any conditions to the purchase must be carefully stated in the offer. For example, if the offer to purchase depends on being able to sell your present home or upon getting financing, these conditions must be stated.

Exhibit 8–12 is a standard purchase agreement form. It is very important to have a qualified attorney assist in the preparation of the purchase agreement.

Financing

Your next step after the offer to purchase will probably be to arrange for financing. The usual arrangement, as discussed earlier, is for the buyer to make a downpayment and to borrow the balance.

Your ability to borrow money will depend upon the lender's evalu-

EXHIBIT 8–12
Offer to purchase

.................., Wisconsin, ..., 19.......

The undersigned Buyer, ...,
hereby offers to purchase the property known as ....
(Street Address)
in the.................. of.................., County of.................., Wisconsin, more particularly described as: ....

having a frontage of about .... feet, with a depth of about .... feet, at the price of .... Dollars ($..................) and on the terms and conditions as follows:

Earnest Money (cash) (check) .... ($..................) Tendered herewith. Additional Earnest Money (cash) (check) .... ($..................) to be paid within .... days of acceptance of offer (or on..................) and the balance in cash at closing or as hereafter set forth.

TIME IS OF THE ESSENCE WITH RESPECT TO ADDITIONAL EARNEST MONEY PAYMENT.

THE BUYER'S OBLIGATION TO CONCLUDE THIS TRANSACTION IS CONDITIONED UPON THE CONSUMMATION OF THE FOLLOWING:

(If this offer is subject to financing, the sale of other property or any other contingency, it must be so stated here. If so state here. If none so state.)

....

Buyer agrees that unless otherwise specified, he will pay all costs of securing any financing to the extent permitted by law, and to perform all acts necessary to expedite such financing.

THE SELLER SHALL, UPON PAYMENT OF THE PURCHASE PRICE, CONVEY THE PROPERTY BY GOOD AND SUFFICIENT WARRANTY DEED, OR OTHER CONVEYANCE PROVIDED HEREIN, FREE AND CLEAR OF ALL LIENS AND ENCUMBRANCES, EXCEPTING: Municipal and Zoning Ordinances and Recorded Easements for Public Utilities located adjacent to side and rear lot lines: Recorded Building and use Restrictions and Covenants; General taxes for year of closing; and .... provided none of the foregoing prohibit present use.

Legal possession of premises shall be delivered to Buyer on date of closing.

Physical occupancy of.................. shall be given to Buyer on..................

If Seller shall occupy premises after closing, Seller shall pay use and occupancy charge of $.................. per day.

Time is of the essence hereto with respect to occupancy. (Strike if not applicable.) It is understood the premises are now occupied by..
under (oral lease) (written lease), which terms are: ....

(If property leased — terms of lease must be stated.)

The sum of $.................. shall be withheld from the purchase price to be escrowed with .... to guarantee delivery of possession to the Buyer AND FOR NO OTHER PURPOSE which sum upon Seller's failure to deliver possession shall be paid to the Buyer as liquidated damages or returned to the Seller if occupancy is delivered to the Buyer on the date of physical occupancy as stated above.

All earnest money paid hereon shall be applied as part payment on the purchase price if this offer is accepted on or before ...., 19.......; otherwise, to be returned to the undersigned Buyer no later than.................., 19....... and this offer shall become null and void.

If this offer is accepted, it shall not become binding upon the Buyer until copy of accepted offer is deposited, postage prepaid, in the United States Mails, addressed to the Buyer at ...., or by personal delivery thereof.

The transaction is to be closed at the office of Buyer's mortgagee, if any, or at the office of.., on or before ...., 19......., or at such other time and place as may be agreed to in writing by the Buyer and Seller.

1. Seller warrants and represents to Buyer that Seller has no notice or knowledge of:

(a) planned or commenced public improvement which may result in special assessments or otherwise affect the property except ....

(b) any government agency or court order requiring repairs, alterations or correction of any existing conditions except ....

(c) ANY STRUCTURAL OR MECHANICAL DEFECTS IN PROPERTY, INCLUDING ADEQUACY AND QUALITY OF WELL AND SANITARY DISPOSAL SYSTEMS, EXCEPT..

The undersigned Buyer has read and fully understands and hereby makes the foregoing Offer to Purchase and acknowledges receipt of a copy of said offer.

THIS CONTRACT INCLUDES THE BALANCE OF TERMS ON REVERSE SIDE.

.... (Buyer)

.... (Buyer)

THE ABOVE OFFER IS HEREBY ACCEPTED. THE WARRANTY AND REPRESENTATION MADE HEREIN SURVIVE THE CLOSING OF THIS TRANSACTION. THE UNDERSIGNED HEREBY AGREES TO SELL AND CONVEY THE ABOVE MENTIONED PROPERTY ON THE TERMS AND CONDITIONS AS SET FORTH AND ACKNOWLEDGES RECEIPT OF A COPY OF THIS AGREEMENT.

....

...., 19....... .... (Seller)

....
(If Seller is married, spouse should sign.) (Seller)

EARNEST MONEY RECEIPT

(Cash) (check) received from..
.... in the amount of..Dollars.
The undersigned hereby agrees to hold same in an authorized Real Estate Trust Account in..
.... Bank in.., Wisconsin,
or transmit the same in accordance with the terms of the above offer.

...., Broker

...., 19....... BY: ....

EXHIBIT 8–12 *(continued)*

THE FOLLOWING TERMS ARE PART OF THE CONTRACT ON REVERSE SIDE.

Included in the purchase price are such of the following items as may be on the premises, which will be delivered free and clear of encumbrances: all garden bulbs, plants, shrubs and trees; screen doors and windows; storm doors and windows; electric lighting fixtures; window shades, curtain and traverse rods, blinds, and shutters; bathroom accessory fixtures; central heating and cooling units and attached equipment; water heater and softener; linoleum cemented to floors; attached carpeting and fitted rugs; awnings; exterior attached antennas and component parts; garage door opener and remote control; fireplace equipment and accessories.

ADDITIONAL ITEMS INCLUDED IN SALE:..

....

....

ITEMS NOT INCLUDED IN SALE:..

....

....

General taxes levied in the year of closing shall be prorated at the time of closing on the basis of the net general taxes for the preceding year.

(**Caution:** -- If property has not been fully assessed, make special agreement.)

(**Caution:** — If area assessments are contemplated, make special agreement.)

Interest, rents and water shall be prorated as of the date of closing. Accrued income and expenses, including taxes for the day of closing, shall accrue to the Seller.

Special assessments, if any, for work on site actually commenced prior to date of this offer, shall be paid by Seller.

Special assessments, if any, for work on site actually commenced after date of this offer, shall be paid by Buyer.

The Seller shall furnish and deliver to the Buyer for examination at least fifteen (15) days prior to the date set for closing, Seller's choice of either:

1. A complete abstract of title made by an abstract company, extended to within thirty (30) days of the closing, said abstract to show the Seller's title to be marketable and in the condition called for by this agreement, except for mortgages, judgments or other liens which will be satisfied out of the proceeds of the sale. The Buyer shall notify the Seller in writing of any valid objection tc the title within ten (10) days after the receipt of said abstract and the Seller shall then have a reasonable time but not exceeding sixty (60) days, within which to rectify the title (or furnish a title policy as hereinafter provided) and in such cases the time of closing shall be accordingly extended; or
2. An owner's policy of title insurance, in the amount of the full purchase price, naming the Buyer as the assured, as his interest may appear, written by a responsible title insurance company licensed by the State of Wisconsin, which policy shall guarantee the Seller's title to be in condition called for by this agreement, except for mortgages, judgments, or other liens, which will be satisfied out of the proceeds of the sale. A commitment by such a title company, agreeing to issue such a title policy upon the recording of the proper documents as agreed herein, shall be deemed sufficient performance.

If this offer provides for a land contract, the same evidence of title shall be furnished prior to the execution of the land contract, and Seller shall furnish written proof, at or before closing, that the total underlying indebtedness, if any, is not in excess of the proposed balance of the land contract, and that the payments on this land contract, are sufficient to meet all of the obligations of the Seller on the underlying indebtedness.

If this offer is the result of a co-brokerage, then all money paid herewith shall be held in the selling Broker's trust account until the acceptance of this offer and shall be transmitted to the listing broker immediately upon such acceptance.

All subsequent payments shall be made to the listing broker and held in the listing broker's trust account.

Should the undersigned Buyer fail to carry out this agreement, all money paid hereunder, including any additional earnest money, shall, at the option of the Seller, be forfeited as liquidated damages and shall be paid to or retained by the Seller, subject to deductions of Broker's commission and disbursements, if any. In the event neither party has commenced a law suit within one (1) year after the closing date set forth in the offer, the Broker is authorized to disburse the earnest money as liquidated damages, and if Seller has not notified Buyer of election to consider the earnest money as liquidated damages within six (6) months of said closing date, Broker is authorized to refund all earnest money to Buyer.

Should the Seller be unable to carry out this agreement by reason of a valid legal defect in title which the Buyer is unwilling to waive all money paid hereunder shall be returned to the Buyer forthwith, and this contract shall be void.

In the event the premises shall be damaged by fire or elements prior to time of closing, in an amount of not more than ten per cent of the selling price, the Seller shall be obligated to repair the same. In the event such damage shall exceed such sum, this agreement may be cancelled at option of Buyer. Should the Buyer elect to carry out this agreement despite such damage, such Buyer shall be entitled to all the credit for the insurance proceeds resulting from damage, not exceeding, however, the purchase price.

....

....

....

....

....

....

....

....

....

....

....

....

ation of your ability to repay the loan. The lender will look at your credit standing, employment record, and earnings record. The amount you can borrow will also be limited by the value and price of the home you wish to purchase and by your ability to repay the loan as evidenced by your current income and expenses. A more complete discussion of credit evaluation is included in Chapter 9.

A lender will require you to sign two types of documents before allowing you to have the money: (1) a statement of the amount of the debt, usually a note or a bond, and (2) a security instrument, usually called a mortgage.

Sources of mortgage money. Savings and loan associations (S&Ls) provide more money for financing home purchases than any other single source. As of the beginning of 1977, S&Ls held 47.3 percent of all nonfarm home mortgage loans. Commercial banks held 26.5 percent of the mortgage financing, and mutual savings banks, located primarily in the New England states, provided 9.6 percent. Life insurance companies have provided 2.9 percent of the mortgage funds, federally supported agencies provided 14.6 percent and credit unions, wealthy individuals, etc., provided the remainder of the money for home mortgage loans.[5]

Types of mortgage financing. Lenders require security for the loan that they make to the home buyer. There are several types of mortgages including the straight, conventional, FHA-insured, VA-guaranteed, and PMI mortgages.

Straight mortgages. Straight mortgages are usually short term, and payments during the life of the mortgage are for interest only. The usual life of a straight mortgage is three to five years, after which it must be paid or renewed. Often there is an understanding that the mortgage loan will be renewed. The straight mortgage has worked to the detriment of many homeowners in the past. When the note is due, the lender can demand the immediate repayment of the full amount borrowed. The large amount due makes it difficult for borrowers to repay in a lump sum. If the borrower is not able to repay or refinance for any reason, such as an economic recession, the lender can take the property in settlement of the debt. These characteristics make the straight mortgage very unattractive for financing the purchase of a home, because most buyers need a longer term for repayment as well as a planned, periodic repayment of the principal.

Conventional mortgages. Conventional mortgages call for a periodic payment of a constant amount that includes the interest and the repayment of principal over the life of the loan. The life of the loan is

---

[5] *Federal Reserve Bulletin.*

usually 20 to 30 years and the loan is said to be "amortized" over that period.

Periodic repayment over the longer period of time is advantageous to both the borrower and the lender. The longer period enables the borrower to spread the payment for the house over its useful life. At the same time, the periodic repayment of principal reduces the amount the lender has at risk in the form of a loan.

FHA-insured mortgages. The Federal Housing Administration (FHA) was established in 1934 to provide insurance to private lenders on insurable mortgage loans for the purchase and/or improvement of homes.

FHA-insured mortgages are merely a hybrid of the conventional mortgage. The difference is that there is a third party introduced to the transaction between the borrower and the lender—namely, the FHA. FHA insures that it will fulfill the mortgage if the borrower does not. The premium paid for FHA insurance is one half of one percent of the loan balance. The interest rate on an insured loan is lower than the rate on a conventional loan because of the reduced risk to the lender.

You can apply for an FHA-insured loan at almost any lending institution. The application is then sent to the FHA office where your qualifications as a mortgagor, estimated value of the property, and conformance of property to FHA standards are evaluated. If you qualify for an insured loan you are notified through the lending institution.

Borrowers with FHA insurance usually are not required to make as large a downpayment as that required for a conventional loan. Recent FHA requirements are as follows:

Value of house	Required downpayment
Up to $25,000	3%
$25,001 to $35,000	10%
$35,001 to $45,000	20%

The local FHA office or lending institutions can give a complete discussion of the current types of loans and qualifications for FHA insurance.

VA-guaranteed mortgage. Veterans Administration (VA) guaranteed mortgages are also hybrids of the conventional mortgage, but are limited to qualified veterans of military service.

The VA does not usually lend the money, but rather guarantees against loss to institutional or private lenders. It will lend directly in rural areas; FHA will not. Limits for the guarantee are stated as a percentage of the appraised value up to a maximum dollar amount. At the present time, the loan itself may be up to $100,000 in many areas, but the guarantee is limited to 60 percent of the appraised value or $17,500, whichever is lower.

If you are a veteran of military service at the time you are buying a home, it is important to contact your VA office for a complete discussion of the current limits and qualifications.

PMI loans. Private mortgage insurance (PMI) loans are also a hybrid conventional loan. A conventional loan from an institutional lender (savings and loan, commercial bank, mutual savings bank, or mortgage banker) is coupled with an insurance policy from a private insurance company (the role played by the government in FHA loans). There are approximately twelve firms that specialize in PMI loans; the largest, representing around two thirds of the total industry, is Mortgage Guarantee Insurance Co. (MGIC) of Milwaukee, Wisconsin.

With a PMI policy a lender can, by law, increase the amount of the loan, up to 95 percent in some cases. The typical PMI loans divide into two types: the ten percent down or 90 percent loan and the five percent down or 95 percent loan. Typically, the charges (premiums) are as follows:

Premium payment method	*95% loan*	*90% loan*
Lump sum	3% of mortgage paid at closing	2% of mortgage paid at closing
Split payment	1% of closing + ¼ of 1% per year	½% at closing + ¼ of 1% per year

Lenders charge more for a PMI loan than a conventional loan to cover the cost of the mortgage insurance premium. The logic for this is that the risk is not totally reduced because a private insurance company is not riskfree as is FHA.

Mortgage discount "points." Points are a one-time charge made by the lender in order to increase the effective interest rate the borrower pays on the loan. Lending institutions generally charge points during periods of tight mortgage money when the rates on mortgage loans are high or on FHA/VA loans because market rates of interest are higher than the limit allowed to be charged on FHA or VA loans.

Each point is equal to one percent of the mortgage principal. Payment for points is made to the lender at the start of the loan period as a part of the closing costs. The number of points that you must pay depends largely upon the availability of mortgage money in your area. For example, suppose mortgage money is tight and you must pay six points in order to get a 20-year, $30,000 mortgage loan at eight percent. This means a payment of $1,800 for points (0.06 × $30,000). The result is an increase in the effective cost of your mortgage loan. In the above example it raises the loan from eight percent to about 8.75 percent.

As you can see, when points are charged on a loan it can greatly increase the amount of money a home buyer must pay at the time of the closing. At this stage you might bargain for fewer points or you might decide to shop around for other financing.

FHA and VA regulation of maximum interest rates is the greatest cause of discount points, but the home buyer is not permitted to pay points. However, no limit is placed on the number of points that a seller may pay to the home buyer's mortgage lender. As a result, the buyer may effectively "reimburse" the seller by paying a slightly higher price for the home. To illustrate, in 1977 the ceiling rate on government-backed loans was 8½ percent and the rate on conventional loans was about 9 percent. The result was that points would have been charged to the seller, or the lender would not make the loan. On a $40,000 loan with a charge of four points, these points total $1,600 (0.04 × $40,000). This cost coupled with a seven percent sales commission (assume the home sold for $45,000, therefore 0.07 × $45,000) of $3,150 reduces the net amount received by the seller to $40,250, a dramatic and painful reduction. Therefore, some sellers of used homes may resist selling if FHA or VA financing is used. Builders, on the other hand, may be agreeable to FHA/VA financing because they spread the cost of the points over all their homes (even those sold on conventional loans) as well as using other techniques to "build" the discount points into the selling price.

Closing

The process of buying a home ends with the act of closing. This is the time when the buyer and seller, their attorneys, and usually the lender meet to do two things. First, financial arrangements between the lender and buyer are concluded. Second, documents transferring title from the seller to the buyer are completed.

Title to property refers to the ownership interest in the property. It grants exclusive possession to the owner and grants recourse to legal power to defend this ownership right. A *deed* is a written document used to transfer the property ownership rights from the seller (grantor) to the buyer (grantee). The deed is written evidence of the transfer and it is often referred to as a deed of conveyance.

There are several types of deeds of conveyance. The safest of these is the *full covenant and warranty deed.* This deed gives the home buyer every possible future guarantee of title by creating a continuing future claim upon the seller. Thus, if other types of deeds, such as *quitclaim* and *bargain-and-sale* deeds are used, they do not provide the same protection to the buyer as does the warranty deed. The quitclaim deed conveys any ownership interest of the seller to the buyer. It is used when the seller cannot or does not warrant any substantial title or possession. This places the risk on the buyer, because if the seller does not have title the buyer receives nothing. Further, there is no legal recourse against the seller.[6]

When making as large a purchase as a house, you will want to be as certain as possible that you have a free and clear title; that is, a title that grants you sole and total ownership rights to the property. As a result, buyers generally demand more than a deed. Other devices that have been developed to provide this protection include the title abstract, certificate of title, and title insurance. The *title abstract* is prepared by an attorney or title guarantee company. It provides a historical account of the property ownership, indicates all activities relating to the title of the property, and lists any unsettled claims against the property. The abstract does not guarantee title, but it provides reassurance.

A second document, the *certificate of title,* is a certification of an attorney's opinion that the buyer is receiving a valid title to the property. Title is not guaranteed by the certification and the attorney cannot be held liable for future claims arising to impair title so long as the search was made with due care (that is, so long as there was no negligence—a difficult fact to prove).

HOW MUCH HOUSING CAN YOU AFFORD?

During the early 1900s, when private lenders were the principal sources of mortgage money, lenders obtained security for a loan by limiting the loan to a small percentage of the value of the property. This practice and other conditions imposed on the loan by individual lenders resulted in many conflicting rules and lending practices.

Two rules of thumb were, and in some cases still are, widely used. The most common of these required that the monthly mortgage payments of principal and interest not exceed a week's take-home pay or 25 percent of the monthly income of the primary wage earner. The other rule required that the cost of the home not exceed 2½ times the

---

[6] William M. Shenkel, *The Real Estate Professional* (Homewood, Illinois: Dow Jones–Irwin, 1976), Chapter 8.

primary wage earner's annual gross income. These rules had merit when the only security that the lender had was the mortgaged property. However, the advent of private and government mortgage insurance and guarantees, and the wider use of credit by consumers has made these indicators much less reliable in evaluating a borrower's ability to pay.

In any analysis of a borrower's ability to pay, consideration must be given to the differences among families in the priorities placed on housing needs. Each family establishes its standard of living by assigning priorities to food, clothing, housing, education, transportation, entertainment and recreation, and many other things. Families with the same income may have widely differing priorities that affect the amount of family income "available" to pay for housing.

While rules and formulas may be useful, these individual differences in spending preferences must be reflected in your housing decision. This is the reason that an analysis of your income and priorities is the only meaningful way to decide what you can afford for housing. This approach is used in the budgeting discussions in Chapters 2 and 17.

ALTERNATIVE FORMS OF HOME OWNERSHIP

Our discussion of home ownership has centered on the single-family dwelling as a solution to shelter needs. With the rapidly rising costs of home ownership, many families have been buying housing other than the traditional house and lot. There are a number of alternatives to the single-family home.

Cooperatives

Co-op housing plans have existed since before World War II but they were of minor importance in this country until 1950, when legislation was passed permitting FHA insurance for co-op housing.

Purchasers of a co-op unit do not directly own their living space. They own membership in the co-op that, as a nonprofit corporation, holds title to the property. Consistent with the co-op organization, each member has one vote, regardless of the size of his or her unit, on affairs to be decided by the membership. Each member signs a three-year occupancy agreement that is automatically renewed unless the member is in violation of the rules or has been given notice to leave.[7]

[7] U.S. Department of Housing and Urban Development, *HUD-FHA Comparison of Co-operative and Condominium Housing,* HUD-321-F(4).

Mortgage payments, real estate taxes, and any other expenses required for the operation of the complex are assumed by the corporation. These costs are then prorated to the members on the basis of the space occupied. To illustrate, if your apartment contains five percent of the housing space in the complex, then your share is five percent of the costs assumed by the corporation. This prorated share of taxes and mortgage interest can be used as an itemized deduction on the member's tax return.

All co-ops that have FHA-insured mortgages permit equity. Equity consists of the modest downpayment, occupancy fee, the value of any improvements that have been approved by the board, and any annual increase as specified in the co-op bylaws. A member receives the amount of this equity when leaving the co-op. Unfortunately, if the co-op has high vacancies and suffers foreclosure, the members lose their equity buildup.

Members may sell their shares to anyone approved by the co-op directors, but usually the co-op has the first option to purchase the shares.

Condominiums[8]

The condominium concept of housing is often viewed as a new idea, but condominiums actually date back to the sixth century B.C. Roman law authorized multifamily housing units in which each family owned its own living space as well as area that was used in common with the other owners.

Condominium ownership is relatively new to homeowners in the U.S., however. The popularity of condominiums has spread so that they can now be found in all fifty states. Legislation was passed in 1961 that permitted the use of FHA-insured mortgages in their purchase. However, fewer than one percent of condominiums purchased since 1961 have FHA-insured mortgages.

Problems for condominium owners. Condominiums are very attractive to and well-suited to meet the housing needs of many families. However, buyers must be very cautious when purchasing a unit. The growing number of buyer complaints about condominiums has led to moves by the federal and state governments to protect owners.

Frequently voiced complaints stem from the fact that most of the owners did not read and understand the Declaration, the legal document that enables the condominium to come into being. To illus-

---

8 U.S. Department of Housing and Urban Development. *Questions About Condominiums*, HUD-365-f.

trate, condominium owners in Fort Lauderdale, Florida, became painfully aware of a clause in their purchase contracts that tied the lease charge for the recreation area to the Consumer Price Index (CPI). Purchase contracts of many complexes in the area contained 99-year leases on recreational facilities that were often owned by the developer or a company owned by the developer. As the CPI began to increase rapidly in the early 1970s, condominium owners discovered that they and any future owners would be required to make monthly payments to developers for such facilities as swimming pools, saunas, etc., and that these payments would increase with but would not decrease with the CPI. Worse still, failure to make these monthly payments could result in foreclosure and loss of the owner's investment.

Complaints also center on issues such as the charging of exorbitant fees for maintenance and grounds leases, inadequate control of the complex by the owners, poor quality construction, and unnecessarily complicated purchase contracts that confound even attorneys.

There appears to be little that can be done by the government for condominium buyers who have already signed legal documents, without running into constitutional issues. Experiences of these owners is a lesson and a warning to all prospective buyers.[9]

The prevalence of these complaints does not say that all condominiums are bad or that the concept has not been successful. Many owners are pleased with their purchases. It is likely that the condominium is destined to increase in importance in the housing industry; mortgage bankers, builders, and the federal government project that half of our population will live in condominiums by the year 2000.

Mobile homes

The mobile home that has evolved over the past twenty years can hardly be called mobile. The Manufactured Housing Institute[10] (MHI) defines a mobile home as a structure that is transportable in one or more units and exceeds either 8 feet in width or 32 feet in length. Mobile homes are constructed on a permanent chassis and can be used as a dwelling with or without a permanent foundation when they are connected to the required utilities. The unit includes plumbing, heating, and electrical systems.

Owners of mobile homes obtain title to the dwelling unit, but this

---

[9] Shirley Scheiba, "Condominium Crackdown," *Barron's*, April 14, 1975, pp. 5, 23–24.

[10] Prior to July 1, 1975, it was the Mobile Home Manufacturer's Association/Trailer Coach Association (MHMA/TCA).

usually does not include a site upon which to locate the home. Such space must be purchased or leased separately.

Estimating cash outlays. The sizes and thus the cost of mobile homes vary considerably. Small, one-bedroom units with less than 600 square feet are available, as are increasingly popular double-wides with more than 1,600 square feet. The trend has been toward a larger size unit. The square footage of living space available in the average size mobile home increased from 780 in 1971 to 1,008 in 1976, as shown in Exhibit 8–13.

EXHIBIT 8–13
Trends in price and size of mobile homes

Year	*Average retail price (all sizes)**	*Average living space (square feet)*	*Cost per square foot*
1971	$ 6,640	780	$ 9.07
1972	6,950	780	8.73
1973	7,770	882	8.84
1974	9,760	910	10.63
1975	11,440	966	11.98
1976	12,750	1,008	13.09

* Includes furniture, draperies, carpeting, and appliances but excludes land as well as cost of steps, skirting, anchoring, and any other applicable set-up charges (approximately 15 percent of home cost).

Source: Manufactured Housing Institute.

Prices of mobile homes range from $6,000 for a small single-wide to approximately $30,000 for a large double-wide unit. Between 1971 and 1976 the average price of all mobile homes increased from $6,640 to $12,750. At least a part of the increase in the average can be accounted for by the trend toward larger units; however, the price per square foot has also increased.

Most new mobile homes are sold fully equipped with kitchen range, refrigerator, furniture in all rooms, carpeting and other floor coverings, curtains, draperies, and lamps. However, the home may be purchased without some (or any) of the general furnishings.

In 1976 the financing of mobile homes was liberalized by permitting VA guarantees of 50 percent of the unpaid balance on mortgages up to $12,500 for a single-wide with a term of 12 years and 32 days; $20,000 for a double-wide with a term of 20 years and 32 days. For the purchase of a mobile home *plus* lot, the loan maximum is $20,000 for a single-wide unit and $27,500 for a double-wide.

Passage of the Housing and Community Development Act of 1974 expanded FHA's authority to insure a loan on a double-wide mobile home and an improved lot up to $22,500; $15,000 for the home and $7,500 for the improved lot or $5,000 for an unimproved lot. The maturity of such a loan may extend to 20 years.

One-time outlays. In addition to a downpayment, which may range from no downpayment under VA regulation to 20 to 30 percent under the installment loan plan with a chattel mortgage, there are other one-time outlays required of the mobile home purchaser. These include the items that are either essential or desirable in making the home usable. Essential extras that will add at least 15 percent to the cost of the mobile home include steps with handrails at each outside door; skirting to conceal the wheels and undercarriage of the home; supports or piers to provide a foundation for holding the home level and stable; over-the-roof ties or anchors in areas of high winds; and concrete strips for the wheels if a base is not provided.

If you move your unit to a mobile home park, utility hookups will be available; otherwise you must provide your own systems. Added outlays will be required for the purchase of a lot (which may be included in a mortgage), connections to electric and gas service, having a well dug, and installation of a septic system. Before a lot is purchased for a mobile home, make certain that regulations of the municipality where you plan to locate permit you to do so.

Monthly outlays. Estimates of monthly outlays should include not only the mortgage payment but also expenses such as rent for a space, insurance, maintenance, repairs, heat, and utilities. Lot rentals for a modern development range from $60 to $125 per month, depending upon the quality of the park and the amenities, such as paved streets and walks.

To illustrate the estimated one-time and monthly outlays for the purchase and ownership of a single-wide mobile home costing $10,000, suppose that it will be placed in a mobile home park. Utility, city sanitation, and water facilities are installed and hooked up. A ten percent downpayment of $1,000 is required with an 11 percent, 12-

Estimated one-time outlay	
Downpayment	$1,000.00
Essential extras (15 percent of cost)	1,500.00
Utility hookups	300.00
Insurance (annual)	70.00
Total	$2,870.00
Estimated monthly outlay	
Mortgage	$ 112.82
Space rental fee	90.00
Utilities and heat	35.00
Maintenance and repairs	20.00
Total	$ 257.82

year mortgage loan on the balance. An annual insurance premium must be paid at the beginning of each year in order to provide needed protection during that time.

Mobile homes require less money for purchase and ownership than do conventional homes. However, a mobile home tends to depreciate in value faster than a conventional home and therefore does not provide the protection against inflation available with conventional home ownership.

SUMMARY

Housing is the hub of the family's private world. The nature of housing has a direct effect on the quality of family life. It affects health, time, and energy required in rearing a family and caring for its members, the way in which family members relate to one another, self-related attitudes, morale, and satisfaction with one's station in life. It also affects the way in which one family relates to another, to the neighborhood, and to the community.

Families do not want, expect, or require dwellings that are identical. Low-income families may be more concerned with securing clean, safe, and reasonably comfortable housing than in, say, finding quarters that are especially psychologically stimulating. At the same time, many families having greater incomes can take basic shelter for granted and proceed to satisfy "higher" level needs in housing.

Families can satisfy their need by renting or owning their dwelling. Whether to rent or buy must be decided by considering the advantages and disadvantages of each in light of the family's needs and income.

Estimates of the costs of renting or buying must consider the one-time as well as the monthly outlays.

The process of acquiring a home involves a logical and orderly plan beginning with a thorough search for and selection of a dwelling through the required financing arrangements. Alternatives to be considered in addition to the conventional home include cooperatives, condominiums, and mobile homes.

DISCUSSION QUESTIONS

1. What are the housing needs that are common to all families? What are the personal needs to be satisfied by housing? Which are satisfied first? Explain.
2. Describe the historical trend in home ownership by American families since the early 1900s. What factors help explain a family's housing status? Discuss.

3. What are the advantages and disadvantages of buying? Of renting?
4. Compare the costs of renting with costs of owning a home. Explain differences between them.
5. What is a deed? A title? What legal devices have been developed to protect an owner's title?
6. How do the fund plan and the direct reduction method of repaying a mortgage loan differ? Which is better? Why?
7. Explain each of the steps to follow when buying a home. What are the market value, cost value, and income value methods of estimating the value of a home?
8. What is the major difference between a VA-guaranteed loan and an FHA-insured mortgage?
9. Explain why "points" are used and how they work.
10. What are alternatives to owning a single-family house? Compare these with regard to property owned, responsibility for the various costs of ownership, and rights to sell the property.

CASE PROBLEMS

1. Dan and Chloe Parker have just graduated from college. They have both obtained jobs in a large city where Chloe will earn $13,000 as an accountant and Dan will receive $12,000 as a teacher, and he feels he could earn $1,500 at a summer job. Dan is tentatively considering going on to graduate school during the next four summers to get a master's degree rather than getting a summer job. While in college, both Parkers had part-time jobs to help pay for their educational costs. Because their part-time earnings did not meet their expenses they had to borrow a total of $7,000, which must be repaid in five annual payments beginning the year after graduation. The Parkers are about to begin shopping for housing.

   What housing alternatives would you recommend for them? Defend your recommendation by identifying important factors for them to consider.

2. Jim and Karen Shepard have been married for the four years since they graduated from college. During this time they have both been working and have been able to build their savings account up to $10,000. Karen is a buyer for a large store that specializes in women's clothing. Her salary is presently about $15,000 per year. Jim has a job in sales where his income depends upon commission. Over the past two years his commissions have been $15,000 and $24,000. A $6,000 portion of this increase is due to a large new account. However, this account is very price conscious and would not hesitate to purchase from Jim's competitors if they offered a lower price. Jim believes that if economic conditions are good his commissions could go as high as $30,000 to $35,000. During a business slowdown, however, he thinks that commissions of $20,000 would be doing well.

   Within the next year the Shepards plan to start their family. They have decided that Karen will continue to work after their children are born. They also recognize that because Jim is doing so well there is a good chance that within the next two years he will be promoted to sales manager of a territory in another state. The Shepards have decided that if this promotion comes through they will move. Because the lease on their present apartment expires in three months, they are wondering what they should do. A new lease on their two-bedroom apartment will require monthly rent of $350 plus utilities, which average $65 per month. Homes with four bedrooms are currently selling for about $50,000. Financing for these homes requires a 20 percent downpayment with an interest rate of 8½ percent for a 25-year mortgage. Closing costs amount to $950. Property taxes have been about $1,200 per year on these houses, and annual maintenance costs about $400 per year. All utilities average $110 per month. The Shepards are in the 35 percent income tax bracket, including both federal and state. Housing values have been increasing six percent per year in the area where the Shepards would buy.

a. Determine the monthly outlay required for each of the alternatives.

b. Given that the property tax and mortgage interest are deductible for income tax purposes (assume annual interest of $3,400 for the first year), determine the after-tax costs of renting and owning for the first year.

c. Recommend the decision that you feel is best for the Shepards. Be sure to include important decision factors in addition to the monthly cost.

SELECTED READINGS

Comarow, Avery. "Ins and Outs of Inspecting a House," *Money,* July 1973, pp. 20–27.

Fowler, G. C., and Mencher, M., eds. *The Fanny Mae Guide to Buying, Financing and Selling Your Home.* New York: Doubleday & Co., Inc., 1973.

Hess, Nancy R. *Home Buyer's Guide.* Englewood Cliffs, New Jersey: Prentice-Hall, Inc., 1976.

Hubin, Vincent J. *Warning! Condominium Ownership May Be Dangerous to Your Health, Wealth, and Peace of Mind.* Homewood, Illinois: Dow-Jones–Irwin, 1976.

Rabb, Judith, and Rabb, Bernard. *Good Shelter: A Guide to Mobiles, Modulars, and Prefabricated Homes,* Scranton, Pa.: Quadrangle/The New York Times Co., 1975.

Rejnis, Ruth. *Everything Tenants Need to Know to Get Their Money's Worth: The Complete Guide to Tenanting.* New York: David McKay Co., Inc., 1974.

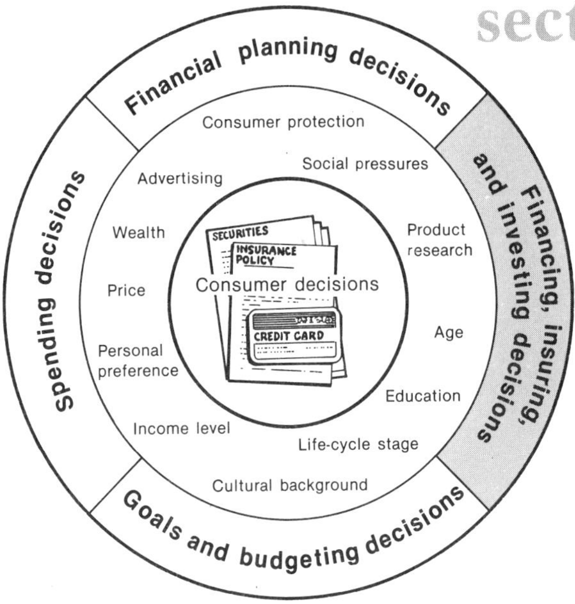

section three

FINANCING, INSURING, AND INVESTING DECISIONS

Being an intelligent consumer involves more than deciding what you want (goal and priority decisions) and then buying it (spending decisions). You must also deal with some rather complex financing decisions which are directly related to priority and spending decisions.

One example of financing decisions is determining how to pay for what you buy. Instead of paying cash, you may choose to finance a purchase through some form of credit. Chapter 9 presents some detailed considerations of the pros and cons of credit use and also explores the very important issues of the cost of credit and the legal rights and duties of a consumer who uses credit.

Another financing decision involves providing financial security against risk. We all face the risk of loss to our persons and property. Chapter 10 outlines the essential nature of the risks we face and suggests a number of ways of handling risk. Chapter 11 deals directly with the question of loss of property and the risk of being sued and discusses how automobile and homeowner's insurance can help manage these risks. Chapter 12 suggests ways of dealing with the personal risks of illness, death, and disability and examines several insurance mechanisms (life insurance, disability insurance, health insurance, and Social Security) as means of coping with personal risk.

The last three chapters of this section are concerned with investing decisions. These investing decisions are designed to build financial security by accumulating and conserving your savings. To these ends, Chapter 13 discusses the overall philosophy of investing and presents the investment pyramid as one outlook on investing. Chapter 14 considers the more specific issue of investing in stocks and bonds and outlines the basic characteristics of these investments. Chapter 15 deals with investment decisions and basic investment strategies. It puts considerable emphasis on the element of risk in investment and the importance of considering your needs and limitations in choosing appropriate investments.

Credit and the consumer

9

OBJECTIVES

This chapter examines how you can make wise use of credit by carefully considering the sources and costs of credit. Wise use of credit also means that you should know the legal rights and duties associated with credit financing. After thoroughly reading and discussing this chapter you should be able to:

. . . Explain the advantages and disadvantages of the major sources and types of consumer credit.
. . . Identify the undesirable clauses in installment contracts.
. . . Explain the factors considered by creditors when evaluating the credit worthiness of a consumer.
. . . Calculate the effective annual percentage rate (APR) of credit.
. . . Describe protection afforded to consumers through the passage of the Consumer Credit Protection Act of 1969.

The use of credit goes back to prehistoric times. Archaeologists have found evidence that ancient societies used consumer credit. The Bible often refers to creditor practices, credit rules, and debtor action.

Consumer credit was widely used in Colonial American times. In a study of the consumer credit in Colonial Philadelphia, William C. Plummer found that the merchants were quite used to selling goods and services on credit. Plummer writes, after examining the records of various business and professional concerns, that ". . . it seems certain that credit rather than cash was the rule."[1]

[1] William C. Plummer, "Consumer Credit in Colonial Philadelphia," *Pennsylvania Magazine*, October 1942, p. 409.

Since the end of World War II consumer credit has grown at an astounding pace. In the period from 1945 to 1950, the amount of consumer credit nearly quadrupled (Exhibit 9–1). The amount of consumer credit doubled in each of the next two decades. By the end

EXHIBIT 9–1
Growth in consumer credit for selected years from 1945 through 1976*

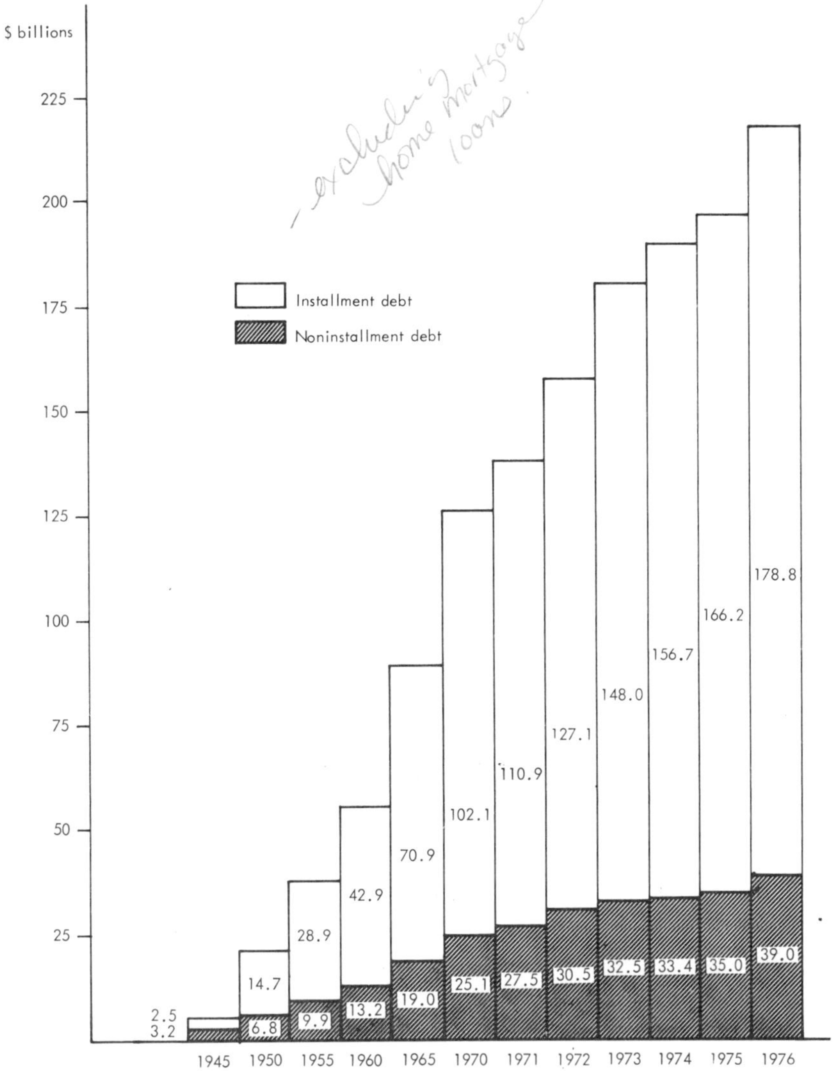

* Data shown are exclusive of home mortgage loans. Series revised by Division of Research and Statistics, Board of Governors of the Federal Reserve System beginning 1970.
Source: *Federal Reserve Bulletins.*

of 1976 the amount of consumer credit outstanding totaled $217.8 billion.

Since the 1950s the vast majority of American consumers have greatly increased their standard of living, and a contributing factor has been the use of credit. Second autos, television sets, dream kitchens, and work-saving household appliances have become common in millions of today's households. Consumer credit paved the way for the mass distribution of these goods from the producers to the homes of the consumers.

AVAILABILITY OF CONSUMER CREDIT

The flexibility of the basic types of consumer credit and of the terms of repayment make credit available to most consumers. There are, however, dangers inherent in easy access to credit. Credit may obscure the need for financial planning, and there is a much higher risk of overspending. Easy credit also encourages impulse buying. However, credit is a fact of modern life. The proper use of credit requires a knowledge of the types of credit available, the sources of credit, and the features and services provided by the various credit plans.

Types of consumer credit

Consumer credit is available in two basic types: (1) direct money loans, and (2) retailer credit. Direct money loans are extended to consumers by lending agencies or financial institutions. The consumer can then use the borrowed money to buy the desired item. When the retailer type of credit is involved, however, the credit is directly related to the sale of the product. Retailer credit is offered by many sellers of goods and services, such as appliance or furniture dealers, automobile dealers, department and specialty stores, physicians, dentists, and many others.

Each of the two types of credit may be further classified by the schedule used for repayment and by the frequency with which approval is required for credit transactions.

The two repayment schedules for credit are the installment and the single, or non-installment, payment. Installment credit usually arises from the purchase of a high-priced item, such as a car, where the buyer does not pay the entire price at once. Payments are then made over several months until the debt is retired. In single-payment credit, the entire debt is scheduled to be repaid in one payment. Some of the sources of credit discussed below may require a specific schedule of repayment, while others are more flexible.

Credit plans may also be classified as open- or close-ended. Open-ended credit is available up to some preset amount without approval for each transaction. You apply for initial approval from a lender, agreeing to the terms of the credit and repayment. Generally, after approval you receive an identifying number or credit card that you can use whenever you need credit.

Close-ended accounts require approval for each transaction. That is, amounts cannot be added to the previous credit financing without a new agreement between you and the lender.

Direct cash loans. Direct cash loans are made in several forms. The loan requirements vary among lenders but they can be put into three main groups: check-credit plans, single-payment loans, and installment loans.

Check-credit plans. Check-credit plans are a form of open-ended credit extended by means of your checking account. In these arrangements the lending institution, usually a bank, approves a predetermined line of credit. When you overdraw your account this automatically triggers the loan. So long as the repayment schedule is met and the authorized limit is not exceeded, you can continue to increase the loan.

Charges for check credit include a finance charge on the outstanding balance and, in some instances, a fee for the credit-checks written.

Single-payment loans. Single-payment loans are loans in varying sizes taken out for a short period of time—usually 30, 60, or 90 days. In most cases there is a collateral requirement based upon the amount of the loan. Finance charges for such loans vary with the size of the loan, the credit rating of the borrower, the amount of collateral provided, as well as the legal rate set by each state.

Installment loans. Installment loans are often used to meet needs over a longer period than the single-payment loans—perhaps even for several years. Periodic payments, whether weekly or monthly, try to match your ability to repay with the size of the loan to be satisfied. Finance charges for these loans depend upon the source, amount, and timing of the loan, as well as the value of any collateral offered. Interest rates may range up to 38 percent per year depending upon the state laws, collateral, etc.

Retailer credit. You may get retailer credit in a variety of charge accounts and credit cards. Such plans range from those set up by a single retailer to those that are international in scope. Credit plans offered by single retailers require payment to each retailer. Those plans that are national or international usually require that payment for credit purchases made at different retail establishments be sent to a single collection point. The most common retailer credit plans include 30-day accounts, revolving credit plans, bank credit cards, and travel and entertainment cards.

Thirty-day accounts. Thirty-day accounts are used by most American families. The amounts owed must be paid within a set time, usually 30 days. The charge for this credit is included in the price of the product or service.

A means of identification may be required for purchases made in retail stores. However, for services including gas, electric, and water utilities, credit is extended as a matter of course. Long-distance telephone calls also fall into this category but the charge for normal service does not. Normal service is usually billed one month in advance; in other words, you are paying for next month's regular telephone service.

Revolving credit plan. The revolving charge account plan enables you to continue charging purchases and paying all or a part of the balance owed each month. Wanamaker's Department Store of Philadelphia introduced this credit plan in 1938. Although their plan was quite different from the revolving credit plan in general use today, the two plans are based on the same concept. The original plan called for complete payment within four months, while today's accounts may take up to one year, depending upon the plan.

Today, the most common revolving credit plan is known as the revolving charge account. This account was introduced in Detroit in 1956 by J. L. Hudson's Department Store, which called the account its "30-Day Account with Optional Terms." Under this type of plan the whole balance can be paid within 30 days with no service charge; or, payments can be made over several months. For accounts outstanding for longer than 30 days, a service charge is made. The plan also provides a schedule of minimum monthly payments based upon ranges of the account balance.

Revolving charge accounts have advantages and disadvantages for the consumer. One advantage is the ability to charge a larger dollar volume of goods than under the regular 30-day account because of the extended repayment period. Second, this account is easy to use. Once the account has been opened, you are free to buy without having your credit rechecked with each purchase.

The disadvantages of the revolving credit plan are in large part a result of its advantages. One danger is that because of the ease and convenience of use of the charge account you may overbuy and thus be continually in debt to the retailer.

Another disadvantage is the high cost of revolving credit. Rates of 1½ percent per month on such accounts are common and usually exceed the cost of several other sources of credit.

A third disadvantage, which is often overlooked, is the statement contained in the revolving credit plan agreement with the creditor that "Title to the merchandise purchased on this account shall remain in you [the seller] until I [the buyer] have paid the purchase price thereof in full. I assume and shall be responsible for all loss or damage to said goods after receipt." This statement is an "add-on clause" and is also discussed with installment debt. This clause leaves open to question when the title to goods bought actually passes to the buyer. If the account is paid in full, there is little question about ownership. But there is a question if there is a continuous balance owed in the account and if at some future time the buyer is unable to make the required payment. How is it determined which goods are not paid for in full? This question is very important if larger, durable items are bought through revolving credit.

Bank credit cards. Bank credit card plans have become increasingly important in providing consumer credit. The first bank credit card of the current type was issued in 1951 by the Franklin National Bank in Franklin Square, New York. By 1953 over a hundred banks had issued their own credit cards. About half of these issuers, however, dropped their cards in a short period of time and the number of banks issuing cards has continued to decline.

In the mid-1960s banks again became interested in the credit card revolving credit plans and late in the decade two giant bank credit card systems emerged as leaders—VISA (formerly BankAmericard) and Master Charge. These cards are convenient because of their wide acceptability and their centralized billing system. Regardless of where a purchase is made, there is only one monthly bill. Many retailers now subscribe to the credit services of one or both of these national bank cards rather than offering their own revolving credit plan. Merchants must pay for this privilege, usually three to five percent of the sales charged on the card, depending on their sales volume. Because of this charge it is unlikely that such plans will be widely used in stores such as supermarkets where there is a low markup.

The Federal Truth-in-Lending Act gives the consumer some protection against having to pay for defective products bought with a bank credit card. If you have a problem with goods or services that you bought with a credit card, you may have the right not to pay the balance due on them. But, you must first try in good faith to return the product or otherwise give the seller an opportunity to correct the problem. There are two limitations to this right:

1. You must have purchased the product in your home state or if not within your home state, within 100 miles of your current mailing address; *and*

2. The purchase price must have been greater than $50.

These limitations do not apply however, if the seller is owned or operated by the bank, or if the bank mailed you the advertisement for the product or service.

A growing number of consumers have accepted the bank credit card as a convenient method of financing a variety of transactions. This is evidenced by the growth in bank credit card balances outstanding. Outstanding balances, almost entirely on VISA and Master Charge, increased from $3.8 billion in early 1971 to over $11 billion in 1976. Estimated purchases on bank credit cards for 1977 were near $30 billion, about 20 percent greater than the $25.5 billion in purchases during 1976. The acceptance of bank credit cards is so widespread that churches of ten religious denominations in Atlanta, Dallas, Kansas City, Los Angeles, and Philadelphia began accepting credit cards as one means of collecting contributions from members.[2]

Many bank credit card holders avoid finance charges by paying each month's billing in full within the prescribed period, usually 25 days from the billing date. If you elect to pay only a part of the balance owed, usually a minimum of ten percent, a finance charge is made as follows:

Balance subject to finance charge	*Monthly rate*	*Annual percentage rate*
$0–$500	1½ %	18%
Over $500	1	12

The actual calculation of the finance charges is discussed in a later section of this chapter.

Travel and entertainment cards. Three nationally known travel and entertainment cards that have been pushed into the background by the rapid growth of the bank cards are American Express, Diners Club, and Carte Blanche. While similarities with bank cards do exist, there are also important differences.

Similarities include their national acceptance by a wide variety of travel- and service-related businesses and their central billing procedures. Also, interest charges are made on balances past due.

One important difference is that the standards to qualify for travel and entertainment cards are generally higher than those for bank card plans. As a result, consumers who are granted a travel and entertainment card generally have credit limits that are higher than they

[2] *Business Week*, August 4, 1975, p. 66.

would have with a bank card plan. A second difference is that these cards make a flat annual charge for membership, usually about $15, in addition to the usual interest charges on accounts.

Exhibit 9–2 shows the relative importance in terms of sales of the five largest bank and travel and entertainment credit cards.

EXHIBIT 9–2
Consumer credit card sales by plan for 1974 (in percent)*

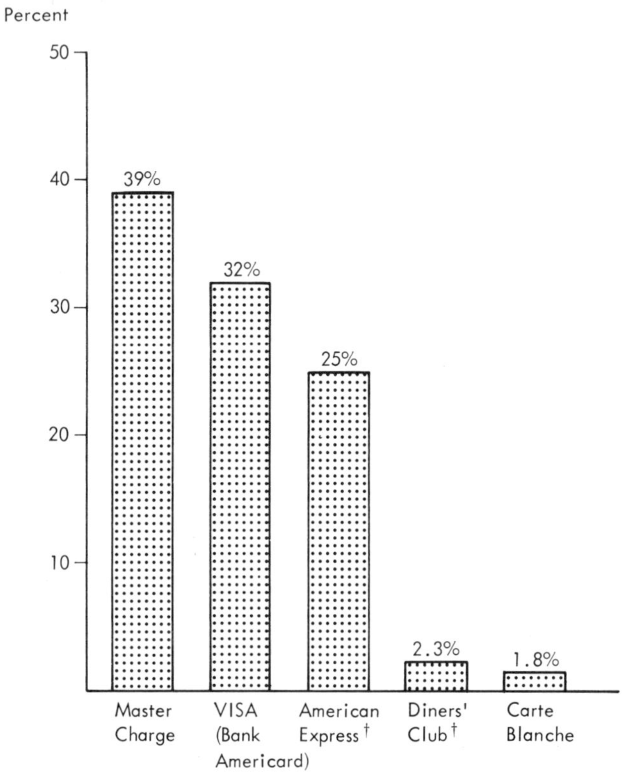

* Percentages may not add to 100 because of rounding.

† Estimate.

Source: Adapted from the August 4, 1975, issue of *Business Week* by special permission.

Sources of direct consumer loans

Direct consumer loans are available from a variety of lenders. The major source is financial institutions whose main business activity is making loans. An important source of income of the institutions is the interest consumers pay for the use of this credit. These financial institutions may be directly or indirectly involved in the credit transaction. Direct involvement results when you visit the lender and get the cash to purchase some specific item from a retailer. A lender is indirectly involved when your debt contract is purchased by a financial institution from the grantor of credit. For example, a car dealer who sells an auto on credit may then sell the installment contract to a bank.

Characteristics of consumer loans vary widely among sources. Differences in eligibility, term to maturity, maximum amount available, collateral requirements, credit investigation, repayment method, and cost may be the result of lender policies or of legal restrictions placed upon the lender.

Six major sources of loans for consumers are commercial banks, consumer finance companies, credit unions, savings and loan associations, life insurance companies, and pawnbrokers.

Commercial banks. Commercial banks offer a wider variety of services than do the other sources of consumer credit. Generally, a better credit record is required to qualify for credit from a commercial bank than is required by other lenders. Loans are available to qualified persons on an unsecured or a secured basis. Unsecured installment and single-payment loans require only a customer's signature on a loan note (a promise to pay). The note details repayment schedules for these loans in terms of amounts due and due dates. The unsecured loan category includes the regular loans, loans through the use of a bank credit card, and so-called check credit.

Secured loans, as the name implies, require some type of collateral. Often the item being financed serves this purpose. For example, auto and furniture purchases may be used as collateral. Other readily accepted collateral includes the cash surrender values of life insurance policies, savings passbooks, or real estate. Banks accept mortgages on real estate for the purchase or the improvement of the property. While a mortgage to buy real estate is not defined as consumer credit, money lent for home improvements is. The maturity on home improvement loans usually runs from five to ten years. Such loans are repaid in installments.

Borrowing from a commercial bank offers you several advantages. First, favorable loan repayment records with a bank are valuable in the establishment of a good credit rating. This is true for any lender, but especially for a commercial bank because much confidence is placed in a banker's evaluation of credit worthiness. Second, the interest rate charged to those who qualify for a loan is usually lower than other alternatives.

A major disadvantage of this source is the rigid requirements to qualify for a loan. This results in limited availability of consumer loans, especially the noninstallment unsecured type of loan. In addition, banks often avoid "small" unsecured loans ($500–$1,000) because they are not profitable for them to handle.

Consumer finance companies. Consumer finance companies specialize in small loans to consumers. Thus, they are also commonly called small loan companies or personal finance companies.

Two factors generally control the size of the loans made by finance companies: the law and the market for loans. State laws determine the maximum loan permitted—the loan ceiling. Loan ceilings range from $1,000 to $25,000 (higher limits usually apply when real estate is involved). Forty-two states now permit loans in excess of $2,000.

The second controlling factor stems from the fact that finance companies generally try to serve consumers who need very small loans. While the average loan granted by finance companies has risen in recent years, the figures in Exhibit 9–3 show the small average size of such loans. Because of the higher cost of small loans, finance companies must charge higher interest rates to cover their costs.

EXHIBIT 9–3
Average loan size, consumer finance companies (selected years, 1959–1976)

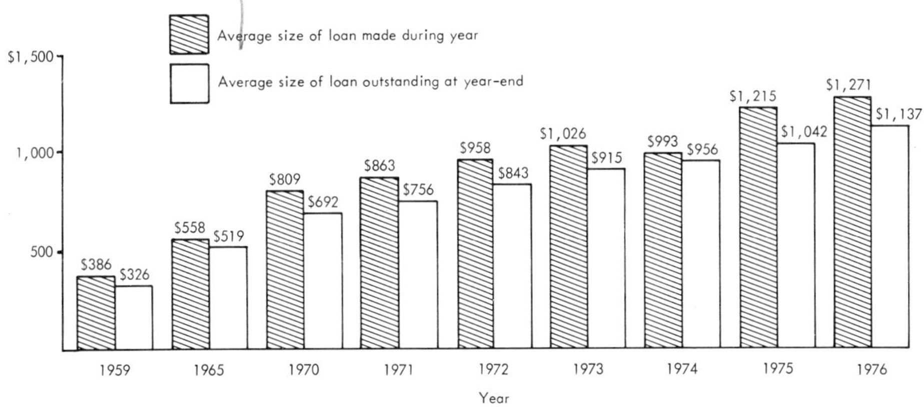

Source: *Finance Facts Yearbook* (Washington, D.C.: National Consumer Finance Association, 1977).

An advantage of consumer finance companies for consumers is that they are willing to make smaller loans than are other sources. Also, you do not need as good a credit rating to borrow from a consumer finance company as you would need to qualify for a loan from another source such as a commercial bank.

But these advantages are also the basis for several disadvantages. One disadvantage is that consumer finance companies charge a higher interest rate than many other lenders. Individual state laws allow small loan companies to charge interest ranging from 12 percent to 36 percent per year.

Credit unions. A credit union is a group of people with a common interest or activity who join together to form a cooperative financial institution for the purpose of making loans to members. These loans are made at rates that commonly are lower than members could obtain elsewhere. In addition to making loans, financial services provided by credit unions often include credit counseling and loan protection life (credit life) insurance. In the event that the borrower dies before repaying a loan, this loan protection insurance can automatically repay debts up to $10,000.

A borrower must be a member of the credit union. Membership involves some minimal amount of savings invested in the credit union, usually as little as $5. Maximum loan limits and loan policies of credit unions are established by government agencies. If the credit union has a federal charter, it is supervised by the National Credit Union Administration. A state-chartered group is usually under the supervision of the state banking commissioner.

Credit unions are attractive sources of loan monies for several reasons. First, interest rates are usually lower than those of other lenders. For many borrowers they are the lowest rates available. The maximum rate allowed by federal or state regulating agencies is usually one percent per month (12 percent annually) on unsecured loans. Secured loans may even be made at a lower rate of three fourths of one percent per month (nine percent annually). Second, small loans are available on a signature-only basis and do not require collateral or cosigners. Some larger credit unions make such loans up to $1,000 on this basis while others have lower limits.

One disadvantage of credit unions is that many people don't like to tell their financial needs to their associates who operate the credit union. Even in the larger groups where a professional is hired to manage the credit union's operations, a committee composed of credit union members will usually formally rule on loan applications. A second disadvantage is the limitation on availability of loans. If you are not or cannot be a member of a credit union, this source of credit is not available to you.

Savings and loan associations. Savings and loan associations (S&Ls) are mainly active in the home mortgage loan market. However, as the result of laws passed in 1972 and 1974, many can now make consumer loans. These laws enabled some federally chartered S&Ls to make unsecured home improvement, home equipment, mobile home, and education loans in states where these loans are permitted for the state-chartered associations. Prior to the passage of these laws, S&Ls could make loans only to people who had savings accounts with the association; the loans were against the accounts (that is, the accounts secured the loans).

Interest rates charged by the S&Ls are generally lower than those charged by a consumer finance company but are higher than those charged by other sources.

Life insurance companies. If a consumer owns a permanent form of life insurance (which will be discussed in Chapter 12), it is possible to obtain a loan in the amount of the cash surrender value, plus any accumulated dividends or interest, from the insurance company. Such loans, called policy loans because the life insurance policy serves as collateral, are available through provisions in the insurance contract.

Borrowing from the life insurance company has several advantages. First, it is relatively simple to obtain the loan. Loans can be obtained by filling out and returning the required forms to the company. Insurance companies will furnish these forms upon request and they will often issue policy loans requested by means of a phone call. Policy loans are easy to obtain because policyholders are in effect borrowing their own money from the company.

A second advantage of a policy loan is the low interest rate. The interest rate is fixed in the insurance contract at the time the insurance is taken out. Policy loan rates commonly range from 4.8 to 6 percent, and during periods of high interest rates, these policy loan rates are typically below other consumer loan rates. A third advantage is that the interest rate on the loan is ordinarily based on the outstanding balance. This practice helps keep the loan charges down.

A fourth advantage of policy loans is that the repayment schedule is very flexible or not even specified. Ordinarily the policyholder is not required to repay the loan, but the interest must be paid as long as the loan is outstanding.

An important disadvantage of policy loans is that the amount outstanding is deducted from benefits paid to the policy beneficiary in the event of the death of the insured. Policy loans reduce the insurance coverage provided to protect against adverse consequences. As the loan is repaid, however, the amount that would be deducted is decreased. To illustrate, if the borrower has a policy with a face value (death benefit) of $30,000 and has a loan of $5,000 on the policy, the beneficiary would receive the difference between the amount of the death benefit and the policy loan outstanding at the time of death, $25,000.

Pawnbrokers. A pawnbroker is a last resort in a money crisis or when the person's credit does not permit borrowing from any other source. Customers get loans by taking personal property to the pawnshop to serve as collateral for the loan. Loans usually amount to less than 50 percent of the appraised market value of the collateral. In return for the collateral, the borrower receives the loan and a pawn ticket needed to redeem the collateral when the loan is repaid. Interest charges on repaid loans may range from about 24 percent to over 100 percent per year plus additional fees in certain cases.

Collateral may be redeemed by making a single payment of principal and interest. Installment payments are not generally used by pawnbrokers as a method of repayment. If the loan is not repaid when due, the pawnbroker has the right to sell the collateral at public or private auction in order to recover the amount of the loan. If the collateral sells for more than the amount of the loan repayment required, the excess proceeds are required to be returned to the borrower. In practice, cases of excess proceeds are almost unheard of.

About the only advantages of this source of consumer credit are that it is quick and it is quiet. The disadvantages are clear—it is very expensive and lacks adequate protection for the consumer.

Installment contracts

Installment credit is usually used to buy durable goods that are major expenditures for the consumer. What represents a major expenditure for a consumer is a relative matter. The purchase of a household appliance selling for $99.95 may be a cash purchase for some families but an installment purchase for others. The percentage of installment credit used to buy major consumer goods is shown in Exhibit 9–4.

Although most sources of installment credit are reputable and honest, you should never sign anything until you completely understand all of the provisions in the contract. This is especially true when someone is urging you to sign "because it's just a standard form containing a lot of legal terms that are only clear to an attorney." What is included in such terminology can be the source of much unhappiness, and you should know what possibilities you are faced with before you sign your name. Many people take this advice lightly because of the "it can't happen to me" feeling and often regret it because it *does* happen to them.

Here are some of the clauses that may be used to place the borrower at a legal disadvantage relative to the lender. These legal provisions

EXHIBIT 9–4
Percentage distribution of consumer installment credit outstanding (selected years, 1940–1977)

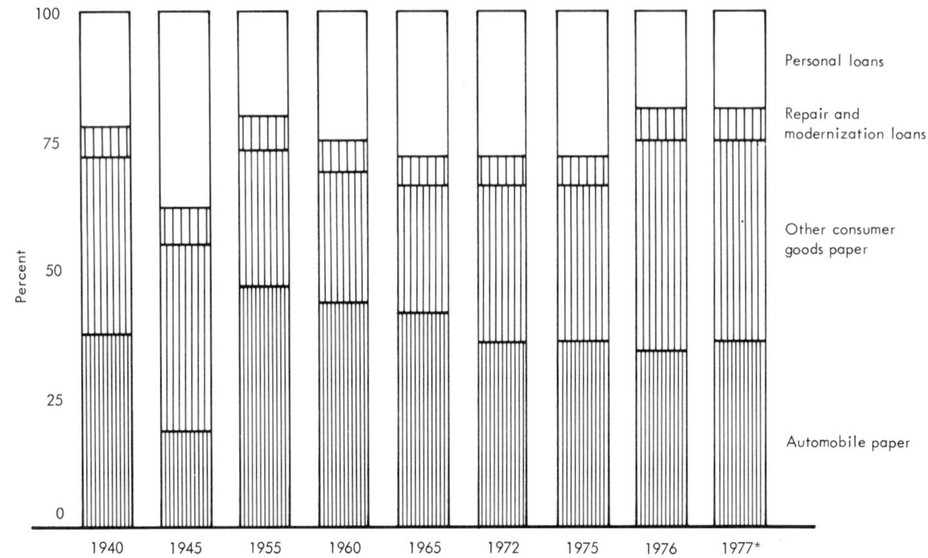

* Installment credit at end of first quarter.
Source: Federal Reserve Chart Book; *Federal Reserve Bulletin.*

can greatly increase the amount paid for credit. The passage of legislation, some of which is discussed below, has limited the use of these tactics in some states, but you still need to be aware of them.

Wage assignment or garnishment. Wage assignment is a means whereby a creditor can collect amounts due by attaching part of the debtor's income directly from the employer. The legal process of attaching a debtor's wages is known as garnishment.

When a debtor's wages have been garnished, the employer can be required by court order to pay up to 25 percent of the debtor's wages to the creditor each pay period until the debt is paid. This is obviously an inconvenience for the employer because of the added accounting routine required. The Consumer Credit Protection Act protects debtors by limiting the garnishment for any work week and by prohibiting the firing of employees just because their wages are garnished. This law is discussed later in this chapter.

Acceleration clause. Acceleration clauses provide that if one or more payments on the debt are missed or in some cases if the payments are delayed for any reason, the entire balance of the debt is due and payable immediately. This makes it possible for the creditor to step up collection procedures before the consumer gets into worse financial trouble and also while there is value in the object originally bought. Be sure that your contract clearly states how many payments can be late or missed before collection procedures can be started.

Balloon balance. Balloon balance refers to a situation where a series of small monthly payments is followed by a much larger final payment. One reason for its use is to reduce the monthly payments, but meeting such a large final payment is undesirable if it causes financial hardship for the family. It may require future refinancing under unfavorable conditions if the full payment cannot be made.

Add-on clause. The add-on clause ties several purchases together. It holds that the title remains with the seller until the account is paid. If you buy a washer, the title remains with the seller until the amount owed is paid. However, if you buy a dryer when you have only one payment left on the washer, the dealer retains title to both appliances until the account is fully paid. If later, while still paying for the dryer, you buy a vacuum cleaner and miss one payment because of some emergency, the seller could repossess all three items to satisfy the remaining debt.

Prepayment and the rule of 78. Prepayment of a loan means that you repay the loan before the maturity date. For example, you might prepay a one-year installment loan after six months. When you do prepay, you should receive a refund of a portion of the interest charge. There are two methods used to calculate refunds—proportional interest and the rule of 78.

Under the *proportional interest* method, interest is refunded in proportion to the time the loan was outstanding. Each month is given equal weighting in the calculation. With a one-year loan prepaid after four months, two thirds ($\frac{8}{12}$) of the interest is refunded, etc.

Under the second method, called the *rule of 78,* the weight placed on each month is varied. To illustrate, suppose you have an installment loan that is to be repaid in twelve monthly installments. At the end of three months you are able to repay the loan. How much interest would be refunded?

Under the rule of 78 the early months in the loan period are given heavier weight in the computation. For a one-year loan, a weight of 12 is given for the first month, 11 for the second, 10 for the third, and so on until the final month, which has a weight of one. The sum of 12 + 11 + 10 + . . . + 1 is 78, thus the name "rule of 78." The lender earns $\frac{12}{78}$ of the interest in the first month, $\frac{11}{78}$ the second, and $\frac{10}{78}$ the third month. After three months, or 25 percent of the loan period, the lender has earned $\frac{33}{78}$ or 42 percent of the interest. The refund would be $^{45}/_{78}$ or about 58 percent of the interest on the contract.

The important difference between these methods is that the rule of 78 makes a loan that is prepaid more expensive. Suppose you had a loan of $100 with an interest charge of $6. You repay the $106 in twelve equal payments of $8.83. The effective interest rate on the loan is about 11 percent. Suppose further that after six months you prepay the balance owed, $53. Under the proportional method the refund is $3 ($^{6}/_{12}$ × $6). Under the rule of 78, however, the lender has earned $^{57}/_{78}$ (12 + 11 + . . . + 7 = 57) of the interest, or $4.38. The remainder of $1.62 is refunded to you. The cost of this loan, as a result of the prepayment and the use of the rule of 78, has gone from 11 percent to 15 percent (the method of calculating the cost of credit is covered in the next section of the chapter). If you believe that there is a good chance that you may be able to prepay a loan, be aware of the method used to figure the amount of interest refunded to you.

Credit life and disability insurance. Credit life and disability insurance is a method of providing for repayment of the debt to the lender if the borrower should die or become disabled. The premium is paid by the borrower and is included in many loans. Special forms of life insurance to cover these loan obligations are available from sources other than the lender at a lower cost to the consumer.

Disability insurance can be quite expensive. It is much like credit life insurance, except that you do not have to die to enable the creditor to collect. Disability insurance pays if you suffer the misfortune of ill health or of disability. It will pay the required amounts until the loan is paid or until you are able to return to work. It sounds like a great idea, but this type of insurance can be expensive.

Who uses credit?

The use of credit can be related to such individual factors as income level and age of the head of the family. Also, as shown in a study of credit card users, consumers tend to spend differently depending on their social class.

Income level. American families of all income levels make use of credit. The extent of usage, however, varies greatly from family to family within any income level. Some families will make the minimum use of credit while others will begin to make extensive use of credit early in life and remain in debt throughout their lifetime.

The Survey Research Center of the University of Michigan conducted a study of consumer finances. Exhibit 9–5 presents a summary of the relationship between income and debt repayment. It was found

EXHIBIT 9–5
Installment debt as a percentage of disposable income (by income)

	No debt	*Less than 10 percent*	*10–19 percent*	*20–39 percent*	*40 percent and over†*	*Not ascertained*
All families	51	27	14	5	1	2
Annual family income						
Less than $3,000 . .	81	7	5	4	2	1
$3,000–4,999	69	12	9	7	2	1
$5,000–7,499	48	24	17	8	2	1
$7,500–9,999	39	30	21	8	*	2
$10,000–14,999 . .	35	41	18	3	1	2
$15,000 or more . .	51	35	10	1	1	2

* Less than 0.5 percent.

† Includes families of zero or negative disposable income.

Source: George Katona, Lewis Mandell, and Jay Schmiedeskamp, *1970 Survey of Consumer Finances* (Ann Arbor: University of Michigan, 1971), p. 25.

that 49 percent of the families owed installment debt, excluding home purchase mortgages, and were making installment payments equal to ten percent or more of their disposable, take home, income.

Families with annual incomes under $3,000 have the lowest ratio of installment payments to disposable income. Of these families, 81 percent had no installment debt, and an additional seven percent had payments equal to less than ten percent of their income. One explanation for this relationship is that the creditors consider low-income families to be poorer risks as a result of their smaller income and do not grant credit. Also, the incomes of this group tend to be rather unstable because they are often employed in unskilled, seasonal, or temporary positions that are very prone to layoffs.

Among the families with incomes of $15,000 and over, 15 percent had no installment payments, and an additional 35 percent had payments equal to ten percent or less of their income. When these families used credit, the amount of credit outstanding tended to be large.

Age of household head. The effect of age of the head of household on the level of commitment to the use of credit is shown in Exhibit 9–6. As you can see, in the households headed by people under 25 years, a larger proportion of the income is used for the repayment of installment debt than in households where the head of the family is older.

The use of credit, as implied by the existence of installment repayments, coincides with the changing needs for consumer goods as the family situation changes. It is common for the family needs to be greatest when there are children growing up. At this same time, however, the family income is not at its peak because the head of the

EXHIBIT 9–6
Installment debt repayment as a percentage of family disposable income (by age of family head)

	No debt	*Less than 10 percent*	*10–19 percent*	*20–39 percent*	*40 percent or more†*	*Not ascertained*
All families	51	27	14	5	1	2
Age of family head						
Younger than 25	41	17	24	14	2	2
25–34	32	36	21	8	2	1
35–44	37	41	15	5	*	2
45–54	44	34	15	2	2	3
55–64	64	42	9	2	1	2
65–74	87	7	3	1	1	1
75 or older	94	3	3	*	*	*

* Less than 0.5 percent.

† Includes families of zero or negative disposable income.

Source: George Katona, Lewis Mandell, and Jay Schmiedeskamp, *1970 Survey of Consumer Finances* (Ann Arbor: University of Michigan, 1971), p. 25.

household is young and inexperienced. So, the need for more funds in order to satisfy the immediate needs of the family is met through the use of credit.

Credit card users. Credit card use and acceptance appears to be somewhat related to the consumer's social class. A study of the use of bank credit cards showed that the lower social classes preferred to use credit cards for durable and necessity goods (appliances, furniture, clothing) whereas the upper social classes preferred to use credit cards for luxury items such as travel, restaurants, and luggage.[3] Also, higher social classes have more favorable attitudes toward credit use.[4]

Another study indicated that the major users of bank credit cards were of higher income and education levels than were nonusers, were of middle age, and were in the professional occupations.[5]

Cost of consumer credit

There is probably no situation in which the old adage "There is no such thing as a free lunch" is more applicable than it is to consumer credit. Users of credit pay for it in one way or another.

---

[3] H. Lee Matthews and John W. Slocum, Jr., "Social Class and Commercial Bank Credit Card Usage," *Journal of Marketing*, vol. 33, January 1969, pp. 71–78.

[4] John W. Slocum, Jr., and H. Lee Matthews, "Social Class and Income as Indicators of Consumer Credit Behavior," *Journal of Marketing*, vol. 34, April 1970, pp. 69–74.

[5] Joseph T. Plummer, "Life Style Patterns and Commercial Bank Credit Card Usage," *Journal of Marketing*, vol. 35, April 1971, pp. 35–41.

Factors determining the cost of credit include the amount of money due, the stated interest rate, additional finance charges incurred, and time.

General cost formula. Consumer credit sources are required by law to inform you of the effective cost of borrowing before the contract is completed. However, because the rate is often not disclosed until this time, it is helpful to know how to estimate the costs of alternative credit sources.

A general formula for estimating the cost of short-term debt to be repaid regularly—weekly, monthly, etc.—in equal amounts is as follows:

$$R = \frac{2MD}{P(N+1)}$$

where

R = estimated effective annual percentage rate (APR);
M = number of payment periods in one year regardless of the number actually made;
D = dollar amount of interest and finance charges;
P = amount available; proceeds of loan or selling price of product;
N = total number of payments to be made.

To illustrate, suppose that you borrow \$300 at eight percent interest for three years. Monthly payments of \$10.34 are required. The dollar amount of interest (D) assumes the use of the original principal for the entire three years. In this example, M = 12, there are 12 months per year; D = \$72 (\$300 × 0.08 × 3 years); P = \$300; and N = 36 (12 monthly payments per year for three years).

$$R = \frac{2 \times 12 \times \$72}{\$300\ (36+1)} = \frac{\$1{,}728}{\$11{,}100}$$
$$= 0.1557 \text{ or } 15.57 \text{ percent.}$$

Notice that the estimated APR is nearly double the stated rate of eight percent. This is the result of paying interest on the full \$300 for the entire three-year period, but because each monthly payment includes interest and repayment of the principal you do not have the use of \$300 for the full three years.

As the number of monthly payments, and thus the time, decreases, the estimated APR also decreases. Suppose that you repay the \$300 in six monthly installments. Now the APR is:

$$R = \frac{2 \times 12 \times \$12}{\$300\ (6+1)} = \frac{\$288}{\$2{,}100}$$
$$= 0.1371 \text{ or } 13.71 \text{ percent.}$$

However, the shorter the repayment schedule, the larger the individual payments will be. Repayment of the loan in six months requires monthly payments of $52 each.

When purchasing a large item on credit, you should choose the financing arrangement that has the lowest rate when other factors, such as time, are equal. To illustrate, suppose that you wish to buy a new color TV that has a cash price of $600. You are trying to decide whether you should use the installment credit offered by the seller or take out a loan from a consumer finance company. A two-year installment loan may be obtained from the Help-U Finance Company at an effective APR of 18 percent. Interest is payable in advance and the principal is to be repaid in equal installments.

Provisions of the retailer installment contract require that you make 24 monthly payments of $29.95 each. The general cost formula can be used to estimate the effective APR. In this case, the calculation of D, the dollar amount of interest or finance charges, is made by finding the difference between the total payments for the appliance and the cash price of the appliance. Therefore, $D = (\$29.95)(24) - \$600 = \$118.80$. The estimated effective APR of the retailer credit is:

$$R = \frac{2 \times 12 \times \$118.80}{\$600\ (24+1)} = \frac{\$2{,}851.20}{\$15{,}000}$$
$$= 0.19 \text{ or } 19 \text{ percent.}$$

The total purchase price of the TV, including financing, is less if you borrow the money from Help-U than if you use the retailer credit. Amounts paid under the two credit plans are as follows:

	Seller credit	*Help-U*
TV purchase price	$600.00	$600.00
Finance charges	118.80	108.00
Total	$718.80	$708.00

The general cost formula can be used only when the regular payments are of equal size. If the payments are unequal, a more sophisticated method of estimating the effective rate on consumer credit is required. Instances of unequal payments are rare in installment consumer credit agreements except where a balloon balance is involved.

Cost of open-ended consumer credit. Estimating the cost of open-ended credit is based upon the same principles discussed above. Because of differences in the methods of calculating the unpaid balance to which the interest rate is applied, the rates and the amounts paid will vary. It is a case where 1½ percent per month may not actually be equal to 18 percent per year.

Differences exist in the interpretation of "unpaid balance" as a result of when and whether partial payments are credited to the account during the month in which payment is made. Three methods of computing the unpaid balance for charge accounts are the previous balance, average daily balance, and adjusted balance methods.

Previous balance method. This method defines the unpaid balance to mean the ending balance on the previous month's statement. The finance charge rate is then applied to this amount regardless of when payment was made during the month. To illustrate, suppose that your balance due on December 28 is $200. If unpaid, this balance is subject to the finance charge of 1½ percent per month on your next statement. On January 4 you pay $150. Your next statement, on January 28, will show a new balance of $53—the unpaid amount plus a finance charge of $3 ($200 × 0.015) based upon the total previous balance even though the amount owed has been $150 lower for nearly the whole month. This works out to an annual rate of about 74 percent. The previous balance method is a very expensive one for the consumer.

Average daily balance method. The average daily balance method is less expensive than the previous balance method. Under this method, the unpaid balance is the arithmetic average of the daily closing balances, excluding your new purchases. That is, the sum of the previous balance less payments—at the end of each day during the billing period—is divided by the number of days in the period. Again, suppose that the closing date on the statement is the 28th of the month, and your previous balance of $200 on December 28 has been reduced by your payment of $150 on the fourth day of the current month, January. The average daily balance for the billing period is $83.87 ($200 for 7 days, plus $50 for 24 days, divided by 31 days). The balance shown on your January 28 statement would be $51.26, including the $1.26 finance charge ($83.87 × 0.015), plus any purchases made during the statement period for which no finance charge is required.

With this method, the date you make your payment affects the amount of the finance charge. For example, if you had made the payment on January 18, the average daily balance would have been $151.61 and the balance on the periodic statement would be $52.27. The larger finance charge of $2.27 resulted from the higher average daily balance as a result of delayed payment. Thus, it is desirable that you promptly pay bills with finance charges calculated using this method.

Many large retailers use the average daily balance method. The

Sears Charge Security Agreement shown in Exhibit 9–7 is one example of this method.

The two largest bank credit cards, VISA and Master Charge, also use the average daily balance method. However, any cash advance loans through these cards is immediately subject to interest.[6] The basis

EXHIBIT 9–7
Sears Charge Security Agreement

SEARS, ROEBUCK AND CO.
SearsCharge Security Agreement

I agree to the following regarding all purchases made on my SearsCharge Identification:

1. I have the following options each monthly billing period:

A. I will pay the entire New Balance within **30** days of the Billing Date shown on the monthly billing statement; or

B. I will pay the deferred payment price for each purchase consisting of the cash price and a **FINANCE CHARGE**.

(1) The **FINANCE CHARGE** will be computed upon the **AVERAGE DAILY BALANCE** of my account in each monthly billing period.

(a) The **AVERAGE DAILY BALANCE** is determined by dividing the sum of the balances outstanding for each day of the monthly billing period by the number of days in the monthly billing period.

(b) The Balance Outstanding for each day of the monthly billing period is determined by subtracting payments and credits from the previous day's balance excluding any purchases added to the account during the monthly billing period and excluding any unpaid **FINANCE CHARGE**.

(2) **FINANCE CHARGE** will be determined by applying a periodic rate of **1.5%** per month **(ANNUAL PERCENTAGE RATE of 18%)** to the first **$500.00** of the **AVERAGE DAILY BALANCE** and a periodic rate of **1%** per month **(ANNUAL PERCENTAGE RATE of 12%)** to any part of the **AVERAGE DAILY BALANCE** in excess of **$500.00**.

(3) No **FINANCE CHARGE** will be assessed:

(a) In a monthly billing period during which there was no Previous Balance;

(b) In a monthly billing period during which payments and/or credits equal or exceed the Previous Balance;

(c) On unpaid **FINANCE CHARGE**; or

(d) On purchases during the monthly billing period in which they are added to the account.

(4) I will pay the deferred payment price for all purchases in minimum monthly payments or more within **30** days of the billing date shown on each monthly billing statement according to the schedule below. The minimum monthly payment will be based upon the Highest New Balance on the account and will change only if subsequent purchases increase the new balance to a bracket of the schedule requiring a higher minimum monthly payment. I have the option of paying more than the minimum payment each month and the right to pay the entire new balance in full at any time without incurring a subsequent **FINANCE CHARGE**.

If the "Highest New Balance" is:	The Minimum Monthly Payment will be:	If the "Highest New Balance" is:	The Minimum Monthly Payment will be:
$ .01 to $ 5.00	Balance	$240.01 to $280.00	$12.00
5.01 to 100.00	$ 5.00	280.01 to 320.00	13.00
100.01 to 120.00	6.00	320.01 to 360.00	14.00
120.01 to 140.00	7.00	360.01 to 400.00	15.00
140.01 to 160.00	8.00	400.01 to 440.00	16.00
160.01 to 180.00	9.00	440.01 to 470.00	17.00
180.01 to 200.00	10.00	470.01 to 500.00	18.00
200.01 to 240.00	11.00	Over $500.00	1/28 of Highest Account Balance rounded to the next higher whole dollar amount.

(5) If I fail to pay any two Minimum Payments when due during any **12** month period, Sears may declare my entire balance due and payable **15** days after giving me written notice of default and after my failure to cure such default.

(6) Sears shall retain title to merchandise purchased under this agreement until paid in full. Each payment shall be applied: first to unpaid **FINANCE CHARGE**; then, as to merchandise and services purchased on different dates, the first purchased shall be deemed first paid; as to merchandise and services purchased on the same date, the lowest priced shall be deemed first paid.

2. My State of Residence is Wisconsin, and I agree to be governed by the Wisconsin Consumer Act with respect to all aspects of all purchases made on this agreement. If I change my State of Residence, I will inform Sears, and Sears will provide me with a new agreement containing the **FINANCE CHARGE** and other credit terms applicable to my new State of Residence.

3. Sears waives the right to retain or to acquire any lien arising solely by operation of law in real property used or expected to be used as my principal residence. This provision is not applicable to judgment liens.

4. Sears is authorized to investigate my credit record and report to proper persons and Bureaus my performance of this agreement.

____
(Customer's Signature)

Accepted:
SEARS, ROEBUCK AND CO. By_______________

Date_______________ Store No._______________

NOTICE: SEE ACCOMPANYING STATEMENT FOR IMPORTANT INFORMATION REGARDING YOUR RIGHTS TO DISPUTE BILLING ERRORS.

14421-418 Rev. 4/28/76
(D 20δ-CHI) WISCONSIN

Source: Reprinted by special permission of Sears, Roebuck and Co.

[6] It is possible to obtain a direct cash loan from subscribing banks by presenting your bank credit card. The loan is then charged to your credit card account.

for the finance charge made by Master Charge, quoted from their monthly statement, is as follows:[7]

> Your account is subject to a FINANCE CHARGE (interest) during any statement period in which you (a) receive or have outstanding a cash advance loan, or (b) fail to pay in full the Previous Balance shown on your statement during the first 25 days of the statement period. The Amount Subject to Interest is the average daily amount of the Previous Balance as reduced by payments you make and credits we apply, and increased by cash advances posted, during the statement period. Interest is calculated on the Amounts Subject to Interest at the periodic rates and corresponding ANNUAL PERCENTAGE RATES shown on the front of this statement. You can avoid FINANCE CHARGES on purchases by paying the New Balance in full within 25 days after the statement closing date. However, any cash advances included in the New Balance will continue to bear interest from their posting date until your payment is received.

Adjusted balance method. The adjusted balance method is the least expensive and offers the greatest flexibility in payment for the consumer. Under this method, the unpaid balance is the ending balance for the period. Amounts paid anytime during the statement period are deducted from the beginning balance, even if the payment is made on the last day of the statement period. Using our previous example, the finance charge based on the adjusted balance of $50 is $0.75 ($50 × 0.015).

Comparison of methods. A comparison of the effective costs of the three methods of calculating the unpaid balance is shown below. Note the relatively high cost of the previous balance method in comparison to the other two approaches.

Method	*Unpaid balance*	*Finance charge*	*Annual rate*
Previous balance	$200.00	$3.00	42.9%
Average daily balance	83.87	1.26	18.0
Adjusted balance	50.00	0.75	10.7

Effect of income taxes on credit cost. Personal income taxes can reduce the net cost of interest paid for credit. For taxpayers who itemize their deductions, any interest paid decreases the amount of taxable income. For example, suppose a married couple files a joint tax return. They have income of $15,000 before any interest deduction. If they have not paid any interest during the year, they owe federal income taxes of $3,010. Now suppose that this same couple has paid $500 in interest during the year.

[7] Reprinted by special permission of Wisconsin Master Charge.

	Without interest deduction	*With interest deduction*
Income less deductions except interest	$15,000	$15,000
Deduct interest	0	500
Taxable income	$15,000	$14,500
Deduct federal income tax	3,010	2,885
Spendable income	$11,990	$11,615

The federal income tax paid decreases by $125 (from $3,010 to $2,885) because of the interest payment of $500. Thus the net cost of the interest to the couple is $375 ($500 − $125).

Income tax deductions do not eliminate the interest cost for the consumer: they only reduce the cost of credit. Money spent for interest is never fully recovered through a reduction in taxes.

A LENDER'S OUTLOOK ON CONSUMER CREDIT

While consumer credit has undergone phenomenal growth, consumers should not view credit as a "money tree." Businesses encourage consumers to use credit in an effort to increase their volume of sales. Such increases in sales volume, and therefore profits, may permit a seller offering credit to sell goods at lower prices than stores with lower volume and no credit program. These business firms fully realize, however, that profits cannot be increased through the granting of credit if the consumer does not repay. Lenders must investigate the credit worthiness of an applicant and grant credit only to those who are likely to repay.

The credit investigation brings together information that through careful analysis can be used to predict future credit behavior—that is, to predict the types and amounts of debts the consumer can be expected to repay. An investigation of this type can be justified only by the belief that past credit behavior can be used to predict future credit behavior.

C's of credit

A credit investigation examines your past credit record. Your credit record is often evaluated on the basis of the "four C's of credit"—character, capacity, collateral, and conditions. Present-day credit executives are finding that while, in concept, relevant information is obtained by following the four C's, a given piece of information often reflects on more than one of the C's. It is not possible to separate the facts that have a bearing on character from those that bear on capacity, and those bearing on capacity from those bearing on collateral, etc.

Character. Of these four C's, character stands out as the most intangible and difficult to assess. Webster defines character as "an individual's pattern of behavior or personality; reputation." What is often accepted as character is, indeed, an individual's reputation, which is really a perception held by others.

Elements entering into a character investigation may be personal. They may include the family situation, personal habits such as drinking or gambling, and virtues such as honesty and courage (or the lack thereof). Character may be inferred from business and professional conduct, including attitude toward and payment of debts and respect for the rights of others. Persons of strong character pay their bills promptly and in accordance with prior agreements.

Character is an inward thing, in effect an intangible quality, that can be inferred only to the extent that it is revealed. It is entirely possible that persons may have reputations for good character as a result of never having been pressed by adversity.

Another problem in assessing character is that information derived from an investigation must be interpreted. Asking questions to get the opinions of others can lead to incomplete and inexact answers. Usually, persons giving opinions provide information in terms of their own standards. For example, one source may view good character as being associated with active membership in a church and may reply in a detracting way if the credit applicant is not an active member. Such responses contain much opinion and little of factual value with regard to the credit worthiness of a person.

Capacity. In a very narrow sense, capacity may mean simply the ability to pay a specific amount of money when it is due. In a wider and more meaningful sense it refers to a measure of the sources of ability to pay, often summarized under the headings of income and employment.

Earning power is the basis for capacity to pay debts. Creditors would be shortsighted, however, if they looked only at income as the basis for granting credit. A more complete investigation of capacity will include the current income and the amount of income that has been earmarked for previously incurred debt, regardless of the size of the income involved. Previously incurred debt may give an entirely different slant to the value of a dollar amount of income. This is not intended to de-emphasize the importance of a credit applicant's having an adequate income, but rather to put income in its proper perspective.

It is generally agreed among credit managers that capacity is second only to character in importance when predicting credit behavior. Much more weight is placed upon each of these two C's than on either of the others.

Collateral. Collateral is some form of tangible property owned by the borrower that is assigned to the lender to act as security for the loan. While the lender plans to be repaid out of the borrower's current income, collateral serves as a "safety valve." In the event that the borrower is unable or unwilling to live up to the provisions of the loan agreement, the lender has the right to sell the collateral and use the proceeds to repay the debt. Often such property must be sold quickly. Thus, the selling price may be less than could be obtained if more time were available. This is a major reason lenders are willing to loan amounts equal to only a fraction of the value of the collateral. Collateral is not often used in retail transactions involving the sale of small or nondurable goods and services. It frequently appears, however, where cash loans are made and in the sale of consumer durables.

Conditions. General economic conditions do have an effect on the willingness of creditors to extend credit. Credit is more freely extended during good economic times than during periods of recession. However, this is one C of credit over which the consumer has virtually no control. As a result, it has little bearing upon our discussion except that you must realize that general economic conditions have an effect on capacity as well as the availability of credit.

Investigating the C's of credit

Our previous discussion of the C's of credit has shown the difficulty involved in defining character, capacity, collateral, and conditions. You should remember that credit judgments are made by individuals. Therefore, it is entirely possible that for a given applicant one creditor may grant credit while another creditor may not. Also, some credit analysts may place more weight on certain factors than will others when making a decision on the granting of credit. Consumers who wish to use credit should pay particular attention to factors such as those discussed below, which have an effect on the availability of credit.

Record of payment. Your record of payment of debts does much to aid a lender in predicting future payment behavior. Many creditors regard this record as the most important single factor revealed by a credit investigation.

Former creditors are a major source of information on your payment record. Important facts include the types of accounts, amounts now owed, amounts past due, and promptness in paying past accounts.

A good record of payment is especially valuable if there is any conflicting or damaging data revealed in the investigation. For instance, if some time ago an account had to be turned over to a collection agency, a good current record would go a long way to offset such information. Creditors usually draw quite a different conclusion from a bad payment record some time ago and a good current record than they do from the opposite sequence.

Consumers sometimes find that they have a family crisis, an emergency occurs, or something happens that would cause them to miss an installment payment. Their credit record can usually remain good if they will just contact the financing agency, explain why their payment will be missed or late, and make arrangements for catching up later. Most businesses don't want the time and expense of repossession, nor do they wish to lose you as a future customer.

Income. Investigation of a person's income is vital because the creditor depends upon income flow for repayment. Important facts about income include the current level of income, its regularity, and the likelihood that it will continue. Employment factors affecting income include the type of business of the employer, the position held, and the length of time with the current employer. Lenders look favorably upon steady employment and long periods (three years or more) with each employer.

Income can be viewed as being available for the repayment of a new debt only if it exceeds the present obligations of the person or family. Therefore, to place income data in a proper perspective, facts about current demands on the family income are essential. Consumers with a steady, secure income that exceeds current debts are the ones most likely to be granted credit.

Housing status. A homeowner is generally considered to be a more permanent member of the local community than is a renter.

References. References are checked to help judge the reputation or character of a credit applicant. Information about honesty, dependability, and trustworthiness is sought. References, reputation, and record of payment reflect a person's character.

Collateral assets. A check of a person's collateral assets is made to determine other sources of repayment that could be relied on if the need arose. Information is sought on the amount of equity (owner's money) the debtor has in the property so that if the property had to be sold to provide the money needed to repay the debt, the lender could expect that there would be money left after any mortgages on the property are paid.

Consumer credit reporting

Individual creditors generally do not conduct their own investigations on credit applicants, especially in large cities. Rather, they get credit information from a centralized source called a credit bureau, which serves as a clearinghouse for consumer credit information. This information about individual consumers is sold to customers of the credit bureau. The bureau's customers (members) include insurance companies, lenders, mailing list companies, prospective employers, government agencies, retailers, etc.

The specialized service offered by the local credit bureau provides a means of identifying persons who may be poor credit risks. It also makes it easier for consumers with good credit records to get credit. Often a call to the credit bureau that confirms the good credit rating of the applicant is enough to permit the credit manager to grant credit on the spot.

Sources of information. Credit bureaus get their credit information from three main sources—members' reports, public records, and direct inquiry. Members report to the credit bureau on their experiences with credit customers. Also, whenever someone applies for credit a copy of the application is sent to the local credit bureau. Information on the forms is checked for content and consistency between applications.

Employees of the credit bureau check the public records for information about consumers that would affect their credit worthiness. The existence of court records for judgments, arrests, convictions, bankruptcies, etc., have an unfavorable effect on the credit rating of the applicant.

Direct inquiry is another method used in obtaining information on an applicant's credit record. Friends, neighbors, colleagues, and employers, as well as those who are listed as references, may be contacted. Contacts are made by personal telephone interview, or by mailing a standard form that can be completed and returned by the informant. Information about morals, reputation, family life, and so forth is often gathered in this way. Clearly, information from these sources reflects the biases, judgments, and standards of those giving it as well as of those interpreting it.

Accuracy of information. In some situations, a consumer may have a poor credit rating as a result of misinterpretation or misinformation. This is not surprising considering the sources of information used, the credit bureau's admittedly limited effort to verify the information, and the exposure of this information to human error and bias.

If inaccurate information or misinterpretation appears in the applicant's credit file, credit may be denied. If this happens, the consumer should be persistent and find out why credit was denied. In spite of all of the complications and difficulties in getting the matter corrected in the record, it must be done or the poor credit rating could cost the consumer future use of credit or even a good job opportunity—a risk far too great to take. Correcting your credit record has been made much easier through the passage of the Fair Credit Reporting Act, a topic that we will discuss in the next section of this chapter.

LEGAL PROTECTION IN CONSUMER CREDIT

Consumers are protected in credit transactions by regulatory agencies of the federal and state governments. They also receive protection through state and federal laws dealing with credit practices. While it is nearly impossible to summarize all the individual state laws, we can describe the protection provided by federal laws.

Consumer Credit Protection Act

The Consumer Credit Protection Act went into effect July 1, 1969. This act contains several important protections for consumers, some of which are better known by individual title names. Title I of the Consumer Credit Protection Act is known as the Truth-in-Lending Act; Title II is concerned with extortionate credit provisions; Title III deals with the garnishment of wages; and Title IV created a National Commission on Consumer Finance. Subsequent to the original passage, two amendments have been passed. One amendment is Title V, the Credit Card Issuance Act passed in 1970, and the second is Title VI, the Fair Credit Reporting Act, passed in 1971.

Truth-in-Lending Act. The objective of the Truth-in-Lending law is to assure that you are given information about credit terms so that you can meaningfully compare credit from various sources. The Act is simply a disclosure law. It provides only that the most important credit information—the finance charge and the annual percentage rate (APR)—must be disclosed; it does not attempt to set limits on the APR charged.

Finance charges to be disclosed include more than just interest. They include any charges that would otherwise not have been incurred such as interest, carrying charges, finder's fees, service charges, and loan insurance costs.

The APR expresses the relationship between the amount of the finance charge and the amount financed. Tables are available that give the accurate APR for both single-payment and installment payments. An earlier method of calculation (general cost formula) was used to estimate this rate; it can be used to closely approximate the APR on any consumer credit.

Another important provision of the Truth-in-Lending Act gives you the right to cancel any credit contract within three business days when the creditor acquires a security interest on your home. While many creditors do not retain a security interest on your home, some do when selling large items such as home improvements.

Federal garnishment law. Garnishment is the right of a creditor legally to claim a part of a person's income directly from an employer to satisfy a debt. Thus, an employer can be required to pay a portion of a debtor's wage to a creditor until the debt is paid. As of July 1, 1970, Title III of the Consumer Credit Protection Act placed federal limitations on garnishment and employer responses toward employees whose wages were garnished.

Federal limitations on garnishment are based upon a consumer's disposable income for any work week. The amount subjected to garnishment is the lesser of (1) 25 percent of take-home pay for that week, or (2) after-tax pay minus 30 times the federal minimum wage at the time earnings are payable. If state laws have more restrictive limitations than does the federal law, the state laws govern, but states can no longer have higher limits than these. For example, in New York the amount subject to garnishment remained at 10 percent, even though the federal limitation is 25 percent.

This law also prohibits employers from firing employees simply because their wages have been subject to garnishment for one indebtedness.

Fair Credit Reporting Act. Title VI amendment to the Consumer Credit Protection Act became effective on April 25, 1971. Because of the great importance of credit reports when applying for credit or for employment, accuracy and fairness of information included in these reports is vital. Prior to this act, the credit report was treated as confidential information that was not available to the person involved. The file was available, however, to potential creditors and employers or almost anyone else. Since April, 1971, credit reports are restricted to those who must evaluate the individual for credit, insurance, or employment purposes.

The purpose of the Fair Credit Reporting Act is to require that consumer reporting agencies adopt reasonable procedures for meeting the information needs of business in matters relating to consumer credit, employment, and insurance. These procedures must be fair and equitable to the consumer with regard to confidentiality, accuracy, relevance, and proper utilization of such information.[8]

---

[8] Section 602(b) of the Fair Credit Reporting Act (Title VI amendment of Consumer Credit Protection Act) effective April, 1971.

The Fair Credit Reporting Act prohibits credit reporting agencies from including obsolete information in a credit file. After seven years, information concerning any suits and judgments, tax liens, unpaid accounts, arrests, indictments or convictions for crimes, or any other adverse information is declared to be obsolete and is removed from the credit record; the single exception is information concerning bankruptcy, on which the time limit is fourteen years. These time limitations are not applicable, however, when the credit report is used in connection with a credit transaction or insurance policy with a principal or face amount of $50,000 or more or when the annual salary from a prospective or current employer may reasonably be expected to equal $20,000 or more.

An important provision of the Fair Credit Reporting Act is your right to know what is contained in your credit file. If you present proper identification, a credit reporting agency must supply you with the nature and substance of all information in your file (except medical information), the sources of the information, and the names of anyone whom it has furnished a report for employment purposes within the past two years or for any other purpose within the past six months. Further, persons who have been denied credit because of a credit report from a credit bureau or have received notice from a collection department affiliated with a credit reporting agency cannot be charged for this information. Any user of credit reports who refuses credit or who takes any adverse action against an applicant whether for credit, insurance, or employment purposes must provide the applicant with the name and address of the credit reporting agency making the report. The applicant is entitled to learn from the user the nature of the adverse information if its source is other than a credit reporting agency, such as information obtained from some person not affiliated with a credit reporting agency. If a reinvestigation of adverse information contained in the file finds the information to be inaccurate or no longer verifiable, the credit reporting agency must promptly delete the information from the credit file. Following any deletion of such information the credit reporting agency must, upon your request, notify any person or business to which they have sent this information that the item has been deleted or provide a statement of the dispute. Such a statement of the dispute is permitted if the consumer and the credit reporting agency are unable to agree on the validity of the information in dispute. The statement is limited to one hundred words and the credit reporting agency must provide assistance in writing a clear summary of the dispute.[9]

These rights hold even if you have not been denied credit, but

[9] Fair Credit Reporting Act, Sec. 611.

simply want to know what is contained in your credit file. In this situation, however, the agency is permitted to charge you a fee for the service. The amount of the charge varies from agency to agency but the maximum charge that can be made is that which the agency would impose on any other recipient of a consumer report. A "reasonable" fee will probably not exceed $25 because the Federal Trade Commission, which enforces the Act, has taken action against charges in excess of this amount.

No consumer may bring any action or proceeding in the nature of defamation, invasion of privacy, or negligence with respect to reporting of information against a credit reporting agency except on the grounds of malice and willful intent to injure. Amounts consumers can collect from such suits are limited to the sum of the actual damages, punitive damages, court costs, and attorney's fees.

Credit Card Issuance Act. Under the Credit Card Issuance Act (Title V of the Consumer Credit Protection Act), consumers gained two important protections. The first of these is that since October 1970, no credit card may be issued to you unless you request or apply for one, except for the renewal and substitution of your existing credit cards. Prior to the effective date of this act, unsolicited credit cards were sent to consumers. These cards could easily land in the wrong hands, and resulting charges could be made to the intended recipient.

Secondly, in addition to stopping unsolicited credit cards the Credit Card Issuance Act limits your liability to $50 in situations where the card is used without permission. Even this liability does not exist unless the card issuer has provided you with a stamped, self-addressed notification that is to be mailed in the event of loss or theft of the credit card. If you report the loss in writing, you also are not liable for the $50.

Under this law it is now a federal offense when a credit card is used for unauthorized purchases of goods or services with a value of $5,000 or more. The maximum penalty for persons convicted of this crime is a $10,000 fine and a five-year prison sentence.

Holder-in-due-course doctrine

The holder-in-due-course doctrine is a legal concept that holds that the liability for a defective product does not follow the financing contract. That is, when a third party, such as a bank, purchases the credit contract from the seller, the liability for the product remains with the seller. Under such an arrangement the consumer is unable to assure fair treatment or satisfaction by withholding payment, for the payment is due to a party other than the seller, a "holder in due course."

Banks, finance companies, and any other purchasers of the contracts are entitled to receive payment. Indeed, if payment is not made for any reason including dissatisfaction with a defective product, the holder in due course may take legal action to collect the debt. Consumers can be forced to pay for even a worthless item.

On May 14, 1976, a federal regulation went into effect that is intended to provide protection against the holder-in-due-course doctrine for consumers in all states. The Federal Trade Commission rule nullifies the holder-in-due-course doctrine and thereby makes the holder of the debt contract liable for any claims and defenses that you could bring against the seller of goods and services. Sellers are required to include the following 48-word legal notice of such liability in the debt contract you sign:

> Any holder of this consumer credit contract is subject to all claims and defenses which the debtor could assert against the seller of goods or services obtained pursuant hereto or with the proceeds hereof. Recovery hereunder by the debtor shall not exceed amounts paid by the debtor hereunder.

Enforcement of this FTC rule is your responsibility either through negotiation with the seller or through legal proceedings, if necessary. The role of the FTC is limited to seeking injunctions and fines against violators as a means of assuring that the required statements are included in the credit agreements.

A somewhat less direct method of enforcing this rule will be through the buyers of credit contracts. Retailers who consistently sell inferior goods or who defraud consumers will undoubtedly find it difficult to locate third parties who are willing to purchase the credit contracts they create. Because many retailers depend on selling these contracts as a means of financing their businesses, responsiveness to consumer expressions of dissatisfaction is likely to improve.

SUMMARY

Since ancient times credit has been used to satisfy today's needs with tomorrow's income. Today, the ready availability of consumer loans and of retailer credit has made it easier for you to obtain and use credit. Major sources of direct consumer loans include commercial banks, consumer finance companies, credit unions, savings and loan associations, life insurance companies, and pawnbrokers. Retailer credit is readily available from, and indeed encouraged by, a wide variety of retail and service organizations.

Credit is closely related to your income and to your age. You need to be able to compare the costs of alternative sources of credit so that you realize the maximum satisfaction from your income.

Lenders evaluate your qualifications for credit by the four C's: character, capacity, collateral, and conditions. An investigation of the C's requires an analysis of your financial and personal record. Many creditors obtain this information from a credit bureau or other centralized source of consumer information rather than conducting the investigation themselves.

State and federal governments regulate consumer credit by controlling the lender's activities and responsibilities to the consumer. Such laws are intended to help protect you from unscrupulous acts by creditors.

DISCUSSION QUESTIONS

1. Exhibit 9–1 shows the rapid growth of consumer credit. What accounts for the great increase in the consumer credit outstanding since 1950?
2. Describe the characteristics of open-ended credit as compared with close-ended credit.
3. Discuss the advantages and disadvantages of each of the sources of retailer credit and of direct consumer loans.
4. What are the C's of credit? Explain each. What information does a creditor need in order to evaluate each of the C's?
5. Suppose that you wish to establish a first-rate credit rating. In light of the factors considered in Question 4, clearly indicate what actions you should take to achieve a good credit rating.
6. Explain how the following clauses in an installment contract can work to the disadvantage of the consumer: (*a*) acceleration clause, (*b*) balloon balance, (*c*) add-on clause, (*d*) rule of 78 for refunding interest when the principal is prepaid.
7. Under the Fair Credit Reporting Act, what is a credit bureau required to do if you request the information in your own file? Who pays for this? When must obsolete information be eliminated from a credit file?
8. Describe the benefits gained by the consumer as a result of the passage of the Truth-in-Lending Act.
9. Define "garnishment." How is it used by creditors? What are the limitations on its usage?
10. What is your maximum liability for a lost or stolen credit card? Under what conditions?
11. What is the holder-in-due-course doctrine?

CASE PROBLEMS

1. Three months ago Kathy and Ken Swenson signed an installment credit

contract in the amount of $500 to finance the purchase of their new refrigerator. Terms of the contract required them to repay the loan in 12 installments of $45.13 each.

What is the estimated effective APR Kathy and Ken are paying?

As a result of an unexpected bonanza, they are able to prepay the loan at the end of the third month. How much interest will be refunded if the proportional method is used? If the "rule of 78" is used? Why does this difference result?

2. Don and Marcia Hill wish to buy some new furniture for their home. They can purchase the furniture for $1,200 cash or they can buy it on an installment plan with the following terms:

   a. Downpayment—20 percent of cash price.
   b. Finance charges—0.75 percent per month on the original amount financed.
   c. 24 monthly payments of equal size.

   It would also be possible for the Hills to borrow 80 percent of the cash price from a consumer finance company. Terms of this loan would require:

   a. Finance charge—8¼ percent per year on the original amount financed plus a credit investigation fee of $28.
   b. Eight quarterly payments of equal size.

   The Hills have savings available for the downpayment.

   What is the total finance charge for the retailer credit? For the finance company loan?

   Which of the two sources of financing has the lower effective APR?

   Which of the sources should they choose? Why?

   Would you buy the furniture under these financing conditions? Explain.

3. A friend of yours has asked you for a six-month loan of $300 to be used to buy a car. You currently have the money in a savings account and do not expect to need it, at least for the next six months. The friend offers to pay you a higher rate of interest than you presently earn on the savings account.

   Describe how you could use the C's of credit in analyzing your friend's loan request.

SELECTED READINGS

Cohen, Jerome B. *Personal Finance.* Homewood, Ill.: Richard D. Irwin, Inc., 1975, chaps. 4, 5, and 6.

"Equal Credit Opportunity," *Federal Reserve Bulletin,* February 1977, pp. 101–107.

Federal Reserve Bank of Philadelphia. *Truth in Lending—What it Means for Consumer Credit,* 1970.

Harter, Ann F., and Harter, Stephen P. *Your Rights to Your Records,* Tampa, Florida: S. Harter, 1977.

Hawver, Carl F. *Basic Principles in Family Money and Credit Management.* Revised edition. Washington, D.C.: Educational Services Division, National Consumer Finance Association, 1974.

McConnell, J. Knox. *How to Get a Loan from Your Bank, Credit Union, or Finance Company.* Hicksville, N.Y.: Exposition Press, Inc., 1976.

Basic insuring decisions

10

OBJECTIVES

This chapter examines the basic principles and mechanics of insurance and suggests how risk management can be used in identifying and managing the risks you face.

After thoroughly reading and discussing the chapter, you should be able to:

. . . Identify and classify property, liability, and personal risks and measure their potential effect on your life.

. . . Describe four means of managing or controlling risk.

. . . Explain the general concept of insurance and the basic principles of insurance concerned with the pooling of risk, insurable interest, and indemnification.

. . . Explain how company, contract, and cost are important factors in deciding on insurance purchases.

Up to this point in the text we have concentrated on how to get more for your money. But another important part of your personal finances is making sure you protect what you get. To do this you must understand the risks that you face and how best to control those risks.

For most people, controlling risk means buying insurance. On the average you will probably spend six to seven percent of your income for insurance. This money will be spent on auto insurance, homeowner's insurance, life, health, and disability insurance, and a variety of other insurances. In the process of buying insurance, you'll have to choose the kinds of insurances, the type of insurance policy, the amount of insurance coverage, the agent, and the insurance company.

THE NATURE OF RISK

Did you ever consider how risky life really is? Risk, which we shall simply define as the chance of financial loss, exists in almost all of our activities. For example, owning a car involves many risks: there is the risk that the car itself will be damaged or stolen. There is the risk of an auto accident in which someone may be killed or seriously injured. There is also the risk that, as a result of an accident, you, the car owner, may be sued.

How can you handle such risks? In the business world, risk is handled by a process known as risk management. Risk management seeks to identify all possible risks, measure their potential impact, and manage risk by insuring it or controlling it. You can apply this process of risk management to your own personal finances.

PERSONAL RISK MANAGEMENT

Identifying risk

Once you begin thinking about it, you quickly realize what a tremendous number of risks you face. There arises a problem of making an orderly list of these events so that you can get a clear picture of all the risks involved. To do that, we suggest classifying risk into three categories: property risks, liability risks, and personal risks.

Property risks. One type of risk that has increased over time is the risk to property. Property risks exist when you may suffer financial loss or damage to your personal or real property as the result of the forces of nature or the perils posed by fellow humans. Our improved standard of living has resulted in a greater accumulation of property such as TV sets, a second or third car, vacation homes, and hundreds of other items. This increase in property means we potentially have more to lose.

Not only do we now have more property to lose, but in many cases our chances of loss have increased. Many existing perils that have threatened us for years have intensified for various reasons. For example, property loss due to crime has accelerated in recent decades. As Exhibit 10–1 indicates, crimes against property increased sharply in the years 1970–75. The reasons for this sharp increase have been attributed to poverty, urbanization, moral decay, and countless other causes. Whatever the real cause or causes, the chance of losing your property from the peril of crime has increased substantially.

Overall, property risks are probably the easiest set of risks to identify. They are generally associated with property that you own, so a

EXHIBIT 10–1
Property losses due to crime (in $ millions)

	Robbery	*Burglary*	*Larceny theft*	*Auto theft*
1970	$ 82	$ 672	$414	$ 873
1971	87	739	461	878
1972	91	722	475	825
1973	100	856	603	1,000
1974	125	1,100	800	1,160
1975	154	1,370	992	1,460

Source: Insurance Information Institute, *Insurance Facts*, 1976.

simple listing of all the items you own gives you a good start on identifying most property risks.

Liability risks. Liability results from situations in which you may be held legally responsible or accountable for damages to another person. Liability is determined in civil courts, which handle noncriminal disputes among individuals. In civil courts one person can sue another and after hearing all the evidence, a jury usually determines any legal liability and the extent or amount of damages.

A large number of potential liability risks arise from this simple relationship in which one person may sue another. Any occurrence in which you may be held legally responsible for injury or loss to another could bring about a legal suit. Generally speaking, there are several types of liability risks that you should be concerned about because they represent typical situations that might arise in your personal or professional life.

The most common liability risk is the chance of being sued for *negligence.* Negligence arises when an individual either acts in a careless manner or fails to take action that is appropriate. For example, an individual whose auto collides with a parked car is generally negligent in driving in a careless manner. Similarly, an individual who fails to give assistance to someone injured in an auto accident might be held negligent for failing to act in coming to the aid of an injured party. In either type of situation, if you act carelessly or "negligently," you can be sued for the resulting damages.

In addition to being responsible for your own actions, you may be responsible for the actions of others. This concept, known as *vicarious liability,* holds that you may be responsible for those who act on your behalf (generally called agents) or who are under your control. Common examples of vicarious liability would include liability for actions of employees, agents, or minor children. In many states, parents are held to be liable, at least to a limited degree, for vandalism or other acts of their minor children. Still another common instance of vicarious liability may exist when you allow someone else to drive your auto.

The extent of your liability perils should be carefully examined. Substantial risk of liability may exist in everyday activities such as owning property or pursuing your occupation or profession. It may also exist in recreational pursuits such as golfing, boating, and hunting, and in any other situation where injury to another may occur. All of your liability risks should be identified and managed in the

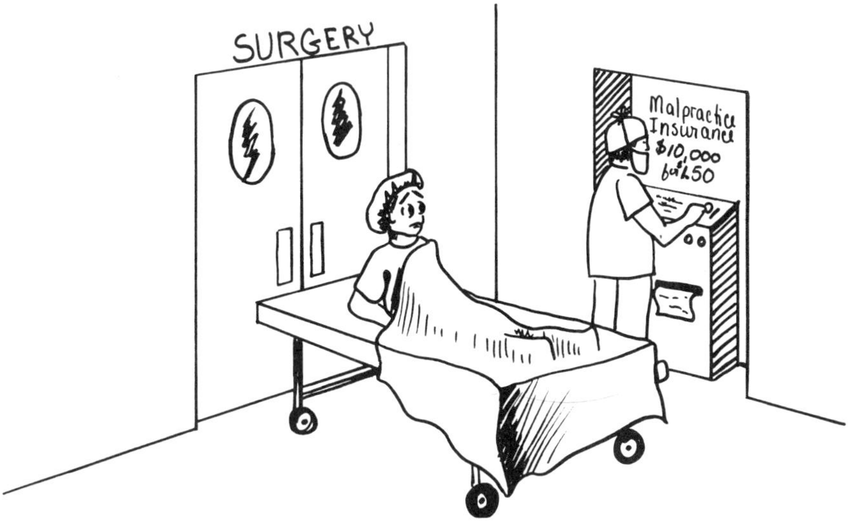

light of increasingly higher court awards that have been coming from our judicial system.

Personal risks. Personal risks exist when you or your family may suffer economic loss or injury to your persons. These personal risk perils would include death, illness, disability, unemployment, and superannuation (old age). Each of these occurrences may damage or destroy the economic value of the individual, deprive the individual or family of a potential source of earning power, and result in costly out-of-pocket expenses.

The plight of a person disabled by heart disease provides a good example of the potential monetary effects of personal risks. The heart disease itself will require out-of-pocket expenses in the form of medical services, therapeutic drugs, and similar medical costs. If the person is totally disabled and thus unable to work, there is also a loss of wages, salary, and fringe benefits and the loss of his or her personal services to the family.

A risk inventory

The discussion so far has attempted to increase your "risk awareness." All too often, the indifference of consumers to the potential impact of risks leads to an unhappy climax in which the unprotected or uninsured individual suffers great financial loss and physical harm. One step in avoiding such an occurrence is to begin planning a strategy to cope with risk. That strategy begins with a thorough identification of all risk exposures, a look at all relevant causes or perils, and an assessment of potential losses that might result. Exhibit 10–2 provides a simple and understandable guideline with which you might inventory the risk exposures you face. It should be pointed out that each individual will have unique types of risk exposures and potential perils; Exhibit 10–2 merely provides a sample treatment of selected risk exposures.

EXHIBIT 10–2
A consumer risk inventory

General type of risk	*Identifiable exposures to risk*	*Potential perils*	*Measurable losses*
Property	Home	Fire, vandalism, flood, earthquake, lightning, etc.	Direct financial loss of property, indirect loss, inconvenience
	Personal property (TV, stereo, clothing, etc.)	Fire, theft, smoke damage, etc.	Direct financial loss of property, loss of sentimental value
Liability	Professional activities	Malpractice suit based on negligence, error or omission	Direct financial loss to settle suit, loss of reputation, etc.
	Automobile ownership	Liability suit based on negligence	Direct financial loss to settle the suit
Personal	Members of the family unit (spouses, children, etc.)	Illness caused by cancer, heart disease, respiratory ailments, accidents, etc.	Medical expenses, loss of income, loss of services, special care expenses
	Spouses in a family unit	Death caused by disease, accident, etc.	Loss of income, loss of personal services, last expenses

Measuring and ranking risk

Once you have identified the risks that you face, you must measure their effect and then rank them in terms of their importance. That is, you'll have to determine which risks will require insurance or other measures and which risks you'll just decide to live with.

The measurement of risk should take account of two factors: (1) the potential severity or consequence of a risk, and (2) the probability that the risk will occur.

To measure the severity of risk, you have to ask yourself, "What will happen if this event occurs?" For example, what will happen if a serious illness like heart disease should strike? Can you list the dollar cost of this event? Will it mean the loss of a job and income? Will it result in costly, prolonged medical treatment? Will there be expensive rehabilitation costs?

In measuring the severity of risk, you must take into account both *direct* and *indirect* losses. Direct losses are outright results of a particular event. For example, if your catalytic converter causes a fire that destroys your car, the direct loss from this event is the value of the car and its contents. But the total loss from this event may also include indirect losses.

An indirect loss is damage that results as a consequence of an event. For example, the loss of your car may force you to rent a car while you shop around for another one. The rental cost is an out-of-pocket expense that you incurred as a result of the direct loss to the car.

The severity of loss should give you some idea of the relative impact of potential risks. Ordinarily you will find the risks like death, illness, and disability have serious financial effects.

A second consideration in assessing risk is the probability that risk will occur. In this instance you're asking the question "How likely is it that this event will really happen?" It is often difficult to judge this aspect of risk, though in some instances there are objective measures. For example, the chance of death can be predicted by using a mortality table. Exhibit 10–3 shows the mortality experience of the U.S. population for selected ages. These figures show that the risk of death generally increases with age.

In looking at such probability figures, you must be sure that you don't use them as excuses for not dealing with potentially unpleasant outcomes. For example, a person who is age twenty-five can refer to the mortality table and see that his or her chances of death are less than two in 1,000. Given those odds, why buy life insurance or plan your estate?

To answer these questions, we can point out two things: (1) While the numbers tell you only two out of 1,000 people will die, you don't know *which* two people are going to die. (2) If death does occur, the economic loss will likely be quite large.

This sort of analysis should be extended to all the risks you dis-

EXHIBIT 10–3
Mortality experience for ages 0–50 (United States total population: 1969–1971)

Age	Deaths per 1,000	Age	Deaths per 1,000	Age	Deaths per 1,000
0	20.02	17	1.17	34	1.95
1	1.25	18	1.28	35	2.09
2	0.86	19	1.34	36	2.25
3	0.69	20	1.40	37	2.44
4	0.57	21	1.47	38	2.66
5	0.51	22	1.52	39	2.90
6	0.46	23	1.53	40	3.14
7	0.43	24	1.51	41	3.41
8	0.39	25	1.47	42	3.70
9	0.34	26	1.43	43	4.04
10	0.31	27	1.42	44	4.43
11	0.30	28	1.44	45	4.84
12	0.35	29	1.49	46	5.28
13	0.46	30	1.55	47	5.74
14	0.63	31	1.63	48	6.24
15	0.82	32	1.72	49	6.78
16	1.01	33	1.83	50	7.38

Source: *Life Insurance Fact Book 1976* (New York: American Council of Insurance), p. 106.

cover. After considering the impact of each risk including its severity and probability, you should be able to rank these risks and determine those that you will insure or control by other means.

Managing risk

There are several basic tools and techniques available for you to use to manage or control your risks. They include retention, avoidance, prevention and reduction, and transfer (insurance). Most consumers are familiar with the term "insurance" and use it in managing risks. We'll discuss the use of insurance in a later part of this chapter. However, consideration should also be given to the other tools and techniques which may prove useful.

Retention of a risk means that the individual retains or keeps the risk and its consequences. Such retention may occur because of the failure to see that some peril exists, or it may occur because a person does not have the time or resources to actively manage the risk. The retention of risk should be an active decision and should be used only where the probable loss or the chance of occurrence is very small, or the use of insurance is prohibitive in terms of cost or availability of coverage.

A second tool used to manage risk is **avoidance.** A necessary part of avoidance is refraining from an activity or condition that is the source or cause of the risk. For example, if you do not want the property or liability risks associated with the ownership of a car, then refusing to own a car may be a way of avoiding that risk. Where an activity may be essential, however, avoidance is not an appropriate risk management technique. For example, those who wish to avoid the risks associated with drinking water or breathing the air cannot in the long run totally avoid the risks associated with these activities.

Loss prevention and reduction represents a third approach to managing risk. This approach involves taking measures to lower the chance that a peril will occur or to reduce its impact in the event that it does occur. Careful housekeeping designed to keep flammables from getting too close to fireplaces and furnaces is an example of prevention applied to the risk of fire. By contrast, a fire extinguisher that would be used to contain or put out a fire would be an example of a means to reduce loss in the event of fire.

An overview of risk management

A personal risk management plan is an important step toward financial security. Exhibit 10–4 suggests a method for drawing this process together. Risk management planning should be done periodically because the risks you face and their relative importance will change as your family situation changes. It is probably a good idea to review your plan every two to three years and whenever important changes such as marriage, divorce, childbirth, or retirement occur.

You should also note that in managing risk, you may use a combination of risk management tools. For example, to cope with possible liability suits arising out of owning an auto, you may want to use prevention (defensive driving) and insurance to handle that risk.

THE BASICS OF INSURANCE

The average consumer depends heavily on insurance as a way of managing the risk of financial loss. Consumers spend billions of dollars each year on premiums to purchase insurance to protect against property risks, liability risks, and personal risks. These premium dollars are used to purchase an expanding number of types of insurance policies: homeowner's insurance, auto insurance, disability income protection, life insurance, health insurance, and professional liability insurance. Within each of these basic types of insurance, there are numerous varieties of policies, each of which may have different contract features. For example, when you decide to buy a life insur-

EXHIBIT 10–4
Personal risk management worksheet

		Risk management strategies			
Identification of risk	*Impact*	*Avoidance*	*Retention*	*Prevention or loss reduction*	*Insurance*
Loss of home due to fire.	Direct loss of property, contents. Indirect loss of additional living expenses.	Avoid financial loss of dwelling by renting.	Retain the risk of small losses through a deductible.	Install fire detection devices. Purchase fire extinguishers. Improve housekeeping.	Purchase homeowner's insurance.
Serious illness of an adult family member.	Possible temporary or permanent disability, loss of income, loss of services, expenses associated with medical care.	Unlikely.	Retain the smaller risks such as the first dollars of medical expense.	Annual checkups and appropriate lifestyle may reduce or prevent serious illness.	Purchase health and disability insurance.
Liability suit arising from the ownership of an auto.	Financial loss incurred in settling a lawsuit.	Don't own an automobile.	Retain risks that have a small dollar impact. Also retain risks that are very unlikely to occur, e.g. lawsuit in excess of $1,000,000.	Drive defensively. Don't drive in hazardous time periods.	Purchase auto liability insurance.

ance policy a choice must be made from among term life, ordinary life, endowment insurance, modified life, a family income policy, family maintenance, variable life, and at least half a dozen others.

After you determine an appropriate type of policy, you have the task of trying to interpret and understand the insurance contract. While insurance companies are trying to simplify insurance contract language, the average policy today is still a very complicated document. One example of this complicated language can be taken from the homeowner's insurance policy that is purchased by most consumers:

> This entire policy shall be void if, whether before or after a loss, the insured has willfully concealed or misrepresented any material fact or circumstance concerning this insurance or the subject thereof, or the interest of the insured therein, or in case of any fraud or false swearing by the insured relating thereto.

This statement covers what the insurance company will do if there is any concealment or fraud in the insurance contract on the part of the insured. While the clause simply says that concealment or misrepresentation by the insured shall void the policy, interpreting the language of this clause presents a challenge to nearly everyone.

Yet another decision to make in purchasing insurance involves the question of how much insurance to buy. For example, in insuring a home, inflation and the rising cost of replacement cause the value of a home to rise over time. Therefore, there is always the question of how much insurance you should put on the dwelling.

A final problem facing you is the selection of an appropriate insurance company. Having determined the type of insurance that is desirable, the type of contract that best fits the situation, and how much insurance to buy, you will find that there are thousands of insurance companies that may sell the type of insurance you desire. These insurance companies may differ in terms of organization and may be called fraternal companies, mutual insurance companies, or stock insurance companies. They may differ in the type of contract offered, the service they provide through their agents, and the basic cost of insurance itself. Thus you must decide how to select an insurance company that will provide you with the greatest amount of insurance for your dollar.

Insuring against risk

The concept of insurance has been around for thousands of years. One of the first reported uses of insurance dates back to 3000 B.C. This use of insurance involved Chinese merchants who had a problem navigating the rapids of the Yangtze River. In navigating these rapids, a good number of boats were lost, and if a merchant happened to be using an unlucky boat that sank, he lost his entire cargo. The merchants soon devised a strategy that would spread the risk. They would gather at a point above the rapids and put part of their cargo in each of the boats. Thus, should any boat be lost going down the rapids, the merchant would lose only a part of his cargo and would not suffer a total loss.

This basic example, which is thousands of years old, illustrates one of the most important concepts of insurance: the *spreading or pooling of risk*. Insurance is designed to spread the risk of loss among many people who trade a small certain loss (the insurance premium) for protection against larger and uncertain losses. The Chinese merchants spread their cargo among the many vessels going over the rapids and, though they were likely to lose part of their cargo, they rarely lost all of it. In a similar manner, you incur a certain loss by paying an insurance premium to the company in exchange for the insurance policy and pooling your risk with many other insureds.

Insurance also depends on a basic principle known as the *law of large numbers* or the *law of averages*. For the insurance mechanism to be effective, risk must be spread over a large number of units. With a large enough number of risks, the insurance company is able to predict with a good deal of accuracy the total amount of loss that will be expected from that group of risks.

This large number of risks must have certain other characteristics. For example, any loss that occurs must be a chance occurrence. The loss must be outside of the control of the insured so that the insured cannot cause the loss and thus perhaps profit from it.

All of these risks must also be largely independent of one another. For example, if a fire insurance company insured only in one city such as the city of Chicago, what would happen if there were another great Chicago fire? Obviously that particular insurance company would be hit so hard that it could not pay all of its losses. Thus insurance companies try to obtain a number of independent risks spread throughout the country either by writing insurance in many different cities and states, or by selling part of their insurance in concentrated risks to another insurance company. This latter process is known as reinsurance.

Finally, there are certain types of risks that are simply uninsurable. For many years the private insurance industry would not underwrite the risk of flood. The reason for that was quite simple: if a company offered flood insurance, people who live in flood-prone areas would choose to take the insurance. This sort of situation gives rise to a phenomenon known as adverse selection, in which high levels of loss require very steep premiums. The high level of premiums discourages insurance, and thus the risk becomes uninsurable. The solution to this type of risk is to get a governmental body to underwrite part of the loss. For example, in the early 1970s the federal government began to subsidize flood insurance and now most individuals may obtain it.

Indemnification is another basic principle of insurance. The word "indemnify" means to compensate for damage or loss sustained. Insurance is designed to indemnify against certain covered risks. The idea of indemnification is to put the insured back to the original economic condition that existed prior to the occurrence of any loss. Inherent in this principle is the idea that the insured should not benefit or profit from insurance; rather, the insured should just be restored to his or her original position. There are many clauses within the insurance contract that are designed to carry out the principle of indemnification.

Another important principle of insurance is known as *insurable interest*. Insurable interest means that you have an economic or personal interest in the object or person being insured. In the case of property, you must have an economic interest. For example, if you own a home you have an economic interest, and thus you can insure the property to the extent of your interest. Insurable interest in life may consist of economic interest as well as bonds of love and affection. A good example of insurable interest in life is the insurable interest of a husband in his wife. The relationship of husband and wife is assumed to have bonds of love and affection.

The idea of insurable interest is designed to prevent people from trying to make insurance a matter of speculation or gambling. For example, if we allowed a person to insure a building in which he or she had no economic interest, there would always be the hazard that the person would try to see that something happened to the building in order to collect the insurance.

The insurance mechanism

Exhibit 10–5 illustrates the basic concept of insurance, using homeowner's insurance as an example. The insurance company, through its agents, sells homeowner's insurance policies to numerous consumers. The insurance company collects the premiums and invests amounts not needed immediately to pay claims. The investment income then comes back to the insurance company and can be used to pay claims as the need arises.

The insurance company is an intermediary in the insurance

EXHIBIT 10–5
The mechanism of insurance

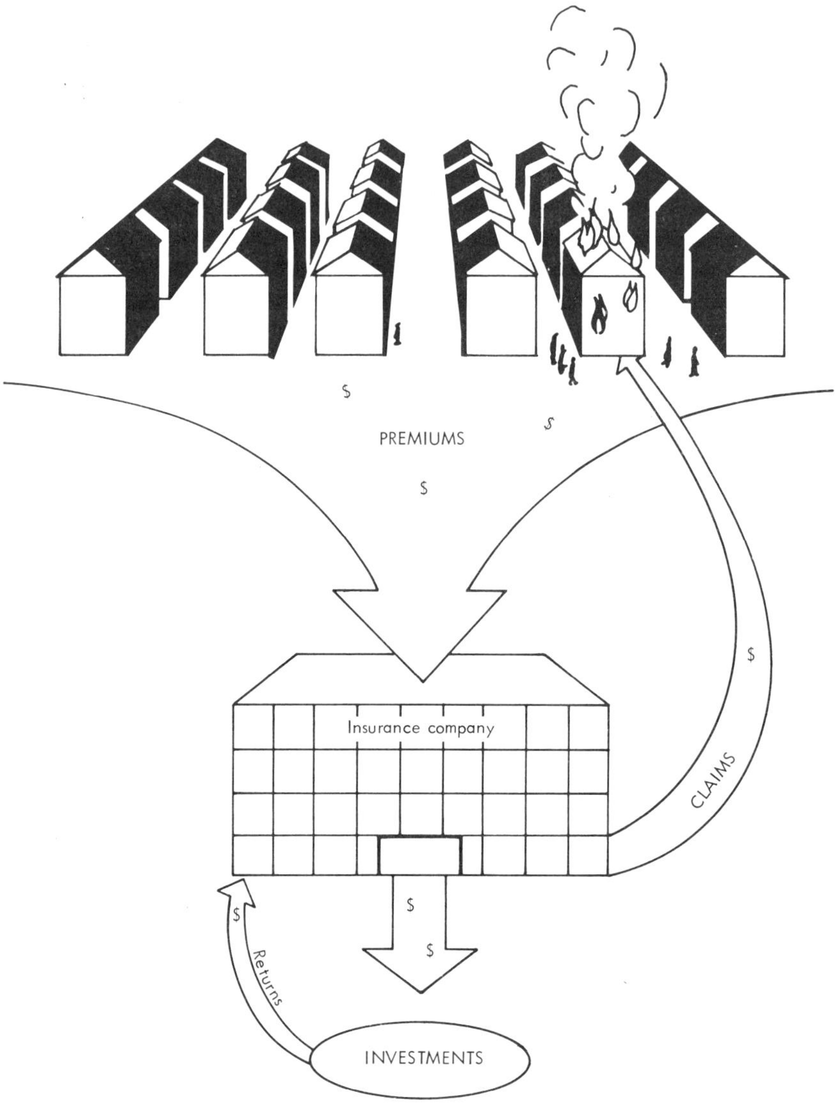

process. This intermediary service costs some money in terms of paying commissions to the insurance agents and paying the operating expenses of the company. The largest expense, however, and the primary purpose of insurance, will be to pay the claims of the unfortunate insureds who experience a loss.

We should all keep in mind this primary purpose of insurance. How often have you heard someone say that they paid insurance premiums for five or ten years and "never got anything for it?" Such individuals miss the main point of insurance: It only pays those who lose! The winners (those who don't suffer a loss) have had coverage against the eventuality of loss but have been fortunate enough not to have suffered any loss. Under the insurance mechanism, they neither deserve nor should they receive any payment.

WHAT TO CONSIDER IN BUYING INSURANCE

Now that we have discussed the basic principles and mechanics of insurance, we can turn our attention to a very practical matter: What factors should you consider in buying insurance? Specifically, after you have decided to insure a risk and you know the amount and type of coverage you need, how should you select the best insurance policy and company?

We'd like to suggest three factors that will help you make that decision. For brevity we can call them company, contract, and cost.

Company

The insurance company is an important part of the insurance arrangement. The company and its agents provide you with needed service. This service includes paying you when you have a loss, advising you on your ongoing insurance needs, and making changes in your insurance amounts and coverages.

You can use several guidelines in evaluating a company's service. Your personal observation of its agents, their general manner in dealing with you, especially if you have a claim with the company, and their professional training will tell you a lot about the company. Professional designations such as CLU (Chartered Life Underwriter) and CPCU (Chartered Property Casualty Underwriter) indicate that an agent has completed additional course work and passed a series of examinations dealing with insurance, economics, and financial planning.

You can also check with consumer organizations such as Consumer's Union for ratings of insurance company service. In addition, you can check with your state insurance commissioner for records of complaints against insurers in your state.

In considering the company, you may also be interested in its organizational structure and financial soundness. Insurance companies are organized as either mutual, fraternal, or stock companies. A mutual insurance company is a type of cooperative that is owned by its policyholders. Each policyholder has a vote in company affairs and a share in any profits the mutual company makes.

A fraternal insurer is also a form of cooperative that is owned by its policyholders. Fraternals are organized to benefit a group of people with a common bond such as religion, ethnic origin, or profession. The fraternal, like the mutual, is a not-for-profit organization that is run for the exclusive benefit of its policyholders.

A stock insurer is owned by stockholders who may or may not be policyholders in the company. The stockholders provide capital to run the company and in return expect a profit.

A final factor to consider in evaluating the company is its financial soundness. A. M. Best Co. and organizations like it provide ratings of financial strength. In recent years, several insurance companies have gone bankrupt because of mismanagement or fraud and this has resulted in losses to policyholders.[1] With this in mind, we would suggest that financial soundness is an important item to check out.

Contract

The insurance policy is a legal contract between the insurance company and the insured that contains provisions dealing with coverage, the conditions of the coverage, and the rights and duties of the insured and the insurer. With the single exception of the basic fire insurance contract, there is no guaranteed uniformity in insurance contracts among insurers. Given this lack of uniformity, it is important to be able to read and analyze the basics of an insurance contract.

The insurance contract can be broken down into three parts: a declarations section, the insuring agreement, and exclusions and conditions.

Declarations section. The easiest thing to find in the insurance contract, almost without exception, is a declarations section. This is usually the first page of any insurance contract. The declarations section states certain things about the insurance policy such as the name of the insured, what is insured (usually a person, activity, or piece of property), the time period for which the insurance is in effect, the amount of insurance purchased, and the premium or cost of the insurance. It may also contain rating information that the insurance company uses to determine the premium or price of the insurance policy.

An illustration of a typical declarations section from a homeowner's insurance policy is contained in Exhibit 10–6. While each type

---

[1] One of the most publicized cases of insurance company failure was the Equity Funding bankruptcy in the early 1970s. The failure resulted from fraud on the part of management and caused substantial losses to company stockholders and insureds.

EXHIBIT 10–6
Sample declaration page for a homeowner's policy

States the named insured. →

DECLARATIONS
Named Insured and P.O. Address (Number, Street, Town or City, County, State, Zip Code)

Describes the time period to which the insurance applies. →

Policy Term: ______ Years ______ Inception ______ Expiration

Describes what is insured. In this case the subject of insurance is a residence. →

The described residence premises covered hereunder is located at the above address, unless otherwise stated herein (No., Street, Town or City, County, State, Zip Code)

States the amount of insurance purchased relative to each type of property or activity concerned. →

Insurance is provided only with respect to the following Coverages for which a limit of liability is specified, subject to all conditions of this policy.

Coverages and Limit of Liability	Section I				Section II		
	A. Dwelling	B. Appurtenant Structures	C. Unscheduled Personal Property	D. Additional Living Expense	E. Personal Liability (Bodily Injury and Property Damage) Each occurrence	F. Medical Payments to Others Each person	Each accident
	$	$	$	$	$	$	$ 25,000

States the total cost or premium and the basic makeup of that premium. →

Premium	Basic Policy Premium	Theft Extension	Additional Premiums		Total Prepaid Premium	Premium if paid in installments	Payable: At Inception (and)	At each subsequent anniversary
	$	$	$	$	$	$	$	$
	Premium for Scheduled Personal Property				$	$	$	$
Form and Endorsements made part of this Policy at time of issue: Insert Number(s) and Edition Date(s)	Form HO- Endorsement(s) HO-			Combined Premium	$	$	$	$

DEDUCTIBLE—SECTION I: Any loss by perils insured against under Section I of this policy is subject to a deductible. Exceptions, if any: ☐ Deductible applicable only to loss caused by the peril of wind-storm or hail (Clause No. 1) ☐ Deductible applicable to loss caused by other perils (Clause No. 2) ☐ Deductible not applicable ☐ Special Loss Deductible Clause $ ______ (Amount)

Special State Provisions: South Carolina: Valuation Clause (Coverage A) $ New York: Coinsurance Clause Applies ☐ Yes ☐ No

Section II—Additional residence premises, if any, located: (No., Street, Town or City, County, State, Zip Code)

Mortgagee(s) (NAME AND ADDRESS)

Countersignature Date Agency at

______ Agent

Contains information needed by the insurance company to determine the appropriate premium. →

Rating Information Only	Dwelling occupied by ☐ 1 ☐ 2 ☐ 3 ☐ 4 families. Code (1) (3) (7) (7)	Tenant ☐ (9)	Deductibles: Type Code	All Perils $	Clause No. 1 $	Clause No. 2 $ Size Code	Zone Code	Not more than ______ feet from Hydrant	Not more than ______ miles from Fire Dept.
Construction of dwelling:	Code (1) ☐ Frame; Code (5) ☐ Frame with aluminum or plastic siding	Code (2) ☐ Brick, Stone or Masonry Veneer		Code (3) ☐ Brick, Stone or Masonry	Code (4) ☐ Fire Resistive	Roof ☐ Approved ☐ Unapproved		Prot. Cl. Code	Premium Group No.
Complete when Form HO-4 is made a part of this policy		Southern States					Fire District		Code
Total Annual Fire and Extended Coverage Rate	Number of Apartments in building	☐ Inside City Limits		☐ Inside Protected Suburban Area		☐ Inside Fire District			

(a) The described dwelling is not seasonal; (b) no business pursuits are conducted on the described premises; (c) the described premises is the only premises where the Named Insured or spouse maintains a residence other than business or farm properties; (d) the Insured has no full time residence employee(s); (e) the Insured has no outboard motor(s) or watercraft otherwise excluded under this policy for which coverage is desired. Exception, if any, to (a), (b), (c), (d) or (e)* of insurance may differ in format and some of the information declared, almost every insurance policy will contain some type of declaration page.

Insuring agreement. The heart of any insurance policy is the section containing the insuring agreement. The insuring agreement states what the insurer promises to do in return for the payment of the premium. It describes the events covered under the contract and usually stipulates the extent of coverage provided by the issuer. Exhibit 10–7 contains a basic insuring agreement from a homeowner's insurance policy.

Exclusions and conditions. Exclusions and conditions limit the extent of insurance coverage and define what conditions must be present before the insurer is obligated to pay. Some policies may have separate sections for this type of information, but typically the exclusions and conditions are sprinkled about in a number of places including the basic insuring agreement.

An example of a typical exclusion contained in an insurance policy is the suicide clause in a life insurance contract. The suicide clause states that the life insurer will not have to pay the face amount of the policy if the insured commits suicide within two years (one year in some policies) after the policy is obtained.

An example of a condition in an insurance contract can be taken from a standard fire insurance contract. The standard fire insurance contract is one of the few insurance contracts that is uniform throughout the United States. This contract contains a condition that suspends or restricts the fire insurance coverage if the insured leaves a described building or residence unoccupied or vacant for a period of 60 consecutive days. You will find that almost every insurance contract has numerous conditions affecting the insurance coverage.

Cost

A third factor to consider in making a decision to buy insurance is cost. In comparing costs, it is important that you give consideration to comparable contract and service features. A low premium on an insurance policy with poor contract provisions may not provide the protection that you need. Similarly, poor service on claims may cost you money by not fully reimbursing your claims.

In general, there are significant differences in premium costs in every line of insurance. It will be worth your time and effort to shop around and get price quotations from several different agents. You should find that the lowest premium costs of property and liability insurance for your home and auto may vary by 20 to 30 percent from the highest quote. The cost differences in life insurance are even

EXHIBIT 10–7
Sample basic insuring agreement

> In Consideration of the Provisions and Stipulations Herein or Added Hereto and of the Premium Above Specified (or specified in endorsement(s) made a part hereof), this Company, for the term shown above from inception date shown above at noon (Standard Time) to expiration date shown above at noon (Standard Time) at location of property involved, to an amount not exceeding the limit of liability above specified, does insure the insured named in the Declarations above and legal representatives, to the extent of the actual cash value of the property at the time of loss, but not exceeding the amount which it would cost to repair or replace the property with material of like kind and quality within a reasonable time after such loss, without allowance for any increased cost of repair or reconstruction by reason of any ordinance or law regulating construction or repair, and without compensation for loss resulting from interruption of business or manufacture, nor in any event for more than the interest of the Insured, against all DIRECT LOSS BY FIRE, LIGHTNING AND OTHER PERILS INSURED AGAINST IN THIS POLICY INCLUDING REMOVAL FROM PREMISES ENDANGERED BY THE PERILS INSURED AGAINST IN THIS POLICY, EXCEPT AS HEREINAFTER PROVIDED, to the property described herein while located or contained as described in this policy, or pro rata for five days at each proper place to which any of the property shall necessarily be removed for preservation from the perils insured against in this policy, but not elsewhere.
>
> Assignment of this policy shall not be valid except with the written consent of this Company.
>
> This policy is made and accepted subject to the foregoing provisions and stipulations and those hereinafter stated, which are hereby made a part of this policy, together with such other provisions, stipulations and agreements as may be added hereto, as provided in this policy.

greater, and you will find that the highest cost policy may cost you twice as much as the lowest cost policy.

Because of the possible extent of cost differences in insurance purchases, we will examine these factors in greater detail in Chapters 11 and 12.

SUMMARY

Part of sound financial planning should include a personal risk management plan that provides a way of achieving financial security from risk. Because risk pervades almost all of your activities, it is essential that you identify, measure, and control risk. You can identify and classify any risk into one of three categories: personal risks, liability risks, and property risks. In assessing the impact of risk, severity and the probability of occurrence are two important factors to consider. To control and manage risk, you can use avoidance, retention, prevention and reduction, and insurance.

Insurance is the most common means of risk management. The basic principle behind insurance is a pooling of risk, in which you trade a certain loss (the insurance premium) for protection against larger losses. Insurance depends upon the law of large numbers. It is a contract of indemnification that compensates only to the extent of your loss. In the insurance arrangement, the insurance company is the intermediary, which collects premiums, invests excess funds, and pays for the insureds' losses.

The decision to buy insurance should include consideration of company, contract, and cost. In evaluating the company, you should look at service, financial strength, and the organizational form. Your analysis of the contract should include an evaluation of the basic contract parts including the declaration page, the basic insuring agreement, and exclusions and conditions. Your evaluation of insurance cost should consider the quality of the contract and the overall strength of the company as well as the premium cost.

DISCUSSION QUESTIONS

1. Drawing upon your own life experiences, compile a list of all the risks that you face. Classify these risks as to whether they are personal risks, property risks, or liability risks.
2. Given the inventory of risks obtained in Question 1, rank all these risks in order of their relative importance. What criteria should you use in ranking risk? Which risk is most important to you? Why? Drawing upon your ranking, what types of risks (personal, property, liability) are most important and least important?
3. With regard to risk measurement, how does the risk of death at age 0 compare to the risk of death at age 40? Does the risk of death always increase with age? Explain.
4. In what way does insurance involve a small certain loss in exchange for protection against potentially larger and uncertain losses?
5. Why is insurance a contract of indemnity?
6. Explain the function of the declaration page in an insurance contract.
7. List several common prevention and reduction techniques that a homeowner could use to handle potential property losses caused by fire.

8. What is the role of the insurance company in the insurance process?
9. What are the similarities and differences among mutual, fraternal, and stock insurance companies?
10. Explain the importance of considering the company when making insurance purchases.

CASE PROBLEM

The following are brief profiles of two households:

Jane Justin is 26 years old and holds a degree in accounting and a CPA. She is currently working for a major accounting firm in Chicago, Illinois. Jane is single, owns her own car, and has a two-bedroom apartment in a suburb of Chicago. She commutes to work with a group of four other professionals, each of them driving one day a week. In her job, Jane frequently travels by plane to distant sites as part of her work as an auditor.

Jane owns her own furniture, appliances, and stereo system and every year she rents a cottage in Michigan where she spends a month's vacation and entertains many friends and relatives. Jane has accumulated a small amount of savings, and she expects to become a partner in her firm within three or four years.

Harold and Emily Richland are each 45 years old and they live in Lawton, Oklahoma. They have four children including daughters aged 21 and 15 and sons aged 17 and 19. Harold is a plant manager for a local bottling plant. Emily manages the household and also works part-time as a legal secretary. The two older children are in college and depend upon their parents for money to pay tuition and room and board.

The Richlands own a home, a 50-horsepower inboard-outboard cruiser, and two cars, which are used by all five family members who are of driving age. One car is currently ten years old. The Richlands have accumulated some savings but expect to exhaust most of this money in paying for college expenses.

Prepare a risk inventory for each of these two households following the guidelines shown in Exhibit 10–2. How do the risks of the Richlands differ from those of Jane Justin?

How would you rank these risks in terms of importance to each household?

SELECTED READINGS

Bickelhaupt, David L. *General Insurance,* 9th ed., Homewood, Illinois: Richard D. Irwin, Inc., 1974, Chapters 1–5.

Greene, Mark R. *Risk and Insurance,* 4th ed., Cincinnati, Ohio: South-Western Publishing Co., 1977, Chapters 1–4.

Oder, Robert W. and Bickley, John S. *Glossary of Insurance Terms.* Santa Monica, California: Insurers Press, Inc., 1972.

Auto and homeowner's insurance

11

OBJECTIVES

The primary function of this chapter is to introduce the common types of auto and homeowner's insurances. These insurances are essential elements of any risk management plan which must deal with liability and property risks.

After thoroughly reading and discussing this chapter, you should be able to:

. . . Identify and explain the major components of a homeowner's insurance policy.

. . . Explain the basic concepts of "fault" and "no-fault" automobile insurance.

. . . Identify and explain the major parts of an automobile insurance policy.

. . . Identify several measures that you may use to evaluate property and liability companies.

Your home and your auto represent very important sources of property and liability risks. Damaged fenders on autos and windstorm damage to roofs and storm windows on homes are common examples of property losses. More importantly, legal suits involving accidents in the home or collisions between autos represent potentially large financial setbacks.

In this chapter we will be concerned with homeowner's insurance, auto insurance, and related insurance coverages as ways of handling these risk exposures. Each type of insurance will be examined in the light of the types of policies available, the basic parts of typical contracts, exclusions and limitations, and policy coverage amounts. The concluding section of the chapter deals with the problem of choosing a good property and liability insurance company.

HOMEOWNER'S INSURANCE

Reasons for buying homeowner's insurance

Almost every one of us owns property in the form of housing or household and personal effects. For those who own a home, condominium, or other type of housing, there is the possibility of loss to the physical structure such as walls, floors, and roof from the threat of fire, wind, and other perils. For both homeowners and renters, there is a need to insure the contents of the dwelling. Contents would include furniture, appliances and personal effects such as clothes, books, jewelry, stereos, and television sets.

Generally speaking, the home and its contents represent the bulk of the average consumer's wealth, and the loss of these possessions would impose a financial hardship. Thus there is the need to protect against their loss by buying insurance.

A second type of insurance needed by the homeowner or renter is liability insurance. This need arises for several reasons. First, your home or apartment can be a source of liability. Friends or relatives who come to visit may injure themselves as a result of what is determined to be your negligence. Other individuals such as the plumber or postal employee may have occasion to enter your home and be accidentally injured. You may even be responsible for trespassers and children who have not been invited into your home or yard but who suffer harm that is the result of your negligence or the condition of the property. Exhibit 11–1 gives some common examples of possible liability risks that may be associated with a dwelling or the ownership of land.

Another general source of liability arises from the activities in which we engage every day. Many apparently harmless activities may result in another person's being injured. What may be a leisurely golf game can turn into a lawsuit if you should happen to drive your golf ball into someone else's head. Likewise, a cookout that you put on for relatives and friends could turn into a very expensive food poisoning case.

The need for insurance against such liability risks is apparent. The size of damage awards has been increasing in recent years and a jury could return a verdict that would bankrupt you or your family. The main solution to this risk of liability is to obtain liability insurance that will cover you against a wide range of legal liability exposures.

For most consumers, the answer to many of these property and lia-

EXHIBIT 11–1
Typical liability exposures of homeowners

Summary of sources of liability	*Legal precedents drawn from case law*
Liability for pets and animals: An individual is responsible for damages caused by pets and domestic animals. It is general common law doctrine that a dog is entitled to one bite before its owner can be held legally liable for damages.	*Smith* v. *Pehal,* 2 Strange, 1264. In the year 1264, a British court held as follows: "If a dog has once bit a man, and the owner having notice thereof keeps the dog, and lets him go about or lie at his door, an action will lie against him at the suit of a person who is bit, though it happened by such person's treading on the dog's toes; for it was owning to his not hanging the dog on the first notice. And the safety of the king's subjects ought not afterwards to be endangered." This case set the famous first bite doctrine rule with regard to pets.
Liability stemming from public officials and licensees (people who must trespass on your property to complete a task such as fire protection, meter reading, etc.) as well as public thoroughfares on your property: Your duty to these individuals is one of ordinary care. You must not create conditions which are dangerous to them and you must warn them of dangers if you know that they are on your premises.	*Mile High Fence Co.* v. *Radovich,* 489 P 2d. 308 (Colo. 1971): The plaintiff Radovich was a police officer who was injured when he fell in a fence hole dug by the Mile High Fence Co. The court held that a landowner must manage his property as "a reasonable man in view of probability and foreseeability." Thus the court upheld the damage award to Radovich and concluded that the landowner must provide safeguards against artificial or manmade hazards. *Adlington* v. *City of Viroqua,* 144 NW 1130 (WI 1914): The owner of property was found negligent for releasing water on his property which then flowed onto a sidewalk and formed ice. A passerby slipped on the ice and incurred a serious injury.
Liability for children: A landowner has a special duty to children and must refrain from creating artificial conditions which are inherently dangerous to children.	*Giacoma* v. *Tapley,* 428 P. 2d 439 (Arizona, 1967): The landowner who maintained an unfenced swimming pool was liable for damages resulting from the death of a small child.
Liability for trespassers: In general you owe a duty of slight care to trespassers. However, you cannot intentionally cause harm to such individuals.	*Katko* v. *Briney,* 183 NW 2d 657 (IA 1971): Katko was injured by a spring gun while trespassing on Briney's property. The court held that the landowner could not protect his property with excessive force and that damages were payable to Katko as a result of the incident.

bility risks lies in homeowner's or renter's insurance. This type of insurance generally contains a package of coverages that meets the needs of most individuals. The packaging of insurance means that different types of insurances are combined within one insurance policy. Thus, instead of buying many separate policies such as fire, theft, and liability, you can get the essential insurances combined in one package policy.

It should be pointed out that a homeowner's policy largely excludes most coverages relating to the ownership of a car. As we shall see in later parts of this chapter, the auto is a source of potential risk that deserves and requires separate insurance coverage.

Policy analysis

The typical homeowner's policy contains five important components following a declaration page: a basic fire contract, property coverages and perils, medical payments coverage, personal liability coverage, and optional endorsements.

Declaration page. The declaration page from the homeowner's policy was reviewed briefly in the previous chapter. The primary purpose of this page is to state the basic facts concerning the insurance contract. Specifically, the declaration page states *who* is insured,[1] *how much* insurance is in effect, *where and when* the insurance is effective, *what property* is insured, and *what perils* are covered.

In addition to this information, the declaration page will tell you if there is a *deductible* on the policy. A deductible is the portion of every loss which you must pay before the company begins to pay. The declaration page will also indicate the amount of the deductible and the perils to which the deductible applies.

One final item on the declaration page is the basic insuring agreement, usually on the very bottom of the page (see Exhibit 10–7). This agreement is a bare-bones statement of the legal insuring contract between the insured and the insurance company. It is an extremely conservative statement that limits coverage to the actual cash value (replacement cost less depreciation) of the insured property. It also limits the number of perils covered to fire, lightning, and "other perils insured against in this policy." The latter statement gives some indication of things to come in the form of expanded coverages contained in later parts of the policy.

Basic fire contract. The second part of most homeowner's policies is the basic fire contract. This contract consists of 165 numbered lines of policy language that spell out in great detail the general conditions of the contract and the specific duties of the insured and the insurance company. With a few exceptions, these 165 lines are uniform in all 50 of the United States. Although this may seem unimportant, in fact the

[1] In most homeowner's policies, the definition of insured includes the named insured and residents of the named insured's household.

EXHIBIT 11–2
Some day 12 wonderful people could destroy you

Some day 12 wonderful people could destroy you.

Meet your jury of peers.

They decide if you owe, and how much, when someone sues.

If you are a professional or top echelon executive, good luck!

In the absence of good luck, what you need is Personal Liability Catastrophe coverage from The St. Paul.

Our Personal Liability Catastrophe Policy can cover you for up to $5 million against almost any kind of liability imaginable. From bodily injury to libel and slander.

It pays the cost of your defense and out of court settlements for covered claims. And Personal Liability Catastrophe coverage is relatively inexpensive. Approximately $100 a year for a million dollars of coverage, depending on where you live and how much you have to lose.

One stipulation. This is excess liability. You must already have $100,000 or so of comprehensive personal liability and $250,000/$500,000 of auto liability protection.

Either way, make your own luck. With Personal Liability Catastrophe coverage from The St. Paul, the company that's been helping folks out of tight spots since before the Civil War.

Talk to an independent agent for The St. Paul today. He's in the Yellow Pages.

THE ST. PAUL
COMPANIES

Serving you around the world . . . around the clock
St. Paul, Minnesota 55102

St. Paul Fire and Marine Insurance Company, St. Paul Mercury Insurance Company, The St. Paul Insurance Company.

standard fire contract is the *only* uniform insurance contract in existence. All other types of insurance contracts may differ from company to company or from state to state.

The standard fire contract lays the groundwork for the entire insuring agreement. It specifically deals with the extent of peril coverage, the legal rights and duties of the insured and the insurer, the rights of third parties such as the holder of a mortgage on the insured's home, and a number of miscellaneous provisions that govern the policy. Exhibit 11–3 contains a sample and a brief summary of a 165-line basic fire insurance contract.

Property coverages and perils. The homeowner's policy covers four types of property losses. In all forms except the HO-4 and HO-6, there is insurance coverage for the dwelling and other structures, such as detached garages. All the homeowner's forms contain coverage for your personal property and additional living expenses. The personal property insurance covers your furnishings, clothing, and other personal effects. Additional living expense insurance covers the additional expenses you incur if you're forced to live away from your home as the result of damage to the home caused by fire, wind, or any other insured peril. For example, if a fire forces you out of your home and you have to live in a motel and eat out, this insurance will pay for your expenses *over and above* your normal living expenses.

The extent of the perils covered on homeowner's insurance depends on the type of policy you choose. You may choose from six types of policies. In most regions these policies are sold as form HO-1, HO-2, HO-3, HO-4, HO-5, or HO-6. (In some regions the designation may be form HO-A, HO-B, HO-C, HO-D, HO-E, and HO-F.) The HO-4 policy is designed for renters who do not have to protect a dwelling. The HO-6 policy is designed for condominium owners. The other types of HO's are designed for owners of single-family homes. Generally speaking, the higher the HO number designation, the greater the extent of additional peril coverages. A summary of the perils covered under each type of HO policy is shown as part of Exhibit 11–4.

In addition to the descriptions of property and peril coverage, you will find other provisions contained in this section of the policy. One very important provision is replacement cost coverage. Until this point in the policy, any loss was to be reimbursed to the extent of actual cash value. Actual cash value is equivalent to the replacement cost of an item less an amount proportional to its expired useful life (sometimes referred to as depreciation). While this type of coverage may be adequate to cover small items such as losses to clothing or furniture, it is inadequate when it comes to losses on a home or dwelling. For example, a home that has a useful life of 100 years may be

EXHIBIT 11–3
Sample basic fire insurance contract

Concealment, fraud. This entire policy shall be void if, whether before or after a loss, the insured has wilfully concealed or misrepresented any material fact or circumstance concerning this insurance or the subject thereof, or the interest of the insured therein, or in case of any fraud or false swearing by the insured relating thereto.

Uninsurable and excepted property. This policy shall not cover accounts, bills, currency, deeds, evidences of debt, money or securities; nor, unless specifically named hereon in writing, bullion or manuscripts.

Perils not included. This Company shall not be liable for loss by fire or other perils insured against in this policy caused, directly or indirectly, by: (a) enemy attack by armed forces, including action taken by military, naval or air forces in resisting an actual or an immediately impending enemy attack; (b) invasion; (c) insurrection; (d) rebellion; (e) revolution; (f) civil war; (g) usurped power; (h) order of any civil authority except acts of destruction at the time of and for the purpose of preventing the spread of fire, provided that such fire did not originate from any of the perils excluded by this policy; (i) neglect of the insured to use all reasonable means to save and preserve the property at and after a loss, or when the property is endangered by fire in neighboring premises; (j) nor shall this Company be liable for loss by theft.

Other Insurance. Other insurance may be prohibited or the amount of insurance may be limited by endorsement attached hereto.

Conditions suspending or restricting insurance. Unless otherwise provided in writing added hereto this Company shall not be liable for loss occurring
(a) while the hazard is increased by any means within the control or knowledge of the insured; or
(b) while a described building, whether intended for occupancy by owner or tenant, is vacant or unoccupied beyond a period of sixty consecutive days; or
(c) as a result of explosion or riot, unless fire ensue, and in that event for loss by fire only.

Other perils or subjects. Any other peril to be insured against or subject of insurance to be covered in this policy shall be by endorsement in writing hereon or added hereto.

Added provisions. The extent of the application of insurance under this policy and of the contribution to be made by this Company in case of loss, and any other provision or agreement not inconsistent with the provisions of this policy, may be provided for in writing added hereto, but no provision may be waived except such as by the terms of this policy is subject to change.

Waiver provisions. No permission affecting this insurance shall exist, or waiver of any provision be valid, unless granted herein or expressed in writing added hereto. No provision, stipulation or forfeiture shall be held to be waived by any requirement or proceeding on the part of this Company relating to appraisal or to any examination provided for herein.

Cancellation of policy. This policy shall be cancelled at any time at the request of the insured, in which case this Company shall, upon demand and surrender of this policy, refund the excess of paid premium above the customary short rates for the expired time. This policy may be cancelled at any time by this Company by giving to the insured a five days' written notice of cancellation with or without tender of the excess of paid premium above the pro rata premium for the expired time, which excess, if not tendered, shall be refunded on demand. Notice of cancellation shall state that said excess premium (if not tendered) will be refunded on demand.

Mortgagee interests and obligations. If loss hereunder is made payable, in whole or in part, to a designated mortgagee not named herein as the insured, such interest in this policy may be cancelled by giving to such mortgagee a ten days' written notice of cancellation.

If the insured fails to render proof of loss such mortgagee, upon notice, shall render proof of loss in the form herein specified within sixty (60) days thereafter and shall be subject to the provisions hereof relating to appraisal and time of payment and of bringing suit. If this Company shall claim that no liability existed as to the mortgagor or owner, it shall, to the extent of payment of loss to the mortgagee, be subrogated to all the mortgagee's rights of recovery, but without impairing mortgagee's right to sue; or it may pay off the mortgage debt and require an assignment thereof and of the mortgage. Other provisions

EXHIBIT 11–3 *(continued)*

relating to the interests and obligations of such mortgagee may be added hereto by agreement in writing.

Pro rata liability. This Company shall not be liable for a greater proportion of any loss than the amount hereby insured shall bear to the whole insurance covering the property against the peril involved, whether collectible or not.

Requirements in case loss occurs. The insured shall give immediate written notice to this Company of any loss, protect the property from further damage, forthwith separate the damaged and undamaged personal property, put it in the best possible order, furnish a complete inventory of the destroyed, damaged and undamaged property, showing in detail quantities, costs, actual cash value and amount of loss claimed; **and within sixty days after the loss, unless such time is extended in writing by this Company, the insured shall render to this Company a proof of loss,** signed and sworn to by the insured, stating the knowledge and belief of the insured as to the following: the time and origin of the loss, the interest of the insured and of all others in the property, the actual cash value of each item thereof and the amount of loss thereto, all encumbrances thereon, all other contracts of insurance, whether valid or not, covering any of said property, any changes in the title, use, occupation, location, possession or exposures of said property since the issuing of this policy, by whom and for what purpose any building herein described and the several parts thereof were occupied at the time of loss and whether or not it then stood on leased ground, and shall furnish a copy of all the descriptions and schedules in all policies and, if required, verified plans and specifications of any building, fixtures or machinery destroyed or damaged. The insured, as often as may be reasonably required, shall exhibit to any person designated by this Company all that remains of any property herein described, and submit to examinations under oath by any person named by this Company, and subscribe the same; and, as often as may be reasonably required, shall produce for examination all books of account, bills, invoices and other vouchers, or certified copies thereof if originals be lost, at such reasonable time and place as may be designated by this Company or its representative, and shall permit extracts and copies thereof to be made.

Appraisal. In case the insured and this Company shall fail to agree as to the actual cash value or the amount of loss, then, on the written demand of either, each shall select a competent and disinterested appraiser and notify the other of the appraiser selected within twenty days of such demand. The appraisers shall first select a competent and disinterested umpire; and failing for fifteen days to agree upon such umpire, then, on request of the insured or this Company, such umpire shall be selected by a judge of a court of record in the state in which the property covered is located. The appraisers shall then appraise the loss, stating separately actual cash value and loss to each item; and, failing to agree, shall submit their differences, only, to the umpire. An award in writing, so itemized, of any two when filed with this Company shall determine the amount of actual cash value and loss. Each appraiser shall be paid by the party selecting him and the expenses of appraisal and umpire shall be paid by the parties equally.

Company's options. It shall be optional with this Company to take all, or any part, of the property at the agreed or appraised value, and also to repair, rebuild or replace the property destroyed or damaged with other of like kind and quality within a reasonable time, on giving notice of its intention so to do within thirty days after the receipt of the proof of loss herein required.

Abandonment. There can be no abandonment to this Company of any property.

When loss payable. The amount of loss for which this Company may be liable shall be payable sixty days after proof of loss, as herein provided, is received by this Company and ascertainment of the loss is made either by agreement between the insured and this Company expressed in writing or by the filing with this Company of an award as herein provided.

Suit. No suit or action on this policy for the recovery of any claim shall be sustainable in any court of law or equity unless all the requirements of this policy shall have been complied with, and unless commenced within twelve months next after inception of the loss.

Subrogation. This Company may require from the insured an assignment of all right of recovery against any party for loss to the extent that payment therefor is made by this Company.

EXHIBIT 11–3 *(concluded)*
Summary of the basic fire contract

Lines 1–6	Make the policy invalid, if the insured willfully conceals or misrepresents any important matter in obtaining the insurance.
Lines 7–10	Exclude certain property (such as paper money or stock certificates) that is highly perishable, mobile, and difficult to reconstruct in a fire loss.
Lines 11–24	Contain a list of perils the insurance company will not cover, e.g., damage caused by "enemy attack."
Lines 25–27	Allow the insurance company to limit or prohibit additional insurance by adding a written endorsement to the policy.
Lines 28–37	Contain a list of events that may suspend or restrict insurance coverage, e.g., knowingly increasing the hazard of loss.
Lines 38–41	Indicate that insurance for any peril other than fire, lightning or removal will be added by a written endorsement.
Lines 42–48	Make provision for possible future changes in the policy, which may be added to the policy in writing.
Lines 49–55	Require written permission of the insurance company in order to waive or abandon any of the conditions contained in the policy.
Lines 56–67	Indicate the insured's and the insurance company's right to cancel the policy.
Lines 68–85	Detail the rights of the holder of a mortgage (mortgagee). Basically this section protects the rights of the mortgagee by giving the holder of the mortgage notice of policy cancellation and the right to file a loss claim if the insured fails to do so.
Lines 86–89	Limit the liability of the insurance company to its proportionate share of all the insurance that covers the home. For example, if a $10,000 home has two $10,000 insurance policies and the home is totally destroyed (a $10,000 loss), then each insurance policy pays $5,000. (The total insurance is $20,000 and each company is responsible for 10/20 of the loss.) This clause discourages the insured from over-insuring and then causing an intentional loss; it is consistent with the general principle of indemnification.
Lines 90–122	List the duties of the insured in case of a loss. Consumers should especially note lines 94–97, which require the insured to provide detailed information for damage claims on any insured property.
Lines 123–140	Indicate an orderly way for settling disputes on claims between the insurer and the insured.
Lines 141–147	Allow the insurance company to settle a claim by paying cash or rebuilding the property.
Lines 148–149	Prevent the insured from abandoning the property to the insurance company.
Lines 150–156	Require the company to pay losses within 60 days after an agreement with the insured.
Lines 157–161	Set forth conditions on the right of the insured to sue the insurance company.
Lines 162–165	Give the insurance company the right to sue and recover from a third party (a party other than the insured) whose negligence may have caused a loss to the insured which the company has had to pay.

EXHIBIT 11–4
Property perils covered in homeowner's and renter's insurance

HO–1	Fire, lightning, removal, windstorm, hail, explosion, riot, civil commotion, aircraft, vehicles, smoke, vandalism, malicious mischief, theft and window breakage.
HO–2	All of those for HO–1 plus falling objects; weight of ice or snow; collapse; bursting, cracking, burning, or bulging of a steam or water heating system, or of appliances for heating water; leakage or overflow of water from a plumbing, heating or air-conditioning system; freezing of plumbing, heating and air-conditioning systems and domestic appliances; injury to electrical appliances, devices, fixtures and wiring (excluding TV, radio tubes, and resistors) from short circuits or other accidentally generated currents.
HO–3	All those for HO–2 plus all risk on buildings except those excluded.
HO–4	All those for HO–2. Does not cover window breakage.
HO–5	All risks on building or personal property except those excluded.
HO–6	All those for HO–2; window breakage may be excluded.

damaged by fire when it is 50 years old. If the replacement cost of the home at the time of loss is $50,000, then actual cash value coverage will pay $50,000 less one-half this amount ($25,000 for depreciation). Thus the homeowner would be faced with having to replace a $50,000 home with only $25,000 of insurance money.

The issue of replacement cost is particularly important in a time of inflationary prices. In recent years, the replacement cost of homes has increased dramatically. As you can see from examining Exhibit 11–5, new home costs, which are a direct indication of how much replacement costs will be, have been rising at more than 10 percent per year in the period 1966–76. At this rate, the replacement cost of a home doubles every seven years!

To deal with the problem of replacement costs, insurers write replacement cost coverage in homeowner's policies *upon the condition* that the homeowner carry an amount of insurance equal to 80 percent of the replacement cost of the home.[2] This 80 percent clause in the contract is commonly referred to as the *coinsurance clause.*

Under the terms of the coinsurance clause, a homeowner recovers on losses according to the following formula:

$$\text{Loss Recovery} = \frac{\text{Amount of Insurance Carried}}{80\% \times \text{Replacement Value of Home at the Time of Loss}} \times \text{Loss.}$$

To show how this works, let's suppose that a homeowner takes out a homeowner's insurance policy that covers the dwelling for

[2] Replacement cost applies only to the home itself. Contents are valued at actual cash value.

EXHIBIT 11–5
Average annual price increases of key consumer items (1966–1976)

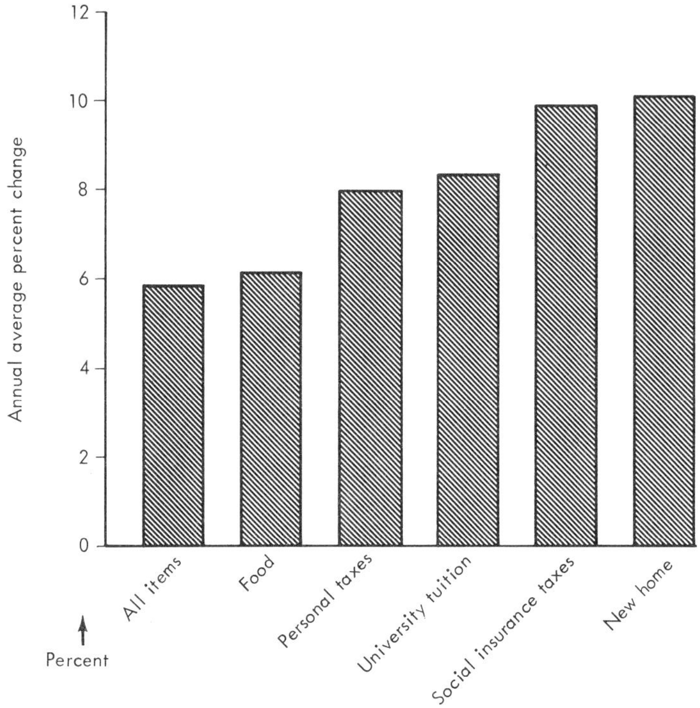

Data: Bureau of Labor Statistics, Commerce Dept., National Center for Education Statistics, MIT-Harvard Joint Center for Urban Studies, BW est.

\$30,000. Several years later, the home is damaged by fire to the amount of \$20,000. If the value of the home at the time of loss was \$50,000, the homeowner would recover as follows:

$$\text{Loss Recovery} = \frac{\$30{,}000}{80\% \times \$50{,}000} \times \$20{,}000$$
$$= \frac{\$30{,}000}{\$40{,}000} \times \$20{,}000$$
$$= \$15{,}000.$$

Because the homeowner did not carry an amount of insurance equal to 80 percent of replacement value, the full replacement value of the loss is not paid for. In this instance, the insurance company will pay \$15,000 and the homeowner will have to stand the other \$5,000.

The obvious problem facing homeowners is to determine what the replacement value will be at the time of loss. The homeowner can add an endorsement (explained more fully later in this chapter) that automatically increases the amount of insurance on the home each year. The rate of increase may vary by type of policy, so even with this inflation protection the consumer should periodically check the value of the home by watching sales of comparable homes or by having the home appraised.

One last provision usually found in the property coverage is a provision for a deductible on certain losses. For example, most homeowner's policies contain a minimum $50 or $100 deductible for wind damage. Thus, if an insured had a $50 deductible and suffered a $400 loss due to wind damage, the insurer would only pay $350, or the difference between the loss and the deductible.

For whatever reason, most consumers find the deductible to be a source of irritation and frequently criticize insurers for "not fully paying for losses." It should be understood that insurers could write policies that paid even the smallest loss. However, it should also be remembered that in settling any loss no matter how small, considerable cost must be incurred in processing the claim. Agents, claims adjusters, and others must be paid for their services. In the case of small claims, the cost of settling the claim may well exceed the amount of loss incurred. If consumers really want every loss covered, they must be willing to pay higher premiums to cover not only the loss but also the cost of settling the loss.

Medical payments. The purpose of the medical payments coverage is to pay medical expenses for persons who are accidentally injured by your activities or on your premises. The insurance coverage is restricted to "reasonable medical expenses" and the limits of coverage are usually quite modest—in the range of $500–$1,000.

The medical payments coverage provides you as a homeowner or renter with immediate coverage for injuries to guests without raising the question of legal liability. That is, guests may be injured through their own careless behavior for which you are not responsible; however, medical payments coverage allows payment for these injuries. This may maintain friendly relations between you and your guests and may also prevent long and unnecessary legal suits.

Personal liability. A second important coverage for most people is insurance for personal liability. Under terms of this coverage, the insurance company agrees to defend you at its own expense and to pay all amounts that you shall become legally obliged to pay for bodily injury or damage to property of others up to the limits of coverage. The liability coverage is extended to legal liability resulting from "an occurrence." Thus you are covered for almost any event (accidental or not) that results in bodily injury *or* property damage to someone else.

Personal liability coverage is extremely important to most homeowners and renters. Not only does it cover occurrences within your home or apartment, but it also provides coverage for most activities away from home. Common examples of coverage away from home might include situations where you might injure someone while hunting, camping, hiking, golfing, or simply walking down the street. The result of any of these occurrences might be an expensive lawsuit with devastating financial consequences. Thus you should recognize the value of personal liability coverage and should consider setting higher dollar limits than are contained in the standard homeowner's policy.[3]

Endorsements. Endorsements add flexibility to the standard homeowner's policy via additional coverages tailored to meet any special needs you may have. In many cases these needs may include insurance coverage for special types of property such as boats, cameras, coin collections, and works of art. In other cases an endorsement may add protection against other perils such as earthquake damage or the mysterious disappearance of property.

Exhibit 11–6 lists typical endorsements that you may wish to add to your policy. Where the endorsement provides you with additional coverage, there will of course be an additional premium charge.

An overview of the homeowner's policy

Exhibit 11–7 summarizes the coverages contained in a typical homeowner's policy. In most forms, coverage amounts for other structures, personal property, and additional living expenses are a percentage of the amount of insurance carried on the dwelling. You may wish to set higher insurance limits for personal property and other structures if the value of your personal property and other structures exceeds this standard amount.

AUTOMOBILE INSURANCE

One of the most obvious risks facing you arises from the ownership or use of an auto. Each year, motor vehicles driven by Americans cause over 40,000 deaths and five million injuries. The gross annual economic cost resulting from this peril amounts to over $20 billion.

---

[3] Most homeowner's policies have $25,000 of basic liability protection. In addition, the insurance company will pay for legal costs incurred in defending you in a lawsuit over and above this basic limit.

EXHIBIT 11–6
A summary of typical optional endorsements that may be added to homeowner's policies

Endorsement	*Coverage provided*
Watercraft	Covers liability exposures for boats over 50 horsepower, inboard-outboards, and sailing vessels over 26 feet. (Boats under 50 horsepower and under 26 feet are covered in most homeowner's policies.)
Farmers' comprehensive personal liability	Covers liability exposures arising from the course of normal farming activities.
Premises alarm system	Gives a discount to the insured who maintains a functioning fire or burglary alarm system.
Secondary residence premises	Adds a variety of basic coverages on cabins, cottages, or other property used as a secondary residence.
Scheduled personal property	Provides coverage for specifically listed property including jewelry, furs, cameras, musical instruments, silverware, golfer's equipment, works of art, postage stamps, and rare and current coins.
Earthquake damage assumption	Adds coverage for direct loss from earthquake and volcanic eruption in excess of a deductible amount (usually 2–5 percent of the property value).
Credit card forgery and depositor's forgery	Covers losses stemming from lost or stolen credit cards and loss resulting from forgeries on checking and savings accounts.
Inflation guard	Automatically increases insurance limits on dwellings by a predetermined annual percentage.
Theft coverage extension	Covers losses resulting from theft from an unlocked vehicle as well as mysterious disappearances of personal property.

The staggering toll of economic losses, coupled with numerous legal suits resulting from accidents, has caused major problems throughout the 1960s and 1970s. Soaring insurance costs and crowded court calendars have been a source of consumer irritation. As a result, laws regulating compensation for auto accident victims are in a state of confusion and change. Basically this problem arises from competing schools of thought, which may be labeled "no-fault" and "fault."

While labeling these schools of thought may be quite simple, explaining the difference between them is not. The fault system of compensation is deeply rooted in the common-law heritage of our legal system. Under this system, compensation to victims of auto accidents is determined on the basis of negligence. While laws of negligence do vary from state to state, one can generally say that the fault system compensates those who are innocent while denying compensation or damages to those who have been largely to blame for an accident. The heart of this fault system is the ability to sue another for wrongful or negligent acts. Thus litigation and the court system form the backbone of the fault system.

The no-fault system was conceived with the notions that the fault system failed to compensate all victims of auto accidents and that, when compensation was awarded to an auto accident victim, the compensation was neither timely nor equitable. No-fault seeks to cure these ills by doing away with most lawsuits and having auto victims compensated for their losses without regard to their degree of negligence or fault in an accident. The no-fault system also proposes to limit recovery to real economic losses such as loss of wages and salary, medical expenses, and other out-of-pocket costs and to eliminate payments for pain and suffering. Exhibit 11–8 summarizes several basic differences between the fault and no-fault systems.

Any discussion of auto insurance must take into account the process of change now evident in the auto insurance field. Because insurance laws vary significantly from state to state, consumers will find that some states have a form of a fault system while a good number of others will have a combination of a fault and no-fault system. As of late 1976, no state has adopted a pure no-fault system that prevents recovery by legal suit in cases involving serious injury or death.[4]

Reasons for buying auto insurance

The most obvious reasons for buying auto insurance are to protect you against liability suits and to insure the value of your car against loss caused by various perils. There are, however, other reasons for buying auto insurance. Individual state laws will frequently encourage or require that you purchase auto insurance as a condition of driving or as a condition of proving your financial responsibility. Some of the following state laws may be applicable to you.

Compulsory insurance. Twenty-two states have adopted compulsory insurance laws that require evidence of insurance prior to licensing. Even with this type of law, many motorists drive around unlicensed and uninsured.

Financial responsibility laws. Some state laws require that a motorist provide proof of financial responsibility (the ability to pay for damages) after an accident has occurred. The amount of proof required is set by state law, and it may be met by a cash deposit, a bond, or auto insurance. Failure to post financial responsibility may mean a

[4] At the end of 1976, 23 states had some form of no-fault insurance law combined with a fault law. Generally the no-fault coverages were restricted to cases where medical damages or economic loss was $5,000 or less.

EXHIBIT 11–7

A summary of property, liability, and peril coverage for homeowner's and renter's insurance

	HO–1	*HO–2*	*HO–3*	*HO–4*	*HO–5*	*HO–6**
Perils covered (see Key)	Perils 1–11	Perils 1–18	Perils 1–18 on personal property; all risks on buildings except those specifically excluded in policy	Perils 1–18	All risks on buildings and personal property except those specifically excluded in policy.	Perils 1–18 except 11
Minimum standard amounts of insurance on:						
House and attached structures	Based on value of property; minimum, $8,000	Based on value of property; minimum, $8,000	Based on value of property; minimum, $8,000	Renter not responsible for building insurance	Based on value of property; minimum, $15,000	Condominium association obtains building insurance
Other structures	10% of amount of insurance on house	10% of amount of insurance on house	10% of amount of insurance on house	No coverage	10% of amount of insurance on house	No coverage
Personal property on home premises	50% of insurance on house	50% of insurance on house	50% of insurance on house	Based on value of property; minimum, $4,000	50% of insurance on house	Based on value of property; minimum, $4,000

Additional living expense	10% of insurance on house	20% of insurance on house	20% of insurance on house	20% of insurance on personal property	20% of insurance on house	20% of insurance on personal property
Comprehensive personal liability—minimum	$25,000	$25,000	$25,000	$25,000	$25,000	$25,000
Damage to property of others	$250	$250	$250	$250	$250	$250
Medical payments	$500 per person up to $25,000 for each accident	$500 per person up to $25,000 for each accident	$500 per person up to $25,000 for each accident	$500 per person up to $25,000 for each accident	$500 per person up to $25,000 for each accident	$500 per person up to $25,000 for each accident

* The HO–6 policy shown in this summary is purchased by the condominium owner to protect his or her personal property and liability exposures. Coverage for the condominium owner's interest in the condominium building itself is usually purchased as a part of a group policy on which all condominium owners contribute a proportionate share of the premium.

Key to perils covered:

1. Fire, lightning
2. Damage to property removed from premises endangered by fire
3. Windstorm, hail
4. Explosion
5. Riots or civil commotion
6. Damage by aircraft
7. Damage by vehicles not owned and operated by people covered by policy
8. Damage from smoke
9. Vandalism, malicious mischief
10. Theft
11. Window breakage (including storm doors)
12. Falling objects
13. Weight of ice, snow, sleet
14. Collapse of building or any part of building
15. Bursting, cracking, burning, or bulging of a steam or water heating system, or of appliances for heating water
16. Leakage or overflow of water or steam from a plumbing, heating, or air-conditioning system
17. Freezing of plumbing, heating and air-conditioning systems, and domestic appliances
18. Injury to electrical appliances, devices, fixtures and wiring (excluding TV, radio tubes, and resistors) from short circuits or other accidentally generated currents

EXHIBIT 11–8
Summary of basic differences between fault and no-fault systems

Basic issue	*Fault*	*No-fault*
What is the basis of compensation to victims of auto accidents?	Based upon the concept of negligence. Basically the innocent may recover while the negligent must provide for themselves.	Based upon a loss sustained in an auto accident. Any such loss enables the victim to recover.
What can an accident victim recover in the form of damages?	Damages may include out-of-pocket costs, pain and suffering, and punitive damages. The latter is an assessment against a wrong-doer for gross misconduct.	Recovery is restricted to economic losses of past and future wages as well as other out-of-pocket costs such as medical expenses and rehabilitation costs.
How are accident cases settled under each system?	The victim must generally deal with the insurance company of the other party to the accident. Failing to reach satisfaction in negotiation, the victim must sue in court.	Victims deal with their own insurance company.
How do insurance and licensing relate under each system?	Generally, insurance is not a condition of licensing, but in most cases, after an accident, a driver must prove financial responsibility in order to continue driving.	Most no-fault laws require insurance as a prerequisite of licensing drivers.
How are benefits paid under each system?	Benefits are usually paid in a lump sum upon a negotiated settlement or following a legal judgment.	Benefits are paid periodically as expenses are incurred.

suspension of driving privileges or even the impoundment of your car until the matter is settled in court.

Unsatisfied judgment funds. Maryland, Michigan, New Jersey, New York, and North Dakota have unsatisfied judgment funds. In situations where an injured motorist cannot collect a judgment against a negligent person because that person has neither money nor insurance to satisfy the claim, the injured party may collect from the state fund within the limits prescribed by law. The party at fault is then indebted to the fund and his or her driving privileges are withheld until he or she can reimburse the fund.

Analyzing the auto insurance policy

The auto insurance policy analysis that follows is based on the premise that most states have automobile accident compensation systems built upon fault laws. In fact, all existing no-fault systems generally cover losses of $5,000 or less. Essentially, all serious auto accident cases are still settled under some form of fault system.

Auto insurance policies usually consist of four basic insurance coverages. These basic coverages include liability insurance, physical damage insurance, medical payments insurance, and uninsured motorist insurance. In most auto policies, liability insurance becomes the basic building block of the policy, and the other three coverages are added at the option of the insured.

In analyzing the auto insurance policy, most consumers will want to examine the following major portions of the policy:

Declaration page. This first page of the auto policy contains a basic summary of all insurance coverages and their costs. These coverages are expressed as maximum limits in thousands of dollars. Premium costs are usually displayed near the summary of coverages.

The declarations page also sets forth numerous basic facts concerning the insurance contract. These basic facts identify the insured and the autos covered by the insurance and include other facts that are essential to the insurance contract.

Liability insurance. The basic building block of most auto insurance coverages is liability insurance. Liability insurance is designed to pay for bodily injury and property damage to another person or persons for which you are legally responsible. For example, if you are responsible for an auto accident that causes property damage to someone's car and personal injury to the occupants of that car, liability insurance is designed to pay for these costs up to the limits of the insurance purchased.

In addition to the basic liability coverage, the liability portion of the auto contract provides the payment of legal defense costs for any suit against the insured. This legal defense is paid for by the insurance company and represents coverage over and above the basic limits of insurance involved.

One of the key problems in liability insurance coverage is the question of how much liability coverage is enough. While most state laws may have minimums such as $25,000 bodily injury coverage per person, $50,000 bodily injury coverage per accident, and $10,000 in property damage coverage (this is usually expressed as 25/50/10 coverage), these minimums may not be enough for all individuals. In light of recent trends toward increasing damage awards in our court systems, many insurance companies are suggesting a minimum coverage of $100,000, with higher limits for people who may have substantial wealth or who may be natural targets for law suits, such as lawyers and doctors.

Physical damage insurance. While liability insurance coverage is designed to pay other people for bodily injury or property damage you cause, there is an obvious need to cover your own property and person for similar events. Part of this need is met by physical damage insurance, which covers physical damage to your property. This insurance comes in the form of two coverages known as collision and comprehensive. Collision covers damage sustained by your car when it runs into another car or a stationary object such as a tree or utility pole. This coverage usually has a deductible such as $50 or $100.

Comprehensive coverage pays for physical damage caused by a variety of perils largely outside the control of the insured. Events such as theft, fire, and flood damage are covered by comprehensive physical damage insurance.

Medical payments insurance. Medical payments insurance will take care of the medical expenses of the insured or guests when injuries are sustained in an auto accident in the insured's car. This coverage also extends to pay medical expenses of you and your family for pedestrian accidents and for accidents in which you are a passenger in someone else's auto.

Medical payments coverage will typically pay for medical, surgical, X-ray, and dental services as well as ambulance, hospital, nursing, and funeral services. It should be remembered that these expenses must result from an auto accident and will be paid even if the insured's negligence has caused the accident.

Uninsured motorist insurance. Uninsured motorist coverage pays for bodily injury suffered by you or your passengers caused by another motorist who is uninsured or who is a hit-and-run driver. This coverage also extends to situations where you suffer bodily injury in a pedestrian accident involving an auto or when you are in someone else's auto. In effect, under this provision the insurance company pays for damages that normally would have been paid for by the liability insurance of the negligent motorist.

Uninsured motorist coverage will pay only for economic losses suffered by the insured. These out-of-pocket costs will generally include medical expenses and loss of wages, but will not include physical damages to your property or payment for pain and suffering.

Optional coverages. In addition to the four basic coverages available in an automobile insurance policy the insured may be able to add other types of coverages to fit personal needs. These optional coverages include towing and labor costs when the insured's auto is disabled and optional theft coverages designed to cover highly vulnerable property such as tape decks and citizen band radios.

Auto insurance packages

Most auto insurance is sold in the form of package insurance policies. Generally, the consumer will find two basic types of package policies, the family automobile policy (FAP) and the special package auto policy (SPAP).

The most common type of auto policy is the FAP. The FAP is built on basic liability coverage and allows you to pick and choose among the other insurance coverages. FAP liability limits are expressed in terms of the conventional coverage per person and per accident or occurrence. For example, an FAP with liability coverage of $100,000 per person with a total single accident limit of $300,000 would express this coverage as 100/300.

The SPAP is a more highly structured auto insurance policy. SPAP's require that you obtain liability, medical payment, and uninsured motorist coverages as a single package. Physical damage coverage is the only basic optional policy element.

The SPAP differs from the FAP in terms of basic liability coverages. Instead of setting up coverages such as 100/300/50 ($100,000 bodily injury per person, $300,000 maximum in any one event, $50,000 property damage coverage), the SPAP applies one limit to be divided as needed in an accident or occurrence. For example, under the SPAP, $300,000 liability coverage might pay for a $200,000 bodily injury loss to a single individual and property damage of $100,000 in the same accident. By contrast, 100/300/50 coverage in an FAP would only pay up to $100,000 per person for bodily injury and $50,000 property damage per occurrence. Thus one of the basic trade-offs in the policies would seem to be one of more flexibility in designing the policy (with an FAP) versus more flexibility in applying the limits of auto liability insurance coverage (with an SPAP).

Auto insurance premiums

The price of auto insurance is a frequent topic of conversation among consumers. In recent years, auto insurance premiums have risen faster than the overall rate of price increase. Part of that rise is caused by the rapid increase in the cost of repair parts and labor (see Chapter 7, Exhibit 7–13), which makes it increasingly expensive to repair an auto.

Auto insurance premiums vary according to a number of factors. For many people, age is a primary determinant of premium cost. By examining Exhibit 11–9, you can see why younger drivers pay more

EXHIBIT 11–9
Accidents by age

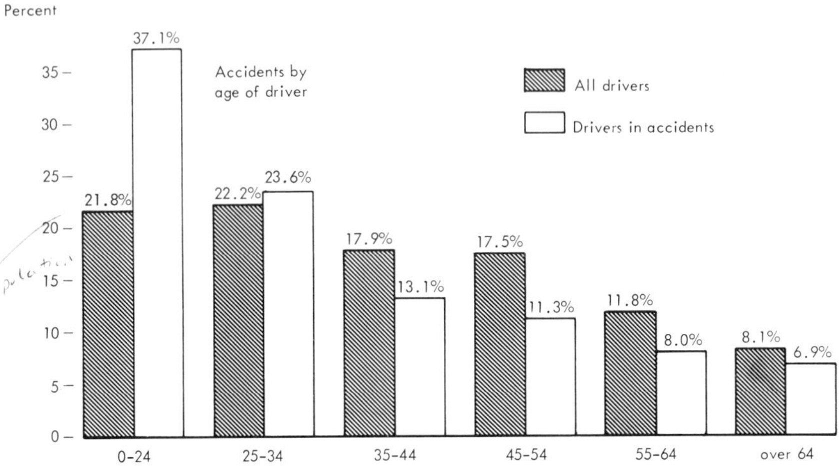

Source: Insurance Information Institute, *Insurance Facts*, 1976.

for auto insurance premiums. The fact is that younger drivers are involved in a greater proportion of all accidents than the proportion of their age group in the driving population. This higher claims cost is the primary cause of high auto insurance premiums for younger drivers.

Many other factors come into play in determining an auto insurance premium. For example, your driving experience and driving record are important. With regard to the latter, speeding tickets and auto accidents within three years of a premium renewal will contribute to higher rates. Other factors that affect the auto rate include:

1. Marital status.
2. Sex.
3. Distance driven to work.
4. Other drivers in a household.
5. Occupation.
6. Make, model, and age of auto.
7. Geographic factors (especially climate and urban density).

Your auto insurance rate reflects these major factors, and to some extent you can offset some of the premium by qualifying for certain discounts. For example, some companies offer discounts for drivers who are nonsmokers or nondrinkers.

Availability of auto insurance

There are many drivers who cannot get auto insurance because they are classified as "bad risks." Their bad risk rating usually results from a poor driving record, a prison record, a history of alcoholism, or some combination of age, make of car, and driving record. These people will generally find insurance unavailable or prohibitive in cost.

This lack of insurance availability can cause very serious problems. In states that have compulsory insurance or financial responsibility laws, a bad risk driver may have the option of not driving or of defying the law by driving without insurance. In the latter case, if he or she causes an accident, there is no insurance to cover the claims of injured parties.

Some states have attempted to solve this problem by establishing auto insurance plans, formerly called assigned risk plans. These plans require that all insurance companies who sell insurance in a state provide auto insurance coverage to high-risk drivers. Each company must take its share of the bad risks and the auto insurance plan acts as the clearinghouse by assigning the bad risks to each company. Motorists insured under this plan pay a considerable surcharge in addition to the regular auto insurance premium.

CHOOSING A PROPERTY AND LIABILITY INSURANCE COMPANY

For most of us, the decision to buy property and liability coverages is probably not a difficult one. However, once that initial decision is made, you must face the complex problem of choosing which insurance company will provide the best policy and service at the lowest cost. With over 1,500 reputable companies to choose from, the uninformed buyer may well make a costly mistake.

One of the primary bases of comparison of insurance policies will be premium cost. Assuming two policies are equal in terms of coverage and service, you may find significant differences in premium costs for auto and homeowner's policies. In fact, shopping around for insurance will reveal differences in premiums of more than 20 percent.

There are several reasons for these cost differences. For one thing, some companies may be highly selective of the people they insure. This selection process, which is termed *underwriting*, may mean that a company will choose only lower risk drivers or homeowners. By being selective, the insurance company's frequency of loss is likely to be lower than the average experience for all insureds; thus the premium charge to their insureds may be lower.

One variation of this selective underwriting theme is for a company to offer special policies designed around one underwriting factor. For example, while young drivers aged 16–24 constitute a higher-than-average auto insurance risk, some auto insurers recognized that certain groups of these young drivers are better-than-average risks. Actuaries point out that young drivers who are honor students are generally good risks. Thus, many companies have "good student" discounts on their auto policies with premium reductions of 10–15 percent for this particular group.

Costs are also lower if an insurance company has been able to reduce its cost of selling policies. Traditionally, property and liability insurance is sold through insurance agents. These agents may be employees of the company and sell only the company's lines of insurance. Such sellers are called exclusive agents.

Still other companies may sell through agents who handle many different insurance companies. These agents are known as independent insurers and may sell insurances from literally hundreds of companies. However, most independents will probably sell the bulk of insurance policies from a limited number of property and liability insurers.

Regardless of whether the insurance is purchased through an exclusive agent or independent agent, the agent must be paid for this service. In general, this cost may be 10–20 percent of the total premium paid, and in most cases the agent's commission on a premium will average close to 17 percent.

One way of cutting this cost is to sell insurance directly to the consumer. One popular form of direct sales is to sell through the mails. The direct mail insurer solicits sales by mailing advertising directly to the consumer. People who elect to purchase from the direct mailer fill in an application form and return it with the appropriate premium. This eliminates the sales costs of an agent and may result in lower premium rates to the insured.

While cost is clearly an important factor, the informed buyer should not buy on cost alone. The service provided by the insurance company and agent is an essential ingredient in helping you build an effective insurance program. Basically this service is provided in two parts.

First, at the time of purchase and renewal of the insurance, the agent and company should assist you in setting dollar limits on coverage, in adding or dropping coverages as personal situations change, and in general in setting up a well-rounded insurance program.

A second area of service involves problems and needs you may have at the time of a claim. You will want cooperation from the insurance company in quickly settling a claim or in providing prompt legal consultation in the case of a third-party suit. The willingness of the company to adjust all losses fairly will strongly influence your satisfaction with the insurance contract.

Although service is an important element, it cannot be compared as prices can—there are few highly reliable service ratings of property and liability insurers. While some data may be provided periodically by consumer groups and the various state insurance commissioners, you may well have to rely on personal experience and word-of-mouth recommendations in evaluating service.

Perhaps the easiest way for you to obtain some overview or general rating of a property liability insurer is to consult *Best's Key Rating Guide: Property-Liability,* which is available in most public libraries. The A. M. Best Company provides this service, which consists of a general policyholder rating and a technical financial rating for use by commercial and consumer purchasers of insurance. Exhibit 11–10 contains a summary of these ratings.

EXHIBIT 11–10
A summary of the rating system used by A. M. Best Co. for property and liability insurers

General policyholder ratings and their meaning		*Financial ratings*	
A+	Excellent	AAAAA	Highest rating
A	Excellent	AAAA+	
B+	Very good	AAAA	
B	Good	AAA+	
C+	Fairly good	AAA	
C	Fair	AA+	
		AA	
		BBBB+	
		BBBB	
		BBB+	
		BBB	
		BB+	
		BB	
		CCC	
		CC	Lowest rating

Source: *Best's Key Ratings: Property and Liability,* A. M. Best Co., New York.

You should look at the general policyholder rating as an overall measure or general index. These ratings are based upon an insurance company's performance in underwriting, economy of management, soundness of investments, and strength of insurance reserves.

SUMMARY

Homeowner's insurance provides a key way of protecting against property losses to the home and its contents and legal suits arising from a wide variety of occurrences. The homeowner's policy comes in six basic forms that fit most consumer situations. The policy can be expanded and modified to fit individual needs by adding endorsements to the basic package policy.

The successive components of the homeowner's policy should be viewed as building blocks. The declarations page expresses the basic facts about the insurance amount, the insured property, and premium rating information. This policy introduction usually concludes with a basic insuring agreement, which is a bare-bones statement of insurance protection against a very small number of risks.

From the declarations page on, the policy adds more coverages and essentially expands upon that basic insuring agreement. In particular, the property coverage and medical payments/personal liability sections greatly expand the types and amounts of coverage. Finally, you may add a wide variety of riders or endorsements that allow you to tailor protection to unique and individual circumstances.

With the homeowner's policy the typical consumer obtains most of the basic coverages needed to protect against loss of property and loss resulting from a liability suit. In all, the homeowner's insurance policy represents an essential element in any good risk management plan.

Auto insurance provides protection against liability risks stemming from auto ownership and also offers several forms of protection against physical damage to the auto. The four basic coverages of the auto insurance policy are liability insurance, medical payments coverage, uninsured motorist insurance, and physical damage insurance. Most auto policies come as package policies known as the Family Auto Policy (FAP) or the Special Package Auto Policy (SPAP). The premium for auto insurance is determined by a number of factors including the driver's age and driving record.

A number of state laws deal with auto insurance and the compensation of auto accident victims. A number of states have adopted a modified form of no-fault insurance that moves away from the negligence concept in paying for accident costs. Other states have adopted compulsory insurance laws and financial responsibility laws to protect consumers.

Because there are over 1,500 insurance companies that sell homeowner's and auto insurance, you have many options as to types of policies and costs. You should shop around for the best premium cost but should also be aware that the service provided by the company and the coverage afforded in the policy are crucial elements in purchasing these insurances.

DISCUSSION QUESTIONS

1. Outline the basic differences between a "no-fault" and a "fault" system for settling auto accidents. What is the status of no-fault auto insurance in your state?
2. A typical complaint of many consumers is that auto insurance rates are very high and the majority of people who are not involved in auto accidents feel that they "never get anything back for all the money paid in." Analyze this attitude. Is it consistent with the insurance principle of indemnification? Explain.
3. In the homeowner's policy, personal liability coverage is designed to cover lawsuits arising out of "occurrences," while the medical payments liability is designed to cover losses arising out of "accidents." Explain the difference between insurance coverage based on accidents and that based on occurrences.
4. The homeowner's insurance policy is said to be a packaged insurance policy. Explain this. What different types of insurance do you find written within the homeowner's package?
5. Explain the concept of an endorsement on an insurance policy. What types of endorsements may be written on a homeowner's policy and what general purpose do endorsements serve?
6. Indicate some ways by which you may be able to differentiate between the thousands of property and liability insurers.
7. Explain the four major coverages in a typical auto insurance policy.
8. What are the primary factors that determine an individual's auto insurance premium?

CASE PROBLEM

In Chapter 10, we presented a case problem that used the household profiles of Jane Justin and of Harold and Emily Richland. Briefly review those profiles before continuing with this case. With the facts you now have, what auto insurance coverages would you recommend for Jane and the Richlands? Would you recommend collision and comprehensive coverage for each household? A very important issue for every consumer who needs auto insurance is determining the appropriate limits of liability.

Based on the Justin and Richland profiles, how much liability coverage should each carry? Explain how you determined these limits.

SELECTED READINGS

Automobile Insurance . . . For Whose Benefit? New York: State of New York Insurance Department, 1970.

Bickelhaupt, David L. *General Insurance,* 9th ed. Homewood, Ill.: Richard D. Irwin, Inc., 1974, chaps. 22 and 23.

Greene, Mark R. *Risk and Insurance,* 4th ed. Cincinnati: South-Western Publishing Company, 1977, chaps. 10 and 16.

Life, health, and disability insurance

12

OBJECTIVES

This chapter identifies the basic personal risks facing consumers and shows how life, health, and disability insurance can be used to manage these risks. After thoroughly reading and discussing this chapter you should be able to:

. . . Identify and list the major personal risks and their potential financial impact.

. . . Explain the two basic forms of life insurance and the significant contract provisions of a typical life insurance policy.

. . . Calculate the cost of life insurance using both the interest adjusted and the net cost methods.

. . . Identify the basic Social Security benefits paid to survivors and show how they integrate with life insurance needs.

. . . Identify the primary sources of disability compensation and the importance of the definition of disability in the disability insurance contract.

. . . Explain both basic medical expense insurance and major medical insurance as well as other sources of health insurance coverage.

Industrialization and increased personal mobility have brought great changes in our economic and social system. One of these changes has been a gradual breaking down of the family and community bonds that had served as important sources of security to individuals. In the past, by providing financial assistance or contributions, the family and community have acted as financial backstops when disaster struck. Many of these traditions are still carried on in rural areas and small towns. For example, it is not unusual for farmers in an area to join to help harvest the crops of a stricken neighbor or to rebuild a barn destroyed by fire.

But a move from the less-populated areas into the urban setting is likely to be marked by a change to an impersonal atmosphere where community bonds are not as strong. In urban settings, individuals and families must become more self-reliant by providing their own means of security from personal risks. In order to deal with some risks, the federal government has created programs such as Social Security, unemployment insurance, and worker's compensation programs. However, these programs do not apply to everyone, and the compensation they provide may prove minimal for those with high-paying jobs or large debts. As a consequence, almost everyone is in need of additional risk management tools such as health and life insurance.

You are faced with the rather complex task of fitting private and social insurances together to form a sensible yet economical plan for financial security. The answer to this problem lies in developing an individually tailored program that recognizes your unique problems and risks.

WHAT CAN HAPPEN?

The question of financial security can be approached by simply asking yourself, "What events can happen *to me* (or my family) that pose a threat to my financial security?" This question should force you to assess both your risks and your financial needs. Setting aside the prospect of damage to property (which was examined in the previous chapter), this analysis focuses attention on the things that might affect your life or health and thus cause financial problems.

The first and most easily recognized risk involves the potential loss of life. The risk of **death** looms as an inevitable event in everyone's mind, but most of us are not sure when that event may strike. Whenever it does occur, death poses a threat to financial security, especially for a family. The death of either spouse may mean a loss of basic income needed to feed, shelter, and clothe a family. It may also mean the loss of valuable services including child rearing, cooking, cleaning, gardening, and maintaining the family home. Such losses of income and services place a financial burden on any family unit; thus, the potentially severe impact of the risk of death must be recognized and managed to assure financial security.

Illness is another risk that we must plan for. When illness is of a short-term nature, the effect on the individual or family may be quite slight. Expenses for hospitalization, medication, and temporary loss of income or services may or may not seriously disrupt the normal pattern of living. But major or longer term illnesses, such as heart disease or cancer, may prove to be quite costly and burdensome. With the high cost of surgery, special care facilities, and complex medical treatments, the daily cost of medical care for major illnesses may be several hundred dollars per day. In addition to these out-of-pocket expenses, a major illness may mean a serious disruption of a career or even make a radical change in careers necessary. Major illnesses can result in a significant decline in income and may also deprive the individual or the family of vital personal services, some of which may have to be provided by someone hired at market wage rates.

Loss of income through illness may also be considered part of a larger personal risk: the chance that **disability** may occur. Disability may be caused by illness or accident and may result in a temporary or permanent condition that prevents or restricts a person's ability to provide income or services. For example, a heart attack suffered by a housewife may restrict her ability to manage the household. Such a condition could be temporary; she might be able to resume her duties after a few months. Were the attack quite severe, however, she might never be able to perform any household duties or she might be able to perform only a portion of her previous tasks. The loss to her family would include the loss of her services and perhaps some long-term special care costs that she might require, such as therapy or rehabilitation services.

Another type of personal risk that hits directly at an individual's personal financial security is **unemployment.** Unemployment usually results from general economic conditions such as recessions, strikes, or shortages—factors over which individuals have no control. Other causes of unemployment may include lack of education and training or similar conditions that an individual might be able to control. Whatever the cause of unemployment, the individual and the family may have to cope with a temporary or extended loss of income.

A fifth category of personal risk is that associated with **old age.** Probably the most serious risk involved with old age is the possibility that individuals may outlive their financial resources. Such an eventuality may then lead to a decline in standard of living and financial independence. With increased medical expenses, generally fixed incomes, and reduced opportunities to earn incomes, the elderly are often confronted with serious challenges to their financial security.

While there are other personal risks that some individuals may face, the five risks we have just covered constitute the normal inventory of significant risks that most people must deal with. Exhibit 12–1 provides a convenient summary and review of these important threats to financial security and their potential impact.

EXHIBIT 12–1
An inventory of personal risks

General category of personal risk	*Types of perils*	*Potential financial impact or loss to individuals or families*
Death	Disease; accident; manmade perils such as wars and homicide; natural perils such as floods, tornadoes, earthquakes, etc.	Total loss of income and/or personal services of the deceased.
Disability	Job-related injuries; household accidents; auto accidents; illness; disease.	Partial or total loss of income and/or personal services; rehabilitation or retraining cost; special care or devices needed to equip home or auto.
Illness	Heart and circulatory ailments; cancer; contagious diseases.	Out-of-pocket medical costs for doctor, hospital and medication; temporary loss of income and personal services.
Unemployment	Recession or depression; strike; shortages; job obsolescence; lack of training or education.	Loss of income and job-related benefits such as pension and health plans.
Old age	Poverty caused by increased medical expenses; inflationary erosion of fixed incomes; forced retirement.	Dissipation of financial resources; reduction in the general standard of living.

Because these personal risks have potentially large financial consequences, you must seriously consider ways of insuring against or otherwise lessening their impact. The problem of organizing such a plan is complicated by the fact that there are many uncoordinated sources of personal risk protection. Social insurances provided by the government, health and disability insurances provided by employers, and your own personal insurance purchases are piecemeal sources of protection. The challenge is to organize a plan that analyzes and coordinates these coverages into a workable plan of protection.

To accomplish this task, you need a working knowledge of the primary tools available. In the remainder of this chapter, we are going to discuss the tools needed to cope with the three major personal risks of death, disability, and illness.

DEALING WITH PERSONAL RISKS: THE PRIMARY TOOLS

LIFE INSURANCE

Life insurance is a financial contract under which you pay premiums to an insurance company, which in turn promises to pay out a specific sum of money upon your death. The insurance company determines its cost or premium for life insurance according to a number of key factors. The most important factor in this calculation is the death or mortality experience that the company projects it will have. For example, suppose the company insures 1,000 females, age 33, for $1,000 each; life insurance actuarial tables based on past years of statistics show that two of these women would die by the end of the policy year. Thus the company would have to pay out $2,000 in death benefits by the end of the year.

In addition to paying for death benefits, the company will also have to add certain costs to the premium amount. For example, the company pays a commission to agents who sell its insurance policies. It will also have to pay costs of issuing insurance policies such as the cost of setting up records or the cost of medical examinations that are used to determine the insurability of its customers. Further costs are added by expenses incurred in running the insurance company and by contributions to the company's profit or surplus account.

A key part of the insurance contract is the ownership and beneficiary arrangement. In all life insurance contracts, there is a designation for the *insured*, the *owner*, and the *beneficiary*. The insured is the person whose life is insured against the peril of death. The owner is the person who pays the policy premium. The beneficiary is the person who receives the payment of the death benefit when the insured dies. In a life contract, there could be three different and distinct parties (insured, owner, beneficiary) or one individual could occupy all three roles. In the typical life insurance policy the owner and the insured are the same person. Where the insured is the beneficiary, the death benefit is paid to the insured's estate. In any case, the owner has all rights to the policy and its cash value and only the owner can designate or change the beneficiary.

It is important to distinguish between two basic types of life insurance. The first type, called *term* insurance, is sometimes described as pure death insurance. Term insurance pays only in the event of death and is written for a specific period of time, such as one, five, or ten years; and at the end of that period the insurance protection expires. It might be said that those policyholders who are living at the end of the insurance period have "won" because their beneficiaries did not collect on the insurance. For those who die during the period of protection, a death benefit is paid to their beneficiaries, who thus receive financial compensation for losses resulting from the death of the insured.

The second basic form of life insurance is called *cash value* insurance. Cash value insurance is designed to provide long-term permanent life insurance protection.

A second distinguishing feature of cash value insurance is that it combines death protection with an accumulating cash savings value, which the policyholder may claim at any time during the life of the policy. The cash value accumulates at modest (2½–3½ percent) but guaranteed rates of interest specified in the life insurance contract and it continues to accumulate over the life of the insurance policy.

In addition to providing the insured with a savings or investment element, the cash value policy is also designed to give longer-term insurance protection. If individuals could only buy one-year term policies, the cost of insurance would rise with the mortality curve (see Chapter 10, Exhibit 10–2). As the death rate increased with age, the price of insurance would soar. By contrast, with cash value insurance, the net amount of pure life insurance decreases as the investment element grows. As Exhibit 12–2 indicates, the investment element provides an increasing amount of protection to offset the higher risk of death at later ages in the life of the policyholder.

Insurance companies have sold dozens of variations of term and

EXHIBIT 12–2
Coverage elements contained in a $10,000 cash value insurance policy*

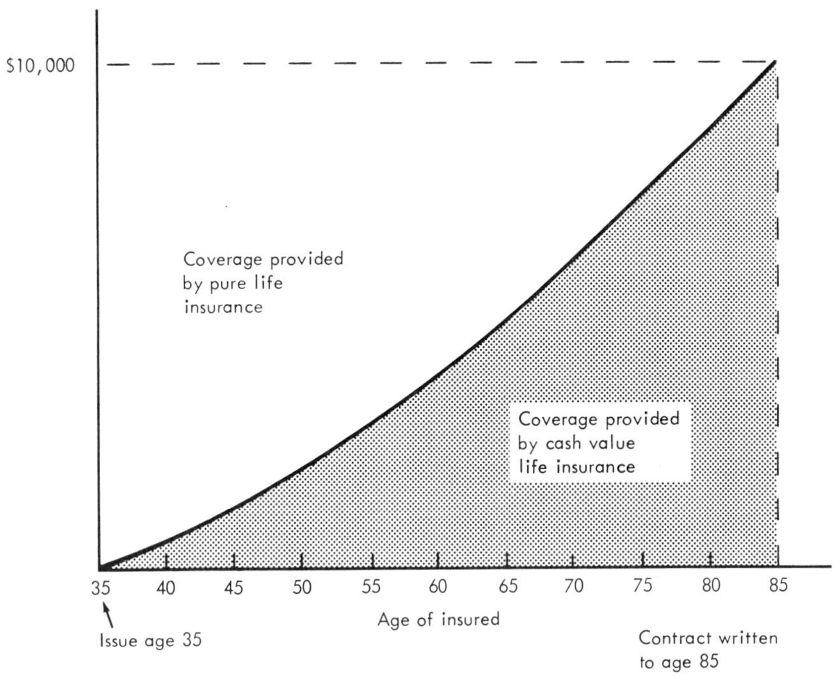

* The exhibit approximates the cash value and pure protection elements in a typical whole life policy issued to a 35-year-old person.

cash value policies. These policies frequently are given different names by different companies. This product proliferation leads to a good deal of confusion on the part of the typical consumer. To clarify this situation, Exhibit 12–3 briefly describes common varieties of each type of contract.

EXHIBIT 12–3
Common types of term and cash value insurance

	Provisions
Term policies	
One-, five-, or ten-year level term	A constant or level amount of life insurance such as $10,000 for the stated policy period. Most level term policies are renewable at the end of the stated period (at a higher premium rate) in which case the policy is usually called a renewable term insurance.
One-, five-, ten-, or twenty-year decreasing term	An amount of life insurance protection which steadily declines over the term of the policy. This type of policy is frequently sold as insurance on a home mortgage because the decline in the outstanding mortgage is matched by a decline in insurance coverage.
Five- or ten-year convertible term	Starts out as a pure or term life policy but provides for a possible conversion of the policy into some form of cash value insurance. This conversion is accomplished without the need of a medical exam or other proof of insurability.
Group term	Life insurance protection for a group of individuals who usually have some common bond in profession or place of employment. Such insurance is written on the group as a whole without considering the individual insurability of each member of the group. Group life insurance is frequently a fringe benefit of employment.
Cash value policies	
Whole or straight life	The most common type of cash value insurance. It combines a slowly rising cash value with a constant amount of insurance protection and a consistent premium over the life of the policy. Most whole life policies are written to mature at advanced ages such as 85, 90, or 100.
Limited payment policies	Have a higher premium than a similar amount of insurance because they provide a faster accumulation of cash values. The faster growth in investment allows an individual to stop paying premiums at an earlier date. Typical limited payment policies provide for 20 years of premium payments or insurance which is paid up at a specified age such as 65.
Endowment insurance	A combination of death protection along with a rapid growth in the cash value investment are the essential elements of an endowment policy. Endowment policies are generally written for periods of 10 or 20 years and at the end of the policy period the cash value of the investment equals the death benefit in the policy. Endowment insurance has very high premium payments in order to provide for the rapid build-up in cash value.

EXHIBIT 12–3 *(continued)*

	Provisions
Cash value policies	
Graduated premium life	Sold under many trade names, but their common element is a low initial premium with gradual increases to a higher premium level in the early years of the policy. This type of policy is generally marketed to younger people because it is tailored to fit the budgets of young, growing families whose incomes will rise substantially as they get experience in the work force.
Combination term and cash value policies	
Family plan	While these policies may be sold under a variety of trade names, they are built on essentially the same principle. The family plan provides a base cash value policy on one of the spouses, with additional smaller amounts of term insurance on the other spouse and the children. Thus the family plan provides protection for all members of the family unit.

Cash value versus term insurance

A key decision in providing life insurance is whether to buy term insurance or cash value insurance. There has been a steady debate for many years over the merits of each. The proponents of cash value insurance claim that it forces the consumer to save and provides "permanent" protection in the sense that the cost of life insurance is level over the life of the policyholder. The proponents of term insurance advocate "buying term insurance and investing the difference." That is, buy term life coverage and use the money you would have invested in cash value insurance to buy higher return investments such as common stock.

The issues and questions raised in this debate are likely to be with us for years to come. It is almost impossible to accurately measure whether buying term and investing the difference is really better than buying cash value. It is also difficult to predict the need for permanent protection as you get older because of the likely changes in your family situation.

We tend to think that the answer lies somewhere in the middle. At younger ages, when there are family obligations, buying substantial amounts of term insurance may be the only way a young family can buy enough insurance protection. Also term insurance makes sense for those financial obligations such as mortgages, which are likely to diminish or disappear over time.

On the other hand, cash value insurance may be a sensible investment for those who can't save or who simply have no skill in investing funds. There is also a good case to be made for having some permanent insurance to pay final expenses and estate taxes.

Endorsements, clauses, and options

The life insurance contract, like any other insurance contract, is a legal document. It contains legal and technical provisions that many people may not understand. While it is probably not essential to know all the contract elements in a life insurance policy, several items are important.

A number of endorsements can be added to the life policy. Two of the more important endorsements are *waiver of premium* and *guaranteed insurability*. The waiver of premium endorsement provides that the life insurance company will pay for the life insurance premium if you become disabled. This provides a convenient form of protection for the continuation of vital life insurance coverage during periods when your income may be disrupted by disability. The cost of this coverage is quite modest and generally is less than $1 per year per $1,000 of life insurance.

An endorsement of special interest to younger people is the guaranteed insurability clause. It allows the policyholder to pay a premium to insure that additional amounts of insurance may be available at set future dates. This means that younger consumers without the necessary funds to purchase their total life insurance requirements can at least guarantee that future insurance will be available without having to pass a medical exam or other test of insurability. This feature is more expensive than waiver of premium (generally two to three times as much), but the cost can be justified in many situations, such as unfavorable family medical history or if other factors such as high blood pressure or weight problems might prevent an individual from obtaining life insurance protection.

A third type of endorsement that an insured might wish to obtain is a *double (or triple) indemnity* clause. This provides for paying two or three times the face value of the policy if the insured is killed accidentally. For example, with a $10,000 policy and a triple indemnity clause, if the insured were killed accidentally the beneficiary of the life insurance policy would receive a $30,000 (3 × $10,000) death benefit. The indemnity clause operates only when an individual dies accidentally. While the risk of accidental death is higher at younger ages, accidents account for about five percent of all deaths.

While the endorsements are generally important additions to the basic contract, there are several elements within the contract itself that should be of particular interest to you. In cash value contracts, you have certain rights within the *nonforfeiture value clause* and the *loan provision clause*. These clauses protect your investment in the cash value contract and offer the insured the following options:

1. *Policy loan*—The insured may borrow money up to the cash value of the policy but continue the insurance contract by paying the normal premium and an interest charge on the policy loan. The interest charge on the policy loan may vary from five to six percent on older policies to eight percent on some newer policies. The insured may repay the policy loan or may simply keep the loan outstanding until the policy expires or the insured dies. In the case of the death of the insured, the policy loan amount is deducted from the total death benefit.
2. *Cash surrender*—The insured at any time may surrender the contract to the company and take a lump sum payment equal to the policy's cash value. The surrender terminates insurance coverage and the contract itself.
3. *Extended term insurance*—The insured may convert the cash value policy into a term life insurance policy. This conversion uses the cash value as the premium payment needed to buy pure death protection in an amount equal to the death benefit in the cash value policy. For example, a typical $10,000 whole life policy on a male, age 24, would have a cash value of $1,090 after ten years. This $1,090 will buy $10,000 of term insurance coverage for about 25 years.
4. *Reduced paid-up insurance*—The cash value may be used to buy paid-up cash value insurance in a reduced amount. Drawing upon the $10,000 policy used in the previous example, at the end of ten years the insured may elect to use the $1,090 cash value to buy $3,080 of paid-up life insurance. This new policy will have a cash value that will continue to grow, and it will not require any additional premium payments.

Yet another feature that may be of some importance in the policy is the *settlement option clause.* This clause offers the owner or the beneficiary (if the owner does not designate a choice) several alternative ways of receiving the death benefit. The following are typical settlement options available in most life insurance policies:

1. *Interest option*—The death benefit is left on deposit with the life insurance company, which in turn pays the monthly interest on the deposit to the beneficiary. The beneficiary, however, may withdraw all or part of the deposit at any time.
2. *Installment option*—The death proceeds are paid to the beneficiary either in equal monthly payments until the death proceeds are exhausted or in equal payments for a specific period of time.

In both cases, the insurance company manages the funds for the duration of the payout.

3. *Life income option*—Quite similar to the installment option except that payments continue for a certain period of time such as ten years. If the beneficiary dies before the end of the ten-year period, the company must continue to pay benefits to the beneficiary's heirs for the duration of the ten-year period. If the beneficiary lives beyond the ten-year certain period, the company will continue to pay over the entire life of the beneficiary.
4. *Life annuity option*—Similar to the life income option except it does not promise any certain period of payments. Thus, the annuity provides a stream of payments that terminates when the beneficiary dies. If a 60-year-old beneficiary started receiving payments in one month and died unexpectedly the next month, no other payment would be made to his or her survivors. On the other hand, if the beneficiary lived to be 150 years old, the insurance company would have to continue to pay even though that person had lived far beyond his or her expected life.

One last important provision of life insurance involves whether or not the policy has a *dividend provision.* A dividend is a payment made by the insurance company to the policyholder. It comes about if the insurance company has a surplus or profit on its business at the end of a policy year. Many critics of life insurance say that dividends are merely a result of the insurance company overcharging on its premiums. Others contend that dividends result from efficient operation of the company. For the most part, dividends are associated with cash value policies, although a few companies will pay dividends on term insurance.

The dividend provision is not automatically included in the policies of all companies. Some companies issue only *nonparticipating* policies, which do not pay dividends, while others offer dividend participation on some or all of their policies.

One other aspect of policy dividends that should be recognized is the way in which the policyholder may use dividends. In almost all cash value policies, the policyholder may take the dividend as a cash payment, leave the dividend with the insurance company as a deposit which draws interest, apply the dividend to offset the annual premium on the policy, or use the dividend to buy additional insurance coverage. This latter option usually allows the insured to buy small amounts of paid-up life insurance and in many companies, it allows the insured to buy substantial amounts of pure death protection in the form of one-year term insurance additions.

The cost of life insurance

The cost of life insurance has been a subject of debate over the last decade. As different methods of evaluating the true cost of life insurance have been developed, considerable attention has been focused on the significant differences in cost among life insurance policies. These cost differentials should provide an incentive for you to find out about sources of cost information and methods of comparing cost.

One method of comparing cost is the *net cost approach*. The price of a life insurance contract over a twenty-year period under this method is calculated as follows:

Total premiums paid over 20 years
− Total dividends received over 20 years
− Cash value in the 20th year
= Net cost for 20 years

As an example, we can calculate the cost of a $10,000 policy that has an annual premium of $150, a projected cash value of $2,000 at the end of twenty years, and projected total dividends of $500 over twenty years. With this information, which you can get from the insurance company or its agent, the twenty-year net cost determination would be as follows:

$3,000 ($150 annual premium × 20 payments)
− 500 (total dividends received over 20 years)
− 2,000 (cash value, which the policyholder could take out in the 20th year)
= $ 500 (the policy's net cost over 20 years)

While the net cost approach gives a reasonably good approximation of cost, several other measures have been developed that generally give a better cost index for insurance policies. These methods, which can be labeled the *interest adjusted approach*, take account of the time value of the amount of money that the policyholder has tied up in this contract. This approach recognizes that in a cash value policy the policyholder ties up money that could have been invested in other sorts of investments.

To illustrate this approach, we can draw upon the policy used in the net cost illustration. In this case, the policyholder is tying up $150 a year over twenty years. Part of this money could be used to purchase term insurance (which would be much cheaper at early ages), and the difference could be invested in the stock market or perhaps in government bonds. Thus the policyholder is giving up the possibility of investing that money in other places by committing it to life insurance premiums. On the other hand, the policyholder is, in most cases, receiving annual dividends for the life policy, which can in turn be invested. By making both of these interest adjustments, we come up with one form of the interest adjusted method of cost comparison. If we assume that five percent represents the true cost or return for money, the general interest adjusted formula would be:

Total premiums paid accumulated at 5 percent
− Total dividends received accumulated at 5 percent
− Cash value in the 20th year
= Interest adjusted cost.

Drawing upon the policy we used in the previous example, the 20-year interest adjusted cost for this policy would be:

	$5,207.89	($150 annual premium invested for 20 years at 5 percent)
−	867.98	(annual dividends invested at 5 percent)
−	2,000.00	(the cash value in the 20th year)
=	$2,339.91	(interest adjusted cost).

In our example, the interest adjusted cost is much higher than the net cost approach. Many authorities in the insurance field feel that the interest adjustment gives a truer picture of the cost of life insurance.[1]

While the merits of each approach will be debated for some years, it is clear that you should be very concerned about obtaining some form of price comparison. Many states including Pennsylvania and Wisconsin have provided cost comparison data or have required insurance companies to furnish such comparisons upon request of the prospective buyer. Lacking these opportunities, you can turn to *Best's Life and Health Edition, Consumer Reports,* or similar sources that periodically update insurance cost information.

Planning for life insurance

One of the most perplexing problems posed by consumers is, "How much life insurance do I need?" The answer to this question is sometimes dismissed by giving a general rule of thumb such as: total life insurance should equal five times your income. Perhaps this type of generalization provides some guidance, but it fails to take into account the vast differences in individual situations.

[1] See for example Joseph M. Belth, *Life Insurance: A Consumer's Handbook* (Bloomington, Indiana: Indiana University Press, 1973).

A more effective approach to life insurance planning involves a determination of financial requirements in the case of death and an assessment of life insurance needs in the light of those requirements. The initial stage of this process requires that individuals and families give serious consideration to the financial consequences of a family member's death. For example, a family would be faced with burial expenses, estate taxes, debt payments, and other income and service needs. Calculating these financial requirements will necessitate some time and research, but the end result will reflect a family's unique situation and will give a dollar measure of family needs.

The second stage of the planning process is to compare the total financial needs with the existing sources that might meet those needs. Suppose for example that a spouse dies and the surviving family members would need $20,000 to settle all debts and expenses and $1,000 a month income to provide for continuing living expenses. Where might the family get the money to fill these needs?

Family assets might be one source of money. Savings and investments and a family home might be sold to raise the needed cash. In most cases, however, the family assets would provide only part of the total required needs.

Social Security payments might also provide income to the survivors, *if* the spouse had worked in a job covered by Social Security. Social Security, which is properly entitled Old Age, Survivors, Disability and Health Insurance (OASDHI), is a mandatory social insurance program that is run by the United States government. The Social Security law covers virtually all non-federal employees and is funded by a payroll tax levied on an employee's earnings with taxes being paid by both employer and employee.

The survivor's benefits paid under Social Security provide income to a spouse caring for minor children, to surviving minor children under the age of 18, to surviving children 18–22 who are pursuing an education, and to the surviving spouse in the retirement years. The size of the payments reaches its maximum in a family with a surviving spouse and two or more children.

Survivor's benefits paid under Social Security are based not only on family size, but more importantly on the deceased spouse or parent's average income subject to the Social Security tax. The amount of benefits paid to survivors under Social Security can be quite substantial; Exhibit 12–4 should give you some idea of the range of these benefits.

The importance of Social Security in planning for life insurance needs cannot be overemphasized. Financial planners have begun to recognize the extent of Social Security benefits and have developed

EXHIBIT 12–4
Selected monthly benefits for survivors under OASDHI (1977)

Average yearly earnings	Retirement benefit to surviving spouse, age				Benefit to surviving child	Benefit to spouse and 1 child	Maximum family benefits
	65	64	63	62			
$923 or less	$ 57.20	$ 52.50	$ 47.70	$ 42.90	$114.30	$171.50	$171.50
1,200	73.60	67.50	61.40	55.20	147.10	220.70	220.70
2,600	108.00	99.00	90.00	81.00	216.00	324.00	324.00
3,000	118.20	108.40	98.50	88.70	236.40	354.60	361.40
3,400	126.80	116.30	105.70	95.10	253.50	380.30	408.30
4,000	139.10	127.60	116.00	104.40	278.10	417.20	475.30
4,400	149.00	136.60	124.20	111.80	297.90	446.90	528.10
4,800	157.70	144.60	131.50	118.30	315.40	473.10	575.30
5,200	165.80	152.00	138.20	124.40	331.60	497.40	622.20
5,600	174.00	159.50	145.00	130.50	347.90	521.90	645.10
6,000	182.30	167.20	152.00	136.80	364.50	547.00	668.60
6,400	190.40	174.60	158.70	142.80	380.80	571.20	692.10
6,800	199.10	182.60	166.00	149.40	398.20	597.30	715.70
7,200	209.40	192.00	174.50	157.10	418.70	628.10	740.70
7,600	218.60	200.40	182.20	164.00	437.10	655.70	764.90
8,000	226.60	207.80	188.90	170.00	453.10	679.70	792.90
8,400	231.40	212.20	192.90	173.60	462.80	694.20	809.90
8,800	237.10	217.40	197.60	177.90	474.20	711.30	829.80
9,200	242.30	222.20	202.00	181.80	484.50	726.80	847.80
9,400	244.30	224.00	203.60	183.60	488.60	732.90	854.80
9,600	246.30	225.80	205.30	184.80	492.50	738.80	861.90
9,800	249.00	228.30	207.50	186.80	498.00	747.00	871.30
10,000	251.00	230.10	209.20	188.30	502.00	753.00	878.50

Source: "Your Social Security" (Washington, D.C.: U.S. Social Security Administration, 1977).

some techniques for integrating life insurance needs with Social Security benefits. Exhibit 12–5, which is drawn from material developed by First National City Bank of New York, details one approach. According to these figures, if the spouse is age 25 and the surviving fam-

EXHIBIT 12–5
The multiples-of-salary chart

Your present gross earnings	Present age of spouse							
	25 years		35 years		45 years		55 years	
	75%	60%	75%	60%	75%	60%	75%	60%
$7,500	4.0	3.0	5.5	4.0	7.5	5.5	6.5	4.5
9,000	4.0	3.0	5.5	4.0	7.5	5.5	6.5	4.5
15,000	4.5	3.0	6.5	4.5	8.0	6.0	7.0	5.5
23,500	6.5	4.5	8.0	5.5	8.5	6.5	7.5	5.5
30,000	7.5	5.0	8.0	6.0	8.5	6.5	7.0	5.5
40,000	7.5	5.0	8.0	6.0	8.0	6.0	7.0	5.5
65,000	7.5	5.5	7.5	6.0	7.5	6.0	6.5	5.0

Source: Citibank, *Consumer Views*, July, 1976.

ily members will need 75 percent of the present gross earnings, then the needed insurance coverage as a multiple of income is shown in the lefthand column of the table. For example, to replace 75 percent of $15,000 (taking into account OASDHI payments to survivors) the insurance needed is 4.5 times $15,000, or $67,500. To replace 60 percent of present gross income, the insurance needed is three times income, or $45,000.

The end product of planning for life insurance needs should be to evaluate the income needs of a household and then to inventory the current sources of income that would be available. This process should point up any gaps in coverage and may signal the need to buy additional life insurance.

DISABILITY INSURANCE

One of the most underrated risks that consumers must manage is that of disability. In the insurance planning process, it is often relegated to last place.

Given the serious nature and potential fiscal losses of the disability risk, it is important to enumerate the sources and types of disability coverage. For purposes of our discussion, we will consider disability insurance as being primarily focused upon replacing or maintaining your stream of income. In this way we can differentiate between disability coverages and health and sickness insurances, with the latter being primarily concerned with paying direct medical expenses.

Sources of disability coverage

There are several basic sources of disability coverage that should be considered in managing the risk of disability. A brief description of each follows.

Social Security. Social Security provides disability benefits for millions of workers who belong to the OASDHI program. To qualify for benefits, the worker must have met the minimum period of coverage set forth under the law.

Most individuals who must contribute to Social Security will qualify for disability benefits. These benefits are monthly income payments that are made *only if the worker is totally disabled.* The maximum benefit now payable to a worker and his or her family is over $1,000 a month. Exhibit 12–6 illustrates benefit levels that prevailed in 1977, but these benefits will change yearly with automatic escalator features that are built into the Social Security law.

The Social Security program provides significant potential disabil-

EXHIBIT 12–6
Selected benefit levels for disabled workers under OASDHI (1977)

Average yearly earnings	*Payments to a disabled worker under 65*	*Maximum payment to worker and dependents*
$923 or less	$114.30	$171.50
1,200	147.10	220.70
2,600	216.00	324.00
3,000	236.40	361.40
3,400	253.50	408.30
4,000	278.10	475.30
4,400	297.90	528.10
4,800	315.40	575.30
5,200	331.60	622.20
5,600	347.90	645.10
6,000	364.50	668.60
6,400	380.80	692.10
6,800	398.20	715.70
7,200	418.70	740.70
7,600	437.10	764.90
8,000	453.10	792.90
8,400	462.80	809.90
8,800	474.20	829.80
9,200	484.50	847.80
9,400	488.60	854.80
9,600	492.50	861.90
9,800	498.00	871.30
10,000	502.00	878.50

Source: "If You Become Disabled" (Washington, D.C.: U.S. Social Security Administration, 1977).

ity benefits, which provide a base income in case of total disability. The test of total disability, which generally means an individual cannot resume employment in any type of job, is somewhat restrictive. For example, Social Security will not cover a partial disability that may reduce but not eliminate an individual's source of income.

Sick leave. This coverage will vary greatly among individuals; sick leave is a fringe benefit offered to an employee, but not all employers offer a sick-leave-with-pay provision. While not all workers have a sick leave benefit, there are a significant number who do. The sick leave benefit usually continues an employee's pay for a limited period of time when illness or disability strikes. This coverage can usually be accumulated if not fully used in a year; but even with the accumulation feature, sick leave is generally a short-term coverage.

Worker's compensation. This program is required by state laws in all 50 states. Benefits may vary from state to state, but generally the employer must provide insurance coverage to pay for lost wages, rehabilitation, and medical expenses *when a worker is injured on the job or has a job-related disability.* In the cases of serious permanent injury or death, Worker's Compensation will provide substantial payments to a worker or survivors.

Group disability policies. Many employees receive the benefit of group disability policies. These policies provide disability payments that, in some cases, supplement Social Security and Worker's Compensation; in other cases, they are made over and above such coverages. In instances where this insurance supplements other coverages, the total monthly income payment to an employee is usually limited to some percentage of the worker's previous earnings. For example, many policies will provide that the combination of group disability benefit and all other disability benefits may not exceed 60 percent of the employee's previous earnings. Group disability policies tend to cover a wide range of disabilities and are not restricted to job-related disabilities.

Waiver-of-premium riders. As we discussed in the previous section on life insurance contracts, policies with waiver-of-premium clauses will pay for life insurance premiums during periods of disability. Waiver-of-premium clauses also may be found in health and disability insurance policies.

Most waiver-of-premium riders require that the insured be totally disabled before the insurer will pay the premium. You will also find that companies will write partial disability or very liberal total disability clauses.

Disability income riders. This optional coverage is usually attached to a life insurance policy to provide for a monthly payment to the insured in the event of disability. This rider or endorsement provides a convenient way of supplementing group and government insurances. The price of this form of coverage is often quite reasonable because it is packaged with another policy and the combination is more economical than two individual policies.

Individual or private disability policies. Many insurance companies sell individual disability policies that provide benefits to a disabled policyholder. In most cases, these policies require that there be a total disability before benefits are paid, but in recent years there has been a trend toward including partial disability benefits. In many cases the partial disability benefit is an incentive for an insured person to try to return gradually to work with combined support from the disability policy and the part-time, job-related income.

Accidental disability insurance. These policies may be issued on a group basis or they may be sold as individual policies. The important thing to note is that this sort of policy *pays only for disability that has been the result of an accident.* In most cases this means that disability resulting from an auto accident or an accident in the home or on the job is covered, while disability resulting from any non-accidental cause such as illness is not covered.

Pension plans. Many employees have pension plans that also provide disability payments. Again, there are great variations among pension plans, and some do not provide a disability benefit. If a plan provides a disability payment, the option to take a disability payment reduces or eliminates any future retirement benefits.

Other things to know about disability insurance

Because the degree and permanence of most disabilities are not clear-cut, it is important to be able to find and interpret the definition of disability in a disability insurance policy and to know the general service record of the company involved. The definition of disability is usually found in the disability clause and will vary greatly from company to company. For example, total disability may be defined as:

a. the inability to work at any and every occupation, or

b. the inability to work at an occupation for which the insured is suited by means of education or experience, or

c. the inability to work at the insured's own occupation.

Considering these definitions, you can see that there is a vast difference in what constitutes disability. In definition (*a*), "any and every occupation" is a very restrictive test. For example, if a "disabled" nuclear physicist could still work as a file clerk, then under this definition he or she would not be disabled. By contrast, definition (*c*) would call any disability that prevents that individual from working in a job as a nuclear physicist a total disability.

A second matter that should concern you is the claims service reputation of the disability insurer. If the insurance company has many disputed claims (a fact that can be uncovered by asking your state commissioner of insurance), this would indicate potential problems with any future claim. Since the degree of disability may well be a matter of judgment, the company's claims service reputation should be a major factor in your choice of a disability insurer.

Because of the serious nature of the disability peril, you should plan for disability coverage just as you would for life insurance coverage. This will mean that an individual or family will have to calculate the costs associated with a disability. These costs may include lost income and services, continuing medical expenses, and rehabilitation costs. Because it is common for a disabled person to need continuing care and medical attention, we should recognize that disability poses a potentially greater financial threat than does death.

Once we are aware of these financial needs, we can sort through all the coverages that may apply. Short-term benefits may be provided by sick leave, Worker's Compensation, group disability coverages, and family savings and reserve accounts. Longer term coverage may come from some of these sources and Social Security and individual disability policies. After melding all these coverage elements and comparing them to the financial requirements, any gaps in disability insurance coverage should become evident.

HEALTH INSURANCE

Faced with rapidly rising medical costs, all consumers must be concerned with the risk of illness. The cost of a day in the hospital in most cities has passed $100 and in some cases $200 a day, making the financial impact of illness staggering. These potential costs make a health insurance plan a necessity in a comprehensive plan of financial security. We define health insurance as that risk management device that pays for costs of illness—including all or part of the doctor's fees, hospital care, drugs, therapy, and related costs.

Health insurance coverages

The array of health insurance coverages available to the consumer is large enough to require some sorting out, but the basic choices or coverages can be summarized as follows.

Basic medical expense insurance. Basic medical expense insurance may be purchased as part of a group insurance policy or as an individual policy. The general coverage provided by basic medical includes *hospital expense insurance* and *surgical expense insurance.* The former covers all or part of the cost of hospitalization including hospital room, board, ordinary nursing care, laboratory fees, X-rays, and other diagnostic procedures. The surgical coverage usually pays for all or part of the physician's fees for surgical procedures, obstetrical services, anesthesia services, radiation therapy, emergency services, oral surgery, and other similar services connected with hospitalization. This combined hospital and surgical coverage is often termed "first-dollar" coverage because it is designed to provide prompt, short-term benefits when an illness occurs.

Medical expense contracts are sold in two basic forms, a *benefit schedule contract* or a *medical service contract.* The benefit schedule contract sets the payment for hospital and surgical services according to a schedule included in the policy. For example, the policy may pay $60 a day toward a hospital room. In cases where the room charges exceed that amount, the policyholder would have to pay the difference. Similarly, the surgical schedule sets forth maximum payments for each surgical procedure; for example, $190 for an appendectomy or $700 for a coronary bypass. Here again, if the charge exceeds the amount set forth in the policy, the policyholder must pay the difference.

The second form of basic medical insurance, the medical service contract, is designed to pay the "customary and usual charges" for hospitalization and surgical expenses. What this generally means is that the insurance company will pay the full cost (less any deductibles or coinsurance) of a hospital room or surgical procedure if that cost is in line with the usual cost of medical services in a given area.

While many insurance companies sell medical service insurance, the most common form of a service contract comes in the form of Blue Cross–Blue Shield policies. Blue Cross and Blue Shield are nonprofit insurance organizations that specialize in selling health insurances. There are Blue Cross and Blue Shield companies throughout the country, each of which sells insurance in a defined geographic area.

In both the benefit schedule and the service contract, hospital and surgical benefits have some payout limit. For hospital coverage, that limit is usually expressed in terms of a number of days of coverage. A typical policy might provide 120 or 160 days of hospitalization per illness, with some policies providing as few as 30 days and others providing as many as 365 days.

Surgical benefits are also limited under each type of policy. The schedule contract has a built-in limitation with the schedule of fees, but it may also have a maximum amount payable per illness or per year. Service contracts usually limit benefit payments by establishing a maximum reimbursement for each illness (such as $1,000) in the contract.

The payments received by a policyholder may be further limited by *deductible* or *coinsurance* clauses. The deductible applies to the first portion of the medical bill for each illness, and the amount of the deductible may vary depending on the insurance company and the preference of the insured.

A second limitation in the basic medical policy may be the coinsurance clause. The coinsurance clause provides for a splitting of costs between the insurer and the insured. For example, a typical policy would provide for 80 percent of medical expenses to be paid by the insurer, leaving 20 percent to be paid by the insured. Thus on a medical bill of $1,000, the insurance company would pay $800 and the insured would pay $200. By paying the $200, the insured would become a "coinsurer" on all medical expenses.

Deductibles and coinsurances represent trade-offs between coverage and price. As the deductible becomes larger or as the coinsurance percentage moves up, the premium on a basic health policy goes down. By contrast, if the policy covers virtually every medical expense, the premium will be higher. For the consumer, an important issue will undoubtedly be the appropriate compromise between price (within budget limitations) and coverage.

Major medical insurance. Major medical insurance is designed to pay for the major or catastrophic costs of illness. It is usually sold in combination with group or individual basic medical insurance, and it provides higher limits of coverage for hospital and surgical expenses. In many cases, major medical will add other coverages not found in the basic contract. Depending on the provisions of specific contracts, major medical may add coverage for prescription drugs and medications, physician's services other than those connected with hospitalization, special care nursing and intensive care hospital services, psychological therapy, and preventive procedures such as an annual physical exam.

Major medical insurance policies usually have payout limits ranging from $10,000 to more than $100,000. Most major medical contracts have some form of deductible and coinsurance on the drug and medication provision.

From the standpoint of risk priorities, major medical insurance should receive serious consideration. Major illnesses with attendant catastrophic medical expenses pose a serious financial threat to every individual and family, and major medical insurance provides a convenient tool for meeting this threat.

Comprehensive medical insurance. The comprehensive policy is a combination of basic medical and major medical coverages. It will generally cover hospital expenses, surgical expenses, and a wide variety of major medical expenses. This type of policy usually has less first-dollar coverage than a basic medical contract because there are usually significant deductible and coinsurance provisions on initial medical expenses. On the other end of the policy, the major medical limit tends to be in the range of $10,000–$25,000, which would provide reasonable major medical coverage but less than the typical major medical policy.

Dental insurance. One of the most recent additions to the variety of health insurances is dental insurance. This coverage is usually written with coinsurance or a large deductible. It ordinarily covers fillings, dentures, extractions, oral surgery, fluoridation treatment, checkups, orthodontal services, and numerous other dental treatments.

Dental insurance coverage tends to be quite expensive because of the relative certainty and frequency of expected dental claims. Because of this expense, the growth of dental insurance coverage has been slow.

Social Security. The Social Security program provides limited health insurance coverage to many people who are covered under Social Security. The primary method of financing medical expenses is Medicare. Medicare provides health benefits for retired individuals who are at least 65 years of age, disabled individuals of any age who are covered by Social Security, and those individuals who need renal dialysis or a kidney transplant.

Medicare provides benefits in two parts. Medicare Part A automatically covers all Medicare recipients and provides limited hospital expense benefits, which include the payment of all costs (less a deductible) for the first sixty days of hospitalization, a partial contribution to any expenses for thirty days thereafter, and some contribution for extended private nursing care for a period not to exceed sixty days.

Medicare Part B requires the insured to pay a premium in order to qualify for medical insurance benefits. These benefits include physician's services, outpatient clinic or emergency room services, home health visits, physical and speech therapy, as well as other medical and diagnostic benefits.

HMOs

In the face of rising medical costs, alternative health care delivery systems have been proposed and implemented in an attempt to provide more economical health care. One such system, the Health Maintenance Organization (HMO), has rapidly developed as a promising alternative to traditional health care delivery.

HMOs are not insurers but are providers of health care services. The HMO is a corporation composed of health care providers such as hospitals and physicians. The HMO sets up a health care plan which is financed by premiums paid by members of the HMO plan.

Under the HMO plan, the HMO is generally responsible for all the health care needs of its members. The member generally chooses a clinic or doctor to take care of his or her health care needs. The doctor or clinic is paid a monthly sum of money (called a capitation rate) for each HMO member and must provide the health care services within that budgeted amount.

One of the key differences between HMOs and traditional health care systems is the financing mechanism. While the HMO retains the private insurer in financing, the method of paying the provider of health care changes from a fee-for-service charge to a prepaid capitation rate or per diem rate for medical services. This method of payment puts the provider of health care at risk and provides a financial incentive to help keep down health care costs.

Another feature of HMOs is the extent and direction of medical benefits. An emphasis on coverage for preventive medical benefits marks a departure from most traditional health insurances. A second emphasis on outpatient treatment and care encourages alternatives to hospitalization for treatment. Finally, HMO basic benefits such as psychiatric care tend to be much longer and broader in coverage than traditional medical insurance.

Health insurance clauses

Certain contract elements in health insurance policies will be of interest to you. Specifically, you will want to watch for clauses that cover *pre-existing conditions, nonduplication of benefits,* and *elimination periods.*

A pre-existing conditions clause usually restricts reimbursement of expenses which are related to conditions that existed before the insurance policy was in effect. Clauses dealing with pre-existing conditions restrict or deny coverage of medical costs for the condition for a specific period of time—sometimes as much as three years.

Another clause to consider is the nonduplication of benefits clause. This provision may limit payout because you have other insurance policies that will pay the same benefit. If you have a group health plan and an individual health plan, the existence of a nonduplication clause in either policy will mean that you are paying for coverage on two policies but only one will provide payment on a claim.

One other clause that may cause some concern is one that deals with an elimination period. The elimination period defines the period of time that must elapse from the start of an illness or hospitalization until the insurance benefits begin. For example, a policy gap in coverage with a five-day elimination period would mean that the insurance would begin to cover expenses after the fifth day of illness. You should be aware of any such provisions and make sure that an elimination clause does not negate much of the coverage value of an insurance policy.

SUMMARY

The personal risks of death, illness, disability, unemployment, and old age pose serious threats to our financial security. Each risk should be examined in terms of the perils that might strike and the potential financial loss that may result.

One of the more serious financial risks we must deal with is the risk of death. A common means of insuring against this risk is life insurance. Life insurance is sold in two general forms, term and cash value insurance, and determining which type to buy is a key decision you must make.

In purchasing life insurance you should be familiar with the basic life contract features and provisions and ways of measuring life insurance costs. Endorsements for double indemnity, guaranteed insurability, and waiver of premium are important features in many contracts. You should also know about nonforfeiture and loan clauses, settlement option clauses, and dividend provisions. The net cost and interest adjusted methods of measuring life insurance costs will be useful tools in helping you decide on insurance purchases.

Planning for the risk of death will require that you integrate many sources of insurance protection. The total of benefits provided by Social Security, family assets, and life insurance should be compared to the total financial needs in the case of death.

Another risk of great consequence is disability. Here too you have many sources of coverage including Social Security, sick leave, Worker's Compensation, and disability policies, which you must integrate into a workable plan to provide financial protection. The general framework for planning disability insurance needs requires that you calculate the benefits derived from these sources and compare them to your financial needs in the event of disability.

Illness is another personal risk that deserves attention. The financial impact of illness may be offset by buying health insurance such as a medical expense contract and major medical insurance. Other sources of coverage including dental insurance, Social Security, and HMOs may also provide financial protection.

DISCUSSION QUESTIONS

1. Explain the potential financial impact associated with the risks of death, illness, and disability. In your opinion, which of these risks poses the greatest financial danger to (*a*) a young family, (*b*) a single career person, and (*c*) a retired married couple?
2. What is the basic difference between term insurance and cash value insurance?
3. Explain the benefits and costs of the guaranteed insurability endorsement on a life insurance policy.
4. What are the nonforfeiture benefits in a cash value life insurance policy?
5. In calculating the cost of life insurance, how does the net cost approach differ from the interest adjusted method?
6. What are the five major sources of disability income compensation?
7. Why can't you count on Worker's Compensation as a disability benefit coverage for all possible disabilities?
8. Explain the importance of the definition of disability in determining your benefits in a disability insurance policy.
9. What are the differences between basic medical insurance, major medical insurance, and comprehensive medical insurance?
10. How does a coinsurance clause work in a medical insurance policy?

CASE PROBLEMS

1. Review the household profiles in Chapter 10. As you will recall, these profiles dealt with a single career person, Jane Justin, and a middle-aged married couple, Harold and Emily Richland. From the profiles presented, prepare an inventory of personal·risks and their potential financial impact for each household.

   Which risks are most important to the Justin and Richland households?

2. Doris and Doug Blount are the parents of three children, ages 5, 8, and 10. At the present time Doris is working full time managing the family household. Doug is employed as a construction laborer, and he earns about $15,000 a year. Doug is fully covered by Social Security, and his wife and children would receive survivor's benefits. The Blounts are looking into their life insurance needs and have come to the point of considering how much life insurance is needed to replace 60 percent of Doug's income in the event of his death.

   Assuming that Doris is 35, explain how much insurance would be needed to replace Doug's income taking into account the Social Security benefits.

   If Doris were 45 years old, would the amount of insurance required change? Explain why.

SELECTED READINGS

Anderson, Dan R. and Nevin, John R. "Determinants of Young Marrieds' Life Insurance Purchasing Behavior: An Empirical Investigation," *The Journal of Risk and Insurance,* vol. 42, no. 3, September 1975, pp. 375–387.

Belth, Joseph M. *Life Insurance: A Consumer's Handbook.* Bloomington, Indiana: Indiana University Press, 1973.

Cohen, Jerome B. *Decade of Decision.* New York: Institute of Life Insurance and the Health Insurance Institute, 1974.

Comparing Life Insurance Costs: The Interest Adjusted Method. New York: Institute of Life Insurance, 1975.

Meyers, Robert J. *Social Security.* Homewood, Ill.: Richard D. Irwin, Inc., 1975.

Investment perspectives and opportunities

13

OBJECTIVES

This is the first of three chapters dealing with personal investment. It is intended to introduce the basic concepts you need to develop a personal investment plan. After thoroughly studying and discussing this chapter, you should be able to:

. . . Explain the concept of an "investment pyramid."
. . . Describe the different types of savings plans available in banking and thrift institutions and in U.S. Savings Bonds.
. . . Describe the advantages and disadvantages of owning real estate or your own business.
. . . Describe the characteristics of investment company accounts.

"How to Become a Millionaire" is the title of a chapter in a recently published book.[1] Scores of authors have dangled such tempting thoughts before a very wealth-conscious and wealth-hungry public. They imply that somewhere there is a magical road to riches. Most of these authors suggest securities as a means to becoming a millionaire (or perhaps a multimillionaire, because we all know that making the *first* million dollars is the hardest). People who want to be instant millionaires are attracted by get-rich-quick "opportunities."

Accumulation of wealth is the central theme of this and the next two chapters. However, you will find no get-rich-quick methods. The purpose of this chapter is to provide a basic understanding of how to

[1] Venita Van Caspel, *Money Dynamics* (Reston, Virginia: Reston Publishing Company, 1975), Chapter 15.

develop an investment plan and of some of the investments that are available. Chapter 14 presents an introduction to investment in stocks and bonds and to the markets for buying and selling them. The final chapter on investments provides a description of the risks in any type of investment and a method of analyzing your investment needs. Investment risk and investor needs are then brought together through a decisionmaking method that focuses on the development of investment policies.

Definitions

There is often confusion over the definition of terms such as investment and speculation. Such confusion is justified, because there is no clear-cut distinction between the two terms. For our purposes, a general distinction will be made. The term *speculation* will be used to refer to situations in which money is committed for the purchase of some wealth-producing investment without adequately investigating the facts; for example, buying on the basis of rumor.

Investment will be used to refer to the commitment of funds after a careful investigation of the facts and analysis of the expected risks and rewards. The distinguishing characteristic between the two activities is the degree of analysis of the facts, including the anticipated risks and returns. This means that an identical commitment of funds by two investors may represent an investment for one but a speculation for the other because of the motivation and preparation for buying. Investors buy because they believe the risks and returns will meet their needs. Speculators buy without making such an analysis.

INVESTMENT PYRAMID

The investment of any part of disposable income means that you have made the decision to postpone using this money until some future time. You may be accumulating funds to buy some large item, such as a home, or to use during your retirement years. However admirable it may be to provide for future financial needs, such plans must take into account the current needs that must be met before funds are available for investment. After taking care of current needs (food on the table, clothing, and other usual living expenses) you can consider an investment plan. One approach to investing is illustrated by the investment pyramid.

The investment pyramid plan shown in Exhibit 13–1 builds upon investments required to meet basic financial needs. This base then provides the foundation for any additional investments that are appro-

EXHIBIT 13–1
Investment pyramid

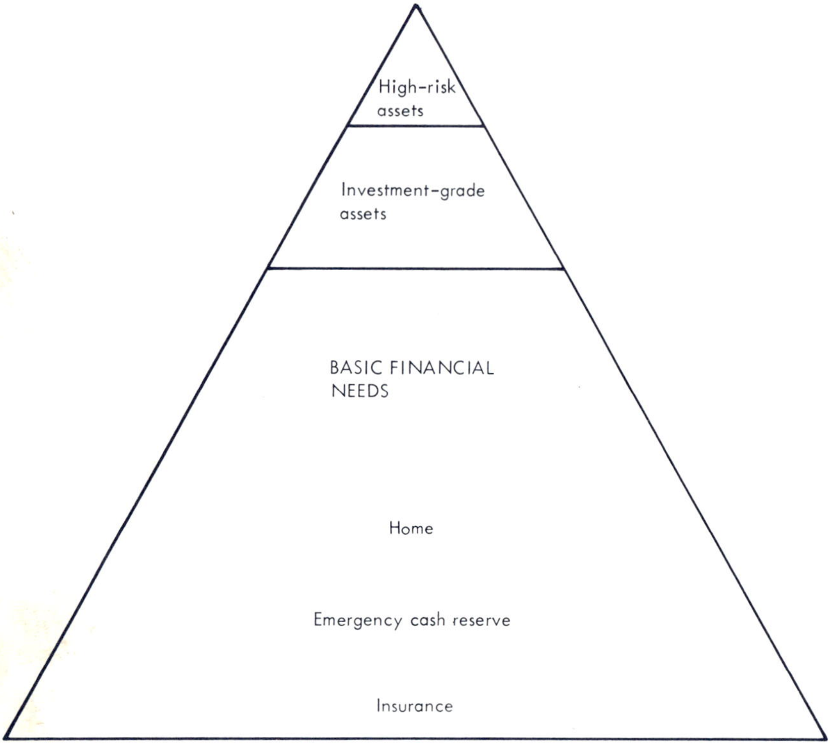

priate. In this plan it is recognized that families need financial protection in the event of an emergency. This protection can be partially provided through the use of insurance (life insurance, medical insurance, etc.) against insurable risks (see Chapters 10, 11, and 12).

In addition, most people need a cash reserve for meeting unexpected expenses or loss of income. The amount of cash reserve required depends upon factors such as stability of income, availability of credit, and the extent of insurance coverage. For example, if you have major medical insurance, the need for a cash reserve to cover large, unexpected medical expenses is far less than if insurance is not available. As a rule of thumb, your cash reserve should be equal to about two to four months of income. If credit is readily available to meet unforeseen major expenses, a smaller reserve of cash is needed. Also, if your income is reasonably stable and secure, there is less chance that you will need the cash reserve for living expenses.

Another layer of the pyramid shown is buying a home. As was discussed in Chapter 8, buying a home represents the largest single outlay for most families.

It is up to you to determine the priority of each of these basic financial needs. Some people will place a higher priority on buying a home than on building an emergency fund or buying insurance. Others will use just the opposite ranking.

Any money that is left after meeting your basic needs for insurance, an emergency reserve, and housing is then available for investment. In choosing investment opportunities, you should be familiar with the risk and return features that will best fit your needs.

In general, there is a direct relationship between the riskiness of an investment and the expected return from it. That is, investments that are very risky are also the ones that can provide the highest returns, while the very safe investments provide lower returns. A more detailed discussion of the risk-return relationship is presented in Chapter 15.

The most frequently used types of personal investment include savings accounts, corporate securities, investment company securities, government securities, and real estate. The discussion of corporate and government securities as personal investments is included in Chapter 14.

SAVINGS AND TIME ACCOUNTS

Savings accounts and other time accounts are used by more people than any other type of investment. In addition to being used as an emergency fund described above, these accounts are frequently used to accumulate money for special purposes (a new car), for future investment somewhere else, and as a safe investment that provides income. They are available in commercial banks, savings and loan associations, mutual savings banks, and credit unions. Each of these institutions has a variety of account arrangements available with yield rates depending mainly upon the length of time the deposit is left with the institution.

Exhibit 13–2 shows the proportions of savings and time accounts held by the four main savings institutions: commercial banks, savings and loan associations, mutual savings banks, and credit unions. Consumers have favored commercial banks and S&Ls to hold their savings deposits and as a result these two institutions have held 80 percent or more of savings in recent years.

Your decision on where to deposit your savings should be based on the following criteria: risk of loss, effective rate of interest paid on savings, and the availability of your funds.

EXHIBIT 13–2
Proportion of savings held by institutions (1970–1976)

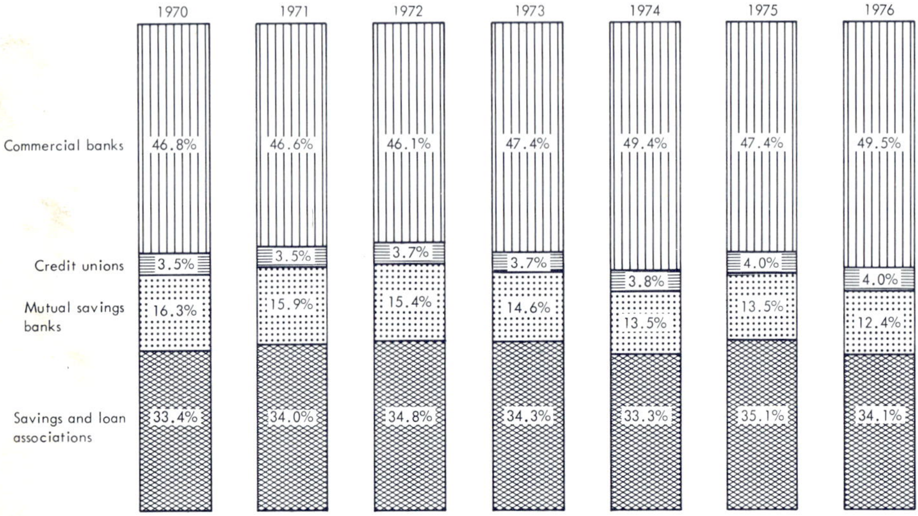

Sources: Federal Home Loan Bank Board; Federal Reserve Board.

Risk of loss is always present because financial institutions do fail. Today, however, most of these savings institutions provide deposit insurance through federal or state agencies. The question then becomes one of the maximum amount that is insured in each account.

The effective rate of interest depends upon two things: the stated rate and the method of calculating the balance upon which interest is paid. For a given rate, you will earn the most interest if you select an account that pays interest from day of deposit to day of withdrawal.

Availability of funds is determined by how much notice must be given in order to withdraw money without incurring an interest penalty for early withdrawal. Some accounts permit withdrawal on demand while others may require a waiting period of 90 days.

Think about each of these criteria as we discuss the savings and time accounts offered by the savings institutions.

Commercial bank savings and time accounts

Banks that are members of the Federal Reserve System are currently required by law to carry insurance for up to $40,000 in each account held in different names. The $40,000 limit applies to the total of all types of accounts held in any one name in any one bank and its branches. You can increase your protection by opening accounts in more than one bank or by opening joint and individual accounts. For example, if you had $100,000 to deposit you could deposit it in three different banks. Or, you and your spouse could open individual accounts and a joint account in the same bank, making sure that no one account had a balance greater than $40,000. Banks that are not members of the Federal Reserve System may also be insured if they meet the requirements of the Federal Deposit Insurance Corporation (FDIC). Most banks provide deposit insurance, but a few do not.[2] The importance of deposit insurance coverage has become more apparent in light of recent failures of large commercial banks.[3]

Savings deposit accounts. The savings account, often called a regular passbook account, is the most flexible in allowing deposits and withdrawals at any time. These accounts usually earn the lowest interest rate among the forms of savings accounts offered by a bank, but for many depositors the flexibility justifies accepting the lower rate. Depositors usually consider these savings as a part of their readily available cash.

Passbooks may or may not be used. Some banks provide ready access to funds through the use of a bank card that can be used to transfer funds from one of the depositor's accounts to another or for the withdrawal of cash from the account at locations other than the bank itself.

Time deposit accounts. The distinguishing characteristic of time accounts is that withdrawals can be made only after written notice except for specified withdrawal periods. These periods usually occur at the end of the quarter when interest is credited to the account. These accounts are offered for depositors who are able to sacrifice some flexibility and commit their money for a period of time ranging from 30 days to six years or more. In return for the reduced withdrawal flexibility, time deposit accounts usually earn one fourth to one half percent higher interest rates than the savings accounts. If you withdraw the funds without adequate written notice or at any time other than the specified withdrawal period, there is a substantial penalty in the form of forfeiture of the higher interest rate. Deposits, however, can be made at any time in this type of account.

Certificates of deposit (CDs) are issued as evidence of longer term

---

[2] As of mid-1977, of the 14,685 commercial banks in the U.S., only about 270 were not insured.

[3] For more on recent bank failures, see: J. F. Sinkey, Jr., "Collapse of Franklin National Bank of New York," *Journal of Bank Research*, Summer 1976, pp. 113–122; R. Karp, "Sleeping Watchdogs; How the American Bank & Trust Co. Went Broke," *Barrons*, December 20, 1976, p. 3; "Hamilton National's Traumatic Monday," *Business Week*, March 1, 1976, pp. 21–22; "What Went Wrong at Herstatt," *Business Week*, August 3, 1974, pp. 13–14; P. Milius, "How the Hamilton Failed," *Bankers Magazine*, Summer 1976, pp. 79–82.

time accounts. The CD states on its face the principal value, interest rate, and date of maturity. The principal amount deposited does not have to be repaid to the depositor until maturity.

CDs are generally issued in amounts ranging from $25 up to $1,000 or multiples thereof. Banks issue larger CDs, over $100,000, which are negotiable, but these are rarely used by individuals.

The maximum rates paid on the various accounts are summarized in Exhibit 13–3.

EXHIBIT 13–3
Savings and time deposit interest rate ceilings* (percent)

	Savings institution			
Type of account	*Commercial banks*	*Savings & loan associations*	*Mutual savings banks*	*Credit unions*
Savings accounts	5	5¼	5¼	7
Time accounts				
90 days to 1 year	5½	5¾	5¾	n.a.†
1 to 2½ years	6	6½	6½	n.a.
2½ to 4 years	6½	6¾	6¾	n.a.
4 to 6 years	7¼	7½	7½	n.a.
6 years or more	7½	7¾	7¾	n.a.

* There are no maximum rates on time deposits in denominations of $100,000 or more. Rates shown effective January, 1978.

† n.a. = not applicable.

Source: *Federal Reserve Bulletin.*

Savings and loan associations (S&Ls)

S&Ls are savings institutions that specialize in receiving savings from individuals and in granting home mortgage loans. Because their capacity to make mortgage loans depends upon the amount of savings held by the association, very competitive rates are paid on savings accounts. Regulation Q, set by a federal agency, permits S&Ls to pay a maximum rate that is one fourth percent higher than the maximum rate allowable for the same type of account in a commercial bank. Maximum rates are shown in Exhibit 13–3.

S&Ls that receive their organizational charters from the federal government are required by law to have their savings accounts insured by the Federal Savings and Loan Insurance Corporation (FSLIC). Insurance coverage is optional for S&Ls chartered by the states, although most of these do protect their deposits with insurance. The maximum coverage by the FSLIC is $40,000 per account. This coverage may be increased by opening accounts in several S&Ls or by opening individual and joint accounts in one S&L, an arrangement comparable with FDIC.

Savings accounts in S&Ls are of two general types: regular passbook accounts and special accounts.

Regular passbook accounts. These accounts are similar to the savings deposits in a commercial bank. Deposits and withdrawals are made by presenting an account passbook. S&Ls have the right to delay withdrawals for up to thirty days, but this option is seldom used.

Special accounts. Special accounts may take the forms of notice accounts, certificate accounts, and the negotiated order of withdrawal account.

Notice accounts require you to provide written notice of your intent to withdraw funds followed by a specified waiting period, such as 90 days. A notice account earns a higher return than a regular savings account.

Certificate accounts are similar to the certificates of deposit issued by commercial banks. These certificates are issued for specified minimum amounts with a fixed maturity date. Very few of these certificates are negotiable, and therefore if you need money before the certificate matures you must depend upon the willingness of the S&L to redeem the certificate. Such a redemption is possible only at a substantial penalty in the form of forfeited interest earnings.

Savers have been making increasing use of S&L certificate and special accounts. During the 1960s the regular passbook account was by far the predominant form of account used by savers. In January, 1973, for the first time, passbook savings accounted for less than 50 percent of total savings deposits in S&Ls. This change occurred because certificate and special accounts were increasing more rapidly than passbook accounts. Proportions of savings held by S&Ls by the type of account are shown in Exhibit 13–4.

Another form of special account is the negotiated order of withdrawal account (NOW). Federal laws explicitly state that savings accounts shall not be subject to check or negotiable orders of withdrawal. The NOW account is an exception to these rules. The move toward such accounts began when the Housing Act of 1968 authorized federal S&Ls to accept orders from depositors to withdraw money from savings accounts and to issue an S&L check to pay a third party. Regulations issued by the Federal Home Loan Bank Board (FHLBB) in early 1971 restricted negotiated orders of withdrawal to periodic or specific third-party payments, primarily for payments related to housing. On April 16, 1975, this rule was changed to permit federally chartered S&Ls to make such payments for any purpose.

Pressures have developed to extend the NOW account and demand-deposit (checking) account nationwide. Illinois-chartered S&Ls were permitted to offer NOW accounts beginning January 1, 1976, but they

EXHIBIT 13–4
Types of accounts in insured savings and loan associations

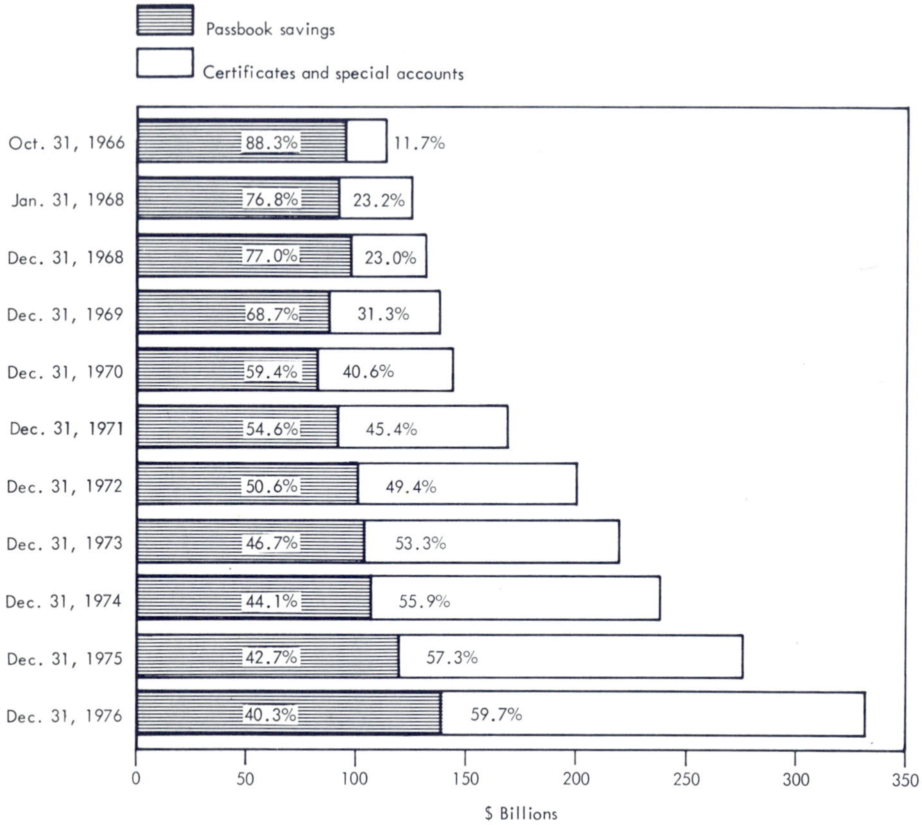

Source: United States League of Savings Associations, *Savings and Loan Fact Book*, 1977.

are not permitted to pay interest on the accounts. Thus, they are sometimes called NINOWs (noninterest-bearing negotiated orders of withdrawal). Such accounts, except in the New England states, must be non-interest-bearing because of federal prohibition against interest on demand deposits. It is easy, however, for you to transfer funds from a separate regular savings account into the NOW account. Since October, 1975, qualified state-chartered S&Ls have been permitted to offer demand-deposit accounts.

Mutual savings banks

Mutual savings banks are owned by their depositors and are organized primarily to encourage savings and thrift. They are found in 17 of the Atlantic coastal states and Puerto Rico.

In addition to ordinary accounts, MSBs offer a wide variety of special high-yield accounts. These special accounts take the form of time or term accounts, certificates, special notice, bonus, systematic savings, and investment accounts. In addition, interest-bearing NOW accounts are available in MSBs located in Massachusetts and New Hampshire, while NINOW accounts are available in New York.[4]

Earnings of MSBs benefit the depositors in two ways. First, dividends are paid at some specified rate. Because the yield is a dividend, however, the rate is subject to change and is not guaranteed. Second, any earnings that are not paid out as dividends are added to the MSB's reserve funds and increase the depositor's protection.

More than 99 percent of all MSBs have insurance covering their savings accounts. Nearly two-thirds of the MSBs are members of the FDIC, which insures individual accounts up to $40,000 each. Other MSBs are covered by state insurance agencies.

Credit unions

A credit union is a cooperative organized by and for members who have a common interest, such as working for the same employer. Credit union members agree to save their money for the purpose of making these savings available as loans to members. Most credit unions are organized along occupational lines. As shown in Exhibit 13–5, at the end of 1976, 55.8 percent of the credit unions had occupation as the common bond. Associational bonds (members of clubs, churches, professional associations, etc.) were second with 17 percent.

EXHIBIT 13–5
Distribution of credit union membership by common bond, 1976

Common bond	*Percentage*
Occupational	55.8
Associational	17.0
Federal, state, county and local government	15.5
Educational services	8.0
Residential	3.7

Source: Credit Union National Association, Inc.

Credit unions were introduced to the United States in 1909 by Alphonse Desjardins, who brought the idea from Western Europe. In that year he started the first credit union in a New Hampshire church

[4] *National Fact Book of Mutual Savings Banking.*

parish. The first deposit was a dime. Desjardins assisted in the passage in Massachusetts of the first general state credit union law in 1909. Since that time the credit union idea has expanded: at the end of 1976 there were 22,608 credit unions in the United States with over 34 million members.

Members accumulate savings in a credit union by purchasing shares, usually in $5 multiples. Generally speaking, savings in a credit union can be considered as ready cash. Withdrawal of funds requires the credit union to repurchase the savings shares. Most credit unions will repurchase the shares at your request, even though they can legally require a waiting period. Some small credit unions may limit the amount any member can deposit in an effort to avoid future problems of large withdrawals.

Credit unions also provide a special account known as the share draft account, which is similar to the NOW account offered by S&Ls. This account, which is eligible to earn dividends, permits the depositor to write drafts in payment of bills.

Dividends are paid to savers out of the credit union's earnings from interest on loans to members. The rates at which dividends are paid range from those of regular commercial bank savings accounts to rates that are somewhat higher than those paid by S&Ls. Maximum rates (see Exhibit 13–3) are established by Regulation Q. In addition to paying dividends on savings, many credit unions also provide term life insurance for members by paying monthly premiums to an insuring agency. There is usually a maximum of $2,000 of life insurance available, but some credit unions provide coverage up to the amount in the saver's account. In the event of death, the saver's estate receives the balance in the account as well as the insurance proceeds.

The National Credit Union Administration provides savers with insurance protection for their accounts. All federal credit unions must, and any state credit unions that apply and qualify may, have individual accounts insured for $40,000. The safety of savers' funds has been very good even in uninsured credit unions as a result of rather strict rules in credit union charters and periodic audits by state examiners.

Advantages and disadvantages of savings and time accounts

Savings and time accounts offer several advantages:

1. Safety. There is little risk of loss of principal or interest if you select an insured account.
2. Savings accounts offer a high degree of availability of your money. Time accounts have a more limited availability, but with the ac-

counts that have shorter notice periods availability is adequate for many people.

3. Convenience and flexibility in making deposits enables you to earn interest immediately from the day you have funds available. There is usually no minimum deposit size.
4. You do not have to pay a fee when you open an account, make deposits and withdrawals, or close the account.
5. The safety and ready availability of the money make these accounts well suited for holding cash reserves and for accumulating money for property taxes, insurance, vacations, etc.

In return for these advantages you must be willing to accept some disadvantages. One disadvantage is the lower rate of return on these accounts than on other types of investments. A second disadvantage is that these accounts are poor protection against inflation. (The effect of inflation will be discussed in Chapter 15.) Third, interest received on your account is fully taxable.

U.S. GOVERNMENT SAVINGS BONDS

These instruments are credit obligations of the U.S. government. Interest rates paid on these obligations have been increased over time to make them more competitive with rates paid by other savings accounts. There are two forms of savings bonds available: Series E and Series H.

Series E bonds

Series E bonds are purchased at 75 percent of face value. They are available in denominations of $25, $50, $75, $100, $200, $500, $1,000, and $10,000. (For a $25 bond you pay $18.75; for a $50 bond you pay $37.50, etc.) Interest then accumulates until at maturity (five years) you receive the face, or maturity, value of the bond. This accumulation of interest represents a six percent rate of return on the amount invested. Because these bonds have an automatic ten-year extension privilege, you can earn the current rate of six percent for a total of 15 years if you so choose.

The interest rate on Series E bonds rises during their life, as shown in Exhibit 13–6. Average returns increase from a low of 3.73 percent if held for only one half year to six percent if held for the entire five-year period. Early redemption costs take the form of reductions in interest earned. For example, if the bond is redeemed at the end of two years,

EXHIBIT 13–6
U.S. Savings bonds, Series E: Approximate investment yields for selected time periods (rates effective July 1977)

Time (years and months after issue)	*Approximate annual yield to beginning of each six-month period (percent)*
0–0	—
0–6	3.73
1–0	4.54
1–6	4.69
2–0	4.76
2–6	4.86
3–0	4.95
3–6	5.03
4–0	5.14
4–6	5.25
5–0*	6.00

* Series E bonds reach maturity value at the end of 5 years.

six months, you will earn 4.86 percent, a rate well below that available at other savings institutions. This provides a strong incentive for you to hold savings bonds to maturity. Savings bonds can be redeemed without notice at financial institutions that are authorized paying agencies, at any Federal Reserve Bank, or at the office of the U.S. Treasurer.

Series H bonds

Series H bonds differ from Series E in that the interest is paid to you by check semiannually, beginning six months after the issue date. They are therefore known as current income bonds. Denominations of H bonds are $500, $1,000, and $5,000. The purchase price and maturity value are both equal to the face amount of the bond. Interest is earned at the annual rate of 4.2 percent for the first year, 5.8 percent for the next four years, and 6.51 percent for the last five years to maturity. This return averages out to six percent for the ten-year period. Savers who need their money can redeem the Series H bonds at face value, without notice, at any time after six months past the issue date. Immediate redemption is a feature unique to these current income bonds. Other issuers of current income bonds, such as corporations, are not required to redeem their bonds until the maturity date—though they may elect to redeem them earlier than the maturity date.

Advantages and disadvantages of U.S. savings bonds

There are several advantages of owning savings bonds:

1. Their rate of return compares favorably with other savings alternatives, if held to maturity, and the safety of this return is unequaled.
2. The bonds can be redeemed without notice.
3. Interest income from these bonds is exempt from state and local income tax and personal property tax.
4. Federal income tax on the interest from Series E bonds can be deferred until they are redeemed. With the automatic extension, it is possible to defer paying taxes on the interest for ten more years. This could defer taxes until after retirement when you will probably be in a lower tax bracket. It is possible to exchange matured Series E bonds for Series H bonds and pay tax only on the interest from the H bonds and defer the tax on the accumulated interest from the E bond even longer. If you expire before the H bonds, the tax is deferred permanently.
5. Savings bonds can be used to build a college fund for your children. If bonds are purchased and the child is listed as owner and parent as beneficiary, *not* co-owner, the annual increases in value of the bonds can be reported as income by the child. A federal tax return may be filed in the child's name the first year, listing the accrued interest as income. Unless the child's income is above the minimum level for federal income tax, no tax will be due. The first year's return establishes intent, and no further returns will be necessary unless total income in any year exceeds the exemption. Then when the bonds are redeemed to provide college funds, the accumulated interest is not taxable.
6. No commission is paid when purchasing or redeeming savings bonds. Authorized agencies, referred to above, sell and redeem them without charge.

Chief among the disadvantages of savings bonds is the relatively low return in the early period of ownership. Interest rates for at least the first year are below other savings alternatives. Second, after you have purchased a savings bond the rate of return is set until maturity or redemption. Other savings institutions can adjust dividend or interest rates upward if conditions warrant (but it should also be recognized that these other institutions can lower their rates). A third disadvantage results from the forfeiture of higher rates of return if you redeem the bonds before maturity. This is especially important if you expect to need the money in a short time.

YOUR OWN BUSINESS

Some investors use ownership of their private businesses as a means of investment. For these people the four words "own your own business" are very important. They have a feeling of pride and satisfaction in being independent. This type of investment usually requires the commitment of a relatively large sum of money for a long period of time. If the business must be sold on short notice or before you have had an opportunity to develop it fully, there is greater chance of loss than when selling an established business. Also, the chance of loss is greater than with several other types of investment because of possible failure of the business and loss of investment. When making an investment decision of this type, you should seek the advice of a good banker and attorney and do some soul-searching to determine whether the business opportunity is a good one and whether you have the ability to manage your own business.

REAL ESTATE

The purchase of the family home, as discussed in Chapter 8, is primarily based upon a consideration of the family's housing needs. Factors such as good location can result in an increase in the value of the house, but generally this investment aspect of the selection decision is secondary.

Besides the family home, there are many other opportunities for the purchase of real estate. Such investment properties can be located in commercial, residential or rural areas. They can be classified as "improved," which implies that there are buildings on the land, or "unimproved," which implies that the land is vacant.

Improved land is often purchased by investors who wish to earn income by renting out buildings. Such investments might include apartment complexes, shopping centers, or office buildings. Investment of this type is the topic of many specialized books.

Unimproved properties usually demand a long-term commitment. These properties are purchased because of their anticipated increase in value—for example, land on the outskirts of a city in an area of probable development, or land near a proposed development such as Disney World in Florida, where land values skyrocketed.

In spite of the attractiveness of real estate investments, there are many disadvantages:

1. Real estate is usually illiquid; that is, it cannot be easily converted back to cash. It is often difficult to sell real estate quickly without losing money.
2. Property must be maintained. Even unimproved lots must be mowed, and property taxes and assessments for street, curb, sidewalk, sewers, etc. must be paid regardless of whether the property is earning income.
3. Real estate is very immobile. Should you become dissatisfied, for example, with the hot, humid climate in which your real estate is located and decide to move to a winter vacationland, you cannot pack your 80 acres of unimproved land or your apartment complex into a suitcase and take it with you.

INVESTMENT COMPANY SECURITIES

Investment companies are organized for the sole purpose of investing in securities and managing their own portfolios. Not only is the business activity of these companies restricted to investment in securities, but it is generally restricted to securities that are regularly bought and sold in the security markets. Capital used for investment is obtained when the investment company sells its own shares to investors. These shares represent a fractional ownership of the securities owned by the company. There are two main types of investment companies. In order of importance, they are the open-end investment company (or mutual fund as it is commonly known) and the closed-end investment company.

Open-end investment companies (mutual funds)

Mutual funds do not limit the number of shares that they will sell. They will issue new shares whenever you wish to buy them and they will repurchase shares whenever you wish to sell. The price at which these transactions occur is determined by the net asset value of the fund. This value is determined by deducting the liabilities of the investment company from the value of all its assets and dividing these proceeds by the number of mutual fund shares outstanding.

In most instances there is a "loading charge" made when you buy the shares. The load is the commission paid to a broker or agent who helps you in the transaction. This charge varies, but usually it ranges from 7½ to 8½ percent of the amount you invest, including the charge. Thus, the true rate that you pay is greater than the stated load. For example, if there is an 8½ percent load and you invest $500 in a mutual fund, $42.50 of that amount is for the loading charge. Your net investment is $457.50. Therefore, the true cost of the load is 9.29 percent ($42.50 ÷ $457.50). Firms usually do not make a charge when the shares are sold, even though some firms have the right to do so.

There are several open-end funds that do not have a loading charge. Shares of these no-load funds are sold by the fund directly to the investor; there is no agent who must be paid a commission. As a result, if you want information on no-load funds, you must find your own because brokers do not provide it. Information is readily available from the fund if you request it. Names and addresses of no-load funds can be found in ads appearing in major financial newspapers such as *The Wall Street Journal.*

No-load funds have gained in importance in recent years, and some firms that previously had a loading charge have transformed to no-load funds. The wide range of no-load funds that is available makes it difficult to justify buying any of the load funds.

Mutual fund managers offer different purchase and dividend distribution plans in an effort to meet different investors' needs. These plans are in sharp contrast to those offered by closed-end funds, where you pay cash for your shares with no withdrawal options except to sell your shares. There are four major types of mutual fund accounts: regular accounts, accounts with automatic dividend reinvestment, accumulation accounts, and withdrawal accounts.

Regular accounts. These are the simplest of the mutual fund accounts. A regular account involves a lump-sum purchase with a specific amount invested at one time. Mutual fund shares are purchased by total dollar amounts; the number of shares is quite immaterial. There are no savings, for example, by purchasing in multiples of 100 shares. Loading charges may be reduced for investments in excess of $25,000—a matter of little consequence for most mutual fund investors.

Within a few days after you purchase mutual fund shares, you should receive either a certificate or a statement indicating the number of shares held for you. Dividend checks are sent to you quarterly, semi-annually, or annually depending upon the policy of the fund. Capital gain distributions, if any, are usually made annually.

Accumulation accounts. An accumulation plan is one that enables investors of even modest means to purchase shares. After making an initial purchase, you can make more purchases when you have funds available. Many mutual funds will even help you arrange an accumulation plan fund. Bank drafts are used to arrange automatic deductions through your savings or checking account, or through payroll deductions.

There are two basic types of accumulation accounts: voluntary—

or informal—and contractual. You begin a voluntary accumulation plan with some minimum investment such as $100 or $500. At the time of purchase you indicate the amount you intend to invest at specified intervals, such as monthly. There is ordinarily a minimum periodic investment of $25 to $50. The regular loading fee, as described above, is charged on each investment. Some funds may credit fractional shares to your account while others credit only full shares. This plan enables you to purchase small amounts when you have funds available. You are, however, under no legal obligation to make the purchases indicated in your original agreement. In fact, you may cancel your account and redeem your shares at their net asset value at any time, thus retaining maximum flexibility.

Contractual accumulation plans differ from the voluntary plans in that the agreement between you and the mutual fund is more formal and includes some built-in incentives to complete your part of the agreement. To begin one of these plans, you agree to purchase some dollar amount of mutual fund shares during a specified time period. Most of these plans run for two years or more and involve an investment goal of $10,000. Purchases are to be made monthly, quarterly, etc., until this goal is reached.

While you may cancel a contractual plan at any time, incentive to complete it is provided by the fact that the loading charge for the entire plan is taken out of the early payments but no such charge is made on later payments. This is known as a "front-end load." Because of the timing of the payment of the load charge, failure to fulfill the agreement results in substantial charges relative to the amount of payment made. If the plan is completed, the charge is usually less than it would have been if the same purchases had been made under a voluntary accumulation plan.

Accounts with automatic dividend reinvestment. Most mutual funds permit you to choose to have all dividend and capital gains distributions reinvested in the shares of the mutual fund. This is done by signing a "dividend reinvestment order."

One advantage of the automatic reinvestment of dividends and capital gains is that it enables you to purchase additional shares without paying added commissions. Dividends are ordinarily reinvested at the current share asking price and capital gains are reinvested at the current net asset value of the company's shares. A shareholder must pay income tax on these funds at the time of reinvestment, however. Later, when the shares are redeemed, there is no tax on the reinvested amounts.

Withdrawal accounts. Withdrawal accounts appeal to investors who want a certain amount of cash income on a monthly, quarterly, or annual basis. These plans are very similar to annuities sold by life insurance companies and to savings accounts that pay interest directly to the depositor.

A minimum amount, such as $5,000 to $10,000, is ordinarily required in an account before regular withdrawals can begin. You can establish a regular withdrawal account by making a cash investment, or you can convert accumulation accounts to withdrawal plans when enough funds have been saved. The periodic withdrawals are made from dividends first. If the dividends are not great enough to cover the withdrawal, a portion of the principal is used to make up the difference. Regular income is received as long as the funds are available from the account. The smaller the withdrawal relative to the size of the account, and the better the investment experience of the fund, the longer the period that you will receive withdrawal payments. For example, suppose you have $50,000 in your account and the fund pays a six percent cash dividend. As long as your withdrawal is $3,000 or less per year, the withdrawal could last indefinitely.

In all cases, you retain complete control of the account. If you so desire, the amount of withdrawal may be increased, decreased, or discontinued. You also have the option of liquidating the account at net asset value. Withdrawal plans are voluntary and flexible arrangements.

Closed-end investment companies

Closed-end investment companies issue a fixed number of shares. Once the fund has sold these it will neither issue more shares nor redeem any shares. If you want your money, you must find someone to buy your shares at prices determined by supply and demand in the marketplace. This is usually done through a securities exchange—a topic discussed in Chapter 14.

Classification of investment companies by investment policy

Investment companies are required to provide a statement of investment goals and policies. A copy of the statement is easily obtainable from a securities broker or from the investment company. Funds have developed with goals designed to meet differing needs for income risk and value of principal. These goals and policies are often stated in terms of the proportions of bonds and stocks held in the mutual fund portfolio. Exhibit 13–7 classifies the types of funds in terms of their relative importance.

EXHIBIT 13–7
Open-end investment companies classified by investment goal (December 31, 1975)

Type of fund	*Number of funds*	*Percentage of total assets*
Common stock		
Maximum capital gain	119	9.4
Growth	153	29.2
Growth and income	95	30.2
Specialized	17	0.6
Balanced	20	9.1
Income	97	12.1
Bond and preferred stock	8	0.9
Money market	34	7.2
Tax-free exchange	12	1.3
Total	556	100.0

Source: Weisenberger Investment Companies Service.

Common stock funds accounted for over 69 percent of the assets held by mutual funds at the end of 1975. As the title implies, these funds invest almost exclusively in common stock and provide the mutual fund shareholder broad diversification. The investment goals of these funds vary in the emphasis placed upon dividend income and capital gains (value of principal) as well as their methods of achieving these goals.

The common stock growth, growth and income, and the maximum capital gains funds differ only in the degree to which they emphasize growth in the value of the security holdings. A means to provide this growth is investment in common stock of companies that are growth companies or are expected to become growth companies. Income is usually a secondary consideration and may be only an incidental goal.

Balanced mutual funds have an investment goal of long-term growth in both income and the value of the securities. These funds hold bonds, preferred stocks, and common stocks in some "balanced" proportions to provide the desired stability of income and principal value.

Income funds emphasize generating a liberal current income from investments. High yields, which are available on bonds and preferred stocks, have encouraged these funds to emphasize these securities in their holdings. Many of the bond and preferred stock funds could be included in this classification.

The high yields on U.S. government securities, especially on the issues with short maturities (known as money market instruments), have substantially increased investor interest in these **money market**

funds. These funds are popular with individual investors who are seeking safety and income.

Dual-purpose funds are closed-end funds with the goal of providing an investment opportunity for two different types of investors. The basic concept upon which dual-purpose funds are founded is quite simple. The fund sells equal dollar amounts of two types of shares: income shares and capital shares. Income shares appeal to investors needing current income, and capital shares may meet the needs of investors whose needs are for capital gains. Owners of the income shares receive all of the income from the entire portfolio. These shares have a minimum stated annual dividend that must be paid for each of the years before any capital shares can be redeemed. Also, these share owners have the right to receive all earnings of the fund in excess of this minimum amount.

Owners of capital shares are entitled to all price appreciation in the investment portfolio over the stated life of the fund, usually 12 to 18 years. As the fund realizes capital gains in the portfolio, these gains are reinvested in more assets. This also benefits the income share owners in that these assets should produce added income.

At the end of the specified life of the dual-purpose fund, the income and capital shares are redeemed. First to be redeemed are the income shares at a predetermined value per share plus any accumulated dividends. Next, all remaining proceeds are distributed to the owners of capital shares on a pro rata basis.

Both classes of shareholders are "leveraged." That is, each class is using the capital of the other in order to attempt to increase the returns on its own. Income share owners receive the income from the capital supplied by both types of share owners. At the same time, capital share owners hope to benefit from price appreciation of those same securities.

Investor advantages of investment company shares

For many investors there are two major advantages to owning shares of an investment company: professional management and diversification. Indeed, these advantages are major reasons for the development and growth of such companies.

Professional managers are employed by the investment company to manage its holdings. However, whether these managers have realized returns for the company greater than those of an individual investor is still open to question. The broad range of objectives stated by various companies makes measurement and comparison of performances difficult.

A diversified portfolio is one whose selection of securities is based on the old proverb, "Don't put all of your eggs into one basket." Diversification means that the funds are spread out by investing in the securities of several companies rather than in just one company. It is quite probable that the investment company can diversify more efficiently than an individual investor.

Selection of a mutual fund requires an analysis of your investment needs—a topic discussed in Chapter 15. This analysis will enable you to select a fund whose goal parallels your own.

SUMMARY

Wealth accumulation and the means to it is the main concern of this chapter. It is our purpose to help you develop a method of analysis that will assist in the development and achievement of your investment goals.

The term investment implies that current funds have been thoughtfully placed so that the amount available will increase over time. Investment differs from speculation mainly in terms of the degree of consideration and preparation that occurs before the available funds are committed.

The investment pyramid is an approach to investing that recognizes that a family's basic needs must be satisfied before funds can be available for use in wealth-producing commitments.

Types of investments discussed in this chapter that are often used for family investments include savings accounts, your own business, real estate, and investment company securities. Savings accounts of varying types and characteristics are available from commercial banks, savings and loan associations, mutual savings banks, credit unions, and in U.S. government savings bonds. These types of accounts differ with respect to withdrawal privileges, but can generally be viewed as a ready source of funds when needed.

Owning a business is important to some individuals in providing a satisfying feeling of pride and independence. If the invested funds are needed for some other purpose, however, the investment may be difficult and costly to convert back to cash.

Real estate investments include both improved and unimproved properties. Such investments are attractive because of the possibility of land value appreciation, particularly if special developments assist in raising valuation. It may be costly to recover funds quickly from a real estate investment, however, if the funds are needed. Also, if you wish to move, you cannot take your real estate with you.

Investment companies are in the business of owning and managing securities holdings. The two main types of investment companies are the open-end (known as a mutual fund) and the closed-end. This distinction is based upon the investment company's ability and obligation to issue new shares and to retire outstanding shares. Since there is a wide variation in the investment policies of these companies, investors are usually able to find one type of fund that meets their needs.

DISCUSSION QUESTIONS

1. Explain the statement, "What may be a speculation for one investor may be an investment for another."
2. Use the investment pyramid as a basis for describing an investment plan.
3. Explain why savings institutions have such a wide variety of savings plans available. Give illustrations of the accounts and how consumers can use them.
4. How do Series E and Series H savings bonds differ from each other? Discuss the advantages and disadvantages of holding these bonds.
5. Explain the difference between open-end and closed-end investment companies.
6. Explain the major difference between the load and no-load mutual funds. What are some reasons for buying load rather than no-load funds? What does it mean if the fund has a "front-end load"?
7. Why would an investor who is interested in appreciation of the value of the principal consider investing in a dual-purpose fund?
8. Compare the deposit insurance offered by each of the savings institutions. If you have deposits in excess of the insured maximum, how can you increase the amount covered by insurance?
9. Compare the interest rate ceilings for the savings institutions. Look up the current interest rate ceilings and compare them with Exhibit 13–3. Explain why changes occurred.

CASE PROBLEM

Steve is a freshman at State University. In order to make it easier to write checks at local businesses he has decided to open a checking account at a local bank. He plans to use this account to pay all of his expenses. Steve finds that one of the banks offers "free" checking to students who maintain a balance of at least $100 at all times. If this balance is not maintained, the service fee would be $2 per month.

This past summer Steve had a job where he earned $1,200 (take-home). He does not plan to work during the school year, at least during his freshman year. In order to help Steve, his parents have agreed to pay for his food and housing for the year, a total cost of $850, and to give him the money at the beginning of the school year. Also, if Steve's required expenses exceed his available earnings, his parents will help him for his freshman year. In January, Steve expects to receive about $350 as a tax refund from his summer earnings. Tuition and books average $550 per semester.

As he was opening his new checking account, Steve wondered whether he should also open a savings account. The bank offered 5 percent on passbook accounts, 5½ on accounts requiring 90-day notice of withdrawal, and 6 percent on one-year certificates of deposit. A local S&L offers similar accounts but the rates are ¼ percent higher.

1. *How could Steve make use of a savings account?*
2. *If he decides to use a savings plan, should he use an account at the bank, S&L, or U.S. Savings Bonds? Explain your decision.*
3. *Does Steve need to provide for an emergency fund? Why or why not?*
4. *Should he place the $100 in his savings plan rather than maintain a minimum balance in his checking account? Why or why not?*

SELECTED READINGS

"How to Pick the Best Savings Account," *Consumer Reports*, February 1975, p. 90.

Lorie, James H. and Hamilton, Mary T. *The Stock Market: Theories and Evidence.* Homewood, Ill.: Richard D. Irwin, Inc., 1973, Chapter 15.

Sauvain, Harry C. *Investment Management*, 4th ed. Englewood Cliffs, New Jersey: Prentice-Hall, 1973.

Van Caspel, Venita. *Money Dynamics.* Reston, Virginia: Reston Publishing Company, 1975.

Widicus, Wilber W. and Stitzel, Thomas E. *Personal Investing*, Revised Edition. Homewood, Ill.: Richard D. Irwin, Inc., 1976.

Investments—Stocks and bonds

14

OBJECTIVES

Stocks and bonds are the second most popular form of investment among consumers. In this chapter we will discuss the characteristics of these securities by type and by issuer and examine how they may be bought or sold. After thoroughly studying and discussing this chapter, you should be able to:

. . . Distinguish between common stocks, preferred stocks, and bonds.
. . . Contrast the characteristics of corporate and governmental securities in terms of what the investor is likely to and legally entitled to receive.
. . . Describe the characteristics of the primary and secondary securities markets.
. . . Identify sources of investment information.
. . . Explain the importance of selecting a broker.
. . . Interpret security price quotations.

There is always someone who is willing to share a tale of how a fortune was made by investing in stocks or bonds. But you will rarely hear stories from people who have lost their money through bad investments. It is the possibility of great gain that attracts many investors to these securities. In the United States, the number of investors who own stocks or bonds is second only to the number who have savings accounts.

Because of the importance of securities as personal investments, our discussion will emphasize the types of corporate and government securities available to investors and the characteristics of each type. An understanding of these characteristics will help you to determine which, if any, of these securities meet your investment needs. An analysis of investor needs is the topic of Chapter 15.

Businesses and governments issue securities to raise the money they need for operations. The money raised by securities is used for replacing or expanding plants and equipment, increasing the amount of inventory carried, constructing new utility plants, defense installations, etc. A common characteristic of such projects is that a relatively large outlay of money is required. Once the project has been completed, the benefits are expected to be realized over a long period of time. For example, a corporation may spend millions of dollars to build a new plant. It expects that the product that is produced in the new plant can be sold at a profit for the firm. Depending upon the type of security used by the corporation to raise the needed funds, these profits can be distributed to the bondholders (creditors) in the form of interest and principal repayment or to the stockholders (owners) in the form of dividends. Thus, investors are actually the suppliers of capital for the various organizations which issue the securities.

Securities are commonly classified in two ways: by type or legal status (debt or equity) and by issuer. Issuers of one or both types of securities include private business corporations, governments, and governmental agencies.

CLASSIFICATION OF SECURITIES BY TYPE OF SECURITY

Debt and equity securities differ from one another in several important ways: in the rights and responsibilities given to investors, in the voice that the investor is given in management's decisions, in the relationship of the investor to the issuer, in the frequency and assurance of interest or dividends, and in the repayment of the invested principal.

Debt securities

Bonds, notes, and bills are evidences of a debtor-creditor relationship between the issuer and investor. When you purchase one of these securities, you receive a certificate to verify the debt that is owed to you; that is, you are a creditor and have loaned money to the issuer. Bonds represent long-term debt, usually five years or more from time of issue to maturity. Notes and bills indicate debts of one to five years and less than one year, respectively, from time of issue. Virtually all debt securities have a maturity, a specific date on which the issuer is legally obliged to repay the principal. Interest on borrowed funds usually must be paid regardless of whether the issuer earns a profit. Failure by the issuer to pay the interest when due is termed a *default*. When the issuer defaults on interest payments, or any other of the provisions in the contract, the investor can take legal action to collect what is due even though the result may be bankruptcy for the issuer. The strong legal position of the bondholder in the event of a default deters the issuer from defaulting. Thus, most issuers will fulfill their part of the contract if at all possible.

Equity securities

Stock represents a share of ownership in a corporation. The most significant distinction among stocks is that between preferred stock and common stock. Common stock is often referred to as the residual or basic ownership security, because these owners are entitled to whatever is left after the claims of all others have been met. Preferred stock is also an ownership security. But, as the name implies, the preferred stock owner receives preference over common stock owners in some situations.

Par value and no-par value

Investors often have questions about the significance of par value of a security. Par value is a value that has been assigned to the shares of stock in the articles of incorporation and may also be referred to as the face or maturity value for a bond. Par value is not an indication of market value.

The original intent of assigning a par value was to provide an indication of the amount of capital that had been raised by the corporation. With the passage of time, however, this intent has not been fulfilled because stock may be issued in exchange for value other than cash. For example, stock may be issued to buy property or services. Thus, it is the market value, not the par value, that is equal to the value of the property or service acquired. It is presently recognized that par value is not serving its intended purpose and most states will permit corporations to issue shares without a par value. As a result, par value, per se, is of no real interest to you as an investor, except as it may indicate the principal value of a debt security.

CLASSIFICATION OF SECURITIES BY ISSUER

There are two major types of issuers of securities: private business corporations and governments or agencies of the government. Nearly all of the private businesses that issue securities are organized as corporations. In the eyes of the law, a corporation is regarded as a legal entity separate from the owners. Its securities are called "corporates."

Governmental bodies on all levels also issue securities. Federal government securities are known as "governments" or as "treasuries." State and local government issues are called "municipals."

Corporate bonds

As was noted, bonds are evidences of debt with a maturity of five years or more. Corporate bonds are commonly issued in denominations or multiples of $1,000. Common usage of the term "a bond" means one bond of $1,000 denomination. Each of these bonds is one of a number of bonds in an entire issue. For example, in a $1,000,000 bond issue there is the equivalent of 1,000 bonds, each with a face value of $1,000.

Interest on corporate bonds is usually paid semiannually on either coupon bonds or registered bonds. Coupon bonds are securities with a series of coupons attached that enable the bondholder to collect the interest. One coupon matures on each of the interest payment dates. To collect the interest you clip the coupon and deposit it in your bank. With a registered bond the name of the holder is recorded with a registrar and the interest is paid by issuing a check to the registered holder of the bonds. A sample of a coupon bond is shown in Exhibit 14–1.

Each bond issue is covered by a contract known as an indenture. The provisions of the indenture specify the rights and obligations of the issuer and of the investor, including when interest and principal are due. This indenture remains in effect until the bonds have either matured or have been otherwise retired. The provisions of the indenture cannot be changed after the bonds have been sold by the issuer except by agreement of the bondholders.

The indenture under which the bonds are issued is made with a trustee, who acts on behalf of the bondholders. The trustee must be a financially responsible third party, usually a large bank or other financial institution. In addition to the responsibility for protecting the bondholders' rights by making sure that the issuer is meeting the conditions set forth in the indenture, the trustee may also be responsible for recording the ownership of the securities and making the interest payments to the registered bondholders. In the event of default by the issuer, the trustee is responsible for bringing legal suit against the company to protect the interests of the bondholders. Bond owners may obtain a copy of the indenture if they wish, but the main features of the contract are contained in the *prospectus*, which is provided to all original buyers of securities.

EXHIBIT 14–1
Corporate bond with coupons

$1000 $1000

No M

WISCONSIN TELEPHONE COMPANY

FORTY YEAR 4⅜% DEBENTURE,
DUE MAY 1, 2002

Wisconsin Telephone Company,
a corporation duly organized and existing under the laws of the State of Wisconsin (herein referred to as the "Company"), for value received, hereby promises to pay to bearer (or, if this Debenture be registered as to principal, then to the registered holder hereof) at the office or agency of the Company in the Borough of Manhattan, The City of New York, the principal sum of

ONE THOUSAND DOLLARS ($1,000),

on May 1, 2002, in such coin or currency of the United States of America as at the time of payment shall be legal tender for the payment of public and private debts, and to pay interest on said principal sum at the rate of 4⅜% per annum, at said office or agency, in like coin or currency, from May 1, 1962, semi-annually on May 1 and November 1, until payment of said principal sum has been made or duly provided for, but only upon presentation and surrender of the coupons for such interest instalments as are evidenced thereby, hereto appertaining, as they shall severally mature.

This Debenture is one of a duly authorized issue of Debentures of the Company, designated as its Forty Year 4⅜% Debentures, due May 1, 2002 (herein referred to as the "Debentures"), limited to the aggregate principal amount of twenty million dollars ($20,000,000), all issued or to be issued under and pursuant to an indenture dated May 1, 1962 (herein referred to as the "Indenture"), duly executed and delivered by the Company to Marine National Exchange Bank of Milwaukee, a national banking association duly organized and existing under the laws of the United States of America, Trustee, to which Indenture and all indentures supplemental thereto reference is hereby made for a description of the rights, limitation of rights, obligations, duties and immunities thereunder of the Trustee, the Company and the holders of the Debentures and coupons.

In case an Event of Default, as defined in the Indenture, shall have occurred and be continuing, the principal hereof may be declared, and upon such declaration shall become, due and payable, in the manner, with the effect and subject to the conditions provided in the Indenture.

The Indenture contains provisions permitting the Company and the Trustee, with the consent of the holders of not less than 66⅔% in aggregate principal amount of the Debentures at the time outstanding, evidenced as in the Indenture provided, to execute supplemental indentures adding any provisions to or changing in any manner or eliminating any of the provisions of the Indenture or of any supplemental indenture or modifying in any manner the rights of the holders of the Debentures and coupons; provided, however, that no such supplemental indenture shall (i) extend the fixed maturity of any Debentures, or reduce the principal amount thereof, or reduce the rate or extend the time of payment of interest thereon, or reduce any premium payable upon the redemption thereof, without the consent of the holder of each Debenture so affected, or (ii) reduce the aforesaid percentage of Debentures, the consent of the holders of which is required for any such supplemental indenture, without the consent of the holders of all Debentures then outstanding. It is also provided in the Indenture that the holders of a majority in aggregate principal amount of the Debentures at the time outstanding may on behalf of the holders of all of the Debentures waive any past default under the Indenture and its consequences, except a default in the payment of the principal of (or premium, if any) or interest on any of the Debentures. Any such consent or waiver by the holder of this Debenture (unless revoked as provided in the Indenture) shall be conclusive and binding upon such holder and upon all future holders and owners of this Debenture and of any Debenture issued in exchange or substitution therefor, irrespective of whether or not any notation of such consent or waiver is made upon this Debenture.

No reference herein to the Indenture and no provision of this Debenture or of the Indenture shall alter or impair the obligation of the Company, which is absolute and unconditional, to pay the principal of (and premium, if any) and interest on this Debenture at the place, at the respective times, at the rate and in the coin or currency herein prescribed.

The Debentures are issuable as coupon Debentures, registrable as to principal, in the denomination of $1,000 and as registered Debentures without coupons in denominations of $1,000 and any multiple of $1,000. At the above-mentioned office or agency of the Company and in the manner, subject to the limitations and upon payment of the charges provided in the Indenture, registered Debentures without coupons may be exchanged for a like aggregate principal amount of coupon Debentures of the authorized denomination bearing all unmatured coupons and any matured coupons in default or for a like aggregate principal amount of registered Debentures without coupons of other authorized denominations, and coupon Debentures bearing all unmatured coupons and any matured coupons in default may be exchanged for a like aggregate principal amount of registered Debentures without coupons of authorized denominations.

As provided in the Indenture, the Debentures may be redeemed, at the option of the Company, as a whole or from time to time in part (selected by lot in such manner as the Trustee may deem appropriate and fair, including the selection by groups as provided in the Indenture), on any date prior to maturity, upon the notice referred to below, at the following redemption prices (expressed in percentages of the principal amount) together with accrued interest to the date fixed for redemption: to and including April 30, 1963, 107.00%; thereafter to and including April 30, 1965, 106.50%; thereafter during the 12 months' periods ending April 30:

1966	106.00%	1973	104.44%	1980	103.19%	1987	101.95%	1994	100.71%
1967	105.50%	1974	104.26%	1981	103.02%	1988	101.77%	1995	100.53%
1968	105.32%	1975	104.08%	1982	102.84%	1989	101.60%	1996	100.35%
1969	105.15%	1976	103.90%	1983	102.66%	1990	101.42%	1997	100.18%
1970	104.97%	1977	103.73%	1984	102.48%	1991	101.24%		
1971	104.79%	1978	103.55%	1985	102.31%	1992	101.06%		
1972	104.61%	1979	103.37%	1986	102.13%	1993	100.89%		

and thereafter, 100%. Notice of redemption to the holders of coupon Debentures to be redeemed as a whole or in part, other than those registered as to principal, shall be given by publication of a notice of such redemption at least four times, each publication to be made in at least two newspapers printed in the English language and customarily published at least once a day for at least five days in each calendar week and of general circulation, in the said Borough of Manhattan, the first such publication to be not less than thirty nor more than ninety days prior to the date fixed for redemption, all as provided in the Indenture. Notice of redemption to the registered holders of coupon Debentures registered as to principal, and to the registered holders of registered Debentures without coupons, to be redeemed as a whole or in part, shall be given either (a) by mailing a notice of such redemption not less than thirty nor more than ninety days prior to the date fixed for redemption to their last addresses as they shall appear upon the registry books, or (b) by publication of a notice of such redemption in the manner provided above, all as provided in the Indenture.

This Debenture shall pass by delivery except while registered as to principal. This Debenture may be registered as to principal upon presentation at the above-mentioned office or agency of the Company, such registration being noted hereon, after which no transfer hereof shall be valid unless made, as provided in the Indenture, at said office or agency by the registered holder hereof or by his attorney duly authorized in writing and similarly noted hereon; but this Debenture may be discharged from such registration by like transfer to bearer noted hereon, whereupon transferability by delivery shall be restored. Such registration, however, shall not affect the transferability by delivery of the coupons for the interest hereon, and such coupons shall continue to be payable to bearer and transferable by delivery. No service charge shall be made for any such registration, transfer or discharge from registration, but the Company may require payment of a sum sufficient to cover any tax or other governmental charge that may be imposed in relation thereto.

The Company, the Trustee, any paying agent and any Debenture registrar may deem and treat the bearer hereof (or, if this Debenture be registered as to principal, then the registered holder hereof) and the bearer of any coupon appertaining hereto, whether or not this Debenture shall be registered as to principal, as the absolute owner of this Debenture or such coupon, as the case may be (whether or not this Debenture or such coupon shall be overdue and notwithstanding any notation of ownership or other writing hereon or thereon made by anyone other than the Company or any Debenture registrar), for the purpose of receiving payment hereof or of such coupon or on account hereof or of such coupon, as the case may be, and for all other purposes, and neither the Company nor the Trustee nor any paying agent nor any Debenture registrar shall be affected by any notice to the contrary.

No recourse shall be had for the payment of the principal of (or premium, if any) or the interest on this Debenture, or for any claim based hereon, or otherwise in respect hereof, or based on or in respect of the Indenture or any indenture supplemental thereto, against any incorporator, stockholder, officer or director, as such, past, present or future, of the Company or of any successor corporation, whether by virtue of any constitution, statute or rule of law, or by the enforcement of any assessment or penalty or otherwise, all such liability being, by the acceptance hereof and as part of the consideration for the issue hereof, expressly waived and released.

Neither this Debenture nor any coupon appertaining hereto shall be valid or become obligatory for any purpose until the certificate of authentication hereon shall have been executed by the Trustee.

In Witness Whereof, Wisconsin Telephone Company has caused this Debenture to be signed by its President or one of its Vice Presidents by a facsimile of his signature and by its Treasurer or one of its Assistant Treasurers by a facsimile of his signature and has caused a facsimile of its corporate seal to be affixed hereunto or imprinted hereon and coupons for interest bearing the facsimile signature of its Treasurer, to be attached hereto.

DATED MAY 1, 1962.

TRUSTEE'S CERTIFICATE OF AUTHENTICATION

This is one of the Debentures described in the within-mentioned Indenture.

MARINE NATIONAL EXCHANGE BANK OF MILWAUKEE,
AS TRUSTEE,

BY SPECIMEN
AUTHORIZED OFFICER

WISCONSIN TELEPHONE COMPANY

Wisconsin Telephone Company,

BY C. E. Wampler
PRESIDENT

SPECIMEN
Moen
TREASURER

WIS. TEL. CO. 4⅜% DEB. OF '02
No. M

EXHIBIT 14–1 *(continued)*

Coupon	Date	Amount
80	MAY 1 2002	$21.87
79	NOV 1 2001	$21.88
78	MAY 1 2001	$21.87
77	NOV 1 2000	$21.88
76	MAY 1 2000	$21.87
75	NOV 1 1999	$21.88
74	MAY 1 1999	$21.87
73	NOV 1 1998	$21.88
72	MAY 1 1998	$21.87
71	NOV 1 1997	$21.88
70	MAY 1 1997	$21.87
69	NOV 1 1996	$21.88
68	MAY 1 1996	$21.87
67	NOV 1 1995	$21.88
66	MAY 1 1995	$21.87
65	NOV 1 1994	$21.88
64	MAY 1 1994	$21.87
63	NOV 1 1993	$21.88
62	MAY 1 1993	$21.87
61	NOV 1 1992	$21.88
60	MAY 1 1992	$21.87
59	NOV 1 1991	$21.88
58	MAY 1 1991	$21.87
57	NOV 1 1990	$21.88
56	MAY 1 1990	$21.87
55	NOV 1 1989	$21.88
54	MAY 1 1989	$21.87
53	NOV 1 1988	$21.88
52	MAY 1 1988	$21.87
51	NOV 1 1987	$21.88
50	MAY 1 1987	$21.87
49	NOV 1 1986	$21.88
48	MAY 1 1986	$21.87
47	NOV 1 1985	$21.88
46	MAY 1 1985	$21.87
45	NOV 1 1984	$21.88
44	MAY 1 1984	$21.87
43	NOV 1 1983	$21.88
42	MAY 1 1983	$21.87
41	NOV 1 1982	$21.88
40	MAY 1 1982	$21.87
39	NOV 1 1981	$21.88

Collateral for bonds. A most important distinction between corporate bonds is made on the basis of the collateral pledged for the payment of the interest and principal. Bonds are known on this basis as either *secured* or *unsecured.*

A secured bond is one that is issued under an indenture that provides a lien on property of the issuer. Interest and principal payments for these bonds are commonly made from the earnings of the issuer. But, should the issuer be unable to make these payments from earnings, the bondholders can force the sale of the collateral in order to collect what is due them. This added backing makes the bonds more attractive to many investors.

Secured bonds are commonly identified by the type of property that serves as collateral for the issue. *Mortgage bonds* are usually secured by a claim or mortgage on the property of the company such as buildings, land, equipment, etc. *Collateral trust bonds* are issued by companies whose property consists mainly of bonds and stocks of other companies. *Equipment trust certificates* are issued by companies in the transportation industry where the collateral is equipment such as locomotives, railroad cars, airplanes, or ships. The title to the equipment is actually placed with the trustee. The equipment involved has a known value and a relatively wide market in the event that it is necessary to sell it.

Unsecured bonds are bonds that are issued under indentures that do not place a lien on any of the property of the issuer. These bonds, commonly called *debentures* or debenture bonds, have only the earning power of the issuer as security for the bond issue. Many large, financially sound corporations are able to issue debentures because their credit rating is so good that there is no advantage to placing a lien on specific assets. In some cases, financially weak companies may issue debentures because they may have no assets to pledge as collateral. Therefore, it is not possible to generalize about the quality of a bond only on the basis of its unsecured nature.

Regardless of whether the bond issue is secured or unsecured, creditors have first claim on both the income and property of the corporation. Owners' (stockholders') claims are secondary to those of creditors.

Retirement provisions. As a bondholder, and therefore a legal creditor, you are entitled to the return of the loan principal. Bond indentures include provisions for the retirement of principal either at maturity or prior to maturity.

Most indentures provide for the periodic retirement of principal, referred to as *amortization* of principal, beginning at some specified time after issue date and continuing until maturity. This is advantageous to the investor because the issuer is more likely to be able to make these periodic payments without financial stress rather than pay the entire principal at maturity.

A common device for amortizing the principal is called a *sinking fund*. The provisions of sinking funds vary widely, but the end result is the same—retirement of principal. Typical provisions provide for the retirement of a specified dollar amount of bonds or of a proportion of the bond issue from funds that the issuer turns over to the trustee.

Retirement of the principal prior to maturity requires a provision in the indenture commonly known as the *call provision*. The call provision permits the issuer to repay the bond prior to maturity by notifying randomly selected bondholders that their bonds are to be redeemed by a specified date. After the specified date, known as the call date, the issuer no longer must pay interest on any such bonds that have not been presented for redemption. Bonds may be made callable only for specific reasons, or they may be callable at any time at the will of the issuer. For example, a firm may be able to refund its bond issue—that is, call its bonds for the purpose of replacing the old issue bearing a high interest rate with a new issue bearing a lower interest rate. In any case, the terms of the call are specifically stated in the indenture. Usually when the bond issue is called for refunding purposes, the call price is greater than the face value. This higher price is known as a call premium and provides you some protection against having the bond called. The premium varies, often depending upon interest rate levels at the time the old bond was issued and the time remaining until maturity. The higher the call premium, the greater the protection afforded the investor. The call provision for the Wisconsin Telephone Company debenture shown in Exhibit 14–1 is expressed on the bond certificate. The provision provides for a decreasing call price each year from 1963 through 1997, when the bond may be called at face value.

The call privilege works to the benefit of issuers, for they can use it to recall bond issues with high interest rates and replace them with issues with lower interest rates. Even though bondholders receive the face value of the bond plus the call premium, the proceeds cannot be reinvested in bonds of similar risk to earn an amount of interest equal to that on the called issue because interest rates have declined. For example, suppose that your triple-A corporate bond with a 9½ percent coupon has been called because interest rates have decreased to 8 percent on similar bonds. That is, this company can now borrow money by paying 8 percent interest rather than the 9½ percent required at the time the old issue was sold. In return for your $1,000 bond you will receive $1,095 (principal plus call premium—often equal to one year's interest), which you can reinvest. As a result of this refunding, your income, assuming you can reinvest the full $1,095 in the new triple-A bond at 8 percent, will now be $87.60 as opposed to the original $95 per year.

Conversion privilege. Some indentures provide for the conversion of the bonds into a specific number of shares of the company's common stock. Conversion is executed at the option of investors who may wish to change their status from creditor to owner. Convertible bonds are attractive because they offer the safety of a creditor's position while at the same time offering, through the conversion privilege, an opportunity to share in any gain from the price appreciation of the common stock. For example, suppose that a $1,000 bond is convertible into 25 shares of common stock; that is, at a conversion price of $40 per share. If the company is successful and the market price of the stock rises to $50, the value of the stock into which the bond is convertible is $1,250. At this point the market price of the bond should also be about $1,250. Thus the bondholder shares in the firm's success through the price appreciation of the bond that resulted from the increased market value of the company's stock.

Investors do not receive this privilege free. The cost usually takes the form of a lower interest rate received on a convertible than on a comparable nonconvertible (straight bond) issue. Convertible bonds are usually callable, and therefore the issuer may be able to force conversion. When the convertible bond has been called, the investor must choose between realizing the call price or the value of stock into which the bond is convertible. Since the value of the stock exceeds the call price of the bond, the bondholder is "forced" to convert. Bondholders do have the opportunity and right to redeem the bond for the call price. This, however, is not a good choice of options.

Common stock

Stockholders are entitled to the rights and responsibilities unique to ownership. A stock certificate is issued to each stockholder indicating the number of shares owned. A sample common stock certificate is shown in Exhibit 14–2. The document defining basic ownership rights is known as the company's articles of incorporation. Rights of shareholders to dividends and voting make common stock an attractive investment.

Dividends that you receive are actually distributions of the company's earnings. The articles of incorporation do not guarantee that you will receive any specific rate or dollar amount of dividend, or that a dividend will be paid even if the company has earnings available.

EXHIBIT 14–2
Stock certificate

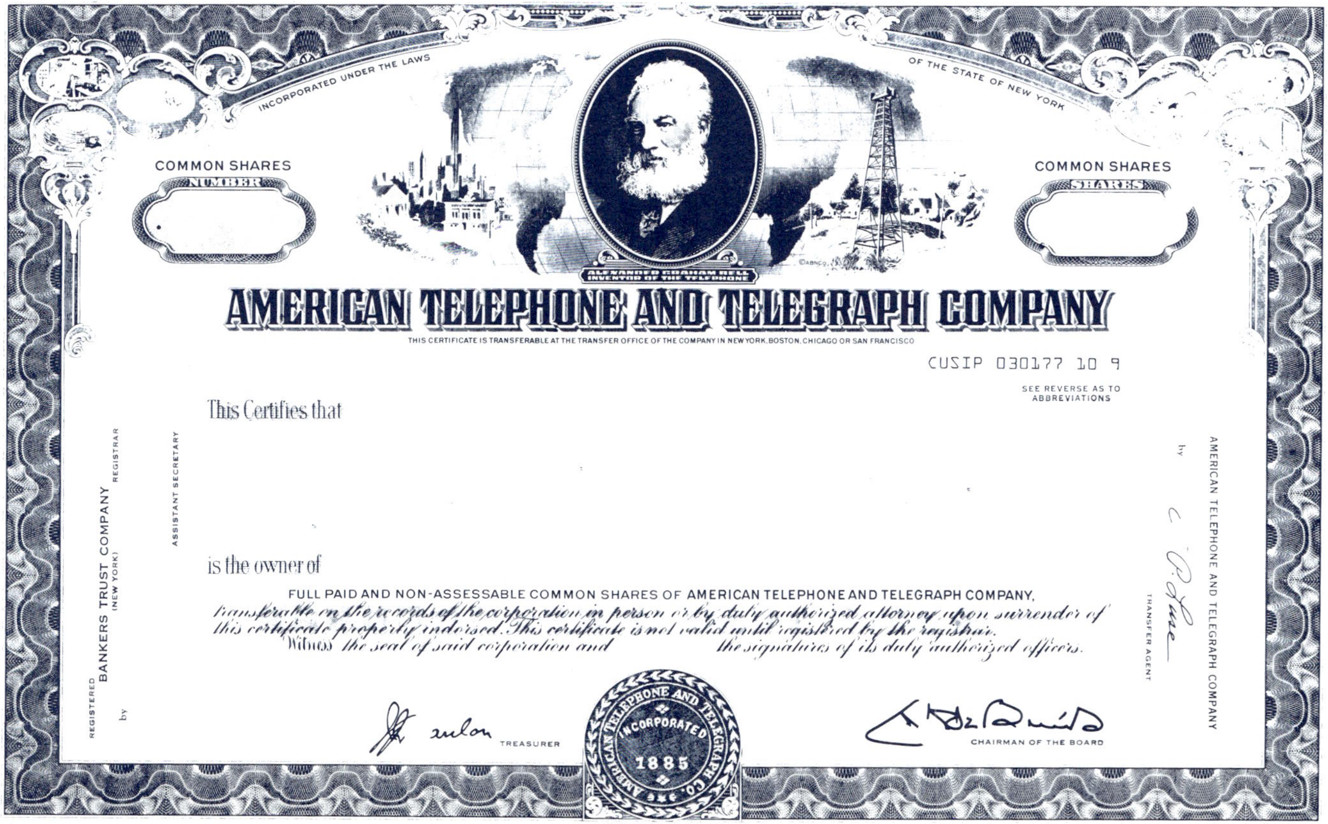

The only right guaranteed is that if the company's board of directors decides to pay (declares) a dividend, each common stockholder will receive the same amount per share. A board of directors is under no legal obligation to declare a dividend, however. Some stockholders have brought legal actions against boards of directors to force the declaration of dividends, but few of these suits have been successful.

It is the prospect of receiving dividends that makes common stock attractive to investors. If a company prospers, large amounts of earnings may be distributed to the owners. The expectation of large dividends means there is potential for large increases in the market price of the stock. But there is also the possibility that the company will not be successful and never declare dividends. And, because the company makes no promise to repay any money invested, investors can recover their principal only by selling to another investor. When the company's prospects are dim, the price of the stock will be low and investors who sell may lose much or all of their invested principal.

Common stockholders also have the right to vote on the election of directors and on various questions of corporate policy (generally one vote for each share they own). Usually common shareholders must approve actions such as mortgaging of property, mergers, acquisitions of other firms or changing the number of shares of stock issued by the corporation. Many stockholders, however, do not take their voting rights seriously enough or are unable to travel to the stockholders' meeting and cast their votes. This is particularly true of investors who own only a few shares. These stockholders sign "proxies" mailed to them by management, transferring to someone else their legal right to vote.

In the event that a corporation is dissolved, common stockholders are entitled to receive a pro-rata share of any proceeds remaining after the claims of all creditors and preferred stockholders are met. There is often an amount to be distributed if the dissolution results from a reason other than bankruptcy. But when bankruptcy is the cause of dissolution, the common stockholder can expect to receive very little, if anything.

There are other stockholder rights that are generally of lesser importance, especially for the average investor. Exercising these rights may involve large legal expenditures. The holder's right to obtain a list of company stockholders' names, inspect corporate books, or bring suit against a director who is believed not to have acted in the best interest of the corporation can be reasonably exercised only by individuals who own major amounts of stock.

Preferred stock

Like common stock, preferred stock represents an ownership interest in the corporation. It differs from common stock, however, in that in exchange for preferential treatment for dividends, preferred stockholders usually do not have voting rights.

Dividends on preferred stock are usually limited in amount per share and may be stated as a percentage of par value or as a dollar amount. Preferred holders are entitled to receive their full dividend before any dividend is paid to the common stockholders. This does not guarantee the payment of a dividend to the preferred stockholders; it simply gives them preference if any dividend is paid. If the dividend is not paid, the preferred stockholders cannot bring legal action to bear on the company to force payment as a creditor can.

In exchange for the preferential dividend treatment, the typical preferred stock does not allow participation; that is, the amount of the dividend is limited to the stated amount. Therefore, if the company is prosperous, preferred owners are not entitled to a larger dividend from the higher company earnings. These higher earnings belong to the common shareholders. Occasionally you can find a participating preferred stock, but it is unusual.

Dividends may be cumulative or noncumulative. Cumulative preferred stock means that if a dividend is not paid (that is, if it is passed), it accumulates. The company must pay all dividends not paid in preceding years before any dividend can be paid to the common stockholder. Even though this is not a legal debt of the issuer, the cumulative preferred stockholder's position is strengthened because of the desire by most companies to pay a dividend to their common shareowners. A noncumulative preferred means that if a dividend is passed it is lost forever by the investor.

Preferred stock owners have a claim on income and on the distribution of property of a dissolved business that must be met before any payment can be made to the common share owners. Amounts of the claim are limited to amounts stipulated in the contract covering the issue.

Other features of preferred stock that are important to you are convertibility and callability. These features in preferred stock work in the same manner as they do with bonds. A convertible preferred share may be exchanged for common stock of the issuing company, thus converting the preferred status of the owner to that of a residual owner. As with bonds, the conversion occurs at the option of the investor. The conversion ratio is specified in the agreement setting forth the rights and limitations of the preferred issue. To illustrate, a preferred share with a par value of $100 is specified to be convertible into five shares of common, a conversion price of $20 per share. At the time the preferred was issued, the price of the common was probably in the neighborhood of $16 per share. If the company is prosperous, the price of the common is expected to rise above the $20 per share conversion price. Dividends may also increase so that the dividends on the five shares of common are greater than the dividend on the one share of preferred stock. This situation makes the conversion attractive to the preferred share owners because they can reap the benefits of being residual owners of a successful company.

Most preferred stock, especially convertible preferred, is callable. Redemption is effected at the option of the issuer at a price stipulated in the agreement covering the issue. Some preferred issues are retired through the use of a sinking fund arrangement similar to the one discussed for bonds. Ordinarily, however, the company has greater flexibility in the retirement of preferred stock than in the retirement of debt.

United States government securities

Obligations of the United States government, commonly called *Treasuries,* are generally considered to be safer than any other security. Because of the government's unlimited power to tax as well as to coin money, there is virtually no possibility of failure to pay interest and principal when due. This does not mean that these securities are risk-free, but this will be discussed in Chapter 15.

All government issues are debt securities. Classification of the debt issues is made in terms of their marketability; that is, whether one investor can transfer the title to the security to another investor through a sale. About 80 percent of the government issues available to investors are marketable issues. Nonmarketable issues, such as savings bonds, account for the other 20 percent of U.S. government debt securities.

Marketable treasuries are divided according to their maturity into three general classifications: bills, notes, and bonds. Treasury bills are of shortest maturity: 13-week, 26-week, and 52-week. A distinctive feature of treasury bills is that interest is paid to investors by having them purchase the bills at a discount (at less than the par value). That is, the interest is collected when the bills are redeemed at par value at maturity.

Treasury notes, which have maturities ranging from one to five years, are initially sold at par value. The Treasury pays interest semiannually to investors and redeems the notes at par value at maturity. Treasury bonds differ from notes in that they have longer maturities, usually 10 to 30 years. Some of the bond issues have special characteristics such as callability, or some may be used at par for the payment of estate taxes even though they may have been purchased in the market for considerably less than par. For example, if an investor pays $800 for a bond of an issue that has been designated by the Treasury as being acceptable at par for payment of estate taxes, the bond can be used to pay $1,000 of estate taxes.

Securities are also issued by agencies or institutions created by the United States government. These agency issues are not direct obligations of, but some issues are guaranteed by, the government. Even those issues not guaranteed are regarded as extremely safe, however, because it is believed unlikely that the federal government would permit these institutions to default. Some of the federal agency issuers include the Federal Home Loan Banks, the Federal Land Banks, and the Government National Mortgage Association.

Municipal government securities

Securities issued by local and state governmental units are commonly called *municipals.* Municipals are attractive investments to investors in high tax brackets because the interest from them is exempt from the federal income tax. This tax exemption has been the topic of much discussion in recent proposals for tax reform before the Congress.

State and local government bonds are classified as being *full faith and credit, revenue bonds, assessment bonds,* or some combination of the three. Full faith and credit bonds, also known as general obligation bonds, have the full taxing power of the issuer backing the bond issue. These securities are regarded as the safest of the types of municipals. In the past, defaults have occurred only during adverse economic periods such as the Great Depression.

Revenue bonds are secured by the success of the project for which the funds were used. They are used to finance housing projects, utilities, stadiums, bridges, and highways. Specific revenues such as rents, fees, and tolls, provide funds to pay principal and interest. In the event that the revenues from the project are not great enough to pay the principal and interest, bondholders cannot legally require the issuer to provide the needed revenues from other sources.

Assessment bonds are used to finance municipal improvements such as streets and sidewalks. Assessments are levied against the property owners, who must then pay for the improvements. Usually the property owner has several years over which payment can be made. As the payments are made, the assessment bond issue is repaid.

THE SECURITIES MARKETS

Active securities markets make it possible and convenient for you to invest your funds in securities and to sell your securities to raise cash. Within these markets there are organizations or institutions that handle the specific transactions involved.

Primary markets

The primary market, or new-issue market, is distinctive in that it includes only the initial sale of securities by the issuer. These sales result in a flow of capital from the investor to the company that issues securities.

You can buy new issues of corporate securities by contacting a securities broker. If the firm with which the broker is associated is a part of the group of firms helping the issuer in the initial sale, there is no commission charged on the transaction.

Purchases of new issues of Treasuries can be made through the Federal Reserve Bank in the district in which you live. To buy these securities you must fill out forms provided by the Bank, on which you indicate the quantity you wish to purchase and the price you are willing to pay. There are no commissions or fees for purchases in these transactions.

While one of the main advantages of this market is the absence of commissions, a disadvantage is that you have less choice of maturities than in the secondary market.

Secondary markets

Securities that have been sold in the primary market may be traded time after time among investors. These trades of existing securities occur in the secondary market. Secondary market transactions are distinguished from those in the primary market by the fact that there is no capital flowing to the issuing corporation or governmental unit.

Secondary markets are divided into two types: organized securities exchanges and the over-the-counter market.

Organized securities exchanges. A securities exchange is a place where a group of individuals gather to trade securities. Traditionally, these are membership associations; only members are permitted to use the exchange facilities for trading and to participate in the management of the exchange.

Securities exchanges that operate in interstate commerce are regulated under the Securities Exchange Act of 1934 and must register with the Securities Exchange Commission (SEC) for permission to operate. The SEC has authority to make rules, examine records, or suspend officers of an exchange if there have been violations of the Act.

There are 14 organized stock exchanges in the United States including 11 outside New York City. Two of the exchanges are national exchanges and dominate the secondary market in that they account for over 90 percent of the trading activity (dollar value of trades) on exchanges. The largest of all these exchanges is the New York Stock Exchange (NYSE), which accounts for about 75 percent of the trading activity. Second in size is the American Stock Exchange (ASE), also located in New York City, which handles about 17 percent of the trading activity on the exchanges. The three largest regional stock exchanges are the Midwest Stock Exchange (Chicago), the Pacific Coast Stock Exchange (Los Angeles and San Francisco), and the Philadelphia-Baltimore-Washington Stock Exchange (Philadelphia). In addition to these, other regional stock exchanges are located in major cities such as Boston, Salt Lake City, and Spokane.

Transactions on an exchange are carried out by auction. Each security traded on the exchange is assigned to a certain "post" (a trading area on the floor of the exchange), and all transactions in that security must be made only at that post. Therefore, at any given time, any exchange member (floor broker) interested in either selling or buying that specific security will be at that post. When one floor broker has shares to sell, other floor brokers who want to buy will compete for the shares. Thus both buyer and seller are assured of the best price. This does not mean that the price remains constant for any period, for the next transaction in the security will likely be at a somewhat different price. It does mean that it is the fairest price available at the time of the transaction.

Over-the-counter markets (OTCs). Security transactions that do not occur on the floor of an exchange are referred to as over-the-counter transactions. There is no centralized facility where trading occurs as there is for an organized exchange, but rather trading occurs over the telephone or through wire transactions.

The securities traded in the OTC are diverse in kind, price, quality, and volume. They range from the common stock of virtually unknown firms to United States Treasury securities. Most of the trading in municipal and treasury bonds and in the stocks of financial institutions occurs in the OTC. It is generally agreed that the dollar volume of trading in the OTC is greater than that on the organized exchanges, but no one knows how much greater.

The OTC operates through wholesale dealer firms that buy and sell securities much as any other wholesalers operate. Individual firms are registered by the National Association of Securities Dealers (NASD) as market makers in one or more issues. These wholesalers deal with each other and with retail brokerage firms that sell to the public. Trading in the OTC is greatly facilitated by the automated system of price quotations provided by National Association of Securities Dealers Automated Quotations (NASDAQ). This system enables subscribing firms to get the current price quotations on any of a large number of issues quoted by the system. Prices for NASDAQ are quoted by the registered dealers making the markets in the securities.

Buying and selling securities

If you know of someone who wishes to sell the security that you wish to purchase, all you have to do is to agree on a price and you can close the deal. By sending the certificate, properly endorsed, to the issuing company's transfer agent, the title to the security will be transferred to you in the company records and a new certificate issued to you. It is not difficult to buy or sell securities if you know someone who will take the opposite side of the transaction.

Buying and selling becomes somewhat more difficult, however, when you have to try to locate the other half of the deal. As a result, stock brokerage firms have been formed that specialize in just this service.

Brokers are licensed to buy or sell securities for clients or for themselves. Brokerage houses vary greatly in size; some firms have offices located in a relatively small geographic area, whereas other firms have offices located nationwide. You must pay for brokerage services in the form of a commission, which is a charge based upon the value of a transaction.

Brokerage houses that are members of an organized exchange are regulated by the Securities Exchange Commission as well as by governmental agencies of the state in which they are located. Activities such as advertising, claims made to clients, and errors made in carrying out an investor's order are closely regulated to lessen the chance that investors will be harmed.

It is important to select a broker who is knowledgeable and in whom you have confidence. Because you are dealing with your present and future financial security, you will want a broker whose investment attitudes are consistent with your own. Too often a broker is more interested in and capable of selling than of advising.

Before making the decision, talk with friends, colleagues, and, most certainly, the broker. Brokers who are interested in you as a client and not just as a source of commissions will usually discuss your investment needs with you. A good question for you to ask is, "What investments do you recommend?" A broker who is interested in commissions will begin naming favorites without first determining your needs. This is not the kind of broker most investors need. A good working relationship with a broker who understands your investment needs and limitations can greatly facilitate the attaining of your investment goals.

Some brokerage firms will also act as dealers. When acting as a dealer, the firm is actually the other party in the transaction; that is, you are either buying from or selling to the dealer. Therefore, if you are looking for someone to help you by representing only your interests, you should be aware of whether the firm you select is acting as a broker or as a dealer in the transaction.

SOURCES OF SECURITIES INVESTMENT INFORMATION

Investors usually find that they lack the time to conduct in-depth research on investment opportunities. In spite of the difficulty of conducting this research, it is necessary if you are going to make an intelligent investment decision. The informational materials you consult must be wisely selected.

As a minimum, investors should depend upon the financial press, brokers, and at least one of the financial services when researching a security. Each of these sources can provide a wealth of information to aid in making a rational decision.

Financial press

Informed investors usually scan or read carefully a significant portion of some financial paper. One of the most widely read financial newspapers is *The Wall Street Journal,* which specializes in providing full coverage of business and economic news as well as news about specific companies—including earnings reports, dividend declarations, new issues, etc. Also included in *The Wall Street Journal* is a listing of various stock market indexes and the price quotations from the NYSE, ASE, and the OTC market. Other newspapers, such as *The New York Times,* commonly have extensive financial sections or just a listing of stock activity and prices.

Stock market averages. As a result of widespread interest in stock market activity, several measures have been developed to indicate both the direction and degree of price movement in the market.

Dow-Jones averages. The Dow-Jones averages have been developed to reflect activity in the stock of three classifications of companies—industrials, transportation, and utilities—as well as for the general market. The best known and most widely used of these indexes is the *Dow-Jones Industrial Average* (DJIA). The DJIA dates back to the mid-1880s when Charles Dow began to measure market activity of industrial companies, using 12 carefully selected firms. Today the DJIA is based upon 30 stocks traded on the New York Stock Exchange. The names of the 30 industrial companies included in the average are shown in Exhibit 14–3.

EXHIBIT 14–3
Companies included in the Dow-Jones Industrial Average

Allied Chemical	INCO
Aluminum Company of America	International Harvester
American Brands	International Paper
American Can	Johns-Manville
American Telephone and Telegraph	Minnesota Mining and Manufacturing
Bethlehem Steel	Owens-Illinois
Chrysler	Procter & Gamble Co.
E. I. du Pont de Nemours	Sears, Roebuck & Co.
Eastman Kodak	Standard Oil of California
Esmark, Inc.	Texaco, Inc.
Exxon	Union Carbide
General Electric	U.S. Steel Corp.
General Foods	United Technologies
General Motors	Westinghouse Electric
Goodyear Tire & Rubber	F. W. Woolworth Co.

The DJIA is calculated by dividing the sum of the closing price on the NYSE of one common share of each of the 30 companies by a divisor that has been adjusted to reflect stock dividends and stock splits over the years.[1] This measure is therefore not an average price per share, but an average price if no stock dividend or split had ever occurred. The divisor used can be found each day on the inside back page of *The Wall Street Journal*. As the prices of the 30 stocks increase, the index will also increase. Changes in the DJIA are quoted in "points." Given the current divisor, a one-point change in the DJIA is

[1] Stock dividends and stock splits result in an increase in the company's number of shares outstanding without any change in total investment by the stockholders. It is no longer possible to calculate the DJIA by using *The Wall Street Journal* because the closing prices shown are a composite of the prices on all of the exchanges, not just the New York Stock Exchange.

equal to a change of approximately five cents in the average price of the stocks included in the calculation.

Other indexes published by Dow-Jones and Company include the transportation average based upon 20 stocks, utility average using 15 firms, composite average (using the 65 firms included in the industrials, transportation and utility averages), and averages for bonds of many types.

Standard & Poor's indexes. Standard & Poor's Corporation (S&P) prepares indexes of stock prices using 1941–43 as the base period. Thus, relative changes in market prices are available. In addition, the importance of each company included is recognized by the use of a weighting technique. The value included for each company in the calculation of the index is the price weighted by the number of shares. A change in the stock price of a large company has greater effect on the index than an identical price change for a smaller company.

Standard & Poor's publishes four common stock indexes using 425 industrial stocks, 25 railroad stocks, 50 utility company stocks, and the composite Standard & Poor's 500. S&P also publishes indexes for preferred stocks, bonds, and groupings such as by industry.

New York Stock Exchange index. This index is the most comprehensive measure of price changes on the NYSE. It is a composite of all of the issues of common stock traded on the exchange. The NYSE is similar to the S&P index in that the value of each stock is weighted by the number of shares outstanding, thus giving a measure based upon the total market value of the shares of each company. The NYSE Index was started in 1966 but has been calculated back to 1939 to provide a historical base.

The American Stock Exchange index is similar to the NYSE Index. It also is a relatively new measure and represents the only comprehensive measure of stocks traded on the American Stock Exchange.

Price quotations. Daily price information is available in the financial press and in many local newspapers. These quotations enable an investor to watch a stock carefully. Exhibit 14–4 is a sample of stock prices as reported in the financial press. Stock price quotations indicate dollars or fractions thereof (the fractions are based on eighths dating back to the Spanish pieces of eight). When a stock price changes 1 point it changes by $1. One eighth of a point is 12.5 cents.

The first two columns of the quotations list the high and low prices at which the stock traded during the year. Companies are identified in an abbreviated form, such as IWG Eq., which stands for IWG Equipment, followed by dividend information. IWG is listed as paying a cash dividend of 12 cents plus a stock dividend, as indicated by the "*b*" (this symbol is explained in the footnotes for the stock quotations).

EXHIBIT 14–4
Stock price quotations

197–									
High	*Low*	*Stocks*	*Dividend*	*P-E ratio*	*Sales 100s*	*High*	*Low*	*Close*	*Net change*
63	50	IWG Eq	.12b	24	645	55	53⅞	53⅞	−1

IWG stock is selling at a price equal to 24 times the current 12-month earnings (Price-Earnings Ratio). On this day, 64,500 shares of IWG stock were traded, some at a price as high as $55 per share and others as low as $53.875 per share. The final trade of the day is $53.875 per share, or $1 lower than the closing price on the day before.

Bond prices are quoted as a percent of par (face) value. Exhibit 14–5 shows price quotations, as published by the financial press, of a corporate bond traded on the New York Exchange. Also shown is a U.S. Treasury issue. The corporate bond issued by PUD Corporation pays interest at the rate of eight percent per year and matures in 1981. The range of prices per bond on the trading day was from a high of $1,028.75 to a low of $1,021.25. The last transaction for the day was at the low price, or $8.75 below the last transaction on the preceding day. Prices of corporate bonds are commonly given in eighths while those of government securities are quoted in thirty-seconds of a percent of face value.

EXHIBIT 14–5
Bond price quotations

New York Exchange Bonds

Bonds	*Current yield*	*Volume*	*High*	*Low*	*Close*	*Net change*
PUD 8s81	7.8	50	102⅞	102⅛	102⅛	−⅞

Government, Agency and Miscellaneous Securities: Treasury Bonds and Notes

Rate	*Mat. date*	*Bid*	*Asked*	*Bid change*	*Yield*
7s	1993–98 May	91.8	92.8	. . .	7.74

The Treasury bond shown pays interest of seven percent per year. The maturity date is May, 1998, but the bond may be called between 1993 and the final maturity. These prices quoted are not prices at which transactions occurred as was the case with bonds traded on the exchange. Rather these are prices at which the bond dealers are interested in doing business. The bid price of 91.8 means that a dealer is willing to buy the bond from anyone who wants to sell at a price of $91\frac{8}{32}$ percent of par, or $912.50 per $1,000 bond. The dealer is willing to sell a $1,000 bond at $92\frac{8}{32}$ percent of par or $922.50. There has been no change in the bid as compared with the closing bid on the preceding day. The yield to maturity on this bond is 7.74 percent. Yields will be discussed further in Chapter 15.

OTC price quotations are also published in a bid-ask manner. These are not actual transaction prices, but rather an indication of the stock value. These stock prices are quoted in dollars or fractions thereof. Price quotations shown in Exhibit 14–6 indicate that LJC Corporation

EXHIBIT 14–6
Over-the-counter quotations

Stock	*Dividend*	*Sales 100s*	*Bid*	*Asked*	*Net change*
LJC Mf	1a	8	25½	26½	+¼

pays a $1 cash dividend plus an additional amount if the company is able. Sales for the day were 800 shares. The current quote is a bid of $25.50 and ask of $26.50 per share. This bid quoted is 25 cents higher than that quoted the day before.

Financial media may also print special sections that include price quotations for foreign securities, local securities not listed on an exchange, and mutual funds.

Brokerage firms

Research departments maintained by many large brokerage houses provide information that can help you select the issues to be bought or sold. This research information deals with industries as well as specific companies within the industries.

Brokerage firms can provide up-to-the-minute price quotations through the use of ticker tapes or quote boards.

Financial services

Financial services are companies that have as their primary activity selling information to investors. There are many services available, but the three leaders are Moody's Investor's Service, Inc., Standard and Poor's Corporation, and The Value Line Investment Survey.

Financial and investment data published by these three companies and others vary in terms of coverage and cost. Coverage of some services is very specialized, such as only speculative common stocks; others provide a broader range of information. While it is quite expensive for an individual investor to subscribe to any of these services, most public libraries will have at least some of the services provided by the companies mentioned above.

SUMMARY

Stocks and bonds are owned by more people in the United States than any of the other personal investments, except savings accounts, and it is easy to find someone who is willing to share a success story with you.

These securities represent a legal relationship between the issuer and the investor and enable the issuer to acquire needed capital.

A bond, or similar security, evidences a debt that is owed by the issuer. Stock, on the other hand, is evidence that the investor owns a share of a corporation.

Securities can be classified in terms of issuer. A general classification is corporate issues and governmental issues. Private business corporations issue bonds, preferred stock, and common stock in order to raise needed capital. Governmental bodies, however, issue only debt securities.

Securities markets have developed that enable investors to buy or sell securities efficiently. The primary market includes those transactions between the issuer and the investor. That is, the capital goes directly to the issuer. In the secondary market the transactions occur between two investors and do not result in increased capital for the issuer. Securities brokers are in the business of bringing together these buyers and sellers so that those who wish to convert cash into securities or securities into cash may do so.

Investment decisions require information. Informed investors generally depend upon several sources for their information, including the financial press, brokers, and one or more financial services.

DISCUSSION QUESTIONS

1. Explain the basic distinction between stocks and bonds. Why are they issued? What rights do holders of each have?
2. What advantages do cumulative preferred stocks offer an investor as compared with common stock? Disadvantages?
3. Compare the Series E bonds discussed in Chapter 13 with the marketable Treasuries discussed in this chapter.
4. Explain the basis for the classification of securities.

5. What is the difference between a mortgage bond and a debenture? Which of these bonds is "better"?
6. Explain how the call provision is used by the issuer. What are the advantages and disadvantages of the call provision for the investor?
7. Compare the characteristics of Treasury bonds, notes, and bills.
8. What are the distinctive features of the primary and secondary security markets?
9. Security market activity is measured by several "averages." Compare the DJIA, S&P 500, and the New York Stock Exchange Index in terms of the numbers of stocks included and the meaning of a change in each.
10. Use *The Wall Street Journal* as a source of security price quotations. Select a preferred stock, corporate bond, U.S. Treasury bond, mutual fund, and a common stock traded on the NYSE and another traded OTC. Interpret each part of each of the complete quotations.
11. Your friend has asked you for advice on whether to select a securities broker or a securities dealer as an intermediary for investing funds. How would you explain the difference between brokers and dealers?

CASE PROBLEM

In order to provide needed income, Eric Roberts has decided to buy bonds with a 15-year maturity. Bonds available for purchase, in addition to new issues yielding 9 percent, include some with a 7 percent coupon selling for 83¾. Interest rates are presently at all-time high levels and are expected to drop to 7½ percent within about 18 months. At that time it is likely that some of the newer, high coupon issues will be refunded.

With regard to the interest rate, what bonds should Eric buy now in order to provide the highest income over the 15-year period? Defend your answer.

SELECTED READINGS

Cohen, Jerome B. *Personal Finance: Principles and Case Problems*, 5th ed. Homewood, Ill.: Richard D. Irwin, Inc., 1975, chap. 13.

Engel, Louis and Wyckoff, Peter. *How to Buy Stocks*, 6th ed. Waltham, Maine: Little, Brown & Co., 1976.

Gold, Roger A. *Can You Be Sure of Your Experts?* New York: Macmillan, 1969.

Personal investment management

15

OBJECTIVES

This chapter examines the risks that are a part of any investment and considers the general relationship of risk and return. The chapter also presents a method for developing investment policies that bring together your needs and the available investments. After thoroughly studying and discussing this chapter you should be able to:

. . . Identify the three major inputs for an investment decision.

. . . Define and explain the major types of investment risks.

. . . Explain how securities and other investments can be evaluated for each of the investment risks.

. . . Identify and analyze investors' needs that act as investment constraints.

. . . Identify and explain defensive and aggressive investment strategies.

. . . Develop basic investment portfolio policies that meet your needs.

The business of "getting rich" by investing can be very complex. You are faced with a large number of possible investments, including common stocks, preferred stocks, bonds, gold, silver, commodities, art work, stamps, coins, real estate, and antiques. Each type of investment has certain unique characteristics. How do you determine which investments are right for you?

A rational approach to personal investment management requires the development of an investment plan. This investment plan should consider all of your financial needs and should be an integral part of your overall family financial plan, as was illustrated by the investment pyramid in Chapter 13. That is, you should consider investments only after your basic family financial needs for an emergency fund, insurance, and a home have been satisfied.

Building an investment plan can be compared with building a house. A careful analysis of your housing needs identifies the amount and type of space you need. It is then up to the architect to design a house, within your financial means, that will satisfy as many of your needs as possible. This usually means that there will be fewer and/or smaller rooms than you might desire and that perhaps fewer luxury items will be used in the construction than if you had no financial constraints.

The development of a personal investment plan requires a similar balancing of needs and constraints. Good investment decisions require three major inputs:

1. An understanding of the types and characteristics of investment opportunities, including the markets in which investments may be bought and sold.
2. An understanding of the investment risks and the effect that these risks have on the value of an investment.
3. An analysis of your investment needs and limitations.

The first of these inputs was discussed in Chapters 13 and 14. It is the purpose of this chapter to discuss the remaining two inputs.

INVESTMENT RISKS AND RETURNS

You choose to invest your money in stocks, bonds, savings accounts, or other options because you are satisfied that the possible return on the investment outweighs the sacrifices you make and the risks you take. This relationship, known as the *risk-return relationship*, is illustrated in Exhibit 15–1. There is a modest rate of return available on low-risk investments such as Treasury bills or fully insured savings accounts, but in order to find an investment that is expected to earn a higher rate of return, it is necessary to take greater risk.

To better understand this risk and return relationship, we must consider what constitutes investment return and what types of risk are present in various investments.

Investment returns

Investment rates of return express the relationship between the periodic amounts you receive and the amount you have invested.

These amounts may be received as dividends if you own stock, or as interest you receive from a bond. Your annual rate of return over the life of the investment may be increased or decreased depending upon whether you recover more or less than your original invested principal at the time the security matures or is sold. If the amount of principal recovered is greater than the original amount invested, you have a capital gain, which increases the total realized return on your investment. Recovery of less than the amount originally invested is known as a capital loss and decreases your realized return. The concept and methods of calculating rate of return can be applied to all investments, and we can use the rates of return on stocks and bonds as an illustration.

EXHIBIT 15–1
General relationship between risk and return

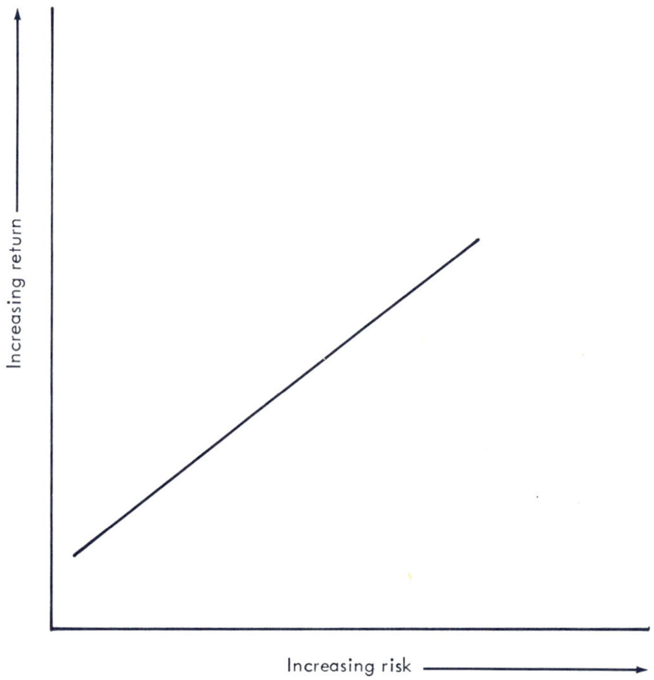

Measure of return on common stock. Returns from common stock are earned in two ways: annual dividends received from the issuer and changes in the value of the stock. These returns are commonly known as *dividend yield* and *capital gain,* respectively.

Dividend yield is calculated by dividing the annual dividend (*D*) by the principal (*P*) invested. For example, suppose that one year ago you paid $25 per share for a stock that pays a $1 annual dividend. The dividend yield is four percent:

$$\text{Dividend yield} = \frac{D}{P} = \frac{\$1}{\$25} = 0.04.$$

Because of potential changes in the market prices of stocks, capital gains are also an important part of the returns expected by owners of stock. Rates of return resulting from capital gains (g) can be estimated by calculating the annual percentage change in the market value of your security. To illustrate, suppose the stock you bought for $25 one year ago now has a market value of $26.50. It is expected that the stock price will continue to increase at this same rate in the future. The return from capital gains that could be realized if you sold the stock is six percent:

$$\text{Capital gains rate } (g) = \frac{\text{Change in price}}{\text{Principal}} = \frac{\$1.50}{\$25} = 0.06.$$

The total annual return from this stock is therefore ten percent, which is the sum of dividend yield and the capital gains rate:

$$\begin{aligned}\text{Total return} &= \text{Dividend yield} + \text{Capital gains rate}\\ &= \frac{D}{P} + g\\ &= 0.04 + 0.06\\ &= 0.10.\end{aligned}$$

Brokerage commissions and other transaction costs and taxes are ignored in the example in order to simplify the calculation. Including these costs in the calculation would reduce the total return.

Measures of returns on bonds. One common measure of the return on bonds is known as the *yield to maturity*. Yield to maturity measures the return that will be earned if you hold the bond until it matures. It is measured by relating time and amount of interest and principal received to the amount invested in the bond. To illustrate, suppose you buy a bond for $1,000. It has 20 years before reaching maturity and an annual interest rate of seven percent. The issuer promises to pay you $35 interest each six months and to repay the $1,000 principal at maturity. Assuming all of these promises are kept and you own the bond until maturity, the yield to maturity is seven percent.

Bond value tables, such as the one shown in Exhibit 15–2, can be used to determine the yield to maturity. Reading down the column of the table for a 20-year maturity, the values shown are prices stated as percentage of face value, that is, 100.00 equals 100 percent. To determine the yield to maturity, read down the column headed "20–0"

EXHIBIT 15–2
Page from a bond value table

7%	YEARS and MONTHS							
Yield	18-6	19-0	19-6	20-0	20-6	21-0	21-6	22-0
4.00	138.95	139.66	140.35	141.03	141.70	142.35	142.99	143.62
4.20	135.77	136.40	137.02	137.63	138.23	138.82	139.39	139.95
4.40	132.68	133.25	133.80	134.35	134.88	135.40	135.91	136.41
4.60	129.68	130.19	130.68	131.16	131.64	132.10	132.55	132.99
4.80	126.78	127.22	127.66	128.08	128.50	128.91	129.30	129.69
5.00	123.96	124.35	124.73	125.10	125.47	125.82	126.17	126.50
5.20	121.22	121.56	121.89	122.22	122.53	122.84	123.14	123.43
5.40	118.57	118.86	119.15	119.42	119.69	119.95	120.21	120.45
5.60	116.00	116.25	116.48	116.72	116.94	117.16	117.38	117.58
5.80	113.51	113.71	113.90	114.10	114.28	114.46	114.64	114.81
6.00	111.08	111.25	111.40	111.56	111.71	111.85	111.99	112.13
6.10	109.90	110.04	110.18	110.32	110.45	110.58	110.70	110.82
6.20	108.73	108.86	108.98	109.10	109.21	109.32	109.43	109.54
6.30	107.58	107.69	107.80	107.90	108.00	108.09	108.18	108.27
6.40	106.45	106.54	106.63	106.72	106.80	106.88	106.96	107.03
6.50	105.34	105.41	105.48	105.55	105.62	105.68	105.75	105.81
6.60	104.24	104.30	104.35	104.41	104.46	104.51	104.56	104.61
6.70	103.15	103.20	103.24	103.28	103.32	103.36	103.39	103.43
6.80	102.09	102.12	102.14	102.17	102.19	102.22	102.24	102.27
6.90	101.04	101.05	101.06	101.08	101.09	101.10	101.11	101.12
7.00	100.00	100.00	100.00	100.00	100.00	100.00	100.00	100.00
7.10	98.98	98.97	98.95	98.94	98.93	98.92	98.91	98.90
7.20	97.97	97.95	97.92	97.90	97.87	97.85	97.83	97.81
7.30	96.98	96.94	96.91	96.87	96.84	96.80	96.77	96.74
7.40	96.00	95.95	95.91	95.86	95.81	95.77	95.73	95.69
7.50	95.04	94.98	94.92	94.86	94.81	94.75	94.70	94.65
7.60	94.09	94.02	93.95	93.88	93.82	93.75	93.69	93.64
7.70	93.16	93.07	92.99	92.92	92.84	92.77	92.70	92.63
7.80	92.23	92.14	92.05	91.96	91.88	91.80	91.72	91.65
7.90	91.32	91.22	91.12	91.03	90.93	90.85	90.76	90.68
8.00	90.43	90.32	90.21	90.10	90.00	89.91	89.81	89.73
8.10	89.55	89.42	89.31	89.19	89.09	88.98	88.88	88.79
8.20	88.67	88.54	88.42	88.30	88.18	88.07	87.97	87.86
8.30	87.82	87.68	87.54	87.42	87.29	87.18	87.06	86.95
8.40	86.97	86.82	86.68	86.55	86.42	86.29	86.17	86.06
8.50	86.14	85.98	85.83	85.69	85.56	85.43	85.30	85.18
8.60	85.31	85.15	85.00	84.85	84.71	84.57	84.44	84.31
8.70	84.50	84.33	84.17	84.02	83.87	83.73	83.59	83.46
8.80	83.70	83.53	83.36	83.20	83.05	82.90	82.76	82.62
8.90	82.92	82.73	82.56	82.39	82.23	82.08	81.93	81.80
9.00	82.14	81.95	81.77	81.60	81.43	81.28	81.13	80.98
9.10	81.37	81.18	80.99	80.82	80.65	80.48	80.33	80.18
9.20	80.62	80.42	80.23	80.04	79.87	79.70	79.54	79.39
9.30	79.87	79.67	79.47	79.28	79.11	78.93	78.77	78.62
9.40	79.14	78.93	78.73	78.53	78.35	78.18	78.01	77.85
9.50	78.41	78.20	77.99	77.80	77.61	77.43	77.26	77.10
9.60	77.70	77.48	77.27	77.07	76.88	76.70	76.52	76.36
9.70	76.99	76.77	76.55	76.35	76.16	75.97	75.80	75.63
9.80	76.30	76.07	75.85	75.64	75.45	75.26	75.08	74.91
9.90	75.61	75.38	75.16	74.95	74.75	74.56	74.38	74.20
10.00	74.93	74.70	74.47	74.26	74.06	73.87	73.68	73.51
10.20	73.61	73.37	73.14	72.92	72.71	72.51	72.32	72.14
10.40	72.32	72.07	71.83	71.61	71.40	71.20	71.00	70.82
10.60	71.06	70.81	70.57	70.34	70.13	69.92	69.72	69.54
10.80	69.84	69.58	69.34	69.11	68.89	68.68	68.48	68.29
11.00	68.65	68.39	68.14	67.91	67.69	67.47	67.27	67.08
11.20	67.49	67.23	66.98	66.74	66.52	66.30	66.10	65.91
11.40	66.37	66.10	65.85	65.61	65.38	65.17	64.96	64.77
11.60	65.27	65.00	64.74	64.50	64.27	64.06	63.86	63.66
11.80	64.20	63.93	63.67	63.43	63.20	62.98	62.78	62.59
12.00	63.16	62.88	62.63	62.38	62.15	61.94	61.73	61.54

Source: Reproduced from *Expanded Bond Value Tables,* Publication No. 83, p. 736, Copyright © 1970, Financial Publishing Company.

until you find 100.00—a price of \$1,000 (1.00 × \$1,000 = \$1,000). The yield to maturity on this bond is determined by reading the figure shown in the "yield" column on the left.

Now suppose the same example as above except that when you bought the bond in the secondary market at a discount (less than face value) you paid only \$901 for it. The price in the bond table is shown as 90.10 (0.901 × \$1,000 = \$901). Because you will receive \$35 interest each six months from a bond that you bought for \$901 and will also receive the \$1,000 face value at maturity rather than just the return of your capital, \$901, your yield to maturity is greater than seven percent. A look at Exhibit 15–2 shows that the yield to maturity on this bond is eight percent.

It is also possible to estimate the yield to maturity through the use of a simple formula. The formula below relates the annual interest on the bond plus the annual share of the discount or premium (value greater than face value) to the average amount invested over the life of the bond.

$$Y = \frac{I + (F - P)/n}{(F + P)/2},$$

where

Y = Estimated yield to maturity
I = Annual interest
F = Face or par value of the bond
P = Price of the bond
n = Years to maturity.

We can use this formula to estimate the yield to maturity of the above bond which was selling at a discount as follows:

$$Y = \frac{\$70 + (\$1{,}000 - \$901)/20}{(\$1{,}000 + \$901)/2} = \frac{\$70 + \$4.95}{\$950.50}$$
$$= \frac{\$74.95}{\$950.50}$$
$$= 0.0788 \text{ or } 7.9 \text{ percent.}$$

Notice that the estimated yield is very close to the more accurate measure of 8 percent shown in Exhibit 15–2.

The estimated yield to maturity for the above bond if it sells at a premium of \$115.60 is:

$$Y = \frac{\$70 + (\$1{,}000 - \$1{,}115.60)/20}{(\$1{,}000 + \$1{,}115.60)/2}$$
$$= \frac{\$70 - \$5.78}{\$1{,}057.80}$$
$$= 0.0607 \text{ or } 6.1 \text{ percent.}$$

Other measures of return on bonds are known as *nominal* and *current yields.* Nominal yield is simply the stated interest rate on the bond, sometimes referred to as the coupon rate. Current yield is calculated by dividing the annual interest received by the price paid. It is a measure used to determine the rate of current income from the bond. In the example above showing the bond selling at a premium, the current yield is 6.27 percent ($70/$1,115.60) and the nominal yield is 7 percent ($70/$1,000).

As you can readily see, yield to maturity would be a more realistic measure for determining whether this investment would give you an adequate return on your capital.

Investment risks

In Chapter 10 when the concept of insurance was introduced, the word "risk" implied a chance of loss, damage, or injury of some sort. In investments, risk is not necessarily a negative term. Risk exists whenever the actual outcome is worse than *or better than* that which was expected; that is, any case in which the actual outcome differs from the expected outcome. It is the possibility of outcomes that are better than expected that makes many investments attractive.

Investment risk has many facets. That is, there are several kinds of investment risk that can result in variability in return from investments. It is possible to isolate these investment risks and to select securities that may increase or decrease your exposure to a given risk. Such an understanding of investment risks is essential in order to develop a sound investment policy. Our discussion will center on separate evaluations of business risk, interest rate risk, purchasing power risk, and a group of factors that affect the desirability of owning various types of securities. These risks and factors will serve as a basis for grading or evaluating investments in order to determine whether they will meet your needs.

It is important for you to recognize both the negative and the positive aspects of risk, but you should also note that for many investors the devastating consequences of a loss of either income or principal is of such great significance that positive aspects of risk become unimportant. For example, you could undoubtedly cope with more income than you expect, but you may find it difficult to adjust to less than you expect. While each of the investment risks to be discussed can result in positive variations from the expected result, for obvious reasons the discussion will be mainly concerned with the negative aspects of risk.

Business risk. Business risk is defined as the uncertainty of future investment returns, either interest, dividends, or capital gains, as a result of changes in the issuer's financial ability.

A firm's ability to meet its financial obligations is of vital importance to its security holders. The expectation of a return gives a security its value. Anything that affects the firm's ability to pay falls into the classification of business risk. If a firm's ability to pay dividends or interest decreases, risk increases. On the other hand, a firm may be more successful than anticipated. This tends to decrease risk in that the firm's financial capacity is strengthened. Securities can thus be evaluated, or ranked, on the basis of their business risk.

Evaluating securities for business risk. Evaluating securities refers to ranking them on the basis of their desirability or strengths. A security that is termed "high grade" is one that has low risk. A system of grading for business risk takes into account the issuer's financial capacity and ability to make income and principal payments.

Those securities with the best claim to principal and income are of the highest grade because they offer the least risk that income or principal will not be paid. As the certainty of the income and principal values diminishes, the level of risk increases and thus the grade decreases.

Several financial services have developed systems of grading securities. Both Moody's and Standard & Poor's have developed rating systems for bonds, preferred stocks, and common stocks. Value Line Investment Survey has a rating system for stocks. Exhibit 15–3 presents Moody's and S&P's bond rating systems, which denote grade

EXHIBIT 15–3
Bond rating symbols used by Standard & Poor's and Moody's

	S&P bond ratings	*Moody's ratings*
Investment grade	AAA	Aaa
	AA	Aa
	A	A
	BBB	Baa
Lower medium grade to speculative	BB	Ba
	B	B
Speculatives	CCC	Caa
	CC	Ca
Pays no interest	C	C
Bonds in default	DDD	Daa
	DD	Da
	D	D

Source: *Standard & Poor's Bond Guide; Moody's Bond Record.*

through the use of symbols ranging from the highest grade of Aaa and AAA, respectively, down to D. These grades indicate quality in terms of business risk. The explanation of the S&P grades as presented in the *S&P Bond Guide* is as follows:

> Bonds rated AAA are the highest grade obligations. They possess the ultimate degree of protection as to principal and interest. Marketwise they move with interest rates, and hence provide the maximum safety on all counts.
>
> * * * * *
>
> Bonds given a BB rating are regarded as lower medium grade. They have only minor investment characteristics. In the case of utilities, interest is earned consistently but by narrow margins. In the case of other types of obligors, charges are earned on average by a fair margin, but in poor periods deficit operations are possible.[1]

United States government issues are not graded. They are assumed to be the safest, highest grade securities available. The ability of the Treasury to meet its obligations has been unquestioned.

The top four bond ratings (AAA, AA, A, BBB) are considered to be investment-grade securities, which means that they are of high enough quality to qualify for commercial bank investment. Bonds rated BB or below are generally regarded as too risky for these institutions as well as for many individual investors.

S&P's systems for grading preferred and common stocks uses seven categories ranging from a high of A+ to a low of C. This system does not grade business risk, but rather it reflects the stability and growth of earnings and dividends. Value Line's rating system uses a numerical scale of 1 to 5, with 5 being most risky and 1 being the least risky. This is also based on past stability of market price and earnings growth rather than the business risk, which has been discussed. It is important that when you are using the security ratings provided by these services, you know what the rating is based on.

Interest rate risk. Interest rate risk is the possibility of changes in the amounts of investment income or in the value of the principal as a result of changes in the rates of return investors are demanding at any given time (market rate of interest). Interest rate risk is of concern mainly for fixed income investments which are of high grade in business risk. For example, price fluctuations in U.S. Treasury securities are caused primarily by changes in market interest rates. Because of the overwhelming importance of business risk, a change in the market interest rate has much less effect on the value of securities that are low grade in business risk.

A discussion of interest rate risk requires a careful distinction be-

[1] *Standard & Poor's Bond Guide.*

tween the effect on the value of principal and the value of income from securities. Changes in interest rates have an effect on the certainty of these values.

After you buy a bond, economic or financial conditions may cause the general level of interest rates to change. Exhibit 15–4 shows the historic yields on long-term bonds. Since 1970 the yields required on AAA corporate bonds have ranged between seven percent and nine percent. Because new bonds become available that promise different rates of return, the market prices of existing bonds will have to adjust so that the expected yield to maturity on these old bonds will be competitive with the new rate. The only way of providing this adjustment is the market price because interest, maturity, and maturity value are fixed in the indenture and are not free to vary.

EXHIBIT 15–4
Long-term bond yields

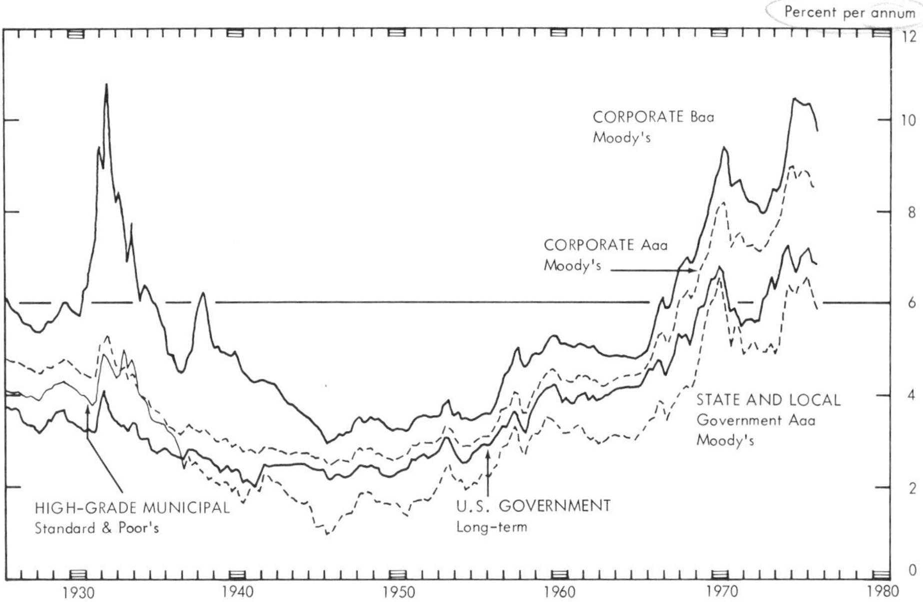

Source: *Federal Reserve Chart Book.*

There is an inverse relationship between the change in the interest rate and the change in the market value of a bond. That is, as the required interest rate increases, the market price of the bond will decrease. Further, it can be shown that the longer the term to maturity of the bond, the greater will be the change in the bond price for a one percent change in the interest rate. For example, suppose that at the time of issue the going interest rate on a bond was seven percent.

Presently, however, the market rate has risen to eight percent for bonds of the same quality. The price decrease of a bond with a maturity of ten years is $68 while the price decrease for a 20-year bond is $99 per $1,000 bond (see Exhibit 15–2 for the price change of the 20-year bond). Therefore, it can be concluded that the longer the term to maturity, the greater the uncertainty of the value of the principal.

Interest rate risk is also of concern in terms of the effect on the value of income. Many investors who own bonds use these securities to provide an income stream. When a bond held by such an investor matures, the principal is commonly reinvested in another bond of similar quality in business risk. As the market rates of interest change, the income realized from the reinvestment will reflect the rates then available in the market. The more frequently the reinvestment of the principal is required because a bond matures, the less stable, or certain, a given income flow will be.

We can conclude, therefore, that the longer the term to maturity of bonds, the more stable will be the income stream from these bonds. To illustrate, suppose that you have two alternatives for the investment of $1,000 to provide an income stream for a 20-year period. You can buy a bond with a one-year maturity and reinvest the principal at the end of each year throughout the 20-year period. Or, you can buy a bond with a 20-year maturity. With the first alternative, the income will vary from year to year, depending upon the market interest rate at the time of reinvestment. The second alternative will provide a constant interest income stream for the entire 20-year period. There is less variability in the income stream from the 20-year bond than from the 20 one-year bonds.

Interest rate risk is generally assumed to be quite unimportant as a variable affecting the price of common stocks. An exception to this may be income stocks.[2] In the case of other common stocks, however, change in the financial ability of the issuer of the stock is a much more important risk for the common stockholders.

Evaluating securities for interest rate risk. A system for evaluating securities for interest rate risk must consider income and principal separately. A high-grade security in terms of interest rate risk is one for which the value of the return is most certain—has least variability.

Since securities having a short maturity are least affected in principal value by changes in market interest rates, they receive a high grade. As the period to maturity becomes longer, fluctuations in interest rates

[2] Income stocks are those issues that have a strong record of paying out a large portion of earnings as dividends, thus providing a stable income for the stockholders. Price appreciation is of secondary concern. Public utility stocks are typical of this type of common stock.

affect the value of the principal more, making long-term instruments low grade in terms of interest-rate risk.

Stability of the value of income return is affected in a manner just the opposite of that for the principal. Short maturities require frequent reinvestment at the interest rate available in the market at that time. Thus, the possibility for variability in the investor's interest income stream increases as the length of maturity of the securities decreases. A long-term bond promises a level interest income for a long period of time. Therefore, long-term bonds are high grade and short-term bonds are low grade in interest rate risk for income. Preferred stocks that are high grade in business risk would also be of a low grade in interest rate risk of principal and high grade in interest rate risk of income.

Purchasing power risk. Purchasing power risk refers to the uncertainty about how much a dollar will buy at some future time when received as income or return of principal.

Inflation, or a rising price level, is a widely recognized economic fact. We see evidence when purchasing products such as food, medical services, autos, or postage stamps. All these items have risen dramatically in price over the last ten years. Rapid rises in the price level of consumer goods and services are ample reason for concern and planning. A common measure of the rate of inflation (rate of price level increase) is the Consumer Price Index. While it is not a perfect device, it is widely accepted as a measure of the cost of living.

We are all affected by increases in the cost of living. While most of us can live with moderate rises of three to four percent per year, people on fixed income are especially vulnerable to rapid inflation. Persistent inflation even at moderate rates has a compounding effect. For example, if the price level increases at a two percent rate per year, it takes about 36 years for prices to double. At a rate of six percent, prices double in about 12 years, and at ten percent prices will double in about seven years. Small wonder that the double-digit inflation of the early 1970s was of major concern, especially to retired people living on fixed incomes.

Inflation is also of concern to investors. We invest in an effort to accumulate wealth. The returns from our investments are ordinarily measured in current dollars, the dollars received at a given time. There is no adjustment made for the fact that because of inflation a dollar buys less today than it did last year or the year before. For example, by the end of 1977 it took about $1.84 to buy the same food that could be bought for $1 as recently as 1967. Thus, it is necessary to measure returns on investments in terms of purchasing power, not just the "current dollar" returns.

The purchasing power of either the income from a security or its principal value is influenced by two factors: (1) the purchasing power of each current dollar, and (2) the number of current dollars received. To illustrate, as the number of current dollars of income from a given security increases, purchasing power increases; but a decline in the amount that each dollar will buy causes purchasing power to decline. The future purchasing power provided by an investment is determined by how rapidly each of these factors is changing. This relationship is illustrated in Exhibit 15–5. Line A of the exhibit illustrates a

EXHIBIT 15–5
Changes in purchasing power

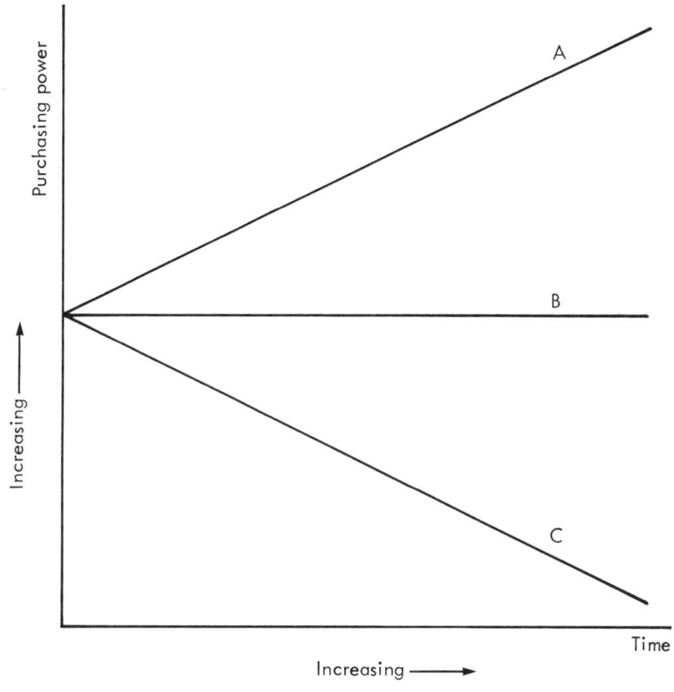

situation where the increase in current dollars is greater than the increase in the price level, resulting in an increase in purchasing power. In the case of line B, both factors move equally so that purchasing power remains constant, whereas with line C the price level is rising more rapidly than the number of current dollars.

It is important to relate this more specifically to the income and principal values of securities. Dividend income from stock can increase as the earnings of the firm increase. As the earnings and dividends increase, the price of the stock is also expected to rise. Thus, during a period of rising prices, common stock is often thought of as a protection against loss of purchasing power, a hedge against inflation. However, the interest stream from a bond remains fixed over the life of the bond. Thus, during a period of rising prices the bondholder loses purchasing power.

Evaluating securities for purchasing power risks. A system of evaluating securities for purchasing power risk should reflect the variability in the value of the income and principal in terms of purchasing power. Those securities with income streams and principal values that can vary with price levels are least susceptible to loss of purchasing power and are therefore the highest grade.

Common stock is considered high grade in purchasing power risk for two major reasons. First, business firms strive to increase their earnings by selling more of their products. This is expected to provide greater profits for the firm, which may result in greater dividends and higher stock prices. A second reason is that the selling prices of a firm's products are not fixed. Selling prices can be increased as costs such as labor or materials rise. Thus increased costs are passed on to the consumer in the form of higher prices. While it is just such activity that causes inflation, the owners of these firms may be offered some protection against inflation.

Securities that have fixed dollar returns are low grade in purchasing power risk. Because bonds, both corporate and government, promise a fixed return of interest and principal, they offer little protection against purchasing power risk. Preferred stock must also be considered to be of low grade because of the promised dividend, usually with no opportunity to have the dividend increased.

With this system of evaluation in terms of a specific risk, strengths and weaknesses of the different types of securities become clearer. Notice, for example, the inverse relationship of the ratings for business risk and those for purchasing power risk; that is, securities that are high grade in business risk are low grade in purchasing power risk and vice versa. This is reasonable because the characteristics that make a security high grade in business risk (strong claim on a fixed amount) also make it low grade in purchasing power risk.

Research has shown that while common stocks appear in general to provide protection against inflation, this is not always true for each individual investor nor for short time periods. Historically, over long periods and large groups of common stocks, the returns on common stock have increased to a degree that more than offsets the effect of inflation. Short-run experience, however, often differs greatly from the average.[3] A discussion with many of the investors who held common stock from 1969 through the mid-1970s will show that during that period of rapid inflation, values of common stocks were declining. When the stock market declines while inflation continues at high levels, investments in stock do not offset losses in purchasing power. Investors caught in the middle watch the cost of meeting their needs rise and the return from their investment fall. This is illustrated by the cost of living measures shown with the measure of stock prices and of dividends in Exhibit 15–6.

Note especially that the changes since 1970 show that while dividends moved upward, as did the cost of living, the stock prices moved downward during this period of rapid inflation. Current dollars available from the value of the principal actually declined, thus compounding the problem of a rising price level.

When we consider the longer time period of 1950 to the present, we find that both dividends and stock prices have generally kept pace with or exceeded the rate at which the cost of living has increased. Thus, to assume that stocks always offer good protection against loss of purchasing power is a misleading assumption at best; but on average they do provide protection against loss of purchasing power.

Other investment qualities

In addition to investment risks, there are some other qualities that have an effect on the desirability of owning securities or other investments. Two of these qualities, important to many investors, are marketability and taxability.

Marketability. Marketability is a term that causes confusion in the minds of investors because it means various things depending upon how it is used. In our discussion, marketability refers to the investor's ability to sell the asset readily at a fair value.

A marketable security is one for which title can be transferred from one investor to another. A highly marketable security usually means that there is a ready market in which the security can be sold without having to sacrifice price. Many of the securities that are actively traded on an exchange are examples of highly marketable securities.

Evaluating securities for marketability. A prime consideration in determining marketability is the relative cost of converting a security

---

[3] See Frank K. Reilly, Glenn L. Johnson, and Ralph E. Smith, "Inflation, Inflation Hedges, and Common Stocks," *The Financial Analysts Journal,* vol. 26, no. 1, January–February 1970, pp. 104–110; Lawrence Fisher and James Lorie, "Rates of Return on Investments in Common Stocks," *The Journal of Business,* January 1964, pp. 3–71; Harry C. Sauvain, *Investment Management,* Fourth Edition (Englewood Cliffs, N.J.: Prentice-Hall, Inc., 1973), p. 127.

EXHIBIT 15–6
Common stock performance as inflation hedge

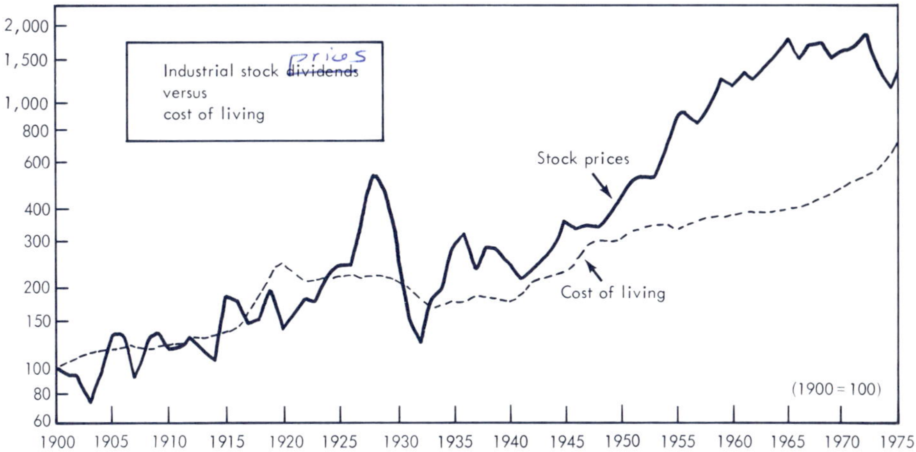

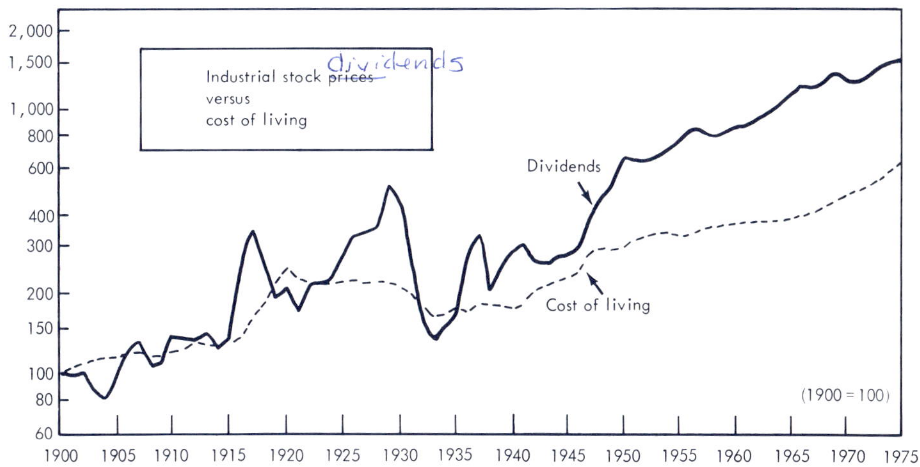

Source: Weisenberger Investment Companies Service, 1976.

to cash. Costs of conversion should include any price concessions that must be made in order to sell on short notice. As the selling costs increase relative to the proceeds, the quality of the security decreases. A security that is high grade in marketability is one that can be sold quickly at an equitable price. An example of a high-grade security would be one that is actively traded on an exchange or OTC where a ready market exists.

Taxability. Investment returns range from being fully taxable to being totally tax exempt. Because of the varying tax treatment of different securities, some may meet an investor's needs better than others.

Dividends from corporate stock are fully taxable for individuals, except for a nominal dividend income exclusion.[4] This is in clear contrast with the income from municipal bonds, which is exempt from federal income tax.

Returns in the form of price appreciation are accorded special treatment as capital gains. For individuals, capital gains of less than $50,000 are generally taxed at a preferential rate, not to exceed 25 percent.[5]

Evaluating securities for taxability. An evaluation system for rating securities in terms of taxability must recognize that the more favorable the tax treatment, the more desirable and thus the higher the grade of the security. Securities with fully taxable income are of lowest grade in taxability for income. When income is tax exempt, the security would be rated as high grade.

For example, dividend or interest income from corporate or Treasury issues is fully taxable, while interest on municipals is exempt from federal income tax. Thus, municipals are high grade while corporates and Treasuries are low grade.

Evaluating investments

An evaluation is valuable in that it enables you to see how the various investments may be used to meet your needs as an investor. Investments that are high grade offer maximum protection. Low-grade ratings indicate that there is little protection against a given risk.

Savings bonds and savings accounts. Exhibit 15–7 presents an approach to evaluating investment alternatives. Savings bonds, savings accounts, and time accounts are of highest grade in business risk because they are either obligations of the federal government or insured by a federal agency. Interest rate risk affects only the income stream of these types. As rates paid by savings institutions change, the income level will change periodically or at the time of redemption of the savings bond. The principal value will not be affected by changes in the market interest rate. Because of the fixed value of both principal and interest, they are low grade in purchasing power risk and are unmarketable.

Proprietary and real estate. Your own business and real estate involve high business risk, because there is usually little diversification

[4] Some exceptions exist in the common stock of some public utilities.

[5] Taxability will be discussed in greater detail in Chapter 16.

EXHIBIT 15–7
Grading investments

Type of Investment	*Grade in terms of investment risks*					
	Business risk	*Interest rate risk*		*Purchasing power risk*	*Marketability*	*Taxability*
		Principal	*Income*			
Savings bonds	Highest	High	Low	Low	†	Low
Savings and time accounts*	Highest	High	Medium	Low	†	Low
Proprietary investments	Low	—	—	High	Low	Low
Real estate	Low	—	—	High	Medium	Medium
Securities:						
Long-term U.S. bonds	Highest	Low	High	Low	High	Low
Short-term U.S. securities	Highest	High	Low	Low	High	Low
Municipals	Med. to high	Low	High	Low	Medium	High
Corporate securities:						
Bonds	Low to high	Low	Medium to high	Low	Med. to high	Low
Preferred stock	Low to med.	Low	Medium	Low	Medium	Low
Common stock	Low	Low	Medium	High	Med. to high	Low
Investment companies	Med.	Low to med.	Medium	Medium	Med. to high	Low

* Up to insured limits.

† These investments are convertible into cash through the issuer.

of products and markets. Also, the success of such ventures is usually directly dependent upon the management ability of one individual. Undeveloped real estate offers high business risk. Development is a risky venture. Developed real estate in a good location with a lessee who is reliable is of medium business risk.

Interest rate risk is ordinarily of little importance with proprietary or real estate investments. Pronounced changes in the market interest rate would be required before there would be any noticeable change in the income or value of these assets. Real estate and proprietary investments are typically good hedges against inflation in that profits and values can increase. These investments are generally low grade in marketability because of the usually limited market. In the event that the principal value is needed quickly, it may be necessary to sell at a sacrifice price in order to attract a buyer.

Securities. Evaluation of securities is based upon the priority of claim on income and assets. As the priority increases, the dollar amount of the claim is typically limited. For example, a bondholder has a claim senior to that of stockholders, but the amount of the claim is limited to a specified amount of interest and principal. Therefore, bonds and preferred stock are of higher grade in business risk than common stock, but common stock is of a higher grade in purchasing power risk.

Interest rate risk is mainly of concern with securities given a high grade in business risk, but short-term instruments are less vulnerable to fluctuations in interest rates. Values of dividend income or principal for common stock are affected little by changes in interest rates. Stocks most likely to be affected by interest rate risk are those often referred to as income stocks. When interest rates increase in the market, prices of these stocks may decrease so that the expected return is comparable with prevailing market returns.

Marketability is medium to high for any securities that are readily traded either on exchanges or over the counter. Infrequently traded securities or securities of family-held companies are low grade in marketability.

This evaluation system can also be applied to other investment opportunities that you may have, enabling you to evaluate their strengths and weaknesses on an objective basis.

ANALYSIS OF INVESTOR CONSTRAINTS

As we said at the beginning of this chapter, designing a personal investment plan is similar to the process of designing a house. It becomes a matter of balancing the desired returns with the investment risks to be accepted or avoided. An analysis of the need for investment income in current and constant dollars, the need for liquidity of principal, and the need for tax protection provide a basis for a statement of investment goals and policies that reflect your financial capacity.

Investment goals are constrained not only by financial capacity, but also by conditions that are peculiar to individual investors. These conditions limit the risk you are emotionally capable of assuming or willing to assume. Psychological constraints require subjective judgments with respect to your ability to manage a portfolio and your general attitude toward assuming risk.

An analysis of your constraints should reflect a consideration of risk in the negative sense. You should be concerned with the outcome if the risks assumed work out poorly. When you consider that there are several possible outcomes from any investment, you should consider the effect if the actual outcome is the worst imaginable. The negative thinking approach is justified by the fact that you will not suffer hardship if the investment return is better than expected, but results poorer than expected could spell financial disaster.

Investor's need for income

The factors that affect the need for investment income vary so much that a generalization is difficult. A discussion of this constraint will center on the average investment requirement in various stages of family life.

Your need for income from investments can be estimated by analyzing the relationship between your *minimum* annual expenses and the level of your income. Emphasis should be placed upon the word "minimum."

Minimum annual expenses should include amounts often referred to as "bare bones" expenses. You can estimate your minimum annual expenses by taking the present level of expenditures and eliminating or reducing expenses that are not essential.

A plan that evaluates necessary expenditures not only accounts for subsistence needs; it assesses the minimal level of expenditure needed to maintain your financial and emotional well-being. You should seek to assure that no undue hardships would be created by an investment decision, even if the worst possibility should come to pass. Some families are able to adjust more easily than others to a lower standard of living.

Young families will ordinarily find reduction of expenses a difficult process. Many of their costs are for essentials such as the mortgage or rent, taxes, insurance, food, clothing, etc. When these expenses are deducted from income, there may be very little left over. Increasing income is required because as the family matures, costs increase. As a result, most of the families in this stage consider their present standard of living a bare bones one.

As the children mature and leave home, family living expenses decrease. Mortgages are frequently paid off and the need for insurance may change, further reducing the minimum annual expenses. Indeed, rather than expenses being equal to or greater than family income, there may be an excess of income.

Income and expenses ordinarily decrease for a retired family. Expenses such as commuting, professional dues, or a second automobile, associated with the business or profession of either or both the retired persons are greatly reduced or eliminated. At the same time, however, this source of earned income also disappears. Thus, for the retired family the sources of income are typically Social Security and a retirement plan from former employers.

Your need for income from investments is determined by comparing your income and minimum annual expenses. If expenses exceed income there is a need to use credit or to provide the added income from investments, depending on the situation. Young families often must depend on credit while retired persons may depend on investments to fill the gap. Where income exceeds expenses there is the possibility of increasing the principal invested, thereby increasing the future investment income available. Therefore, income and expenses should be estimated through the several stages of family life.

Another factor affecting need for investment income is change in the purchasing power (real value) of the dollar. Many of the sources of income expected to begin during retirement, such as pensions, are of a rather fixed amount, and therefore inflation decreases their real value. Thus it will take more dollars to buy those things needed for a bare bones living during retirement years. Therefore, the level of inflation in living costs is very important to the development of a financial plan.

A common error made in managing investments is expecting too much income from too little principal. Suppose that your expected need for income from investments in order to meet your minimum annual expenses is $2,000 per year. If you have a principal amount of $200,000, this would require an average return of only one percent, not at all difficult to achieve. However, if your principal is only $20,000, it would require a ten percent rate of return. Given the positive relationship between return and risk, it is evident that the situation that would require you to assume the greater risk would likely be the one where you would be least able to do so. If the rate of return required on the principal is greater than is feasible within an acceptable level of risk, it is necessary either to revise the minimum annual expenses, to plan for the accumulation of a larger principal, or to plan to consume part of the principal to supplement the income.

Investor's need for liquidity

Liquidity is more than just being able to convert an asset to cash. To be liquid means to be able quickly to recover the principal in its entirety or with only a small loss relative to the original investment.

A need for liquidity can usually be estimated by examining the level of obligations that must be met or supported by the investment portfolio, such as serving as collateral for a debt, and the required rate of return to provide needed investment income.

Liquidity to support debt. Substantial personal debts may require liquidity so that, if necessary, the debt could be retired by selling the assets. Such amounts of personal debt often arise as a result of borrowing to finance proprietary-type investments. In arranging such a loan, the lender may be willing to accept a lien only on the business property, but quite often the lender will also look to other assets, such as securities, for collateral to repay the loan if the business fails. If the business is prosperous, it may never be necessary to sell the collateral to pay the debt. Consistent with the negative approach, however, the possibility of failure does exist and could spell financial disaster if not taken into account when developing the plan.

Another claim that will come due at some time even for those of moderate wealth is associated with estate settlement costs. Taxes and funeral expenses must be paid and medical costs are likely if there has been a prolonged illness. Each investment plan must include a means of meeting these expenses.

Other borrowing arrangements may require that securities used as collateral must be equal to at least a given percentage of the loan. In the event their worth falls below that value, either more collateral is required or a reduction of the loan is needed. Those securities that provide the greatest liquidity are less subject to price fluctuation and thus may be more readily acceptable as collateral.

Liquidity to provide income. Liquidity needs are also tied closely to the need for investment income. When the required rate of return on principal is low, the investor does not have to be very concerned with the liquidity of the principal. All of the required income can be easily provided.

But, when the required rate of return would call for taking great risk in order to provide the needed income, it may be necessary for the investor to depend upon a portion of the principal to meet the minimum annual expenses. In order to minimize the loss of principal, these funds should be in a more liquid form.

Liquidity is also needed by the investor whose debt obligations and income requirements would not be a constraint. Even for the investor who does not depend upon investment income to meet minimum annual expenses, liquidity may be desirable in order to take advantage of future investment opportunities.

Investor's need for tax protection

The extent to which tax protection is needed depends upon the applicable federal and state income tax rates. Taxes will be discussed more fully in Chapter 16, but for now note that certain issues of securities can provide an advantage in terms of income and estate taxes. These securities generally provide an advantage only for those investors who are in the higher tax brackets.

To the extent that tax protection is needed, the types of securities available are limited. It may well be that because of the progressive structure of our federal income tax rates, only a portion of the portfolio would need the tax protection.

You can analyze your need for tax protection by comparing the returns available on taxable securities with those on securities from which income is tax exempt. Suppose that a tax-exempt municipal is available that yields six percent and corporate bonds of comparable quality yield 8.57 percent. As shown in Exhibit 15–8, if the tax rate on your income is 20 percent, you will maximize your return by choosing the taxable corporate bonds. When the tax rate on income is 40 percent, the return is greater on the municipal bond.

EXHIBIT 15–8
Comparing taxable and tax-exempt yields

Security	Yield at purchase price	After-tax yield: 20% tax rate	After-tax yield: 40% tax rate
Municipal	6.00%	6.00%	6.00%
Corporate	8.57%	6.85%	5.14%

The tax rate that makes the two bonds provide an identical after-tax yield is 30 percent ($0.06 = 0.085[1 - t]$, where t = tax rate). Given the relative yields used in the example, whenever the tax rate applicable to an amount of investment income exceeds 30 percent, you can improve your return by using the tax-exempt security.

The value of tax exemption becomes more difficult to determine for investments that are partially tax exempt or those that are subject to preferential tax rates. Such may be the case with distributions from investment companies or from capital gains.

An investor's needs for tax protection vary over time. The changing market rates of interest available on both taxable and tax-exempt issues make it worthwhile to reexamine periodically the need for tax protection.

Investor's ability to manage a portfolio

The ability to manage a portfolio has an important influence upon the types of securities that are appropriate. Generally speaking, the less qualified you are to manage the portfolio, the more severe the constraint on your ability to assume investment risks. If, on the other hand, you have an interest and aptitude for managing a portfolio, you may increase the amount of risk you assume.

Portfolio management ability may be limited for various reasons. You may estimate the severity of this constraint by looking at your record. The record considered should include a time period long enough to cover good and poor markets. An evaluation of the performance could include a comparison of your performance and that of some indicator of the average performance of the market.

Another limitation often imposed is lack of time to manage a portfolio. People who are employed full time may find that they do not have the time required to manage a portfolio, especially one that assumes high risk.

Psychological constraints

Many choices we make are difficult to justify on a purely rational basis. Each of us has a personal set of values and preferences within which we make decisions.

When we consider the returns available from an investment in various types of securities, we know that in general common stocks could provide the greatest return. This would logically imply that investors who are financially able should invest in common stock for a greater return. But, for psychological reasons, common stocks are not appropriate for all investors. The potential price fluctuations of common stock such as those shown in Exhibit 15–9 may be more than some people can stand and therefore they won't want common stock. Some investors do not feel comfortable unless they have their money in a savings account.

EXHIBIT 15–9
Price fluctuations of selected common stocks

Security	High price 1968–69	Low price 1970	Percentage decline
Four Seasons Nursing Centers of America . . .	90¾	0.20	99
National Environment Corp.	27	⅜	99
National Student Marketing	35¾ *	⅞	98
Performance Systems . . .	23	⅛	99

* Adjusted for subsequent stock split.

However rational or irrational an investor's temperament may appear to others, it should be carefully considered when developing an investment policy. This may well be the most severe investment constraint for many investors.

STATEMENT OF PERSONAL INVESTMENT POLICIES

It is through the statement of personal investment policies that investment needs and constraints are brought together. A sound investment policy should do two things:

1. It should define your needs and desires, and
2. It should specify how these goals are to be met within the recognized constraints—amount available for investment, what risks are acceptable, and what level of emotional strain can be tolerated.

The statement should explicitly set forth the appropriate investments to be used in terms of the investment risks, the other investment qualities, and the return expected. Policies should be stated specifically enough so that it is possible to determine whether or not they are being achieved.

Consider the policy pertaining to the family emergency fund as an example. Suppose that Bruce and Donna McBride have determined—in light of their insurance coverage, job security, stability of income, and the ages of their four young children—that they need an emergency fund equal to a minimum of three months' living expenses. They know that short-term credit is available from a bank if more than the minimum is required.

The appropriate investment for the emergency fund must be high grade in business risk for principal because the McBrides can ill afford to lose these funds. Any returns generated by these funds, however, can help to offset loss of purchasing power. Any further required adjustment for loss of purchasing power can be made through additions to the funds to maintain the three-month reserve. Interest rate risk of principal is also of concern because of the effect it may have on the value of the principal. Since this is an emergency fund, the McBrides do not know when it will be needed in cash. Thus, decreases in the value of the principal cannot be tolerated. The stability of the income stream as a result of interest rate risk is a secondary consideration; stability of principal is of primary concern. Further, the funds must be liquid so that they are readily available in the event they are needed. Taxability is of some concern because the McBrides are presently in the 40 percent marginal tax rate for federal income taxes.

Because the McBrides are busy with job, family, and community obligations, they do not have much time to spend in the management of the investment of these funds.

A policy statement covering the McBride family's emergency fund can be expressed as follows: emergency funds equal to three months' living expenses should be maintained in savings accounts, half of which may be in a 90-day notice time account in whichever insured savings institution pays the highest interest. Income is to be reinvested in the account to help offset the effects of inflation. The amount in the emergency fund is to be evaluated each year and adjusted to an amount equal to three months' living expenses.

This specific statement of investment policy covering the emergency fund provides the McBrides with a clear understanding of what they need, the type of investment to be used to provide for the need, and a standard to evaluate the results.

Investors commonly err by stating their policies in terms that are too general to be useful. An investment policy statement to "provide maximum investment income from a portfolio of high-grade bonds" may seem clear, but there is little indication of the investor's constraints with respect to risk. Further, there is no way to determine whether the policy is being carried out.

Investment strategies

An investment strategy is closely related to the investment policies discussed above. The statement of investment policies defines the types of securities and the extent of risk permitted by your constraints. Investment strategies are concerned with decisions made in the management of the portfolio. Clearly, any desired changes in the makeup of the portfolio should be carried out within the provisions of the stated investment objectives.

For purposes of discussion, investment strategies can be categorized as defensive or aggressive. Defensive strategies include those that seek to preserve principal and the stability of income flows. Aggressive policies are intended to result in greater increases in both the value of the principal and in yield; investors accept added risks in return for possible increases in value.

Just as investment objectives should be written out so performance can be evaluated, a written statement of investment strategies enables you to make decisions that are consistent with investment needs. Only if they are written out is it possible to evaluate how well these strategies are working. Unwritten strategies often become very fluid and frequently result in unrecognized shifts in emphasis. While shifts in strategies are often necessary and justified by changing investor needs, changes should be made only after you have carefully reexamined your circumstances.

Investment strategies require you to make two decisions: first, determine the number and type of securities to be held in the portfolio, commonly called diversification. Second, decide on the timing of changes in the portfolio.

Diversification. Probably the best-known strategy for attempting to control the risk to which you are subject is diversification. To diversify means to spread the risk. For example, a diversified securities portfolio is one that holds the securities of more than one company. That way if one of the companies is unsuccessful, all investment returns will not be lost. However, the negative side of diversification is that if one of your companies is very prosperous, your gains will be offset by the other companies that are not as successful.

Diversification can also apply to the combination of different types of investments in an effort to reduce risk. You may own your own business and also own Treasuries.

A defensive policy for security investments uses diversification to assure an average rate of return on investments of a particular risk grade. There is a question about how many different issues must be owned to provide the average return. There are no specific numbers available to serve as a general rule, but generally the lower the grade in business risk of the securities, the larger the number required to provide average returns. The low-grade business risk rating means that there is greater variability in the returns from the individual issues, thus requiring more issues for the averaging effect than would be needed if high-grade securities were held.

An aggressive policy would concentrate on holding fewer issues in the portfolio in an effort to increase returns by taking advantage of the greater price variability. Such a policy may be referred to as **con-**

centration. The extreme in aggressiveness would be to concentrate the entire securities portfolio in the common stock of a small, little-known, speculative company. The investment return would be a total loss of the investment if the company (such as National Student Marketing or National Tape) fails, but it could be a real bonanza if the company (such as IBM, Xerox, and 3M) becomes very prosperous. In any case, in a concentration strategy the expected variability of returns is very great.

Investment timing techniques. A number of methods have been developed in an effort to predict changes in the values of securities. About the only sure thing that has been learned is that market prices do indeed fluctuate. Attempts to increase investment returns by making investments when prices are expected to rise or selling when prices are expected to fall are categorized as aggressive policies. Every investor will agree that the desired principle is to "buy low, sell high." It is not as simple to achieve this timing as it may appear at first glance. Though forecasting can greatly improve returns, inaccuracies can result in substantial losses. These inaccuracies can result in the undesirable situation of "buy high and sell low."

Timing techniques have been developed in an effort to help you assume a more defensive posture. Two of these techniques are known as dollar-cost averaging and formula plans. These strategies are designed to offset the euphoria that an investor experiences in an up (bull) market or the natural conservatism created by a down (bear) market.

Dollar-cost averaging. Dollar-cost averaging is a strategy whereby you invest equal dollar amounts at predetermined intervals. The success of such a strategy is based upon the fact that the fixed amount invested will purchase more shares of stock when the price is low than when the price is high. Given that market prices will fluctuate, this strategy enables you to acquire shares over time at an average cost that is less than the average market price per share.

An important aspect of the dollar-cost averaging strategy is for you to continue to invest regular and equal dollar amounts, even in a declining market. Psychologically, this is difficult to do and is one of the bases for adopting a formula timing investment plan, as discussed below.

Exhibit 15–10 presents an example of a hypothetical dollar-cost averaging strategy. Suppose you plan to invest $1,000 each time period. This money is to be invested in the stock of one company. The market price is assumed to fluctuate around $40 per share. Even with the fluctuations assumed, notice that after the first period the average cost per share is less than the average price paid per share. This is the result

EXHIBIT 15–10
Dollar-cost averaging strategy—an example*

Time period	*Market price per share*	*Number of shares purchased in period*	*Total number of shares held*	*Total amount invested*	*Market value of shares held*	*Average cost per share*	*Average market price*
1	$40	25.00	25.00	$1,000	$1,000.00	$40.00	$40.00
2	$30	33.33	58.33	$2,000	$1,749.90	$34.29	$35.00
3	$40	25.00	83.33	$3,000	$3,333.20	$36.00	$36.67
4	$45	22.22	105.55	$4,000	$4,749.75	$37.90	$38.75
5	$40	25.00	130.55	$5,000	$5,222.00	$38.30	$39.00
6	$35	28.57	159.12	$6,000	$5,569.20	$37.71	$38.33
7	$40	25.00	184.12	$7,000	$7,364.80	$38.02	$38.57

* Broker's fees are excluded.

of investing an equal amount during each time period; the invested money purchases a different number of shares of stock each time—more when the price is low, fewer when the price is high. This strategy will produce a gain for the investor except when the market price of the stock generally declines throughout the whole investment period.

In spite of its attractiveness, there are several difficulties with the dollar-cost averaging strategy. One difficulty is that it is still necessary for you to select a good security. The simplified example shown above assumes the purchase of the stock of a single company. However, if you adopt a more defensive approach and diversify, several appropriate securities must be selected. If each periodic investment is used to buy small amounts of each of the securities in the portfolio, commissions will be relatively great and cancel much of the benefit to be gained from this strategy. This disadvantage may be overcome to some extent by buying the stock of a diversified company or shares of a no-load mutual fund.

A second disadvantage is that while decisions to purchase securities are made in a mechanical manner, there are no conditions stated for determining when to sell the securities. For many investors the decision to sell is far more difficult to make than the decision to buy.

Formula timing strategy. The formula timing strategies are designed to provide a mechanical basis for determining when to buy a security as well as when to sell. These strategies often take the form of a constant ratio plan or a variable ratio plan.

The simpler of the two is the constant ratio plan. With this strategy, you determine the makeup of your portfolio in terms of stock, bonds, cash or savings, depending upon your needs and constraints. Then you maintain this relationship by buying and selling as required. If the stock prices rise, you sell stock to buy bonds or increase cash or savings and vice versa. Ordinarily the timing of these adjustments is determined by a certain percentage change in the ratios or by certain time intervals.

The variable ratio plan is based upon changes in the ratios of stock to bonds to cash, etc., depending upon expected market activity. Thus, it tends to be more aggressive than the constant ratio plan. For example, when you judge that the stock market is near a peak, the predetermined ratios may indicate that you should hold 10 percent stock, 50 percent bonds, and 40 percent savings. When the market declines, and perhaps there is also a decline in the general economy and interest rates, the price of bonds goes up and the price of stocks goes down. When it is believed that the market indicators point to a bottoming out for stock prices, the ratios may direct that the portfolio should consist of 60 percent stock, 30 percent bonds, and 10 percent savings. These ratios are predetermined and are ordinarily tied to some measure(s) of securities market activity. The objective is to buy the securities when the prices are low and sell when the prices are high.

This objective causes great difficulty for many investors. The terms "high" and "low" are relative. Prices are high after they have risen above purchase costs, but they may still be low in terms of an expected future price. Or, prices are low after they have declined but they may be high relative to expected future prices. Predicting when stock prices and interest rates will reach highs and lows is not a simple matter.

In spite of the difficulties with these mechanical timing strategies, it can generally be said that on the average they are more successful than a more emotional approach. But then, if you stand with one foot in a tub of 180-degree water and the other foot on a block of ice, on the average you should be quite comfortable.

These investment strategies are not intended to be the perfect solution for all investment decisions. Rather, they are intended to provide guidelines to follow. Since these guidelines are developed before the emotional intensity of a crisis is felt, they can help you make decisions that are consistent with your needs and investment constraints.

SUMMARY

Three major inputs are needed to make an investment decision. One input is an understanding of types of investments, the second is information, and the third is an analysis of investor needs and constraints.

Constraints generally appear as limitations on the ability to assume investment risks. Investment risks include business risk, interest rate risk, purchasing power risk, and the qualities of marketability and taxability. Each type of investment can be graded in terms of each of these risks and qualities.

Your needs can be analyzed within guidelines that consider your need for income, liquidity, and tax protection as well as psychological needs relating to management ability and your capability to take risk.

Investment policy statements must be specific enough to enable you to evaluate performance. This requires a specific statement of investment objectives for each portion of the portfolio. Strategies for achieving these objectives must also be predetermined to avoid undue influence of emotionality when making decisions.

Investment strategies must deal with the construction of the portfolio as well as the timing of changes, if any, in the portfolio. Diversification lessens the risk in the portfolio while concentration increases risk. Mechanical timing strategies become more aggressive, assume more risk, when they depend upon a forecast of market activity to initiate changes in the portfolio. Investment timing strategies include dollar-cost averaging and the formula plans.

DISCUSSION QUESTIONS

1. Explain the role of each of the three major inputs to the investment plan. Can you think of any dangers to the investor if one of these inputs is left out?
2. Explain the statement, "There is a positive relationship between the risk and return of an investment."
3. Calculate the estimated yield to maturity, current yield, and the coupon rate on a bond that has 25 years to maturity, pays $60 per year interest, and has a market price of 85.
4. Calculate the expected rate of return on a common stock that has a market price of 60½, pays a dividend of $3.10, and sold for 55 one year ago. (The price increase is equal to the average growth rate expected in the future.)
5. What is "risk"? What are the investment risks and qualities that affect the desirability of securities? Explain the basis for evaluating securities in terms of each of these risks as it affects principal and income.
6. What are the investor needs that must be analyzed in order to determine investment constraints? Why is a negative approach justified when analyzing investor constraints?
7. How should you analyze your need for investment income?
8. What factors determine a need for liquidity?
9. Why is it important to consider more than just financial ability when analyzing needs?
10. Explain the need to be specific when stating personal investment policies. What should be included in such a statement?
11. "Diversification is a defensive investment strategy while concentration is an aggressive strategy." Explain.
12. Describe dollar-cost averaging as an investment strategy. What are its advantages and disadvantages?
13. Why is the formula timing strategy superior to dollar-cost averaging? How does it work?
14. Explain why the variable-ratio plan is more aggressive than the constant-ratio plan.

CASE PROBLEMS

1. Paul and Linda Simon are a young couple in their late 20s with two children, ages 5 and 7. They have been living within their income and

have been able to provide the necessary emergency fund and insurance for their family. Linda and Paul are buying a home and have a balance of $20,000 on the mortgage. Just recently they found out they will receive $40,000 from the estate of an uncle. They have never invested money in anything except a savings account but are not overly concerned about possible short-term fluctuations in the value of investments.

a. *Examine Paul and Linda's need for:*
   1. *Investment income during the next ten years.*
   2. *Investment income during the children's college years.*
   3. *Liquidity of principal.*

b. *Recommend an investment policy that meets the Simons' needs.*

2. Ms. Sara Ellendorf, a friend of your family, has just retired and has come to you for advice. She is very emphatic about wanting a stable investment income with a high degree of safety. (Further discussion with her rules out common stock because of the business risk involved.) You recommend that she should buy triple-A corporate bonds due in 20 to 25 years. She replies that she doesn't expect to be around that long and doesn't like the long maturity. You then suggest that she buy triple-A bonds with a three-year maturity. She likes this suggestion and says she thinks it's exactly what she needs.

   What is the effect of interest rate risk on this policy? Explain this to Ms. Ellendorf.

3. Martha and Dan Richards had been married 20 years when Martha was widowed as the result of an auto accident. She received $75,000 from the life insurance company. Martha must now provide for their two children, ages 14 and 16. The family will receive Social Security benefits, but Martha has determined that this will not be enough for them to live on. A comparison of their minimum required expenses and their income from Social Security shows that right now they need $5,000 of income from investments. Martha has decided that she will limit her investments to securities. She has never owned securities before and is somewhat concerned about the fluctuations in market prices, especially of common stock, but she does not rule out holding some stock. Martha says that she would like to hold long-term (20-year maturity), high-grade bonds because the market price should always be close to what she paid. Then, when the children need financial help to go to college she would be able to get her money back by selling the bonds.

a. *Analyze Martha's investment constraints. Which appear to be most restrictive at present? In the future?*

b. *Evaluate Martha's desire to hold long-term, high-grade bonds. What dangers exist for her in such a policy?*

c. *In light of your analysis, recommend a policy to meet Martha's needs. Support your recommendation.*

SELECTED READINGS

Cohen, Jerome B.; Zinbarg, Edward D.; and Zeikel, Arthur. *Investment Analysis and Portfolio Management,* 3d ed. Homewood, Ill.: Richard D. Irwin, Inc., 1977.

Lorie, James H. and Hamilton, Mary T. *The Stock Market.* Homewood, Ill.: Richard D. Irwin, Inc., 1973.

Malkiel, Burton G. *A Random Walk Down Wall Street.* New York: W. W. Norton & Company, Inc., 1973.

Sauvain, Harry C. *Investment Management,* 4th ed. Englewood Cliffs, N.J.: Prentice-Hall, Inc., 1973.

Widicus, Wilbur W., and Stitzel, Thomas E. *Personal Investing.* Rev. ed. Homewood, Ill.: Richard D. Irwin, Inc., 1976.

section four

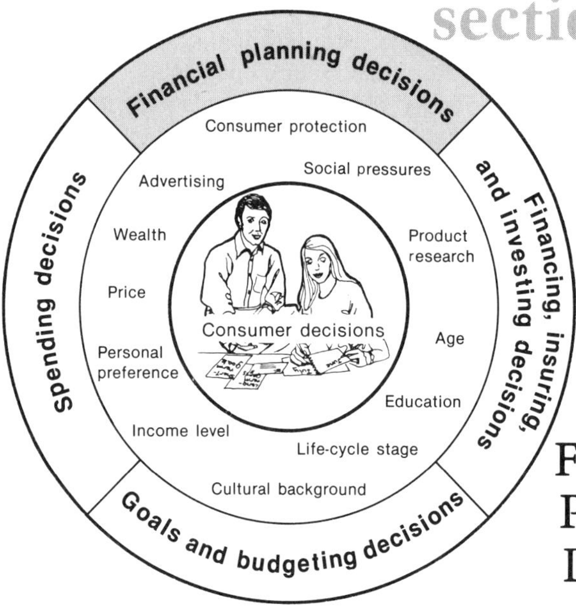

FINANCIAL PLANNING DECISIONS

Most of the consumer decisions we make are related to our immediate wants and needs. The bulk of our spending decisions relate to buying the necessities of life such as food and housing. And if we become too preoccupied with making these short-term decisions, we often overlook the need to plan ahead for future events.

In this section of the text we will examine the need to make financial planning decisions. Financial planning decisions may be thought of in terms of how they affect our future financial position. They are essentially decisions made at the present time that affect the future outcome of events.

Chapter 16 discusses the need for planning ahead to minimize taxes. It points out the general planning principles to follow and suggests sources of expert tax planning.

Another basic part of personal financial planning involves the ability to analyze your current financial position. Chapter 17 examines techniques that you can use to determine your financial weaknesses and strengths. This information provides a valuable starting point from which you can begin to make plans to strengthen your personal finances.

Chapter 18 provides an opportunity to learn how longer range financial planning decisions can help provide a sound future financial situation. The chapter suggests specific methods by which you can plan for the future and highlights the need to use budgeting as a primary planning tool.

Tax planning

16

OBJECTIVES

The primary purpose of this chapter is to introduce the idea of tax planning for federal income and estate taxes as a means of minimizing your taxes. This introduction covers the elemental parts of the tax planning process and provides general tax guidance as opposed to a highly technical in-depth approach.

After thoroughly reading and discussing this chapter, you should be able to:

. . . Identify the principal forms of taxes paid by consumers and their relative importance as tax burdens.

. . . Distinguish between tax avoidance and tax evasion.

. . . Explain the general process for deriving your net income tax.

. . . Identify sources of professional help for planning estate and income taxes.

. . . Outline the process of determining an individual's taxable estate.

. . . Identify the basic ways in which property may be transferred at death.

According to the old saw, the only sure things in life are death and taxes. Over the years governments have devised many ingenious ways of extracting money from the pockets of taxpayers. You are familiar with taxes on income, property, and gas, but you may not be aware of state, local, or federal taxes on beekeeping, boxing clubs, and mink farms.[1] Ultimately, of course, whether these taxes are on corporations and businesses, or directly on the individual, you pay all taxes as part

[1] For examples of state taxes, see *Taxes 1976* (Madison, Wisconsin: Wisconsin Taxpayer's Alliance, 1975), pp. 2–5.

of the price of products and services or as a direct payment to a governmental unit. Whatever form the tax levy takes, one sure thing is that taxes represent a large financial obligation for most consumers.

TAX BURDEN

Tax burden refers to the relative amount of income that a person pays in taxes. In general, the overall tax burden averages about 30 percent of income. By comparison the tax levies in most Western industrial countries are higher. For example, the tax burdens in Norway, Denmark, Sweden, and the Netherlands take an average of more than 40 percent of a person's income.

Taxes are the price paid for a variety of governmental services ranging from garbage collection to national defense. It is our contention that you should try to minimize your tax cost by planning just as you would minimize the cost of food, autos, and the like by careful shopping. This chapter, then, will be devoted to tax planning. Before we start on the planning itself, we should take a look at the principal taxes facing you.

Income taxes

One of the most familiar taxing tools is a tax on the income of individuals and corporations. This device is used by the federal government and, to an increasing extent, by state and local governments as a primary source of revenue. In the case of the U.S. individual income tax, the tax is designed to increase as income increases; thus, it is termed a *progressive* income tax.

At the federal level, income tax rates range from a minimum of 14 percent to a maximum of 70 percent. The determination of what income is taxable and the application of the appropriate tax rate is, of course, the puzzle facing taxpayers each Spring as they prepare their U.S. tax returns. Though more shall be said about the matter later in this chapter, handling the problems and complexities of the income tax laws may be the most important planning activity you can undertake.

Property taxes

One of the oldest forms of taxation is a tax on property. In the United States, the most common form of property tax is levied by local towns and cities on real estate. The real estate tax is usually expressed as a rate per $1,000 of assessed property value; for example, a rate of

$32 per $1,000 means that the taxpayer pays $32 for every thousand dollars' worth of assessed value.[2] Thus, if a home and the land it is on is assessed at $25,000 and the tax rate is $30 per $1,000 of assessed value, the taxpayer would have a real estate property tax of $750.

The property tax is used by local governments to raise money to pay for services such as police and fire protection, streets and highways, and public schools.

Sales taxes

State and local governments have increasingly relied on sales taxes as a major source of revenue. The sales tax is a percentage levy upon the gross sales of retail and service establishments. For example, if a state has a five percent sales tax on clothing, a retailer who sells a $50 coat must collect a $2.50 tax, raising the total cost to $52.50. Most sales tax laws provide for taxes on almost all goods and services, but some states do exempt essential items such as food and medical services.

A frequent criticism of the sales tax is that it is unfair because it is regressive. That is, the tax burden on lower income taxpayers is proportionally higher than the burden on upper income taxpayers.

User taxes

The idea behind user taxes is to put the financial burden of a specific government service on those who use that service. For example, both federal and state governments levy a tax on each gallon of gas that is sold for use in autos and trucks. This tax money is then kept in a separate fund, which in most states is used to pay for highway construction and repair. Other forms of user fees include hunting license fees, sewerage taxes, and motor vehicle license fees.

Estate and inheritance taxes

The history of estate taxes under the English common law can be traced back to feudal times when a king or lord had all rights to his serfs' property upon their deaths. This type of death tax now takes the form of estate and inheritance taxes. Estate taxes are levied by the federal government on all property that the deceased owned at the time of death. This includes all real estate, stocks, bonds, other securi-

[2] The property tax may also be expressed as so many mills per $1.00 of assessed property value. In the above example, a rate of $32 per $1,000 is expressed as a mill rate of 32 mills per $1 of assessed value.

ties, cash, and in most cases, life insurance. Estate taxes are paid directly out of an estate before any money is transferred to the heirs.

Inheritance taxes are imposed by state governments on the transfer of property from the deceased's estate to an heir. This tax is generally paid by the one who inherits the property. Every state except Nevada levies an inheritance tax in one form or another, but the tax rates among these states vary tremendously. Arizona (which levies the tax on the estate itself) and Florida are known for extremely low inheritance taxes, while Wisconsin and New York have relatively high rates.

Gift taxes

Another tax on the transfer of property and wealth is the gift tax. The federal government and many state governments charge a tax on the value of gifts between individuals. Under the Tax Reform Act of 1976, the federal government combined the gift tax and the estate tax to form one combined tax on gifts and estates.

Social insurance taxes

The social insurance programs created by federal and state governments are financed by social insurance taxes. These taxes are earmarked for a specific use and are usually kept in segregated trust accounts. On the federal level, the Social Security system is supported by payroll taxes paid by employers and employees. In 1978, the Social Security tax was 6.05 percent on the employer and 6.05 percent on the employee. Thus, for every $100 of payroll up to the maximum specified by law, the employer must contribute $6.05 and the employee must pay another $6.05. In 1978, the maximum taxable income was $17,700, but this figure will climb to $31,800 by 1982. Exhibit 16–1 details the proposed increases in the maximum Social Security tax and maximum wage subject to tax.

Most state social insurance taxes are levied on the employer and

EXHIBIT 16–1
Projected Social Security taxes

	1977	*1978*	*1979*	*1980*	*1981*	*1982*
Tax rate (percentage of taxable wage)	5.85%	6.05%	6.13%	6.13%	6.65%	6.70%
Maximum wage taxed (proposed)	$16,500	$17,700	$22,900	$25,900	$29,700	$31,800
Maximum tax (proposed)	$ 965	$ 1,071	$ 1,404	$ 1,588	$ 1,975	$ 2,131

Source: Social Security Administration.

are not directly levied on the employee. Typical state programs include unemployment insurance contributions to support state funds that pay benefits to unemployed workers.

TAX PLANNING FOR CONSUMERS

The certainty of taxes is a generally accepted fact of life. In a few places in the world (the Cayman Islands, for example), there may be tax havens where individuals pay virtually no taxes. But for the rest of us, dreams of lower taxes or no taxes at all fly in the face of reality.

This is not to say that we cannot do anything about taxes. There are legitimate ways of saving tax dollars. In doing so, we must clearly distinguish between tax avoidance and tax evasion. Tax avoidance involves legal methods of reducing taxable income. For example, older taxpayers may qualify for additional deductions, exemptions, and credits that may reduce taxable income and taxes payable. These sorts of deductions are provided for in the Internal Revenue Code, which is the result of Congressional legislation.

By contrast, tax evasion involves illegal methods of reducing or eliminating taxes. Failing to report income and listing nonexistent deductions are examples of tax evasion. As a reflection of its criminal character, the penalties for tax evasion include jail sentences and heavy fines.

Given the alternatives, tax planning based on tax avoidance would seem to be the clear choice. We must, of course, realize that certain taxes do not lend themselves to the planning process. For example, sales taxes are unavoidable, although a resident of one state may avoid the sales tax in another if the sales transaction is carried out directly by mail.[3]

Of the taxes we have discussed, both income and estate taxes are excellent examples of taxes that deserve tax planning consideration. The rest of this chapter will be devoted to discussing income and estate tax planning for the average consumer. We should point out that tax law and tax planning can become quite complicated. No single chapter in any book will make you an expert on taxes. But what we can do is point out the general approach to tax planning and additional sources of information and expert knowledge that you can utilize.

Planning for federal income taxes

For over 125 years the federal government derived its operating revenues from an assortment of excise and import taxes. By the early

[3] The law in this matter may vary from state to state, but most states exclude sales taxes on direct mail selling to out-of-state residents.

1900s, the financial needs of government began to exceed these traditional sources of revenue, and efforts to increase the revenue base led to the passage of the 16th Amendment to the Constitution of the United States. The 16th Amendment, which is the constitutional foundation of the government's right to tax a person's income, states that:

> Congress shall have the power to lay and collect taxes on income, from whatever source derived, without apportionment among the several states, and without regard to any census or enumeration . . .

Congress apparently took this charge seriously, for it has enacted a large number of tax bills since 1913 that tax almost every source of income. In fact, the income tax has become a mainstay of federal government revenues: it accounts for over 40 percent of all revenues collected. The federal income tax bite on consumers is quite substantial. The average federal income tax rate in 1977 was 9.6 percent of consumer income.

Before you can begin to do tax planning, you must understand how the federal income tax works. The federal income tax equation shown in Exhibit 16–2 illustrates how you determine your taxable income. As you can see, adjustments, deductions, and tax credits can legitimately reduce your taxable income.

EXHIBIT 16–2
The federal income tax equation

	Gross taxable income
−	Adjustments
=	Adjusted gross income
−	Deductions in excess of flat standard deduction
=	Tax table income
−	Tax credits
=	Net income tax

Gross taxable income. The starting point for determining your taxes is gross taxable income. Taxable income includes all sources of income that are not expressly exempt from tax. In general, compensation for your services is taxable income. This includes salary, wages, fees for services, commissions, bonuses, and tips. Interest, rent, and miscellaneous income are also generally taxable income. Interest income includes interest on corporate bonds, notes, and bank deposits. Rental income, royalties, dividends on common and preferred stock, gambling income, and alimony are other taxable sources of income.

Certain income and cash you receive is not taxable income. The following items are generally not subject to the federal income tax:

Interest on state and municipal bonds and notes.

Interest on obligations of U.S. possessions.

Life insurance proceeds paid by reason of death of the insured.

Social Security benefits.

Worker's Compensation payments.

Unemployment insurance benefits.

Welfare and public assistance payments.

Policy dividends on life, health, and disability insurance contracts.

Gifts and inheritances.

The first $100 ($200 for a couple) of dividends on common and preferred stock.

Money received to settle a damage or injury suit.

Health insurance premiums paid by your employer.

Pension and disability payments to members of armed services.

Scholarships and fellowships.

Capital gains income. For many years, our tax system has had special provisions for capital gains and losses. A capital gain or loss occurs when you sell an asset such as a business or investment securities. When you sell a capital asset and get more or less than you paid for it, one of the following four gains or losses occurs:

1. When you buy an asset, sell it within twelve months, and get less than you paid for it, you have a *short-term capital loss.*
2. When you buy an asset, sell it within twelve months and get more than you paid for it, you have a *short-term capital gain.*
3. When you buy an asset, sell it after holding it for at least twelve months, and get less than you paid for it, you have a *long-term capital loss.*
4. When you buy an asset, sell it after holding it for at least twelve months, and get more than you paid for it, you have a *long-term capital gain.*

Short-term capital gains and losses are considered ordinary income and are included in the determination of gross taxable income. Short-term capital gains increase gross taxable income, and you must add the full amount of the short-term gain to your ordinary income. You may use up to $3,000 of short-term losses to offset your ordinary income. Any amount in excess of $3,000 may be used to offset future short-term gains, then long-term gains, then up to $3,000 of gross income.

Long-term capital gains and losses are not fully included in ordinary income and are taxed differently. Long-term capital gains receive favorable treatment under the tax law.

To illustrate, if a person bought a farm for $100,000 and sold it two years later for $200,000, the capital gains tax can be calculated in either of two ways with the taxpayer paying the smaller tax:

1. The $100,000 is reduced by 50 percent to $50,000 and this amount is added to the taxpayer's ordinary income and taxed at the tax table rate.
2. Alternatively, all gains up to a maximum of $50,000 are taxed at 25 percent and the remaining $50,000 is taxed at 50 percent of the unearned income tax rate to a maximum rate of 35 percent.

In the case of long-term capital losses, you may use them to offset long-term gains or you may use 50 percent of the loss, up to $3,000, to reduce your ordinary income. Any remaining loss can be used to offset up to $3,000 of gross income in future years or to offset first future long-term gains, then future short-term gains.

Adjustments. Adjustments, properly called deductions for adjusted gross income, are important because they reduce your gross taxable income. These adjustments are usually made up of necessary expenses associated with your business or the production of income. In general you can reduce your gross taxable income through the following adjustments:

Expenses for carrying on your trade or profession.

Meal, travel, and lodging expenses while away from home and on business.

Reimbursed expenses of an employee.

Expenses attributable to rent and royalty property.

Moving expenses.

Contributions to qualified retirement plans.

Premature time deposit withdrawal penalties.

Losses allowed on sales or exchanges of property.

Long-term capital gain deduction.

Each of these adjustments has limits and conditions as to what can be deducted and how much the adjustment may be. For example, the Tax Reform Act of 1976 amended the adjustment for moving expenses by allowing deductions for a net move of 35 miles (versus 50 miles under the old law) and raising the amount of the deductions from $2,500 to $3,000.

One of the more significant adjustments to your income can be contributions made to qualifying retirement plans. The tax law has been arranged to allow a person to deduct such payments from current income for the purpose of starting a plan that will provide income in the retirement years. In general, the earnings or investment income on these retirement accounts escapes immediate taxation. When retirement benefits are withdrawn, the retirement benefits are taxed in the year they are received.

You can use qualified retirement plans as part of your overall strategy to lower your tax bill. They allow you to set aside funds while you are employed and subject to higher income tax rates. When you retire, your taxable income will likely be much lower, and thus your retirement benefits are subject to a lower tax rate.

The two most common retirement funds are Keogh Plans and Individual Retirement Accounts (IRAs). Keogh Plans allow self-employed individuals to set up a tax-deferred retirement account. They benefit professional people such as doctors, lawyers, and architects, and also may be used by farmers, sole proprietors, and business partners.

Keogh Plans must meet the following requirements:

1. An individual cannot begin to collect retirement benefits before age 59½ but must begin collecting benefits by age 70½. Funds withdrawn from retirement accounts prior to age 59½ are subject to a ten percent penalty tax unless the individual withdrawing them is disabled.
2. Where a Keogh Plan is used by a proprietorship, partnership, or other organization with employees, the plan must also be set up for fulltime employees who have worked at least three years.
3. Contributions to a Keogh Plan must be invested in an approved manner. Current tax law allows investments to be managed by banks, trust companies, savings and loans, annuities and endowment life insurance, and mutual funds.
4. The contributions to the plan under the current tax law allow a minimum deduction of $750 or 100 percent of earned income up to $750 and a maximum deduction of 15 percent of earned income up to a limit of $7,500 annually.

The IRA is primarily designed to benefit individuals who are not self-employed but who work for employers that do not have retirement plans.

The IRA law also allows a working spouse with an IRA to set up and contribute to an IRA for a nonworking spouse. This arrangement can be set up in one joint account or separate IRA accounts.

To qualify for an IRA, you must meet the following conditions:

1. You must have earned income from full-time or part-time work and not be able to join a retirement plan at the place of employment.
2. You cannot begin drawing benefits before age 59½ but must begin taking benefits by age 70½. Withdrawals prior to age 59½ are subject to penalty taxes similar to those that apply to premature Keogh withdrawals.
3. Annual contributions can amount to 15 percent of earned income up to a maximum of $1,500. For joint accounts, the maximum contribution is 15 percent of the working spouse's income up to a maximum of $1,750.

The total of all adjustments is subtracted from gross taxable income to get adjusted gross income. Adjustments are an important category of deductions. They may be used whether or not you choose to use the itemized or the standard deduction.

Deductions. Deductions, technically called deductions from adjusted gross income, generally consist of amounts you pay for state and local taxes, interest, contributions, and medical expenses. Under our present tax law, you may individually itemize each legitimate deduction or you may choose to use the flat standard deduction. If you use the flat standard deduction, you may deduct the amounts shown in Exhibit 16–3 from your adjusted gross income.

EXHIBIT 16–3
Flat standard deductions for taxpayers

Filing status	*Flat standard deduction*
Married filing joint return	$3,200
Married filing separate return	1,600
Single taxpayers and heads of households	2,200
Surviving spouse	3,200

The provisions for standard deductions have been changed frequently by new tax legislation. The flat standard deduction figures shown in Exhibit 16–3 were set under the Tax Reduction and Simplification Act of 1977.

The Tax Reduction and Simplification Act of 1977 directed the IRS to prepare tax tables that incorporate personal exemptions and the flat standard deduction. Thus if you don't itemize deductions, you can turn directly to the tax table after you subtract any adjustments from your gross taxable income. This saves you the trouble of computing your standard deduction.

The second option on deductions involves itemizing each major category of deductions and then totaling the categories to arrive at the total itemized deductions. Under our current tax structure, there are literally hundreds of possible tax deductions. The following are some of the deductions you may take:

Interest paid on home mortgages and other real estate mortgages.
Finance charges on credit cards.
Interest on installment purchases.
Foreign taxes.
Sales taxes.
Property taxes.
Contributions to charitable organizations.
Medical expenses including doctor fees, hospital costs, medical aids and supplies, transportation and travel associated with an illness, medical care insurance, and home improvement costs required by an illness.
Drugs and medicines.
Casualty and theft losses.
Fees for tax preparation and planning.
Investment expenses.
Union dues.
Child care expenses.
Professional dues and subscriptions.
Fees paid to obtain employment.
Alimony.

Deductions, like adjustments, are subject to certain limitations. For example, you may only deduct medical expenses in excess of three percent of your adjusted gross income. Thus, if your adjusted gross income is $12,000 and your medical expenses are $1,500, you may deduct $1,140 [$1,500 − (0.03 × $12,000)] from your adjusted gross income.

Under the Tax Reduction and Simplification Act of 1977, the taxpayer deducts only the amount by which his or her itemized deductions exceed the flat amounts shown in Exhibit 16–3. For example, if a married couple has itemized deductions of $4,000, they will deduct $800 (that is, $4,000 − $3,200) from their adjusted gross income to determine tax table income. The tax table they then use will reflect credit for the $3,200 flat deduction.

Exemptions. The final category of reductions in taxable income involves personal exemptions. Exemptions are set amounts (currently $750 per person) that are figured into your tax table. An exemption is allowed for the taxpayer and each dependent. For example, a husband, wife, and four children would be entitled to six exemptions, and this would be reflected on the tax table.

The tax law also provides for counting additional exemptions for special situations. If a taxpayer or dependent spouse is 65 years or older, an extra exemption is allowed. For example, a husband and wife, each age 65, would qualify for four exemptions. The same double exemption applies to any taxpayer or dependent spouse who is blind, regardless of age.

Computing the tax. After you have determined your tax table income, you can generally compute your tax from the IRS tax tables. If your income exceeds the ceiling amount in the tax table, you will have to compute your tax by using the IRS tax rate schedules such as those shown in Exhibit 16–4.

Tax credits. After computing the gross tax, you may be entitled to certain credits against the amount of tax. A credit is a dollar-for-

EXHIBIT 16–4
Tax rate schedules for 1977 and later years

Married taxpayers filing jointly and surviving spouses			*Single individuals*		
Taxable income	*Tax on Column 1*	*Percent on excess*	*Taxable income*	*Tax on Column 1*	*Percent on excess*
$ 3,200	$ 0	14	$ 2,200	$ 0	14
4,200	140	15	2,700	70	15
5,200	290	16	3,200	145	16
6,200	450	17	3,700	225	17
7,200	620	19	4,200	310	19
11,200	1,380	22	6,200	690	21
15,200	2,260	25	8,200	1,110	24
19,200	3,260	28	10,200	1,590	25
23,200	4,380	32	12,200	2,090	27
27,200	5,660	36	14,200	2,630	29
31,200	7,100	39	16,200	3,210	31
35,200	8,660	42	18,200	3,830	34
39,200	10,340	45	20,200	4,510	36
43,200	12,140	48	22,200	5,230	38
47,200	14,060	50	24,200	5,990	40
55,200	18,060	53	28,200	7,590	45
67,200	24,420	55	34,200	10,290	50
79,200	31,020	58	40,200	13,290	55
91,200	37,980	60	46,200	16,590	60
103,200	45,180	62	52,200	20,190	62
123,200	57,580	64	62,200	26,390	64
143,200	70,380	66	72,200	32,790	66
163,200	83,580	68	82,200	39,390	68
183,200	97,180	69	92,200	46,190	69
203,200	110,980	70	102,200	53,090	70

Source: Internal Revenue Service.

dollar reduction in the tax bill and is a very important means of reducing the tax bite.

Tax credits are a quick way of reducing taxes and stimulating our economic system. Congress has in the past enacted tax credit allowances that apply for a short span of time. For example, in 1975 Congress passed a tax credit of five percent of the purchase price of a home that was built or under construction by March 26, 1975. This one-time credit, which was limited to a maximum of $2,000, was designed to boost consumer spending and thus stimulate the economy.

Other examples of tax credits (which appear to be more or less permanent parts of our income tax laws) include the retirement income credit, the credit for federal gas and oil taxes, and a credit for contributions to political candidates.

The retirement income credit is designed to reduce the tax on taxable pension income of retired people. The credit for federal gas and oil taxes is a refund to taxpayers who use fuels or oil for nonhighway purposes and may apply to fuel and oil used in farm equipment, power boats, and lawnmowers. Finally, the tax credit on political contributions gives a taxpayer a limited credit for contributions to political candidates and campaign committees.

Filing your income taxes

The first step in preparing your taxes is to determine whether or not you have to file; many people with small incomes do not. If you have any question as to whether you have to file, you can call your local IRS office.

Even if you have very little income, you still may choose to file. If you had income tax withheld or if you are eligible for a tax credit payment, you should file to get your refund.

For those who do have to file, Exhibit 16–5 shows what you should report and what form you should use. For individuals, the basic tax filing form is the Form 1040 or 1040A. The 1040 form is used by those who itemize or have adjustments and for people with larger incomes. The 1040A, known as the short form, can be used by those who meet the income level set in the law and who do not wish to itemize deductions.

Approaching the income tax problem

Many people find income taxes a source of never-ending confusion and mystery. Others may simply need a little help in locating the

EXHIBIT 16–5
Filing your federal income taxes: an overview

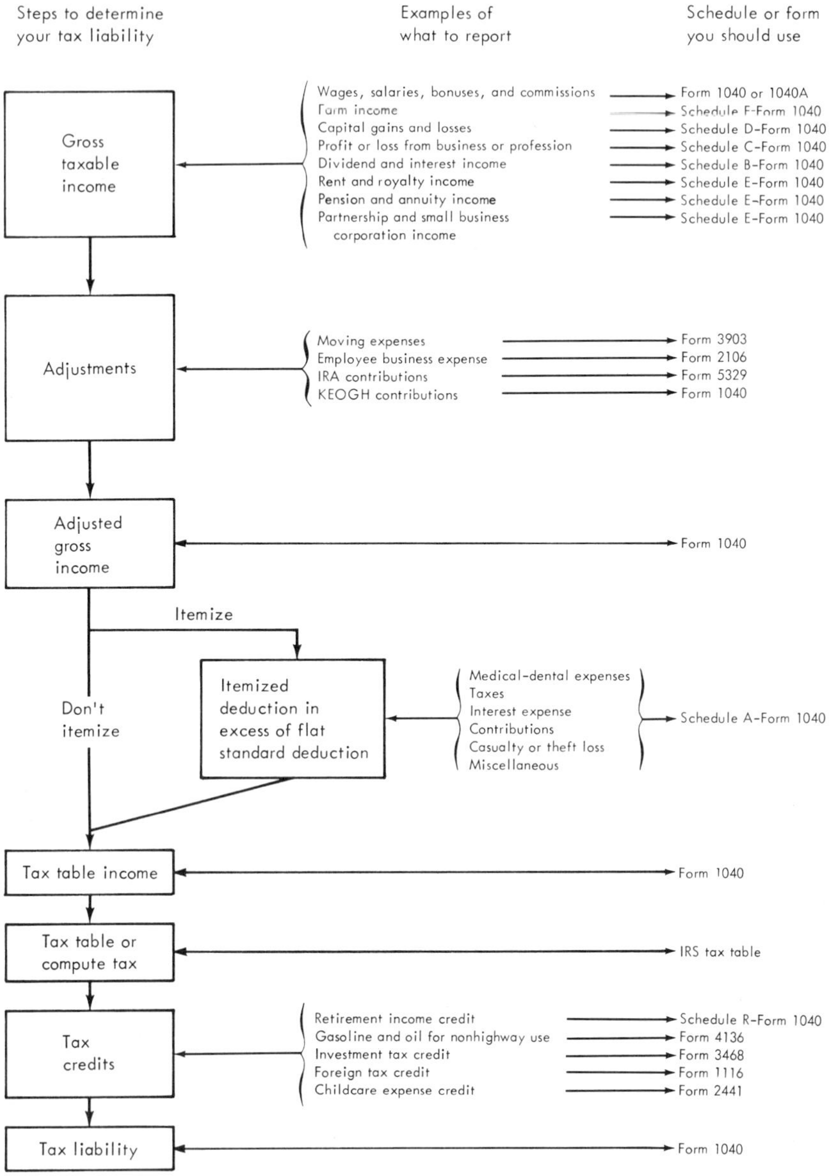

best devices for reducing income taxes. Few are tax experts who need no help at all.

For those who feel hopelessly lost, the best alternative is to turn to professional help in preparing tax returns and planning future tax strategies. The taxpayer will find many sources of tax preparation including large businesses with nationwide offices, certified public accountants (CPAs), tax lawyers, and an assortment of individuals with varying degrees of commitment (part-time vs. full-time) and expertise. CPAs and tax lawyers tend to charge the most for tax preparation and advice, but they usually have a higher level of training and education. The large tax preparation firms will often charge less than a CPA, but the bulk of their personnel are seasonal employees who are more versed in the mechanics of tax preparation than they are in the details of the tax laws. At the bottom of the list are individuals who hang out shingles as tax preparers. These people have widely varying skills and education levels, so you should be quite careful in choosing this form of assistance.

We should point out that the process of preparing a tax return simply deals with what has already happened. Tax preparation is really only one-half of the tax planning process. More importantly, you need someone to point out possible adjustments, deductions, exemptions, and credits at a time when you are in a position to plan ahead and take advantage of future situations. Tax planning prior to a major change in life can often save substantial sums. Retirement, for example, usually means extra exemptions and a retirement income credit. Planning ahead may allow the retiree to take gains on stocks or sell a vacation home at a time when the exemptions and credit provide some tax shelter.

In general, tax planning requires a much higher level of expertise than tax preparation. Tax planning may encompass estate planning, the use of trusts, and an advanced knowledge of complicated tax laws involving deferred income, tax shelters, and other tax devices. The best sources for this type of planning are the tax lawyer and the CPA. Both of these professionals have a good deal of formal education in taxation and both deal with taxes every day.

For those people who like working out their taxes or would rather do it themselves, tax preparation and planning can and probably should be aided by a one-time session with a tax expert (the tax lawyer or CPA) who can point out the best tax strategies. You can then devote time to learning more about how to use these ideas. For example, you can buy or borrow a number of magazines and subscription services that will provide periodic updates on changes in the tax laws. There are many government publications dealing with income taxes that are usually available free of charge at local Internal Revenue Service offices.

Whether you decide to have someone else do it or do it yourself, keep in mind that the tax law changes very rapidly. The Tax Reform Act of 1976 and the Tax Reduction and Simplification Act of 1977 contained several thousand pages of changes and additions to the tax statutes. You can expect changes of this magnitude about every other year, and you must be ready to respond to them.

TAX AUDITS

The United States is one of the few countries in the world to rely on voluntary compliance in the payment of income taxes. This means that the government depends on the individual to file income taxes each year and that the government spends very little on the process of collecting taxes.

Voluntary compliance does not mean that the government never checks up on the taxpayer. Indeed, every year the Internal Revenue Service (IRS) audits millions of tax returns and calls many taxpayers in for an in-depth look at their tax returns. The taxpayer must then bring in his or her records for examination. The initial examination is conducted by an IRS agent in the IRS office closest to the taxpayer. In most instances, this initial conference will reveal that the tax return is OK or that the taxpayer has made an error and must pay an additional tax.

In some cases, however, the taxpayer and the IRS agent will not agree on the points at question. The taxpayer may then appeal the case to the senior officer (district director) in that office. If there is still disagreement, the taxpayer can move the case to a conference at the regional IRS office. From there the case may go to U.S. Tax Court or the U.S. District Court for a formal trial. Beyond that, the taxpayer may appeal the case to the U.S. Court of Claims, the U.S. Court of Appeals, and finally to the U.S. Supreme Court. Needless to say, as the taxpayer gets into the regional conference and the courts, he or she should hire a competent lawyer who specializes in tax matters.

At some time in your life, you will likely be subject to a tax audit. Before breaking into a cold sweat, you should keep the following points in mind:

Taxpayers' rights. As we said earlier, you do not have to accept the decision of the examining agent. You should not be intimidated by this individual or the prospect of additional appeals if you think you have a legitimate point.

Records. The IRS is quite specific on the need for substantiation of deductions and adjustments. Written records or other evidence of expenses which you are deducting is a must. You can help yourself on this point by keeping receipts and a daily log of your mileage and other expenses.

A gray area. Although the federal tax laws occupy several volumes, the law is vague on many points. Over the years, deducting educational expenses and maintaining a business office at home have been subjects of considerable dispute. In many cases, you (and your lawyer) and the IRS may disagree over the interpretation of the law. Such disagreements are common, and if you pursue the matter, the outcome will frequently be in your favor.

PLANNING FOR PROPERTY TRANSFERS: ESTATE AND GIFT TAXES

As the result of the Tax Reform Act of 1976, taxes on the transfer of property through gifts and inheritances are now subject to unified tax treatment. Prior to this law, gift taxes were 25 percent less than estate taxes and this encouraged the transfer of property prior to death to save on taxes.

Under the provisions of the Tax Reform Act of 1976, all gifts in excess of the annual exemption made after December 31, 1976, will be included in the donor's (giver's) estate and will be taxed under a new unified rate schedule. The Tax Reform Act of 1976 still allows you to give up to $3,000 ($6,000 for a married couple) per year, tax free, to as many people as you wish. These annual exemptions make it advantageous to transfer property by gifts prior to your death.

The new schedule shown in Exhibit 16–6 applies to the net taxable estate, a concept we will explore later in the chapter.

The new unified federal estate and gift tax applies to all property owned by the decedent at the time of death and gifts in excess of the annual exemption. This includes real estate, stocks, bonds, savings, most life insurance (even though payable to a beneficiary), and any other interests in property, business, or other forms of wealth. The essence of planning for these property transfers involves determining how this property should be handled in the light of probate costs, administrative costs, and most importantly, estate taxes.

Property transfers at death

Property transfers provide the mechanical means whereby property is distributed upon a person's death. These transfers may be useful in

EXHIBIT 16-6
Federal unified estate and gift tax rates—1977 and after

*Amount with respect to which the tentative tax is to be computed**	*Tentative tax*
Not over $10,000	18 percent of such amount.
Over $10,000 but not over $20,000	$1,800, plus 20 percent of the excess of such amount over $10,000.
Over $20,000 but not over $40,000	$3,800, plus 22 percent of the excess of such amount over $20,000.
Over $40,000 but not over $60,000	$8,200, plus 24 percent of the excess of such amount over $40,000.
Over $60,000 but not over $80,000	$13,000, plus 26 percent of the excess of such amount over $60,000.
Over $80,000 but not over $100,000	$18,200, plus 28 percent of the excess of such amount over $80,000.
Over $100,000 but not over $150,000	$23,800, plus 30 percent of the excess of such amount over $100,000.
Over $150,000 but not over $250,000	$38,800, plus 32 percent of the excess of such amount over $150,000.
Over $250,000 but not over $500,000	$70,800, plus 34 percent of the excess of such amount over $250,000.
Over $500,000 but not over $750,000	$155,800, plus 37 percent of the excess of such amount over $500,000.
Over $750,000 but not over $1,000,000	$248,300, plus 39 percent of the excess of such amount over $750,000.
Over $1,000,000 but not over $1,250,000	$345,800, plus 41 percent of the excess of such amount over $1,000,000.
Over $1,250,000 but not over $1,500,000	$448,300, plus 43 percent of the excess of such amount over $1,250,000.
Over $1,500,000 but not over $2,000,000	$555,800, plus 45 percent of the excess of such amount over $1,500,000.
Over $2,000,000 but not over $2,500,000	$780,800, plus 49 percent of the excess of such amount over $2,000,000.
Over $2,500,000 but not over $3,000,000	$1,025,800, plus 53 percent of the excess of such amount over $2,500,000.
Over $3,000,000 but not over $3,500,000	$1,290,800, plus 57 percent of the excess of such amount over $3,000,000.
Over $3,500,000 but not over $4,000,000	$1,575,800, plus 61 percent of the excess of such amount over $3,500,000.
Over $4,000,000 but not over $4,500,000	$1,880,800, plus 65 percent of the excess of such amount over $4,000,000.
Over $4,500,000 but not over $5,000,000	$2,205,800, plus 69 percent of the excess of such amount over $4,500,000.
Over $5,000,000	$2,550,800, plus 70 percent of the excess of such amount over $5,000,000.

* The tentative tax applies to the sum of (*a*) the amount of the taxable estate and (*b*) the amount of the adjusted taxable gifts.

reducing estate taxes, but they are also useful in the overall estate planning process.

Wills. Our current laws provide for a number of ways in which an individual can transfer property in the event of death. The most familiar path is to designate heirs (who shall inherit the property) and the specific property that they are to receive through a last will and testament. The will is a legal document that must be executed according to the laws of the state in which an individual has established residence.

In general, your will should contain the following features:

1. An introductory statement indicating your name, place of residence, and general condition at the time you make the will; for example, "being of sound mind and not acting under duress." This statement should also indicate that you are revoking any and all previous wills.
2. A section providing for payment of your legal debts and expenses of last illness, funeral, and burial.
3. Provisions for the disposal of your real and personal property and any residual estate. These provisions might include direct bequests to your heirs or charitable institutions. They might also include provisions for setting up a trust to manage your assets for the benefit of your heirs. You may wish to be very specific in designating your property (my gold watch to my son John, my rocking chair to my daughter Julie) or you may simply leave a portion of your estate (one third of my estate to my son John) and trust that property will be appropriately distributed.
4. A provision naming the trustee, personal representative, or executor of your estate. This person or organization, such as a bank or trust department, will be responsible for administering your affairs while your estate is being settled. You may wish to give this person broad powers to lease, rent, sell, and otherwise manage your property in carrying out your wishes.
5. Provisions relating to appointing guardians for your minor children in the event there is no surviving spouse.

You should get expert legal advice in making your will. An experienced lawyer can draft the proper language for your will and may also be able to point out things that you haven't thought of. The lawyer will also know the technicalities involved in executing your will in accordance with state laws.[4]

Intestacy. For persons who die without a will (intestate), every state has a law on intestate succession. Most intestate succession laws designate that the deceased's property shall go to the closest blood relative or relatives. For example, most state laws provide that a husband's property is shared by his wife and children upon his death. Thus if an

---

[4] There are significant differences in laws governing wills and estates among the 50 states. For example, a few states allow an individual to make out a handwritten will, while most do not allow this practice.

individual does not plan for property transfers at death, the state assumes that role through the laws of intestate succession.

Survivorships. Survivorships represent a very common way in which property can be designated. *Joint tenancy, tenancy in common,* and *tenancy by the entirety* are three forms of joint ownership that can be used to transfer property to survivors. Joint tenancy is an arrangement where two or more people own a piece of property. In joint tenancy, an owner retains the right to sell his or her share of the property without the permission of the other owners. Upon the death of one owner, his or her share passes to the surviving owners.

Tenancy in common means that two or more people own a piece of property and that they each have the right to dispose of their share of the property without getting the permission of the other owners. When an owner dies, his or her share of the property goes to his or her rightful heirs who may or may not be the other owners of the property.

Tenancy by the entirety may be used only by married couples. Tenancy by the entirety means that the husband and wife each own a share of the property but may not sell their share without the permission of the other. Upon the death of either spouse, the share of the deceased spouse's property goes to the surviving spouse.

Beneficiaries. Even more common than survivorships is the transfer of property through a beneficiary designation. This transfer device is largely confined to life insurance contracts and allows the owner of the life insurance policy to designate the individual or party who will receive the death benefit.

Trusts. In addition to these common forms of property transfer, there are more sophisticated ways of designating property. Property transfers through trust agreements (other than trusts set up in wills) are legal devices that allow a person to designate how a trust will be distributed at death.

While estate tax planning is an essential part of the overall estate planning process, it is helpful to get an overview of the estate planning process. We shall therefore consider the overall problem before dealing with one of its parts.

Probate

All estates are settled through a process known as probate. The term "probate" technically means to prove a will or last testament. But probate courts in each state handle all matters regarding the settling of the estate, including estates of persons who died intestate. In most cases, you will need a lawyer to handle the probate process.

The process of probate typically involves the following steps:

1. A formal petition to the probate court requesting that legal proceedings be started to settle the estate.
2. An initial court hearing where the court appoints and instructs an executor or personal representative. At this stage all potential heirs to the estate are usually notified of the proceedings.
3. The executor or personal representative inventories and appraises all the deceased's assets.
4. Creditors are notified by published legal notice that they may submit any claims against the deceased.
5. Where there is a will, the will is proven (determined to be legal) and the legal heirs are determined.
6. Creditors are paid and then any estate and inheritance taxes are settled.
7. The proceeds of the estate are distributed among the heirs.

While the procedures of probate courts in each state may vary, the general steps outlined above are uniform in most states. The process of probate may take a few months, but in instances where the estate is large or the will is questioned, the proceedings may last for years.

Reasons for estate planning

One of the main reasons for estate planning is to minimize the tax bite on property transfers. We have already observed in Exhibit 16–6 that estate taxes represent a substantial charge on property transfers. Careful planning can substantially reduce or eliminate that problem.

A second reason to consider estate planning involves administrative and probate costs. The more complex and dragged out this process is, the higher the probate and administrative costs. These costs include court costs, lawyer's fees, and fees charged by executors and personal representatives of an estate. Comprehensive estate planning can reduce these costs and avoid most of the probate process.

A third rationale for setting up an estate plan is to distribute property in accordance with an individual's wishes. Whether these wishes involve the distribution of a favorite watch, a set of tools, or ten million dollars, unless a specific plan is formulated and set up, the property of a deceased individual will be distributed according to provisions in state law or by the estate's executor. Because an individual's wishes carry no weight after death, there can be no assurance that property will be appropriately distributed unless a formal legal plan is in effect.

A final reason for estate planning involves the avoidance of estate management problems. These problems may include the question of whether the heirs have the time or knowledge to settle the estate and continue to manage their inheritances. Another management problem may involve bickering among relatives over inheritances when one of the relatives serves as the administrator or executor of the will. These and other potential problems can be resolved before an individual dies by simple estate planning.

/**The estate planning team.** Estate planning draws upon many fields of study. The planning process is complex and requires legal, financial, insurance, and accounting expertise. For most individuals this means assembling a team of experts to help out in the process.

The head of that team is likely to be a lawyer with skills in estate planning. The lawyer can help you decide whether or not a will is necessary (in most cases it is) and what special problems might have to be solved. The lawyer can begin the process of gathering the basic facts. For example, you may have dependents to provide for in the event of your death. Post-secondary education for children, an adjustment income for a spouse, and money to support your dependent mother may be examples of the basic needs that will determine how you go about setting up your estate plan. The lawyer can also work on an overall tax strategy that can save on estate shrinkage. Finally, the lawyer can plan the best way to transfer property at death with the lowest possible tax, the fewest management problems, and the shortest probate period.

For people with larger estates it may also be advisable to involve a CPA, bank trust officer, and insurance expert. The CPA has insights into estate tax planning and may also help you assess your current and future financial condition. The CPA may be very important if you own part of a business whose value or continued operation may be in question in the event of your death. The bank trust officer can work with you and your lawyer in involving the bank trust department in several key areas of estate management. The trust department can provide investment management services and can also serve as executor or personal representative of the estate. The bank trust department is a neutral party that may help avoid family disputes over inheritances and the administration of the estate.

The life insurance agent can also provide input into this process by making suggestions on the estate plan, providing basic aids such as life insurance and annuity contracts, and drawing upon estate planning services in the home office of the life insurance company. Most life insurance agents who are CLUs (Chartered Life Underwriters) have considerable training and expertise in the estate planning process.

The degree to which all these people become involved in your estate planning will depend upon the complexity of your estate. For most estates, the lawyer and life insurance agent can provide the essential services. As the estate becomes more complicated, the trust officer, the CPA, and an estate tax expert (usually a tax lawyer) may be needed.

What about estate taxes?

The Tax Reform Act of 1976 brought about a number of major changes in the federal estate tax. Prior to this legislation, federal estate taxes ranged from three percent to 77 percent, and the first $60,000 of an estate was exempt from estate taxes. There was also a difference in rates between the federal estate tax and the federal gift tax, the gift tax being 25 percent less than the estate tax. Thus gifts were used to reduce a person's taxable estate prior to death. The 1976 tax legislation changed most of this. Tax rates now vary between 18 percent and 70 percent. The $60,000 exemption was replaced with a tax credit that will be gradually increased to $47,000 as shown in Exhibit 16–7 by January 1, 1981. Finally, the distinction between gift and estate taxes has been eliminated, and now both gift and estate transfers are taxed at the same rate.

EXHIBIT 16–7
Unified credit and equivalent estate level (1976–1981)

For decedents dying in	*Unified credit*	*Unified credit covers tax on all estates up to*
1977	$30,000	$120,667
1978	34,000	134,000
1979	38,000	147,333
1980	42,500	161,563
1981	47,000	175,625

Source: "Tax News" (Chicago, Ill.: Haskins and Sells, September 22, 1976).

Estate taxes and the recent changes in estate tax laws should be examined in the light of their effect on the typical consumer. In order for each of us to appreciate the need for tax planning, we must be somewhat familiar with the basics of estate taxes. The following three questions form a basis for looking at this problem: (1) What determines an individual's taxable estate? (2) At what point is estate tax planning necessary? (3) What strategies can be used to reduce estate taxes?

The taxable estate. The first step in determining the taxable estate is to lump together all property and wealth that is subject to estate taxes. This amount is called the gross taxable estate, and it consists of all interests in real estate, investments, personal property, and the face amount of all life insurance policies that a person owns.

Once the gross estate is established, the estate tax laws allow certain deductions and exemptions. All of the deceased's debts are deducted from the gross taxable estate. These debts include mortgages on real estate, charge accounts, notes owed to financial institutions, and any other amounts that constitute legal debts. The law also allows deductions for funeral expenses, expenses of the last illness, appraiser's fees, court fees, executor and attorney fees, and property, income, and gift taxes due. There is also a category of charitable exemptions that excludes all bequests to religious, charitable, scientific, and educational organizations from estate taxes.

After subtracting all the exemptions and deductions, the net taxable estate is taxed at the rates shown in Exhibit 16–6. This gross tax is offset by the new unified estate and gift tax credit. What remains is the net estate tax.

To summarize and illustrate this process, we can look at a particular case. Suppose we look at the estate of Alan Bernstein, who has real estate worth $100,000, life insurance of $150,000, and other property worth $50,000. In addition he has debts of $60,000, last expenses of $4,000, probate costs of $5,000, and a bequest to his Alma Mater, Behemoth U, of $20,000. His net estate tax would be derived as follows:

Gross estate:		
Real estate	$100,000	
Life insurance	150,000	
Other	50,000	
Total gross estate		$300,000
Deductions:		
Debts	$ 60,000	
Last expenses	4,000	
Probate costs	5,000	
Total deductions		$ 69,000
Exemptions:		
Bequest	$ 20,000	20,000
Total deductions and exemptions		$ 89,000
Net taxable estate		$211,000
Gross tax		$ 58,320
Tax credit (as of 1981)		$ 47,000
Net estate tax payable		$ 11,320

As we can see, the process of determining the taxable estate and the tax are not complicated. This step is very important, however, because it will show the size of the tax bill and it will also point out any need for estate tax planning.

At what point is estate tax planning necessary? While we would advise you to do basic estate planning to make sure that your wealth is transferred according to your wishes, estate tax planning is not necessary for everyone. Tax planning is important only if an estate is large enough to have a substantial estate tax or if substantial future growth of the estate appears imminent. All of this boils down to the simple question: At what dollar level is tax planning necessary?

One way of measuring this is to look at the current estate tax laws to determine when the estate tax begins to take effect. With the new tax credit, we have to determine how much of an estate escapes taxation. Exhibit 16–7 shows the unified estate tax credit established in the Tax Reform Act of 1976 and the equivalent estate level that would escape taxation.

When the unified credit reaches its maximum in 1981, estates of $175,625 or less will not have to pay federal estate taxes. You should begin to consider tax planning as your net taxable estate approaches the $175,000 level, remembering that state inheritance taxes may also be an important factor.

Estate planning strategies: The marital deduction. Once the need for estate tax planning is apparent, the immediate question becomes: What can be done to lessen the tax? A common method of arranging estates for married couples is to set up a marital deduction. The marital deduction is set up in the last will and testament of each spouse and takes effect upon the death of one of the spouses.

The principal feature of the marital deduction is that it reduces the taxable estate by allowing a deduction for property passing to the surviving spouse. The current tax law allows a marital deduction of up to $250,000 or one half of the decedent's adjusted gross estate (the adjusted gross estate equals the gross estate less deductions and expenses but not exemptions), whichever is greater. In effect, this means that $250,000 or one-half of the adjusted gross estate may be passed tax-free to a surviving spouse. If we apply this principle to the Alan Bernstein illustration (assuming he left all his property to his wife), his net taxable estate would be as follows:

Gross estate		$300,000
Deductions:		
Debts, last expenses, etc.	$ 69,000	
Marital deduction	250,000	
Total deductions		319,000
Exemptions	$ 20,000	20,000
		$339,000
Net taxable estate		0

In Bernstein's case, the marital deduction wipes out the $11,320 tax liability and allows the full estate (less deductions and exemptions) to pass to his wife.

The key to setting up the marital deduction is a session or two with a lawyer to take care of the appropriate legal work. The cost of this work will depend upon the complexity of the estate, but the total planning cost should be quite small compared to the eventual tax savings.

FINAL THOUGHTS ON INCOME AND ESTATE TAX PLANNING

As you probably realize by now, this chapter raises a lot of important questions. In many cases you may think it raises more questions than it answers. If so, you're probably right, but that's as it should be. We indicated at the outset of this chapter that tax questions are extremely complex and that the tax laws change rapidly. No chapter (or even group of chapters) can give you all the tools needed to completely do your own tax planning and preparation.

What we've tried to do is to point out the crucial areas that will require your attention as you proceed through life. We've also tried to point out who can help you with your tax problems and when such help should be sought. However you decide to take care of taxes in your lifetime, we think that tax assistance will help you legally minimize your tax bills.

SUMMARY

Every American consumer faces the annual cost of a multitude of taxes. The payment of real estate, sales, income, estate, gift, inheritance and user taxes consumes up to 30 percent of the average family's budget.

Consumers can try to minimize tax costs by planning for income and estate taxes. Income taxes levied by the federal government constitute the heaviest single tax on most individuals and families. The key to minimizing taxes lies in reducing gross taxable income and maximizing deductions, exemptions, adjustments, and tax credits. For many individuals, help in income tax planning should be sought from qualified professional tax lawyers and CPAs.

Estate taxes are another form of taxation for which you can plan. Planning for estate taxes should be part of the overall estate planning process. Estate planning should deal with tax problems, estate management problems, and distributing property according to your wishes. The Tax Reform Act of 1976 made substantial changes in estate taxes and eliminated many of the gift-giving strategies for tax planning. There is now a unified tax structure governing gifts and estates, and there are tax credits and changes in the marital deduction. Like income tax planning, estate tax planning is an ongoing process and is sufficiently complex to require expert help.

DISCUSSION QUESTIONS

1. Explain why the federal income tax is called a progressive tax.
2. Identify three user taxes and explain the rationale behind the user tax.
3. What is the difference between tax avoidance and tax evasion?
4. What are adjustments in the federal income tax system and how do they fit into the federal tax equation?
5. How do the Keogh and IRA retirement plans differ in terms of who may benefit from them?
6. What is the difference between tax planning and tax preparation?
7. If a taxpayer is audited by an IRS agent, must he or she accept the IRS agent's decisions? Explain.
8. Explain the main reasons for estate planning. For estate tax planning.
9. What is the function of the insurance agent on the estate planning team?
10. What is the basic idea behind a marital deduction? How does it lower tax rates?

CASE PROBLEMS

1. John and Mary Richards are both self-employed professionals just out of graduate school. John is setting up a dental practice and Mary is a CPA. They currently have two children, ages 3 and 5. In the current year, their joint income will be $45,000. They have gathered their tax information for the year, and figure that they have the following deductions, adjustments, and credits:

Investment tax credit on John's dental office	$ 1,800
State income taxes paid	3,500
Interest on home mortgage	5,000
Charitable contributions	500
Moving expenses	1,200
Business expenses	11,000
Other deductions	4,000

Classify each of the above as an adjustment, an itemized deduction, a tax credit, or an exemption.

2. John and Mary Richards expect to increase their income at the rate of 20

percent per year as their practices grow to maturity in about ten years.

Based on these facts, the information in Case 1, and the tax rate schedule shown in Exhibit 16–4, do you think they could use some tax advice? Do they qualify for an IRA or Keogh Plan? If so, would such a plan be advantageous to them?

SELECTED READINGS

Barlow, Robin, and Coe, Richard. "The Incidence of Selected Taxes by Income Classes," Chap. 8 in Vol. 2 of *Five Thousand American Families—Patterns of Economic Progress.* Ann Arbor: Institute for Social Research, 1974.

Coe, Richard. "A Note on the Short and Long-Run Equity of the Federal Individual Income Tax," Chap. 10 in vol. 3 of *Five Thousand American Families—Patterns of Economic Progress.* Ann Arbor: Institute for Social Research, 1974.

Prentice-Hall Federal Tax Handbook (Annual). Englewood Cliffs, N.J.: Prentice-Hall, Inc.

Your Federal Income Tax. Published annually by the Internal Revenue Service.

Personal financial analysis

17

OBJECTIVES

This chapter explores techniques you can use to analyze your own financial situation and shows you how to use a balance sheet for personal financial planning.

After thoroughly reading and discussing this chapter, you should be able to:

. . . Explain the need for a financial profile as a basis for planning.
. . . Construct a personal balance sheet.
. . . Analyze a personal balance sheet.
. . . Identify symptoms of financial problems.

Decisions to save your money, to spend all of your money, or to borrow and spend more than your current income are usually influenced by your age and stage in the family cycle. If you feel you are constantly short of money, you share with the majority of mankind. Our wants always seem to exceed our resources. What you really need is more than the feeling you never have enough money: you need a system that will identify those needs of highest priority and that will use the available funds to satisfy them. This process is known as personal financial planning.

Advantages of personal financial planning

One of the major advantages of personal financial planning is that it enables you to gain the greatest satisfaction from your income. By placing priorities on your needs and wants and by channeling your available income to those needs with highest priority, you are able to gain the greatest satisfaction.

Another advantage of planning is that it provides a means of developing a sound financial condition. A sound financial condition means that you are able to meet your financial obligations without undue stress.

Families who do not plan their spending are often faced with financial distress or disaster. A Family Service Association of America study revealed that one of the characteristics of families who had declared bankruptcy was a lack of personal financial planning. The families did not realize that they were getting in over their heads until it was too late.[1]

Development of a personal financial plan

The development of a personal financial plan requires a comparison of the present financial position or profile with your financial goals. This comparison is made clearer through the development of a personal balance sheet. Results of the comparison serve as a basis for developing the long-range financial plans that we discuss in Chapter 18.

THE BALANCE SHEET—A PICTURE OF CURRENT FINANCIAL CONDITION

A balance sheet is a method of showing the values of what you own (assets) and the amounts you owe (liabilities) at a specific point in time. This information is important to you, because it provides you with a current picture of your own financial situation. As such, it is a necessary beginning step in developing a plan. It will help identify the actions required to reach your financial goals.

To illustrate, we may compare this process with planning a trip. If your goal is to go to Aspen, Colorado, your planned direction of travel will depend upon your starting point: if you don't know the starting point of your trip, you may never arrive at your desired destination.

Constructing your balance sheet

Your balance sheet is a picture of the cumulative effect of your past financial activities. The picture shows a value for all of the things that you own (your assets), how much of this value has been provided

[1] *Family Credit Counseling—An Emerging Community Service* (New York: Family Service Association of America, 1967).

by using funds from creditors (your liabilities), and how much of the funds have been provided by you (your net worth).

Notice that in the balance sheet for the David Dirth family shown in Exhibit 17–1, the total assets equal the sum of funds borrowed from creditors plus the net worth of the Dirth family. The totals balance; therefore, the name "balance sheet." Assets are classified as current or fixed, while liabilities are classified as current or long-term.

Current assets. Current assets are those assets that can be quickly converted to cash. Items such as checking and savings accounts, cash value of insurance policies, and securities are current assets.

Cash. Cash includes amounts on hand plus amounts held in checking or savings accounts. This should include amounts held for special reasons, such as money in an emergency fund.

The Dirth family has $40 on hand to meet the general expenses of the household plus $456 in its checking account. Savings accounts have been established for use as an emergency fund and for money being accumulated to help pay for the car the family expects to purchase as a replacement for its present second car.

U.S. government savings bonds. Savings bonds should be listed at their current redemption value. This value can be readily determined by asking any authorized redemption center. According to the balance sheet, at present the Dirths do not hold any savings bonds.

Cash surrender values. Permanent life insurance has an investment (or cash surrender) value if the insured wishes to discontinue the policy coverage. This amount increases over the time the policy is in effect. To determine the cash surrender value for your policies, turn to the table included in the policies.

David Dirth has two policies with a combined cash surrender value of $2,072.

Securities. The balance sheet value of your securities should reflect their current market value. Prices of many securities traded over the counter and those that are listed on exchanges can be found in financial newspapers such as *The Wall Street Journal.* If the price of any of the securities you own is not included in the newspaper listings, a call to your broker should get the information for you.

Dave and Judy Dirth currently hold two corporate bonds with a combined value of $1,500, 100 shares of stock with a current value of $23.25 per share, and 100 shares of a mutual fund with a net asset value of $27.59 per share.

Other current assets. Any other current assets should be listed at their estimated value. The Dirths loaned $150 to a friend, Bruce Davidson. They expect him to repay the $150 within the next month.

Fixed assets. Fixed assets are those that usually take a longer period to convert to cash. They include assets that have a useful life longer

EXHIBIT 17–1

DAVID DIRTH FAMILY
Balance Sheet
June 30, 1978

Assets		
Current Assets:		
Cash		
On hand	$ 40	
Checking account	456	
Emergency fund	2,100	
Other savings accounts	1,076	
Total Cash		$ 3,672
U.S. Savings Bonds		—
Cash surrender value of insurance		2,072
Securities (market value)		
Bonds	$ 1,500	
Stocks	2,325	
Mutual funds	2,759	
Total Market Value		6,584
Other Current Assets (specify)		
Loan to Bruce Davidson		150
Total Current Assets		$12,478
Fixed Assets:		
Automobiles	$ 3,300	
Personal property	2,500	
Real estate—homestead	45,000	
Real estate—other	6,000	
Proprietary investments (specify)	—	
Total Fixed Assets		56,800
Total Assets		$69,278

Liabilities		
Current Liabilities:		
Current Bills		
Charge accounts	$ 516	
Insurance premiums owed	360	
Taxes owed	—	
Utilities	55	
Other (specify)	—	$ 931
Loans—Short-term (balance)		
Bank		
Car	$ 300	
Furniture	1,000	
Nonbank	—	1,300
Total Current Liabilities		$ 2,231
Long-Term Liabilities (balance):		
Mortgage Loans		
Real estate—homestead	$29,492	
Real estate—other	4,000	
Other (specify)		
Education	2,000	
Insurance policy loan	200	
Total Long-Term Liabilities		35,692
Total Liabilities		$37,923
Net Worth		31,355
Total Liabilities and Net Worth		$69,278

than one year, such as real estate, home furnishings, autos, and proprietary investments.

Automobiles. A reasonable estimate of the value of your car can be made by comparing the blue book price with prices contained in newspaper advertising.

The Dirths have two cars. Their first car is two years old and is estimated to be worth $2,700. Their second car, which is six years old, is estimated to be worth $600.

Personal property. Any personal possessions that are salable should be listed at their estimated value.

Dave and Judy estimate that they could sell an antique desk, a grandfather's clock, other furniture, and their jewelry for about $2,500.

Real estate—Home. Estimate the value at which your house and lot would sell in the current market. (Methods of estimating the value of real property were discussed in Chapter 8.) Be sure that your estimate includes the value of the land.

Dave and Judy's home is eight years old and is located in a new area of the city. Comparable homes in the area are selling for about $45,000, and the Dirths believe that there would be little difficulty in getting the same price for theirs.

Real estate—Other. Estimate the value the same way you did for your home.

The Dirths own three acres of wooded land on a small lake. They are currently using it for weekend and vacation camping trips but plan to build a cottage on the property. Realtors in the area have estimated the value of the land at $6,000.

Proprietary investments. Estimate the market value of any proprietary investments you hold. Proprietary investments are those investments in which you have ownership rights and participate in the management. For example, if you are in a partnership that owns a McDonald's restaurant and you act as the manager, this would be a proprietary investment.

The Dirths do not have any proprietary investments.

Total assets. The total of the estimated values for the current and fixed assets is a measure of what is owned. Because these are estimates for assets other than cash and U.S. Savings Bonds, there is a chance that an amount greater or less than the estimate may be recovered if the assets were actually sold.

Dave and Judy Dirth have assets with an estimated value of $69,278.

Current liabilities. A liability is an amount that is owed to someone else. Liabilities are incurred whenever you borrow money or purchase goods or services on credit. Liabilities are legal obligations; therefore, they have an important place on your balance sheet. Current liabilities are those amounts due in a short time, usually within one year. Included in this classification are short-term loans and bills received but unpaid.

Current bills. List the bills that have been received but are as yet unpaid. Bills that are anticipated several months from now but are not currently due should not be included.

The Dirths currently owe $516 on charge accounts, $360 on an annual life insurance premium, and they have received their monthly utility bill of $55.

Loans—Short-term. Determine the amount of loan repayments that are due during the next year. These loans may be from either bank or nonbank sources.

Dave and Judy have bank loans of $300 for their car and $1,000 for furniture, which must be repaid within the year. They have no short-term loans from nonbank sources.

Long-term liabilities. Loans with maturities of longer than one year are classified as long-term liabilities.

Mortgage loans. List the balance due on the mortgage loan. Monthly statements provided by many lenders make this figure readily available.

Dave and Judy owe $29,492 on their home mortgage loan and $4,000 on the mortgage loan for their three acres of lakefront property.

Other loans. Include the balance due on any other loans that you have outstanding.

While going to college the Dirths had to borrow $2,200 to help finance their educations. Of this amount the Dirths borrowed $2,000 through their university student financial aids office and $200 from the life insurance company as a policy loan.

Total liabilities. Dave and Judy have incurred $37,923 in liabilities. Their total liabilities represent the exact amount owed, because they have made contractual agreements that specify the amount due to each creditor.

Net worth. This section of the balance sheet shows how much of the stated asset value belongs to you. It is measured as the difference between total assets and total liabilities.

If the assets were all sold, $37,923 of the proceeds would go to pay the Dirth's creditors. The remaining proceeds, $31,355, belong to the Dirths; this constitutes their net worth.

Interpreting your balance sheet

The types of assets and the proportion each represents of the total reflect where the needs priorities of the family have been placed. Some families may place a higher priority on owning a large home and new car than on maintaining an emergency fund or owning other wealth-producing assets. Or, the priorities may be reversed. The composition of assets is also influenced by the stage in the family life cycle. Younger families will ordinarily have a larger proportion of their assets in the form of a home and car. Older families have had a longer period in which to accumulate assets and therefore, in addition to the home and car, will usually have greater value in assets of other types, such as securities.

Liabilities and net worth are also influenced by the family cycle. Young families will typically have a larger percentage of their assets financed with debt, while retired families may be free of long-term debt. Young families may see credit as the only way to satisfy their need to own a home. Waiting to purchase the home, car, or furniture until enough money has been saved is not acceptable to them. Thus, they create large liabilities on their balance sheets by using credit.

A personal balance sheet is useful only when you assess what it tells you. To begin, look at the figures that have been listed. Are you surprised by any of them? Do any of the figures appear out of proportion in relation to the rest of the items? How have you used your money? What type of holding makes up the largest proportion of assets? Are all of the assets necessary? Is the emergency fund large enough to meet your basic needs in the event that income stops for a few months? This inspection can tell you whether your needs and priorities are being followed when spending decisions are being made.

Then look at the liabilities. Are current liabilities of reasonable size in relation to the current assets? Are the liabilities the result of borrowing for specific assets, or were the funds required for ordinary living expenses?

These questions, and others like them which you may have, are sometimes difficult to answer. Some answers depend in large part upon your priorities. Other answers can be based on somewhat more objective information.

A more objective approach to interpreting the balance sheet is to look for relationships between assets, liabilities, and net worth. These selected relationships can be analyzed through the use of financial ratios.

Ratio analysis. Ratios can be used to evaluate your liquidity (ability to meet current liabilities) and to evaluate your debt position. The current ratio is a common measure of liquidity. Useful measures of your debt position include the debt ratio and debt coverage ratio.

Current ratio. The current ratio is calculated by dividing total current assets by total current liabilities. This important measure shows whether in an emergency current liabilities could be met through the liquidation of the current assets. There is no "magic" number that assures safety, but the figure should be in excess of 1.0. A current ratio equal to 1.0 means that if you use all of your cash and can sell your other current assets at the value stated on the balance sheet, you will just be able to pay your current liabilities. But this is a dangerously low ratio because the values shown for assets, such as securities, are estimates while the liabilities are known with great accuracy. It is therefore good to provide a cushion by planning for a current ratio greater than 1. Many businesses say that a minimum for their current ratio is 2. With a current ratio of 2, if you could dispose of your current assets at the rate of 50 cents for each dollar shown on the balance sheet, you could still pay your current liabilities.

The Dirths have a current ratio of 5.59 ($12,478/$2,231). Further analysis shows that the total cash exceeds the amount of current liabilities. This means that Dave and Judy Dirth should have little difficulty meeting their current liabilities.

Debt ratio. The debt ratio is calculated by dividing total debt by total assets. It indicates the extent to which credit is being used to finance new assets or other expenditures. A high percentage of debt indicates that creditors have a large claim and any adverse development that reduces family income could put the family in a precarious financial position. Frequently borrowers with high debt ratios find it difficult to get additional credit because creditors are afraid they won't be able to collect.

Dave and Judy have a debt ratio of 0.54:1 ($37,923/$69,278). Just over half of their assets are financed with debt. All creditors could be paid if the assets could be disposed of for about 54 percent of the value shown on the balance sheet.

Families in the early stages of the family cycle are likely to have high debt ratios. These families commonly use credit to purchase a home (for which they may borrow 80 percent or more of the purchase price), furnishings and appliances, and cars, all of which increases the debt ratio.

Because much consumer debt is installment debt, it is important to estimate your debt capacity by analyzing the required installment payments in light of the income available to make the payments. These ratios are known as *debt coverage ratios.*

To illustrate, suppose that the Dirths have mortgage payments totaling $275 per month and that when all other essential living expenses have been paid there is $330 available to meet the mortgage obligations. The mortgage debt coverage ratio is 1.2 ($330/$275). This ratio provides a measure of the Dirths' ability to meet their mortgage obligations. As the coverage ratio gets closer to 1.0, it means that any decrease in income makes it more difficult to meet the debt payments. If the coverage is at or below 1.0, an unexpected bill can mean that some bills must remain unpaid.

THE BALANCE SHEET FOR STATING GOALS

Your goals may be expressed in financial terms by defining the target levels of the assets, liabilities, and net worth on future balance sheets. These targets should reflect your needs in the near future and several years ahead. For example, suppose that your short-term goal is to accumulate $1,000 to be used for a family vacation next year. You plan to accumulate the money in a savings account. By specifying the level of the account at the end of each month, you are stating a short-term goal for the use of the family income.

Long-term goals may also be stated in financial terms. Emergency funds for situations such as loss of income or large medical bills can be set at two to four months' income. Or, looking ahead to retirement years may encourage you to begin accumulating a nest egg in the form of added investment in wealth-producing assets such as securities or real estate. Specifying the desired levels of these investments at various points in time are expressions of financial goals.

Defining the assets required to meet your goals also requires a definition of how these assets are to be financed. That is, is it necessary for you to borrow money, as may be needed for the purchase of real estate, or can the asset be acquired from your current income, as with an emergency or vacation fund or with funds accumulated specifically for that purpose?

Family net worth also follows the family cycle. Exhibit 17–2 illustrates a pattern of family net worth over the family cycle. Young families have a low, perhaps even decreasing, net worth in relation to total assets. As the family matures and the liabilities are paid, the family net worth increases.

Family net worth may also increase as a result of increasing values of assets. For example, your net worth may increase if the home you purchase increases in value because of inflation or other causes.

Family net worth usually reaches a peak just prior to retirement. People ordinarily try to have their long-term debts repaid so that during retirement they will no longer be faced with debt repayment. During retirement, net worth may be a major source of funds for living expenses. As a result, any change in net worth will depend upon the relationship between retirement income and the required living expenses. If living expenses are greater than retirement income, some

EXHIBIT 17–2
Family net worth over family cycle

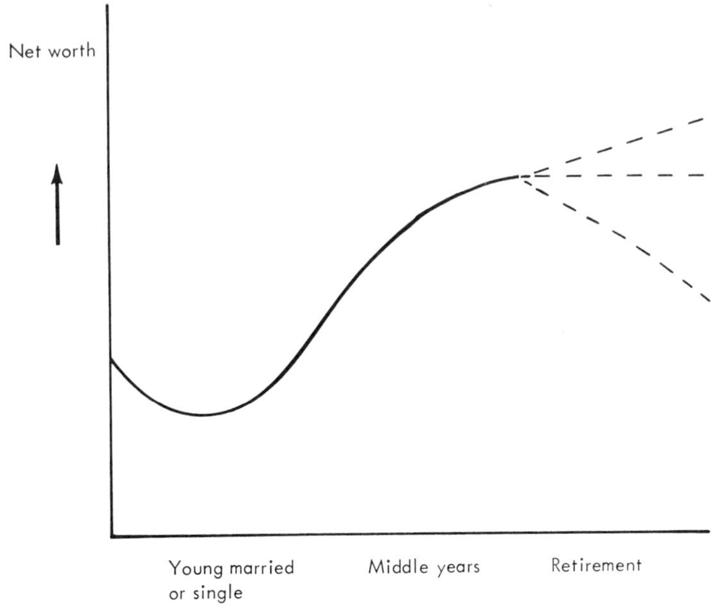

assets must be sold to provide the needed funds. Thus, net worth will decrease. However, if income exceeds living expenses, net worth may continue to increase even after retirement.

As actual balance sheets are prepared in the future and compared with your goals, it is quite easy to see whether your goals are being met. If there is a difference between the desired and actual levels of the assets, liabilities, or net worth, you should determine the reason. Because of changes which may have occurred, it may be necessary to review your goals to make them more compatible with current family conditions.

FAMILY DEBT MANAGEMENT

Debt limits

There is no simple formula that you can use to determine the extent to which you can "safely" be in debt. Studies conducted by the United States Department of Agriculture, however, show the average income, expenditure, debt and liquid assets for four broad age groups in the 1960s, the latest years for which such data are available. Financial relationships, based upon average ages of the family heads, as presented in Exhibit 17–3, showed that the ratio of total debt (excluding home mortgages) to current annual income decreases from 81 percent for a young family (head is under 35 years) to 78 percent for a growing family (head 35–54 years) to 41 percent for a contracting family (head 55–64 years) to 38 percent for the retired family (head 65 years and over). While these ratios are general, they do indicate that debt changes with age, occupation, wants and needs, and financial resources.

EXHIBIT 17–3
Average financial ratios of families by age groups

	Age of family head			
Ratio	*35 and under*	*35–54*	*55–64*	*65 and over*
Current expenditures to current income	1.01	0.97	0.80	0.99
Total debt to current income	0.81	0.78	0.41	0.38
Current assets to total debt	0.39	0.86	3.64	9.86

Source: U.S. Department of Agriculture.

Every balance sheet will include some debt, if only for current bills. The use of some debt is a matter of convenience and can be handled by almost all families. Problems arise, however, when families create more debt to pay for their assets than they are financially able to repay. The use of too much debt usually results in financial distress or bankruptcy.

Characteristics of families in financial distress

A Family Service Association of America study developed a profile of people who were in serious financial difficulty. One common characteristic of these families was the youth of the family heads: over 75 percent were between 25 and 35 years of age. These ages represent the period of family formation when earning power is lowest and the need to purchase goods, especially durables, is at its greatest level.

A second common characteristic was the blue-collar occupation of the family head. Income was generally below the national or state average, and 25 percent of the wives were working in an attempt to relieve the financial strain.

The largest creditors of these financially distressed families were finance and loan companies, retail stores, and banks, respectively.

About 36 percent of the families had debt payments that exceeded 75 percent of their income. Another 33 percent of the families had debt payments that ranged from 50 to 74 percent of their income. The remaining 31 percent of the families had debt payments equal to less than 50 percent of their income.[2]

A private study conducted recently by a finance company manager reveals an interesting profile of families that have declared bankruptcy. The study analyzed 180 bankruptcies from ten consumer loan offices located in the Midwest. Eighteen recently bankrupt accounts for consumer loans from each office were selected for the analysis.

The age profile of the bankrupts showed that about 73 percent were between the ages of 21 and 38. Within this age bracket, 31 percent were between age 21 and 26. This result supports the findings of the Family Service Association of America study. Age appears to be a predictor of possible financial distress.

A second predictor of financial problems from the viewpoint of the finance company was the intended use of the loan proceeds by the borrower. Of the 180 bankrupt accounts, about 60 percent had used the loan proceeds to renew or consolidate old debts.[3] This indicates that current spending is too great for current income and that refinancing will provide only temporary relief.

Symptoms of financial problems

It is important to be able to identify when you are in financial trouble and heading for financial distress. This can help you avoid getting in deeper.

One of the symptoms of financial distress is that debt payments exceed 20 percent of your income. Ordinary living expenses (food, clothing, shelter, etc.) usually require about 80 percent of disposable income. If more than 20 percent is required for debt payments, someone isn't going to get paid.

Another guideline is the relationship between total debts, excluding home mortgages, and the family's gross income (before taxes). When debts exceed 40 percent of gross income, it is usually difficult to pay off the debts. Debts end up being extended and/or defaulted.

A third symptom of financial distress is assuming new debts to handle existing debts. Consistent borrowing to either extend or consolidate loans is an indication that financial distress will exist when these loans are due to be repaid. When current income is not sufficient to pay living costs and existing debts, financial disaster is imminent.

---

2 *Family Credit Counseling—An Emerging Community Service.*

3 "Individual Bankruptcy," unpublished manuscript.

It is these dangers of debt combined with instability in the income stream that lead to financial distress for many families. Reductions in family income often occur as a result of the pregnancy of a working wife or as a result of layoffs. The reduced income stream is insufficient to take care of all of the debts that have been incurred—a situation of financial distress.

SUMMARY

Family spending decisions should reflect age of family head and the individual family needs, wants, prospects, and financial resources. Personal financial planning enables you to satisfy your needs of highest priority while at the same time developing a sound financial condition.

A balance sheet is a useful tool in analyzing the family financial condition. Construction of a family balance sheet requires the identification and evaluation of the family's assets and liabilities. The difference between the assets and liabilities is the family's net worth, the asset value actually owned by the family.

The interpretation of the balance sheet is a most important step in determining the family's financial profile. The balance sheet should reflect your needs and priorities. A comparison of the family needs and priorities with the balance sheet items will show whether the priorities have been observed in making spending decisions. If you find yourself borrowing in order to meet ordinary living expenses, you are headed for financial disaster.

An analysis of your balance sheet through the use of ratios provides added insight into your current financial profile.

Your financial goals may be expressed in financial terms and presented in the form of desired levels of assets, liabilities, and net worth on future balance sheets. Specific statement of the goals makes it possible to determine clearly whether you are meeting your goals.

No simple formulas are available that can be used to tell when a family has a "safe" amount of debt. In general, debt capacity depends upon the age of the family head, occupation, and stage in the family cycle.

One study of the financial profiles of families in financial distress situations indicated that over 75 percent are families of which the head is between 25 and 35 years of age. Many of these families have incomes that are below average in size and jobs that are unstable, resulting in unexpected layoffs and decreased income.

Symptoms of financial trouble include: 1) debt payments in excess of 20 percent of disposable income, 2) total debt in excess of 40 percent of gross income, and 3) need for loans to meet current expenses.

DISCUSSION QUESTIONS

1. What is the meaning of "net worth" on a balance sheet?
2. Construct a balance sheet for the Thompson family based on the following items, which the Thompsons either own or owe:
   a. A home mortgage of $25,000
   b. A checking account balance of $350
   c. A short-term loan of $3,000 for 180 days payable to First Bank
   d. A home valued at $40,000
   e. Savings bonds worth $1,500
   f. Cash value of life insurance worth $2,000
   g. Current bills of $1,200
   h. An automobile worth $2,500
   i. Property taxes due of $1,000
3. How would you explain the relatively high debt ratios of younger families where the spouses are ages 20–40 when compared to older families where the spouses are ages 50–70?
4. Explain how the current ratio and debt coverage ratio can be used in planning.
5. What is the general relationship of net worth to the family cycle? What explains the rapid increase in net worth during the "middle years"?
6. According to the Family Service Association study, what are the common characteristics of people who are likely to get into serious financial difficulty?
7. As a rule of thumb, why should debt payments be 20 percent or less of household income?
8. Explain why extending and consolidating existing debts may be a sign of forthcoming financial problems.
9. The Fred Bith family owns a $30,000 home, a $1,000 savings account, personal property of $2,000, and life insurance cash values of $2,000. In addition, the Biths owe $800 in taxes, $1,000 in current bills, and a $20,000 mortgage.

   Calculate the net worth of the Biths.

CASE PROBLEMS

1. Mary and Tom Sigel are currently considering the purchase of a new camper-trailer that sells for $5,000. If they buy this unit, they plan to finance it on a three-year installment contract at 12 percent. This will mean monthly payments of $166. The Sigels' combined annual income is $18,000 per year. Their monthly fixed expenditures for housing, utilities, food, clothing, insurance, and other necessities are $1,000 per month. In addition, income, property, and Social Security taxes are $300 per month. The

Sigels are currently paying $100 a month in car installments and $50 per month on a furniture installment contract.

Analyze the Sigels' situation. Would you recommend that they buy the camper? If so, explain how the camper will fit into their budget. If you don't think they should buy it, explain your reasoning.

2. From the narrative below construct a personal balance sheet for the Tom Lange family:

   The Tom Lange family lives in an apartment in Dallas, Texas. They own two autos, each valued at $1,500. Mr. Lange has a portfolio of securities currently valued at $10,000 and $8,000 of family personal property. The Lange family debts consist of a $3,000 installment contract on one auto, a $5,000 collateral loan for securities, $5,000 for installment notes on furniture and personal property, and $3,000 on a signature loan.

   After analyzing the balance sheet, comment on what problem or problems seem to need attention. What would you recommend as financial advice to the Lange family?

SELECTED READINGS

A Date with Your Future. New York: Institute of Life Insurance and Health Insurance, Publication #166.

Bemis, Jacob. "Income Instability," Chap. 6 in Vol. 1 of *Five Thousand American Families—Patterns of Economic Progress,* Ann Arbor: Institute for Social Research, 1974.

Helfert, Erich A. *Techniques of Financial Analysis,* 3d ed. Homewood, Ill.: Richard D. Irwin, Inc., 1976.

"Planning for Inflation," A Personal Business Supplement. *Business Week,* September 14, 1974, pp. 175–183.

Sherwin, Sidney. *What to Do When Your Bills Exceed Your Paycheck.* Englewood Cliffs, New Jersey: Prentice-Hall, Inc., 1974.

Planning for the future

18

OBJECTIVES

Making plans to take care of future emergencies and to achieve future goals should be a part of your financial planning. This chapter suggests the need for such planning and explores several basic techniques that you may use.

After thoroughly reading and discussing this chapter you should be able to:

. . . Identify the major shocks and transitions in the life cycle that may require financial planning.

. . . Explain and construct a spending profile.

. . . Explain how zero-base budgeting may be applied to personal finances.

. . . Construct a long-range financial plan using projected income and expense budgets and projected personal balance sheets.

Quite early in the book we discussed some basic principles for setting goals and budgeting income. In the intervening chapters we've examined the important decisions that you have to make in order to reach these goals. By now you have a good idea of the variety of spending and financing decisions you may face in the course of managing your personal finances.

With this background in mind, it is time to turn again to the importance of financial planning. Financial planning can be used to get a better perspective on the impact of future events on your personal fortune.

WHY PLAN?

Life cycle shocks

In the course of each of our lives we will experience events that will disrupt our lives and affect our economic wellbeing. These events, which we will refer to as life cycle shocks, will be largely outside of our control and will tend to be chance events.[1]

A recent study of the impact of these disruptions has highlighted the importance of planning for life cycle shocks. This study, conducted by the Institute for Social Research at the University of Michigan, examined the shock connected with the following events:

1. Firings—including layoffs, strikes, lockouts, business folding, and firings.
2. Unemployment.
3. Underemployment—meaning being unable to locate additional work.
4. Evictions—forced relocation due to outside forces.
5. Emergency expenditures.
6. Unplanned children.
7. Illness.

Each of these seven items caused a deterioration in family wellbeing, and each event posed varying degrees of trauma or shock to families that experienced them. The shock varied depending upon income source, income level, class or status, and personality type. For example, those people who derived their income from sources such as alimony or family gifts were less affected by life cycle shocks than were those who derived their income from accumulated wealth or assets. What this seems to suggest is that these life cycle shocks have greater impact on those who are wealthier than those who are poorer and perhaps more used to such shocks.

The seven shocks examined in the Institute for Social Research study provide some good reasons for thinking about financial planning. But there are additional disruptive events connected with the life cycle that may pose problems.

---

[1] Much of the material in this section is drawn from "Involuntary Disruptions of 'Life-Cycle' Plans," by Everett Ehrlich, which appears as Chapter 5 in Volume III of *Five Thousand American Families—Patterns of Economic Progress* (Ann Arbor: Institute for Social Research, 1975).

Life cycle transitions

At various points in your life cycle, you will come to times of transition and change. These events will be marked by changes in your family structure, sources of income, goals, spending decisions, and financing decisions.

One of the first transitions you may face is associated with reaching your legal majority and striking out on your own. Leaving the family setting may begin by directly joining the work force and setting up a separate household. It may also occur more gradually as you go away to technical school or university, return to live at home during summers, graduate, and then move out completely to take a fulltime job and establish an independent household. However this process comes about, this change will mean more responsibility for earning an income and making spending decisions. This transition may well mark your first opportunity to make independent personal financial decisions.

A second transition you may encounter involves the decision to marry. Marriage generally means some drastic changes in your personal financial goals and spending patterns. It often requires decisions to spend large amounts of future income to pay off debts incurred in buying a home and its furnishings. It may also mean that the sources of family income will change over time with both spouses working at times and at other times one spouse staying at home to take care of children. Marriage may also mean making some important long-range financial decisions such as providing for the future education of your children and making an orderly estate plan.

A third type of transition involves separation from a spouse through death or divorce. In either case, the separation has social and economic consequences for a family, especially where there are minor children. The death of a spouse may mean an important change in the family's source of income and may drastically affect personal finances. Divorce also may change the nature of family income and may cause one spouse or the other to make important decisions on educational and career matters.

A fourth transition that may have great effect on the family is the change from active participation in the work force to a retired status. The transition to retirement may bring about decisions to change homes or relocate, and it raises important estate and tax planning decisions. It will also bring about important changes in the level and source of income.

All four of these transitions and the seven life cycle shocks discussed earlier will be easier to handle if you manage them through financial planning. To some degree, at least, you can anticipate and plan for each of these events.

HOW TO APPROACH FINANCIAL PLANNING

Financial planning involves bringing together all aspects of your personal finances in an effort to achieve your goals. It is more than just budgeting. It also includes consideration of your past spending patterns and your present financial condition. It must also take account of your plans for investing, insuring, financing, spending, and your tax and estate planning. The budget, however, ties all this together and reflects your decisions in all other planning areas.

Exhibit 18–1 presents an overview of financial planning. The various plans and the budget are interrelated and must reflect your day-to-day living needs and fixed payments such as housing and utilities.

Financial planning should begin with a clear definition of what you want to accomplish in the upcoming weeks, months, and years. The need to have positive goals that can be changed to meet changing personal situations was explored in some detail in Chapter 1. Once your goals are defined, you can proceed with your financial planning by analyzing your past spending habits. This information serves as a basis for making plans for the future.

Analyzing the past

Information about your past spending behavior can be of great help in making your future plans. How have you spent your money in the past *as evidenced by actual expenditures?*

EXHIBIT 18–1
Overview of personal financial planning

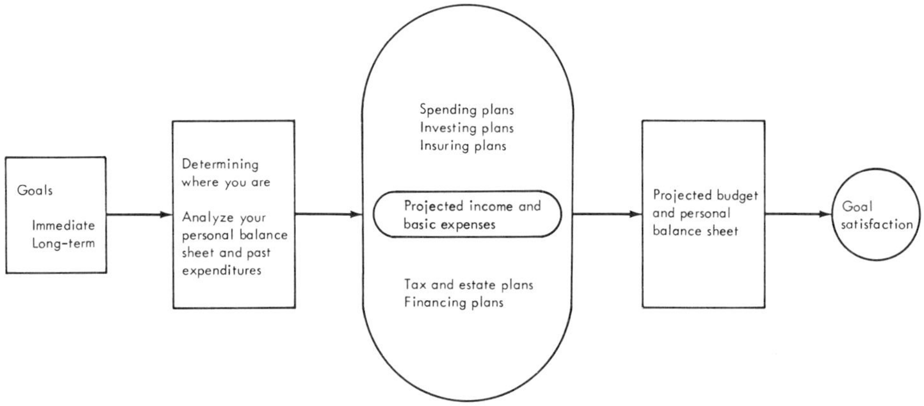

This latter point is quite crucial. There may be a great difference between how you think you spent your money and how you actually spent it. The only way to be sure is to examine your spending records.

For those people who do most of their spending through checking accounts and credit cards, the analysis of past expenditures may be quite easy, providing they've kept past receipts and credit card billings. If this information is available, the main problem will be to classify your expenditures in order to get a spending profile.

Exhibit 18–2 suggests one way of building a spending profile. It is a good idea to look at your spending over a period of at least one year, and it may be better to examine expenditures for several years. In building the spending profile you should examine both the amount and the percentage of income spent on each category.

EXHIBIT 18–2
Monthly expenditure profile

	Month #1		*Month #2*		*Month #3*	
Type of expenditure	*Dollars spent*	*Percent of income*	*Dollars spent*	*Percent of income*	*Dollars spent*	*Percent of income*
Housing						
Food and beverage						
Clothing						
Medical						
Transportation						
Household supplies						
Personal care supplies						
Recreation and entertainment						
Savings						
Miscellaneous						
Totals						

The spending profile should give you some concrete idea about what you have done in the past. You may well find out that your actual past spending differs greatly from how you thought you spent your money.

You can check to see whether your past spending is consistent with the goals you have in mind. The spending profile can show you what your spending behavior was in relation to any increases in your level of income. One of the prime benefits of an analysis of the past is that it provides a basis for deciding what changes you want to make in future spending.

Analyzing the present

Analyzing spending in the past can give you insight into what you might do to improve future finances. But you should also consider your present financial situation and its bearing on what you can and can't do in the future.

One of the best ways of analyzing your present situation is to use the personal balance sheet and analytical techniques that were developed in Chapter 17. The balance sheet will give you a picture of your current obligations and net worth and can be used as another part of the information base for future plans.

Planning for the future

Your analysis of past and present conditions should provide information that will be helpful in determining what can be accomplished in the future. We'd like to suggest several ways of looking at your financial future.

One planning technique you can use is zero-base budgeting (ZBB). ZBB has been a "buzz word" in government and business in recent years, but it is also applicable to your family financial planning.

To begin, you must determine a level of minimum or survival expenditures. These expenditures will include food, housing, clothing, and other such necessities needed to survive. This is comparable with the process of determining the minimum monthly expenses as discussed in Chapter 15.

Beyond these survival expenditures, all other expenditures must be justified. To do that you can list on index cards the expenditures you'd like to make in the next year and then rank them in terms of your priorities. These expenditures might include spending $1,000 on a vacation, $900 for eating out three times a month during the year, and saving $1,000 for the future purchase of a vacation home.

The ranking process can be an opportunity for family members to talk about spending priorities. Each spouse or family member may rank things differently, and this will allow you to discover these differences and to resolve them.

Once you have completed your ranking you should add up your wants and compare total expenditures with total income. The likely result will be that your wants will exceed the available funds. In this case you can begin to make adjustments as follows:

1. You can scale down your spending on various priorities.

2. You can eliminate or greatly reduce spending on low-priority items.
3. You can find cheaper ways of reaching some of your goals by doing the labor yourself or by some other means.

The ZBB approach requires you to rethink your spending every year and to justify nonsurvival expenditures. This process is likely to help you bring your goals into focus and get you thinking about longer term planning.

LONG-TERM FINANCIAL PLANNING—A CASE EXAMPLE

To accomplish long-range goals, you must begin to think about a long-range plan that will provide enough money to carry out your objectives. The long-range plan should take into account projected income and expenditures over the period of time you estimate it will take to accomplish your goals.

It is perhaps easier to illustrate this process with a case example. In this example we'll follow the progress of Nancy and Jack Andrews. Nancy and Jack graduated from the University of Washington last year. Nancy is currently teaching music in the Minneapolis school system. Her salary is $11,000 per year. Jack majored in engineering and is now employed by a local computer manufacturer. His current salary is $15,000 per year.

Nancy and Jack have decided to have two children. They have opted for a traditional set of family roles and anticipate that Nancy will devote most of her time to caring for the children but will be able to work part-time in her home by giving piano lessons. She estimates that she will earn about $3,000 a year through her part-time work.

The Andrewses' goals

Nancy and Jack have discussed what they want to accomplish in the next five years. Their primary objective is to save enough money for a downpayment of 20 percent on a three-bedroom home in the city. That type of house now sells for $40,000 and housing prices have been rising seven percent per year. A second objective is to pay off $5,000 in loans that Jack and Nancy took out to complete their educations. A third objective is to build up an emergency fund of $5,000 to take care of contingencies such as short-term disability and illness.

Analyzing past and present conditions

Because the Andrewses are just completing their first year of marriage, their spending in the past year reflects a heavy investment in setting up their household and completing their education. They do, however, know that they need basic spending of $1,000 per month to provide food, housing, clothing, insurance, and other essentials. They currently need 20 percent of their annual income to meet federal, state, and other taxes. They also plan to spend about $200 per month on incidentals and entertainment.

The Andrewses have examined their current financial status by preparing a personal balance sheet. After one year of marriage, their financial condition is reflected in the balance sheet shown in Exhibit 18–3.

EXHIBIT 18–3
Balance Sheet

JACK AND NANCY ANDREWS
Balance Sheet
September 1, 197–

Assets		*Liabilities*	
Cash	$ 300	Current bills	$ 300
Savings bonds	500	Installment loan on auto	800
Savings account	1,000	Educational loans	5,000
Family auto	2,000	Total Liabilities	$6,100
Furniture and miscellaneous	2,500	Net Worth	200
Total Assets	$6,300	Total Liabilities and Net Worth	$6,300

By applying the analytic techniques we discussed in the last chapter, the Andrewses can get some idea of their relative financial position. Their current ratio (current assets divided by current liabilities) of 1.64 would seem to be adequate but not outstanding. Their debt ratio (total debt divided by total assets) of 0.97 indicates that they are not in a position to rely on more debt financing. Thus in order to achieve their goals, they will have to accumulate money out of future earnings.

Projected income and basic expenditures

Jack and Nancy have made some estimates of their future income and expenses. Regarding income, they expect that Nancy will work full-time for two more years and then will begin part-time work. They anticipate that her salary will increase by seven percent over the remaining two years. Their projected income for Jack assumes some advances for the first five years with his income increasing at ten percent per year.

Their base expenditures will remain quite stable until the anticipated birth of children in years 3 and 5. With the birth of each child they expect their base expenses to rise 20 percent and 10 percent, respectively. Inflation will also take its toll, and they expect base expenditures and incidentals to increase a minimum of five percent per year.

Jack and Nancy have prepared a projection of future income and expenditures, which is illustrated in Exhibit 18–4. This exhibit shows that they should be able to save quite a bit in their next two years, but when Nancy begins part-time work they will have to dip into savings.

EXHIBIT 18–4
Five-year plan for Jack and Nancy Andrews

	Year #1	*Year #2*	*Year #3*	*Year #4*	*Year #5*
Income					
Jack	$16,500	$18,100	$20,000	$22,000	$24,100
Nancy	11,800	12,600	3,000	3,000	3,000
Interest*	55	410	900	895	977
Total income	$28,355	$31,110	$23,900	$25,895	$28,077
Expenses and loan repayments					
Basic expenses	12,000	12,600	15,800	16,600	19,200
Incidentals	2,400	2,500	2,600	2,800	2,900
Taxes	5,700	6,100	4,600	5,000	5,400
Repay educational loans	1,000	1,000	1,000	1,000	1,000
Auto installment	800	—	—	—	—
Payment to emergency fund	1,000	1,000	1,000	1,000	1,000
Savings for downpayment	5,455	7,910	−1,100	−505	−1,423
Total expenses and loan repayments	$28,355	$31,110	$23,900	$25,895	$28,077

* Interest is calculated at 5.5 percent annual rate on the beginning of year balance in the savings account plus the emergency fund.

Integrating financial planning considerations

After the Andrewses have a good grasp of projected income and basic expenditures, they can begin to refine their financial plan. They will have to make a number of policy decisions as to how they will achieve their goals.

For example, they have decided to accumulate money for a house downpayment and an emergency fund. Given these objectives they must then decide where to invest these funds. Following the investment pyramid approach set forth in Chapter 13, they should realize that these funds are part of their basic financial needs. As such they will not want to lose these funds and their investment policy will likely center around safe, fairly low return investments such as savings accounts and savings bonds.

Another thing they should consider is a plan to manage all the risks they face. Given their small amount of net worth and heavy future dependence on Jack's income, they should make plans to handle any future crisis brought on by death, disability, illness, unemployment, or other events. This will probably mean that they should consider life insurance on both spouses and will have to integrate Social Security and Jack's fringe benefits (such as disability and health insurance) as well as personal assets such as their emergency reserve into a well-coordinated risk management plan.

The Andrewses should also consider future estate and tax planning. Drawing up a will may become especially important when the Andrewses have children. As their net worth grows they will also want to plan to minimize estate taxes. Given their current financial condition, estate tax planning would not be necessary for many years.

Jack and Nancy should also review their spending plans, especially those relating to big-ticket items. They should take into account the possible replacement of the family auto or major appliances and should consider how they will finance these items. Overlooking these replacement costs may upset their future financial plans.

Projecting a personal balance sheet

If Jack and Nancy follow the plan shown in Exhibit 18–4, and assuming their savings earn 5.5 percent per year and that their earnings on the emergency account will go into their general savings, their projected financial position five years hence is shown in Exhibit 18–5.

EXHIBIT 18–5

JACK AND NANCY ANDREWS
Projected Balance Sheet
September 1, 198–

Assets		*Liabilities*	
Cash	$ 300	Current bills	$ 300
Savings bonds	650	Net Worth	19,237
Emergency fund	5,000		
Savings account	11,337		
Family auto	1,000		
Furniture	1,250		
Total Assets	$19,537	Total Liabilities and Net Worth	$19,537

The value of the savings bonds assumes a six percent annual increase. The emergency fund has been built up at the rate of $1,000 per year for the five-year period.

The savings account used to accumulate the money for the home downpayment will have a balance of $11,337 determined as follows:

Year	*Balance at beginning of year*	*Net change in savings for downpayment**	*Balance at end of year*
1	$ 1,000†	$ 5,455	$ 6,455
2	6,455	7,910	14,365
3	14,365	−1,100	13,265
4	13,265	− 505	12,760
5	12,760	−1,423	11,337

* From Exhibit 18–4.

† From Exhibit 18–3.

The balance sheet also reflects a 50 percent depreciation in the auto and furniture.

Fulfilling goals

At the end of five years the Andrewses appear to have achieved most of their goals. They have paid off the loan and have built an emergency fund of $5,000. They have also built up a savings account of $11,337, which is about 20 percent of the escalated cost of the home they wish to purchase.

The Andrewses should also pay close attention to the trends shown in Exhibit 18–4. The amount of money "available for savings" declines when they have their first child and in fact they must use savings to achieve their budgets in years 3, 4, and 5. By extending this analysis to year 6, they should find that their savings flow will become positive because they will no longer have to pay into the emergency fund and their educational loans will be repaid.

SUMMARY

Planning for the future incorporates all the positive aspects of your goal setting, priority rankings, spending, financing, insuring, and investing decisions. The importance of planning for the future is made more urgent by the possibility that during your lifetime you may experience one or more life cycle shocks and a number of life cycle transitions. You may be fired or unemployed for some other reason, evicted from your home, become ill, or face the arrival of unplanned children or emergency expenditures. The transitions in your life cycle occur as you progress through school, graduate, choose to marry and have children, and retire from the work force. Other transitions may occur as a result of loss of your spouse. Financial planning will help to cushion the shock of these events. On the more positive side, it will enable you to achieve the goals you desire in life.

Logical steps to financial planning for the future include setting or clarifying your goals, analyzing and learning from your past financial experiences, analyzing your present financial condition, and then making use of this information to plan for the future in a realistic fashion.

Zero-base budgeting (ZBB) is one tool that may be of great help to you in your planning. You begin by listing your minimal needs for survival and the accompanying expenditures, then adding hoped-for expenditures and ranking them according to your priorities. When comparing these expenditures with your estimated income, you will probably find it necessary to make certain downward adjustments in the expenses.

The case example of Nancy and Jack Andrews, a young couple just facing the establishment of their family and home and planning all the incumbent financial needs, shows how overall financial planning can be used.

The payoff from overall financial planning comes from knowing that you are achieving your short- and long-range personal financial goals.

DISCUSSION QUESTIONS

1. What is zero-base budgeting? Explain how this concept can be applied to personal finances.
2. List the seven life cycle shocks and explain how they may vary in impact with your level of income.
3. In terms of the life cycle shocks and the disruptions in the life cycle, which do you think would have the most effect on a middle-aged couple with two children?
4. Outline the steps in the general process of long-range personal financial planning.
5. Explain how you would construct a spending profile and indicate how this tool can be used to assist you in financial planning.
6. After looking at the Andrews case in this chapter, do you agree with their conservative investment policy? Explain.
7. Analyze the Andrewses' projected personal balance sheet in year 5. Calcu-

late both the current ratio and the debt ratio and indicate whether they are adequate.

CASE PROBLEMS

1. *In the Andrews case presented in this chapter, would you recommend that they go ahead with their house purchase? Analyze this move in full detail and show why you would or would not recommend such a move.*
2. *Drawing upon the Andrews case, explain the effect of each of the following events on their five-year plan:*
   a. *Home building costs rise at 10 percent instead of 7 percent.*
   b. *Nancy decides to work an extra year as a teacher.*
   c. *An emergency expenditure of $2,000 is required to replace the family auto.*

SELECTED READINGS

A Guide to Budgeting for the Retired Couple, rev. ed. U.S. Department of Agriculture, October, 1973.

Porter, Thomas and Alhire, Durwood. *Wealth: How to Achieve It!* Reston, Va.: Reston Publishing Company, Inc., 1976, chaps. 1–4 and 18–19.

Stillman, Richard J. *Guide to Personal Finance,* 2d ed. Englewood Cliffs, New Jersey: Prentice-Hall, Inc., 1975, chaps. 1–2.

Glossary

acceleration clause A clause found in most debt contracts that states that in the event of any default by the debtor the balance owed is immediately due.

actual cash value In insurance policies, a measure of loss that is equal to the replacement cost of an item less depreciation.

add-on clause A clause often found in an installment contract that enables creditors to repossess items purchased from them and paid for, if the purchaser defaults on payments for additional items.

agent One who acts on behalf of another person or business. Insurance and real estate agents are common examples of such agencies.

amortization Method of gradually repaying the principal amount of a loan through periodic payments of equal amounts.

annuity A contract issued by an insurer in which the insurer agrees to make periodic payments that continue during the life of a person (annuitant) or for a specified period of time.

appraisal An evaluation of property to determine its value.

APR Annual percentage rate of interest on debt.

assets Items that people or businesses own, including real property, cash, securities, and other things of value.

assigned risk plan A pooling arrangement usually set up by state law whereby those who cannot ordinarily get insurance are assigned to insurers who are required to or who voluntarily participate in the pool.

balance sheet A financial statement that shows the general financial condition of a person, family, or business in terms of assets, liabilities, and net worth at a particular point in time.

balloon balance In an installment contract, a situation where the balance to be retired by the final payment is substantially larger than any of the previous payments.

bankruptcy A state of insolvency in which an individual or business cannot pay its bills and has little prospect of doing so in the future.

beneficiary A person who may become eligible to receive or is receiving benefits under a life insurance policy.

bequest A transfer of property through a will or a gift of property made while a person is still alive.

bond An interest-bearing certificate of public or private indebtedness, usually with a maturity of five years or more at the time of issue.

book value Purchase cost less accumulated depreciation.

broker One who acts as a middleman (agent) in transactions involving securities, insurance, or real estate.

business risk The uncertainty of the size of investment returns due to the issuer's ability to pay.

C's of credit Four factors that are important in determining an applicant's credit worthiness—character, capacity, collateral, and conditions.

capital gain A gain derived from the sale of real estate, securities, and other capital assets.

capital loss A loss resulting from the sale of real estate, securities, and other capital assets.

cash value life insurance A life insurance policy with an investment or cash value element.

certificate of deposit (CD) A time deposit that normally requires a greater minimum, pays a higher interest rate, and has a longer period before withdrawal than other bank accounts. CD's of small denominations are often referred to as guaranteed income bonds, bank bonds, or savings certificates.

Chartered Life Underwriter (CLU) A designation granted by the American College of Life Underwriters, which signifies that an individual has successfully completed a series of exams in insurance, economics, life and health insurance, estate planning, etc.

Chartered Property and Casualty Underwriter (CPCU) A designation granted by the American Institute for Property and Liability Underwriters, which signifies that an individual has successfully completed a series of exams covering property and liability insurance, economics, management, finance, etc.

closed-end lease A lease agreement in which the lessee is responsible only for the rental payment and does not guarantee the value of the leased asset at the end of the lease period.

closing costs Sometimes called settlement costs. Costs in addition to the price of a house including mortgage service charges, title search, insurance, and transfer of ownership charges.

coinsurance clause (1) In property insurance policies, a clause that specifies a minimum coverage (such as 80 percent of replacement cost) that is required for the insured to receive payment for the full value of losses up to the policy face. (2) In health insurance policies, a clause that specifies the sharing of any loss between the insured and the insurance company.

collateral Security for a loan provided by the borrower in the form of pledged assets or an endorsement of a cosigner. If the borrower defaults, the lender may sell the pledged asset or require the cosigner to complete the payments.

collateral trust bond A bond for which collateral takes the form of securities of other companies owned by the issuer.

common stock Securities representing an ownership interest in a corporation.

concentration An investment policy of selecting one or a few investments; the opposite of a policy of diversification.

condominium Individual ownership of a dwelling unit and an undivided interest in the common areas and facilities that serve the multi-unit project.

conspicuous consumption Spending for the purpose of sensation or show.

consumer fraud Deceitful practices, such as bait and switch and referral sales schemes, that are used to cheat consumers.

consumerism The social movement seeking to achieve greater rights, safety, and information for consumers.

cooperative housing An apartment building or a group of dwellings owned by residents and operated for their benefit by their elected board of directors. Residents occupy but do not own their units; rather they own a share of stock in the total enterprise.

credit bureau A business that specializes in accumulating personal information about individuals for the purpose of selling the information to prospective employers, creditors, etc.

credit rating A measure used by credit bureaus to indicate a person's ability or willingness to pay debts.

credit union An organization composed of members with a common interest who bind together to make loans to members.

current asset An asset that can be quickly converted to cash without a serious loss in value.

current dollars Dollars received at any point in time without regard to their purchasing power.

current liability An obligation or debt payment that is due and payable now or within a period of one year.

current ratio Current assets divided by current liabilities.

debenture A bond for which the earning power of the issuer serves as collateral.

debt ratio Total debt divided by total assets; this measure shows the extent to which credit is being used to finance assets.

declaration That portion of an insurance contract that states information as to the person or property insured, the period and amount of insurance, premiums, and other relevant data.

deductible That portion of an insured loss assumed by the insured.

deed A legal document used to transfer a property title from one person to another.

default Failure to fulfill the conditions of a contract.

depreciation A decrease in the value of tangible property over time caused by use, wear and tear, and obsolescence.

discretionary expenditures Spending for nonessential items. Also spending subject to an individual's freedom of judgment or choice.

discretionary income The amount of personal income left after paying taxes, food, shelter, clothing, and other essential expenditures.

disposable personal income Take-home pay. That income available after income and Social Security taxes have been deducted.

diversification The principle of reducing risks by spreading your money among several different investments.

dividend (1) The return of a part of the insured's policy premium in a participating insurance policy. (2) A payment to preferred or common stockholders representing a distribution of a corporation's profits.

dividend yield For stocks, the annual cash dividend divided by the current market price of a security and expressed as a percentage.

dollar cost averaging A method of buying stocks by investing equal dollar amounts of money periodically in the same security.

double indemnity An option in a life insurance policy that provides for the payment of twice the basic death benefit in the event the insured's death is the result of an accident.

durables Goods that are expected to last or be consumed over an extended period of time.

earnest money The deposit of money given to the seller by the potential buyer to show intent to buy the real estate.

emergency fund An amount of money kept in a liquid investment as a reserve to handle possible financial calamities.

endorsement A written or printed form attached to an insurance policy that alters the insurance policy in matters relating to property covered, perils insured, locations covered, etc.

equipment trust certificates Debt issues that have the issuer's equipment as collateral. The title to the equipment is held by a trustee.

escrow Money or papers representing financial transactions that are given to a third party to hold until all conditions in a contract are fulfilled.

estate tax A tax assessed on the transfer of wealth in an estate.

exclusion A contractual provision that denies coverage for certain perils, properties, persons, or locations.

exclusive insurance agent An agent who sells and services insurance under a contract that usually limits representation to one insurer.

Family Automobile Policy (FAP) An insurance policy that provides a package of property and liability insurances to insure against perils associated with owning an auto.

family income Total personal income from spouses and other employed family members.

financial responsibility laws Statutes that require a motorist to provide proof of financial responsibility to pay damages arising out of past or future auto accidents.

fixed assets Assets that have a useful life longer than a year and that are not readily convertible into cash.

fixed costs Costs that are fixed in total for some time period regardless of usage; for example, the premium for an auto insurance policy.

food grading Grading is intended to identify quality. It is indicated through a system of letters or numbers.

food inspection Means of protecting the consumer by assuring that food is processed under sanitary conditions to provide safe and unadulterated food.

foreclosure The legal process by which, in the event the borrower defaults, a lender can force the sale of property in order to recover money loaned on it.

formula timing plans A method of making buy and sell decisions using some predetermined criteria based upon changes in securities prices.

garnishment A legal procedure that enables a creditor to collect unpaid debts by requiring the debtor's employer to apply a part of the debtor's wage toward the retirement of the debt.

gift tax A tax levied on the value of property transferred as a gift.

guaranteed insurability An option in life insurance policies that allows the insured to buy additional, predetermined amounts of insurance at set intervals without evidence of insurability.

Health Maintenance Organization (HMO) A corporation made up of health care providers that offers comprehensive health care plans.

holder-in-due-course A doctrine that holds that the liability for a defective product does not follow the financing contract.

homeowner's insurance An insurance policy that comes in six basic forms (HO–1, HO–2, HO–3, HO–4, HO–5, and HO–6) and contains a package of property and liability insurance designed to protect the insured against most property and liability perils associated with owning a home or condominium or renting an apartment.

impulse spending Purchasing of goods and services on the spur of the moment with little deliberative thinking.

income tax A tax levied on individual and business income.

indemnify To restore loss by payment, repair, or replacement.

indenture The contract that contains the provisions defining the rights and responsibilities of the investors and issuers of a bond.

independent insurance agent An agent who sells and services insurance under contract with numerous insurers and who has general control, ownership, and use of policy records.

Individual Retirement Account (IRA) A tax-deferred retirement plan for employed individuals whose employers do not provide retirement plans.

inflation A condition of increasing prices.

inheritance tax A tax levied on the value of wealth received by an heir.

installment loan A debt that is repaid in two or more payments made at regular intervals.

interest adjusted cost A method of determining the cost of life insurance that takes into account the time value of money.

interest rate risk The uncertainty of the size of investment returns attributable to changes in interest rates.

intestacy The state of dying without having made a will.

investment Buying securities or other assets after a careful investigation of the facts and an analysis of the expected risks and returns.

investment company (closed-end) Investment companies that limit the number of shares they issue and which do not repurchase their shares.

investment company (open-end) A company that uses the proceeds from the public sale of its shares in order to invest in various securities for the benefit of its public shareholders. The number of shares issued is not limited and they will be repurchased by the company whenever the shareholder wishes to sell them. Also known as a mutual fund.

Keogh Plan Tax-deferred retirement plan available to self-employed individuals.

law of large numbers The basis for predicting the chance of loss, this law states that the predictability of loss improves as the number of observations or units insured increases.

lease An agreement entered into whereby the lessor makes certain property available to the lessee under specific conditions for a rental fee.

leverage The use of someone else's money to attempt to increase your rate of return.

liability The state of being legally responsible or answerable. Also an obligation or debt owed to someone else.

liability insurance Insurance that pays on behalf of an insured for losses to others arising out of the insured's negligence or omission.

life-cycle cost The total of all purchase, operating, and maintenance costs incurred over the useful life of a product.

long-term liability An obligation or debt payment that is not due and payable for at least one year.

maintenance agreement An agreement whereby in return for a fixed annual premium a seller promises to provide all needed service on a specific appliance for a specified time.

marginal tax rate The percentage of the last dollar of income that is paid in taxes.

marital deduction Provision in the federal tax law that allows a substantial deduction for property transferred to a surviving spouse.

maturity The period of time for which a contract is written.

medical payments insurance A type of coverage often provided in auto and homeowner's insurance policies that provides for payment for medical expenses resulting from an accident or other insured peril, without regard to liability.

mortgage A document indicating a claim against property.

mortgage bond A bond whose collateral is evidenced by a mortgage on the issuer's assets.

mortgage discount points In regard to a mortgage loan, a one-time charge assessed by a lending institution to increase the yield from the mortgage loan.

mortgage loan A special kind of long-term loan for buying a house in which the house serves as collateral for the loan.

municipals Debt obligations issued by a state or local governmental agency. The interest from these bonds is exempt from federal income taxes.

mutual fund See investment company (open-end).

negligence The state of being held legally answerable or responsible for acts of omission or commission.

negotiated order of withdrawal (NOW) An account that enables financial institutions that are not commercial banks to offer "checking accounts."

net cost A method of determining the cost of life insurance.

net worth The difference between assets and liabilities, which indicates extent of your ownership or wealth.

nondiscretionary expenditures Spending for the essentials of life such as food, clothing, and shelter. Also, spending in which an individual has little or no freedom of choice or judgment.

nonduplication of benefits A clause in some health insurance policies that specifies that benefits will not be paid for losses reimbursed by other insurers.

nondurable good Product that is used within a short time period or in a single usage.

nonforfeiture value Values contained in a life insurance policy (occasionally a health insurance policy) that belong to a policy owner even if he or she ceases to pay the policy premium.

open-end lease A lease agreement whereby in addition to the rental payment the lessee guarantees the value of the leased asset at the end of the lease period.

out-of-pocket costs Costs that involve the actual outflow of cash.

over-the-counter (OTC) A secondary market for securities in which transactions are arranged through a telephone or telegraph network, rather than through bidding (*see* securities exchange).

par value The face value assigned and printed on a security certificate.

peer group Any group of individuals who are of equal status in terms of age, occupation, social status, or other characteristics.

personal income Gross income before payment of taxes and any other essentials.

point In regard to securities, a unit used in quoting prices and market averages. (See also mortgage discount points.)

policy loan A loan made by an insurance company to a policyholder on the cash surrender value of a life insurance policy.

portfolio The investments held by an individual or by an organization.

pre-existing condition A health or physical condition that existed prior to the effective date of an insurance policy and that is generally not fully covered in a policy.

preferred stock An ownership security that gives its holders certain preferences over common stockholders, usually in terms of dividends. In return for these preferences the preferred holder does not have the right to vote on corporate matters.

primary securities market The means whereby new securities are offered for sale to investors and the net proceeds go to the issuing organization.

private brands Product brands usually owned by retailers rather than by the manufacturer.

probate The judicial process used to establish the validity of a will and carry out its terms. Also, the judicial proceedings needed to settle an estate.

prospectus A document that describes the securities to be issued and the conditions under which they are to be offered as well as the prospects for company performance.

purchasing power risk The uncertainty of the value of investment returns attributable to price level changes.

replacement cost The cost of replacing property with like kind of material and construction and with no deduction for depreciation.

risk (1) With regard to insurance, the chance of loss now or in the future. (2) With regard to investing, the chance that actual investment returns will vary from expected returns.

rule of 78 A method that places greater weight on earlier months in the repayment schedule when determining what amount of finance charges should be refunded if an installment loan is repaid before the maturity date.

sales tax A tax levied on the value of a sales transaction.

secondary securities market A system including organized securities exchanges and the over-the-counter market in which investors buy and sell securities among themselves. None of the proceeds go to the issuer.

securities exchange A centralized location where securities are bought and sold among, or for, investors.

security deposit An amount of money required by a lessor at the beginning of a lease to serve as protection against property damage caused by the lessee.

services Time and labor purchased from others such as a doctor's services, a plumber's services, etc.

settlement options A clause that contains alternative options regarding the payment of the proceeds or cash value of a life insurance policy.

Special Package Auto Policy (SPAP) A form of auto insurance containing a package of required coverages with available options and designed to cover most of the perils associated with automobile ownership.

speculation Buying securities or other assets without first investigating or understanding the facts and expected risks and returns.

straight life insurance A type of cash value insurance policy for which one pays premiums (1) for life, (2) to a specified age such as 85, or (3) until the policy is surrendered. Also may be called ordinary or whole life.

tax avoidance Reduction of a person's tax bill by legal methods.

tax credit A direct offset against an individual's tax liability.

tax evasion Reduction or elimination of taxes by illegal methods.

term life insurance Life insurance issued for a specific term of years after which it expires without value.

title The evidence of a person's legal right to possession of property.

title insurance Special insurance that protects against loss of one's equity investment in real property if a flaw in the property's title is found.

trust A legal arrangement whereby people contract for the management and control of certain assets for the benefit of themselves or other individuals.

underwriting The process of selecting and classifying risks according to the degree of their insurability.

uninsured motorist coverage An insurance coverage contained in an auto insurance policy under which the insurer will pay for the insured's damages for which another motorist is liable but unable to pay.

unit pricing Method of pricing that calculates the cost per common unit of measurement; for example, cents per ounce.

U.S. Treasury securities Debt securities—bonds, notes, and bills—issued by the United States government.

variable costs Costs that vary in total amount usually in relation to usage; for example, gasoline for an auto or the monthly utility bill.

waiver of premium An option in life and health insurance policies that waives or forgives premium payments during periods when the insured is disabled.

will A legal declaration (usually a written document) of a person's wishes as to the disposition of his or her property at death.

zero-base budgeting (ZBB) A budgeting technique that requires an annual justification of all expenditures.

Index

F

J

K–L

N

O

P

V

W

Y–Z

This book has been set in 10 and 9 point Trump Mediaeval, leaded 2 and 3 points. Section numbers are 24 point Trump Mediaeval bold and section titles are 18 point Trump Mediaeval. Chapter numbers are 54 point Palatino and chapter titles are 18 point Trump Mediaeval bold. The size of the type page is 27 by 44½ picas.